Causal Cognition

SYMPOSIA OF THE FYSSEN FOUNDATION

Causal Cognition

A Multidisciplinary Debate

Edited by

Dan Sperber, David Premack, and
Ann James Premack

A Fyssen Foundation Symposium

CLARENDON PRESS · OXFORD

Oxford University Press, Walton Street, Oxford OX2 6DP

Oxford   New York

Athens   Auckland   Bangkok   Bombay
Calcutta   Cape Town   Dar es Salaam   Delhi
Florence   Hong Kong   Istanbul   Karachi
Kuala Lumpur   Madras   Madrid   Melbourne
Mexico City   Nairobi   Paris   Singapore
Taipei   Tokyo   Toronto
and associated companies in
Berlin   Ibadan

Oxford is a trade mark of Oxford University Press

Published in the United States
by Oxford University Press Inc., New York

A catalogue record for this book is available from the British Library

Library of Congress Cataloging in Publication Data
Causal cognition : a multidisciplinary debate / edited by Dan
Sperber, David Premack, and Ann James Premack.
(Symposia of the Fyssen Foundation)
Includes bibliographical references.
'Sixth Fyssen Symposium, held at the Pavillon Henri IV à St
-Germain-en-Laye from 7 to 10 January 1993' – Pref.
1. Cognition – Congresses. 2. Causation – Congresses.
3. Attribution (Social psychology) – Congresses. 4. Cognition and
culture – Congresses. I. Sperber, Dan. II. Premack, David.
III. Premack, Ann J. IV. Series: Fyssen Foundation symposium.
BF311.C35 1994   153–dc20   94–28383

ISBN 0 19 852314 9 (Hbk)
ISBN 0 19 852402 1 (Pbk)

Printed in Great Britain by Biddles Ltd,
Guildford & King's Lynn

Preface

This is the report of the Sixth Fyssen Symposium, held at the Pavillon Henri IV at St-Germain-en-Laye from 7 to 10 January 1993 in the presence of Mme Fyssen, President of the Fyssen Foundation. The theme of this symposium, 'Causal understanding in cognition and culture', is central to the aim of the Fyssen Foundation which is 'to encourage all forms of scientific inquiry into cognitive mechanisms, including thought and reasoning, underlying animal and human behaviour, and their ontogenetic and phylogenetic developments'.

The Scientific Committee of the Foundation had entrusted three of its members, Gilbert Lewis, David Premack, and Dan Sperber, with the organization of this symposium. Gilbert Lewis, who helped give the conference its initial impetus and define its contents, had to resume anthropological fieldwork in Guinea Bissau (with a break in order to attend the meeting) and could not participate in the editorial work. Ann James Premack joined the two other conference organizers to form the editorial team.

The general organization of the meeting was similar to that of previous Fyssen Symposia. Draft manuscripts were pre-circulated to participants. Final papers were swiftly prepared after the meeting. Most questions put during the meeting were also recorded in writing at the time, and were used by the authors as a basis either for modifications of their papers or for written answers which appear after their papers.

We are extremely grateful to Mme Colette Kouchner who helped with the conference planning, Mme Colette Leconte who was responsible for the administration and the organization of the meeting itself, and Mme Monique Lucas who provided secretarial assistance during the editorial process. All the participants join us in expressing our deepest gratitude to the Fyssen Foundation, and in particular to Mme Fyssen, who have made possible a symposium that we shall remember not just for its intellectual stimulation, but also for its lavish hospitality.

Paris
April 1994

D. S.
D. P.
A. J. P.

Contents

Participants

Daniel Andler
CREA-Ecole Polytechnique, 1, rue Descartes, 75005 Paris France.

Scott Atran (contributor)
Department of Anthropology, 1054 L.S.A. Building, University of Michigan, Ann Arbor, MI 48109–1382, USA.

Renée Baillargeon (contributor)
Department of Psychology, University of Illinois at Urbana-Champaign 603 East Daniel, Champaign, IL 61820, USA.

Maurice Bloch
Department of Anthropology, London School of Economics, Houghton Street, London WC2A 2AE, UK.

Pascal Boyer (contributor)
Department of Anthropology, King's College, Cambridge CB2 1ST, UK.

Francesca Bray
Department of Anthropology, University of California, 341 Haines Hall, Los Angeles, CA 90024, USA.

Susan Carey (contributor)
Department of Psychology, Massachusetts Institute of Technology, Cambridge, MA 02139, USA.

Patricia W. Cheng (contributor)
Department of Psychology, University of California at Los Angeles, 405 Hilgard Avenue, Los Angeles, CA 90024–1563, USA.

Anthony Dickinson (contributor)
Department of Experimental Psychology, University of Cambridge, Downing Street, Cambridge CB2 3EB, UK.

Frank Doring
Groupe de Recherche sur la Cognition, CREA-Ecole Polytechnique, 1, rue Descartes, 75005 Paris, France.

C. R. Gallistel
Department of Psychology, University of California at Los Angeles, 405 Hilgard Avenue, Los Angeles, CA 90024–1563, USA.

Rochel Gelman (contributor)
Department of Psychology, University of California at Los Angeles, 405 Hilgard Avenue, Los Angeles, CA 90024–1563, USA.

Vittorio Girotto
Via Valgimiglio, 4, 35100 Padua, Italy.

Ian Hacking (contributor)
Department of Philosophy, University of Toronto, Victoria College, Toronto, M5S 1K7, Canada.

Denis J. Hilton (contributor)
Professeur à l'ESSEC, Avenue Bernard Hirsch, BP 105, 95021 Cergy-Pontoise Cedex, France.

Robert A. Hinde
The Master's Lodge, St John's College, Cambridge CB2 1TP, UK.

Lawrence A. Hirschfeld (contributor)
Department of Anthropology, 1054 L.S.A. Building, University of Michigan, Ann Arbor, MI 48109–1382, USA.

Keith Holyoak
Department of Psychology, University of California at Los Angeles, 405 Hilgard Avenue, Los Angeles, CA 90024–1563, USA.

Michel Imbert
Laboratoire des Neurosciences de la Vision, Université Pierre et Marie Curie, 9, Quai Saint-Bernard, 75252 Paris, Cedex 05, France.

Pierre Jacob (contributor)
CREA-Ecole Polytechnique, 1, rue Descartes, 75005 Paris, France.

Pierre Jaisson
Laboratoire d'Ethologie Expérimentale, Université Paris-Nord, Avenue Jean-Baptiste Clément, 93430 Villetaneuse, France.

Frank C. Keil (contributor)
Department of Psychology, Cornell University, 228 Uris Hall, Ithaca, NY 14853, USA.

Marc Kirsch
Assistant de Sciences Cognitives, Université de Paris XI, 91000 Orsay, France.

Max Kistler
CREA-Ecole Polytechnique, 1, rue Descartes, 75005 Paris, France.

Hans Kummer (contributor)
Ethologie und Wildforschung, Universität Zurich — Irchel, Gebäude 25, Winterthurerstrasse 190, 8057 Zurich, Switzerland.

Bruno Latour
Centre de Sociologie de l'Innovation, Ecole Nationale Superieure des Mines, 62, Boulevard Saint-Michel, 75006 Paris, France.

Alan M. Leslie (contributor)
Center for Cognitive Science, Rutgers University, Psychology Building—
New Wing, Busch Campus, Piscataway, NJ 08855, USA.

Gilbert Lewis (contributor)
Department of Anthropology, University of Cambridge, Free School Lane,
Cambridge CB2 1TP, UK.

Geoffrey Lloyd (contributor)
Darwin College, Cambridge CB3 9EU, UK.

Jacques Mehler
Directeur d'Etudes à l'EHESS, Laboratoire des Sciences Cognitives et
Psycholinguistique, EHESS, 54, Boulevard Raspail, 75270 Paris, France.

Michael W. Morris (contributor)
Department of Organizational Behavior, Graduate School of Business,
Stanford University, Stanford, CA 94305, USA.

Richard Nisbett (contributor)
Institute of Social Research, University of Michigan, Ann Arbor,
MI 48109–1382, USA.

Ira Noveck
Département de Psychologie, Université de Paris VIII—Saint-Denis, 93526
Saint-Denis Cedex, France.

Philip Pettit (contributor)
Research School of Social Sciences, Australian National University,
Canberra, AC7 2614, Australia.

Guy Politzer
Chargé de Recherche, Département de Psychologie, Université de Paris
VIII—Saint-Denis, 93526 Saint-Denis Cedex, France.

Ann James Premack (co-editor and contributor)
Laboratoire de Psychologie de l'Enfant, CNRS, 41, rue Gay Lussac, 75005
Paris, France.

David Premack (co-editor and contributor)
Laboratoire de Psychologie de l'Enfant, CNRS, 41, rue Gay Lussac, 75005
Paris, France.

Elizabeth S. Spelke (contributor)
Department of Psychology, Cornell University, Uris Hall, Ithaca,
NY 14853–7601, USA.

Dan Sperber (co-editor and contributor)
CREA-Ecole Polytechnique, 1, rue Descartes, 75005 Paris, France.

Leonard Talmy
Department of Linguistics, University of New York at Buffalo, 628 Baldy
Hall, Buffalo, NY 14260, USA.

Michael Waldmann
Psychologisches Institut, Universität Tübingen, Frieddrichstrasse 21, 2400
Tübingen, Germany.

Amanda L. Woodward (contributor)
Department of Psychology, Cornell University, Uris Hall, Ithaca,
NY 14853-7601, USA.

Introduction

DAN SPERBER

The existence of cognition in nature is an outcome of biological evolution. The overall function of cognition is to give the organism some control over its environment. Such cognitive control calls for the ability to represent causal regularities. Therefore the idea of an evolved cognitive system that did not provide, first and foremost, some causal knowledge makes little sense. Reflecting on the role and forms of causal knowledge, both in animal and human cognition, was the first aim of this symposium. In the human case, individual causal understanding is largely derived from interaction with other humans and from culturally developed causal theories. Reflecting on the relationship between individual and cultural aspects of causal understanding was our second main aim.

Until the 1960s, the psychological study of causal cognition remained underdeveloped. Studies such as those of Piaget (1927), Michotte (1946), or Heider (1944, 1958) were exceptions. Since then, there have been two main waves of study on the topic. The first and largest, often labelled 'attribution theory', is mostly the work of social psychologists and of psychologists of reasoning. It has focused on general properties of causal inference on the one hand, and of causal attributions in the interpersonal and social domain on the other (see Hewstone (1989) for a recent review, Schustack (1988) for a review on causal reasoning, and Hilton (1988) for a collection with a focus on some of the issues discussed in this book). The second wave is mostly the work of developmental psychologists. It has focused on forms of causal understanding specific to different cognitive domains, such as common-sense physics and common-sense psychology, and on their innate bases (see Carey and Gelman (1991), Gelman and Byrnes (1991), and Hirschfeld and Gelman (1994) for recent collections).

Both psychological approaches to causal understanding derive many of their concepts and questions from much older philosophical work. While Aristotle's ideas on causality are somewhat alien to us, Hume's are not. From Hume onwards, the metaphysics of causality and the psychology of causal understanding have been closely intertwined.

It is in the First Book of his *Treatise of human nature* (1739–40), entitled 'Of the understanding', that Hume put forward his doctrine about causality. Our idea of causality, Hume claimed, is that of a necessary connection among things. However, this sort of connection cannot be observed – the only relevant relations that can be observed are those of contiguity and succession — nor can it be rationally inferred. Causal beliefs are both indispensable to human understanding and unfounded.

The very premises of Hume's challenge have sometimes been questioned. Thus some philosophers have denied that causal beliefs are indispensable. Bertrand Russell likened the law of causality to the British monarchy, both surviving, he claimed, because they are 'erroneously supposed to do no harm' (Russell 1918, p. 180). Similarly, Henry Kyburg has argued that 'the epistemological role [of the notion of causality] is nil; and that the psychological role is of mainly pathological interest' (Kyburg 1988, p. 22) Other philosophers have, on the contrary, claimed that causation is much less problematic than Hume maintained. Thus C. J. Ducasse maintained that 'the causal relation, when correctly defined is as directly observable as many other facts, and that the alleged mysteriousness of the causal tie is therefore a myth' (Ducasse 1926, p. 57; see also Anscombe 1971).

The first anti-Humean idea, that causal thinking is an unnecessary illusion, has not attracted psychologists despite their interest in cognitive illusions. After all, psychologists themselves are in the business of providing causal explanations. Their experimental and statistical methods are intended to establish causal explanatory claims. Thus, to deny the epistemic role of causal considerations would be, for psychologists, to undermine their own enterprise.

On the contrary, the second anti-Humean idea, that causal relations may be perceived and not just inferred, has been espoused, developed, and experimentally tested by the Belgian psychologist André Michotte (1946) and is elaborated in several of the contributions to this book. However, the psychologist's notion of perception is not necessarily the same as the philosopher's. Whereas, in the philosopher's sense, one can only perceive what there is, in the psychologist's sense, illusions, misperceptions, and cases of 'filling in' count as perceptions. Actually, in Michotte's experiments, what subjects experienced was an illusion of causality! Therefore, strictly speaking, Michotte's experiments and others in the same vein do not prove Hume wrong. The question remains: when we perceive, in the psychologist's sense, causation at work, what are the objective properties of the stimulus that cause this perception? And, in normal conditions, is actual causality one of these properties?

Most philosophers have accepted Hume's two premises: that causal beliefs are essential to human understanding, and that they result from non-demonstrative inference or induction. Much work has been focused on the meaning of causal claims and on the methods by which they are, or should be, arrived at (see the readings in Sosa and Tooley (1993)). The dominant view has been that a relation between two events can be said to be causal if it instantiates an appropriate regularity or, better, a causal law.

Establishing a causal claim thus conceived is a matter of discovering the combination of causal laws and circumstances at work in a given case, a combination often thought of as a 'mechanism'.

Another common view of causal claims and causal inference is that a relation between two events can be said to be causal if the occurrence of the first is a condition of an appropriate kind for the occurrence of the second. What kind of condition is appropriate? Sufficient condition, necessary condition, and some articulation of the two (such as Mackie's INUS conditions — see Mackie (1974)) have been argued for by various authors. Establishing a causal claim thus conceived involves establishing that the appropriate kind of condition is satisfied. John Stuart Mill (1843) was a precursor in providing explicit methods for such inference. The characterizations of causation in terms of regularities and in terms of conditions look very different but they can be made to cohere. For instance, it can be argued that causal claims are claims about the instantiation of regularities, but that arriving at these claims involves reasoning on conditions.

Today, under the influence of the development of probabilistic thinking and of quantum mechanics, the idea that causation involves a necessary relation is being questioned. New probabilistic views of causation have been developed (Suppes 1970; Salmon 1984, Humphreys 1989). They may involve ideas of (probabilistic) laws. They tend to give an important place to the notion of a mechanism as a tool for sorting causal from non-causal correlations. Causal inference may then be viewed as some combination of probabilistic reasoning and theorizing about mechanisms.

Although some philosophers have argued that push–pull causation and intentional causation are crucially different (Hart and Honoré 1959), most have aimed at giving a unitary account of causation and causal induction. Much early psychological work on causal inference also aimed at characterizing it in a unitary fashion, with the stress on either mechanism or conditions, and often with a probabilistic viewpoint.

A unitary view of causal inference has, of course, always been compatible with the idea that domain-specific beliefs play a role in actual inference as premises. Most attribution theorists combine a unitary view with the recognition of domain-specific biases such as Ross's 'fundamental attribution error', (which consists in overestimating individual dispositions and underestimating situational factors in explaining social behaviour (Ross 1977)). Generally, there has been a growing willingness among psychologists favouring a unitary approach to causal inference to acknowledge the role in causal inference of *acquired* domain-specific schemas or models (Gentner and Stevens 1983; Holland *et al.* 1986).

Some psychologists have gone even further and explored the possibility that the procedures of causal inference differ substantially from one conceptual domain to the next, and do so by virtue of *innate* dispositions.

From the biological and naturalistic point of view characteristic of much current cognitive science, induction had better be, if not strictly speaking, logically valid, at least cognitively sound. This follows from the idea that the enduring existence of cognitive mechanisms in nature is a feedback effect of their relative success at performing their functions. The very difficulty of establishing the soundness of induction when its procedures are conceived in a unitary fashion motivates the exploration of an alternative 'modular' approach. Human knowledge — and in particular causal knowledge — is then better viewed as the output, not of a general purpose intelligence, but of a number of autonomously evolved, genetically determined, domain-specific competences (Barkow *et al.* 1992; Hirschfeld and Gelman 1994). This, we noted, is the approach currently explored by many developmental psychologists.

While there have been many conferences on attribution theory, this is the first conference on causal understanding where the new developmental domain-specific approaches have been given centre stage and confronted by older domain-general approaches. One of our aims, in staging this confrontation, was to assess the degree to which the more recent approaches renew our understanding of causal cognition.

Psychologists who accept a domain-specific approach to the development of causal understanding differ as to the number, organization, and role of the relevant domains. While the existence of a physical domain and a psychological domain is generally accepted, that of a biological domain and a social domain is much more controversial. Other issues are in debate. To what extent are domain-specific abilities truly modular? In what manner and how rigidly are their specific domains defined? In what manner and to what extent is the knowledge that they determine susceptible of revision? Another of our aims was to confront different points of view on these issues.

The problem of understanding how sound causal induction is possible might also be illuminated by the social sciences. Causal understanding has long been of interest to historians of ideas and anthropologists. After all, most causal beliefs are partly or wholly derived from cultural sources. To that extent, they are the product of long-term collective enterprises rather than of our individual cognitive resources. Arguably, the epistemic reliability of a collective extending over many generations might be greater than that of an individual. Social scientists, however, have been less concerned with the cognitive soundness of causal representations than with their social relevance and their place within each particular culture. They have documented the diversity of causal explanations found across cultures, a diversity which raises issues of soundness on its own. They have studied how, even within the same culture, quite different views of causality are invoked in, for instance, the religious, scientific, and legal spheres.

The relation between culturally developed forms of causal understanding and fundamental cognitive dispositions has generally been ignored. This is in part due to the idea that cultural representations, because of their very diversity, cannot be explained or even illuminated by cognitive invariants. This view of the relationship – or lack of relationship – between the cognitive and cultural sciences has recently been challenged (Sperber 1985*a*, *b*). A few anthropologists have adopted a perspective close to that of the developmental psychologists, and argued that domain-specific forms of causal understanding are also at work in culturally transmitted knowledge. One of our aims was to confront these different approaches to cultural representations of causality, both among themselves and with psychological approaches.

Other perspectives, other competences do contribute to our understanding of causal understanding, but alas could not be represented in this symposium if we wanted to keep it small enough for optimal interaction. The history and philosophy of science, ethnography, linguistics, and social psychology were under-represented. Legal scholars, with their interest in responsibility, and students of technology with their interest in efficiency and control, were altogether absent. Still, we felt that this meeting brought out novel issues and controversies in a particularly challenging manner.

The book is divided into eight parts. Part I is on causal representation in non-human animals. Parts II–V are on causal understanding in different domains. Part VI discusses the legitimacy of domain-specific causal understanding from a philosophical point of view. Part VII is on domain-general approaches to causal understanding. Part VIII is on causal understanding in cross-cultural perspective. There has been an unavoidable element of arbitrariness in allocating chapters to parts, since many chapters contribute to the themes of several parts. Each part has its own foreword where the papers in the section are introduced.

REFERENCES

Anscombe, E. (1971). *Causality and determination.* Cambridge University Press.

Barkow, J. H., Cosmides, L. and Tooby, J. (1992). *The adapted mind: evolutionary psychology and the evolution of culture.* Oxford University Press.

Carey, S. and Gelman, R. (1991). *Epigenesis of mind: biology and cognition.* Erlbaum, Hillsdale, NJ.

Ducasse, C. J. (1926). On the nature and the observability of the causal relation. In *Causation* (ed. E. Sosa and M. Tooley), pp. 125–36. Oxford University Press.

Gelman, S. A. and Byrnes, J. P. (1991). *Perspectives on language and thought: interrelation and development.* Cambridge University Press.

Gentner, D. and Stevens A. L. (ed.) (1983). *Mental models.* Erlbaum, Hillsdale, NJ.

Hart, H. L. A. and Honoré, A. M. (1959). *Causation and the law*. Clarendon Press, Oxford.

Heider, F. (1944). Social perception and phenomenal causality. *Psychological Review* **51**, 358–74.

Heider, F. (1958). *The psychology of interpersonal relations*. Wiley, New York.

Hewstone, M. (1989). *Causal attribution: from cognitive processes to collective beliefs*. Blackwell, Oxford.

Hilton, D. (1988). *Contemporary science and natural explanation: commonsense conceptions of causality*. Harvester Press, Brighton.

Hirschfeld, L. and Gelman, S. A. (1994). *Mapping the mind: domain-specificity in cognition and culture*. Cambridge University Press.

Holland, J. H., Holyoak, K. J., Nisbett, R. E. and Thagard, P. R. (1986). *Induction: processes of inference, learning, and discovery*. MIT Press, Cambridge, MA.

Hume, D. [1739–40] (1888). *A treatise of human nature* (ed. L. A. Selby-Bigge). Oxford University Press.

Humphreys, P. (1989). *The chances of explanation: causal explanation in the social, medical and physical sciences*. Princeton University Press.

Kyburg, (1988). Cognition and causality. In *Cognition and representation* (ed. S. Schiffer and S. Steele). Westview Press, Boulder, CO.

Mackie, J. L. (1974). *The cement of the universe: a study of causation*. Oxford University Press.

Michotte, A. (1946). *La perception de la causalité*. Editions de l'Institut Supérieur de Philosophie, Louvain. English translation: *The perception of causality*. Methuen, London, 1963.

Mill, J. S. [1843] (1874). *A system of logic* (8th edn.). Harper, New York.

Piaget, J. (1927) *La causalité physique chez l'enfant*. Alcan, Paris. English translation: *The child's conception of physical causality*. Kegan Paul, London, 1930.

Ross, L. (1977). The intuitive psychologist and his shortcomings: distortions in the attribution process. In *Advances in experimental social psychology* (ed. L. Berkowitz), Vol. 10. Academic Press, New York.

Russell, B. (1918). *Mysticism and logic*. Longmans, London.

Salmon, W. (1984). *Scientific explanation and the causal structure of the world*. Princeton University Press.

Schustack, M. W. (1988). Thinking about causality. In *The psychology of human thought* (ed. R. J. Sternberg and E. E. Smith). Cambridge University Press.

Sosa, E. and Tooley, M. (ed.) (1993). *Causation*. Oxford University Press.

Sperber, D. (1985a). *On anthropological knowledge*. Cambridge University Press.

Sperber, D. (1985b). Anthropology and psychology: towards an epidemiology of representations. *Man (NS)*, **20**, 73–89.

Suppes, P. (1970). *A probabilistic theory of causality*. North-Holland, Amsterdam.

Part I

Causal representation in animal cognition

Foreword to Part I

Dickinson and Shanks, working in the Humean tradition, argue that the basic mechanism of 'goal-directed instrumental action' is causal belief in both the human and, as they put it, 'the "humble" rat pressing a lever for food'. Hume would have endorsed this claim with pleasure, having said as much himself.

To defend the position, Dickinson and Shanks pursue three questions.

1. Are animal actions intentional, mediated by a representation of the action–outcome association?

2. Are human causal judgement and instrumental performance affected by the same parameters?

3. Are both human causal judgements and animal actions mediated by comparable causal processes?

To all these questions, they reply positively.

For example, they show that the variation under several parameters is the same for instrumental responding as it is for judgement of causal relations. Further, both the human judgement of causal relations and instrumental responding in animals are affected by the same parameters, including, impressively, those that create an illusion of causality.

An intentional action, they argue, both produces an outcome and is directed at a goal. If the outcome that the act produces satisfies the goal, the act will continue. However, if the act no longer produces a satisfying outcome, or else the goal itself is eliminated (for example by feeding a hungry rat), the act will not continue. Using this simple test, Dickinson and Shanks are able to distinguish goal-directed instrumental action, such as the lever pressing of the rat, from Pavlovian conditioning and other non-intentional behaviour. This fecund paper, part of a closely reasoned program on intentionality in animal action that Dickinson and his distinguished colleagues began 10–15 years ago, contains twists that would have titillated Hume.

Kummer accepts the responsibility that psychologists invariably impose upon the biologist: to provide an evolutionary account, in this case of causal knowledge. Kummer considers the genetic program for associative learning, arbitrary or 'weak causality' as he prefers, to be universal, found in brainless micro-organisms as well as in humans. However, he argues that beyond this universal program, one must expect to find causal interpretations specific to special environments and modes of life.

He suggests, for instance, that Michotte's 'object impulse' causality may be a speciality of tool-using species, for only they hit one object with another. He points out that animal detectors of what humans call causality are for the most part '... not precursors of our causal perceptions and concepts, but original solutions of their own design'.

He provides a number of examples of devices that cope with causal relations which would go unrecognized because the critical events are not contiguous. The circadian rhythm is itself one solution to this problem because it enables the time of most profitable foraging to be predicted. Another example he provides are the 'decision rules' that males use to determine whether offspring are theirs. A male who shares his mate with other males needs such rules because, with the advent of internal insemination, he loses the ability to monitor his paternity directly, and cannot easily know which of the offspring are his and whether he should assist in their care. Kummer's examples remind psychologists of the world of alternatives that go beyond those that they have taken into the laboratory!

D.P.
A.J.P.

1

Instrumental action and causal representation

ANTHONY DICKINSON AND DAVID SHANKS

From a functional perspective, cognitive resources for representing causality should be intimately tied to the behavioural capacity for goal-directed instrumental action—action by means of which we manipulate and control the environment to serve our needs and desires. Without such a capacity, causal knowledge would be impotent, locked within the mind and without impact upon the world. Consider a 'purely' Pavlovian agent, equipped only with a set of innate anticipatory reactions to signals of important events in the world, reactions which evolution (rather than experience) has ensured are adapted to these events. To engage these anticipatory responses, an agent needs to detect merely the *predictive* rather than the *causal* association between potential signals and the impending events, and as a consequence the representation of any causal relation is redundant to the function of these pre-selected responses. The process of evolution, rather than the agent's cognitive resources, ensures the selection of responses having appropriate consequences and thus harmony between behaviour and environment.

However, such a Pavlovian agent is at the mercy of the stability of the causal relations between its behaviour and events in the world. This point can be illustrated by one of the simplest behavioural capacities—the ability to approach signals of valuable resources. Having fed chicks at a distinctive food bowl, Hershberger (1986) found that when they subsequently moved some distance from the bowl, not surprisingly they immedlately ran towards it. For a second group, however, Hershberger reversed the normal relation between locomotion and spatial translation by placing the chicks in a 'looking glass' world where the bowl receded twice as fast as they ran towards it, and approached them at twice the speed that they ran away from it. This reversal of the normal relation between locomotion and relative spatial translation requires that the chicks learn to run away from the bowl in order to reach it. The chicks never successfully adapted to the reversal, even across 100 m of training, suggesting that their 'approach' behaviour is a simple conditioned response elicited by the attractive stimulus of the food bowl. Given the Pavlovian nature of its 'approach' behaviour, any knowledge that a chick might have of the causal consequences of locomotion is redundant, for there seems to be no mechanism which can bring such causal knowledge to bear on the control of its spatially directed behaviour.

In contrast with the case of Pavlovian conditioning, the capacity for instrumental action provides the agent with a behavioural medium through which causal knowledge can be expressed with profit. Instrumental actions are effective just to the extent that they allow agents to control the causal processes that determine access to resources and avoidance of harmful situations. Intentional folk psychology recognizes the central role of causal cognition in instrumental behaviour. Under an intentional interpretation, the psychological antecedent of an instrumental act is the interaction of a belief (or representation) that there is a causal relation between the action and its outcome, with a desire for that outcome through a process of practical inference. Thus, for example, the act of switching on a light is explained in terms of the agent's desire for illumination and his or her belief that pressing the switch causes the light to come on.

One implication of this naive intentional psychology is that goal-directed instrumental action may be a basic behavioural marker of causal cognition. The tendentious nature of the claim is obvious from the very fact that many animals to whom we may be reluctant to attribute causal beliefs are capable of such behaviour. The prototypical example of instrumental action in the animal conditioning laboratory is that of the hungry rat pressing a lever for food. But can we really attribute to the 'humble' rat the capacity to represent the causal consequences of lever pressing on the basis of such a simple competence? This is precisely the issue that we shall examine in this chapter.

Our analysis addresses three issues. The status of instrumental action as a marker of causal knowledge is predicated on the intentional thesis that these actions are, in fact, mediated by causal beliefs. We examine this claim by investigating the concordance between human causal judgements and instrumental performance across variations in the parameters of an action–outcome relation. The second issue concerns whether or not animal action exhibits the necessary prerequisite for an intentional account, namely that it is mediated by some representation of the action–outcome association. Unless we can establish that the instrumental action of an animal is more than a simple stimulus–response habit, its status as a marker of causal cognition is not even open to debate. Finally, we take up the issue of whether human causal judgements and animal actions are mediated by comparable processes, an issue that we address in terms of their susceptibility to causal illusions. To the extent that we can find dissociations between causal judgements and either human or animal action, the thesis must be in doubt. In contrast, concordance in both cases would provide converging evidence favouring goal-directed instrumental action as a marker of causal cognition, albeit of the most primitive kind.

CAUSAL JUDGEMENT AND ACTION

The main challenge to the intentional theory of action has come from traditional studies of 'conditioning without awareness', and more recently from claims to have demonstrated so-called 'implicit' learning in instrumental tasks. A number of studies have reported behavioural learning in tasks in which agents appear to be unaware of the instrumental contingencies, that is, of the causal consequences of their actions. Typically, such studies have either employed a complex or obscure contingency (Berry and Broadbent 1984) or have attempted to mask the actual contingency with a task demand that identifies another relation as critical (Svardtal 1991). However, these demonstrations do not speak to the role of cognition in simple instrumental behaviour of the type studied in animal conditioning.

For this reason, the instrumental task that we used to assess the concordance between action and causal belief employed simple unmasked instrumental relations. In this task, originally developed by Wasserman and his colleagues (Wasserman *et al.* 1983), human subjects have the opportunity to perform the simple action of pressing the space bar on a microcomputer keyboard and observing the outcome, a brief illumination of an outline figure on a video screen. We chose this task because of its formal similarities with the standard free-operant procedures used with animals in the conditioning laboratory. We assume, of course, that the rat does not have knowledge and theories about the causal processes that may mediate the relation between pressing a lever and the delivery of a food pellet, and so we arranged to make our human subjects equally ignorant.

Demonstrations of instrumental learning without 'awareness' have assessed an agent's causal knowledge in post-training questionnaires, a procedure that has led Brewer (1974) and Shanks *et al.* (1994) to question the adequacy of the cognitive assessment in relation to the behavioural changes observed. Ideally, to be a compelling challenge to an intentional account of action, the dissociation between behaviour and cognition should be demonstrated with a procedure in which the agent's belief about the relevant contingency is assessed at the time of action, i.e. at the time when the belief is assumed to be active in the generation of the action. But such an assessment procedure may well preclude the possibility of observing the dissociation, in that it would require the agent to tolerate an obvious discord between cognition and action. By its very nature, cognitive assessment at the time of action may well bring about behavioural control by causal knowledge that would not have occurred otherwise.

Given these problems, we adopted the strategy of investigating the concordance between cognition and behaviour across variations in the major parameters of instrumental relation in separate groups of subjects. Within the context of our task, we already know that the temporal contiguity between action and outcome has a major effect on judgements of the causal relation (Shanks *et al.* 1989; Shanks and Dickinson 1991). In these studies we gave subjects a number of periods in which each press of the space bar produced the outcome with a probability of 0.75. Although the outcome never occurred without a press, its occurrence could be delayed for a fixed time after the press that caused it. At the end of each period, the subjects were asked to judge the strength of the causal relationship between action and outcome using a scale on which '100 indicates that pressing the SPACE BAR always caused the triangle to light up, and zero indicates that pressing the SPACE BAR had no effect on whether or not the triangle lit up'.

To ensure that judgements were sensitive to the causal relationship between action and outcome, we included non-contingent periods in which the action had no effect on the occurrence of the outcome. In fact, in each non-contingent period we played back the exact temporal pattern of the outcomes that had been generated by the subject's performance during the matched contingent period (in which the causal relation was in effect). Consequently, judgements from the non-contingent periods provided a baseline against which to assess the subject's sensitivity to the causal relation.

Figure 1.1(a) illustrates the judgements from the study by Shanks and Dickinson (1991). The first point to note is that judgements were sensitive to the presence of a causal relation: whereas subjects gave judgements close to zero in the non-contingent (non-causal) conditions, the mean rating in the contingent (causal) condition with an immediate or contiguous outcome (zero delay) was 78, thus approximately matching the actual probability with which the action caused the outcome. More important, however, is the fact that the ratings declined systematically in the contingent condition as the action–outcome delay was increased across a few seconds, even though, of course, the relevant causal property of the relation remained constant. Whatever the delay, pressing had the same effect on the likelihood of an outcome.

Given this pattern of judgements, the basic tenet of the intentional theory, namely that actions are mediated by causal beliefs, predicts that performance for a desired outcome should show a similar sensitivity to temporal contiguity. To investigate this prediction we ran a second group of subjects under the same condition, but in this case the task demand was

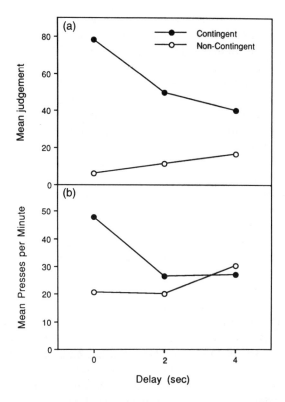

Fig. 1.1. (a) Mean causal judgements and (b) mean rate of pressing as a function of the action–outcome delay in the contingent and non-contingent conditions of the study by Shanks and Dickinson (1991).

to maximize the number of 'points gained' rather than to judge the causal relation. The pay-off was such that each outcome gained three points, but each press cost one point. As Fig. 1.1(b) illustrates, the rate of pressing was also sensitive to the presence of a causal relation when the outcome occurred immediately following the action, but failed to discriminate between the contingent and non-contingent conditions when the outcome was delayed.

In comparing the profiles of judgement and rate of pressing, it is noticeable that performance appeared to be more sensitive to delay. In contrast with the performance profile, the presence of a delay, while reducing the judged strength of the causal association, did not abolish the ability of the subjects to detect the contingency; they simply rated it as weaker when the outcome was delayed. This apparent dissociation probably reflects the actual pay-off structure of the performance task—a structure in which pressing could only achieve a net gain of points if each press increased the probability of the outcome by more than 0.33. Thus, even if one believes that an action has a weak causal influence on the outcome (as apparently the subjects did in the delay conditions), the intentional account does not predict that such weak beliefs should produce performance under the constraints of the pay-off structure. The dissociation that would be particularly problematic for intentional theory would be a demonstration of 'implicit' learning or 'conditioning without awareness', namely a demonstration that performance discriminates between the contingent and non-contingent schedules at a delay which yields comparable judgements for these two conditions.

Of course, the major parameter of an instrumental relation is the strength of the causal association between action and outcome, or in other words the degree to which acting actually increases the frequency of the outcome. The effect of this parameter can be investigated, unconfounded by variations in temporal contiguity, by keeping constant the probability $P(O/A)$ of the outcome occurring immediately following the action and varying the probability $P(O/-A)$ of the outcome in the absence of an immediately preceding action. If $P(O/A)$ is greater than $P(O/-A)$, there is a positive causal relation between the frequency of the action and the number of outcomes, in that more outcomes can be gained by acting rather than not acting. Further, the absolute number of additional outcomes that can be gained by acting decreases as $P(O/-A)$ is raised until, when $P(O/A) = P(O/-A)$, there is *no* causal association between action and outcome frequency. Under such a non-contingent schedule, a subject who presses frequently gains no more outcomes than one who never presses.

It is well established that causal judgements are sensitive to the causal association between action and outcome on the type of free-operant schedule that we used to study the effects of temporal contiguity (Wasserman *et al.* 1983; Shanks 1987). This sensitivity is illustrated by the results of a study, displayed in Fig. 1.2(a), in which we kept the probability of an outcome contiguous with a press of the space bar constant at 0.875 and varied the likelihood of the outcome in the absence of an immediately preceding press (Shanks and Dickinson 1991). As can be seen, judgements of the causal effectiveness of pressing reflected the strength of the causal relation, decreasing systematically as $P(O/-A)$ was raised.

In a comparable study, Chatlosh *et al.* (1985), as well as requiring their subjects to make causal judgements, also imposed the performance task demand of maximizing the number of outcomes. In accord with the intentional theory of action, performance exhibited a parallel sensitivity to the strength of the causal association, an effect that we replicated (Fig. 1.2(b)) under the same pay-off structure as that employed in the contiguity study (Shanks and Dickinson 1991). The only difference was that in our study

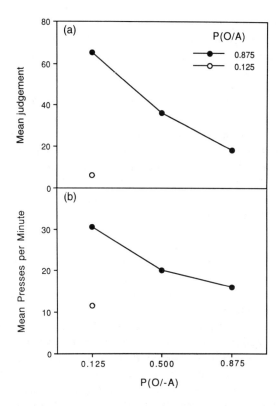

Fig. 1.2. (a) Mean causal judgements and (b) mean rate of pressing as a function of the probability $P(O/\text{-}A)$ of non-contiguous outcomes in the study by Shanks and Dickinson (1991).

the performance subjects were not required to make causality judgements (in order to preclude the possibility that such a request would bias them towards maintaining performance–judgement concordance).

In summary, causal judgements and instrumental performance exhibit a comparable sensitivity to variations in action–outcome contiguity and causality, a concordance that is predicted by the claim that an instrumental belief about the strength of the causal relation is an antecedent to action. It must be recognized, of course, that this evidence is no more than correlational, and that the concordance may well reflect the operation of independent psychological processes developed under the requirement that both cognition and action should veridically reflect causal associations in the world. It is true that, from a normative point of view, temporal contiguity should be without effect; as we have pointed out, for a fixed probability that an action will produce an outcome, the action is just as

effective in producing outcomes whatever the delay. Sensitivity to contiguity, however, may well be a prerequisite for detecting variations in
causality produced by differences in the likelihood of contiguous and non-
contiguous outcomes.

More compelling evidence for a common process would come from a
demonstration that judgements and performance manifest the same causal
illusions. One such illusion is seen when the absolute probability of the
outcome is varied on a non-contingent schedule under which, of course,
there is in *no* causal association: the higher the absolute outcome probability, the greater is the causal judgement (Alloy and Abramson 1979;
Dickinson *et al.* 1984; Shanks 1987). This illusion is illustrated in Fig. 1.2(a)
by a comparison of the judgement for the non-contingent schedule when
the outcome probability was high ($P(O/A) = P(O/-A) = 0.875$) with that
when the probability was low ($P(O/A) = P(O/-A) = 0.125$). The important
observation in this study, however, is the fact that a tendency to exactly
the same illusion was found in the performance condition (see Fig. 1.2(b)).
Since this illusion serves no obvious functional purpose, it is unclear why
independent processes for cognition and action should have developed
comparable and non-veridical sensitivity to overall outcome frequency.

Finally, we must consider the possibility that the interaction between
judgement and action is just the reverse of that posited by intentional
theory. However, we think it unlikely that our subjects' causal judgements
were based on their performance rather than the other way round. For this
account to work, it must be the case that the performance of subjects in
the judgement group was sensitive to the causal relation in a way that
paralleled the performance profile of those who worked under an explicit
pay-off structure. But this was not so. In the judgement group, in fact,
the subjects pressed at comparable rates in the conditions that produced
the highest and lowest judgements: when $P(O/-A)$ was 0.125 per second,
the subjects performed at a rate of 26 presses per minute in the presence
of a causal association ($P(O/A) = 0.875$) and only slightly less, 23 presses
per minute, in the absence of any association ($P(O/A) = 0.125$) (see also
Chatlosh *et al.* 1985). Thus these subjects, at least, could not have based
their judgements upon differential performance.

In conclusion, we find that the concordance between causal judgement
and performance provides sufficient justification for regarding human
instrumental action as a behavioural marker of causal belief. The question
that we now wish to consider is whether or not there are grounds for
extending this claim to animal action.

INSTRUMENTAL REPRESENTATIONS IN ANIMALS

The intentional account of action maintains that instrumental performance is based upon a representation of the relation between action and outcome, specifically a belief about the causal association between these events. Consequently, there is little point in considering this account as a candidate for animal action unless we can show that such actions are in fact based upon some representation of the action–outcome relation, rather than being just simple stimulus–response habits reinforced by the outcome.

The most compelling evidence for the role of action–outcome representation in the control of animal action comes from studies of outcome devaluation. Adams and Dickinson (1981) trained hungry rats to press a lever using two types of food pellets with different flavours; one, the positive outcome, was delivered immediately following a lever press with a probability of approximately 0.10 (positive contingency), whereas to receive the negative outcome the animals had to refrain from pressing for a short period (10 seconds) (negative contingency). Each outcome was presented equally frequently; what differed was its causal relation to the act of pressing the lever.

In the second stage, one of the outcomes was devalued. The devaluation procedure capitalized on the fact that if consumption of a flavoured food is followed by gastric illness (induced in the present case by an injection of a mild toxin), animals develop an aversion to the food. Thus, immediately after instrumental training, an aversion was established to the positive outcome for one group and to the negative outcome for a second group. It is important to note that the lever was not present during this aversion conditioning and that food pellets were presented to the animals independently of any instrumental behaviour.

The question at issue is to what extent this devaluation treatment affected the propensity of the animals to press when the lever was once again made available in a final test stage. The predictions of intentional theory are clear. During instrumental training, the animals should have learned that there was a positive causal relation between lever pressing and the positive food pellets (and possibly even that there was a negative relation in the case of the negative pellets). Performance would then be determined by the interaction between these beliefs and the relative desirability of the two outcomes. To the extent that the devaluation treatment attenuated the relative desirability of the positive outcome, subsequent lever pressing should have been reduced. Thus the rats with the aversion conditioned to the positive outcome should have been the least inclined to press the lever in the final test.

In contrast, if lever pressing was no more that a simple habit, the devaluation treatment should have been without effect; if the presentations of the positive pellets had done no more during instrumental training than to strengthen or reinforce the tendency to press the lever, a subsequent change in their reinforcing property should not have affected the strength of this tendency. Of course, if the pellets were presented contingent upon the instrumental action during the test, devalued pellets would not act as a reinforcer and might even punish pressing. For this reason Adams and Dickinson conducted the test of instrumental performance after the devaluation treatment in the absence of any outcomes.

The results of this test unequivocally favour the intentional account in that animals for whom the positive outcome had been devalued pressed less than those who received equivalent devaluation of the negative outcome. So far, no explanation of this devaluation effect has been offered that does not appeal to control of the action by some form of representation of the action–outcome relation experienced during instrumental training. What remains at issue, however, is the feature of the relation encoded by this representation.

While dismissing stimulus–response habit theory (but see Dickinson 1985, 1989), one may still wish to argue that what is encoded by the instrumental representation is that the outcome 'follows' the action — in other words the temporal contiguity between the two events, rather than the causal relationship. It is true that instrumental learning by rats is sensitive to temporal contiguity (Dickinson *et al.* 1992), as are human performance and causal judgements. Thus a further prerequisite for an intentional account of animal action should be its sensitivity to the *causal* rather than just to the *contiguous* relation between action and outcome.

In our discussion of the concordance between human causal judgements and performance, we pointed out that instrumental causality could be manipulated, while keeping action–outcome contiguity constant, by varying the likelihood of non-contiguous outcomes. A fixed probability $P(O/A)$ of a contiguous outcome ensures that the likelihood of an outcome immediately following an action remains constant, while the strength of the causal relation can be manipulated by altering the probability $P(O/-A)$ of an outcome in the absence of an action. Raising $P(O/-A)$ reduces the strength of the causal association until when $P(A/O) = P(O/-A)$ performance of the action has no effect on the likelihood of the outcome for just as many outcomes are received whether or not the agent acts.

In a seminal experiment, Hammond (1980) trained thirsty rats to press a lever for water before investigating the effect of varying the action–outcome relation on performance, just as we subsequently did in the case of human performance (Chatlosh *et al.* 1985; Shanks and Dickinson 1991). Figure 1.3 displays the rate of lever pressing by Hammond's rats on their final session of training under the various contingencies. With $P(O/A)$ set at 0.12, performance declined systematically with increments in $P(O/-A)$,

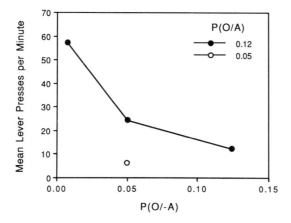

Fig. 1.3. Mean rate of lever pressing by rats in the Hammond (1980) study as a function of the probability $P(O/-A)$ of non-contiguous outcome. These data points represent the performance on the last session of each condition and were estimated graphically from the figures published by Hammond (1980).

indicating that animal performance is sensitive to the strength of the causal relation between the frequencies of the action and the outcome.

CAUSAL ILLUSIONS IN ANIMAL ACTION AND HUMAN JUDGEMENT

So far we have established two points about animal instrumental action (in the case of the rat's lever press): (1) it is mediated by some form of representation of action–outcome relation; (2) performance of the action is sensitive to the causal association between the frequencies of these events. Given these prerequisites for an intentional account, we now wish to examine the prime prediction of intentional theory within the context of animal action.

In evaluating the intentional account of human action, we focused on the concordance between causal judgements or beliefs and instrumental performance predicted by the thesis that such beliefs mediate action. Moreover, we attached particular importance to causal illusions as evidence for such mediation on the grounds that, although independent cognitive and behavioural processes may have developed comparable sensitivity to valid parameters of action–outcome causality, there is no reason to expect them to yield the same illusions. We shall now apply the same strategy to the evaluation of an intentional account of animal action but, of necessity, in this case we focus on the concordance between animal action and human judgement. In fact, Hammond (1980) presented evidence relevant to the causal illusion that we discussed in the human case. Recall that both human performance and judgements under non-contingent schedules are affected by overall outcome frequency, with higher frequencies producing greater levels of performance and more positive causal judgement in the absence of any causal association. Hammond (1980) reported the same illusion for his rats; as Fig. 1.3 shows, his animals tended to press the lever more under a non-contingent schedule when the probability of a water presentation was 0.12 rather than 0.05 per second.

A more compelling parallel arises from the study of the effects of signalling non-contiguous outcomes on non-contingent schedules. However, in order to understand the rationale for this manipulation we shall have to consider briefly theories of the sensitivity of causal judgements to non-contiguous outcomes (Shanks 1993). According to rule-based accounts, agents are assumed to estimate the frequency of both co-occurrences of the putative causal event and the outcome, and non-contiguous outcomes during their interaction with, or observation of, a causal process. To arrive at a judgement, these frequencies are then compared by some rule which ensures that, as the probability of non-contiguous outcomes increases, judgements decrease.

In applying this rule, a question arises concerning when a particular non-contiguous outcome should contribute to the estimate of the relevant frequency. For example, in trying to assess the causal relationship between operating a particular switch and the onset of a light, spontaneous illuminations that occur without the operation of the switch should clearly contribute to the estimate. However, if a second switch is present, illuminations preceded by its operation should not contribute to the estimate. In this latter case, both switches could be causally effective. Given the problem of identifying the relevant non-contiguous outcomes, Cheng and Novick (1991, 1992) introduced the notion of a 'focal set' of events, i.e. the set of events that are relevant to evaluating the effectiveness of a target cause. The basic idea here is that outcomes that are not contiguous with the putative cause should be included in the focal set only if (1) they are identical with those that are paired with the putative cause, and (2) they occur in exactly the same context except for the absence of this target cause.

This 'focal set' account predicts that we should be able to induce an illusion of instrumental causal control by manipulating the context of non-contiguous outcomes. This prediction can be illustrated by reconsidering our simple instrumental task. (Shanks and Dickinson, 1991). Recall that in this task subjects were required to judge the causal effectiveness of an action (pressing the space bar on a microcomputer keyboard) in producing an outcome, (the flash of an outline figure on the computer monitor). As Fig. 1.2(a) shows non-contingent schedules, in which the probabilities $P(O/A)$ and $P(O/-A)$ of contiguous and non-contiguous outcomes are equal, yield low and therefore appropriate judgements. As the non-contiguous outcomes in this study were the same as those paired with the action and occurred in the same context, they should have entered into the 'focal set' and thus through application of a contingency rule served to reduce judgements.

However, if these non-contiguous outcomes could be removed from the 'focal set' in some way without in fact bringing about a causal relation between action and outcome, it should be possible to induce the illusion of causal control. Shanks (1989) attempted to do this by signalling the occurrence of each non-contiguous outcome. In each condition of this study pressing the space bar produced an immediate contiguous outcome with a probability of 0.50. What varied across conditions was the probability of non-contiguous outcomes; in the contingent condition (Con) the outcome never occurred in the absence of an immediately preceding press, whereas in the non-contingent condition (Non) the outcome was just as likely to occur in the absence as in the presence of a press. As Fig. 1.4(a) shows, this study replicated the basic effect of non-contiguous outcomes on causal judgement in that the contingent condition consistently yielded higher judgements of causal control by the action than did the non-contingent condition.

The novel feature of this study was the inclusion of a third non-contingent signal condition (Sig) in which each presentation of the outcome, in the absence of a press, was preceded by and therefore signalled by a brief auditory stimulus. This signal should have marked these outcomes as different from those associated with pressing and thus removed them from the 'focal set', which in turn should have have elevated the subjects' causal judgements. A comparison of the mean judgements for the signal and non-contingent conditions in Fig. 1.4(a) reveals that just such an elevation occurred in the study by Shanks (1989).

For the present purposes, the significance of this signalling effect does not lie with the credence that it gives to rule-based, 'focal set' accounts of causality judgements. In fact, the effect is also predicted by the alternative class of accounts (which, incidentally, we have favoured (Shanks and Dickinson, 1987, 1988)) that appeals to the process of selective attribution embodied in associative learning processes. Rather, its importance, for our comparative analysis, is that it represents another example of a causal illusion against which we can assess the concordance between judgement and instrumental performance. The fact is that the subjects have no more control over the occurrence of the outcome in the signalling condition than under the simple non-contingent schedule; in both cases whether or not the subject presses the space bar has no effect on outcome frequency.

Dickinson and Charnock (1985) (see also Hammond and Weinberg 1984)

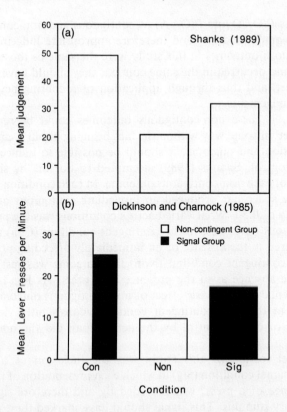

Fig. 1.4. (a) Mean causal judgements in the study by Shanks (1989) and (b) mean rate of lever pressing by rats on the last session of each condition in the study by Dickinson and Charnock (1985) for the contingent (Con), non-contingent (Non), and signalling (Sig) conditions.

sought to determine whether rats are subject to the same causal illusion. Initially thirsty animals were trained to press a lever under a schedule in which the probability of an outcome (a sugar solution) after each press was 0.05. This contingent condition (Con) sustained a high rate of lever pressing (Fig. 1.4(b)). Thereafter, half the animals were switched to a non-contingent condition (Non) in which the outcome occurred with the same probability in the absence of a preceding press. As would be expected, the change of schedule produced a profound reduction in performance. The remaining animals in the signalling condition (Sig) were also switched to the non-contingent schedule, but in this case each non-contiguous outcome was signalled by a short stimulus. As in the case of human causality judgements, this signalling operation attenuated the decremental effect of the non-contingent schedule. Although some reduction from the contingent baseline level of performance was observed, it was not as profound as in the non-continuant condition.

The similarity of the relative profiles across the contingent, non-contingent, and signalling conditions in Fig. 4 suggests that similar psychological processes underlie human causality judgements and simple instrumental performance by rats. The occurrence of the signalling effect in both measures is particularly compelling, for this causal illusion is predicted by specific theories of the processes mediating the acquisition of causal beliefs. Unless one is willing to argue for the operation of functionally similar but psychologically distinct processes in the two cases, the most straightforward account of the judgement–performance concordance is to assume that both animal instrumental action and human causality judgements are the product of similar representations of the causal relation between action and outcome. For this reason we should argue that goal-directed instrumental action is a behavioural index of causal cognition.

CAUSAL REPRESENTATIONS

Our analysis so far has had little to say about the nature of the content of the causal knowledge underlying instrumental action. By appealing to an intentional account, we have assumed, at least implicitly, that this knowledge takes a representational form in which some general causal predicate relates an action A to an outcome O in a way that rationalizes the process of practical inference (Heyes and Dickinson 1990). Such a representational form is appropriate for what Premack (1995) has referred to as 'arbitrary' causal relations, i.e. relations that are presented to the agent in a form that manifests no evidence about the specific generative processes that instantiate the causal association. In the absence of generative evidence, any two arbitrarily selected events can be placed, at least in principle, within a causal relation. Clearly, the causal relations that we have considered so far fall within this category; in our studies of causality judgement we deliberately selected a task which presented the subjects with little or no evidence about the nature of the underlying generative process by which a key press actually produced the flash on the computer monitor in an attempt to match the arbitrary nature of the relation to that which we assume holds between lever pressing and food presentation in studies of instrumental conditioning in animals.

Premack (1994) (see also Premack 1976) contrasts such arbitrary relations with what he calls 'natural causality' which concerns a particular generative relationship between a special highly restricted set of events. The example he cites of natural causality is that of the mechanical interaction manifest in the collision of a moving and a stationary object, followed by the subsequent movement of the initially static object. Although the analysis of the relation between arbitrary and natural causation has had a long and involved philosophical history, ever since Hume (1739) argued for the primacy of the arbitrary, our concern here is whether fundamentally different psychological processes are involved in the representation of the two classes of causation. To the extent that they are, we must restrict our claims about the status of goal-directed instrumental action as a marker of causal cognition to the arbitrary case.

On the basis of his classic studies of the launching effect, Michotte (1963) argued for the psychological differentiation between arbitrary and natural causation. When presented with an illusory collision between a moving and a stationary visual stimulus, subsequent, contiguous rectilinear motion of the initially stationary stimulus produces an immediate phenomenological impression that the collision caused this motion. One reason, Premack (1995) argues, for believing that representations of natural causation differ from arbitrary causal beliefs is that their manifestations, such as the launching effect, occur at full strength on a single episode, whereas representations of arbitrary relations are assumed to be based on multiple samples of the causal process.

Although we may have reason to doubt that this factor is critical—Skinner (1938) demonstrated that hungry rats are sensitive to a single pairing of a lever press and food—judgement of 'natural' and 'arbitrary' causality can be dissociated within the context of Michotte displays. Recently, Schlottmann and Shanks (1992) examined the effect by varying both the contiguity and contingency between the putative cause C (the collision of the two visual stimuli) and the outcome O (the motion of the initially stationary stimulus). Contiguity was manipulated by varying the time between a collision and the motion of the second stimulus, whereas the effect of contingency was studied by interspersing trials on which a collision occurred with trials on which the first stimulus remained stationary, thereby precluding a collision. In the contingent condition the second stimulus also remained stationary in the absence of a collision so that the effect (movement of the initially stationary stimulus) never occurred without the putative cause (a collision), i.e. $P(O/\text{-}C) = 0$. In contrast, in the non-contingent condition the second stimulus moved on trials both with and without a collision, i.e. $P(O/\text{-}C) = 1$. Consequently, in this condition the effect was as likely to happen in the absence of the cause as its presence.

Subjects were required to make two kinds of ratings. Following selected collisions, they were asked to rate their perception of the relation between cause and effect on that specific episode using instructions that emphasized the natural causal relation. The instructions for the other rating, the causal judgement, encouraged subjects to treat the cause–effect relation as

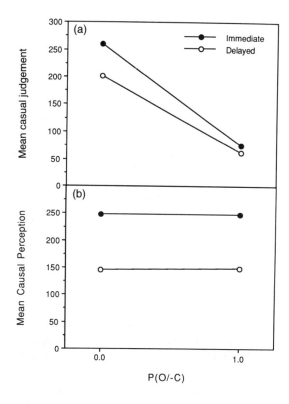

Fig. 1.5. (a) Mean causal judgement and (b) mean causal perception as a function of the probability $P(O/\text{-}C)$ of the outcome (O) in the absence of the putative cause (C) in the study by Schlottmann and Shanks (1992).

arbitrary, and to base their judgements on the events occurring across a series of trials. As Fig. 1.5 shows, variations in both contiguity between the putative cause and effect and contingency dissociated these two forms of ratings. Whereas the causal perceptions were unaffected by contingency (Fig. 1.5(b)), this variable had a profound influence on causal judgements (Fig. 1.5(a)). The reverse pattern was seen across variations in contiguity: delaying the effect greatly attenuated causal perception, but had only a moderate influence on judgement and then only in the contingent condition.

Clearly, given this double dissociation, it would be difficult to maintain that 'natural' causal perceptions and 'arbitrary' causal judgements are mediated by a common representation. This is most clearly illustrated by the immediate non-contingent condition ($P(O/\text{-}C) = 1.0$); the subjects perceived a strong causal influence on these episodes while at the same time believing that they were not the product of an enduring causal relation. To the extent that this dissociation can be generalized to other examples of natural causality (Shultz 1982), we cannot assume that capacity for goal-directed instrumental action speaks to the question of whether the agent can represent natural generative causal relationships, and we do not wish to claim this cognitive ability for the 'humble' rat.*

Given this caveat, a sceptic may claim that our rationale does no more than equate the capacity for causal representation with that for associative learning. The answer to this charge is not simple, and depends upon appreciating the fact that representations cannot be characterized independently of the processes that operate upon them (Anderson 1978). This point can be illustrated by considering the prototypical example of predictive learning in the animal conditioning laboratory — Pavlovian conditioning. Recall that Pavlov (1927) signalled the presentation of food to his hungry dogs by a neutral stimulus such as a tone or light. Across a series of such pairings, the dogs started to salivate to the signal in anticipation of the food. Pavlov explained this form of learning by assuming that the pairings of the signal and food formed an association or connection from the brain centre activated by the signal to that excited by the food. As a result, presentations of the signal could now indirectly activate the food centre, thus producing salivation. In one form or another, this associative or connectionist account of Pavlovian conditioning has stood the test of time (Dickinson 1980).

The question at issue, however, is whether or not we should regard such a Pavlovian associative connection as functioning as a cognitive representation of the predictive relation between signal and food in the production of the conditioned response of salivation. Our answer is that we should not. In order for the associative connection to function as a predictive representation, the processes operating on it to control behaviour would in one way or another have to deploy and respect the representational relation between the connection and the actual signal–food association in the world. Thus, if the connection was deployed by a process that implemented an inference that rationalized the resulting behaviour with respect to a predictive content of the connection, we should argue that this connection acts as a representation of the predictive relation for the agent. Clearly, this is not the case in the Pavlovian explanation outlined above; according to this theory the light or tone does not act as a *predictive* signal for the food in the production of the conditioned response, but rather, in Pavlov's words, as a 'surrogate' or 'substitute' for the food; all the connection does is to extend the range of stimuli that can elicit salivation.

---

* This is not to say that non-human animals are incapable of representing natural causality. Premack (1976) has presented compelling evidence that chimpanzees can comprehend certain forms of natural causality.

Unfortunately, this analysis does not allow any firm conclusion about the representational status of an associative connection in the case of instrumental action. A number of authors (Colwill and Rescorla 1986) have argued that goal-directed instrumental action is mediated by the formation of a connection between a psychological element (or a pattern of activation across elements) activated by the performance of the action and one excited by the presentation of the outcome. Indeed, we ourselves have argued that human judgement of arbitrary causality is also governed by associative principles (Shanks and Dickinson 1987; Shanks 1993). The problem with determining the representational status of such an associative connection, however, is that as yet no one has offered a satisfactory mechanism to explain the production of the instrumental action itself (Dickinson 1989; Dickinson and Balleine, 1993). If such a mechanism effectively implemented the practical inference process specified by intentional theory, as we suspect must be the case, then we should be fully justified in regarding the action–outcome association as a representation of the causal relationship between these events. To the extent that this mechanism conforms to the rationality of practical inference, it must treat the action–outcome association, at least implicitly, as possessing causal content.

Thus the nature of the mental vehicle that carries relational learning, such as an associative connection, is not the critical determinant of its cognitive status, and indeed it may well be similar for cognitively mediated behaviour and simple conditioned reactions. What endows a particular vehicle with representational power is its function within the machinery of the mind. Adherence to an associative theory of instrumental learning does not, of necessity, vitiate the cognitive basis of actions mediated by such learning.

In conclusion, we argue that the converging evidence from the concordance between the determinants of human causality judgement and animal performance indicates that the capacity for goal-directed instrumental action is the most basic behavioural marker of causal cognition. Just as Piaget (1954) argued that the ontological foundations of causal cognition lies in action, so, we should argue, does the phylogenetic origin. It was the enhanced fitness, endowed by the capacity to control rather than just react to the environment, that provided the genetic impetus for the evolution of a mind and nervous system capable of representing causality.

ACKNOWLEDGMENTS

The work reported in this paper was supported by grants from the Science and Engineering Research Council (SERC) to A. Dickinson and by the Medical Research Council (MRC). We should like to thank R. A Boakes for his comments on a draft of this paper.

REFERENCES

Adams, C. D. and Dickinson, A. (1981). Instrumental responding following reinforcer devaluation. *Quarterly Journal of Experimental Psychology* **33B**, 109–22.

Alloy, L. B. and Abramson, L. Y. (1979). Judgement of contingency in depressed and nondepressed students: sadder but wiser? *Journal of Experimental Psychology: General* **108**, 441–85.

Anderson, J. R. (1978). Arguments concerning representations of visual images. *Psychological Review* **85**, 249–77.

Berry, D. C. and Broadbent, D. E. (1984). On the relationship between task performance and associated verbalizable knowledge. *Quarterly Journal of Experimental Psychology* **36A**, 209–31.

Brewer, W. F. (1974). There is no convincing evidence for operant or classical conditioning in adult humans. In *Cognition and the symbolic processes* (ed. W. B. Weimer and D. S. Palermo), pp. 1–42. Erlbaum, Hillsdale, NJ.

Chatlosh, D. L., Neunaber, D. J., and Wasserman, E. A. (1985). Response-outcome contingency: behavioral and judgmental effects of appetitive and aversive outcomes with college students. *Learning and Motivation* **16**, 1–34.

Cheng, P. W. and Novick, L. R. (1991). Causes versus enabling conditions. *Cognition* **40**, 83–120.

Cheng, P. W. and Novick, L. R. (1992). Covariation in natural causal induction. *Psychological Review* **99**, 365–82.

Colwill, R. C. and Rescorla, R. A. (1986). Associative structures underlying instrumental learning. In *The psychology of learning and motivation* (ed. G. H. Bower), Vol. 20, pp. 55–104. Academic Press, New York.

Dickinson, A. (1980). *Comtemporary animal learning theory*. Cambridge University Press.

Dickinson, A. (1985). Actions and habits: the development of behavioural autonomy. *Philosophical Transactions of the Royal Society of London Series B* **308**, 67–78. In *Animal intelligence* (ed. L. Weiskrantz), pp. 67–78. Clarendon Press, Oxford.

Dickinson, A. (1989). Expectancy theory in animal conditioning. In *Contemporary learning theories: Pavlovian conditioning and the status of traditional learning theory* (ed. S. B. Klein and R, R. Mowrer), pp. 279–308. Hillsdale, NJ.

Dickinson, A. and Balleine, B. (1993). Actions and responses: the dual psychology of behaviour. In *Problems in the philosophy and psychology of spatial representation* (ed. N. Eilan, R. A. McCarthy, and M. W. Brewer), pp. 277–93. Blackwell, Oxford.

Dickinson, A. and Charnock, D. J. (1985). Contingency effects with maintained instrumental reinforcement. *Quarterly Journal of Experimental Psychology* **37B**, 397–416.

Dickinson, A., Shanks, D. R. and Evenden, J. L. (1984). Judgement of act-outcome contingency: the role of selective attribution. *Quarterly Journal of Experimental Psychology* **36A**, 29–50.

Dickinson, A., Watt, A. and Griffiths, W. J. H. (1992). Free-operant acquisition with delayed reinforcement. *Quarterly Journal of Experimental Psychology* **45B**, 241–58.

Hammond, L. J. (1980). The effect of contingency upon appetitive conditioning of free-operant behavior. *Journal of the Experimental Analysis of Behavior* **34**, 297–304.

Hammond, L. J. and Weinberg, M. (1984). Signaling unearned reinforcers removes the suppression produced by a zero correlation in an operant paradigm. *Animal Learning and Behavior* **12**, 371-7.

Hershberger, W. A. (1986). An approach through the looking glass. *Animal Learning and Behavior* **14**, 443-51.

Heyes, C. and Dickinson, A. (1990). The intentionally of animal action. *Mind and Language* **5**, 87-104.

Hume, D. [1739] (1978). *A treatise on human nature* (ed. L. A. Selby-Brigge) (2nd edn revised by P. H. Nidditch). Clarendon Press, Oxford.

Michotte, A. (1963). *The perception of causality*. Methuen, London.

Pavlov, I. P. (1927). *Conditioned reflexes*. Oxford University Press.

Piaget, J. (1954). *The construction of reality in the child*. Basic Books, New York.

Premack, D. (1976). *Intelligence in ape and man*. Erlbaum, Hillsdale, NJ.

Premack, D. (1995). Cause/induced motion : intention/spontaneous motion. In *The origins of the human brain* (ed. J. P. Changeux and J. Chavaillon), Chapter 18. Clarendon Press, Oxford.

Schlottmann, A. and Shanks, D. R. (1992). Evidence for a distinction between judged and perceived causality. *Quarterly Journal of Experimental Psychology* **44A**, 321-42.

Shanks, D. R. (1987). Acquisition functions in causality judgement. *Learning and Motivation* **18**, 147-66.

Shanks, D. R. (1989). Selectional processes in causality judgment. *Memory and Cognition* **17**, 27-34.

Shanks, D. R. (1993). Human instrumental learning: a critical review of data and theory. *British Journal of Psychology* **84**, 319-54.

Shanks, D. R. and Dickinson, A. (1987). Associative accounts of causality judgment. In *The psychology of learning and motivation* (ed. G. H. Bower), Vol. 21, pp. 229-61. Academic Press, New York.

Shanks, D. R. and Dickinson, A. (1988). The role of selective attribution in causality judgment. In *Contemporary science and natural explanation* (ed. D. J. Hilton), pp. 95-126. Harvester Press, Brighton.

Shanks, D. R. and Dickinson, A. (1991). Instrumental judgment and performance under variations in action–outcome contingency and contiguity. *Memory and Cognition* **19**, 353-60.

Shanks, D. R., Pearson, S. M. and Dickinson, A. (1989). Temporal contiguity and the judgment of causality by human subjects. *Quarterly Journal of Experimental Psychology* **41B**, 139-59.

Shanks, D. R., Green, R. E. A. and Kolodny, J. (1994). A critical examination of the evidence for unconscious (implicit) learning. In *Attention and performance XV: conscious and nonconscious information processing*. (ed. C. Umilta and M. Moscovitch), pp. 837-60. MIT Press, Cambridge, MA.

Shultz, R. R. (1982). *Rules of causal attribution*. Monograph 47 (1, serial no. 194), Society for Research in Child Development.

Skinner, B. F. (1938). *The behavior of organisms*. Appleton-Century-Crofts, New York.

Svardtal, F. (1991). Operant modulation of low-level attributes of rule-governed behavior by nonverbal contingencies. *Learning and Motivation* **22**, 406-20.

Wasserman, E. A., Chatlosh, D. L. and Neunaber, D. J. (1983). Perception of causal relations in humans: factors affecting judgments of response–outcome contingencies under free-operant procedures. *Learning and Motivation* **14**, 406-32.

2

Causal knowledge in animals
HANS KUMMER

INTRODUCTION

An evolutionary perspective of causality rests on the assumption that the causal connection is not a 'real' thing but an 'interpretation'. True conceptual interpretation may be a human specialty. Evolution, having begun with brainless micro-organisms, could not start at that level, but in its course designed alternatives with similar functions. The genetic programme for associative learning treats two contiguous events as 'causally connected', a useful concept to consider in the environments of most species of animals. However, beyond this universal interpretive program, we must expect to find causal interpretations specific to special environments and modes of life, for example knowledge akin to hydrodynamics in jet swimmers, hydroballistics in archer fish, and solid body mechanics in digger wasps. The 'object impulse' causality found by Leslie and Keeble (1987) in human infants may be a specialty of tool-using species (or merely the first-choice hypothesis of a researcher of that species). Trees and conspecifics do not usually bump into one another, and so launching may not be a relevant form of causality in species other than the human.

Causal knowledge is one way to influence certain parts of one's environment through prediction and action. While all animal species exert some control by using their knowledge of interdependent events, only humans are known to have explicit causal reasoning. It is hardly necessary to mention that animal detectors of what humans call causality are for the most part not precursors of our causal perceptions and concepts, but original solutions of their own design. We cannot assume a priori that any of them involve anything akin to our causal understanding (but see Chapter 1), nor that human reasoning is necessarily more correct than its animal analogues; for example many animals relate intestinal illness to the ingestion of a novel food, but in no known case to the magic action of a conspecific. Nevertheless, for simplicity we shall apply the term 'causal knowledge' to all the above cases.

Knowledge about connections of events appears in two forms which behave differently in the course of phylogeny, but on closer inspection they may simply be extreme forms on a continuum.

Weak causal knowledge ('arbitrary' *sensu* Premack (1995)) is the result of associative learning: event x is frequently followed by event y. Since no pre-existing knowledge tells the animal which events are likely to follow others, the animal requires many repetitions before it can extract the reliable connections from the multitude of actual stimuli. The content of weak knowledge is merely: 'If two events often occur in virtual synchrony they will do so again'. One-trial associative learning is possible (Mahoney and Ayres 1976) in conditioning chambers where the events to be linked by conditioning are probably the only events that can occur. Only tests executed under a natural density of irrelevant events could tell us whether the animal indeed has a true predilection for associating the two particular events tested in the chambers.

Weak causal knowledge apparently occurs in all species including our own and permits the connection of any two events in temporal order as long as both are perceived or performed in the same motivational state. It is most likely to occur if the two events are closely contiguous. The fact that *contiguity* is the dominant cue for causality in so many species requires an explanation. First, it may reflect the fact that contiguous events are more often correlated than are more distant events in the world for most organisms; what is heard, seen, and felt are aspects of the same movement of another body, or the immediate effects of the movement of one's own body. This seems particularly true of the inanimate world, where the energy encased in a stimulus disperses across space and fades across time; it seems less generally true for the animate environment where causes such as insemination, parasitic infection, or death can produce major later effects within a group. Second, contiguity is a major cue of weak cause detectors because, without stronger knowledge concerning what events can or cannot have been the cause of a particular event, the number of candidate environmental events that occurred (even in the preceding five minutes before the effect) is too large to be analysed from an acceptable number of repetitions.

Even the most important causal connections cannot be discovered with weak knowledge if the effect is delayed, such as is the case of birth following a mating or illness following the eating of a certain food.

Strong causal knowledge ('natural' *sensu* Premack (1995)), in contrast, does not depend on close contiguity and a large number of repetitions. Its base is an a priori 'interpretation' of certain specific events, based on specific programs: the animal 'knows' that a causal connection between these two events is highly probable. The inclination to form these particular connections is so strong that some are formed even when the two events are widely separated in space and/or time.

Strong causal knowledge predicts event B from event A, but not vice versa, as suggested by the reversals in the study of Leslie and Keeble (1987), and perhaps it never 'retrodicts', since a *post hoc* inference to a past cause is not useful for an organism unable to form a theory. Strong causal knowledge can be encoded in a hard-wired gene-supported program and can be unconscious. Its most elementary form is the unconditioned reflex. The eye-blinking reflex 'expects' a high probability of an impact to the eye from a passing visual stimulus. The innate releasing mechanisms found by ethologists in insects, fish, and birds 'tell' the animal to address, say, courtship to a conspecific wearing the right external marks. These mechanisms detect the animate object that will respond profitably to the subject's action, and they detect causation along with other kinds of correlation, without giving it any special treatment. Most such contents of strong knowledge are specific to a species and are particularly adaptive in certain domains of its environment. If learned, one (or a few) repetitions are sufficient.

Genetic programs are generally shaped by selection to support the particular professional skills of each species in its habitat, and we can expect that causality programs are no exception. The selective response of human infants to an object that launches another (by hitting it) may be partly learned, but is probably supported by a program encoding strong causal knowledge specific to our species. A theory of impulse mechanics is also strong causal knowledge. Despite its different origin, it does for humans what gene-supported programs do for humans and animals, indicating the types of events among which causal relationships are highly probable.

We prefer the labels 'weak' and 'strong' knowledge to Premack's 'arbitrary' versus 'natural' because association learning is as much based on a natural genetic learning program that reflects causal connections in the natural environment as are mechanisms that detect the connections between temporally distant events. The difference is that the latter are far more selective about candidate events for the specific type of connection that they are designed to detect, whereas the former accept a large number of seemingly arbitrary pairs of events. (One constraint on this arbitrariness has been reported by Sevenster (1973) from stickleback fish. A male fighting response cannot be reinforced by the presentation of a ripe female; response and reward must be motivationally compatible.)

LONG INTERVALS BETWEEN RECURRENT EVENTS

Weak causal knowledge fails to detect causal connections among events more than an instant apart. A partial solution that has evolved to overcome this insufficiency is the circadian rhythm, an internal pacemaker that shapes the hormonal and physical activity of the organism in a periodicity of roughly 24 hours. The pacemakers, typically located in parts of the optical system that vary across taxa, are found from unicellular organisms to mammals, and are kept in phase with the actual day cycle by external *Zeitgebers*. The location of specific external events on the cycle is the probable mechanism, in many species, for predicting the time of most profitable foraging. It informs the individual when to return to a particular food location. For example, nectarivorous birds make circuits between flowers at a rate which allows for the replenishment of nectar, and shorebirds correctly predict local low tides that expose their major food source, arriving early when winds delay the time of the tide and late when they advance it. Beyond the daily cycle, brent geese return to the same sward at intervals of 4–5 days, which is the interval after which regrowth has produced optimum protein content and digestibility (Drent 1982). Knowledge about periodicity of external events lies between weak and strong knowledge.

LONG INTERVALS BETWEEN DIVERSE EVENTS: PATERNITY

Genetic programs can do more than just measure the duration of an external process not directly monitored by the animal; some programs, encoding strong knowledge, can connect an outcome with a specific past action even though no contiguity or similarity exists between them. Two examples follow.

With the phylogenetic advent of internal insemination, a male animal loses direct monitoring of his paternity. In species where he shares the same female with competing males, he cannot easily know whether any of the female's offspring are also his own. Yet, such knowledge importantly affects whether or not he will benefit his own fitness by helping to raise the offspring. Selection must be expected to promote any form of causal knowledge connecting matings with the appearance of young. Western humans may or may not solve the problem by causal reasoning, nowadays by applying DNA fingerprinting, but animals use what behavioural ecologists call 'decision rules'.

The Dunnock (*Prunella modularis*) is a species of small brown bird with a variable mating system. In the polyandrous variety, two males occupy the same territory with one female and compete for her. Davies *et al.* (1992) have identified the rules which govern the amount of food a male provides to the young in the common nest. Males are unable to recognize their own offspring among the nestlings (if they feed at all, they feed all nestlings); instead they use indirect cues. Their first rule: feed the brood if you have mated with the female during her egg-laying period, i.e. between the time you saw the first egg in the nest to the time that the female begins to brood; disregard matings before and after that period. Their second rule: if another male is in the territory, adjust your proportion of feeding to the percentage of time that you spent alone with the female (of the total of such exclusive access time enjoyed by you and the other male). DNA fingerprinting has shown that these rules are good predictors of paternity. The rules are not optimal, however, since a male gives equal value to the last day of the egg-laying period, even though it is less productive. Furthermore, a male can be cheated in his reckoning by an artificial egg placed in the nest prematurely.

Another male program for assessing paternity was discovered by Perrigo *et al.* (1990) in house mice. When a male mouse encounters a neonate in his territory, he normally kills it, but he abruptly switches to infant care during the period when the neonate might be his offspring. Here, the 'decision rule' is: switch from kill to care 18–22 light–dark cycles after you have mated and ejaculated. This rule is followed regardless of the female with which the male has mated, whether the mated (or any) female is with the male during this period, or whether or not the neonates are his offspring. When experimenters change the natural light cycle to artifical day lengths of 22 or 27 hours, the males still 'count' the cycles, not the actual time; once again, males applying the rule can be cheated.

Analogous causal reasoning by a human male would read as follows. Here is an infant. Some male must have fathered it about 265 days ago. I did not mate then. Therefore the infant is not my child and must not be housed in my territory. But whether the mouse represents the two connected events, whether he even remembers his copulation in some other context, is not known.

There is, at present, only one interpretation of these findings: an evolved program directs the coupling between two very specific events among the thousands of others, even though they are not contiguous in space or time. The animal has a correct 'prejudice' in a very literal sense. Few examples of such strong causal knowledge have as yet been discovered, but the general principle of adaptive genetic programs is well known.

In both examples, a more efficient program would simply enable males to *discriminate* their genetic offspring from others. Some insects and mammals can indeed recognize close kin, probably by genetic odour labels (Holmes and Sherman 1982; Page *et al.* 1989). Equipped with such a program, dunnocks could feed only those nestlings they fathered, but evolutionary chance (or constraints) has steered dunnocks and mice to another less efficient program.

Species-specific programs also direct special types of animal *learning* in contexts where the correct coupling of cause and effect is critically

Table 2.1 *Characteristics of weak and strong causal knowledge*

	Weak (artificial)	*Strong (natural)*
Generality across species	Similar learning program in many species	Program highly specific to species
Generality of contents (classes of events)	Program accepts all events perceived in given motivation	Program accepts only highly specific events
Exposures required for learning	Many	Few or none
Contiguity required	Only closely contiguous events accepted	Accepts events widely separated in space and time

important for survival and reproduction — where weak causal knowledge cannot handle the association because the two events are not contiguous and/or because a mistake is too damaging to permit repeated exposures. The coupling of a novel food taste with delayed illness is a well-known example (Garcia *et al.* 1974), as is, possibly, the use of medical plants by chimpanzees in the wild (Huffman 1989).

PHYLETIC DISTRIBUTION OF WEAK AND STRONG CAUSAL KNOWLEDGE

Table 2.1 summarizes the characteristics of weak and strong programs for the detection of causal connections. The weak kind, associative learning, has been found in a large number of animal species ranging from single-cell organisms to mammals, suggesting first that the *immediate* effects of a causal event are common in all environments and can be detected without a centralized nervous system. Weak causal knowledge may well be the most ancient mechanism for causality detection evolved in phylogeny, according to the speculation on p. 27. Relevant connected events are more generally contiguous in the inanimate environment, and primeval organisms presumably had nothing to learn about long-term biological causation.

Strong versions of causal knowledge are poorly known. Zoologists have not specifically searched for them; they looked for genetic programs for adaptive behaviour in general. The programs for imprinting and song-learning in birds, for example, are not detectors of external causality. Here, the causal processes proceed *within* the animal. All they do is ensure that the individual develops appropriate behaviour, picking up external information from the right source at the right time and then addressing the behaviour to the right object at the right time. In sexual imprinting, for example, the form and colour of parents lead adult offspring to select sexual partners of the same appearance. However, this is a long-term response and not the detection of cause.

In the present context, these non-causal programs are useful only because they tell us something about how a program changes by evolution to accommodate a new species and its new environment. A male songbird, for example, has a sensitive period during which it accepts and stores a certain range of song types sung at that time in its environment. This general principle is varied across species primarily in two parameters: the age at which its sensitive period occurs, and the range of songs that it accepts. Depending on these parameters, the nestling of one species learns the song of its father, and the subadult of another species learns the songs of its neighbours in its final range; one species learns only its own dialects, while another may imitate other species. No doubt the dunnock's mode of determining paternity is itself a variant of a more widely distributed program.

The future search for strong causal programs may be guided by asking which causal connections among non-contiguous events are likely to be crucial for a species. Heavy rain preceding a flood, magnetic storms preceding earthquakes, migrations of predators, early signs of numerical development of food organisms or parasites—all are candidates in addition to those mentioned. Long-term food hoarding by animals is a well investigated example, demonstrating precise hippocampal spatial memory of up to 1000 sites in birds (vander Wall 1990), but the connection between cause and effect is qualitatively simple in this case.

Whether strong causal knowledge exists in lower invertebrates may depend on whether sufficiently relevant and precise non-contiguous causal connections occur in their environments.

STRONG CAUSAL KNOWLEDGE IN PRIMATES

Primates have a reputation for lacking specific adaptive behavioural programs. These include strong causal knowledge. One case of paternity recognition in *Macaca nemestrina* was not confirmed (Wu *et al.* 1980). Accordingly, pronounced paternal care is found only in monogamous species. A similar impression comes from field observations of the ability of primates to make retrograde inferences from effect to cause. Carnivores can follow traces by olfaction, but vervet monkeys respond neither to prey carcasses left in trees by leopards nor to the tracks of pythons, even though both leopards and pythons are major vervet predators (Cheney and

Seyfarth 1990). No genetic program or reasoning seems to inform a vervet that these traces indicate the probable proximity of a predator.

Chimpanzees, however, have been observed to investigate abandoned tools and to destroy fresh sleeping nests made by neighbouring groups of conspecifics (Goodall 1986). Here, as well as in technical abilities such as nest construction and tool use, primates, with the exception of chimpanzees (and, in zoos, orang-utans), are remarkably poor performers. The consensus is that the technical abilities of great apes do not stem from detailed behavioural programs such as those of termites and sea otters, but from largely unaided learning and from intelligence. The use of hammer stones (in nut-cracking) among wild chimpanzees is a slow process that does not begin until the age of 5, and reaches top performance only in adulthood (Boesch and Boesch 1984). A strong causal program for the technique would induce a more rapid development.

The causal perception of human infants (Leslie and Keeble 1987), however, is the effect of strong causal knowledge. While there are no comparable studies on lower primates, an observational study triggered by spontaneous tool use in our study group of the long-tailed macaque (*Macaca fascicularis*) gives hints at the very loose programs directing the development and propagation of a launching technique in a primate species that has not been known to use tools in the wild.

Two male macaques, one of them the alpha male, have begun using sticks to rake apples (fallen from a tree outside the wire fence) to within their reach. The development of such tool use was followed closely. In the early months, the males would try to reach the apples by hand. In so doing they grasped herbs, small stones, and sticks, only to release them again. This is no more than 'redirected' behaviour aimed at a substitute. Occasionally, however, they grasped two sticks and rubbed them against each other, or they threw sticks and stones near the apples. Eventually, they used the sticks, worrying an apple chaotically and pushing it away as often as pulling it closer. Their causal rule seemed to be: move things near the apple, and it may approach — a correct but inefficiently general rule in comparison with the findings of Leslie and Keeble (1987) and Brown (1990). That it was necessary to touch the object with the stick, and to give the touch a certain direction, was evident to young children after three successful trials. In the macaques the knowledge emerged only after about 50 sessions of 30 minutes each (Kummer *et al.*, unpublished).

The program that could have promoted onlookers to acquire the technique from the models was equally loose. During the periods when a model poked a stick at an apple, the onlookers picked up sticks and began to chew and break them, making no attempt to direct either their gaze or their sticks at the apple. All they 'learned' from the model was 'handle sticks'. This 'stimulus enhancement' (Galef 1988), which was not extended to stones, may only slightly increase the probability that an onlooker discovers stick use. Studies by Visalberghi and Fragaszy (1990) have shown that even the highly manipulative capuchin monkeys cannot imitate specific tool techniques.

These loose programs may be similar to those that primates possessed when they evolved tool use. Chimpanzees in the wild are observed to use a number of tool techniques, but their number and types vary markedly across populations. This intraspecific diversity of techniques suggests that chimpanzee techniques are not necessarily based on more precise strong genetic programs than those of lower primates.

If not by genetic programs, can non-human primates generate strong causal knowledge by causal reasoning? Chimpanzees familiar with human tools correctly identify the tool that leads from a pre- to a post-state of a target object (Premack and Premack 1988). Premack (1993) also reported an experiment which suggests causal reasoning in pre-school children and juvenile chimpanzees. In one test, the subject could observe that an apple and a banana were placed in two different containers in an enclosure. Then the subject's view was briefly obstructed. Next it saw a trainer appear midway between the containers, eating either an apple or a banana. When released, all children (and some chimpanzees) went to the container holding fruit different from the one eaten by the trainer. The 'smart' subjects obviously reasoned that the fruit eaten by the trainer was the same apple (or banana) originally placed in the containers. The remaining chimpanzees did not reason that the fruit eaten must have been the fruit first placed in the container, and simply went to the container whose fruit matched the fruit eaten by the trainer. In a variant of the test, the fruit eaten could not be the one hidden in the container because the interval between event one (placement of fruit in container) and event two (trainer eating fruit) was too short, i.e. the trainer could not possibly have retrieved the fruit from either container. Four-year-old children were able to take the temporal calculations into account, but the 'successful' chimpanzees behaved as before. This seems to be the only work on causal reasoning in non-human primates.

Primates are considered to be experts in the detection of social causality (Byrne and Whiten 1988). For example, since a threat takes effect over a distance, and since a fight or a reconciliatory grooming bout alters inter-actions of the participants as much as several minutes later (Cords 1992), weak causal knowledge based on contiguity cannot accurately detect such causal connections. Research into strong detectors of social causality in non-human primates has yet to begin (Stammbach 1988; Cheney and Seyfarth 1990). Since such programs are likely to be costly in evolutionary terms, weak knowledge on the basis of contiguity can be expected to be used as an approximative rule of thumb.

The following example shows how long-tailed macaques (*M. fascicularis*) rely on a *weak* cue of spatial contiguity in a social sequence that would require more elaborate stronger detectors: when a juvenile screams, dominant group members attack subordinates preferentially if they happen to be close to the screamer, and even if they did not cause the screaming. In this case, proximity stands for social causation (Kummer and Cords 1991).

SUMMARY

Causal reasoning is only one way of achieving causal knowledge, and may be mostly restricted to our species. In the course of evolution, animals evolved alternatives. Associative learning among contiguous events leads to 'weak causal knowledge'—weak because it is restricted to effects that immediately follow causes, and because it is largely unaided by previous knowledge about what types of events in the environment are likely to be causally connected. In contrast, 'strong' causal knowledge performs the functions of causal reasoning; it is based on evolved programs that encode one class of important events as the probable or certain cause of another class. Its strengths are that it requires little or no repetition, and that it can link events separated in space and time such as mating and the birth of young. Its weaknesses are that such programs have evolved only for pairs of very important and sufficiently frequent events, and that decision rules produced by such programs are often inexact and can be misled by unusual circumstances. Research on such strong programs is incipient, particularly with primates, but so far has not yielded convincing examples except in the human case.

REFERENCES

Boesch, Ch. and Boesch, H. (1984). Possible causes of sex differences in the use of natural hammers by wild chimpanzees. *Journal of Human Evolution* **13**, 415–40.

Brown, A. L. (1990). Domain-specific principles affect learning and transfer in children. *Cognitive Science* **14**, 107–33.

Byrne, R. and Whiten, A. (ed.) (1988). *Machiavellian intelligence. Social expertise and the evolution of intellect in monkeys, apes, and humans*. Clarendon Press, Oxford.

Cheney, D. L. and Seyfarth, R. M. (1990). *How monkeys see the world*. University of Chicago Press.

Cords, M. (1992). Post-conflict reunions and reconciliation in long-tailed macaques. *Animal Behaviour* **44**, 57–61.

Davies, N. B., Hatchwell, B. J., Robson, T., and Burke., T. (1992). Paternity and parental effort in dunnocks *Prunella modularis*: how good are male chick-feeding rules? *Animal Behaviour* **43**, 729–45.

Drent, R. H. (1982). Risk–benefit assessment in animals. In *Animal mind – human mind* (ed. D. R. Griffin). Springer, Berlin.

Galef, B. G. (1988). Imitation in animals: history, definition and interpretation of data from the psychological laboratory. In *Social learning. Psychological and biological perspectives* (ed. T. R. Zentall and B. G. Galef). Erlbaum, Hillsdale, NJ.

Garcia, J., Hankins, W. G., and Rusiniak, K. W. (1974). Behavioral regulation of the milieu interne in man and rat. *Science* **185**, 824–31.

Goodall, J. (1986). *The chimpanzees of Gombe*. Harvard University Press, Cambridge, MA.

Holmes, W. G. and Sherman, P. W. (1982). The ontogeny of kin recognition in two species of ground squirrels. *American Zoologist* **22**, 491–517.

Huffman, M. A. (1989). Observations on the illness and consumption of a possibly medicinal plant *Vermonia amygdalina* in the Mahale Mountains National Park, Tanzania. *Primates* **30**, 51–63.

Kummer, H. and Cords, M. (1991). Cues of ownership in long-tailed macaques, *Macaca fasciularis*. *Animal Behaviour* **42**, 529–49.

Leslie, A. M. and Keeble, S. (1987). Do six month old infants perceive causality? *Cognition* **25**, 266–88.

Mahoney, W. J. and Ayres, J. J. B. (1976). One-trial simultaneous and backward fear conditioning as reflected in conditioned suppression of licking in rats. *Animal Learning and Behavior* **4**, 357–62.

Page, R. W., Robinson, G. E., and Fondrk, M. K. (1989). Genetic specialists, kin recognition and nepotism in honey-bee colonies. *Nature, London* **338**, 576–9.

Perrigo, G., Cully Bryant, W., and von Saal, F. S. (1990). A unique neural timing system prevents male mice from harming their own offspring. *Animal Behaviour* **39**, 535–9.

Premack, D. and Premack, A. J. (1988). *The mind of an ape*. Norton, New York.

Premack, D. (1993). Prolegomenon to evolution of cognition. In *Exploring brain functions: models in neuroscience* (ed. T. A. Poggio and D. A. Glaser). Wiley, New York.

Premack, D. (1995). Cause/induced motion: intention/spontaneous motion. In *The origins of the human brain* (ed. J.-P. Changeux and J. Chavaillon), Chapter 18. Clarendon Press, Oxford.

Sevenster, P. (1973). Incompatibility of response and reward. In *Constraints on learning: limitations and predictions* (ed. R. A. Hinde and J. Stevenson-Hinde). Academic Press, London.

Stammbach, E. (1988). Group responses to specially skilled individuals in a *Macaca fascicularis* group. *Behaviour* **107**, 241–66.

vander Wall, S. B. (1990). *Food hoarding in animals*. University of Chicago Press.

Visalberghi, E. and Fragaszy, D. (1990). Do monkeys ape? In *Comparative developmental psychology of language and intelligence in Primates* (ed. S. Parker and K. Gibson). Cambridge University Press.

Wu, H. M. H., Medina, S. R. and Sackett, G. P. (1980). Kin preference in infant *Macaca nemestrina*. *Nature London* **285**, 225–7.

DISCUSSION

Participants: D. Hilton, F. Keil, G. Lloyd, R. Nisbett, E. Spelke, L. Talmy

Hilton: There are studies in human sociobiology which suggest cyclical causes of behaviour of which people are often unaware. Thus young women at the peak of fertility in their menstrual cycle typically feel better, dress more attentively, wear more jewellery, and expose more flesh in discos. However, it is unlikely that they have an explicit awareness of the biological causes of this behaviour. Do you think that many, if not all, of the 'strong' causal perceptions you talk about may be like this, i.e. domain-specific synchronizations of behaviour without conscious appreciation of causes, as opposed to the conscious 'phenomenologically compelling' causal beliefs triggered by Michotte's experiments?

Kummer: There are two aspects to this question. First, the cyclical displays of young women do not originate from any kind of causal knowledge of the subject. The causal process is entirely internal and works without being simulated in the subject's brain. By causal knowledge I mean knowledge of a nexus between events of which at least one is external, not part of the subject's physiology or maturation. Second, strong causal knowledge seems mostly domain-specific and possibly unconscious in animals. However, a mature human causal theory also includes strong knowledge but, if powerful, is neither domain-specific nor unconscious. By strong knowledge I mean that the detection of the particular causal nexus requires considerable background knowledge beyond 'contiguity is relevant', regardless of how it is encoded.

Keil: You carefully suggest that the animal detection abilities of causal relations are analogous to our cases of causal knowledge. But perhaps many of our own strong detectors are not so different, especially in young children. We can also see bizarre mistakes in infants. Perhaps the apparent differences are later glosses created by overlaid cognitive operations.

Launching knowledge might well be linked to tool use; true launching may be extremely rare in a non-manipulated world.

Are animals ever pure contiguity detectors in simple associative terms, or are there always some boundary conditions that make them exclude easily perceivable correlations?

It seems that, even in short time intervals, the number of possible correlations is too high. Perhaps there is a continuum from arbitrary to natural or weak to strong.

Kummer: It seems very likely that humans also have animal-like strong detectors. No sharp dichotomy was intended between humans and animals or between weak and strong knowledge.

There are indeed constraints even on associative learning. As mentioned in the chapter, two events that are *not* both responded to in a given motivation are *not* connected (Sevenster 1973). Animal motivation causes the subject to admit only stimuli, rewards, and types of his own behaviour that are relevant to its present need. Specialists in learning probably know about many other constraints. However, not all of them may be as adaptive as the motivational selection just mentioned, and only the adaptive ones can be termed knowledge in the widest sense of the word.

Nisbett: Is it not the case that the existence of various forms of 'preparedness' for learning associations reduces the sharp differences you suggest between humans and animals?

Kummer: Yes, indeed; see the first part of the answer to Keil.

Lloyd: The notion that explicit causal reasoning develops from the types of (analogues of) causal reasoning discussed in relation to animals and to human children is only one of a number of possible hypotheses. The fact that existing causal reasoning of a *formalized* kind develops in certain societies only at certain historical junctures may suggest that there are other factors at work.

Kummer: I am sorry that this was not made clear. In the chapter I suggest that — like mechanisms for, say, navigation — strong cause detectors in animals other than primates are probably for the most part *not* precursors of our causal perceptions (see for example the paternity detection mechanisms). Otherwise they would not be analogues but homologues. There will be exceptions, but we still seem to be far away from tracing the phylogentic developments of any one strong cause detector on any branch of the animal pedigree.

Spelke: The question of whether human systems of knowledge of physical objects is shared by other animals is fascinating and seems to remain largely open. Your interesting observation of the macaque may not suggest a difference here. Children also find the task of using a stick to retrieve an object difficult. Long before they can act on this knowledge they are able to recognize violations. It would be interesting to learn whether animals also recognize these violations. In general, the relation is between the ability to recognize/understand causal relations and the ability to act on such knowledge. I believe that this kind of comparative research may shed important light on the nature of the knowledge systems we find in humans.

Kummer: If the ability to recognize violations but not to act on such knowledge does not merely reflect the difficulty of the motor performance (as when we observe a tight-rope walker), this is a most promising result. Could it be related to the child's ability to imitate — here to represent causal essentials of the task observed — which has not yet been found in monkeys?

Talmy: What struck me most about your description of the alpha male was that he persevered with the task of pulling an apple towards him for over a year despite repeated failure. If the monkey were motivated simply by some form of associative cause–effect pairings, he would have presumably given up early on. The fact that he persevered suggests that he had some kind of pre-existent causal conception. This might consist of some protoconception that acting on something might affect it in a desired way, although without any clear understanding of what those actions might be. More specifically, such a protoconception might involve the notion that working away at some task with a succession and variety of actions might lead to refinements which will eventually succeed in the desired effect.

Kummer: The alpha male went through many long and failing attempts but nevertheless succeeded once or twice in most of the sessions, and we know that irregular rewards can be powerful reinforcers. Nevertheless your idea is an interesting alternative which we shall keep in mind.

Part II

Causal understanding in naïve
physics

Part II

Causal understanding in naïve physics

Foreword to Part II

What does the infant know about the physical world? The work of Elizabeth Spelke and her associates, and of Renee Baillargeon and her associates, has shown the resolving power of looking-time studies. These studies have uncovered the unexpected competences of the infant and demonstrated the value that developmental studies have for cognition in general.

According to Spelke, Ann Phillips, and Amanda Woodward, infants have a set of innate beliefs concerning the basic properties of a physical object. For example objects are internally cohesive, and thus when they move do not come apart, change their boundaries, or collect other objects (as one drop of water collects another). Further, they move on paths that are continuous in both time and space. These core beliefs represent the infant's initial *theory* of the physical world and stand at the centre of the adult's intuitive understanding of that world.

Baillargeon, Linda Kotovsky, and Amy Needham dispute the notion of core beliefs and argue instead that the infant recognizes types of inter-actions between objects, in each case transforming an initially primitive concept into a precise one. For example, in the case of support, the infant recognizes that an object needs contact with another, but does not distinguish appropriate from inappropriate contact, accepting as support contact from the side as well as from below. It then rejects support from the side, and eventually quantifies the amount of support needed from below. This pattern is not unique to support, they claim, but is found in all interactions including containment, collision, etc.

Spelke and her associates have recently turned their attention to shadows and people, asking whether infants distinguish them from physical objects. Young infants do not have a good grasp of shadows; they have a better grasp of people. People perceive, want, and think— i.e. have mental states—and communicate the content of their mental states to one another. Do young infants recognize any of these states? Spelke and her associates answer by both reviewing the literature and contributing studies of their own.

D.P.
A.J.P.

3

Infants' knowledge of object motion and human action

ELIZABETH S. SPELKE, ANN PHILLIPS, AND
AMANDA L. WOODWARD

OVERVIEW

What is the intuitive conception of a human being, and how is it related to the intuitive conception of an inanimate material object? Is the system of knowledge underlying common-sense reasoning about human action distinct from that underlying common-sense reasoning about the motion of an inanimate object? What aspects of intuitive psychological and physical conceptions are inevitable and universal across cultures, and what aspects are variable and subject to change?

Studies of early cognitive development provide one approach to these questions. A wealth of observations of infants' actions on objects and interactions with people suggest that young infants distinguish people from inanimate objects and are sensitive to differences between human action and inanimate object motion. In addition, experiments have shed some light on infants' knowledge of how inanimate objects move, and the methods developed have begun to be used to probe infants' knowledge of how people act. The findings of this research suggest that infants begin to reason about human action during the first year and that the knowledge underlying this reasoning differs, in some ways, from the knowledge underlying reasoning about inanimate object motion. Ultimately, we hope that these studies will shed light on mature systems of knowledge of people and objects by illuminating their foundations in early development.

We begin by reviewing the methods and findings of studies of infants' reasoning about inanimate object motion. Because human action appears to violate some of the constraints on inanimate objects, we next ask whether infants are sensitive to violations of constraints on objects by considering briefly how they reason about shadows. Finally, we turn to infants' reasoning about human action. First, we describe a study investigating whether infants understand that human action cannot be predicted solely on the basis of mechanical considerations. We then turn to the literature on social interaction and communication in infancy as a source of suggestions concerning infants' positive knowledge of human action, and we present the methods and findings from our own initial research on this topic.

REASONING ABOUT INANIMATE OBJECT MOTION

Recent experiments provide evidence that infants reason about the behaviour of inanimate objects by drawing on knowledge of constraints on object motion. Infants' knowledge has been revealed through the work of a number of investigators (see particularly Chapters 4 and 5), whose methods are based on the finding that infants tend to look longer at novel or surprising events than at familiar and expected events (Bornstein 1985; Spelke 1985; Baillargeon 1993). In many scores of studies, infants have been presented with events that either accord with or violate different constraints on objects, and their looking times have been measured (Ball 1973; Baillargeon 1986; Leslie and Keeble 1987; Leslie 1991; Baillargeon *et al.* 1990; Spelke *et al.* 1992; Wynn 1992; Xu and Carey 1992; S. Carey, L. Klatt, and M. Schlaffer, unpublished manuscript). With only a few exceptions, the findings of these studies are in broad agreement concerning infants' physical knowledge. Young infants appear to reason about objects in accord with three principles, each encompassing two constraints on object motion.

Figure 3.1 summarizes these principles and constraints. According to the *principle of cohesion*, objects are connected and bounded bodies that maintain both their connectedness and their boundaries as they move freely. This principle encompasses the symmetrical constraints of 'cohesion' (moving objects, unlike sand piles, do not disperse) and 'boundedness' (moving objects, unlike drops of water, do not coalesce). Evidence that infants are sensitive to this principle comes from a number of experiments (von Hofsten and Spelke 1985; Kestenbaum *et al.* 1987; Spelke 1988; Spelke *et al.* 1989; S. Carey, L. Klatt and M. Schlaffer, unpublished manuscript). An experiment by Spelke *et al.* (1993) serves as an example.

This experiment focused on infants' looking times for the outcomes of visible events in which an object either moved as a whole or broke apart. Three-month-old infants were familiarized with an object standing on a surface and were then presented with two alternating test events in which a hand grasped and lifted the top of the object. In one event, the whole object rose into the air, consistent with the cohesion principle. In the other event, the top half of the object rose into the air while the bottom of the object remained on the table, in violation of the cohesion principle (Fig. 3.2). Looking times for the outcomes of these events were measured,

(a) The principle of cohesion: a moving object maintains its connectedness and boundaries

Motion in accord with cohesion

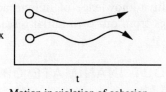

Motion in violation of cohesion

Connectedness violation   Boundedness violation

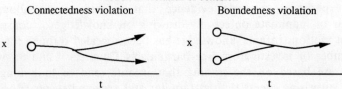

(b) The principle of continuity: a moving object traces exactly one connected path over space and time

Motion in accord with continuity

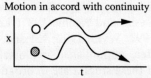

Motion in violation of continuity

Continuity violation   Solidity violation

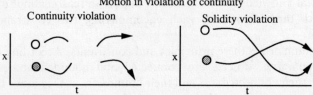

(c) The principle of contact: objects move together if and only if they touch

Motion in accord with contact

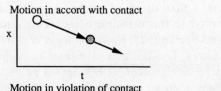

Motion in violation of contact

Action on contact violation   No action at a distance violation

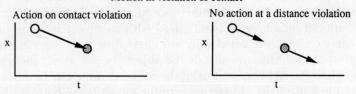

Fig. 3.1. Principles guiding infants' physical reasoning.

Experimental Condition

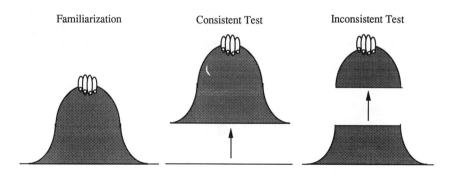

Familiarization   Consistent Test   Inconsistent Test

Control Condition

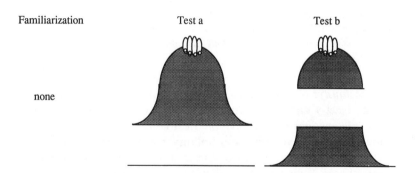

Familiarization   Test a   Test b

Fig. 3.2. Schematic depiction of the outcome displays for a study of infants' knowledge of the cohesion principle. Arrows indicate an object's previous path of motion. (After Spelke *et al.* 1993.)

beginning when all or part of the object came to rest in mid air and ending when the infant looked away from the display. These looking times were compared with each other and with the looking times of infants in a baseline condition, who were presented only with the static outcome displays. The infants in the experimental condition looked reliably longer at the inconsistent outcome display. This difference did not stem from an intrinsic preference for that display, because it was not shown by the infants in the baseline condition. Therefore the experiment provides evidence that young infants are sensitive to the cohesion principle.

The second principle guiding infants' physical reasoning is the *principle*

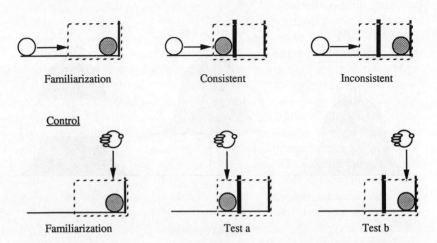

Fig. 3.3. Schematic depiction of displays for a study of infants' knowledge of the continuity principle. Arrows indicate the path of visible motion from an object's initial position (open circles) to the occluder (broken lines); shaded circles indicate the object's resting position when the occluder was removed. (After Spelke *et al.* 1992.)

of continuity: objects exist and move continuously, such that each object traces exactly one connected path over space and time (Fig. 3.1(b)). This principle encompasses the symmetrical constraints of 'continuity' (objects move on connected paths) and 'solidity' (objects move on non-intersecting paths, such that two distinct objects never occupy the same place at the same time). A number of studies provide evidence for sensitivity to this principle (Baillargeon 1986; Baillargeon and Graber 1987; Baillargeon *et al.* 1990; Baillargeon and DeVos 1991; Leslie 1991; Wynn 1992; Xu and Carey 1992; Spelke *et al.* 1994; M. M. Sitskoorn and A. W. Smitsman, submitted; Wilcox, Rosser, and Nadel, submitted) including the following study by Spelke *et al.* (1992).

The experiment focused on infants' looking times for the outcomes of events in which an object moved from view toward a hidden obstacle and reappeared on either the near or the far side of the obstacle. Infants aged just under 3 months were familiarized with an event in which a ball rolled on a horizontal surface, disappeared behind a screen, and then was revealed, by the raising of the screen, at the far end of the surface (Fig. 3.3). Looking time was recorded only after the raising of the screen, when the stationary object appeared at its final position. After interest in this event had declined, infants were tested with two events in which a barrier was placed on the surface, the screen was lowered to cover the barrier, the ball was rolled as before, and the screen was raised to reveal the ball at rest either against the barrier (a novel position that is consistent with the continuity principle) or at the far end of the display (a familiar position that is inconsistent with the continuity principle because the ball could have arrived at that position only by passing through the hidden barrier or by moving discontinuously). Looking times for these two outcomes were compared with each other and with the looking times of infants in a control condition, in which the same outcomes were preceded by uniformly consistent events in which the ball was lowered to its final position. The infants in the experimental condition looked reliably longer at the inconsistent event outcome. The equal looking times of infants in the control condition suggested that this difference did not reflect an intrinsic preference for that outcome display. Therefore the experiment provides evidence that young infants are sensitive to the continuity principle.

The third principle guiding infants' reasoning, and the focus of this chapter, is the *principle of contact*: objects act upon each other if and only if they touch (Fig. 3.1(c)). This principle encompasses the symmetrical constraints of 'action on contact' (objects act upon each other if they come into contact) and 'no action at a distance' (objects do not act upon each other if they do not come into contact). Research by Leslie and his colleagues provides a wealth of evidence that infants reason about object motion in accord with this principle (Leslie 1982, 1984; Leslie and Keeble 1987) (for reviews, see Leslie (1988) and Chapter 5 of this volume), and their findings are corroborated by research from other laboratories (Borton 1979; Oakes 1993; Van de Walle and Spelke 1993; Chapter 4 of this volume); for partly contrary evidence see Oakes and Cohen (1990). We illustrate these findings by describing what may have been the first study of infants' knowledge of the contact principle (Ball 1973).

Children ranging in age from 9 weeks to 2 years were presented with an event in which two objects moved in succession behind a screen under spatio-temporal conditions that elicit, for adults, an impression that the first object set the second object in motion (Michotte 1963) (Fig. 3.4). After familiarization with this event, the screen was removed and the children were presented with fully visible events in which the first object either hit the second object (consistent with the contact principle) or stopped short of it (inconsistent with that principle). Looking times for the two test events were compared with one another and with the looking times of children in a no-familiarization baseline condition. Relative to baseline, the subjects in the experimental condition showed a reliable preference for the inconsistent event. A reanalysis of Ball's data (Spelke and Van de Walle 1993) provides evidence that this preference was significant not only for the sample as a whole but for the subset of children who were less than

Habituation

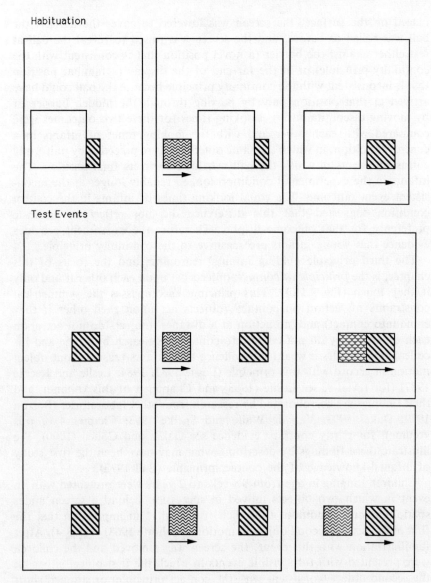

Fig. 3.4. Schematic depiction of displays for a study of infants' knowledge of the contact principle at the beginning (left), middle (centre), and end (right) of each event. (After Ball 1973.)

7 months old. A recent study obtained the same preference with 6-month-old infants (Van de Walle *et al.* 1994). Infants evidently inferred that the two objects met behind the screen, in accord with the contact principle.

In summary, young infants appear to know that inanimate objects move cohesively, exist and move continuously, and act upon each other on contact. Infants exhibit their knowledge in a variety of situations involving both visible and hidden objects. Indeed, a comparison across different studies reveals a convergence between infants' reactions to events involving visible objects and infants' reactions to events involving hidden objects. For example, infants apply the contact principle to both hidden events (Ball 1973; Borton 1979) and visible events (Leslie and Keeble 1987; Chapter 4 of this volume).

The convergence of findings from studies presenting different events and using different methods suggests that knowledge of the principles of cohesion, continuity, and contact is relatively robust and general in infancy. Nevertheless, these principles do not apply to all perceptible entities. In particular, the contact principle is violated by animate objects, including people, and by shadows. We ask next whether infants are sensitive to violations of this principle.

REASONING ABOUT SHADOWS

The motions of shadows violate all the constraints that infants apply to objects. Shadows do not move cohesively or continuously: when a shadow moves off the edge of a surface, it neither maintains its connectedness nor traces a continuous path; when two shadows move together on a surface, they lose their boundaries and coincide in space and time. Shadow motions also violate the contact principle: a shadow moves with the object that casts it and not with the surface on which it is cast. One series of studies has begun to investigate whether infants attend to shadow motions and appreciate that these motions differ from the motions of objects (J. Rubenstein, G. Van de Walle, and E. S. Spelke, in preparation).

The first experiment investigated whether infants perceive and attend to shadow motions. Infants aged 5 and 8 months were familiarized with a stationary display consisting of a shadow, a ball that appeared to adults to cast the shadow, and a box on which the shadow appeared to be cast (Fig. 3.5). (The shadow was actually produced by a hidden object and hidden lighting inside the box, camouflaged by shading on the visible surfaces in the display.) Infants were then tested alternately with the same stationary display and with an otherwise identical display in which the shadow moved laterally (Fig. 3.5(a)). Each of the 12 infants in this study

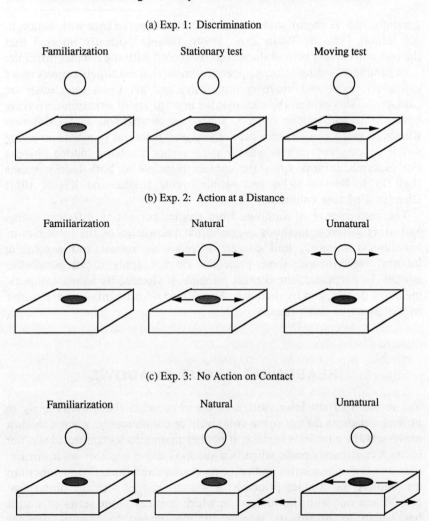

Fig. 3.5. Schematic depiction of the events for studies of (a) infants' sensitivity to shadow motions, (b) infants' knowledge that shadow motion violates the constraint of no action at a distance, and (c) infants' knowledge that shadow motion violates the constraint of action on contact. Arrows indicate the direction and extent of motion of the shadow and objects. (After J. Rubenstein, G. Van de Walle, and E. S. Spelke, in preparation.)

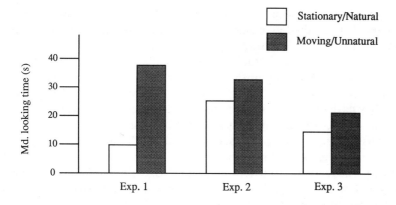

Fig. 3.6. Median looking times at displays in which a shadow is either stationary or moves and in which its motion is either natural and inconsistent with the constraint of action on contact or unnatural and inconsistent with that constraint. (After Rubenstein, G. Van de Walle, and E. S. Spelke, in preparation.)

looked longer at the display in which the shadow moved (Wilcoxon $z = 3.06$, $p < 0.005$) (Fig. 3.6), providing evidence that they detected and attended to the shadow's motion.

The next experiment began to probe infants' understanding of shadow motions, by investigating whether 5- and 8-month-old infants appreciate that a shadow moves with the object that casts it even when the object and shadow are spatially separated. Infants were familiarized with the same stationary display as in the first study and then were tested with two events in which the ball moved (Fig. 3.5(b)). In one event, the shadow moved with the ball—a natural motion for shadows, in violation of the constraint of no action at a distance. In the other event, the shadow remained at rest—an unnatural motion for shadows, in accord with this constraint. Thirteen of the 16 infants in this study looked longer at the *natural* event in which the motion of the shadow violated the contact principle (Wilcoxon $z = 2.10$, $p < 0.02$) (Fig. 3.6). This finding suggests that infants incorrectly inferred that the shadow would remain at rest, in accord with the constraint of no action at a distance.

The third experiment investigated whether infants appreciate that a shadow does not move with the surface on which it is cast. Infants were familiarized with the stationary display and then were tested with two events in which the box moved (Fig. 3.5(c)). In one event, the shadow remained at rest—a natural motion for shadows, in violation of the constraint of action on contact. In the other event, the shadow moved with the box—an unnatural motion for shadows, in accord with this constraint. Eleven of the 16 infants looked longer at the natural event in which the shadow remained at rest (Wilcoxon $z = 1.79$, $p < 0.05$) (Fig. 3.6). Infants appeared to infer that the shadow would move with the surface, in accord with the constraint of action on contact.

Taken together, these studies suggest that 5- and 8-month-old infants make false inferences about the behaviour of shadows. To the extent that the motions of detached shadows are familiar to infants, all the motions that they have seen have violated the contact principle. Nevertheless, infants appear to react to such motions as novel or unnatural, relative to shadow motions that accord with the contact principle. These findings suggest that infants overextend principles governing object motion to other perceptible entities. The tendency to overextend knowledge of material objects appears to persist well into childhood, leading to systematic errors in children's judgments about shadow phenomena (De Vries 1987).

Studies of infants' reasoning about shadows raise questions concerning infants' reasoning about human action. It has been proposed that infants categorize an entity as self-propelled, and therefore animate, by applying principles governing the motions of inanimate material objects to the entity and testing for violations of those principles (Premack 1990; see also Steward 1984; Gelman 1990). The above studies may pose difficulties for this view. Although infants attend to the motions of shadows, at least in certain visual displays, and although shadows disobey all the constraints that infants apply to material objects, infants nevertheless appear to over-generalize mechanical constraints to shadows. This finding casts doubt on the thesis that infants test all perceived motion patterns for violations of mechanical constraints. It remains possible, however, that infants distinguish people from inanimate objects in their reasoning about action and motion, and that they appreciate that human action is not subject to all the constraints on inanimate objects.

REASONING ABOUT HUMAN ACTION

Like inanimate objects, people move as connected and bounded wholes on continuous and unobstructed paths. Unlike inanimate objects, however, people do not appear to act in accord with the contact principle. Although human action may be as constrained by the contact principle as is inanimate object motion at a neurophysiological level, it is not so constrained at the level of perceptible objects. People and other animals have perceptual systems that allow them to detect and respond to objects at a distance, steering a course around distant obstacles and toward distant goals. People have motivational systems that direct their actions and cognitive systems that allow them to make plans, choose actions, and pursue enduring goals. People communicate, influencing one another's actions, intentions, and

Table 3.1 *Possible principles underlying reasoning about human action*

Principles that apply to the motions of all material objects
1. Cohesion: people move as connected bounded wholes
2. Continuity: people move on connected unobstructed paths
3. Gravity: people rest and move on supporting surfaces

Principles that are specific to the actions of animate objects
4. Self-propelled motion: human action is not constrained by the contact principle
5. Social responsiveness: people respond contingently to the actions of social partners
6. Social reciprocity: people react in kind to the actions of social partners
7. Communication: people supply social partners with information
8. Emotion: people's actions are influenced by their motivational and emotional states
9. Goal-directedness: people act to attain goals
10. Perception: people's actions are guided by their perceptions

states of knowledge; therefore one person's actions can be coordinated with the actions of other people, whether or not the people are in immediate contact. All these factors enable people to behave in ways that are not predictable from a consideration of their immediate physical environment.

The existence of perceptual, motivational, cognitive, and communicative systems has both a negative and a positive consequence for reasoning about human action. On the negative side, one cannot infer what people are doing by analysing the contact relations among objects. For example, if an action by one person appears to cause a reaction in a second person, one cannot infer that the first person touched the second. On the positive side, one can often infer a person's actions by drawing on information about the person's perceptions, emotional states, goals, and interactions with other people. For example, if a person looks desirously at one object while ignoring a second object, he or she is more likely to act on the first object. If one person smiles at a second person, the second person is likely to smile as well. Table 3.1 provides a list of candidate principles for reasoning about human action, drawn from our own intuitions and from a number of theoretical proposals about initial concepts of persons or animate objects (Gelman 1990; Premack 1990; Mandler 1992; see also Chapters 5, 6, and 7 of this volume). We focus in turn on each of the principles that are specific to reasoning about animate objects, asking first whether infants appreciate that human action is not predictable from an analysis of contact relations.

DO INFANTS SUSPEND THE CONTACT PRINCIPLE IN REASONING ABOUT HUMAN ACTION?

To investigate whether infants apply the contact principle to events involving people, we conducted an experiment that was patterned after the study by Ball (1973) described above and that used events involving people or large inanimate objects (Woodward *et al.* 1993) (Fig. 3.7). In the experimental condition with inanimate objects, 7-month-old infants were presented with videotaped events involving objects 5 and 6 feet high with bright contrasting colours and patterns, and distinctive meaningless shapes. Each object was moved from behind by a hidden person walking at a normal pace. First infants were familiarized with an event in which the objects moved behind a large central occluder. On each trial, one object moved fully into view on the left side of the television screen and disappeared behind the occluder, and then after an appropriate time interval the second object began to move in the same direction and disappeared at the right side of the television screen. This event was then repeated in reverse, beginning when the second object moved into view on the right and ending when the first object disappeared on the left. Repetitions continued until the infant looked away from the display, ending the trial. A succession of familiarization trials were given until the infant's looking time declined to half its initial level, and then the infant was presented with two test events involving fully visible objects undergoing the same configuration of visible motion. In one event, the two objects came into contact at the centre of the display and their motion changed at the point of contact. In the other event, the moving object stopped short of the stationary object, which began to move after a short pause such that the objects' changes in motion were separated in space and time.

The events for the experimental condition with people were the same, but they involved a man and a woman who walked naturally. Like the objects, the people began moving and reversed direction out of the infant's sight, beyond the edges of the television screen; therefore their behaviour did not indicate whether they could change their motion spontaneously. In the familiarization event, the man held both arms up close to his body and moved toward the half-hidden stationary woman, who faced leftward toward the man at the start of the event and turned her head and body to face rightward when she began to move. In the test event with contact, the man collided with the woman, making contact along most of the upper body and appearing to set her in motion. In the test event without contact, the man walked forward in the same posture but stopped short of the woman, who appeared to begin moving spontaneously. As for the events with inanimate objects, each event with people was then repeated in reverse and presented continuously for as long as the infant looked at it.

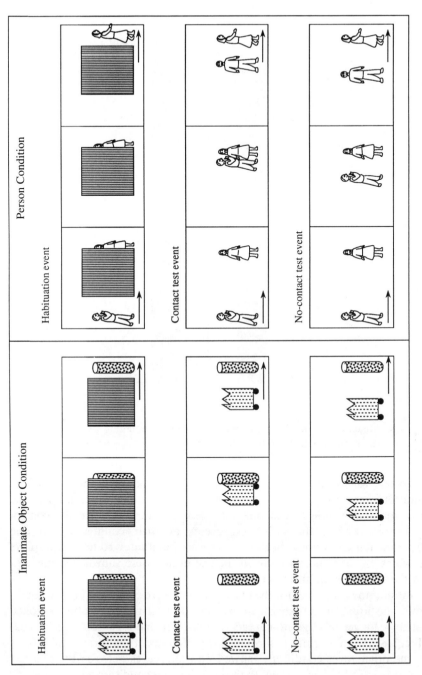

Fig. 3.7. Schematic depiction of the events for a study of infants' inferences about the contact relations between inanimate objects or people. (After Woodward *et al.* 1993.)

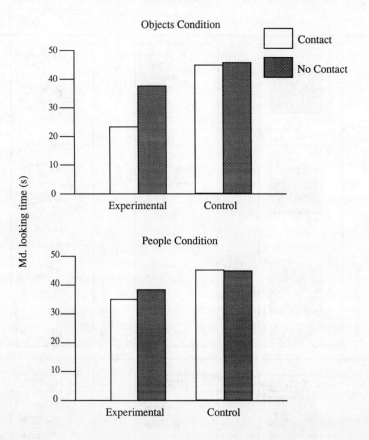

Fig. 3.8. Median looking times for events in which inanimate objects or people change their motion with or without contact. (After Woodward *et al.* 1993.)

To test for differences in the intrinsic attractiveness of the test events, additional groups of infants participated in two control conditions, one with inanimate objects and one with people. The infants in the control conditions viewed the same test events as their counterparts in the experimental conditions, but first they were habituated to neutral displays in which the objects to appear in the test events were shown standing still on the two sides of the screen.

Infants' looking times for the two test events were compared in each condition. The infants in the experimental condition with inanimate objects looked reliably longer at the no-contact event (Wilcoxon $z = 2.25$, $p < 0.02$) (Fig. 3.8); 12 of 16 infants showed this preference. In contrast, the infants in the other three conditions showed no preferences between the two test events (each Wilcoxon $z < 1$). In the experimental condition with people, six of 16 infants looked longer at the no-contact test event; in the control condition with inanimate objects, seven of 16 infants showed this preference; in the control condition with people, eight of 16 infants showed this preference.

Further analyses compared the looking preferences of infants in the different conditions. Because of high variability in all the conditions, the difference between looking preferences in the experimental and baseline conditions with inanimate objects was only marginally significant (Wilcoxon–Mann–Whitney $z = 1.49$, $p < 0.07$, one-tailed). Thus the present study weakly replicates Ball's (1973) original finding. (An experiment by Van de Walle *et al.* (1994) provides a stronger replication.) The difference between looking preferences in the experimental and baseline conditions with animate objects did not approach significance (Wilcoxon–Mann–Whitney $z < 1$). In contrast, the looking preferences in the experimental condition with inanimate objects differed from those in the experimental condition with people (Wilcoxon–Mann–Whitney $z = 1.68$, $p < 0.05$). This effect is not attributable to differences in the intrinsic attractiveness of the test events with people versus objects, because the preferences in the two control conditions did not differ ($z < 1$).

These findings provide evidence that 7-month-old infants do *not* apply the contact principle to people. In the presence of information for a causal relationship between two perceptible entities, infants tend to infer contact between the entities if they are inanimate objects but not if they are people. In this respect, infants appear to reason differently about people and objects. As suggested by Premack (1990) and Gelman (1990), infants appear to appreciate that people are capable of self-propelled motion.

Our findings accord with the findings of experiments using other methods (Legerstee 1992). Research from the laboratory of Poulin-Dubois (D. Poulin-Dubois, A. Lepage, and D. Ferland, unpublished manuscript) compared the reactions of 9- and 12-month-old infants to a robot and an unfamiliar person both when they were standing still and when they were undergoing self-propelled motion. Children at both ages reacted with most negative affect in the condition in which the robot appeared to move itself around the room. Their reaction may reflect the expectation that the robot would not move spontaneously; the absence of negative affect in the condition in which the person moved suggests that this expectation is not applied to an unfamiliar person. In addition, an experiment by Carlson-Luden (reported by Golinkoff *et al.* (1984)) compared the abilities of 10-month-old infants to learn to push a lever in order to set either an inanimate object (a picture) or a person in motion. Although infants learned to make the picture move by pushing the lever, they did not learn to make the person wave and smile. A similar pattern was observed with younger infants in an experiment by Legerstee (1994). Legerstee compared the reactions of 4-month-old infants to events in which a person or an inanimate object disappeared behind a door. Whereas the infants responded to the disappearance of the object by touching the door, they responded to the disappearance of the person by vocalizing to the person without contacting the occluder. All these experiments suggest that infants reason differently about the motions of people than about the motions of inanimate objects.

Although infants appear to suspend the contact principle in reasoning about human action in the above studies, none of these studies sheds light on infants' positive understanding of human action. Infants may suspend the contact principle because they appreciate that human action is directed to goals or guided by perceptions, or because they appreciate that humans communicate and interact at a distance. Alternatively, infants may lack any positive conception of human action; they may view human behaviour as unpredictable. We turn to other research to distinguish these possibilities.

COMMUNICATION AND SOCIAL INTERACTION IN INFANCY

Research from a large number of laboratories has charted the development of infants' social interactions. Although not all of this research was conducted with our questions in mind, it provides a place to look for suggestions concerning infants' understanding of human action. We review parts of this research as it bears on infants' understanding that human action is socially responsive, coloured by emotion, directed to goals, and guided by perception.

People interact

By the time that they are a few months old, infants participate in well-orchestrated contingent interactions with their parents (Brazelton *et al.* 1974; Stern 1974; Trevarthen 1977, 1979; Tronick 1981; Field 1982; Stevenson *et al.* 1986; Cohn and Tronick 1988). Therefore early conceptions of human beings may involve an understanding of the ways in which people interact. Three aspects of human interaction that are accessible in principle to young infants are contingency (humans react to one another), reciprocity (humans respond in kind to one another's actions), and communication (humans supply one another with information). A variety of studies of early social interactions suggest that infants are sensitive to these properties. In each case, however, clear evidence that infants understand the social character of human action has been difficult to obtain.

A number of researchers have investigated infants' understanding of humans as socially responsive actors using the 'still-face' procedure

(Tronick *et al.* 1978; Field *et al.* 1986*b*; Cohn and Elmore 1988; Gusella *et al.* 1988; Ellsworth *et al.* 1993; Muir and Hains 1993). In this procedure, an experimenter or parent interacts with the infant for several minutes and then stops reacting to the infant and stands motionless with a neutral facial expression. By 3 months, infants show decreases in smiling and increases in grimacing in the still-face phase of the procedure (Field *et al.* 1986*b*; Gusella *et al.* 1988). This effect does not appear to reflect a simple reaction to the cessation of an interesting event, because changes in smiling are reduced if infants are presented with an inverted face (Rach-Longman and Muir 1990) or with an interacting inanimate object that elicits equally high levels of attention (Legerstee *et al.* 1987, 1990; Ellsworth *et al.* 1993). Nevertheless, infants appear to show similar reactions in a still-face procedure involving a person who responds contingently to their actions and one who responds non-contingently (Muir and Hains 1993). Therefore it is not clear whether infants' emotional reactions to a still face reflect their expectation that people will behave contingently.

Further studies provide evidence that infants are sensitive to the contingent character of social interactions. Young infants can learn about contingencies, both those involving people (Pelaez-Nogueras and Gewirtz, 1993) and those involving inanimate objects (Watson 1972; Rovee-Collier *et al.* 1989). Moreover, young infants who are presented with a video image of a socially interactive adult have been found to show greater positive affect if the adult's behaviour is contingent on their own actions than if it is not (Hains *et al.* 1992). Like the still-face studies, these investigations fall short of establishing that infants have definite expectations about the behaviour of their social partners. Nevertheless, they provide evidence that infants are sensitive to the contingent responsiveness of a social partner and respond to their partners with appropriate social expressions.

Studies of games such as 'peek-a-boo' and give-and-take routines in which babies and their adult partners switch roles may serve to investigate whether infants have expectations about the reciprocal character of human interactions. Infants begin to play these games systematically at about 9 months of age (Bruner 1975; Trevarthen 1979). Research by Ross and Lollis (1987) suggests that infants at this age understand the roles involved in games such as peek-a-boo and work to maintain their reciprocal structure. In their longitudinal study, babies were taught two-person games involving objects in which the infant and an adult experimenter each played a specific role. After the baby was engaged in the game, the adult stopped fulfilling her role. Even at 9 months, infants responded to this break in the action in ways that suggested that they understood the structure of the game: they looked back and forth between the adult and the objects and were likely to repeat their turn or assume the turn of the adult. These findings suggest that 9-month-old infants expect their partners to continue to act in their reciprocal role. To our knowledge, however, no experiment has investigated infants' sensitivity to the reciprocal character of interactions in which they do not participate. In particular, we do not know whether infants who see one person engage in a given action predict that his or her social partner will also engage in a similar or complementary action.

Studies of imitation may serve to investigate younger infants' understanding that people respond in kind to one another's actions. Even newborn infants imitate the facial movements and emotional expressions of an adult (Meltzoff and Moore 1977, 1983; Field *et al.* 1982, 1986*a*; Vinter 1986; Reissland 1988; Legerstee 1991) and they respond with interest to an adult who imitates their own actions (Field 1977). In addition, an analysis of mother–infant dialogues provides evidence that maternal vocalizations increase the likelihood of infant vocalizations (Stevenson *et al.* 1986). Meltzoff and Moore (1992) have speculated that early imitation is an information-seeking activity, by which infants attempt to elicit actions from a social partner. If this interpretation is correct, then imitation would appear to reflect a tacit understanding that humans interact reciprocally.

A third characteristic of human interactions is that they involve the transfer of information from one person to another. Bates and colleagues (Bates *et al.* 1979; Bretherton *et al.* 1981) have suggested that infants first understand the communicative aspect of human interaction at about 9 months of age. At this age, three types of behaviour appear that suggest that infants intend to communicate: (1) they persevere in the face of failure to transmit their message and vary the form of the message until they succeed (see also Scollon 1976); (2) when requesting an object, they shift their gaze from the object to their addressee as if to check whether the message was understood; (3) they begin to use ritualized gestures in their interactions (Bates *et al.* 1979). Although Bretherton *et al.* (1981) interpret these developments in terms of the emergence of an 'implicit theory of interfaceable minds', that interpretation can be questioned on two grounds. On the one hand, it is possible that younger infants understand the communicative character of human interactions but lack the resources to act upon this understanding in the above ways. Some studies of naturally occurring social exchanges involving young infants may suggest an earlier understanding of communication (Tronick 1981). On the other hand, it is possible that 9-month-old infants still lack this understanding and have learned a set of routines for manipulating the actions of others (Shatz 1983).

People experience and express emotion

Young infants are sensitive to expressions of emotion. One-day-old infants show discrimination of happy versus sad living faces (Field and Walden 1981), and 5-month-old infants show discrimination between vocal expressions which are happy versus sad (Walker-Andrews and Grolnick 1983) or happy versus angry (Walker-Andrews and Lennon 1991). These abilities appear to reflect more than a sensory analysis of emotional displays, because 4-month-old infants show no discrimination of happy and sad faces when the faces are presented upside down (Oster 1981), 5-month-old infants generalize from one set of actors portraying happy or sad emotions to new actors portraying these emotions (Caron *et al.* 1988), and 5-month-old infants are able to match facial expressions with their congruent vocal expressions (Walker 1982). Moreover, young infants respond appropriately to certain emotional expressions. Two-month-old infants imitate facial expressions of happiness, sadness, and surprise (Field *et al.* 1986*a*), and react in systematic and appropriate ways to maternal expressions of joy, sadness, and anger (Haviland and Lelwica 1987). At slightly older ages, infants respond with negative emotion to their mothers' depressed affect (Tronick *et al.* 1986), and they respond appropriately to the emotional content of praise or prohibition even if the speech is not in their native language (Fernald 1993). From an early age, then, infants appear to be sensitive to the emotional tone of a voice or an expressive face, and they react appropriately to these signals.

For adults, emotional expressions convey information both about the state and probable actions of the person expressing the emotion and about the objects towards which the emotion is expressed. A person who evinces disgust at one object and pleasure at another object is more likely to approach the latter object. Moreover, if someone expresses disgust or alarm while looking at an object, this behaviour suggests that the object may be unpleasant or dangerous. Studies of pre-school children's memory of emotional events suggest that they are also aware of these linkages (Liwag and Stein 1993). Are infants able to use a person's emotional expressions as information about his or her probable actions? Conversely, can they use a person's actions as information about his or her probable emotional state? Research by Wellman and Woolley (1990) shows that 2.5-year-old children can predict the emotional state (happy versus sad) of a character in a simple story from a consideration of the character's actions and their consequences. For example, children at this age predict that a character who wants her mittens will be happy if she finds them and sad if she does not. Given this ability, it seems reasonable to expect that children can use information about emotions to predict behaviour, but this question has not been addressed directly for toddlers or infants. However, there is a large body of evidence relevant to infants' use of emotional expressions in reasoning about states of the world — research on 'social referencing' in infants.

By the end of the first year, infants tend to look at the faces of their parents when confronted with an ambiguous situation, and they use information from a parent's facial and vocal expressions to regulate their behaviour (Campos and Stenberg 1981). In a variety of settings, infants' approach and avoidance behaviours towards people and objects are influenced by the positive and negative messages that their parents express toward those objects. In particular, a parent's emotional expressions influence the degree of interaction of 10-month-old infants with a stranger (Feinman and Lewis 1983) and the probability that 12-month-old infants will cross a visual cliff (Sorce *et al*. 1985) or touch an unfamiliar toy (Hornick *et al*. 1987; Walden and Baxter 1989; Rosen *et al*. 1992). Some researchers report similar effects in younger infants, although their findings are less clear. In a study by Walden and Ogan (1988), 6- to 9-month-old infants avoided a toy which had been the target of a negative emotional expression by a parent, but they did not check the parent's expression reliably. More dramatically, Pelaez-Nogueras (1993) was able to condition social-referencing type responses in 4- to 5-month-old infants. However, it is not clear whether infants' conditioned responses draw on the same underlying understanding as does the social referencing of older children.

Studies of social referencing provide evidence that older infants are sensitive to emotional expressions in other people, and that this sensitivity guides their actions on objects. The findings of these studies cannot be explained in terms of a direct effect of a perceived expression of emotion on the infant's own affective state, because the changes in infants' actions that occur in response to the expressions of another person are specific to the objects to which the person's expressions are directed (Hornick *et al*. 1987; Walden and Ogan 1988). Nevertheless, none of these studies reveals whether infants use information from a person's emotional reactions to an object to predict how the person will act towards that object.

People pursue goals

Because human action is goal directed, it is often possible to predict what a person will do from behavioural evidence concerning his or her intentions and goals. Do young children appreciate the goal-directed character of human action, and do they use behavioural information about a person's goals to predict his or her future actions?

There is ample evidence that 2.5-year-old children understand human action in terms of goals and intentions. By this age, children predict the behaviour of story characters from information that they are given about the characters' goals (Wellman and Woolley 1990), they talk about the behaviour of themselves and others using intentional action verbs (Huttenlocher and Smiley 1990) and mental verbs such as 'want' or 'think' (Bretherton *et al*. 1981; Shatz *et al*. 1983), and they interpret new verbs as referring to intentional as opposed to accidental acts (Tomasello 1993). Studies of children's memory of unfamiliar actions suggest that, when there is a clear goal, children as young as 15 months remember the structure of a person's actions in relation to that goal (Bauer and Shore 1987; Bauer and Mandler 1989; Travis 1993). For example, young children are more likely to remember an action that was instrumental in completing a goal than an action which was irrelevant to that goal (Travis 1993). Observations of 9-month-old infants' persistent requests for action on the part of others invites the interpretation that they are also aware of others' goals (Bates *et al.* 1979; Bretherton *et al.* 1981); for a contrary interpretation of this evidence see Shatz (1983). The 9-month-old infant's developing understanding of pointing (Murphy and Messer 1977) invites a similar interpretation. To our knowledge, however, there is no direct evidence bearing on infants' ability to understand human action as goal directed. Methods by which this question may be addressed are suggested in Chapter 7.

People perceive

Human action is guided by perception: people move so as to approach perceived goals and avoid perceived obstacles. Although perception itself is an internal process, behavioural signs of perception such as the direction of gaze are an important part of the information that adults use to predict what other people will do. Are infants sensitive to the linkage between action and perception, and can they use information about what people perceive to predict their actions?

Two-year-old children have some understanding of the conditions under which adults are able to witness events and of the effects of witnessing an event on adults' knowledge and behaviour. For example O'Neill (1993) found that such children's instructions to their mothers about retrieving a hidden object varied depending on whether the mother had seen the object being hidden. The children's verbal instructions were longer and more specific when the mother either left the room or was blindfolded during the hiding of the object than when she was present and witnessed the hiding. These children appeared to appreciate that the mother could not act, unaided, to retrieve a toy she had not seen.

Two experiments suggest that younger children also have some understanding of linkages between looking and acting. First, 16- to 19-month-old children's word learning is reliably influenced by a speaker's direction of looking. When an experimenter introduced a new object and offered a name for the object, children learned the object's name if the speaker looked at the object while speaking but not if she looked away (Baldwin 1991). The infants evidently used the direction of the speaker's gaze as information about what the person was talking about. Second, both 10-month-old and 18-month-old children who are facing away from the mother have been found to turn more often to look and smile at her when she was previously seen to be looking at the infant than when she was previously seen to be reading a magazine (Jones *et al.* 1991). Careful analyses of the timing of the infants' actions suggested that infants were not responding directly to the mother's own signals or to an internal state of affect engendered by the mother's attention. Rather, the infants appeared to appreciate that the mother was more open to communication when she faced the infant. Nevertheless, these studies fall short of showing that infants can use information about a person's direction of gaze to predict what the person will do.

What of younger infants? When 3-month-old infants view a photograph of a face in a frontal orientation, their response to the photograph is reliably influenced by the face's direction of gaze. Infants respond with more negative emotion if the eyes are directed away from the infant than if they are directed to the infant (Ehrlich 1993). Evidently, young infants are sensitive to some of the information indicating what a person perceives.

Studies of infants' ability to follow the gaze of another person suggest that gaze direction is meaningful for infants. When infants interact with a person who looks at an object, they tend to follow the person's direction of gaze to the object (Scaife and Bruner 1975). The ability to follow an adult's line of regard increases in accuracy over the course of the first year. At 6 months, infants turn to look at an object in the direction that the adult is looking, but they typically look at the first object that they encounter in that direction, even if the adult is looking at a more distant object. By 12 months, infants follow the adult's line of regard to the correct object (Butterworth and Grover 1988). These looking patterns may reflect changes in infants' understanding of gaze direction and perception.

In summary, infants appear to be sensitive to a variety of aspects of human action. However, it is not clear what knowledge underlies this sensitivity or whether infants can use this knowledge to infer what a person will do. These questions have proved difficult to answer using studies of infants' spontaneous social and communicative behaviour. We have begun to approach them using different methods in which infants observe fully visible or partly hidden events in which they do not participate.

DO INFANTS MAKE POSITIVE INFERENCES ABOUT HUMAN ACTION?

Our first experiment (A. Phillips, A. L. Woodward, and E. S. Spelke, in preparation) used the same method as in previous studies of physical reasoning to investigate whether infants can infer the hidden actions of a person by drawing on information about about the person's affect and

Fig. 3.9. Schematic depiction of the events for studies of infants' knowledge that the direction of a person's action is predictable from the direction of his or her gaze. (After A. Phillips, A. L. Woodward, and E. S. Spelke, in preparation.)

expression. First, infants were presented with an actor, a table, and two stuffed animals in two corners of the table (Fig 3.9(a)). On each of a series of familiarization trials, the actor looked at the child, established eye contact, and then looked away towards one of the toys (for half the children, this was the toy on the left) with an expression of joy and interest. After the infant had looked at this display for 3 seconds, a large curtain was drawn, occluding the entire stage. When the curtain was opened a few seconds later, the actor's head was centred, she was looking down, and she was holding the toy at which she had been looking. Looking time to this outcome display was recorded, and trials were continued until the infant's looking time had declined to half its initial level.

A test sequence followed, consisting of two events presented on six alternating trials. Both test events ended with the same outcome display: the curtain opened to reveal the experimenter holding and looking at the toy that was opposite the one that she had looked at and acted on during familiarization. In one test event, the experimenter began by looking and smiling at this toy; this event was consistent with the principle that people act on things that they see and approach things that they like. In the other test event, the experimenter began by looking at the toy at which she had looked during the familiarization period. Because the experimenter looked desirously at one object but picked up a different object, this event appeared to be inconsistent with the principle that human actions are guided by their perceptions and desires.

The first experiment was conducted with 8- and 12-month-old infants. The younger infants showed no preference between the two test events (Wilcoxon $z < 1$) eight of 16 infants looked longer at each event outcome. In contrast, the older infants looked reliably longer at the event outcome in which the actor held the toy at which she had not been looking (Wilcoxon $z = 2.07$, $p < 0.02$); 11 of 16 infants showed this preference (Fig. 3.10(a)). However, the change in looking preferences from 8 to 12 months was not significant (Wilcoxon–Mann–Whitney $z = 1.15$), nor was the preference for the inconsistent outcome across the two ages combined (Wilcoxon $z = 1.45$, $p = 0.07$). Therefore the findings of this experiment provide evidence that one-year-old children infer that a person will reach for the object at which she is looking with positive affect, but they do not clearly suggest how this tendency develops between 8 and 12 months.

The next experiment investigated infants' ability to infer a person's actions from behavioural signs of perception and emotion when both her actions and her gaze direction are continuously visible. Infants aged 8 and 12 months were presented with fully visible events in which an actor looked and smiled at one object while reaching for that object or for a different object (Fig 3.9(b)). As in the previous study, infants were familiarized with an event in which the actor looked at and reached for one toy, and then they were tested with events in which the actor reached to the second toy either while looking at that toy (consistent) or while looking at the first toy (inconsistent). The actor looked and reached at the same time, and she did so repeatedly on every trial for as long as the infant watched the display. Infants' total looking times for these events were recorded and compared. The results were weaker than those of the previous study: infants showed no differential looking at the consistent versus the inconsistent events at either 8 months or 12 months, (both Wilcoxon $z < 1$) (Fig 3.10(b)). The change in looking preferences from 8 to 12 months was not significant (Wilcoxon–Mann–Whitney $z < 1$), and an analysis of the two ages combined revealed no reliable preference between the events (Wilcoxon $z < 1$). Nevertheless, 11 of 16 12-month-old infants looked longer at the inconsistent event compared with eight of 16 8-month-old infants. Combining the results of the two experiments revealed a strong preference at 12 months for the events in which the person reached for one object during or after the time that she looked and smiled at another object (Wilcoxon $z = 2.52$, $p < 0.01$). Although no such preference was observed

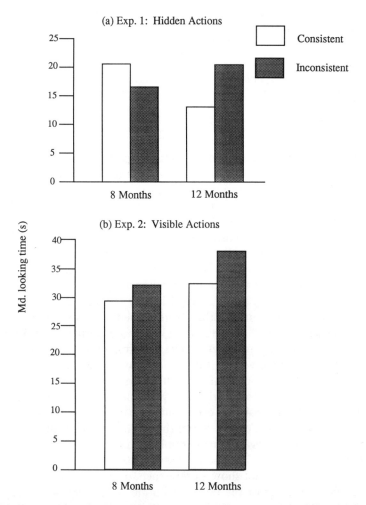

Fig. 3.10. Median looking times at (a) the outcomes of events or (b) fully visible events that are consistent or inconsistent with the principle that the direction of action follows the direction of gaze. (After A. Phillips, A. L. Woodward, and E. S. Spelke, in preparation.)

at 8 months ($z < 1$), the combined analyses still revealed no significant change in preferences between the two ages ($z = 1.26$, $p > 0.10$).

These studies provide evidence that 12-month-old infants infer a person's behaviour from information about her line of regard and emotional expression. This effect was not obtained for 8-month-old infants, but the difference in performance of the two age groups never attained significance. It is

Table 3.2 *Number of infants preferring the inconsistent versus consistent event outcomes who followed or did not follow the actor's line of regard*

Preference on test trials	8 months		12 months	
	Followers	*Non-followers*	*Followers*	*Non-followers*
Inconsistent	5	0	8	2
Consistent	2	3	4	1

possible that the 8-month-old infants' performance was heterogeneous, such that some infants were able to make this inference whereas others were not. This possibility is strengthened by the evidence that the ability to follow line of regard improves between 6 and 12 months (Scaife and Bruner 1975; Butterworth and Grover 1988).

To assess whether sensitivity to line of regard influenced infants' performance in our studies, we conducted a further analysis. On each of the first six familiarization trials of the first experiment, we coded whether an infant followed the actor's direction of gaze.* Infants were scored as correctly following line of regard if they looked first at the toy to which the experimenter turned; they were scored as incorrect if they looked at the other toy first. Infants who had more correct than incorrect trials were counted as 'followers'. The looking preferences of the followers and the non-followers in the test trial were then compared (Table 3.2). For the 12-month-old infants, the tendency to follow the actor's line of regard during familiarization was unrelated to the tendency to look longer at the inconsistent event outcome during the test phase (chi-square $(1, n = 15) = 0$). For the 8-month-old infants, in contrast, the tendency to follow line of regard during familiarization predicted infants' preference on the test trials. Eight-month-old infants who did not follow the actor's line of regard did not show a preference for the inconsistent event outcome; in contrast, most of the infants who did follow her line of regard looked longer at that outcome (chi-square $(1, n = 10) = 4.29, p < 0.05$). Because of the small number of subjects included in this analysis, these findings are not conclusive. They suggest that infants who can follow a person's line of regard can also use this information to predict the person's actions.

In summary, two lines of experiments provide evidence that children

* This analysis could only be conducted for the first experiment because the ability to follow the actor's line of regard could not be assessed in the second study; since the actor continually moved the object at which she looked, infants might have looked at the appropriate object because they detected its motion. In addition, because of lost video records, only 10 of the 8-month-old infants and 15 of the 12-month-old infants could be coded and entered into the analysis.

begin to distinguish in their reasoning between the actions of human beings and the motions of inanimate objects during the first year of life. By 7 months, infants' inferences about a person's actions are not guided by the contact principle, in contrast with their inferences about inanimate object motion and in accord with the notion that human actions are self-propelled. By 12 months, infants' inferences about a person's actions are guided by behavioural indicators of what the person sees or wants. Although these studies do not tell us that infants understand perception or emotion, infants use of these indicators accords with the principle that people act on the things that they perceive and the principle that people approach the things that they desire. Therefore studies of infants' reasoning using preferential looking methods converge with studies of infants' spontaneous social behaviour to suggest that infants differentiate between people and inanimate objects and develop specialized knowledge of human behaviour.

We do not know what changes take place in infants' understanding of human action during the first year. The findings of our gaze-following study and of studies by other investigators suggest that there may be important developments between 8 and 12 months. At around this age, pointing and following of points first emerge and the ability to follow line of regard improves. This is also the time when intentional attempts to communicate are first evident, when infants begin to communicate using gestures, and when infants first show signs of understanding language (Benedict 1979). Finally, social referencing and interactive games are first noted at about this age. These abilities might reflect an advance in infants' understanding of intentions and, perhaps related to this, the attainment of an understanding of reference.

DOMAIN-SPECIFIC SYSTEMS OF KNOWLEDGE

The findings that we have reviewed are consistent with the view that reasoning depends on domain-specific systems of knowledge. By the end of the first year, infants reason about human action by drawing on information about aspects of human behaviour — direction of gaze, expression of emotion — that do not apply to the behaviour of inanimate objects. Symmetrically, infants reason about inanimate object motion in accord with constraints — action on contact, no action at a distance — that they withhold from their reasoning about human actions. These findings accord with the suggestions arising from naturalistic studies of infant behaviour, from experimental manipulations of naturally occurring social behaviour, and from a number of theoretical accounts of early cognitive development (Mandler 1992; Chapters 5, 6, 7, and 10 of this volume).

Much remains to be learned about the system of knowledge underlying infants' reasoning about persons and about the relation of this system to the system of knowledge underlying infants' reasoning about inanimate objects. Although observations of early developing social behaviour are suggestive, they do not show clearly whether young infants reason about people in accord with conceptions of human actions as directed to goals, guided by perceptions, co-ordinated with the actions of other people, and coloured by emotions. Conclusions about infants' reasoning are difficult to draw from observational studies because of ambiguities that arise in interpreting social behaviour as reflecting expectations on the one hand or responses to social signals on the other. Studies using preferential looking methods could provide a complement to observational studies in this respect. By assessing infants' inferences about a person's hidden or future actions and by focusing on infants' understanding of events in which they are not active participants, these methods may help to reveal infants' understanding of people and of the ways in which people differ from inanimate objects.

Although research with infants implies that infants distinguish people from inanimate objects on some basis, we do not know how infants categorize an entity as a person or an inanimate object or how infants reason about entities such as animals and self-propelled machines that do not fall neatly into the category 'human' or the category 'inanimate' (see Chapters 6 and 7 for suggestions). A suggestion that arises from our studies of shadows, in contrast with some proposals (Gelman 1990; Premack 1990), is that infants do not categorize entities as animate by detecting violations of constraints on inanimate objects. Infants may single out persons by detecting motion patterns that are specific to the class of animate objects (see Chapters 6 and 7).

Studies of the early development of knowledge of persons and objects may provide clues to the nature and organization of this knowledge in its mature state. Adults in Western cultures appear to waver between a conception of persons as physical objects that are deeply subject to all mechanical constraints and a conception of persons as intentional agents who are not subject to the contact principle or perhaps to any physical constraints. Long-standing debates over the existence of free will and the nature of personal identity suggest that these two conceptions are deeply in conflict, but they do not reveal the essence of each conception or the relations between them. Do humans view themselves and others as physical objects who happen to have some mental properties, or as entities of a different kind who happen to have some of the properties of material objects? In either case, what are the physical or mental properties that stand at the centre of the concept 'person'? Studies of the earliest conceptions of people and objects, and of their subsequent development, offer one approach to these questions.

REFERENCES

Baillargeon, R. (1986). Representing the existence and the location of hidden objects: object permanence in 6- and 8-month-old infants. *Cognition* **23**, 21–41.

Baillargeon, R. (1993). The object concept revisited: new directions in the investigation of infants' physical knowledge. In *Visual perception and cognition in infancy*, *Carnegie-Mellon Symposia on Cognition*, Vol. 23 (ed. C. E. Granrud). Erlbaum, Hillsdale, NJ.

Baillargeon, R. and DeVos, J. (1991). Object permanence in young infants: further evidence. *Child Development* **62**, 1227–46.

Baillargeon, R. and Graber, M. (1987). Where's the rabbit? 5.5-month-old infants' representation of the height of a hidden object. *Cognitive Development* **2**, 375–92.

Baillargeon, R., Graber, M., DeVos, J., and Black, J. C. (1990). Why do young infants fail to search for hidden objects? *Cognition* **36**, 255–84.

Baldwin, D. A. (1991). Infants' contribution to the achievement of joint reference. *Child Development* **62**, 875–90.

Ball, W. A. (1973). The perception of causality in the infant. Presented at the Meeting of the Society for Research in Child Development, Philadelphia, PA.

Bates, E., Benigni, L., Bretherton, I., Camaioni, L. and Volterra, V. (1979). *The emergence of symbols: cognition and communication in infancy*. Academic Press, New York.

Bauer, P. J. and Mandler, J. M. (1989). One thing follows another: effects of temporal structure on 1- to 2-year-olds' recall of events. *Developmental Psychology* **25**, 197–206.

Bauer, P. J. and Shore, C. M. (1987). Making a memorable event: effects of familiarity and organization on young children's recall of action sequences. *Cognitive Development* **2**, 327–38.

Benedict, H. (1979). Early lexical development: comprehension and production. *Journal of Child Language* **6**, 183–200.

Bornstein, M. H. (1985). Habituation of attention as a measure of visual information processing in human infants: summary, systematization, and synthesis. In *Measurement of audition and vision in the first year of life* (ed. G. Gottlieb and N. A. Krasnegor), Ablex, Norwood, NJ.

Borton, R. W. (1979). The perception of causality in infants. Presented at the Meeting of the Society for Research in Child Development, San Francisco, CA, March 1979.

Brazelton, T. B., Koslowski, B., and Main, M. (1974). The origins of reciprocity: the early mother–infant interaction. In *Origins of behavior* (ed. M. Lewis and L. Rosenblum), Wiley, New York.

Bretherton, I., McNew, S., and Beeghly-Smith, M. (1981). Early person knowledge as expressed in gestural and verbal communication: when do infants acquire a 'theory of mind'? In *Infant social cognition* (ed. M. Lamb and L. R. Sherrod). Erlbaum, Hillsdale, NJ.

Bruner, J. S. (1975). From communication to language: a psychological perspective. *Cognition* **3**, 255–87.

Butterworth, G. and Grover, L. (1988). The origins of referential communication in human infancy. In *Thought without language* (ed. L. Weiskrantz). Clarendon Press, Oxford.

Campos, J. J. and Stenberg, C. R. (1981). Perception, appraisal, and emotion: the onset of social referencing. In *Infant social cognition* (ed. M. E. Lamb and L. R. Sherrod). Erlbaum, Hillsdale, NJ.

Carey, S., Klatt, L. and Schlaffer, M. (1992). Infants' representations of objects and nonsolid substances. Unpublished manuscript, Massachusetts Institute of Technology.

Caron, A. J., Caron, R. F., and MacLean, D. J. (1988). Infant discrimination of naturalistic emotional expressions: the role of face and voice. *Child Development* **59**, 604–16.

Cohn, J.F. and Elmore, M. (1988). Effect of contingent changes in mothers' affective expression on the organization of behavior in 3-month-old infants. *Infant Behavior and Development* **11**, 493–505.

Cohn, J. F. and Tronick, E. Z. (1988). Mother–infant face-to-face interaction: influence is bidirectional and unrelated to periodic cycles in either partner's behavior. *Developmental Psychology* **24**, 386–92.

DeVries, R. (1987). Children's conceptions of shadow phenomena. *Genetic Psychology Monographs* **112**, 479–530.

Ehrlich, S. (1993). Infant perception of gaze direction. Presented to the Meeting of the Society for Research in Child Development, New Orleans, LA.

Ellsworth, C. P., Muir, D. W., and Hains, S.M.J. (1993). Social competence and person–object differentiation: an analysis of the still-face effect. *Developmental Psychology* **29**, 63–73.

Feinman, S. and Lewis, M. (1983). Social referencing at 10 months: a second order effect on infants' responses to strangers. *Child Development* **54**, 878–87.

Fernald, A. (1993). Approval and disapproval: infant responsiveness to vocal affect in familiar and unfamiliar languages. *Child Development* **64**, 657–74.

Field, T. (1977). Effects of early separation, interactive deficits, and experimental manipulation on infant-mother face-to-face interaction. *Child Development* **48**, 763–71.

Field, T. (1982). Infant arousal, attention, and affect during early interactions. In *Advances in infancy research,* Vol. 1, (ed. L. Lipsitt). Ablex, Norwood, NJ.

Field, T. and Walden, T. (1981). Production and perception of facial expressions in infancy and early childhood. In *Advances in child development and behavior* (ed. H. W. Reese and L. P. Lipsitt). Academic Press, New York.

Field, T. M., Woodson, R., Greenberg, R., and Cohen, D. (1982). Discrimination and imitation of facial expressions by neonates. *Science* **218**, 179–81.

Field, T., Goldstein, S., Vega-Lahr, N., and Porter, K. (1986*a*). Changes in imitative behavior during early infancy. *Infant Behavior and Development* **9**, 415–21.

Field, T., Vega-Lahar, N., Scafidi, F., and Goldstein, S. (1986*b*). Effects of maternal unavailability on motion–infant interactions. *Infant Behavior and Development* **9**, 473–8.

Gelman, R. (1990). First principles organize attention to and learning about relevant data: number and the animate–inanimate distinction as examples. *Cognitive Science* **14**, 79–106.

Golinkoff, R. M. (1983). Infant social cognition: self, people and objects. In *Piaget and the foundations of knowledge* (ed. L. S. Liben). Erlbaum, Hillsdale, NJ.

Golinkoff, R. M., Harding, C. G., Carlson, V., and Sexton, M. E. (1984). The infant's perception of causal events: the distinction between animate and inanimate objects. In *Advances in infancy research* (ed. L. P. Lipsitt and C. Rovee-Collier). Ablex, Norwood, NJ.

Gusella, J. L., Muir, D. W., and Tronick, E. Z. (1988). The effect of manipulating maternal behavior during an interaction on 3- and 6-month-olds' affect and attention. *Child Development* 59, 1111-24.

Hains, S. M. J., Rehkopf, B., and Case, A. (1992). Facial orientation of parents and elicited smiling by infants. *Infant Behavior and Development* 15, 444.

Haviland, J. M. and Lelwica, M. (1987). The induced affect response: 10-week-old infants' responses to three emotional expressions. *Developmental Psychology* 23, 97-104.

Hornick, R., Risenhoover, N., and Gunnar, M. (1987). The effects of maternal positive, neutral, and negative affective communications on infant responses to new toys. *Child Development* 58, 937-44.

Huttenlocher, J. and Smiley, P. (1990). Emerging notions of persons. In *Psychological and biological approaches to emotion* (ed. N. Stein, B. Leventhal, and T. Trabasso). Erlbaum, Hillsdale, NJ.

Jones, S. S., Collins, K., and Hong, H. (1991). An audience effect on smile production in ten-month-old infants. *Psychological Science* 2, 45-9.

Kestenbaum, R., Ternine, N., and Spelke, E. S. (1987). Perception of objects and object boundaries by three-month-old infants. *British Journal of Developmental Psychology* 5, 367-83.

Legerstee, M. (1991). The role of person and object in eliciting early imitation. *Journal of Experimental Child Psychology* 51, 423-33.

Legerstee, M. (1992). A review of the animate–inanimate distinction in infancy: implications for models of social and cognitive knowing. *Early Development and Parenting* 1, 59-67.

Legerstee, M. (1994). Patterns of 4-month-old infant responses to hidden silent and sounding people and objects. *Early Development and Parenting* 3(2), 71-80.

Legerstee, M., Pomerleau, A., Malcuit, G., and Feider, H. (1987). The development of infants' responses to people and a doll: implications for research in communication. *Infant Behavior and Development* 10, 81-95.

Legerstee, M., Corter, C., and Kienapple, K. (1990). Hand, arm and facial actions of young infants to a social and non-social stimulus. *Child Development* 61, 774-84.

Leslie, A. M. (1982). The perception of causality in infants. *Perception* 11, 173-86.

Leslie, A. M. (1984). Spatiotemporal continuity and the perception of causality in infants. *Perception* 13, 287-305.

Leslie, A. M. (1988). The necessity of illusion: perception and thought in infancy. In *Thought without language* (ed. L. Weiskrantz). Clarendon Press, Oxford.

Leslie, A. M. (1991). Infants' understanding of invisible displacement. Presented at the Meeting of the Society for Research in Child Development, Seattle, WA.

Leslie, A. M. and Keeble, S. (1987). Do six-month-old infants perceive causality? *Cognition* 25, 265-88.

Liwag, M. D. and Stein, N. L. (1993). The effects of retrieval instructions on children's memory for emotion episodes. Presented at the Meeting of the Society for Research in Child Development, New Orleans, LA.

Mandler, J. M. (1992). How to build a baby II: conceptual primitives. *Psychological Review* 99, 587-604.

Meltzoff, A. N. and Moore, M. K. (1977). Imitation of facial and manual gestures by human neonates. *Science* **198**, 75–78.

Meltzoff, A. N. and Moore, M. K. (1983). Newborn infants imitate adult facial gestures. *Child Development* **54**, 702–9.

Meltzoff, A. N. and Moore, M. K. (1992). Early imitation within a functional framework: the importance of person identity, movement, and development. *Infant Behavior and Development* **15**, 479–505.

Michotte, A. (1963). *The perception of causality* Basic Books, New York.

Muir, D. W. and Hains, S. M. J. (1993). Infant sensitivity to perturbations in adult facial, vocal, tactile, and contingent stimulation during face to face interactions. In *Developmental neurocognition: speech and face processing in the first year* (ed. B. de Boysson-Bardies, S. de Schonen, P. Jusczyk, P. McNeilage, and J. Morton). Kluwer, Dordrecht.

Murphy, C. M. and Messer, D. J. (1977). Mothers, infants and pointing: a study of a gesture. In *Studies in mother–infant interaction* (ed. H. R. Schaffer). Academic Press, London.

Oakes, L. M. (1993). The perception of causality by 7- and 10-month-old infants. Presented at the Meeting of the Society for Research in Child Development, New Orleans, LA.

Oakes, L. M. and Cohen, L. B. (1990). Infant perception of a causal event. *Cognitive Development* **5**, 193–207.

O'Neill, D. (1993). Two-year-olds' ability to provide their mothers with knowledge. Presented at the Meeting of the Society for Research in Child Development, New Orleans, LA.

Oster, H. (1981). 'Recognition of emotional expressions in infancy? In *Infant social cognition: empirical and theoretical considerations* (ed. M. E. Lamb and L. R. Sherrod), pp. 85–125. Erlbaum, Hillsdale, NJ.

Pelaez-Nogueras, M. (1993). Infant learning to reference maternal emotional cues. Unpublished doctoral dissertation, Florida International University.

Pelaez-Nogueras, M. and Gewirtz, J. L. (1993). Mothers' contingent imitation increases infant vocalizations. Presented at the Meeting of the Society for Research in Child Development, New Orleans, LA.

Poulin-Dubois, D. and Schultz, T. R. (1988). The development of the understanding of human behavior: from agency to intentionality. In *Developing theories of mind* (ed. J. W. Astington, P. L. Harris, and D. R. Olson), pp. 109–25. Cambridge University Press.

Premack, D. (1990). The infant's theory of self-propelled objects. *Cognition* **36**, 1–16.

Rach-Longman, K. and Muir, D. W. (1990). Three-month-olds' responses to televised upright and inverted faces of their mothers and a stranger during face-to-face interactions. *Infant Behavior and Development* **3**, 576.

Reissland, N. (1988). Neonatal imitation in the first hour of life: observations in rural Nepal. *Developmental Psychology* **24**, 464–9.

Rosen, W. D., Adamson, L. B. and Bakeman, R. (1992). An experimental investigation of infant social referencing: mothers' messages and gender differences. *Developmental Psychology* **28**, 1172–8.

Ross, H. S. and Lollis, S. P. (1987). Communication within infant social games. *Developmental Psychology* **23**, 241–8.

Rovee-Collier, C. K., Earley, L. and Stafford, S. (1989). Ontogeny of early event memory: III. Attentional determinants of retrieval at 2 and 3 months. *Infant Behavior and Development* **12**, 147-61.

Scaife, M. and Bruner, J. S. (1975). The capacity for joint visual attention in the infant. *Nature, London* **253**, 265.

Scollon, R. (1976). *Conversations with a one-year-old*. University of Hawaii Press, Honolulu, HI.

Shatz, M. (1983). Communication. In *Handbook of child psychology*, Vol. 3, *Cognitive development* (ed. J. H. Flavell and E. M. Markman), pp. 841-89. Wiley, New York.

Shatz, M., Wellman, H. M. and Silber, S. (1983). The acquisition of mental verbs: a systematic investigation of the first reference to mental states. *Cognition* **14**, 301-21.

Sitskoorn, H. M. and Smitsmon, A. W. (submitted). *Infants' perception of object relations: passing through a support?*

Sorce, J., Emde, R., Campos, J. and Klinnert, M. (1985). Maternal emotional signaling: its effect on the visual cliff behavior of 1-year-olds. *Developmental Psychology* **21**, 195-200.

Spelke, E. S. (1985). Preferential looking methods as tools for the study of cognition in infancy. In *Measurement of audition and vision in the first year of postnatal life* (ed. G. Gottlieb and N. Krasnegor). Ablex, Norwood, NJ.

Spelke, E. S. (1988). Where perceiving ends and thinking begins: the apprehension of objects in infancy. In *Perceptual development in infancy. Minnesota Symposium on Child Psychology*, Vol. 20 (ed. A. Yonas). Erlbaum, Hillsdale, NJ.

Spelke, E. S. and Van de Walle, G. (1993). Perceiving and reasoning about objects: insights from infants. In *Spatial representation* (ed. N. Eilan, W. Brewer, and R. McCarthy). Blackwell, New York.

Spelke, E. S., von Hofsten, C. and Kestenbaum, R. (1989). Object perception and object-directed reaching in infancy: interaction of spatial and kinetic information for object boundaries. *Developmental Psychology* **25**, 185-96.

Spelke, E. S., Breinlinger, K., Macomber, J. and Jacobson, K. (1992). Origins of knowledge. *Psychological Review* **99**, 605-32.

Spelke, E. S., Katz, G., Purcell, S. E., Ehrlich, S. M. and Breinlinger, K. (1994). Early knowledge of object motion: continuity and inertia. *Cognition* **51(2)**, 131-76.

Spelke, E. S., Breinlinger, K., Jacobson, K. and Phillips, A. Gestalt relations and object perception in infancy: a developmental study. *Perception* **22**, 1483-501.

Stern, D. N. (1974). Mother and infant at play. In *The effect of the infant on its caregiver* (ed. M. Lewis and L. Rosenblum). Wiley, New York.

Stevenson, M. B., Hoeve, J. N. V., Roach, M. A. and Leavitt, L. A. (1986). The beginning of conversation: early patterns of mother-infant vocal responsiveness. *Infant Behavior and Development* **9**, 423-40.

Stewart, J. (1984). Object motion and the perception of animacy. Presented at the Meeting of the Psychonomic Society, San Antonio, TX.

Tomasello, M. (1993). Acquiring words in non-ostensive context. Paper presented at the Meeting of the Society for Research in Child Development, New Orleans, LA.

Travis, L. L. (1993). Goal-based orizanization of event memory in toddlers. Presented at the Meeting of the Society for Research in Child Development, New Orleans, LA.

Trevarthen, C. (1977). Descriptive analyses of infant communicative behavior. In

Studies in mother–infant interaction (ed. H. R. Schaffer). Academic Press, London.

Trevarthen, C. (1979). Communication and cooperation in early infancy: A description of primary intersubjectivity. In *Before speech: the beginning of interpersonal communication* (ed. M. Bullowa), pp. 321–47. Cambridge University Press.

Tronick, E. (1981). Infant communicative intent: the infant's reference to social interaction. In *Language behavior in infancy and early childhood* (ed. R. E. Stark). Elsevier, New York.

Tronick, E., Als, H., Adamson, L., Wise, S. and Brazelton, T. B. (1978). The infant's response to entrapment between contradictory messages in face-to-face interaction. *Journal of the American Academy of Child Psychiatry* **17**, 1–13.

Tronick, E. Z., Cohn, J. and Shea, E. (1986). The transfer of affect between mothers and infants. In *Affective development in infancy* (ed. T. B. Brazelton and M. W. Yogman, pp. 11–25. Ablex, Norwood, NJ.

Van de Walle, G. and Spelke, E. S. (1993). Integrating information over time: infant perception of partly occluded objects. Presented at the Meeting of the Society for Research in Child Development, New Orleans, LA.

Vinter, A. (1986). The role of movement in eliciting early imitations. *Child Development* **57**, 66–71.

Van de Walle, G., Woodward, A. L. and Phillips, A. (1994). Infants' inferences about contact relations in a causal event. Presented at the IXth Biennial Meeting of the International Society for Infant Studies, Paris.

van Hofsten, C. and Spelke, E. S. (1985). Object perception and object-directed reaching in infancy. *Journal of Experimental Psychology: General* **114**, 198–212.

Walden, T. A. and Baxter, A. (1989). The effect of context and age on social referencing. *Child Development* **60**, 1511–18.

Walden, T. A. and Ogan, T. A. (1988). The development of social referencing. *Child Development* **59**, 1230–40.

Walker, A. S. (1982). Intermodal perception of expressive behaviors by human infants. *Journal of Experimental Child Psychology* **33**, 514–35.

Walker-Andrews, A. S. and Grolnick, W. (1983). Infants' discrimination of vocal expressions. *Infant Behavior and Development* **6**, 491–8.

Walker-Andrews, A. S. and Lennon, E. (1991). Infants' discrimination of vocal expressions: Contributions of auditory and visual information. *Infant Behavior and Development* **14**, 131–42.

Watson, J. S. (1972). Smiling, cooing, and 'the game'. *Merrill-Palmer Quarterly* **118**, 323–40.

Wellman, H. M. and Wooley, J. D. (1990). From simple desires to ordinary beliefs: the early development of everyday psychology. *Cognition* **35**, 245–75.

Wilcox, T., Rosser, R., and Nadel, L. (submitted). *Location memory in young infants.*

Woodward, A. L., Phillips, A. and Spelke, E. S. (1993). Infants' expectations about the motion of animate versus inanimate objects. Proceedings of the Fifteenth Annual Meeting of the Cognitive Science Society, Boulder, CO, pp. 1087–91. Erlbaum, Hillside, NJ.

Wynn, K. (1992). Addition and subtraction by human infants. *Nature* **358**, 749–50.

Xu, F. and Carey, S. (1992). Infants' concept of numerical identity. Presented at the Boston University Language Acquisition Conference.

4

The acquisition of physical knowledge in infancy

RENEE BAILLARGEON, LAURA KOTOVSKY, AND AMY NEEDHAM

INTRODUCTION

What role does causality play in the development of infants' physical reasoning? The answer to this question naturally depends on *how* we define causality. On the one hand, we might characterize causal reasoning at a very general level in terms of the construction of conceptual descriptions that capture regularities in the displacements of objects and their interactions with other objects. On the other hand, we might take causality to mean something far more specific associated with the formation of sequences in which one event is understood to bring about another event through the transmission of force or some other generative process.

In this chapter we focus primarily on the first of the two definitions listed above. There is now considerable evidence that, in learning about physical events, infants construct increasingly elaborate descriptions that enable them to arrive at increasingly accurate predictions about the events. How does this construction process take place? Over the past few years, we have begun to build a model of the development of infants' physical reasoning. This model is based on the assumption that infants are born, not with substantive beliefs about objects, as Leslie (1988; Chapter 5 of this volume) and Spelke and her colleagues (Spelke 1991; Spelke *et al*. 1992; Chapter 3 of this volume) have proposed, but with a highly constrained mechanism that guides infants' acquisition of knowledge about objects. The model is derived from findings concerning the development of infants' intuitions about different phenomena (for example support, collision, unveiling, arrested-motion, occlusion, and containment phenomena). Comparison of these findings points to a developmental pattern that recurs across ages and phenomena. We assume that this pattern reflects, at least indirectly, the nature and properties of infants' innate learning mechanism.

In what follows, we describe the developmental pattern identified in the model and review some of the evidence supporting it (readers are referred to Baillargeon (in press *a*, *b*, *c*) for further discussion of the model). Finally, we contrast the present approach with that adopted by Spelke and her colleagues (Spelke 1991; Spelke *et al.* 1992; Chapter 3 of this volume) and by Leslie (1988; Chapter 5 of this volume). In this context, we return to the second, more specific, definition of causality mentioned earlier and ask whether this definition, with its focus on notions of force or generative transmission, can shed further light on the findings discussed in this chapter.

INITIAL CONCEPTS AND VARIABLES

Current evidence suggests that, when learning about a physical phenomenon, infants first form a preliminary all-or-nothing concept that captures the essence of the phenomenon but few of its details. In time, this *initial concept* is progressively elaborated. Infants slowly identify discrete and continuous *variables* that are relevant to the phenomenon and incorporate this accrued knowledge into their reasoning, resulting in increasingly accurate interpretations and predictions over time.

To illustrate the distinction between initial concepts and variables, we shall summarize experiments on the development of young infants' reasoning about support, collision, and unveiling phenomena.

Reasoning about support phenomena

Evidence from our laboratory
Adults possess sophisticated intuitions about support relations between objects. These intuitions enable them to place objects safely on tables and shelves, stack objects in cupboards and trunks, carry armfuls of groceries and dishes, improvise makeshift shelters and ladders, and balance ornaments at the top of Christmas trees and wedding cakes.

At what age do infants begin to develop an understanding of support phenomena? To address this question, we conducted a series of experiments in which infants aged from 3 to 6.5 months were presented with simple support problems involving a box and a platform.

Initial concept: contact between the box and platform   In our first experiment (Needham and Baillargeon 1993*a*) we asked whether 4.5-month-old infants appreciate that a box can be stable when released *on* but not *off* a platform. The infants saw the possible and impossible events depicted in Fig. 4.1. In the possible event, a gloved hand deposited a box on a platform and then retreated a short distance, leaving the box supported by the

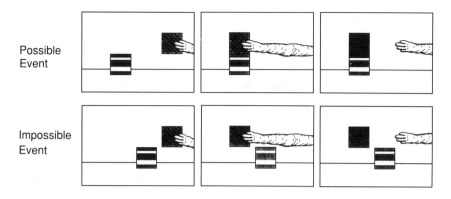

Fig. 4.1. Schematic drawing of the test events used by Needham and Baillargeon (1993a).

platform. In the impossible event, the hand deposited the box beyond the platform and then retreated, leaving the box suspended in mid-air with no visible means of support. Additional groups of 4.5-month-old infants were tested in two control conditions. In one, the infants saw the same test events as the infants in the experimental condition except that the hand never released the box, which was therefore continuously supported. In the other control condition, the infants again saw the same test events as the infants in the experimental condition except that the box fell when released by the hand beyond the platform.

The results showed that the infants in the experimental condition looked reliably longer at the impossible than at the possible event, whereas the infants in the two control conditions tended to look equally at the events they were shown. Together, these results indicated that the infants expected the box to fall when it was released beyond the platform and were surprised that it did not.

The results of this first experiment suggested that, by 4.5 months of age, infants expect objects to fall when released in mid-air. The next experiment asked whether 3-month-old infants also possess intuitions about support phenomena (Needham and Baillargeon, 1993b). The infants watched test events in which the extended index finger of a gloved hand pushed a box from left to right along the top surface of a platform (Fig. 4.2). In the possible event, the box was pushed until its leading edge reached the end of the platform. In the impossible event, the box was pushed entirely off the platform and stayed suspended in mid-air. Prior to the test events, the infants saw familiarization events that were similar except that a longer platform was used so that the box was always fully supported (Fig. 4.2).

Familiarization Events

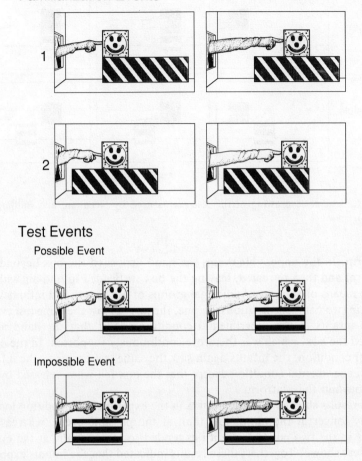

Fig. 4.2. Schematic drawing of the events used by Needham and Baillargeon (1993*b*, experiment 1).

A second group of infants was tested in a control condition identical to the experimental condition except that the hand grasped the box, which was therefore continuously supported.

The infants in the experimental condition looked reliably longer at the impossible than at the possible event, whereas the infants in the control condition tended to look equally at the test events that they were shown. These results suggested that the infants in the experimental condition expected the box to fall when it was pushed off the platform and were surprised that it did not.

Hand-in-Box Condition

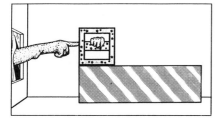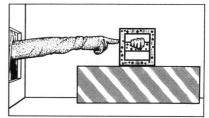

Empty-Box Condition

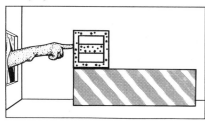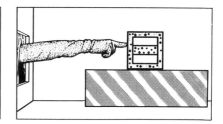

Fig. 4.3. Schematic drawing of the events used by Needham and Baillargeon (1993*b*, experiment 2).

This interpretation was supported by the results of another experiment with 3-month-old infants (Needham and Baillargeon 1993*b*). The infants in this experiment saw the same familiarization and test events as the infants in the experimental condition in the first experiment. However, prior to seeing these events the infants received an additional trial that was similar to the familiarization trials except that the front of the box was removed, creating a large opening (Fig. 4.3). For half the infants (hand-in-box condition), a second hand could be seen through the opening, holding the back of the box. For the other infants (empty-box condition), no hand was visible inside the box.

The results indicated that the infants in the empty-box condition looked reliably longer at the impossible than at the possible event, but that the infants in the hand-in-box condition tended to look equally at the two events. Together, these results pointed to two conclusions. The first was that the infants in the empty-box condition preferred the impossible event, not because they were intrigued to see the box suspended in mid-air, but because they were surprised that the box remained stable after it lost contact with the platform. The second conclusion was that the infants in the hand-in-box condition were able to take advantage of the information given at the start of the experiment to make sense of the impossible event;

Possible Event

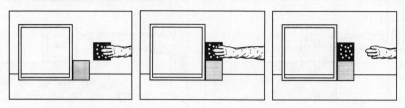

Impossible Event

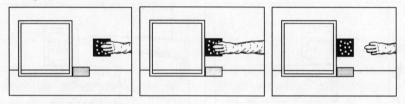

Fig. 4.4. Schematic drawing of the test events used by R. Baillargeon, H. Raschke, and A. Needham (in preparation).

specifically, they realized that the box did not fall when pushed off the platform because it was held at the back by a second hidden hand.

Discrete variable: type of contact between the box and platform   The results of our initial experiments indicated that, by 3 months of age, infants understand that a box must be in contact with a platform in order to be stable. In our next experiment (R. Baillargeon, H. Raschke, and A. Needham, in preparation) we asked whether infants also appreciate what *type of contact* is needed between a box and a platform for the box to be stable. In the experiment, 4.5-month-old infants saw the possible and impossible events depicted in Fig. 4.4. In the possible event, a gloved hand placed a small square box against the side of a large open platform on top of a smaller closed platform. The impossible event was identical with the possible event except that the closed platform was much thinner so that the box lay well above it.

The results indicated that the female infants looked reliably longer at the impossible than at the possible event, suggesting that they (a) realized that the box was inadequately supported when it contacted only the side of the open platform and hence (b) expected the box to fall in the impossible event and were surprised that it did not. A control condition in which the hand retained its grasp on the box provided evidence for this interpretation.

In contrast with the female infants, the male infants in the experimental condition tended to look equally at the impossible and the possible events, suggesting that they believed that the box was adequately supported in both events. Because female infants mature slightly faster than male infants (Haywood 1986; Held, in press), sex differences such as the one described here are not uncommon in infancy research (Baillargeon and DeVos 1991; L. Kotovsky and R. Baillargeon, in preparation). Given this evidence, it is likely that, when tested with the same experimental procedure, slightly younger female infants (i.e. infants aged 3.5 months) would perform like the 4.5-month-old male infants, and slightly older male infants (i.e infants aged 5.5 months) would perform like the 4.5-month-old female infants. An experiment is under way to confirm this last prediction.

Continuous variable: amount of contact between the box and platform   The results of the last experiment indicated that, by 4.5 months of age, infants have begun to realize that a box can be stable when placed on but not against a platform. Our next experiment examined whether infants are aware that, in judging the box's stability, not only the type but also the amount of contact between the box and the platform must be considered (Baillargeon *et al.* 1992). Subjects were 6.5-month-old infants. The infants were assigned to either the 15 per cent or the 70 per cent condition. The infants in the 15 per cent condition watched test events in which a gloved hand pushed a box from left to right along the top of a platform (Fig. 4.5). In the possible event, the box was pushed until its leading edge reached the end of the platform. In the impossible event, the box was pushed until only the left 15 per cent of its bottom surface remained on the platform. The infants in the 70 per cent condition saw similar test events except that the box was pushed until the left 70 per cent, rather than the left 15 per cent, of its bottom surface remained on the platform. Prior to the test events, the infants in the two conditions watched familiarization events involving a longer platform (Fig. 4.5).

The results indicated that the infants in the 15 per cent condition looked reliably longer at the impossible than at the possible event, whereas the infants in the 70 per cent condition tended to look equally at the events that they were shown. These results suggested that the infants (a) realized that the box was adequately supported when 70 per cent, but not 15 per cent, of its bottom surface lay on the platform and hence (b) expected the box to fall in the impossible event and were surprised that it did not. This interpretation was confirmed by the results of a control condition identical with the 15 per cent condition except that the hand grasped the box, thereby ensuring its support.

In a subsequent experiment, 5.5-month-old infants were tested using the 15 per cent condition procedure (Baillargeon *et al.* 1992). Unlike the 6.5-month-old infants, these younger infants tended to look equally at the impossible and the possible events, as though they judged that the box

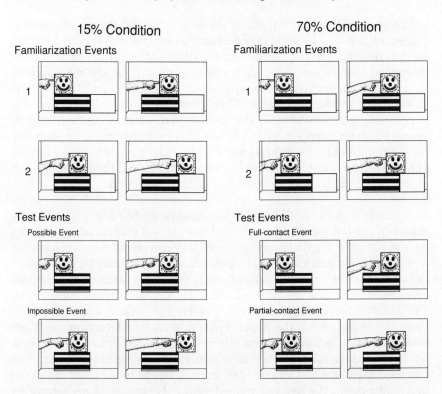

Fig. 4.5. Schematic drawing of the events used by Baillargeon *et al.* (1992).

was adequately supported even when only its left corner remained on the platform. This negative result was replicated in a later experiment (Needham and Baillargeon 1993*b*).

Conclusions   The results reported in this section suggest that, in reasoning about support problems involving a box and a platform, infants progress through the following developmental sequence. By 3 months of age, if not before, infants expect the box to fall if it loses contact with the platform and to remain stable otherwise. At this stage, any contact between the box and the platform is deemed sufficient to ensure the box's stability. At least two developments take place between 3 and 6.5 months of age. First, infants become aware that the type of contact between the box and the platform must be taken into account when reasoning about the box's stability. Infants initially assume that the box will remain stable if placed either on or against the platform. By 4.5 to (presumably) 5.5 months of age, however, infants come to distinguish between the two types of contact and recognize that only the former ensures support. The second development is that infants begin to appreciate that the amount of contact between the box and the platform affects the box's stability. Initially, infants believe that the box will be stable even if only a small portion (e.g. the left 15 per cent) of its bottom surface rests on the platform. By 6.5 months of age, however, infants expect the box to fall unless a significant portion (e.g. 70 per cent) of its bottom surface is supported.

One way of describing this developmental sequence is that, when learning about the support relation between two objects, infants first form an initial concept centred on a distinction between contact and no contact. In time, this initial concept is slowly elaborated. Infants identify first a discrete (type of contact between the objects) and later a continuous (amount of contact between the objects) variable and incorporate them into their initial concept, leading to increasingly successful predictions over time.

Evidence from Spelke's laboratory

The evidence reviewed in the preceding section indicates that young infants possess intuitions about support phenomena. This evidence contrasts with reports from Spelke's laboratory (Spelke *et al.* 1992; E. S. Spelke, K. Jacobson, M. Keller, and D. Sebba, submitted; E. S. Spelke, A. Simmons, K. Breinlinger, and K. Jacobson, submitted) that young infants either lack such intuitions, or possess intuitions that are best characterized as exceedingly fragile and limited. These reports involve six different experiments, most of which yielded negative results. In what follows, we describe these various experiments and consider alternative explanations for their findings.

Experiments with a falling object that stops in mid-air

In the first experiment we discuss (Spelke *et al.* 1992, experiment 4), 4-month-old infants were habituated to an event in which a hand released a ball in mid-air and the ball then fell some distance until it disappeared behind a screen. After a few seconds, the screen was removed to reveal the ball resting on a horizontal surface above the floor of the apparatus. Following habituation, the horizontal surface was removed, and the infants saw a possible and an impossible test event. In the possible event, the ball was revealed on the apparatus floor when the screen was removed. In the impossible event, the ball was revealed in the same position that it had occupied in the habituation event; however, because the horizontal surface was no longer present, the ball now appeared to be floating in mid-air. The infants tended to look equally at the impossible and the possible events, suggesting that they were not surprised to see the ball suspended in mid-air when the screen was removed.

How can we account for these negative results? One possibility is suggested by a comparison of the impossible event used by Spelke *et al.* (1992, experiment 4) with that shown in the first support experiment described above (Needham and Baillargeon 1993a). In the impossible event devised by Spelke *et al.*, a hand released a ball which then fell behind a screen; after a few seconds the screen was removed to reveal the ball floating in mid-air. In the impossible event used by Needham and Baillargeon (1993*a*), a hand released a box which remained suspended in mid-air (Fig. 4.1). Thus a subtle difference between the violations shown in the two experiments was that the latter involved a dynamic event in which an object lost its support and yet failed to fall, whereas the former involved a static display in which an object was revealed already suspended in mid-air.

Evidence for the importance of this distinction was provided by an additional experiment conducted by Needham and Baillargeon (1993*a*) using the same box and platform as before (Fig. 4.1). The infants in this experiment saw a possible and an impossible static test display. In the possible display, the box rested on the platform, as in the possible event shown in the initial experiment. In the impossible display, the box stood suspended in mid-air to the left of the platform, as in the impossible event used in the initial experiment. The results indicated that the infants tended to look equally at the two displays as though they were not surprised in the impossible display to see the box suspended above the apparatus floor with no visible source of support.

What should be made of the fact that the infants in both the experiment of Spelke *et al.* (1992, experiment 4) and the above experiment failed to respond to the impossible static displays that they were shown? At least two hypotheses come to mind. One is that, unlike dynamic events in which objects are observed to lose their supports, static displays involving suspended objects fail to engage infants' reasoning about support. It could be that infants initially reason about support relations only in situations where they can identify two clear participants: an object and a support (e.g. a hand and a platform). In such situations, infants would readily demonstrate an expectation that the object should fall when inadequately supported (Needham and Baillargeon 1993*a*, *b*; R. Baillargeon, H. Raschke, and A. Needham, submitted). In contrast, situations in which an object floats in mid-air without a visible support (and infants have been given no hint of a hidden support) would fail to engage or bring forth infants' intuitions about support, leading to unsuccessful performances.

A second (and perhaps not unrelated) hypothesis is associated with the nature of the data available to infants concerning support phenomena. From birth, infants no doubt experience countless situations whose outcome is consistent with the notion that objects fall when they lose contact with their supports. Thus infants may notice that their dummies fall when they open their mouths, and that toys fall when they open their hands. Similarly, infants may observe that objects typically fall when released (or are swept off tables) by their parents and siblings. In addition to these situations, however, infants may also experience situations involving stable and yet apparently unsupported objects: shades on floor-lamps, ceiling fans, lamps suspended in front of a wall, hanging plants, or even doorknobs could all seem to be free-floating in space when viewed in such a way that their supports are not visible. It could be that, by 4 or even 3 months of age (Needham and Baillargeon 1993*b*), infants have formed definite expectations about the first type of situation: they expect objects to fall when they lose their supports. At the same time, infants might possess no expectations about the second type of situation, as though the latter did not yet fall within the purview of support phenomena.

Whatever the explanation for young infants' consistent lack of response to static displays involving apparently unsupported objects, there is evidence that, by 6 months of age, infants already show reliable surprise at such displays. In another experiment, Spelke *et al.* (E. S. Spelke, A. Simmons, K. Breinlinger, and K. Jacobson, submitted, experiment 1) tested 6-month-old infants with the same procedure that they had used with their 4-month-old subjects (Spelke *et al.* 1992, experiment 4). The results indicated that these older infants looked reliably longer at the impossible than at the possible event. This positive finding was later confirmed in an experiment (E. S. Spelke, K. Jacobson, M. Keller, and D. Sebba, submitted, experiment 2) conducted with a similar procedure except that the screen was absent; thus the infants saw the ball fall in full view to the horizontal surface (habituation event), the apparatus floor (possible event), or a point in mid-air corresponding to the position of the horizontal surface in the habituation event. The infants again showed a reliable preference for the impossible over the possible event, suggesting that they were surprised to see the ball suspended in mid-air with no apparent support. Additional results (E. S. Spelke, K. Jacobson, M. Keller, and D. Sebba, submitted; E. S. Spelke, A. Simmons, K. Breinlinger, submitted) provided further evidence for this interpretation.

Experiments with an object released in mid-air   In the preceding sub-section, we discussed two experiments conducted by Spelke and her colleagues (E. S. Spelke, K. Jacobson, M. Keller, and D. Sebba, submitted, experiment 2, 1993*b*, experiment 1) with 6-month-old infants that yielded positive results. In contrast with these two experiments, three additional experiments carried out by Spelke *et al.* (E. S. Spelke, K. Jacobson, M. Keller, and D. Sebba, submitted) with 6-month-old infants produced negative findings. Surprisingly, the method of these three experiments was very similar to that of the two successful experiments described above. For example, in one experiment (E. S. Spelke, K. Jacobson, M. Keller, and D. Sebba, submitted, experiment 4) the infants were habituated to an event in which a hand lowered a ball to a horizontal surface above an apparatus floor and then released the ball. Following habituation, the surface was removed and the hand released the ball after lowering it either to the apparatus floor (possible event) or to a point in mid-air corresponding to the surface's position in the habituation event (impossible event). Another experiment (E. S. Spelke, K. Jacobson, M. Keller, and D. Sebba, submitted, experiment 7) was similar to the last except that the hand moved the ball forward in depth instead of lowering it from above. Finally, a third experiment (E. S. Spelke, K. Jacobson, M. Keller, and D. Sebba, submitted, experiment 6) again examined infants' responses to test events in which a ball was released after being lowered to a surface (possible event) or to a point in mid-air (impossible event); however, no habituation event was shown in this experiment.

How can we account for the discrepancy between the positive and negative results obtained by Spelke *et al.* (E. S. Spelke, K. Jacobson, M. Keller, and D. Sebba, submitted; E. S. Spelke, A. Simmons, K. Breinlinger, and K. Jacobson, submitted) in these five, superficially very similar, experiments? The most probable explanation is related to infants' ability to detect that the hand had released the ball. In the two experiments that yielded positive results (E. S. Spelke, K. Jacobson, M. Keller, and D. Sebba, submitted, experiment 2; E. S. Spelke, A. Simmons, K. Breinlinger, and K. Jacobson, submitted, experiment 1), the hand dropped the ball, making it very easy for the infants to notice that the hand no longer held the ball. However, in all three of the experiments that produced negative results, the hand moved the ball to its final position and then released it, presumably by opening its fingers (there is no mention in the papers that the hand moved away from the ball). It may be that this form of release was too subtle for 6-month-old infants. Yonas and his colleagues (Yonas and Granrud 1984; Yonas *et al.* 1987) have demonstrated that depth perception develops according to a regular sequence: kinetic cues are used by infants at birth, binocular cues at about 4 months, and pictorial cues at about 7 months. In the experiments under discussion, an important cue as to whether the hand was holding or had released the ball may have been pictorial in nature: the occlusion or non-occlusion of the ball by the hand's fingers (the figures in Spelke *et al.* (E. S. Spelke, K. Jacobson, M. Keller and D. Sebba, submitted; E. S. Spelke, A. Simmons, K. Breinlinger, and K. Jacobson, submitted) suggest that the hand held the ball from the back, with only the fingers visible). Lacking the ability to interpret this occlusion cue, the 6-month-old infants in the experiments would have been unable to determine whether the hand was holding or had released the ball, and hence would have failed to detect the violations that they were shown (for further situations in which infants fail to show surprise at impossible events because of limited depth perception, see Baillargeon (in press *a*)).

Experiment with an object rolling across a gap   Spelke *et al.* (E. S. Spelke, A. Simmons, K. Breinlinger, and K. Jacobson, submitted, experiment 3) reported one further experiment with 6-month-old infants that had negative findings. The infants were habituated to an event in which a ball rolled from left to right along the upper of two horizontal surfaces and disappeared behind a screen that hid the right end portion of the two surfaces. After a few seconds, the screen was removed to reveal the ball resting on the upper surface against the right wall of the apparatus. Following habituation, a gap considerably wider than the ball was created in the upper surface, behind the screen, and the infants saw a possible and an impossible test event. The possible event was similar to the habituation event except that the ball rolled along the lower of the two surfaces. The impossible event was identical to the habituation event: the ball rolled along the upper surface and disappeared behind the screen; when the screen was removed, the ball was revealed on the same surface to the right of the gap. The infants did not show a reliable preference for the impossible over the possible event, suggesting that they were not surprised, when the screen was removed, to see the ball resting past the gap in the apparatus's upper surface.

To what should these negative findings be attributed? One possibility is that the infants lacked the physical knowledge necessary to interpret the test events correctly; their knowledge of displacement, as opposed to support, phenomena might have been too limited for them to appreciate the conditions under which a moving object can 'jump' across a gap (e.g. a golf ball that rolls across a hole instead of falling into it). A second possibility is that the infants possessed the knowledge required to detect the violation shown in the impossible event, but failed to demonstrate this knowledge because they did not attend to the gap's presence (for examples of attentional failures in infants' physical reasoning, see Baillargeon (in press *a*)). Yet a third possibility, and the one we believe is most likely, is related to the design of the experiment. Recall that the impossible event was perceptually more similar than the possible event to the habituation event: the ball rolled along the upper surface in the habituation and the impossible events, and along the lower surface in the possible event.

The type of cross-design used in this experiment is frequently used (Baillargeon *et al.* 1985; Baillargeon 1987; Spelke 1991; Spelke *et al.* 1992), no doubt because it presents obvious advantages: if an impossible event is perceptually more similar than a possible event to a habituation event, then a higher response to the impossible event cannot be interpreted as a superficial novelty response. Nevertheless, data from our laboratory have led us to suspect that such a design may not be appropriate for infants aged 6 months and older. In a series of experiments on arrested-motion phenomena, infants aged 5.5, 4.5, and 3.5 months were habituated to a screen that rotated through a 180° arc (Baillargeon *et al.* 1985; Baillargeon 1987). Following habituation, a box was placed behind the screen, and the infants saw a possible and an impossible test event (Fig. 4.6). In the possible event, the screen rotated until it reached the box (112° arc); in the impossible event, the screen rotated through a full 180° arc, as though the box were no longer behind it. The results indicated that the 5.5- and

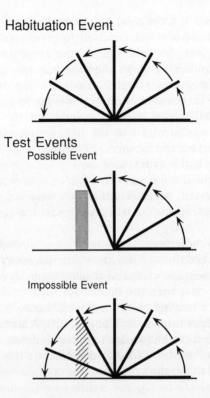

Fig. 4.6. Schematic drawing of the events used by Baillargeon (1987).

4.5-month-old infants, and even some of those aged 3.5 months, looked reliably longer at the impossible than at the possible event, suggesting that they expected the screen to stop when it reached the box and were surprised that it did not in the impossible event. Control data obtained without a box behind the screen provided evidence for this interpretation.

In a subsequent unpublished experiment, we also tested 6.5-month-old infants using the same procedure. Much to our surprise, however, the data collected with these older infants were negative: the infants tended to look equally at the two test events. In our quest for an explanation of this puzzling finding, we were led to examine more closely the infants' responses to the first pair of test trials in which they were presented with the impossible and the possible events. Data analyses indicated that the infants looked reliably longer at whichever event they were shown first. This result led us to the hypothesis that the 6.5-month-old infants looked equally at the two test events because they were responding simultaneously to both the physical novelty of the impossible event and the perceptual novelty of the possible event. Recall that the screen moved through a full 180° rotation in the habituation and the impossible events, but underwent a shorter 112° rotation in the possible event. To examine this hypothesis, we tested an additional group of 6.5-month-old infants using the same procedure as before, except that the infants received a single habituation trial. The infants now showed a reliable preference for the impossible event, presumably because the single habituation trial was not sufficient to lead them to perceive the possible event as more novel than the impossible event.

Given our claim that cross-designs may be not be suitable for testing infants aged 6.5 months and older, readers may wonder how we explain the two positive results that Spelke *et al.* (E. S. Spelke, K. Jacobson, M. Keller, and D. Sebba, submitted, experiment 2; E. S. Spelke, A. Simmons, K. Breinlinger, and K. Jacobson, submitted, experiment 1) obtained with 6-month-old infants. Recall that, in both experiments (described above), a ball fell to a surface above the apparatus floor in the habituation event. In the test events, the surface was removed and the ball fell to the same position in mid-air (impossible event) or to a novel position on the apparatus floor (possible event). Our intuition is that the infants encoded the ball's position in the habituation event not in absolute terms (e.g. 'the ball is occupying *x* location in space'), but rather in relative terms (e.g. 'the ball is on the surface'). In the test events, the surface was removed so that both positions of the ball appeared relatively novel. Research with older children has also found that, when landmarks are available, subjects are more likely to encode and remember objects' locations in terms of the landmarks rather than in absolute terms (Acredolo 1978).

Knowledge about collision phenomena

Evidence from our laboratory

Initial concept: impact between a moving and a stationary object   Our research on infants' reasoning about collision phenomena has focused on simple problems involving a moving and a stationary object. Our first experiment (L. Kotovsky and R. Baillargeon, in preparation) asked whether 2.5-month-old infants expect a stationary object to be displaced when it is hit by a moving object. The infants in the experiment sat in front of an inclined ramp, to the right of which was a track (Fig. 4.7). The infants were first habituated to a cylinder that rolled down the ramp; small stoppers prevented it from rolling past the ramp onto the track. Following habituation, a large wheeled toy bug was placed on the track. In the possible event, the bug was placed 10 cm from the ramp. In this event, the bug was not hit by the cylinder and remained stationary after the cylinder rolled down the ramp. In the impossible event, the bug was placed directly at the bottom of the ramp. In this event, the bug was hit by the cylinder but again remained stationary. Adult subjects typically expected the bug to be

Habituation Events
Far-Wall Event

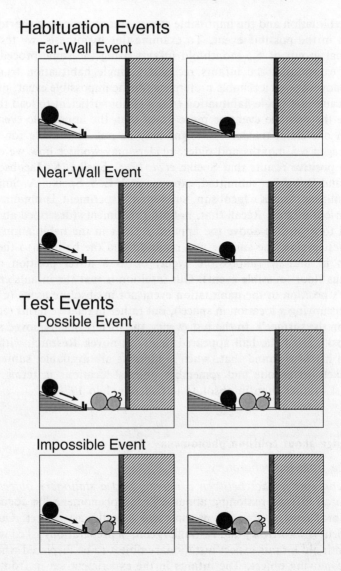

Near-Wall Event

Test Events
Possible Event

Impossible Event

Fig. 4.7. Schematic drawing of the events used by L. Kotovsky and R. Baillargeon (in preparation, experiment 1).

displaced when hit by the cylinder; the experiment thus tested whether 2.5-month-old infants would possess the same expectation.

A second group of 2.5-month-old infants was tested in a control condition identical to the experimental condition with one exception. In each test event, the right wall of the apparatus was adjusted so that it stood against the front end of the bug, preventing its displacement.*

The infants in the experimental condition looked reliably longer at the impossible than at the possible event, whereas the infants in the control condition tended to look equally at the two test events that they were shown. Together, these results pointed to two conclusions. One was that the infants in the experimental condition expected the bug to be displaced when hit and hence were surprised that it remained stationary in the impossible event. The second conclusion was that the infants in the control condition realized that the bug remained stationary when hit because its displacement was prevented by the wall.

A second experiment provided support for the findings of this initial experiment (L. Kotovsky and R. Baillargeon, in preparation). The infants saw habituation events similar to those used in the previous experiment, except that a tall thin barrier was added. On alternate trials, this barrier stood across the ramp, where it blocked the cylinder's path, or behind the ramp, out of the cylinder's path (Fig. 4.8). Following habituation, the bug was placed at the bottom of the ramp. In the possible event, the barrier stood behind the ramp; the cylinder rolled down the ramp and hit the bug, causing it to roll down the track. In the impossible event, the barrier stood across the ramp so that the cylinder now hit the barrier rather than the bug; nevertheless, the bug again rolled down the track, as in the possible event.

The infants tended to look equally at the two habituation events, but looked reliably longer at the impossible than at the possible test event. These results suggested that the infants preferred the impossible event, not because they were intrigued to see the barrier standing across as opposed to behind the ramp, but because they were surprised to see the bug move when the cylinder hit the barrier rather than the bug. An experiment is in progress to provide further support for this interpretation.

Continuous variable: size of the moving object   The results of our initial experiments indicated that, by 2.5 months of age, infants expect a stationary object to be displaced when hit by a moving object. Our next experiments asked whether infants realized that how far a stationary object is displaced, when hit by a moving object, depends on the moving object's

---

* To equate the test events shown to the infants in the experimental and the control conditions more closely, the right wall of the apparatus was also moved in the experimental test events: in each event the wall was positioned 10 cm from the front end of the bug. The infants were also shown the two wall positions on alternate habituation trials (see Fig. 4.7). Analysis of the habituation data revealed no reliable preference for either wall position.

Habituation Events

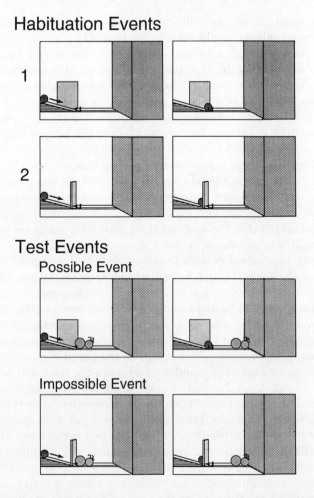

Fig. 4.8. Schematic drawing of the events used by L. Kotovsky and R. Baillargeon (in preparation, experiment 2).

size or, more precisely, mass (however, because our data are insufficient to judge whether infants based their predictions on the moving object's size or mass, we shall refer only to its size). Subjects in the experiments were 11-month-old infants (Kotovsky and Baillargeon, 1994) and 6.5-month-old infants (L. Kotovsky and R. Baillargeon, in preparation). However, because similar findings were obtained with the two age groups, only the experiment with the younger infants will be described.

The apparatus and stimuli in this experiment (L. Kotovsky and R. Baillargeon, in preparation) were similar to those used in the previous experiments, except that the track was much longer (Fig. 4.9). The infants in the mid-point condition were habituated to a blue medium-size cylinder

Mid-point Condition
Habituation Event

End-point Condition
Habituation Event

Test Events
Large-Cylinder Event

Test Events
Large-Cylinder Event

Small-Cylinder Event

Small-Cylinder Event

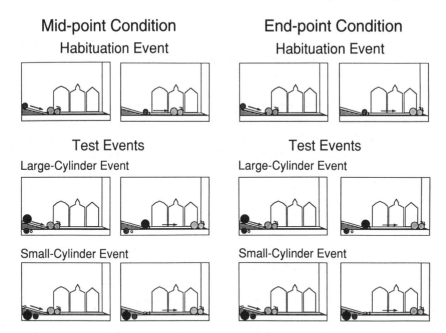

Fig. 4.9. Schematic drawing of the events used by L. Kotovsky and R. Baillargeon, (in preparation, experiment 1).

that rolled down the ramp and hit the bug, causing it to roll to the middle of the track. Two new cylinders (constructed of the same material as the habituation cylinder) were introduced in the test events: a yellow cylinder that was larger than the habituation cylinder, and an orange cylinder that was smaller than the habituation cylinder. Both cylinders caused the bug to travel farther than in the habituation event: the bug now stopped only when it reached the end of the track and hit the right wall of the apparatus.

When asked how far the bug would roll when hit by any one cylinder, adult subjects were typically reluctant to hazard a guess: they were aware that the length of the bug's trajectory depended on a host of factors (for example the weight of the cylinder and bug, the smoothness of the ramp and track, and so on) about which they had no information. However, after observing that the bug rolled to the middle of the track when hit by the medium cylinder, adult subjects readily predicted that it would roll farther with the larger cylinder and less far with the smaller cylinder, and were surprised when this last prediction was violated. The experiment thus tested whether 6.5-month-old infants, like adults, (a) would understand that the size of the cylinder affected the length of the bug's displacement and (b) would be able to use the information conveyed in the habituation event to calibrate their predictions about the test events.

A second group of infants (end-point condition) were tested in a condition identical to the mid-point condition except that they were given a different calibration point in the habituation event. As shown in Fig. 4.9, the medium cylinder now caused the bug to roll to the end of the track, just as in the test events.

After seeing that the bug rolled to the end of the track when hit by the medium cylinder, adult subjects (a) expected it to do the same with the large cylinder and (b) were not surprised to see it do the same with the small cylinder (subjects simply concluded that the track was too short to show the effects of cylinder size). The experiment thus tested whether 6.5-month-old infants, like adults, would perceive both the end-point condition test events as possible.

The results indicated that the infants in the mid-point condition looked reliably longer at the small cylinder event than at the large-cylinder event, whereas the infants in the end-point condition tended to look equally at the two events. Together, these results indicated that the infants (a) were aware that the size of the cylinder should affect the length of the bug's trajectory and (b) used the habituation event to calibrate their predictions about the test events. After watching the bug travel to the middle of the track when hit by the medium cylinder, the infants were surprised to see it travel farther with the smaller but not the larger cylinder. In contrast, after watching the bug travel to the end of the track with the medium cylinder, the infants were not surprised to see it do the same with either the small or the large cylinder.

In a subsequent experiment, 5.5-month-old infants were tested with the procedure used in the mid-point condition (L. Kotovsky and R. Baillargeon, in preparation). The performance of the female infants was identical to that of the 6.5-month-old infants, suggesting that they were surprised to see the bug roll to the end of the track with the small but not the large cylinder. This interpretation was supported by an additional experiment in which 5.5-month-old female infants were shown the end-point condition events. Like the 6.5-month-old infants, they now looked equally at the small- and large-cylinder events.

In contrast with the female infants, the male infants who were shown the mid-point condition events tended to look equally at the small- and large-cylinder events. These negative results suggested that the infants were not surprised, after seeing the medium cylinder cause the bug to roll to the middle of the track, to see the small cylinder cause it to roll to the end of the track. At least two interpretations could be advanced for this negative finding. One was that the male infants were still unaware that the size of the cylinder could be used to reason about the length of the bug's displacement. The other was that the male infants had difficulty in remembering how far the bug had travelled in the habituation event and hence

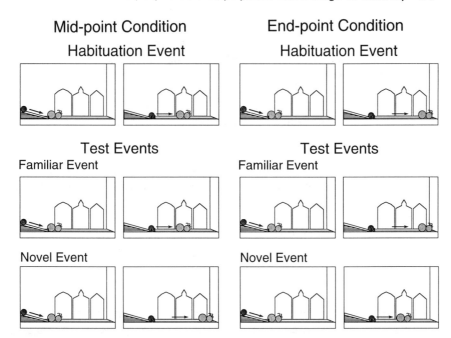

Fig. 4.10. Schematic drawing of the events used by L. Kotovsky and R. Baillargeon (in preparation, experiment 3).

lacked the necessary information to calibrate their predictions about the small and large cylinders.

To examine this second interpretation, two groups of 5.5-month-old male infants were tested in a simple memory experiment (L. Kotovsky and R. Baillargeon, in preparation). As before, the infants in the mid-point condition were habituated to the medium cylinder rolling down the ramp and hitting the bug, causing it to roll to the middle of the track (Fig. 4.10). Following habituation, the infants saw two test events. One (familiar test event) was identical to the habituation event. In the other event (novel test event), the medium cylinder now caused the bug to roll to the end of the track. The infants in the end-point condition saw similar habituation and test events, except that the bug rolled to the end of the track in the habituation event, so that which test event was familiar and which was novel was reversed.

The results revealed a significant overall preference for the novel over the familiar test event, indicating that the infants had no difficulty recalling how far the bug had rolled in the habituation event. Data from a pilot experiment provided further support for this conclusion. The infants in this experiment saw the same habituation event as the infants in the mid-point condition above. During the test events, two novel medium cylinders were introduced, one yellow and the other orange; both caused the bug to roll to the end of the track. The infants' looking times indicated that they found both events surprising, suggesting that they (a) remembered that the blue medium cylinder in the habituation event caused the bug to roll to the middle of the track and (b) expected it to roll the same distance when hit by the yellow and orange medium cylinders, and were surprised that it did not.

Together, the findings obtained with the 5.5-month-old male infants suggest the following conclusion. After observing that the medium cylinder causes the bug to roll to the middle of the track, 5.5-month-old male infants expect it to do so again when hit by a cylinder of the same size, but have no expectation as to how far it should roll when hit by cylinders of different sizes. Infants seem unaware that they possess information that they can use to reason about the novel cylinders.

Conclusions Together, the results of the collision experiments reported above point to the following developmental sequence. By 2.5 months of age, infants expect a stationary object to be displaced when hit by a moving object; however, they are not yet aware that the size of the moving object can be used to predict how far the stationary object will be displaced. For example, if shown that a medium cylinder causes a bug to roll to the middle of a track, infants have no expectation that it should travel farther when hit by a larger cylinder and less far when hit by a smaller cylinder. By 5.5–6.5 months of age, however, infants not only recognize that a stationary object should be displaced when hit by a moving object, but also appreciate that how far the stationary object is displaced depends on the size of the moving object.

One interpretation of these findings is that, when learning about collision events between a moving and a stationary object, infants first form an initial concept centred on a distinction between impact and no impact. With further experience, infants begin to identify variables that influence this initial concept. By 5.5–6.5 months of age, infants realize that the size of the moving object can be used to predict how far the stationary object will be displaced.

Evidence from other laboratories
Because collision events constitute prototypical causal sequences for adults, infants' responses to such events have long been of interest to researchers interested in the development of causal reasoning (Leslie and Keeble 1987; Oakes and Cohen 1990). These investigations have established that infants readily distinguish between collision events that adults perceive as causal and non-causal.

In one experiment, Oakes and Cohen (1990) habituated 6- and 10-month-old infants to one of three videotaped events: (a) a causal event in which a moving toy contacted a stationary toy, which immediately moved off; (b) a non-causal event in which a 1-second delay separated the motion of the first and the second toy; (c) another non-causal event in which a spatial gap of 2.5 cm separated the motion of the two toys. Following habituation, the infants were presented with the two events not shown in habituation. The results indicated that the 10-month-old infants who had been habituated to the causal event dishabituated to the two non-causal events, whereas those habituated to either of the non-causal events dishabituated only to the causal event. In contrast, the 6-month-old infants tended to look equally at the events. The authors concluded that, by 10 months of age, infants are already able to differentiate between causal and non-causal events.

Additional evidence obtained with a different method suggests that 6-month-old infants are also sensitive to causality in event sequences. Leslie and Keeble (1987) habituated 6-month-old infants to an animated film depicting either a causal or a non-causal collision event. In the causal event, the infants saw a red brick move from left to right and collide with a green brick, which immediately moved off. The non-causal event was identical except that the movement of the green brick was delayed by 0.5 seconds. Following habituation, the infants saw the same event in reverse. The authors reasoned that, whereas only spatiotemporal direction was reversed in the non-causal test event, both spatiotemporal and causal direction were reversed in the causal event. Therefore, if the infants were sensitive to causality, they should dishabituate more to the causal than to the non-causal test event. The results indicated that the infants looked reliably longer when the causal rather than the non-causal event was reversed. These and control results suggested that, by 6 months of age, infants are already sensitive to the causal properties of events.

How should the findings of Oakes and Cohen (1990) and Leslie and Keeble (1987) be integrated with the results of the collision experiments reported in the previous section? We might be tempted to conclude that the 6.5- and 11-month-old infants (Kotovsky and Baillargeon 1994; L. Kotovsky and R. Baillargeon, in preparation) in our experiments not only (a) expected the bug to move when hit by the cylinder and (b) realized that the size of the cylinder affected the length of the bug's displacement, but also (c) perceived the relation between the cylinder's and the bug's motion in causal terms. Such a causal relation might be defined in terms of abstract conceptual roles (i.e. 'agent', 'patient'), or in terms of a physical force transmitted from one object to the other, with a greater force resulting in a greater effect.

However, it is not entirely clear whether such a conclusion would be appropriate. A rather surprising aspect of the findings reported by Oakes and Cohen (1990) and Leslie and Keeble (1987) concerns their habituation

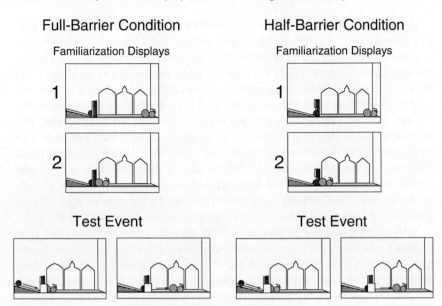

Fig. 4.11. Schematic drawing of the test events used by L. Kotovsky and R. Baillargeon (in preparation).

data. Both sets of authors reported that, in the habituation phases of their experiments, the infants tended to look equally at the causal and the non-causal collision events that they were shown. Thus, even though a spatial or a temporal gap separated the motion of the first and the second object in the non-causal events, the infants showed little or no surprise at the events. Such negative findings appear at odds with those obtained in the present experiments. Recall, for example, that even 2.5-month-old infants were found to look reliably longer when a spatial gap (created by a barrier) separated the motion of the cylinder and the bug than when no such gap existed and the cylinder hit the bug directly (L. Kotovsky and R. Baillargeon, in preparation).

Data from a further collision experiment might help bring this issue into sharper focus (L. Kotovsky and R. Baillargeon, in preparation). In this experiment, 7.5-month-old infants were assigned to a full- or a half-barrier condition. The infants in the full-barrier condition were first shown the two static familiarization displays depicted in Fig. 4.11. In the first display, the infants saw a tall thin barrier standing at the bottom of a ramp; a medium cylinder lay on the ramp, against the left side of the barrier. In the second familiarization display, a bug was added and stood against the right side of the barrier. It was hoped that examination of the two displays would lead the infants to realize that the barrier prevented contact between the cylinder and the bug. The infants in the half-barrier condition saw identical displays except that the lower half of the barrier was removed, so that contact between the cylinder and the bug was possible (the half-barrier was supported by a post located on the far side of the ramp). Following the two familiarization trials, a small screen was positioned at the bottom of, and parallel to, the ramp. The screen hid the rear portion of the bug as well as the lower portion of the barrier; with the screen in place, the full and the half barrier appeared identical. The infants in the two conditions watched, on four successive trials, a test event in which the medium cylinder rolled down the ramp and the bug rolled to the middle of the track.

Even though the infants in the full- and half-barrier conditions saw exactly the same test event, those in the full-barrier condition were found to look reliably longer than those in the half-barrier condition. These results suggested that the infants (a) remembered which barrier was present behind the screen, (b) understood that the cylinder could contact the bug when the half but not the full barrier was in place, and hence (c) were surprised in the full-barrier condition to see the bug move off after the cylinder rolled down the ramp. Data from a control condition in which the bug remained stationary with both the full and the half barriers confirmed this interpretation.

The design of this last experiment was similar in many ways to the habituation portions of the experiments conducted by Leslie and Keeble (1987) and Oakes and Cohen (1990). In each case, different groups of infants were shown collision events that adults might describe as causal (the first object causes the motion of the second object) or non-causal (the first object cannot be the cause of the motion of the second object because the motions of the two objects are separated by a temporal or a spatial gap). However, despite the similarity in their designs, the experiments yielded very different results.

We believe that such a discrepancy is important because it raises questions about the generality of the findings obtained by Leslie and Keeble (1987) and Oakes and Cohen (1990). The causal and non-causal events used by these authors involved filmed or videotaped events very different from the live events shown in the present experiments. Recall that in our events the infants saw an object that was set in motion by a hand roll down a ramp and loudly hit another object, which then rolled to a stop. Many of these features differed in the events shown by Leslie and Keeble and by Oakes and Cohen: the objects initiated their own movements, showed little or no deceleration, and so on.

These observations suggest the following speculations. It may be that, when shown stylized collisions, infants readily perceive non-causal events as arbitrary and make little attempt to understand them. However, when

Possible Event

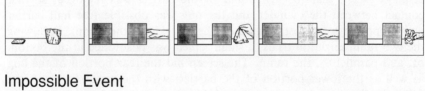

Impossible Event

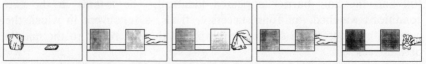

Fig. 4.12. Schematic drawing of the test events used by Baillargeon and DeVos (1993, experiment 1).

shown more natural collisions, infants may adopt a more inquisitive attitude toward non-causal events. Such an attitude might stem from two distinct sources. On the one hand, infants might dismiss the first object's motion as the cause of the second object's motion and scrutinize the event for an alternative cause. On the other hand, infants might still perceive the first object's motion as the cause of the second object's displacement, but be puzzled as to how this effect could have been accomplished. The interest of the second interpretation is that it would indicate that the conditions under which infants perceive events as causal or non-causal differ for different stimuli.

Knowledge about unveiling phenomena

Initial concept: presence of a protuberance in a cloth cover

Our experiments on unveiling phenomena have involved problems in which a cloth cover is removed to reveal an object. Our first experiment examined whether 9.5-month-old infants realize that the presence (absence) of a protuberance in a cover signals the presence (absence) of an object beneath the cover (Baillargeon and DeVos 1993). At the start of the possible event, the infants saw two covers made of a soft fluid fabric; the left cover lay flat on the floor of the apparatus, and the right cover showed a marked protuberance (Fig. 4.12). Next, two screens were pushed in front of the covers, hiding them from view. A hand then reached behind the right screen and reappeared first with the cover and then with a toy bear of the same height as the protuberance shown earlier; the hand waved the bear gently to the side of the screen until the computer signalled that the trial had ended. The impossible event was identical except that the location of the

Possible Event

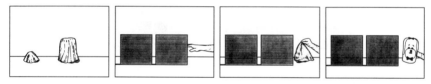

Impossible Event

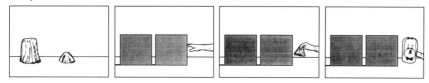

Fig. 4.13. Schematic drawing of the test events used by Baillargeon and DeVos (1993, experiment 2).

two covers at the start of the event was reversed, so that it should have been impossible for the hand to retrieve the bear.

The infants looked reliably longer at the impossible than at the possible event, suggesting that they understood that the bear could have been hidden under the cover with a protuberance but not the flat cover. This interpretation was supported by the results of a second condition in which the hand reached behind the left as opposed to the right screen so that the bear's position in the impossible and the possible events was reversed.

Continuous variable: size of the protuberance

The results of our first experiment indicated that, by 9 months of age, infants can use the existence of a protuberance in a cloth cover to infer the existence of an object beneath the cover. Our next experiment (Baillargeon and DeVos 1993) investigated whether infants could also use the size of the protuberance to infer the size of the object under the cover (Fig. 4.13). At the start of the possible event, the infants saw two covers made of a soft fabric; on the left was a small cover with a small protuberance and on the right was a large cover with a large protuberance. (The small protuberance was 10.5 cm high and the large protuberance 22 cm high thus the difference between the two was easily detectable.) Next, screens were pushed in front of the covers, and a gloved hand reached behind the right screen twice in succession, reappearing first with the cover and then with a large toy dog 22 cm in height. The impossible event was identical to the possible event except that the location of the two covers at the start of the event was reversed, so that the hand now appeared to retrieve the large dog from under the cover with the small protuberance.

Possible Event

Impossible Event

Fig. 4.14. Schematic drawing of the test events used by R. Baillargeon and J. DeVos (in preparation).

Unlike the infants in the last experiment, the infants in this experiment tended to look equally at the impossible and at the possible events, suggesting that they believed that the large dog could have been hidden under the cover with either the small or the large protuberance. The same result was obtained in a subsequent experiment in which a slightly different procedure was used (Baillargeon and DeVos, 1993). How should these negative findings be explained? At least two hypotheses could be proposed. One was that the infants were not yet aware that the size of the protuberance in each cover could be used to infer the size of the object hidden beneath the cover. The other explanation was that the infants recognized the significance of the protuberance's size, but had difficulty remembering this information after the cover was hidden from view.

The results of another experiment provided evidence for the first of these two interpretations. The infants in this experiment (R. Baillargeon and J. DeVos, in preparation), who were aged 9.5 and 12.5 months, were reminded of the size of the protuberance in the cover behind the screen (Fig. 4.14). At the start of the possible event, the infants saw the cover with the small protuberance; to the right of this cover was a second identical cover. After a brief pause, the first cover was hidden by the screen; the second cover remained visible to the right of the screen. Next, the hand reached behind the screen's right edge and removed first the cover and then a small toy dog 10.5 cm in height. The hand held the small dog next to the visible cover, allowing the infants to compare their sizes directly. The impossible event was identical with the possible event, except that the hand retrieved the large toy dog (22 cm in height) from behind the screen.

The 12.5-month-old infants looked reliably longer at the impossible than at the possible event, suggesting that they realized that the small but not the large dog could have been hidden under the cover behind the screen. This interpretation was supported by the results of a control condition in which the infants simply saw each dog held next to the visible cover (as in the rightmost panels in Fig. 4.14); no reliable preference was found for the large-dog over the small-dog display.

In contrast with the 12.5-month-old infants, the 9.5-month-old infants tended to look equally at the impossible and the possible events. Thus, despite the fact that the infants had available a reminder — an exact copy — of the cover behind the screen, they still failed to show surprise at the retrieval of the large dog. It might be argued that infants less than 12.5 months of age are simply unable, when reasoning about hidden objects, to take advantage of reminders such as the visible cover. However, evidence from other experiments (Baillargeon 1991) indicates that even young infants can make use of visual reminders to make predictions concerning hidden objects.

Conclusions

The results summarized above suggest the following developmental sequence. By 9 months of age, infants realize that the existence of a protuberance in a cloth cover signals the existence of an object beneath the cover; they are surprised to see an object retrieved from under a flat cover but not from under a cover with a protuberance. However, infants are not yet aware that the size of the protuberance can be used to infer the size of the hidden object. When shown a cover with a small protuberance, they are not surprised to see either a small or a large object retrieved from under the cover. Furthermore, providing a reminder of the protuberance's size has no effect on infants' performance. However, under the same conditions 12.5-month-old infants show reliable surprise at the large object's retrieval.

One interpretation of these findings is that, when learning about unveiling phenomena, infants first form an initial concept centred on a distinction between a protuberance and no protuberance. Later on, infants identify a continuous variable that affects this concept: they begin to appreciate that the size of the protuberance in a cover can be used to predict the size of the object hidden under the cover.

Other phenomena

In the preceding sections, we have examined the development of infants' intuitions about three distinct phenomena: support, collision, and unveiling phenomena. In each case, we have argued that infants' knowledge develops in a regular sequence beginning with the identification of a core event, followed in time by the addition of discrete and continuous variables (for a discussion of how variables are revised in time, see Baillargeon (in press *a*)).

Habituation Events

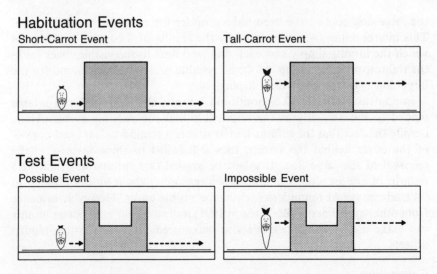

Fig. 4.15. Schematic drawing of the events used by Baillargeon and DeVos (1991).

Would other physical phenomena lend themselves to similar developmental descriptions? Research already in the literature provides encouraging hints for future investigations.

Occlusion phenomena

In an earlier experiment we examined whether 3.5-month-old infants are aware that the height of an object affects whether it will be visible when passing behind a screen with a window (Baillargeon and DeVos 1991). The infants were habituated to a toy carrot that slid back and forth along a horizontal track whose centre was occluded by a screen; the carrot disappeared at one edge of the screen and reappeared, after an appropriate interval, at the other edge (see Fig. 4.15). On alternate trials, the infants saw a short or a tall carrot slide along the track. Following habituation, the mid-section of the screen's upper half was removed, creating a large window. The infants then saw a possible and an impossible test event. In the possible event, the short carrot moved back and forth along the track; this carrot was shorter than the window's lower edge and so did not appear in the window when passing behind the screen. In the impossible event, the tall carrot moved along the track; this carrot was taller than the window's lower edge and hence should have appeared in the window but did not in fact do so.

The results showed that the infants tended to look equally at the short- and the tall-carrot habituation events, but looked reliably longer at the impossible than at the possible test event. These results indicated that the infants (a) realized that the height of each carrot determined whether it should be visible in the screen window and hence (b) were surprised that the tall carrot failed to appear in the window in the impossible event.

In a subsequent experiment, 3-month-old infants were tested using the same procedure (Baillargeon and DeVos 1991). However, unlike the 3.5-month-old infants, these younger infants tended to look equally at the impossible and the possible test events. Together, these results might be taken to suggest that, by 3.5 months of age, infants have already identified one variable that affects the outcome of occlusion events: they realize that whether an object is fully or partially visible when passing behind an occluder depends on the height of the object relative to that of the occluder. However, younger infants may not have identified this variable.

These data give rise to intriguing questions regarding the development of infants' intuitions about occlusion phenomena. Do infants go through an initial stage in which they expect any object to be invisible when passing behind any occluder? Do infants then go on to identify both object variables (e.g. height and width of the object) and occluder variables (e.g. presence and location of windows) that are relevant to occlusion events? In collaboration with Andrea Aguiar, we have recently begun experiments that address these questions. Although preliminary, our results suggest that the answers to the questions are likely to be positive.

Containment phenomena

In one experiment, Sitskoorn and Smitsman (1991) presented 6-month-old infants with a possible and an impossible containment test event. In both events, a large box with an open top rested on the apparatus floor and a block was lowered into the box. In the possible event, the block was narrower than the box and hence could be contained in it; however, in the impossible event, the block was wider than the box and hence should not have been contained in it. The authors found that the infants looked longer at the impossible than at the possible event, suggesting that they were aware that the width of the block relative to that of the box determined whether one could fit into the other.

Future experiments could ask the following questions. Do infants go through an initial stage in which they expect that any object can be inserted into any open container, regardless of their respective dimensions? Also, at what age do infants become aware that the height, width, and compressibility of an object affect whether it will fit inside a given container? In collaboration with Andrea Aguiar, we have recently undertaken experiments that bear on this question. The data collected so far suggest that, at 5.5 months of age, infants are still unaware that the size of an object can be used to predict whether it can be contained in another;

unlike the infants tested by Sitskoorn and Smitsman (1991), our younger subjects failed to be surprised when shown a large ball being lowered into a much smaller container.

Passing-through phenomena

In a recent experiment, Spelke *et al.* (1992) habituated 4-month-old infants to an event in which a hand dropped a medium-sized ball behind a screen; after a few seconds, the screen was removed to reveal the ball resting on the lower of two horizontal surfaces beneath a gap in the upper surface that was wider than the ball. Following habituation, the infants saw a possible and an impossible test event that were identical to the habituation event except that two new balls were introduced. In the possible event, the ball was smaller than the habituation ball; in the impossible event, the ball was larger than both the habituation ball and the gap in the upper surface of the apparatus. The infants looked reliably longer at the impossible than at the possible event, suggesting that, by 4 months of age, infants are aware that the width of an object relative to that of a gap affects whether one can pass through the other (for another example of an arrested-motion phenomenon in which 4.5-month-old infants appear aware of a size variable, see Baillargeon (1991)).

Further experiments could ask the following questions. Is there an initial stage in which infants expect any object to pass through any surface that presents a gap, regardless of their respective dimensions? At what age do infants become aware that these dimensions matter?

Mechanisms of change

In the preceding section, we have described striking parallels in the development of infants' knowledge of support, collision, and unveiling pehnomena. We have also hinted, on the basis of various findings, that similar patterns may be found in the study of other phenomena such as occlusion, containment, and passing-through phenomena.

How can these various developmental sequences be explained? We believe that they reflect, not the gradual unfolding or progressive enrichment of innate beliefs about objects, but rather the application of a highly constrained innate learning mechanism to available data. In the present approach, the problem of explaining the age at which specific initial concepts and variables are understood is that of determining (a) what data (observations or manipulations) are necessary for learning and (b) when these data become available to infants.

To illustrate this, consider the developmental sequence revealed in the support experiments described above (pp. 86-7). One might propose that 3-month-old infants have already learned that objects fall when released in mid-air (Needham and Baillargeon 1993*b*) because this expectation is consistent with countless observations (e.g. watching their carers drop peas in pots, toys in baskets, clothes in hampers) and manipulations (e.g. noticing that their dummies fall when they open their mouths) available virtually from birth.

Furthermore, one might speculate that infants do not begin to recognize what type of contact is needed between objects and their supports until 4.5 months (R. Baillargeon, H. Raschke, and A. Needham, in preparation) because it is not until this age that infants have available pertinent data from which to abstract this variable. Researchers have found that unilateral visually guided reaching emerges at about 4 months of age (White *et al.* 1964; Newell *et al.* 1989). With this new-found ability, infants may have the opportunity deliberately to place objects against other objects, and to observe the consequences of these actions. According to this account, the sex difference revealed in our experiment would be traceable to female infants' engaging in these manipulations slightly ahead of male infants.

In a similar vein, one could suggest that it is not until 6.5 months that infants begin to appreciate how much contact is needed between objects and their supports (Baillargeon *et al.* 1992) because, once again, it is not until this age that infants have available data from which to learn such a variable. Investigators have reported that the ability to sit without support emerges at about 6 months of age; infants then become able to sit in front of tables (e.g. on a parent's lap or in a high-chair) with their upper limbs and hands relieved from the encumbrance of postural maintenance and thus free to manipulate objects (Rochat and Bullinger, in press). For the first time, infants may have the opportunity to deposit objects on tables and to note that they tend to fall unless a significant portion of their bottom surfaces is supported.

In the natural course of events, infants would be unlikely to learn about variables such as type or amount of contact from visual observation alone because carers rarely deposit objects against vertical surfaces or on the edges of horizontal surfaces. However, there is no a priori reason to assume that infants could not learn such variables if given appropriate observations. We have recently undertaken a new research programme to investigate this possibility. This programme involves experiments that attempt to teach infants initial concepts and variables that they have not yet acquired.

To illustrate, consider once again the finding that 6.5-month-old but not 5.5-month-old infants are aware that the amount of contact between a symmetrical box and a platform affects whether the box will be stable (Baillargeon *et al.* 1992). We speculated above that infants identify the variable 'amount of contact' when they begin to generate, through their own manipulations, data from which to learn it. But what if the data were made available to infants in a different way, through exposure to a carefully constructed set of observations? Would infants aged less than 6.5 months be able to learn, on the basis of such observations, that the amount of contact between a box and a platform must be taken into account when predicting the box's stability? To examine these questions, we have recently begun an experiment in which 5.5-month-old infants are tested with events similar to those used in the 15 per cent condition in the experiment conducted by Baillargeon *et al.* (1992) (see Fig. 4.5). Prior to seeing these test events, however, the infants receive training trials in which they see a hand deposit a box on a platform and then withdraw a short distance, as in Needham and Baillargeon (1993*a*) (see Fig. 4.1). On alternate trials, the box is deposited in such a way that either 100 per cent or only 15 per cent of its bottom surface is in contact with the platform. In the first situation, the box remains stable when released; in the second, the box falls. Our hope is that, after seeing such training trials, infants will for the first time show surprise when, in the impossible test event, the finger pushes the box until only 15 per cent of its bottom surface rests on the platform.

In the course of conducting this and related experiments, we hope to determine precisely what type of observations, and how many, are necessary for infants to abstract the variable 'amount of contact'. The interest of such teaching experiments is that they will provide useful insights into the nature and properties of infants' innate learning mechanisms.

CONCLUDING REMARKS

The approach to infants' physical reasoning described in this chapter differs from that adopted by Spelke and her colleagues (Spelke 1991; Spelke *et al.* 1992; Chapter 3 of this volume) and Leslie (1988, Chapter 5 of this volume) in several respects. In these brief remarks, we shall focus on one major difference between these approaches, namely the nature and content of infants' innate endowment.

Spelke and her colleagues (Spelke 1991; Spelke *et al.* 1992) have argued that infants are born with certain core beliefs about objects, such as the belief that objects move along connected unobstructed paths. Non-core beliefs, such as the belief that objects require support to remain stable, would be acquired through observations and manipulations of objects. One prediction suggested by this distinction is that core principles would be demonstrated earlier than non-core beliefs, and would be revealed uniformly in all situations in which they are implicated. Non-core principles, in contrast, would yield more fragile piecemeal patterns, with performance varying widely across situations and infants.

The present approach differs from that of Spelke in that it assumes that infants are neither born with nor acquire general beliefs about objects. Rather, infants are thought to identify types of interactions between objects, and to learn in each case first initial concepts and variables. Thus infants are expected to learn separately about barrier phenomena, passing-through phenomena, containment phenomena, and unveiling phenomena, even though all such phenomena reflect the same fundamental principle that two objects cannot occupy the same space at the same time. The evidence, reviewed in this chapter, that infants learn about some of these phenomena long before others is of course consistent with this view; recall, for example, that infants have been shown to be aware that the size of an object affects whether it can pass through a given gap before they realize that the size of an object affects whether it can be inserted in a given container, or that the size of a protuberance in a cloth cover signals the size of the object hidden under the cover.

Of course, it is possible that in the course of development infants or children eventually come to integrate their knowledge of related phenomena into a single unified structure, but we believe that these developments are initially quite separate. Infants, we suspect, go about the world identifying basic ways in which objects behave or interact. These types of interactions are akin to conceptual roles, i.e. infants reason about objects and occluders, objects and gaps, objects and supports, objects and barriers, objects and containers, objects and soft fluid covers, and so on. A key research question, from this perspective, is that of determining how infants' innate learning mechanism leads them to identify, on the basis of available observations and manipulations, these distinct conceptual categories.

Let us now turn to the approach adopted by Leslie (1988, Chapter 5 of this volume). He has suggested that, from birth, infants' reasoning about physical objects is guided by a notion of agency that focuses on mechanical force relations between objects. A straightforward way of reconciling Leslie's perspective with our own would be to propose that one of the fundamental constraints on infants' innate learning mechanism is an intuitive notion of force. From this viewpoint, infants' identification of and learning about different types of physical phenomena would be tantamount to their learning about how force relations are expressed or implemented in different physical contexts. Thus infants' learning about displacement, collision, or arrested-motion phenomena would be described in terms of objects bearing, transmitting, or resisting forces.

At the start of the chapter, we distinguished between two definitions of causality. We suggested that causal reasoning could be characterized at a general level in terms of the construction of conceptual descriptions that capture regularities in objects' displacements and interactions with other objects. However, causality could also be taken to mean something more specific associated with the formation of sequences in which events are linked through force relations. In describing our research in the preceding section of this chapter, we opted implicitly for the first of these definitions: infants' reasoning was discussed in terms of the identification of increasingly sophisticated regularities in the ways in which objects behave and interact. If we were to adopt Leslie's assumption that an intuitive notion of force lies at the core of infants' representations of objects' displacements and interactions, we would be shifting towards the second definition.

At the present time, we are still uncertain whether the data available to us warrant such a shift. Much of Leslie's research with infants has focused on collision events (see discussion of Leslie and Keeble (1987) on pp. 100-4). Such events naturally lend themselves to discussions of force relations. But what of other events such as support or unveiling events? Should we assume that infants represent such events in terms of objects passively exerting or resisting forces? And what of events such as occlusion events, where force descriptions seem inapplicable?

No doubt future research will help us to determine which, if any, of the three approaches discussed here most closely captures the development of infants' physical reasoning. Given the merits of each approach, however, it is plausible that our final model of physical reasoning in infancy will represent a combination of all three approaches. How might such a model be characterized? One possibility is that infants will be thought to be born with an innate learning mechanism that guides their identification of and learning about distinct physical phenomena — distinct conceptual ways in which objects behave and interact. Among the constraints on this learning mechanism will be a few core intuitive notions. One such notion may be related to a definition of an object — a definition less involved than but nevertheless akin to some of the core beliefs posited by Spelke to be innate (for example a tendency to view connected surfaces or surfaces that move together as wholes). Another such notion might be the force notion proposed by Leslie. However, such a notion would no longer operate as the central or key element in infants' physical representations; rather, it would operate as one of several constraints on these representations. In this broad perspective, infants' causal reasoning would thus come to encompass both definitions of causal reasoning mentioned earlier.

ACKNOWLEDGEMENTS

The research presented in this chapter was supported by grants to RB from the Guggenheim Foundation, the University of Illinois Center for Advanced Study, and the National Institute of Child Health and Human Development (HD-21104). We thank Jerry DeJong and Judy DeLoache for helpful comments and suggestions, Elizabeth Cullum for her help with the data analyses, and Andrea Aguiar, Elizabeth Cullum, Lincoln Craton, Julie DeVos, Marcia Graber, Myra Gillespie, Valerie Kolstad, Helen Raschke, and the undergraduate assistants at the Infant Cognition Laboratory, University of Illinois, for their help with the data collection. We would also like to thank the parents who kindly agreed to allow their infants to participate in the research.

Correspondence concerning this article should be sent to: Reneé Baillargeon, Department of Psychology, University of Illinois, 603 E. Daniel, Champaign, IL 61820, USA.

REFERENCES

Acredolo, L. (1978). Development of spatial orientation in infancy. *Developmental Psychology* **74**, 224–34.

Baillargeon, R. (1987). Object permanence in 3.5- and 4.5-month-old infants. *Developmental Psychology* **23**, 655–64.

Baillargeon, R. (1991). Reasoning about the height and location of a hidden object in 4.5- and 6.5-month-old infants. *Cognition* **38**, 13–42.

Baillargeon, R. (In press *a*). A model of the development of infants' physical reasoning. In *Advances in infancy research*, Vol. 9, (ed. C. Rovee-Collier and L. Lipsitt) Ablex, Norwood, NJ.

Baillargeon, R. (In press *b*). How do infants learn about the physical world? *Current Directions in Psychological Science*.

Baillargeon, R. (In press *c*). Physical reasoning in infancy. In *The cognitive neurosciences* (ed. M. S. Gazzaniga). MIT Press, Cambridge, MA.

Baillargeon, R. and DeVos, J. (1991). Object permanence in young infants: further evidence. *Child Development* **62**, 1227–46.

Baillargeon, R. and DeVos, J. (1993). The development of infants' intuitions about unveiling events. (In press).

Baillargeon, R., Spelke, E., and Wasserman, S. (1985). Object permanence in 5-month-old infants. *Cognition* **20**, 191–208.

Baillargeon, R., Needham, A., and DeVos, J. (1992). The development of young infants' intuitions about support. *Early Development and Parenting* **1**, 69–78.

Haywood, K. M. (1986). *Lifespan motor development*. Human Kinetics, Champaign, IL.

Held, R. Development of cortically mediated visual processes in human infants. In *Neurobiology of early infant behaviour* (ed. C. von Euler, H. Forssberg, and H. Lagercrantz) Macmillan, London.

Kotovsky, L. and Baillargeon, R. (1993*b*). Qualitative and quantitative reasoning about collision events in infants. In preparation.

Kotovsky, L. and Baillargeon, R. (1993*c*). Reasoning about hidden barriers: 7.5-month-old infants' responses to possible and impossible collision events. In preparation.

Kotovsky, L. and Baillargeon, R. (1993*d*). Should a stationary object be displaced when hit by a moving object? Reasoning about collision events in 2.5-month-old infants. In preparation.

Kotovsky, L. and Baillargeon, R. (1994). Calibration-based reasoning about collision events in 11-month-old infants. *Cognition* **51**, 107–29.

Leslie, A. M. (1988). The necessity of illusion: perception and thought in infancy. In *Thought without language* (ed. L. Weiskrantz). Oxford University Press.

Leslie, A. M. and Keeble, S. (1987). Do six-month-old infants perceive causality? *Cognition* **25**, 265–88.

Needham, A. and Baillargeon, R. (1993a). Intuitions about support in 4.5-month-old infants. *Cognition* **47**, 121–48.

Needham, A. and Baillargeon, R. (1993b). Reasoning about support in 3-month-old infants. (In press).

Newell, K. M., Scully, D. M., McDonald, P. V., and Baillargeon, R. (1989). Task constraints and infant grip configurations. *Developmental Psychobiology* **22**, 817–32.

Oakes, L. M. and Cohen, L. B. (1990). Infant perception of a causal event. *Cognitive Development* **5**, 193–207.

Rochat, P. and Bullinger, A. Posture and functional action in infancy. In *Francophone perspectives on structure and process in mental development* (ed. A. Vyt, H. Bloch, and M. Bornstein). Erlbaum, Hillsdale, NJ.

Sitskoorn, M. M. and Smitsman, A. W. (1991). Infants' visual perception of relative size in containment and support events. Presented at the International Society for the Study of Behavioral Developmental, Minneapolis, MN, July 1991.

Spelke, E. S. (1991). Physical knowledge in infancy: reflections on Piaget's theory. In *The epigenesis of mind: essays on biology and cognition* (ed. S. Carey and R. Gelman). Erlbaum, Hillsdale, NJ.

Spelke, E. S., Breinlinger, K., Macomber, J., and Jacobson, K. (1992). Origins of knowledge. *Psychological Review* **99**, 605–32.

White, B. L., Castle, P., and Held, R. (1964). Observation of the development of visually directed reaching. *Child Development* **35**, 349–64.

Yonas, A. and Granrud, C. (1984). The development of sensitivity to kinetic, binocular and pictorial depth information in human infants. In *Brain mechanisms and spatial vision* (ed. D. Ingle, D. Lee, and M. Jeannerod). Nijhoff, Amsterdam.

Yonas, A., Arterberry, M. E., and Granrud, C. E. (1987). Space perception in infancy. In *Annals of child development* (ed. R. Vasta). JAI Press, Greenwich, CT.

Part III

Causal understanding in naïve psychology

Foreword to Part III

Readers heartened by agreement may wish to linger over this section; they will find, despite keen differences in style, greater consensus than in other sections. For instance, all three chapters agree on the starting point of naïve psychology: infants distinguish categorically between objects whose motions are internally and externally caused.

Alan Leslie divides the concept of agency into three hierarchically ordered subtheories, each of which activates the other, and deals with agency on an increasingly internal level. The first, dealing with outward mechanical properties, pivots on the concept of force and stresses that agents (unlike physical objects) have internal and renewable sources of force. The second notes that agents are not merely internally motivated self-propelled systems; they also perceive the environment, pursue goals, and interact with one another. The final component moves inside the agent and treats agents' beliefs about the world, representing their propositional relations to information with a meta-representational data structure that is specific to this subsystem.

In this neat set of interlocking subtheories, Leslie captures the three principal levels of an organism: physical, motivational, and cognitive. The reader will find a truly profound agreement between parts of his system and that of Gelman, Durgin, and Kaufman, as well as little disharmony with that of Premack and Premack. Moreover, in the case of the latter two, each fills out the part underplayed by the other. For example, Leslie gives a full account of the mechanical level showing the explanatory merit of his concept of force, while Premack and Premack dwell on the motivational level, showing the explanatory merit of the concepts of value and power.

Rochel Gelman, Frank Durgin, and Lisa Kaufman argue that infants use causal principles in distinguishing animate from inanimate objects. These 'first' principles concern 'requisite energy sources' and the 'stuff' of which an object is made. The cause of animate motion, they argue, comes from internally controlled release of stored chemical energy, whereas the cause of inanimate motion is external force and involves a transfer of energy from one object to another. It is this knowledge, they contend, and not perceptual information that enables the infant to distinguish animate from inanimate. Parts of Gelman's 'first principles' and the first two of Leslie's 'subtheories' are siblings if not twins in different attire.

Gelman and her colleagues discount a hypothesis by Steward (1984), according to which infants identify animate objects by their failure to move according to Newtonian principles. That hypothesis may sink without assistance, however, for it not only defines a major ontological category on negative grounds, but also presupposes (unrealistically) an exquisite mastery of Newtonian principles by the infant. When calling into question the informativeness of spatio-temporal analysis, why fix on deviations from Newton? There are livelier alternatives. Action at a distance and goal directedness are also spatiotemporal analyses.

The ontological category of Gelman and her associates is that of animacy, which presupposes the distinction between alive and not alive and thus has one foot in pyschology and the other in biology. It is a more complex category than that of either agency or intentional, which does not presuppose the distinction and has both feet in psychology.

An intentional object, in the model proposed by David Premack and Ann James Premack, is one that is both self-propelled and goal-directed. Although, in their view, infants lack both a general concept of goal and a well-formed motivational theory, they can recognize three kinds of goal-seeking. Infants interpret goal-directed action as intentional, i.e. internally caused.

Value is the fundamental property that infants attribute to the interaction between intentional objects. Recognition of power—that some intentional objects can control the movement of others—leads the infant to distinguish between free and forced co-movement, inter-preting the former as group and the latter as possession. The older infant 'explains' the properties that it attributes in terms of states of mind. Thus Premack and Premack join Spelke in assigning 'theory' to the infant, but include the most basic of human dispositions, the disposition to explain.

D.P.
A.J.P.

5

A theory of agency
ALAN M. LESLIE

INTRODUCTION

I shall outline a 'tri-partite' theory of our core understanding of Agency. More specifically, I shall discuss a theory of the core constraints that organize our early learning about the behaviour of Agents.

To clear the ground a little, I should mention two things I do *not* mean by 'Agency'. Sometimes, 'agency' means just any cause of an event. However, what I mean by Agency is a particular class of *object*. Often the term 'agent' is used to denote the entity that is momentarily the cause of some other event, for example the stone that breaks the window. This is *not* how I shall use the term. Instead, an Agent (with a capital letter) is a type of object and Agency an enduring property of that object. Clearly, people are examples of things which are enduringly Agents, even though, from time to time, they may be the passive victims of some particular event. In this sense, Agency is a property of objects rather than a property of motion.

The second thing that I do *not* mean by Agency is animacy. The type of model I shall develop appeals to a notion of modular design (Marr 1982). In the context of core commonsense conceptual knowledge, modular design translates into the notion of 'subtheory'. Core knowledge is divided into subtheories to the extent that an information processing system is organized into modules. From this point of view, the concept *animate being* carries biological connotations — is living, reproduces, grows, etc. — that are, by hypothesis, extrinsic to our core notion of Agency. The system I describe does not make explicit information of a biological character. It is left as an open empirical question whether some other part of core systems, not explored here, represents biological information (see Chapters 9 and 10).

The central part of the theory of cognitive development deals with core cognitive architecture: it characterizes those properties of the information processing system that provide the basis for development, as opposed to those properties that are the result of development. For example, in classical associationism core cognition is assumed to consist purely of statistical associative processing over elementary 'sensations'. In other views, core architecture is assumed to have a more varied componential character. In the main, core structure will reflect specialization for carrying out particular information processing tasks as a result of adaptive evolution. From this point of view, Agents have provided a potent source of adaptive pressure in human evolution with obvious 'benefits' in terms of enhanced social intelligence flowing from a sophisticated capacity to explain, predict, and interpret their behaviour.

The tripartite theory of Agency begins with the idea that Agents are a class of objects possessing sets of causal properties that distinguish them from other physical objects. The next assumption is that, as a result of evolution, we have become adapted to track these sets of properties and to learn efficiently to interpret the behaviour of these objects in specific ways. I begin by identifying three classes of distinctive properties of Agents that determine their behaviour. Each of these classes of properties sets Agents apart from mere physical objects, and each produces its own special problems for a processing system whose task is to understand the behaviour of Agents.

Three subtheories of Agency

Three classes of real world properties distinguish Agents from other physical objects.

1. **Mechanical properties**: Agents have mechanical properties that mere physical objects do not have. I shall characterize the main difference in terms of having an internal and renewable source of 'energy' or FORCE versus not possessing such a source and thus having to rely on external sources.

2. **Actional properties**: Agents do not simply move and take part in events. Agents *act* in pursuit of goals and re*act* to the environment as a result of perceiving. Mere physical objects do not act in pursuit of goals and do not perceive their environment. Furthermore, the acting and reacting Agent can come together with another Agent and inter*act*.

3. **Cognitive properties**: the behaviour of Agents is determined by cognitive properties, for example holding a certain attitude to the truth of a proposition. Mere physical objects do not have cognitive properties.

My claim is that tracking each of these three classes of properties poses to some extent distinct information processing problems that require to some extent distinct solutions. My hypothesis is that, as the result of the evolution of a modular design, our core notions of Agency reflect three distinct processing mechanisms arranged hierarchically. Succeeding mechanisms interpret Agents' behaviour at succeeding levels of representation. Each level corresponds to a different 'subtheory' of Agency. Description at one level provides the principal relevant input for inferring the appropriate description at the next level. These three mechanisms with their respective 'subtheories' introduce in turn the three causal *paradigms* that form the core of human commonsense: 'mechanical causality', 'teleological causality', and 'psychological causality'.

MECHANICS AND THE FORCE REPRESENTATION

Marr (1982) pointed out that any representational system makes explicit certain kinds of information at the expense of relegating other kinds of information to the background. Marr illustrated this idea by comparing Roman and Arabic numeral systems in terms of the extent to which they make arithmetic relations explicit. The key question to ask about a representational system is what sort of information it makes explicit in contrast with the other kinds of information that it leaves implicit. For example, I suggested earlier that our core representations of Agency left it implicit whether Agents possessed biological properties. In this section I shall argue, contrary to the traditional assumption which reduces all physical knowledge to spatiotemporal information, that there is a level of representation which is basic to human intelligence that makes mechanical information explicit.

David Hume (1740) was to a large extent responsible for the diversion of attention from commonsense mechanics that has characterized much of modern psychological thought. Hume's programme of doing away with a core level of mechanical understanding was to become a central plank of the empiricist programme. Core understanding, according to this view, comprised essentially two things: first the registration of spatiotemporal properties, and second the statistical association of spatiotemporal properties with one another. Mechanics was squeezed out of the system (cf. Mandler 1992). Hume begins his analysis by considering the launching event.

Here is a billiard ball lying on the table, and another ball moving toward it with rapidity. They strike, and the ball which was formally at rest now acquires a motion. This is as perfect an instance of the relation of a cause and effect as any which we know either by sensation or reflection. (Hume, p. 292)

Hume goes on to argue that the only thing that we see in such an event is its spatiotemporal properties, namely the spatial contact between the two objects and the movement of the second object without delay after impact by the first. We cannot, Hume argued, see, i.e. *observe*, the causal relation. This meant to Hume that our idea of causal relation had to be the result of statistical associations formed within this recurring spatiotemporal pattern. I believe that Hume was right about the first part of his analysis, namely that we *see* only the spatiotemporal properties in this event. He was right about seeing only spatiotemporal properties – not because his theory of *observation* was right, but simply because that is the job of *vision*. Vision makes explicit information about space and spatial arrangement over time. This is what Marr (1982) called the 'quintessential fact about vision'. But Hume was wrong to conclude that our idea of causal relation must therefore be based on statistical association. As we shall see, what makes launching seem 'perfect' to us as an instance of cause and effect, is that it instantiates a mechanical interaction with a perfect transmission of 'FORCE'.

Launching and FORCE

FORCE is a primitive mechanical notion, invoked by attention to three-dimensional bodies and their arrangements. It must be stressed that FORCE is not to be identified with the scientific notion of energy or force or any other scientific notion. The FORCE representation is the result of evolutionary adaptation and not the product of a scientific theory developed culturally. The general idea behind the FORCE representation is that (a) when objects move, they possess or bear FORCE, and (b) when objects contact other objects, they transmit, receive, or resist FORCE. Talmy (1988) has discussed a similar notion of 'force dynamics' discernable in patterns of lexicalization and verb argument structure in natural language.

The FORCE representation has an important role in determining the sorts of things that infants know or assume about the physical world. Let me begin by looking at three phenomena from my own work on infancy which support and illustrate this idea. I shall then point to some key findings from the research of Spelke and of Baillargeon that also support the assumption of a core FORCE representation.

In a series of experiments some years ago (Leslie 1982, 1984*b*; Leslie and Keeble 1987), I showed that 6-month-old infants were sensitive to the causal structure of the kind of billiard ball launching effect David Hume had described. In the critical experiment (Leslie and Keeble 1987) infants were habituated to a film of a direct launching event (Fig. 5.1). A second group were habituated to a variation on this launching event in which a short time delay was interposed between the impact of the first object and the movement of the second object. Michotte (1963) had shown that, for adults, the interposition of this short delay destroyed the impression of causality or pushing that was clear when viewing the direct non-delayed event. When both groups of infants had been habituated to their respective events, they were each tested on exactly the same respective event, but played backwards in time.

Causal Sequence

Forward

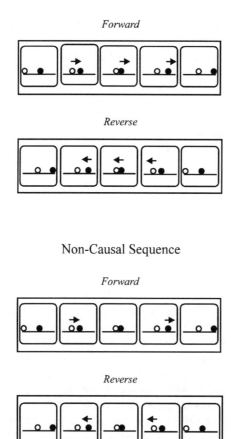

Reverse

Non-Causal Sequence

Forward

Reverse

Fig. 5.1. Six-month-old infants were habituated to either a causal or non-causal sequence and then tested with the same sequence reversed. In the non-causal sequence there is a 0.5 second delay between impact and reaction. Infants recover their attention more when the causal sequence is reversed. (After Leslie and Keeble 1987.)

From a *spatiotemporal* point of view, both groups of infants saw equal changes on testing. For both groups of infants their test event occurred in an opposite spatial direction. Also, for both group, the event played with an opposite temporal order. Likewise, for both groups, whatever degree of motion continuity was present during familiarization was present once again during the test. Finally, the contingency between the motions in the familiarization events was present again in the test events. All this stems from the fact that both groups of infants simply saw the same film that they had seen previously but with the projector running in reverse.

From the point of view of *mechanics*, however, there was an important difference between the effect of reversal on the two initial films. In the causal direct launching event, the two objects appear to have different mechanical roles: the first object is a transmitter of FORCE, a pusher, while the other is the recipient of FORCE, an object which is pushed. When this event is reversed these mechanical roles are also reversed: the pusher becomes the pushed. In the case of the non-causal event, however, there is no such apparent mechanical relation between the objects; there is no pusher and no pushed. Thus when this event is reversed there is still no pusher and no pushed, and consequently no reversal of roles. If the infants construe these events from a mechanical point of view, then the direct launching event in reverse will be more interesting than the non-causal delayed event in reverse. Therefore, even though the spatiotemporal changes and the contingency properties are equated in the test for the two groups, the causal group should recover attention more. This is exactly what we found.*

The above results are immediately understandable in terms of a mechanical or FORCE representation which infants deploy tacitly. Furthermore, a FORCE description allows us to understand, where Hume could not, why launching should seem 'perfect' to us as an instance of cause and effect. Consider how the FORCE representation describes the behaviour of the objects in the launching effect. The event begins with object A moving and object B stationary. Therefore object A rather than object B has to be the initial bearer of FORCE. When object A impacts on object B and becomes stationary, it transmits all its FORCE to object B. Object B, which is now in motion, has gained the FORCE formerly borne by object A.

The above findings with 6-month-old infants depend upon the infants seeing a particular causal, presumably mechanical, *direction* in the launching event. Our results showed that the causal direction is conceptually distinct from the spatiotemporal direction. However, having a definite causal direction is not the inevitable result of just any kind of mechanical construal. In fact, there is a causal symmetry[†] if the event is

---

* Cohen and coworkers (Oakes and Cohen 1990; Cohen and Oakes 1993) have criticized the claim that these results demonstrate a 'modular perception' in infants. Cohen seems to me to misconstrue some aspects of the problem. For example, he obtained evidence of a causal perception in 10-month-old but not in 6-month-old infants. However, the striking finding is that whenever the infants in his study showed sensitivity to the spatiotemporal properties of the particular stimuli he used, they also showed sensitivity to causal properties. Having said that, the particular version of the 'modular theory' that Cohen attacks (Leslie 1988) is not the same in important respects as that argued for here. It may be that some of Cohen's recent results fit better with the present 'theory of body' view.

[†] I am indebted to Elizabeth Spelke for this point.

construed in terms of Newtonian mechanics: when object A impacts on object B and causes B to move off, there is an opposite and equal reaction from B to A. Under reversal the same symmetrical relationship would hold again. However, common-sense intuition is that being stationary and moving at a constant velocity are fundamentally different states. The results on the perception of launching suggest that infants share this intuition. We cannot tell for sure from these results in which direction the infants apprehend that the causal direction runs: whether it is B's moving away from A's impact that causes A to stop, or, what seems much more likely, that A's impact causes B to move away. I put forward the following hypothesis. The infant's 'theory of body' (ToBy) tacitly employs the idea that FORCE is transmitted from one object to another in a particular direction, from the moving to the stationary, like a baton being passed on in a relay race. There is no opposite and equal reaction as far as ToBy is concerned. This defines *mechanical* direction—the direction of FORCE transmission. Mechanical directionality in turn gives rise to the asymmetrical notions of mechanical role that seem so ubiquitous in common sense. Our sensitivity to launching, as both adults and infants, is in part structured around the notion of mechanical role, which in turn reflects the direction of FORCE transmission.

The mechanics of containment

My second example illustrating the FORCE representation is of a simple hidden mechanism. Six-month-old infants apparently make a mechanical construal of invisible displacement by container (A. M. Leslie and P. Das Gupta, submitted). Infants apparently expect an object that has been entrained by an inverted cup to reappear in its new position when the cup is lifted up (Fig. 5.2). According to Piaget (1955), this is one of the last events to be understood by the infant in the course of object concept development. Although the 12-month-old infant has solved the $A\bar{B}$ error, she has done so because these problems involve only 'visible hidings': on its way to being hidden, the object's displacement is visible. Beyond 12 months, infants still have problems with hiding tasks that involve invisible displacement. This is Piaget's other 'classic hiding task'. A small object is enclosed by a hand; the infant then watches as the clenched hand moves under a screen. After a few seconds, the clenched hand emerges. The infant searches in the hand but finds nothing. Where is the object? Typically, infants will not go on to search under the screen until they are about 18 months old, despite the fact that they have searched under screens from 8 months and solved 'visible hiding' tasks with screens from 12 months.

It is only with the solving of invisible displacement problems that Piaget credits the infant with a formed object concept. This is because, in order to understand invisible displacement, the child must represent an absent object as having an objective existence in space – something which is not required, according to Piaget, in order to solve simpler hiding tasks such as the A$\overline{\text{B}}$ task.

Our test of invisible displacement simplifies Piaget's task in two ways. First we dispense with the final hiding screen. Having a hiding screen at the end of an invisible displacement requires the infant to understand an embedded hiding. First, the object is hidden within the container that performs the displacement and then the container itself is hidden behind a screen. It may be that this kind of nested hiding requires too much from limited processing capacity. Second, we used visual attention measures rather than manual search. Instead of showing the infant that the object is not in the first hiding place and asking her to search for it, we show the infant that the object is not in the second 'hiding' place and ask if the infant is surprised.

Figure 5.2 displays one of the conditions in our study. Infants were habituated to a containment event and then tested on one of two test events. The first test event depicted an impossible outcome in which the contained and entrained object fails to reappear in position 2. We called this the vanish event. The other test event, which we called no-object, involves the component movements of the containment event but with no object present on the table. If the infant simply responded to meaningless subcomponents of the containment event, then the infants should either look slightly longer at the no-object event, because this shows fewer subcomponents compared with the Vanish event and is thus more novel, or, on weaker assumptions, should simply continue to habituate to both vanish and no-object. Likewise, if the infant simply viewed the containment event as a series of meaningless 'displays' appearing in positions 1 and 2, then the infants should recover looking as much or more to the no-object event as to the vanish event. In contrast, if the infants construe the event as involving the mechanical containment and transport of a substantial object, then they will be surprised at the 'impossible' vanish event.

We added a second condition to this experiment which we called the no-containment condition. The infants were habituated to the no-containment event as shown in Fig. 5.3. These infants received no training during habituation on the disappear–reappear contingency involved in the containment event. We then tested their reactions to vanish in the absence of such training. If infants simply respond to the presence or absence of an object on stage rather than to the mechanically anomalous vanishing of an object, then again they should prefer the no-object event. Conversely, a mechanical interpretation without contingency training will lead them to prefer the anomalous vanish event. Our results showed that even 6-month-old infants

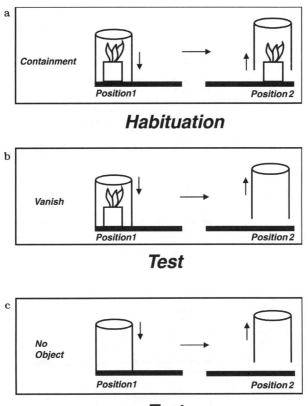

Fig. 5.2. Infants were habituated to an event in which an opaque inverted container covered an object and then entrained it to new position. This cup was then lifted up, revealing the object. Infants were tested either on an 'impossible' event in which the entrained object had apparently vanished, or on a new event in which there was no object throughout.

prefer the vanish event in both conditions. Figure 5.4 shows the looking patterns that we found.

When the infants responded to the non-appearance of the object in position 2 as the container was lifted up, they were presumably surprised that it was not there sitting on the table top. Apparently, infants do not expect the inverted container to support the object—for the object to be stuck up inside the cup. Although the solid sides of the container can and do entrain the object sideways, the aperture of the inverted cup cannot entrain the contained object upward. Of course, an aperture cannot bear, receive, or transmit FORCE. The FORCE representation provides a

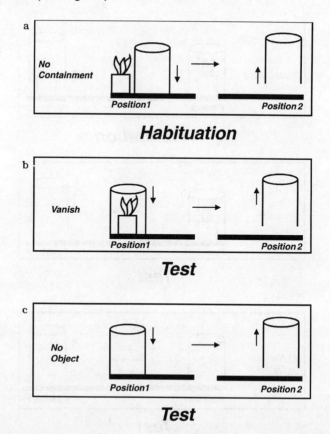

Fig. 5.3. Infants were habituated to an event similar to that in the previous figure except that the object was not covered or entrained by the opaque container. Again the infants were surprised by the impossible test event.

natural account of how infants can make useful assumptions regarding simple mechanisms, such as the inverted container, and rapidly learn about them. In each case, learning about elementary mechanisms will involve relating the geometry of solid three-dimensional objects to their FORCE dynamical properties as they come into contact with other bodies.

Mechanical Agency

My third example concerns the infant's appreciation of mechanical Agency. In terms of the FORCE representation, Agents are that class of physical object that possess an *internal and renewable* source of FORCE. Because objects move as a result of FORCE, and because Agents have an internal

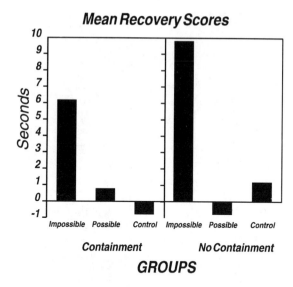

Fig. 5.4. Looking scores for 6-month-old infants show they were surprised at the 'impossible' vanish event in both the containment and no-containment conditions.

and renewable source of FORCE, Agents are free to move about on their own—what Premack (1990) calls 'self-propelledness'. Mere physical objects, however, lack an internal and renewable source of FORCE and therefore move only as a result of receiving FORCE externally from Agents or other objects that bear FORCE transiently. This simple FORCE dynamical assumption, relating patterns of motion to the force properties of the objects exhibiting the patterns, provides a powerful learning mechanism for infants.

Some years ago, I carried out a series of experiments which probed whether infants perceive a mechanical interaction between a hand and another physical object as the hand picks up the object (Leslie 1982, 1984a). In these experiments, infants were shown to be sensitive to the spatial relationship between the hand and object, but only when the hand and object moved together. Furthermore, an analogous spatial relationship between two physical objects, neither of which were Agents but which moved together as the hand and object had done, did not produce recovery of interest. Fig. 5.5 illustrates the stimuli used. The infants apparently considered the contact relation to be significant only in the case of active hands. Presumably this was because only in the case of the active hand does the spatial contact mediate a mechanical relation, i.e. allow the transmission of FORCE.

Consider the following. A hand moves around a lot on its own. A mere

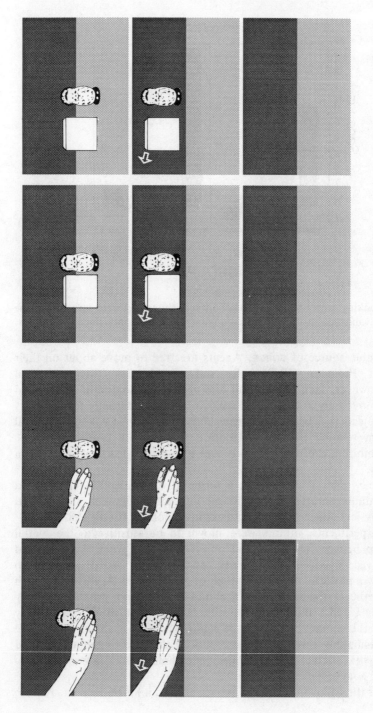

Fig. 5.5. Reading the strip from top to bottom, infants were habituated, for example, to a hand picking up a doll. They were then tested on a sequence showing the hand 'picking up' the doll again but with a small gap between hand and object. Infants recovered attention to this change but not to a similar change when there was no hand, but only another object making the same movements. (After Leslie 1984a.)

physical object does not move around a lot on its own. Suppose that the infant registers these two spatiotemporal patterns of motion. It does not follow from these spatiotemporal patterns alone that, when the infant sees the hand and object moving together with *symmetrical* spatiotemporal patterns, it must of necessity be the hand that is picking up the object rather than the object that is pushing the hand backwards. The mere fact of previously associated spatiotemporal patterns should not, in and of itself, produce a perception of *asymmetrical* mechanical roles in an event in which the hand and object move together. However, an asymmetrical interpretation of mechanical roles does follow if the FORCE representation is applied. Because the hand moves around a lot on its own, it provides ample evidence for **ToBy** that the hand has an internal and renewable source of FORCE. The passivity of the object, in contrast, indicates to **ToBy** that the object depends on external sources of FORCE. Having arrived at a FORCE dynamical description of hands as Agents, it does follow that when hands and objects move together it will be the hand that transmits FORCE and the object that receives. From this mechanical point of view, it will be the hand that picks up and pulls the object rather than the object that pushes the hand backwards. The FORCE dynamical interpretation leads the infant naturally to attend to the contact relation, since spatial contact is required for the transmission of FORCE and, more generally, for the mediation of all FORCE dynamical relationships.

Further evidence for the FORCE representation

In order to indicate the possible scope of the FORCE representation, I shall briefly indicate a range of other mechanical phenomena understood by infants. Many of the findings of Baillargeon (Chapter 4) and of Spelke (Chapter 3) fall under the rubric of the FORCE representation.

The FORCE representation plays a role in defining the mechanical object. There is an important psychological distinction between the mechanical object and the 'purely visual object' (see Leslie (1994b) for a discussion of this distinction). The purely visual object is the output of visual processes that recognize objects visually by shape, i.e. according to the disposition of their surfaces or shaped parts in space (Marr 1982). Purely visual processes probably do not make explicit any information about the mechanical properties of objects (see the discussion of the case of solidity in Leslie (1988)). Vision is confined to representing the visible properties of surfaces. However, the mechanical object is constituted by properties of its interior as much as by the visible properties of its surfaces.

From the point of view of the FORCE representation, the most basic property of a physical body is its *hardness*: to be a body and to enter into the system of FORCE dynamical relationships, an entity must have a non-zero degree of hardness. A simple thought experiment suggests that, if something entirely lacks hardness, our common-sense intuition is that it is not, by virtue of that fact alone, a physical body. However, a purely visual object does not have to possess any degree of hardness. Imagine entering a room in which a superb three-dimensional hologram of a cup is displayed sitting upon a table. As long as one is restricted to examining it visually, one is convinced it is a cup. Those visual processes that recognize objects by shape, immediately recognize this apparition as a cup. However, when one tries to grasp it, one's fingers pass through the visible surfaces with no resistance whatsoever. Now one will say that, after all, there is 'nothing there'. However, the apparition will continue to be a perfectly good visual object.

If non-zero *hardness* is the prerequisite for something to count commonsensically as a physical body, it is because this condition must be met if an entity is to enter into the system of FORCE relations. Without some degree of hardness, an entity can have no contact mechanical interactions with anything else.

The innate principles of objecthood that Spelke has identified (Spelke 1988; Spelke *et al.* 1992) can be seen against the background of these remarks. Thus the mechanical object constituted in terms of *boundedness* resists intrusion along its boundaries by other FORCEful objects to the extent that it is *hard* along its boundaries. It resists deformation by FORCEful objects to the extent that it is rigid, and rebounds from deformation by FORCEful objects to the extent it is elastic or compressible. In a contrasting case, a mass of sand, which has a non-zero degree of hardness and thus has mechanical properties and qualifies as a body, does not qualify as a (count) object because it has no hard boundaries.

A mechanical object is *cohesive* to the extent that it remains a continuous whole when subjected to FORCE. Whereas a visual shape description will make explicit, for example, that a pyramid is on top of a cube forming a continuous *shape*, it will not reveal whether the pyramid is *attached* to the cube forming a single object. Attachment is a mechanical relation: whether two entities are part of a single object or form two distinct objects depends upon the FORCE required to separate them. More elaborate notions of attachment, breakage, fixing, and so on can be developed within this representational system, allowing the construction of a mechanical object catalogue (cf. Corballis (1992) on the human capacity to create artefacts). Finally, *solidity* appears to be related to hardness in a general sense, as well as having a more particular sense of *being filled*, i.e. having a hard interior. The solid object resists occupation by another FORCEful object unless its inside is empty and there is an aperture in its outer surface through which the other object can pass into its empty interior. Objects like this can function as mechanical containers.

The FORCE representation allows objects to be described as simple mechanisms. Perhaps the simplest 'mechanism' of all is the movement of an object. The blocking of one object by another (Baillargeon *et al.* 1985; Baillargeon 1986; Spelke *et al.* 1992) illustrates the *resisting* of FORCE. The launching of one object by another (Leslie and Keeble 1987) illustrates *transmission* and *reception* of FORCE. Transport by mechanical containment illustrates *resistance* and *entraining* (A. M. Leslie and P. Das Gupta, submitted). Even the static relation of support studied by Needham and Baillargeon (1993) may illustrate an implied FORCE in the supported object which is resisted through contact with the support.

Finally, there is a particular class of mechanical object which is distinguished by having its own internal and renewable source of FORCE, i.e. the class of Agents. This characterization of Agents within the FORCE representation determines that Agents will be the source of FORCE in interactions with mere objects, i.e. determines the direction of causation; therefore a hand will be perceived as playing the active mechanical role in events such as pick-up (Leslie 1984*a*). Agents enter ubiquitously into FORCE mechanical descriptions by moving freely, and by being a source of support, blocking, pushing, transport, and so forth. This notion of the mechanical Agent falls out naturally from the FORCE representation.

It is beyond the scope of this chapter to compare the FORCE representation with the mechanical theories that children and adults come to hold as a result of prolonged reflection or formal instruction. Carey (1986) has described some of the differences between the common-sense construals of physical phenomena that children make and scientific accounts of the same phenomena, as well as some of the difficulties that children have in responding to instruction in these scientific ideas. No doubt it will be important to distinguish between core representational systems and the common-sense theories that later develop around this core, and yet later resist replacement by scientific ideas. The later 'peripheral' developments, while perhaps reflecting aspects of the core, will tend to focus on the areas where the core notions cast least light. For example, McCloskey (1983) discusses parallels between 'naïve' adult notions and medieval impetus theories. The impetus theory of motion stated that an object that has been set in motion has acquired a FORCE that keeps it moving and then gradually dissipates. Many adults today apparently hold some version of this view. My guess is that the parallels are not wholly relevant to the FORCE representation. This is because the domain of the FORCE representation is contact mechanical interactions between objects, whereas the central problems for impetus theory are the behaviour of objects in 'free flight' — projectiles, rising and falling objects, and so on. One might speculate that core mechanics focuses rather narrowly on the moment of contact: the FORCE dynamics of a motion are specified less and less definitely the further away from the moment of contact the objects travel.

In summary, in this section I have postulated a specialized adapted learning mechanism **ToBy**, which, deploying the FORCE representational system, makes explicit information about the mechanical properties of objects and events. The notion of the mechanical Agent springs naturally from this representational system, as do representations of the mechanical interactions between Agents and mere physical objects. What the FORCE representation will not do is capture the next two levels of understanding Agency.

ToMM AND INTENTIONAL AGENCY

If we considered only the mechanical level, we would fail to notice the other distinctive properties of Agents, for Agents are not merely involved in mechanical events. Agents also *act* in pursuit of goals. Tracking the actional properties of Agents means relating Agents to the environment at a distance in time and a distance in space. This contrasts sharply with the contact mechanical concerns of **ToBy**. The FORCE representation focuses **ToBy** on contiguous relationships in time and space. However, when an Agent acts in pursuit of a goal, the goal state is a state of affairs that has not yet come about; it is, as it were, 'at a little distance in time'. In fact the goal may never be realized, in which case the goal state remains, as it were, 'at a little distance in time'. Agents not only act in pursuit of goals, but also react to the environment through perception. Such reaction to the environment takes place at a distance in space. Agents act and react in relation to circumstances at a distance in space and time. This is the fundamental principle of the second level or subtheory of Agency: Actional Agency.

This mode of attending to Agents, i.e. at the level of action, creates a quite different information processing task from tracking the contiguous relations of mechanics. It seems reasonable to assume that this work is carried out by a quite different brain mechanism from **ToBy**. Accordingly, in my model, actional Agency is tracked by a mechanism which I call **ToMM**, for 'theory of mind mechanism'. The properties of Agents which are tracked by **ToMM** also differ in another quite fundamental way from those properties tracked by **ToBy**. **ToMM** is concerned with the *intentional* properties of Agents. Whereas objects and physical events are simply *in* the world, the intentional states of Agents are *about* the world. **ToMM**'s task is to provide a spontaneous grasp of such states — to provide a system for representing how meaning enters into the determination of behaviour. Whereas **ToBy** provides an object-centred description of a given scenario, **ToMM** provides an intentional or Agent-centred description.

The actions of Agents are not simply reducible to a mechanical pattern of motion any more than mechanical patterns of motion are simply reducible to spatiotemporal patterns. The intentional level reflects the fact that the behaviour of Agents is *about* circumstances that are at a distance from the behaviour itself.* In fact, my model recognizes two subtypes of intentionality. Accordingly, I shall talk about **ToMM** *system$_1$* and **ToMM** *system$_2$*. **ToMM** *system$_1$* has the job of making explicit information about the state of affairs that the Agent is *acting* to bring about or *trying to bring about*. **ToMM** *system$_2$* has the job of making explicit the *attitude* that the Agent takes towards the truth of a given piece of *information*. I shall be brief in my exposition of **ToMM**. For further discussion of **ToMM** *system$_1$* see Leslie (1994*b*) and for discussion of **ToMM** *system$_2$* see Leslie (1987, 1994*a*) and Leslie and Thaiss (1992).

My model provides for two subtheories of intentional Agency: Agent and Action, and Agent and Attitude. The Action subtheory illustrates the second causal paradigm, that of 'teleological causality'. The Attitude subtheory introduces the third and final causal paradigm, 'psychological causality'. In the course of development, these subtheories are distinct and hierarchically organized. *System$_1$* provides the input descriptions of Agent's goal-directed actions that *system$_2$* requires to carry out its task of inferring Agent and Attitude descriptions, just as **ToBy** provided *system$_1$* with the right kind of information to enable it to infer Agent and Action descriptions.

ToMM *system$_1$* makes explicit information concerning principally three things: first, that a given Agent acts in pursuit of a given goal; second, that a given Agent reacts to a given aspect of the distant environment through sensing; third, that two or more given Agents interact when the pursuit of goals meshes in given ways. I believe that there is some evidence to suggest that the understanding of actional Agency begins during the first year of life, probably in the second half of the first year. This may be reflected in the patterns of interaction to which infants apparently become sensitive during this period. Such patterns of goal interaction may include *helping* and *harming* (cf. Premack 1990; Chapter 7 of this volume), *refusal*, and *instrumental requests*. The *system$_1$* action representation provides a natural way of capturing such patterns. For example, helping occurs when the goals of one Agent's action enhance the achievement of the goals of another. Harming occurs when the goals of one Agent oppose or diminish the achievement of the goals of another. Refusal occurs when one Agent's goal involves another Agent and is blocked by the second Agent. Instrumental requests occur when a gesture is directed at another Agent in an

---

* In hitting a nail into a piece of wood my goal might be to build a house or it might be to build a boat. Whichever it is, the motion of hitting the nail is exactly the same.

effort to recruit that Agent to the pursuit of the requester's own goal. Elementary examples of these actions and interactions can be observed beginning in the latter half of the first year. For example, the infant refuses food or a toy, and requests an object with a reach toward it and a look at mother. Also appearing during this time are reversible role interactions like give-and-take games (Bruner 1976). The infant also begins to follow another person's eye gaze during this period (Butterworth and Grover 1988). It seems plausible that these developments depend upon the recognition of the actional properties of Agents.*

We come now to the last level of the tripartite theory of Agency. This level tracks the *cognitive* properties of Agents. Tracking cognitive properties requires a sensitivity to the relationship between Agents and *information*. I have argued in a series of papers (Leslie 1987, 1994*a*; Leslie and Thaiss 1992) that there are a set of key notions that allow the child to understand behaviour in terms of the Agent's relationships to information. The 'informational relations' represent the Agent as taking or holding an attitude to the truth of a proposition, for example *believing* this or that. Because the 'information' may in fact only be a fiction, the child gains the capacity to do something that at first sight appears almost useless: he or she can begin to understand the role of fictional circumstances in producing Agents' behaviour.

Of course, it is absurd to explain the actual behaviour of mere physical objects as issuing from circumstances which one knows are purely fictional. Yet this is a hallmark pattern of explanation in so-called 'theory of mind'. For example, John jumped into the shop doorway. Why did he do this? To avoid the rain. Was it raining? No! John merely thought it was raining. Here the fictional circumstance of 'it is raining' is used to explain John's actual behaviour, although it could never be used to explain why John was wet. Such 'fictional causes' pose unusual problems for an information processing system whose job it is to track the behaviour of Agents. Fictional circumstances create a unique learnability problem. One cannot learn about fictional causes in the 'ordinary' way—by looking at the circumstances, correlating circumstances with outcomes, and so on—if the circumstances do not exist.

This learnability problem is partly solved by a particular data structure that is specific to **ToMM** *system*$_2$. This is the representational system that I have called the 'metarepresentation' (Leslie 1987). The metarepresentation captures information necessary for expressing propositional attitude

---

* I think that there is reasonably good evidence that the great apes understand aspects of the actional properties of Agents (Premack and Woodruff 1978; Gomez 1991) (see also Whiten and Byrne's (1988) anecdotal evidence although the latter authors do not give this interpretation to the observations that they report). In comparison, the evidence that great apes understand propositional atitudes seems much flimsier.

concepts. In this representational system attitudes are represented as three-place relations between an Agent, an aspect of reality, and a proposition or piece of information describing a fictional situation. The first clear evidence of the use of attitude concepts in infant development occurs in the second half of the second year of life with the emergence of the ability to pretend and to understand pretence in others (Leslie 1987).

ToMM *system*$_2$ may begin its development in the months immediately leading up to the emergence of pretence. During this period, more sophisticated forms of communication than those seen in the first year of life become evident. For example, the instrumental pointing of the first year is supplemented by informative pointing during the first part of the second year. Baldwin (1993) has shown that from about 18 months of age infants take into account the focus of attention of an Agent during the ostensive definition of words. Rather than take the referent of the novel word to be the object that the infant herself is attending to at the moment the word is heard, the infant instead checks to see what object is the focus of attention for the speaker and takes *that* to be the referent of the novel word. In this the infant reveals a construal of the Agent as an object which is sensitive to, and thus can convey, information. As well as discovering *linguistic* meaning by attending to the direction of Agents' attention during ostensive acts, around this time infants become sensitive to the *speaker's* meaning during pretence. Thus, when in the course of play mother hands baby a banana saying, 'The telephone is ringing. It's for you', the infant does not conclude that 'telephone' is a word for bananas, but correctly interprets mother's actions as relating to mother's pretence that the banana is a telephone.*

SUMMARY

The integrated cognitive systems described in this three-part theory of Agency constitute a powerful learning device that lays the foundation for a formidable social intelligence as well as for a causal view of the world of considerable richness and subtlety. Three distinct forms or paradigms of causation are contained within the three representational systems deployed in the course of infancy. I suspect that many domains of knowledge and belief which are culturally elaborated later are based on extensions of these three paradigms, and that productive tensions may arise between them when they compete to capture phenomenon.

There are also aspects of the cognition of Agency that are left out of this

* These and related issues are discussed at length elsewhere and I refer the interested reader to Leslie (1987, 1988a, 1994a), Leslie and German (in press), and Leslie and Roth (1993).

picture, for example affective evaluation and moral judgement. As regards basic moral evaluative judgement (see Chapter 7) my feeling is that this 'belongs to', or at least is related to **TOMM** *system*$_1$ and the subtheory of Actional Agency. This is suggested by, for example, the notions of helping and harming in particular, and the need to evaluate goals and interactions in general. In the syndrome of childhood autism there is a specific impairment in *system*$_2$ notions alongside a relative sparing of *system*$_1$ notions (Leslie 1992; Leslie and Roth 1993). R. J. R. Blair (unpublished) has recently shown that autistic children are able to distinguish between actions that transgress moral injunctions from those that merely contravene convention. This interesting neuropsychological result fits nicely with the picture of core architecture for the cognizing of Agency that has been emerging over the last decade.

REFERENCES

Baillargeon, R. (1986). Representing the existence and the location of hidden objects: object permanence in 6- and 8-month old infants. *Cognition* **23**, 21–41.

Baillargeon, R. (1993). The object concept revisited: new directions in the investigation of infants' physical knowledge. In *Visual perception and cognition in infancy*, (ed. C. Granrud), pp. 265–315. Erlbaum, Hillsdale, NJ.

Baillargeon, R., Spelke, E. S., and Wasserman, S. (1985). Object permanence in five month old infants. *Cognition* **20**, 191–208.

Baldwin, D. A. (1993). Infants' ability to consult the speaker for clues to word reference. *Journal of Child Language* **20**, 395–418.

Bruner, J. S. (1976). From communication to language – a psychological perspective. *Cognition* **3**, 255–87.

Butterworth, G. and Grover, L. (1988). The origins of referential communication in human infancy. In *Thought without language* (ed. L. Weiskrantz), pp. 5–24. Oxford University Press, Oxford.

Carey, S. (1986). Cognitive science and cognitive education. *American Psychologist* **41**, 1123–30.

Carey, S. (1988). Conceptual differences between children and adults. *Mind and Language* **3**, 167–81.

Cohen, L. B. and Oakes, L. M. (1993). How infants perceive a simple causal event. *Developmental Psychology* **29**, 421–33.

Corballis, M. C. (1992). On the evolution of language and generativity. *Cognition* **44**, 191–226.

Hume, D. [1740] (1962). *An abstract of a treatise of human nature*. Reprinted in *David Hume: on human nature and the understanding* (ed. A. Flew). Collier-Macmillan, 1962.

Leslie, A. M. (1982). The perception of causality in infants. *Perception* **11**, 173–86.

Leslie, A. M. (1984a). Infant perception of a manual pick-up event. *British Journal of Developmental Psychology* **2**, 19–32.

Leslie, A. M. (1984b). Spatiotemporal continuity and the perception of causality in infants. *Perception* **13**, 287–305.

Leslie, A. M. (1987). Pretense and representation: the origins of 'theory of mind'. *Psychological Review* **94**, 412–26.

Leslie, A. M. (1988). The necessity of illusion: Perception and thought in infancy. In *Thought without language* (ed. L. Weiskrantz), pp. 185–210. Oxford Science Publications, Oxford.

Leslie, A. M. (1992). Autism and the 'Theory of mind' module. *Current Directions in Psychological Science* **1**, 18–21.

Leslie, A. M. (1994a). *Pretending* and *believing*: issues in the theory of ToMM. *Cognition* **50**, 211–38.

Leslie, A. M. (1994b). **ToMM, ToBy,** and Agency: core architecture and domain specificity. In *Mapping the mind: domain specificity in cognition and cultural* (ed. L. Hirschfeld and S. Gelman), pp. 119–48. Cambridge University Press, New York.

Leslie, A. M. and German, T. P. (In press). Knowledge and ability in "theory of mind": one-eyed overview of a debate. In *Mental simulation: philosophical and psychological essays* (ed. M. Davies and T. Stone). Blackwell, Oxford.

Leslie, A. M. and Keeble, S. (1987). Do six-month-old infants perceive causality? *Cognition* **25**, 265–88.

Leslie, A. M. and Roth, D. (1993). What autism teaches us about metarepresentation. In *Understanding other minds: perspectives from autism* (ed. S. Baron-Cohen, H. Tager-Flusberg, and D. Cohen), pp. 83–111. Oxford University Press).

Leslie, A. M. and Thaiss, L. (1992). Domain specificity in conceptual development: neuropsychological evidence from autism. *Cognition* **43**, 225–51.

McCloskey, M. (1983). Intuitive physics. *Scientific American* **248**, 122–30.

Mandler, J. M. (1992). How to build a baby, II: Conceptual primitives. *Psychological Review* **99**, 587–604.

Marr, D. (1982). *Vision*. W. H. Freeman, San Francisco, CA.

Michotte, A. (1963). *The perception of causality*, Methuen, Andover.

Needham, A. and Baillargeon, R. (1993) Intuitions about support in 4.5-month-old infants. *Cognition* **47**, 121–48.

Oakes, L. M. and Cohen, L. B. (1990). Infant perception of a causal event. *Cognitive Development* **5**, 193–207.

Piaget, J. (1955). *The child's construction of reality*. Routledge & Kegan Paul, London.

Pinker, S. and Bloom, P. (1990). Natural language and natural selection. *Behavioral and Brain Sciences* **13**, 707–84.

Premack, D. (1990) The infant's theory of self-propelled objects. *Cognition* **36**, 1–16.

Premack, D. and Woodruff, G. (1978). Does the chimpanzee have a theory of mind? *Behavioral and Brain Sciences* **4**, 515–26.

Spelke, E. S. (1988). The origins of physical knowledge. In *Thought without language* (ed. L. Weiskrantz), pp. 168–84. Oxford Science Publications, Oxford.

Spelke, E. S., Breinlinger, K., Macomber, J. and Jacobson, K. (1992) Origins of knowledge. *Psychological Review* **99**, 605–32.

Talmy, L. (1988). Force dynamics in language and cognition. *Cognitive Science* **12**, 49–100.

Whiten, A. and Bryne, R. W. (1988). Tactical deception in primates. *Behavioral and Brain Sciences* **11**, 233–73.

DISCUSSION

Participants: S. Carey, D. Hilton, F. Keil, M. Morris, E. Spelke, L. Talmy

Spelke: I like your idea that the mechanical system for representing objects and their interactions is distinct from the visual system for representing surfaces. There are good reasons for this: one needs the visual system to represent *whatever* happens—things dissolving, things interpenetrating. However, one needs the other system to underlie inferences about what will happen/what should have happened out of view. But does the notion of FORCE in itself help in supporting predictions/inferences about interactions among inanimate objects? (a) Why does the infant see the moving object as the Agent instead of the stationary object? (b) Why do infants appear to make some predictions about object motion (e.g. solidity) but not others (e.g. inertia)? Will the FORCE notion ultimately explain this, or does it need to be supplemented by further principles and constraints?

Leslie: The FORCE notion can draw together and make sense of otherwise disparate phenomena. Objects which move are (typically) seen as bearing FORCE; those that do not are (typically) seen as lacking FORCE. For a FORCE transaction to occur there must be contact between objects. This provides powerful assumptions for learning about object interactions. For example, in launching, the moving object must be the cause because it is the bearer and therefore the transmitter of FORCE on contact with the stationary FORCE less object. The respective roles that the different objects play in this encounter follow from the FORCE representation. (Notice that I do not say that the moving ball in launching is an Agent—it is momentarily the cause, but it is a mere physical object throughout because it lacks an internal and renewable source of FORCE.) The only alternatives to this sort of account that I know of rely upon simply describing the spatiotemporal patterning of motion or appeal, *à la* Hume, to statistical properties of the event. None of these alternatives, as far as I can see, account for or do justice to the empirical data. For example, they do not tell us why infants see launching as an event with a particular causal direction over and above its spatiotemporal direction.

These simple FORCE assumptions also extend to mechanical Agents. (Let me re-emphasize that 'mechanical Agent' means an Agent described at the mechanical level — alternatively, an entity which is an Agent by virtue of its mechanical properties — and not simply any physical object that happens momentarily to be mechanically active.) Because Agents move around freely and without the external acquisition of FORCE, they must have an internal and renewable source of FORCE. Assuming the infant has sufficient exposure to a given Agent, this is the only description compatible with the FORCE representation. It also fits nicely with **ToBy**'s concern with internal properties, to which I drew attention. Therefore it seems to me that your first question is answered decisively by the FORCE notion.

Why is inertia (and possibly gravity effects and acceleration) harder for infants to comprehend? My guess is that this stems from the FORCE dynamical interest in contact. If FORCE can only be carried by bodies, then it can only pass between bodies through contact. A property of object motion such as inertia may not be construed as a unitary property of motion but instead partly in terms of mechanical role — for example whether one object resists another in an interaction — while other aspects of our cultural notion of inertia may not fall under the FORCE representation at all. If so, this would be an important empirical finding with regard to our core representations. **ToBy** may have no in-built specifications for 'free-flight' motion patterns (gravity, acceleration, etc.), and these patterns may simply have to be learnt by gradually internalizing spatiotemporal analogues. In this connection one might raise the case of *support*. Some of your own results suggest that infants lack an appreciation of support relations, while other work by Baillargeon and collaborators (Needham and Baillargeon 1993) suggests that infants can appreciate support. If **ToBy** has little or no specification for 'free-flight' patterns, then an object stopping suddenly in mid-flight might not seem surprising even though it lacks visible support. Perhaps this is no more surprising than other events in which objects suddenly start to move or suddenly stop moving without there being a visible external cause. In Baillargeon's tests of support, there are contact mechanical relations between one object and another: an object is pushed over the edge of a support. It may be that these contact mechanical relations engage the FORCE representation in a way in which 'free flight' does not.

Other findings coming out of Baillargeon's laboratory may also indicate the sort of contribution that network tuning may make to the infant's reasoning about the physical world. It seems that infants apply fairly general mechanical principles to understanding elementary mechanisms but are relatively poor at problems which demand *metrical* reasoning. Thus, whereas the baby assumes that one object cannot pass through another object, he or she is unsure where exactly on its trajectory the first object will contact the other (Baillargeon 1993; Chapter 4 of this volume). This sort of metrical information probably relies on analogue representations, while mechanical role (FORCE dynamical) representations are well suited to predicate–argument representation. If this is so, then there are interesting implications for the internal architecture of **ToBy**, implying a close connection between two different kinds of architecture within a single system. Something similar appears to be true within the language system, within, in fact, a tiny subpart of language concerned with the morphophonemics of past tenses. S. Pinker and P. Prince (unpublished) have argued that regular and irregular past tenses are handled by systems with quite different architectures: one is rule-based and structure dependent, and the other is associative and 'metrical'.

Keil: Is the idealized representation provided by the FORCE system truly ideal in its abstraction nature such that it would induce the infant actually to prefer the pure idealized launching *more* than the imperfect friction-full sorts of launching so common in the real world? Indeed, it could be argued that, apart from infants who haunt billiard halls, most have never seen anything approaching an idealized launching event. If you think that infants would not prefer the idealized over the more natural event, what then do you mean by saying that the FORCE representation is idealized?

Does the FORCE system enable understanding of things like a container or Spelke's primitive notions, or does it take those as arguments and expand on them? One can have two-dimensional notions of containment, and the notion of spatiotemporal continuity seems to be perhaps given new implications by FORCE but not explicated or understood in such terms.

Leslie: The effect of the ubiquitous friction on real world motions raises interesting questions for the representation of FORCE. For example, perhaps it appears to infants that mere objects suffer a spontaneous loss of FORCE in contrast with Agents who move freely with a renewable (internal) source of FORCE. I have no idea whether or not spontaneous loss of FORCE is construed by infants. However, it is interesting that Michotte found that launching events where the second object slowed down after its initial impulse seemed to produce a stronger causal impression in adults. I am not sure that I said that the FORCE representation is 'idealized'. I did argue that the FORCE representation could explain why a launching event should appear as a 'perfect instance of cause and effect', quoting from Hume, whereas Hume was not able to offer any explanation for this at all.

With regard to your second set of questions, I do believe that the FORCE representation plays an important role in understanding containment *qua* mechanism. It is true that one can have two-dimensional containment like a circle with a cross in the middle. But here the containment is purely spatial without any mechanical significance whatsoever (see the discussion of this point by Leslie (1994*b*)). However, when the containment is provided by a three-dimensional object, then there are mechanical implications which have to be understood in terms of FORCE and related notions (for example see my earlier discussion of hardness). For example, a three-dimensional container can entrain or transport another object placed within it, while a two-dimensional container cannot (do not confuse the three-dimensional piece of paper with the two-dimensional circle and cross upon its surface!). A. M. Leslie and P. Das Gupta (submitted) have obtained evidence that infants as young as 6 months understand some of the mechanical implications of such containment, as I outlined earlier.

Spatiotemporal continuity is not likely to be explicated in terms of FORCE, nor should we expect it to be. My assumption is that spatiotemporal properties are described prior to the operation of **ToBy**, and indeed these descriptions form **ToBy**'s main input (Leslie, 1994*b*). What you may have in mind is spatiotemporal continuity in relation to object identity. It seems unlikely that the FORCE representation is fundamental to object identity (in the sense of numerical identity). However, there are cases where FORCE considerations play some role; for example how identity is determined is affected by whether or not an entity is a countable object or a mass. It is necessary to describe the FORCE properties of an entity (e.g. its cohesion) to determine whether or not it is countable or simply an incohesive mass. One way of doing this might be to apply minimal FORCE to the entity by, for example, poking it gently with one's finger. However, I do not wish my message to be that somehow 'everything' reduces to the FORCE representation.

Carey: There are two distinct senses of 'explicit': (a) on the surface of the representation that is the output of some stage of processing and (b) available to the central reasoning process, i.e. on the surface of the output of the last stage of processing before reasoning. Which do you mean? To focus this question: Would you predict that 18-month-old infants, for example, would be able to make explicit judgements on the basis of the output of **ToBy** (for example verbally expressed predictions or predictions by pointing to a photograph choice of what will be found behind a screen in a Spelke–Baillargeon scenario)?

Leslie: I was using 'explicit' in the first sense, i.e., in the sense, following Marr (1982), of information being put in the foreground by a representational system. This use of 'explicit' leaves open as an empirical question whether or not the output of **ToBy** is explicit in the second sense, for example available to a given central reasoning process at a given age, in a given task, under given circumstances, etc. It seems to me that such questions will turn out to be quite complex. For example, is central reasoning a single unstructured process? I doubt it. I think that **ToBy** and **ToMM** together function as a kind of interface system between input

and more central processes (cf. Premack's pertinent remarks about 'interpretation' processes (Premack 1990)). If, instead of asking about verbal
prediction at 18 or 24 months, you had asked about manual search
responses at 12 months, the answer would be that the action-planning
system either has limited access to **ToBy**'s output or is not always able to
make good use of it. All these questions about knowledge versus ability in
development can only receive clear answers in relation to a blueprint for
cognitive architecture. I have made related arguments in connection with
difficulties that 3-year-old children encounter with solving certain false
belief problems (Leslie and Thaiss 1992; Leslie and Roth 1993; Leslie
1994*a*). There are limits to the attempt to describe 'what the child knows'
because neither the 'child' nor 'knowing' are psychologically indivisible, and
to that extent are not the appropriate entities for psychology study.

In short, the theory of **ToBy** leaves as an open question whether and
under what circumstances children can verbally access the output of **ToBy**.
Other views in the study of development have stressed, indeed insisted on,
the homogeneity of cognitive architecture. Such views would, as a matter
of principle, conclude that **ToBy**'s knowledge is continuous with central
processes and encyclopaedic knowledge. However, as far as I am concerned,
these are empirical questions.

Talmy: Your use of Michotte's 'launching effect' in your research raises
the question of why this effect is thought of as 'launching', which refers
to the later occurring motion of the second display dot, instead of as
something like 'stopping dead', which would refer to the earlier occurring
motion of the first display dot. One can posit as a reason for this a
systematic perceptual bias — both among subjects and among the professional psychologists who name the effect — to attend preferentially to the
later event, the result, rather than to the earlier event, the cause.

An explanation for this asymmetry in the distribution of attention in
perception is a parallel asymmetry that can be observed encoded in the
structure of language as I have described in a recent paper, 'The windowing
of attention in language'. In referring to a causal sequence that is initiated
by a volitional Agent and that ends with the desired result, there is a
universal tendency among languages to favour a construction which
explicitly represents only the initiator and that final resulting subevent. For
example, if I as an initiating Agent want to break a vase, and effectuate
this by bending down, lifting a rock, swinging the rock, launching the rock,
and propelling the rock through the air so that the rock then hurtles through
the air, impacts with the vase, and then the vase breaks, this entire sequence
can be represented in English as 'I broke the vase', which names solely the
initiating Agent 'I' and the final resulting subevent 'the vase broke'. The
point is that all the intermediary causal subevents are omitted from explicit

mention. Of these intermediary subevents, the next most favoured one is the penultimate subevent, that i.e., the immediate cause of the final event, which in some languages must be explicitly mentioned, while in others is available for optional mention. An example of the latter is English, with its 'by' clause. For example, one can say 'I broke the vase by hitting it with a rock', but any earlier subevent in the entire causal sequence cannot be readily expressed in the 'by' clause. For example, it is impossible to say 'I broke the vase by bending down/by picking up a rock/by swinging a rock/by propelling a rock'. In being structured in this way, language would seem to be reflecting general cognitive structure with respect to how attention is distributed over Agentively effectuated results.

In general, the intuition is that once one has proficiency, one's foreground attention is almost entirely on the final subevent — the desired result or effect — and minimally, or only in the background, on any of the intervening causal subevents. The reason that such a distribution may have evolved into this pattern is that a volitional Agent's intended goal or result can be treated psychologically as an invariant held across the variation of the range and variety of means that might be marshalled to accomplish the intended result.

Leslie: An alternative account of the attentional bias with regard to the launching event might be the principle 'attend to the FORCE'. Given **ToBy**'s notion of FORCE and the resulting asymmetrical FORCE transaction in launching, we have a bias to follow the progress of the FORCE as it is carried away by the second object. With regard to your very interesting observations on language structure, I am attracted to the idea that there has been a co-evolution of grammatical (e.g. verb–argument) structure and the representational systems employed by **ToBy** and **ToMM**. Pinker and Bloom (1990), for example, have made parallel arguments. If I am right in understanding your examples, then where there is a volitional Agent, it can be mentioned as the initiator of an extended sequence; where there is no volitional Agent, then only a direct cause (i.e. the penultimate event in the sequence) can be mentioned. Thus if I (a volitional Agent) detonated a dynamite charge sending a huge boulder rolling down a mountain which smashed into a dam releasing large amounts of water which then flooded Jim's house, I can readily say, 'I flooded Jim's house'. However, if the huge boulder in question had been sent down the mountain by the eruption of a volcano, it would be odd to say, 'The volcano flooded Jim's house'. I would not be surprised if such facts about language are related to the different 'conceptual' contributions of **ToBy** and **ToMM**, in particular to the contrast between the contiguous relations of contact mechanics and the 'at a distance' action of goal-directed Agency (see discussion on p. 136). For example, in the case of **ToBy**'s contact mechanical FORCE transactions the focus is necessarily on immediate cause. In contrast, the contribution of **ToMM** is to focus attention on the 'at a distance' link between Agent and goal (what you called the 'desired result').

If language has evolved (in part) to express and communicate efficiently the conceptual structures generated by **ToBy** and **ToMM**, then we should expect there to be interrelationships of this sort. Basic aspects of verb–argument structure appear well suited to express **ToBy**'s mechanical relationships (and less well suited to represent the appearance of individual faces for example). **ToMM** $system_1$ requires that the basic 'mechanical' sentence structures be extended to allow mention of the Agent in its typically 'distant' goal-directed initiating role. Verb–argument structure then requires one more extension, this time to reflect **ToMM** $system_2$, where one of the arguments is an entire sentence. With this extension, the metarepresentation can now be expressed linguistically by means of verbs of attitude and argument. Together with an object catalogue and a store of nouns, these systems form a major part of core conceptualization that is in place by the third birthday.

Hilton: In the case of the hand moving the object (entraining), the perception of causality may be affected by the orienting response. We know from Michotte that where the eye is fixated affects the perception of causality. Could an explanation of seeing the hand as the cause simply be that we orient to what is moving, track it with our eye, and therefore see it as causal? No attribution of 'intentionality' would be needed.

Leslie: I need to make some clarifications in response to your points. I did not argue in the case of my hand experiments that an attribution of 'intentionality' was implied. Instead I used that as evidence to support the apprehension of *mechanical* Agency by an infantile **ToBy**. In describing mechanical Agency, no intentionality is attributed. On my modular assumptions, that is the job of the next stage of representation which is carried out by **ToMM**. As regards your suggestion of a role for the orienting response, it is not at all clear why tracking with the eyes would make you see something as a cause. Furthermore, it leads to paradox in the case of the launching event, where tracking the second object as it moves away would lead one to perceive it somehow as the cause rather than the effect.

The point that I tried to make with regard to my hand experiments was that simply tracking a moving object would not carry implications for any particular mechanical role when that object is in interaction with another object such that they move together. If they move together, presumably they are tracked together. Therefore one of the events that the infant saw began with a hand grasping an object with both stationary. The hand and the object then move off together. The equivalent pattern is shown where the hand and object are slightly out of contact. In cases like these, the infant sees the hand and the object moving with the same spatiotemporal pattern.

The question is why prior perception of the hand moving freely and on its own should lead to the representation now and the inference now that, when the hand and the object are moving together, it is the hand and not the object that is the cause. My suggestion for this is that a prior perception of the hand moving freely on its own has already led to a certain 'conclusion', or rather to a certain FORCE representation, namely of the hand as a mechanical Agent (i.e. as an entity which is an Agent by virtue of its enduring mechanical properties). Agency in this sense is a property of the hand and consequently of particular motions that the hand undertakes. This results in a particular directional FORCE representation when a hand and object move together, namely the hand picks up the object.

Morris: You propose that a concept of FORCE rather than, say, transfer of kinetic energy is primitive in causal cognition about the physical domain. A virtue of this more abstract concept FORCE is that it can also describe people's causal intuitions about psychological and social domains, as Talmy has argued. Do you think that a common notion of FORCE underlies causal reasoning in physical, psychological, and social domains? Or do you think that notions of psychological or social FORCE are mere metaphors from the physical domain?

Leslie: I do not think that the notion of FORCE is so abstract that exactly this notion simply shows up again in the folk psychological domain. To that extent, what Talmy has drawn attention to is a 'metaphor'. Maybe there are notions in other domains which are 'descendants' of **ToBy**'s FORCE (see Carey (1988) for a discussion of conceptual descendancy in development). If so, there might be two different kinds of descendancy at work. One type of descendancy might arise during the evolution of core architecture where neural circuits which have provided solutions to old problems are duplicated and adapted to solve new problems. Adaptation might introduce new characteristics. For example, one might think here of a descendancy between **ToBy**'s mechanical Agent who, with its own internal resources, moves freely, producing contact effects on objects, and **ToMM**'s actional Agent who strives freely toward distant goals.

The other kind of descendancy might be psychogenetic, i.e. arise through psychological processes in development. For example, perhaps the child develops biological ideas that employ something like a notion of 'vital force', say, by extending the FORCE notion of a mechanical Agent into the biological domain and the array of concepts like energetic–tired, healthy–sick, alive–dead, and so on. Pointing to what appear to be intriguing generalizations and calling them 'metaphors' or 'conceptual descendants' or whatever is fine; however, we are a very long way from being able to construct explanatory theories. But these are among the deep questions that developmental psychology can ask.

6

Distinguishing between animates and inanimates: not by motion alone

ROCHEL GELMAN, FRANK DURGIN, AND LISA KAUFMAN

INTRODUCTION

In this chapter we present an account of the origins and development of our ability to classify moveable entities as either animate or inanimate. The account builds on the known abilities of young infants to find three dimensional objects (Kellman and Spelke 1983) and to reason about some of their fundamental physical characteristics, for example that they occupy space, move as a whole, cannot pass through each other, etc. (see Chapters 3, 4, and 5). We argue that infants' abilities to find and reason about objects are complemented by skeletal causal principles. First-causal principles lead infants to attend to and interpret both an object's composition and its motion path in ways that are relevant to the distinction between animate and inanimate objects. They do so because they support interpretations of motion and transformation with respect to the requisite energy sources and the material types involved in the object's composition and motion path.

Our account of young infants' differential treatment of animate and inanimate objects is fundamentally conceptual and therefore diverges from those that limit infants' abilities to the perceptual level. The latter class of accounts of animacy are based on the assumption that the perceptions of particular kinds of movements can, alone, yield veridical animate or inanimate attributions (Bassili 1976; Mandler 1992; Stewart 1984; Chapters 7 and 20 of this volume). Our account, which focuses attention on abstract causal principles, is not unique. It is consistent with the argument of Heider and Simmel (1944) that the motion paths of objects and their interactions are interpreted in terms of schemata (Goffman 1974; Hochberg 1978). Related views have been developed by Leslie, Talmy, Spelke and her colleagues, other authors in this volume who attribute infants' (and beginning language learners') interpretations of objects and/or semantic relations to force-dynamic conceptual primitives or implicit theories about physics.

We favour the idea that an underlying conceptual scheme serves infants' selection and interpretation of inputs for several reasons. Data about motion paths are often ambiguous. In addition, motion path information is neither necessary nor sufficient for the correct identification and interpretation of novel instances. Therefore perceptions about trajectories cannot be sufficient data for the veridical identification of objects and events as animate or inanimate. Further, since correct identifications and attributions occur even when a novel object is static (Massey and Gelman 1988), information about the path is not even necessary. Finally, it is not clear how a perception-only account of the sources of infants' abilities can explain the evidence that infants are capable of causal interpretations of motion paths, whereas these findings are readily explained by a theory that grants infants skeletal causal principles.

On first causal principles

Gelman (1990) proposed that attending to and learning about relevant characteristics of animate and inanimate objects benefits from certain processing mechanisms. These are informed by causal principles that correspond to deep and fundamental distinctions about an object's composition and its sources of motion or change. Animate objects can cause themselves to move or change; inanimate objects cannot. These differences go hand in hand with the fact that animate objects are composed of biological matter and honour biological principles, whereas inanimate objects are composed of non-biological material and honour principles of inanimate causation. The cause of animate motion and change comes from the internally controlled and channelled release of stored chemical energy that is characteristic of biological entities. The cause of inanimate motion is an external force, and there is always a transfer of energy from one object to another, or a conversion of potential to kinetic energy. Animate motions have a quality of function (purpose). This is a direct consequence of their governance by control mechanisms that makes it possible for animates to respond (adjust) to environments — be they social or non-social — and adapt to unforeseeable changes in circumstances (Gallistel 1980).

The foregoing considerations underlie Gelman's (1990) proposal that learning about animates and inanimates is guided by first principles regarding the energy sources that enable the motion and change of each class of objects. The **innards** principle draws attention to and interprets perceptual information about those natural objects that move on their own; the **external agent** principle supports the processing and interpretation of data about objects that move as a function of external energy sources. In general the idea is 'attend to information about sources of energy and their consequences'. In this context, two points deserve comment.

First, we do not endow infants with a modern notion of energy, or even any particular theory of energy. Processing mechanisms that are constrained by the innards principle process objects and related events as if certain natural objects have something inside that enables their own motion and change. The principle is neutral with respect to the nature of what a child might think about the 'inside' of self-propellable objects. Since the ideas about 'insides' vary with the belief system of a culture (at a given place and time in history), they must be learned as a function of experience in one's culture. Similarly, processing mechanisms that embody the external agent principle process events as if an external agent contributes to the energy needed for non-biological objects to accelerate and move/change in certain ways. However, the principles do not carry with them a commitment to a particular account of energy or theory of physical causality. Therefore both causal principles are neutral with respect to the ultimate explanation systems developed about animate and inanimate objects. As **skeletal** principles, they serve to render salient information that pertains to the motion paths and the conditions that support them for animate and inanimate objects. The external interaction principle organizes conceptual–perceptual processing of information that is relevant to inanimate objects and their motions. The innards principle organizes the conceptual–perceptual processing of, and learning about, the characteristics of real world animate objects.

Potential information about a source of energy includes information about the entity itself, particularly whether it is composed of living 'stuff' and possesses characteristics that are biological. Information about these is yoked to the difference between the innards and external agent causal principles. Causal principles are not applied in the abstract; they are related to the class of entities that interact with the principles, just as entities in other domains are related to the principles that define the domain. Given that the material composition of an object is closely related to the energy conditions that support its path of movement through time and space, causal principles help render salient those features of objects that are related to their motions. This can be expanded as follows. Since biomechanical motions are performed only by biological entities, learners will attend to and learn about characteristics of the objects that co-occur with and are relevant to observed motion paths. Similarly, learners will attend to and process those details of inanimate objects that bear on the nature of its motion path. Information about an object's surface characteristics—its smoothness, shape, and size—as well as its source of movement, the barriers that it encounters, its direction with respect to the ground, and so on are all salient. Causal principles render them salient if the observer uses motion cues to classify novel objects and events as animate or inanimate.

Evidence that motion paths are causally interpreted by infants

Baillargeon and her colleagues have provided evidence that infants interpret motion paths in ways that are consistent with the external agent causal principle. One example is the demonstration by Baillargeon *et al.* (1985) of object permanence in 6- to 8-month-old infants. In this experiment infants saw the same motion path at two different times. During the habituation phase, they saw a screen rotate towards and away from them through a 180° arc. Nothing was behind the screen. When their interest in the moving screen declined, i.e. when the infants habituated, the stage was set for creating the viewing conditions of the same 180° rotating screen for a second time. To do this, the experimenter showed infants an object placed to the left side of the screen. While infants watched, the experimenter moved the object behind the screen and the post-habituation phase of the experiment was started. Once again the screen rotated toward and away from the infant. On alternating trials it either traversed a novel 120° arc in its rotation or the familiar 180° arc. Given the physics of the situation, the screen should have stopped at about the 120° position of its rotation, but when it continued through an 180° arc (by the use of trick mirrors and invisible doors), it contributed to the adult perception of an impossible event, an unseen block being repeatedly crushed and uncrushed as the screen circumscribed the arc. The event is identified as impossible by adults because they are aware that, except in the world of spirits and ghosts, one solid object cannot move through another. If infants are restricted to the perceptual analyses of motion paths, they should see no difference between a 180° arc rotation shown in both the habituation and post-habituation phases. They should continue to be uninterested in the event, and prefer to look at the 120° event, which generates a novel perception. However, if infants interpret the motion paths in terms of causally relevant variables, they should treat the second showing of the 180° event as different from the first. In fact, they attended more to the 180° event, leading to the conclusion that they interpreted the perceptual information about the motion path in ways that we know are causally relevant.

A subsequent series of experiments by Baillargeon (1987) demonstrated that 7-month-old infants relate the path of the rotating screen to causally relevant characteristics, for example the height and compressibility of the object to be hidden in the second part of the experimental paradigm discussed above. Infants expected the rotating screen to stop sooner for the taller of two similarly shaped objects that they saw hidden behind the screen. Similarly, given a few seconds to manipulate a hard and a soft compressible object, they expected the screen to stop sooner when it hid the hard object as opposed to the compressible object. The work reported by Baillargeon and her colleagues and by Spelke and her colleagues in this volume (Chapters 3 and 4) provide evidence that even 3- and 4-month-old infants attend to and interpret variables that are relevant to the causal conditions underlying the generation of an object's motion path in time and space.

The Baillargeon studies offer some support for our key assumption that motion paths are causally interpreted. As noted by Leslie and Keeble (1987), infants shown film of a launching event behaved as if they took into account the different mechanical roles of two moving 'objects', the pusher (the transmitter of 'energy') and the pushed (the recipient of 'energy'). Again, the relevant data come from the conditions that lead infants to dishabituate following a habituation phase. In this case, two separate groups of infants watched different pairs of events during habituation and post-habituation trials. The first group watched a pair that consisted of a film of Michotte's launching event (Michotte 1963) and its reversal (we denote these events 1A and 1B). The reversal was obtained by running the film of event 1A backwards. The second group watched a pair of events, denoted 2A and 2B, that differed from the first pair in the following way. In event 2A, there was a half second delay between the pusher's reaching the pushed object and both moving on together. Since the delay removes the causal impression of launching, there is no reason to assign causal roles to the perceived objects. Again, the second event for the subjects in the second group was made by running 2A backwards.

Leslie and Keeble (1987) habituated infants to an A event and then showed them the B event, to make up what we shall call an AB pair of events. If infants could not interpret the perception of launching with respect to causal roles, there should have been no difference between the ways that infants in the two conditions reacted to their respective reversals. If they could consider the mechanical roles of the objects, then it should matter to them that event 1B illustrated an event that was both conceptually and perceptually reversed but event 2B was just perceptually reversed. In fact, infants in group 1 looked longer at their reversed event than did those in group 2, a result that provides further support for our claim that motion paths are interpreted and that causal principles direct attention to information about energy sources.

The foregoing reviews some of the evidence for our central claim that different skeletal causal principles organize attention to and learning about the animate–inanimate distinction. The work of Spelke and her colleagues presented in this volume (Chapter 3), which controlled for the fact that animates and inanimates tend to differ in size and surface characteristics, demonstrates that 7-month-old infants know that, whereas two inanimate objects have to contact each other if a causal event is to occur, the same is not true for two people. The authors contrasted infants' reactions to two pairs of videotaped displays. The inanimate pairs of stimuli were two objects of heights 5 and 6 feet which had distinctive shapes and contrasting bright colours and patterns. The animate pairs consisted of two people. In the inanimate test condition, infants watched two events: (i) the objects moved towards each other, touched each other, and changed direction; (ii) the objects moved towards each other, stopped briefly before reaching the point of contact, and changed direction. In the people condition the structure of the two events was identical with that of the inanimate events. For example, the parallel event for the person contact condition showed a person holding her arms up and close to her body as she brushed alongside another person. During test conditions, infants looked reliably longer at the no-contact inanimate event; they showed no such preference in the animate event trials. This is what one should observe if the innards and external agent causal principles aid infants in interpreting the motion paths of animate and inanimate objects. Converging evidence that infants interpret a given motion path differently, depending on whether or not the object is animate, can be found in Golinkoff and Harding (1980) and Poulin-Dubois and Schultz (1988).

Evidence that infants interpret the same motion path differently depending on whether the path is generated by an animate or an inanimate object, is particularly troublesome for theorists who favour non-conceptual accounts of initial abilities to respond differently to animate and inanimate objects. For such accounts to work, the spatiotemporal information about the motion paths should not be ambiguous, i.e. it should not be consistent with more than one interpretation. Otherwise, the perceptual inputs cannot lead to the correct classification of an object or an event as animate or inanimate. In what follows we discuss this problem in more detail and show that it is not unique to infants.

CONCEPTUAL COHERENCE: NOT BY MOTION ALONE

Our arguments for a conceptually based account of the early ability to distinguish between animate and inanimate objects parallel those made against the classical definition of concepts (Armstrong *et al.* 1983). The characteristics of redness and roundness are neither necessary nor sufficient identification criteria for a tomato. Both are characteristic of apples, as well as many other objects, and tomatoes can be yellow and oval. To deal with the problems posed by these examples, theorists have proposed that concepts are organized around a core implicit theory or set of conceptual principles that function to outline the kinds of information that are relevant to these cores (Carey 1985; Murphy and Medin 1985). These problems do not diminish in an account of concepts of animacy and inanimacy; turning to motion patterns as the critical sources of input does not alleviate the problem of indeterminancy. Perceiving that something accelerates in the absence of a source for the acceleration does not guarantee identification of the unknown object as animate, any more than does the perceiving of redness and roundness guarantee correct identification of an object as a tomato.

When perceptual information is ambiguous, one way to disambiguate it is to interpret it within a conceptual framework. The abstract causal principles serve this function for both the infants in the above experiments and the adults in the experiments presented in the next section. They lead one to interpret motion paths in terms of the causal conditions of the motion. Implicit causal principles underlie the information processing that leads to the attribution of causal source(s). They focus processing on those aspects of the situation that are indicative of a mechanical or biomechanical interpretation of the object and its motions and/or the changes it undergoes in form, colour, etc. These include clues about material composition, speed, change in direction, surface characteristics of both the object and its environment, etc.

Animates cannot be distinguished from inanimates simply on the basis of motion because the cues of motion, like the static cues of colour and shape, are ambiguous. A wide range of trajectories can be interpreted as the motions of either an animate or an inanimate object. Our general ability to keep implicit track of the predictive validity of a cue, or combination of cues, leads to knowledge about the kinds of motion paths that tend to go with given object kinds. In a similar way, knowledge about the appearance of objects in each class, the surface cues that tend to distinguish the substances of the two kinds of objects, the environmental factors that are relevant to the motions and reactions of the different objects, and so on is acquired. Such knowledge then functions to help us make educated guesses about the identity of new objects and events. However, a purely cue-driven learning account will not work. Should we discover that our guess is contradicted when we encounter information about the composition and movement conditions of the unknown object, we shall be quick to update our assignment.

Implicit causal principles allow learning like the foregoing to proceed rapidly for the same reason that any learning benefits from available mind structure. Like all mental structures, no matter their origin, causal principles function to combine what is just learned with what is known already. This sets the stage for fast learning about the cues that, on average, distinguish between animate or inanimate items. Armed with such knowledge, even very young children should be able to make good guesses about the category assignment of novel items. Evidence that they can is presented later in this chapter. (For further discussion of the parallel function between first principles and acquired structures, see Gelman and Brenneman (1993).)

The studies presented in the following sections buttress our position. In the next section we show that motion paths are ambiguous for adults, not just infants. Part of the presentation is based on analyses of some of Stewart's unpublished work* which is being cited in the literature in favour of perception-first accounts (Mandler 1992; Chapter 20 of this volume). This section ends with a report of studies by Durgin and Gelman that reinforce our conclusions about the Stewart data. We then return to developmental issues. A review of preschool children's abilities to assign representations of objects to animate and inanimate categories sets the stage for a discussion of the learning model.

ADULT RESPONSES TO MOTION PATHS

Stewart reconsidered and extended

Stewart (1982, 1984) proposes that we perceive a moving object as inanimate when its motion path is consistent with Newtonian laws of motion. If the motion path violates Newtonian principles, then we perceive animacy. Attributions such as intentions, desires, hunger, affection, etc. follow. To obtain evidence for her theory, Stewart showed college students a computer-generated ball that moved on the screen in ways that were either consistent or inconsistent with Newtonian mechanics. Examples of these motion trajectories are shown schematically in Fig. 6.1. Some of these are labelled with Stewart's characterization of the animacy cue(s) in a display (e.g. 'Avoidance' in Fig. 6.1(f)). All of them are labelled with Stewart's predictions regarding the expected perception (Animate, Inanimate, Neutral). Figures 6.1(a) and 6.1(b) show one object colliding with another in accord with the laws of elastic collision. Stewart predicted that these would be perceived as inanimate events. However, she predicted that perceptions of displays like Figs 6.1(c) and 6.1(d) would be neither animate nor inanimate but neutral. She argued that an object moving at a constant velocity along a straight motion path offers no information about what initiated the motion and therefore little or no information for animacy or inanimacy.

Stewart's work (Stewart 1982, 1984) is beginning to attract the attention of authors who prefer models of animacy that are not initially conceptual (Mandler 1992; Chapter 20 of this volume). There are results in the work that are consistent with Stewart's account. However, there are some outcomes that are not as predicted; for example individuals do not perceive

---

*We thank Judith Stewart for providing us with such full access to her unpublished data and writings.

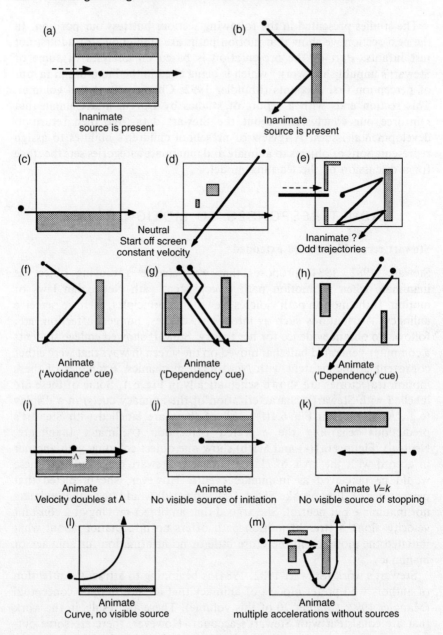

Fig. 6.1.

an object that moves along the motion path shown in Fig. 6.1(f) as animate. Further, there are possible problems with the data analyses. Stewart assigned categorical judgements to an interval score in some of her statistical analyses. For example in one study subjects responded by choosing between the attributions of 'alive creature', 'non-alive object', 'can't tell'. These in turn were assigned degrees of inanimacy scores of 0, 1, and 2 for use in parametric analyses. However, 'non-alive' is a predicate that has multiple meanings, including 'dead' which is a predicate that can be used sensibly with animate noun phrases (Carey 1985). Second, it is unlikely that 'can't tell' lies half-way between the animate and inanimate anchors on a psychological scale of animacy. Instead, it is possible that a mean score of 1 masks the fact that some subjects used the animate category and others used the inanimate category. Additionally, the requirement that subjects classify a display into one of the conceptual categories could have encouraged interpretations that fit within this classification scheme; if so, it is hard to exclude the possibility that subjects interpreted what they saw to achieve their answers.

Stewart was well aware of these concerns. Indeed, the rating criterion problem led her to perform a series of unpublished studies on the effects of instructions. In one, she used an open-ended response mode and asked college students ($N = 21$) to report 'what came to mind', what the display 'reminded them of'. In subsequent studies, Stewart encouraged her subjects to 'see' all the represented objects and their motion paths in a certain way. In one of these studies, 10 additional students were told that everything represented the motion of an animate object, generated by a person or an animal; in another study with yet another sample of 10, subjects were told that everything they would see represented the motion path of an inanimate object such as a ball. Fortunately, the same displays were used across all three of these instruction conditions, which we denote here the unconstrained, animate constrained, and inanimate constrained groups. Stewart's generosity with her data makes it possible for us to present analyses of these, the outcome of which is a body of evidence that illustrates the ambiguity of objects' trajectories.

The new Stewart studies

The subjects in the unconstrained, animate constrained, and inanimate constrained groups saw the displays shown in Fig. 6.1. The stimuli were created and shown on a Commodore computer. The program first painted between 0–4 orange background strips in haphazardly selected places around the outer portions of the screen (these appear as black bars and squares in Fig. 6.1). When this was complete a black roundish ball (one sprite in size) followed the trajectory programmed for that trial. Sprites moved across the screen at a constant velocity of about 1 inch per second. Accelerations either doubled or halved the speed of the sprite. The total duration of a display varied from 6 to 25 seconds. Answers were recorded for later transcription. We decided to code only the first response recorded, on the grounds that these were the least likely to reflect interpretations (our hypothesis) as opposed to cue-driven perceptions (the bottom-up hypothesis).

Coding   Each respondent's first reply for each display was scored in two ways, first with respect to the kind of *object* seen and then with respect to the kind of *event* reported. For the object-kind, we coded whether the noun or pronoun used to describe the ball (actually, the computer sprite) referred to an *animate*, *inanimate*, or *mechanical* object (e.g. tourist, ball, and jet plane respectively). A fourth category, *other*, was used when an answer was ambiguous, incomplete, or did not fit into one of the above three categories. Examples of *other* answers included graph, computer game, and skating. Skating was ambiguous because it was not clear whether the observer was talking about a person who was skating or just the skates. When an answer referred to a well-known inanimate event, as when many subjects described the Michotte-like collision in Fig. 6.1(b) as 'pool' or 'a pool game', we assumed that the object was not stated owing to conversation constraints against stating the obvious. In this case, we assumed that had the subject referred to an object, it would be the standard one that fitted the known game or script. In the example under discussion, this means that our object-kind code scored the response as inanimate as opposed to *other*.

Codes of event-kinds were based only on the kind of motion path ascribed to the display. In some cases, this is all that a respondent talked about, for example a tennis ball hitting a wall. In other cases, the event was embedded in a more complex script, for example where the curved trajectory display (Fig. 6.1(e)) led an observer to say that someone was carrying a balloon that 'was released'. In the latter case, both the object-kind and the event-kind were scored as inanimate. The fact that the perceived motion path was embedded in a causal account is clearly of interest. However, since the latter referred to entities that were not part of the display, to code the perceived motion path itself as animate would be to confound issues of perception and interpretation of the display. We shall return to the issues raised by this example.

When we scored event-kinds, it was necessary to expand the criteria for the other category to include complex descriptions of computer games ('that's an old Pong computer game'), mathematical and scientific talk about the displays ('a drawing of a parabolic curve' or 'It looks really sticky ... when it hits every wall it's not using the laws of physics'), comments on the displays, metaphorical answers ('a stable relationship'), and literal descriptions ('It moved along a diagonal, then it moved in another direction').

Use of the event-kind code for a description was usually straightforward, as for 'That person is going fast', which was classified as animate. However, there were problem cases, particularly in data sets from the two constrained instruction conditions. For example, one subject in the inanimate constrained group said that the display in Fig. 6.1(m) was 'a vacuum cleaner doing a lousy job', and subjects in the animate constrained group told us about animate objects being bounced or pushed through walls after seeing collision displays. In these cases, although the case of the noun phrase (NP) and verb phrase (VP) do not agree, one senses that the VP encodes the intended answer. It is as if the respondents have found a way to meet the demand characteristics of the task and at the same time tell us what they 'really' saw.

Three lines of evidence supported our decision to focus on the VP when classifying reported events as animate, inanimate, mechanical, or other. First, verbs are often very selective about the meaning of the nouns with which they pair (Pinker 1989; Gleitman 1990). For example, if we hear 'That dax is frightened', 'The zifs are walking', or 'The tral is investigating', we are inclined to assume that the NP is animate. These facts justified our decision to accept psychological verb phrases (ones that referred to knowledge states, volition, desire, motivation, motivational states, emotions, perceptions, and goal-oriented plans of action) as evidence that subjects saw an animate event, despite their use of an inanimate NP. Therefore, although the *it* in 'it knew where it wanted to go' and 'It gets frightened' was coded *inanimate* in the object-kind analyses, the events in which the object participated were scored as *animate*.

Use of sociolinguistic devices can mitigate or exaggerate the animacy of an agent. This can be accomplished by using the verb in the passive tense as did the animate constraint subject who said 'The child was thrown' after watching a collision display. In addition, English speakers can use indefinite pronouns, or 'you' and 'they', in an indefinite function to depersonalize or render an agent neutral or nondescript, for example 'They were pushed'. Results of this kind (Weiner and Labov 1983) supported our decision to pay attention to the details of verb use when coding for event-kind. See also Beedham (1987), Lamb (1991), and Stanley (1975).

Finally, we obtained new data to validate our reliance on the VP in order to classify descriptions in which the class (animate, inanimate, etc.) of NP and VP disagreed. We presented a group of introductory honours psychology students at the University of Pennsylvania with a variant of the fill-in-the-blank task. In our version, passages with a blank occurred in the NP. Some of these were created by deleting the item(s) that were in conflict with the structure and semantics of the VP. For example 'That is a vacuum cleaner doing a lousy job' became 'That is a ------ doing a lousy job', 'The ball couldn't decide' became 'The ------ couldn't decide' and 'The animal is being thrown' became 'The ------ is being thrown'. Others were created by deleting material in the NP that was consistent with the VP, for example 'a leaf being blown around' was rendered 'A ------ was blown around'. These control sentences were included to verify our judgement that the NP and VP classes agreed semantically and structurally.

As expected, all 21 students filled in the vacuum item with animate nouns, including worker, janitor, student, cook, businessman, carpenter, and painter. Similarly the original 'The ball couldn't decide' generated nothing but animate answers, including man, boy, debater, mother, Danish Prince, judge, and jury. The original 'The person was bounced off something' was paired with nouns that were all inanimate except one, a bird. Answers included ball, rock, golf ball, superball, and spring. Finally, the example control sentence elicited nouns that were referents for light objects like leaves, feathers, etc. These data were used to check our coding assignment on the basis of the linguistic cues detailed above or when such cues were not present because subjects had compromised the syntactic and semantic rules of agreement.

Coding of both the object-kind and event-kind was reliable. A sample of 54 per cent of the data was scored twice, once by one author in consultation with an independent rater and once by another author. Agreement between raters was obtained for 93 per cent of scored object-kinds and 92 per cent of the event-kinds. The raters continued to score the remaining protocols on their own until all were coded. Unless noted to the contrary, the results presented below are based on event-kind data. There are two reasons for this decision. Focus on the event-kind analyses is probably more consistent with Stewart's scoring procedure; it appears that her results were based on codes that included details regarding event descriptions. Second, as already indicated, the object-kind answers were more likely to reflect demand characteristics. For example, when animate constraint subjects saw the odd collision path (Fig. 6.1(e)), all but 20 per cent complied with the instructions to interpret the display as animate by giving an animate NP but 60 per cent generated inanimate event descriptions.

Baseline considerations

The overall pattern of results from the unconstrained group are shown in Fig. 6.2. They are consistent with Stewart's earlier reports which means that we can treat them as a baseline against which to compare results from the groups that were constrained by instructions to attempt to give animate or inanimate interpretations. In this section we ask whether the detailed pattern of results matches the predictions made by the Stewart model. To anticipate, there are enough departures for us to conclude that the results are better accounted for by the kind of account that we favour.

Figure 6.2 shows the percentage of subjects who offered a given kind of

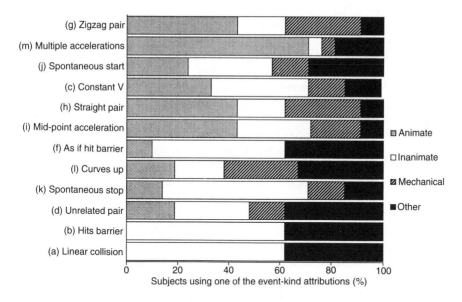

Fig. 6.2.

event description for each display. The displays are arranged from bottom to top in order of their tendency to elicit animate descriptions. Clear collision events were seen as inanimate by most of the subjects and never elicited animate attributions. The display that contained multiple stops and starts in the absence of any source for these was the one most likely to elicit animate attributions. The displays with a mid-point acceleration or paired and co-ordinated motion paths were reasonably good inputs for animate attributions.

Although the foregoing details of the results are all consistent with Stewart's account of animacy, others are not. Contrary to Stewart's prediction, the display that traced a collision 'avoidance' path (Fig. 6.1(f)), i.e. did not hit a barrier, was not particularly seen as animate. Many of the motion paths that violated Newtonian mechanics were ambiguous: some subjects saw them as inanimate and some saw them as animate. This is not what is expected if the perception of animacy is like 'a perceptual illusion' (Stewart 1982) and therefore not subject to conceptual interpretation (cf. Chapter 5). Two displays should have been preferentially judged as animate—the one that showed an object traversing an upwardly curved motion path (Fig. 6.1(l)) and the one that showed the object starting to move on the screen without a causal source (Fig. 6.1(j)). However, they elicited animacy judgements in only 25 per cent and 20 per cent of the subjects respectively.

Some might argue that there is a way of viewing the problematic data points we cite that will be more consistent with Stewart's model than we allow. Perhaps 'mechanical' attributions are used for weaker animate percepts. The idea would be that perceived mechanical and animate events are interchangeable; both solve the perceptual problem of accounting for acceleration in the absence of an external source. However, given the subjects' use of mechanical scripts, it would be a mistake to collapse these. Consider the data for displays where the object started to move on the screen (Fig. 6.1(j)) or accelerated at the mid-point (Fig. 6.1(i)). Although some observers gave mechanical attributions to a display that should be animate, others used inanimate attributions. As can be seen in Fig. 6.2, this tendency is particularly strong when the display object started on its own (Fig. 6.1(j)) or stopped without slowing or contacting another object (Fig. 6.1(k)). More generally, there is too much variability across displays in the use of mechanical event accounts to hold that these are interchangeable with animate attributions. These considerations, together with others presented later in this chapter, encourage us to keep the mechanical and animate categories separate. The evidence fits better with the conclusion that machines are in a hybrid category of their own.

The fact that so many of the Stewart displays are best described as ambiguous is consistent with our account. The information from a limited segment of the motion path of a novel object is often insufficient to render an attribution. The perceptual information is interpreted with reference to the possible causal conditions consistent with what is observed. When a motion path is not unique to a class of objects, we should expect more than one outcome of the interpretative processes. For example, as our subjects showed, the perception of a particular curving path lends itself to a wide range of causal interpretations including '... a cyclist going around a corner', '... a balloon and the wind was blowing and it went like this, this, like a helium balloon. It got caught up in the air', '... a horse climbing a mountain', and '... some kind of magnetic ball that encountered a field that pushed it away'.

The results from the display where there was an abrupt collision-like change in direction even though the ball never made contact with the barrier (Fig. 6.1(f)) are particularly interesting. Contrary to Stewart's prediction, subjects treated this as inanimate. In our view this is what they should have done because the trajectory does not have high validity for an 'avoidance' event. In avoidance paths, it is seldom the case that the angle of incidence is equal to the angle of reflection. This is characteristic of elastic collision events. However, the anomalous causal information means that observers should give reasonably novel interpretations of the event or even suggest that they misperceived it. In fact, many individuals either noted the fact that the ball failed to hit the wall, appealed to invisible barriers or clear walls, or suggested that electromagnetic forces were at work. Some asked why the ball did not hit the barrier and one person claimed that his eyes were playing tricks on him.

Our position differs from Stewart's in another rather subtle way. We have no reason to treat trajectories that offer little information about the animacy or inanimacy of an object as neutral, i.e. they will lead to descriptions that are neither animate or inanimate. Instead, such trajectories should be particularly ambiguous, i.e. they should encourage rich interpretations that supply considerable detail to relate the perceptual input to a causal account. This is what happened with the Stewart neutral displays (Fig. 6.1(c)) and 6.1(d)). Display 1(c) led to accounts like 'some kind of train going along a track', 'A swimmer swimming in a pool', '. . . something going over ice . . . like scooting over ice', 'Something rolling along in a gutter', 'A rabbit running along, like when you see the horse races, and the rabbits on the fence . . .', and 'A father sending a ball across the floor'.

These responses embed within them an account of how the seen object could have moved at a constant velocity, either because of a tracking device, characteristics of the surface, or a particular kind of actor in a particular kind of setting. This is the kind of evidence that we need to conclude that the data are not neutral — eliciting no impression, one way or another — but are instead fodder for the causal principles, encouraging interpretation of what is perceived in terms of the possible agents and conditions that generated the trajectory. Put another way, this is further evidence for our belief that attributions of animacy reflect the workings of mutually constraining perceptual and conceptual processes. We can expand this as follows.

Individuals' perceptions of the spatiotemporal characteristics of the motion paths (trajectories) shown schematically in Fig. 6.1 were almost always veridical in the unconstrained group, i.e. object-kind and event-kind attributions were consistent with what was shown regarding the speed, acceleration, and path of the object. However, the attributions were not based solely on these characteristics. What was perceived was interpreted with reference to the conditions that could cause such a trajectory, even if it meant inventing invisible barriers, unseen tracking devices, and meanings for the rectangles and bars that happened to be on the screen. In other words, veridical perceptions were related to ideas about the kinds of environments in which an event could have occurred. In turn, all this was related to causal considerations, i.e. to one's hypotheses about the kinds of things and conditions that could cause the trajectory in question. Thus causal principles constrained what was perceived. Conversely, causal interpretations were constrained by what was perceived. For example, the interpretative freedom given the perception of an object rapidly traversing a path wherein the angle of incidence equals the angle of reflection was less than the interpretative freedom allowed by an object moving at a constant velocity. Therefore we conclude that the causal interpretation of the data is deeply related to the input, even though what is perceived does not, on its own, generate a perception of animacy or inanimacy. The results from the groups whose interpretations were constrained by our instructions support these ideas.

Constrained instructions as setting conditions

If, as Stewart suggested, the perception of animacy is akin to an illusion, then telling someone to 'see' such events in another way should have no more effect than do instructions not to see the Muller–Lyer illusion. However, if perceptions of animacy and inanimacy are both constrained by and able to constrain causal reasoning about the data, there are conditions under which instructions should alter respondents' reports. If subjects are asked to 'see' a display as animate, they should be able to do so if this interpretative set is consistent with the constraints given by the perceptual inputs. Otherwise, they should not succeed in meeting our request. More generally, individuals' success with constrained instructions should be related to the extent to which a display includes information that is consistent with the request. Therefore individuals should find it harder to 'see' motion paths that typically index collisions as being associated with animate events. Similarly, observers should have difficulty in finding inanimate solutions for displays with multiple accelerations. In contrast, they should be able to find animate solutions where an object's motion path stops in the middle of the display, even though the baseline bias, as revealed in the unconstrained group, is for an inanimate event. This is because the data include information that is relevant to the abilities of inanimate objects to start and stop themselves. Put differently, the instructions can be thought of as setting subjects to pay attention to those aspects of a display that are relevant to a certain kind of causal account. Subjects should follow instructions better when given displays that contain more such features.

The top and bottom panels of Fig. 6.3 summarize the results from the inanimate instruction and animate instruction groups respectively. As can be seen, observers in both groups responded as expected. They were not very good at finding acceptable animate solutions for collisions (Figs 6.1(a) and 6.1(b)); similarly, they resisted the experimenter's request for an inanimate solution for the display with multiple accelerations (Fig. 6.1(m)) and twinned zigzag trajectories (Fig. 6.1(g)). Otherwise, they were rather adept at 'seeing' displays in ways that met the constraints of the instructions that they received. We end with some samples of what kinds of events

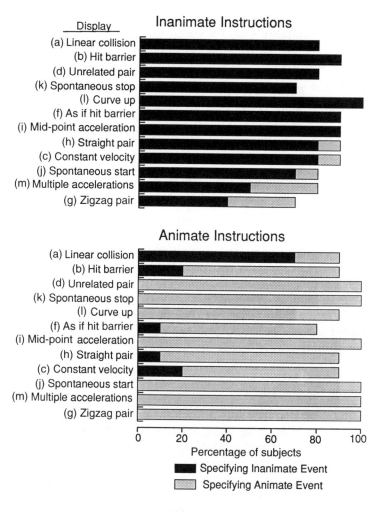

Fig. 6.3.

observers reported under these experimental conditions. More importantly, they actually work; that is, they reflect solutions that involve a combination of a veridical perception and a causally acceptable interpretation. They illustrate our point that abstract causal principles focus attention on information that can be related to a reasonable causal account of an object's movements.

Examples of some of the answers from the constrained conditions help to illustrate this point. Answers (a) and (b) were obtained in response to the trial during which the sprite moved horizontally across the screen and seemingly stopped on its own (Fig. 6.1(k)). As can be seen in Fig. 6.3, this was not a very animate display for unconstrained subjects. Answers (c) and (d) are examples that satisfied the constraints of the multiple acceleration display (Fig. 6.1(m)) as well as the inanimate instructions.

(a) It looks like my mum shopping and stopping right in front of a store.

(b) That was a figure skater that fell down.

(c) (long pause). Gosh, I don't know . . . let's try just a windblown object. You're in an area where it is swirling and stopping and changing direction. . . .

(d) Kind of reminded me of some sort of balls in a track that can only go in certain. . . .

All these examples include clear information about the causes of one or more accelerations, despite the fact that no such information was represented in the motion path: someone's mother stops abruptly to look at a shop window; a skater falls unexpectedly; a path which usually has high validity for animacy is rendered inanimate by an unseen wind or tracking device, the kind of causal agents that can cause erratic changes in direction. Similar features characterize the Durgin–Gelman transcripts discussed below, even though they were obtained with somewhat different displays that moved more slowly across the screen.

The Durgin–Gelman studies

The studies presented here support our conclusion about Stewart's data — that attributions of animacy reflect the operation of mutually constraining perceptual and conceptual processes. Principles of causality direct and modulate attention towards relevant aspects of objects and their motions. They conceptually constrain the interpretation of novel objects such that those objects with cues that have high predictive validity for animacy are likely to be classified as animate, while those with characteristic cues for inanimacy are more likely to be given inanimate attributions. Furthermore, the 'cues' suggesting animacy or inanimacy are sometimes more conceptual than perceptual (e.g. goal-directed activity). The film recorded by Heider and Simmel (1944), which is often cited by those favouring a direct perception account of animacy, shows a rich supporting environment that clearly constrains answers, for it is unlikely that talk about people chasing each other in and out of a house would be forthcoming if the shapes were not moving in and out of a square with an opening. Interestingly, much of the supporting role of the static environment is de-emphasized, or even ignored, in bottom-up theoretical accounts (Bassili 1976). The present studies were undertaken to investigate the possible interaction of a moving object and

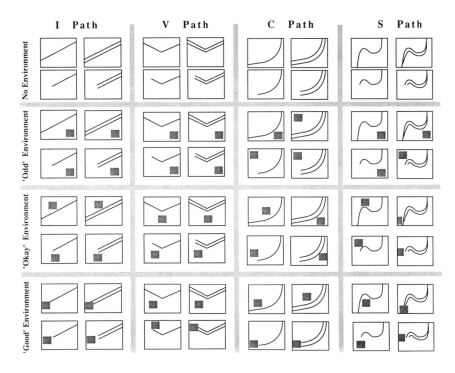

Fig. 6.4.

its environment under conditions in which interpretation is unconstrained by perceptually available information. Our studies thus bear on our interpretation of Stewart's findings, and on the role of conceptual principles that we believe are used in organizing perceptual evidence.

The Durgin–Gelman studies have much in common with the Stewart studies. Like Stewart, we presented computer-generated displays of one or two small balls (sprites) moving on a video terminal* and, again like Stewart, we collected both descriptions (unconstrained) and rating data. However, we used a combinatorial design to analyse the effects of various features and we adopted a continuous rating scale of animacy to supplement our coding of verbal descriptions of the displays. Schematic drawings of the 64 displays are shown in Fig. 6.4. The design for the creation of these displays called for the combination of straight or curved segments with or without inflections to produce four types of trajectories which we label,

---

*Our displays were produced and displayed on a Macintosh SE with a frame-by-frame sprite program Videoworks II® synchronized with the screen refresh using a Videoworks Accelerator® and presented by means of a Hypercard® interface.

according to their shape, I, V, C, and S. The four types of trajectories were combined with combined with three variables: (a) four levels of environment quality (none, odd, okay, or good) defined by the presence of a single grey rectangle at some location on the screen, (b) stopping on or moving off the screen or not remaining on the screen, and (c) number of sprites (one or two).

Design details

Because the displays are rather similar, we decided against a full factorial experiment. Instead, a quasi-latin-square design (Cochran and Cox 1957) was used to present the 64 displays according to a balanced plan, which meant that we presented subjects with a different sample of eight displays in each phase of the experiment. Fifty-six subjects (undergraduates from the Universities of Pennsylvania and Virginia) first gave descriptions of eight displays (phase 1). Forty of these subjects then gave ratings of animacy to a different set of eight displays (phase 2). Thus each of these participants saw, at most, 16 displays, and each of the 64 individual displays was described by seven subjects and rated by five (different) subjects.

The two-phase experiment lasted about 35–40 minutes. The first phase required an open-ended response and therefore paralleled the Stewart unconstrained condition. The second phase required ratings of the degree of 'aliveness' of the object/event shown in each display. The description task was presented first, so that the explicit animacy instructions of the rating scale task did not bias the open-ended responses. By saving the rating task until last, we circumvented the need to familiarize subjects with samples of the displays to anchor the points on the rating scale. Subjects were alone during the study; they were run in by and responded to a computer-generated experiment. All stimulus presentation and data entry was subject controlled. Individuals typed their phase 1 attributions on the computer keyboard, and 'painted' their phase 2 ratings (from 'not at all') to 'very alive') on the screen using a mouse. The length of the bar gave us scores that ranged from 0 to 400. The overall mean animacy rating was 158.

Some expectations

Our primary expectation was that interactions, in both senses of the word, would be important. Animate objects can respond and adjust to their environments in ways that are unavailable to inanimate objects. Thus, although we expected objects moving on curved trajectories to evoke a higher animacy rating than those moving on straight paths, we also expected that more meaningful environments would add to the impression of animacy (by meaningful environments we mean environments that support interpretations of a moving object(s) interacting with its environment). However, the presence of inflections, or changes in the direction in which the object was heading (as in the S- and V-shaped paths), was expected to

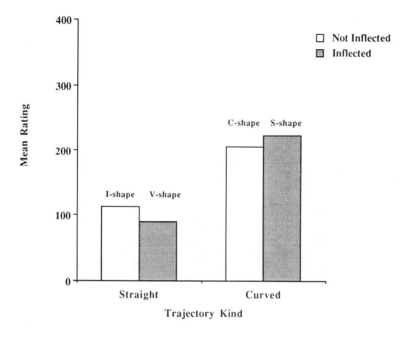

Fig. 6.5.

interact with the local path shape (curvilinear or rectilinear) because the inflected straight line which formed the V-shaped path contained information specifying a collision which was countersuggestive of animate attributions. Moreover, we have learned from Stewart's data that environmental variations have little effect on attributions given to collision-like trajectories. The V-shaped path is so characteristically inanimate that Stewart's observers preferred to invent environments in order to explain better a causal script involving collision rather than assimilate it to an animate event involving avoidance.

Given that co-ordinated activity is much more characteristic of animate action principles, we also expected that path twinning would encourage animate attributions and boost animacy ratings. However, once again we were prepared for interactions between this variable and others, for we expected individuals to integrate all information when interpreting their perceptions. If they have perceptual inputs that are particularly characteristic of inanimate events, then they might well find an inanimate causal script that is consistent with both this information and the presence of twinning. It should be remembered that Stewart's subjects could assign inanimate scripts to co-ordinated motion paths. They did this by appealing to causal conditions like tracking devices and transparent connectors.

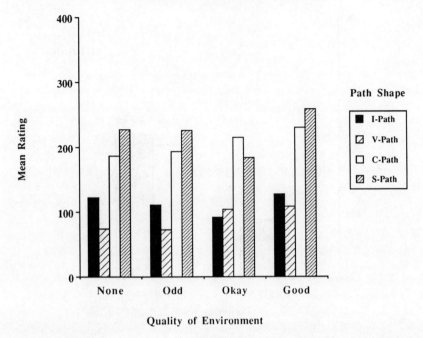

Fig. 6.6.

Rating data

The effect of segment shape (curvilinear versus rectilinear) on the animacy ratings, which is shown in Fig. 6.5, was significant ($F(1,39) = 170$, $p < 0.01$). The anticipated interaction of the presence of an inflection and segment shape was also found ($F(1,39) = 5.6$, $p < 0.05$), reflecting the fact that the presence of an inflection enhanced the rated animacy of the curved path but decreased the rated animacy of the otherwise straight path (Fig. 6.5). More important to the main hypothesis of the study, there was a significant environmental effect (Fig. 6.6), which is reflected in enhanced animacy ratings provided by the 'good' environment ($F(3,37) = 3.8$, $p < 0.05$). Moreover, there was a significant interaction between path type and a portion of the environment variable ($F(3,37) = 5.0$, $p < 0.05$) which can best be understood by examination of Fig. 6.6. Although the odd environment is the same as an absence of environment for all types of path, the I- and S-shaped paths are extremely sensitive to the relative goodness of the 'okay' and the 'good' environments. Both show a relative decline in animacy when the environment is only 'okay'. There were no main effects of stopping or of having more than one object. However, there were patterns of interaction involving these variables, which we shall discuss below.

Free-response data

The descriptions produced during phase 2 of the experiment were coded according to the scheme developed for the Stewart studies. As shown in Fig. 6.7, the pattern of animate event attributions across the four kinds of trajectories are consistent with the rating results. Observers were most likely to attribute animate events to curved paths and inanimate events to V-shaped paths. Despite these tendencies, all trajectories were ambiguous. Even though S-shaped paths received more animate than other kinds of attributions, the fact remains that some people did interpret these as evidence for an inanimate event, for example 'Moves similar to a feather caught in the wind' or 'A smoke particle as seen from above in a wind tunnel' or 'a falling snowflake'. Similarly, some observers paired V-shaped paths with animate events, for example bird flying above a house' or 'A person walking up to a building to see if it's open. It wasn't so he walked away' or '. . . a vulture flying down to the ground to get its prey'.

The fact that even the curved displays were ambiguous is consistent with an important feature of the rating data. Although the displays in question were judged to have reasonable cue-validity for animacy, they did not receive particularly high animacy ratings. This is what one would expect if simple trajectories like ours and Stewart's do not, on their own, guarantee an animate percept. Intermediate level ratings are consistent with our view that information can have reasonable cue validity for animacy without being defining.

Attributions, like ratings, were influenced by the expected interaction between kind of environment and path direction. To show this, we start with distributions of animate and inanimate attributions for the four different environments. As can be seen in Fig. 6.8, subjects favoured animate over inanimate interpretations for okay and good environments. In contrast, inanimate attributions dominated, given either an odd environment or no environment. Animate interpretations for an object that moved in the context of an okay or good environment included 'A bee going into a bee hive' or 'A baseball player running back to the dugout'. These are very different in character from the two animate attributions that were assigned to the same motion path shown without an environment or with an odd environment. In neither case do the actors move on their own: 'Someone riding a sled down a steep slope' or 'It looked like an object, for example a skier, headed down a steady incline'. Instead, they use an inanimate object that is suited to the presumed inclined plane in the environment. No such crutch appears in the attributions offered when the same motion path was set in a Good environment. The scripts generated here always involve self-initiated goal-oriented actions that interact with a particular place. These qualitative differences are particularly interesting and help

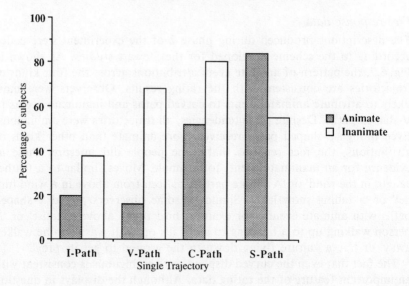

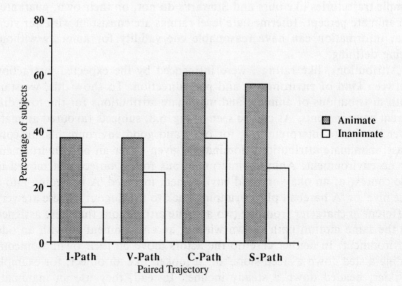

Fig. 6.7.

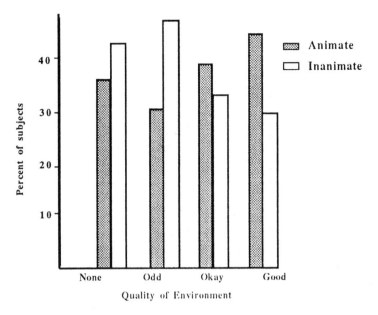

Fig. 6.8. The effects of environment on event attributions in the Durgin–Gelman Study.

account for the relationship between environment quality and event-kind attributions.

The capacity for self-generated actions is closely related to the ability to respond and adjust to the environment. Hence, when a moving object is in an environment in which it might come close to but avoid, enter, etc. an object, the constellation of information should be readily assimilated to interpretations that are consistent with the innards principle. Therefore, on average, attributions should be more animate. For similar reasons, given a path that has good cue-validity for inanimacy, the external agent inanimate principle should encourage attention to those aspects of the environment that bear on the calculation of its speed and trajectory, for example the surfaces of an object, the medium on (in) which it moves, its relative position with respect to the ground, its size, and its shape. Interpretation of these inputs can proceed with a rather narrow sampling of the environment around the path. If nothing is proximate, as in the odd and no environment conditions, there is no reason to alter an ongoing interpretation of the perceived information. Therefore it is not surprising that ratings of inanimacy are more likely when there is no environment or the environment is at a distance.

Our account of the quality of environment effect also applies to why twinned motion paths should, on average, encourage animate ratings and

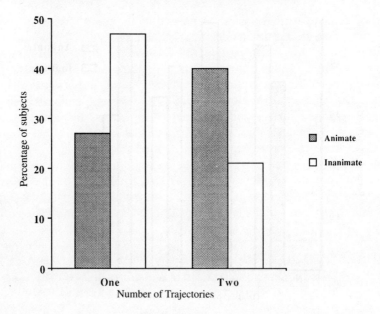

Fig. 6.9.

event-kind attributions. When the environment is social, animates can respond in kind, co-ordinate their acts with others, oppose others, and so on.
Ratings reflected an interaction between change of direction and pairing.
The qualitative effects of path number on event-kind attributions as a function of path shape are shown in Fig. 6.9.

Figure 6.9 shows the overall tendency for observers to write about
animate as opposed to inanimate events depending on whether the display
had one or two paths and whether the path was straight or not and changed
direction or not. Since the rate of mechanical attributions was comparable
across conditions, only animate and inanimate attributions are represented
in the figure. Setting aside consideration of the S-shaped path findings for
the moment, a common generalization can be made about the data shown
in Fig. 6.9. The single versus pair variable had the effect of switching
observers from a preference for inanimate attributions to a preference for
animate attributions. For example, although observers favoured inanimate
attributions for a single C-shaped path, they preferred animate attributions
for twinned C-shaped paths. However, as with our rating results, the extent
of the pair effect is not constant across the different path shapes. The different pattern of answers for the straight and V-shaped paths illustrates this
point. Further, although animate attributions were favoured for both single
and paired S-shaped paths, it is important to point out that the overall

level of animate attributions was depressed by the paired displays. Results like these tend to exclude models that assume that cues for animacy are additive (see Chapter 20), particularly because subjects' comments show that the repeated finding of interactions between variables indexes a strong tendency for individuals to relate and interpret their percepts to causal principles. Individuals' attributions are full of comment about the speed, weight, size, and surface characteristics of an object. In turn, these are placed in media (usually invented) and related to environments that can support the observed characteristics of the trajectories.

In summary, the characteristics of the trajectory influence the interpretation, but they do not determine it. The interpretation of the event is generated by the interaction between the principles that guide a causal analysis of the event and the characteristics of the observed trajectory.

PRESCHOOL CHILDREN CAN ASSIGN ANIMATE AND INANIMATE PREDICATES TO STILL PHOTOGRAPHS OF NOVEL STIMULI

We have been developing the position that, on its own, simple trajectory information is ambiguous. Such information is not sufficient for the identification of a novel object as animate or inanimate. We turn now to another problem — information about the path of motion is not necessary. L. B. Smith, D. Heise, and S. Rivera (in preparation) have shown that 12-month-old infants discriminate a set of displays that are made by pasting together pieces of photographs of animate material from a set of displays that are made by pasting together pieces of inanimate material. By the time that children are 3 years old, they can reason appropriately about unfamiliar animate and inanimate objects presented in photographs. For example, Massey and Gelman (1988) found that 3- and 4-year-old children were able to look at photographs of novel mammalian and non-mammalian animals, statues, wheeled inanimates, and complex rigid inanimates and correctly infer whether each could go both up and down a hill on its own.

Monochrome line drawing reproductions of some of the photographs used by Massey and Gelman are shown in Fig. 6.10. Neither these nor any of the other 14 items could be labelled correctly by separate groups of children of the same age. Despite the evidence that these were unfamiliar objects and despite the fact that they were shown in a still photograph, the children performed very well. They correctly answered that both mammalian and non-mammalian animals could move up and down the hill by themselves, that the wheeled objects could appear to move down but not up the hill by themselves, and that the statues and complex rigid objects could neither go up nor down the hill on their own. It is particularly

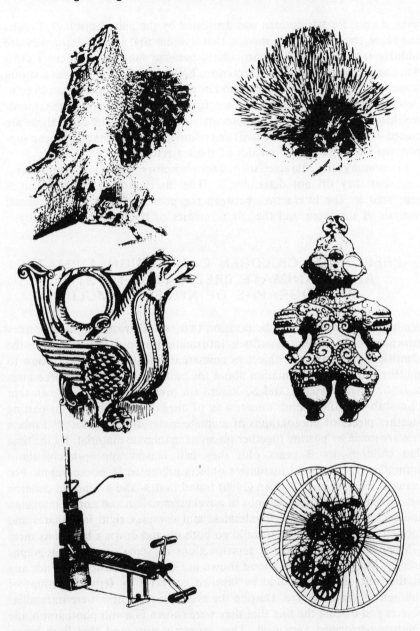

Fig. 6.10. Line drawings of some of the photographed objects used by Massey and Gelman (1988). Starting on the top row and going from left to right, the samples are a displaying lizard, an echidna, a vessel made to look like a mythical creature, an insect-eyed figurine, an exercise device, and an old-fashioned two-wheeled bicycle. Massey and Gelman did *not* use line drawings in their study.

interesting that the children did not attribute animacy to the statues or simple machines, even though they were selected to look like familiar animals or to represent objects that sometimes move on their own. The gross shapes of the statues often resembled those of familiar humans or animals more than did the shapes of the unfamiliar animals. Thus the children were already attuned to subtle features of shape and surface character. Similarly, we see that very young children do not assimilate machines to the animate category. We now return to why we believe that machines are conceived of as a separate hybrid category, i.e. neither animate nor inanimate.

Massey (1988) provides additional evidence that shifts from one conceptual goal to another are paired with shifts in the kinds of object characteristics that are treated as relevant. To demonstrate this, Massey compared the way that groups of 3- and 4-year-old children (as well as adults) organized triads of the Massey–Gelman photographs in two different task conditions. In one task the children were asked to pick the two pictures that looked most alike; in the other, the same children were told to pick the two that could go up a hill by themselves. The particular Massey–Gelman stimuli for this study were chosen on the basis of a sample of adults' perceptual similarity ratings of them. Given the ratings, Massey could select appropriate experimental and control triads, i.e. triads that contained pairs that looked alike but crossed the animate–inanimate classification (e.g. the echidna and statue shown in Fig. 6.10). Massey assumed that children would choose these pairs during the look-alike task, but not during the up-hill–down-hill task.

When analyzing her data, Massey asked whether the children's choices from the look-alike task could predict the answers on the causal task better than an animate–inanimate rule on the causal task. She reasoned that if the up-hill choices were based on judgements of perceptual similarity, as opposed to considerations of an object's animate status, children should select the two items that looked most alike even when deciding which could (or could not) go up the hill on its own. This gave her a principled way of comparing the same choices in the up-hill task with same choices in the perceptual similarity task.

Since the items within the animate and inanimate categories tended to look more alike than unalike it is not surprising that Massey reported that the perceptual similarity rule had some predictive validity for both adults and children. Despite this, she found that the conceptual animacy model predicted the causal task choices better than did the look-alike model. This was true for all age groups. Therefore surface cues that controlled similarity judgements did not control answers to the causal questions. More importantly for the discussion here, since the stimuli were of static objects, it is clear that animacy decisions can be rendered even when an object is not moving.

Other details of the Massey–Gelman study show that the children looked for animate-relevant information in the pictures, even if this meant attending to minute and seemingly non-salient details. For example, they focused on the antennae of a crustacean when explaining why it could move up a hill, and seemed to ignore the fact that it had a large shiny surface. In contrast, the same children stated that statues could not move because they were too shiny! Some children even claimed that an unknown animate object could move itself because it had legs, a rather startling claim for objects like the echidna whose limbs were not visible in the photograph. However, 'limbs' *per se* did not suffice for a child: statues with limbs were not able to move themselves because they lacked 'real' feet, they were 'furniture animals', 'pretend', or 'marked-up' (i.e. patterned on the surface), or they were made of the 'wrong stuff', be the 'stuff' metal, wood, or plastic (Gelman 1990).

The children's claims that statues did not have 'real' feet or that animals had limbs when none were visible are consistent with the idea that the information in the pictures was interpreted with reference to causal principles. Metal feet cannot serve as an agent of self-initiated motion, no matter how much they resemble what the children call 'real' feet. However, the capacity for self-initiated motion is typically realized through limb action, so why not assume that these are part of the animal in the picture, whether or not they are shown?

Kremer (1989) confirms the early salience of subtle cues in photographs for motion-pose and type of material. When shown, one at a time, a series of pairs of photographs of live animals and quality three-dimensional copies (Lenox porcelains), 4-year-old children readily identify each as 'real' or 'fake'. A similar trend for 3-year-old children was mitigated by their problems with the ambiguous terms real, fake and pretend. In an ongoing study by Gelman and Meck that is designed to minimize such ambiguity, we are finding that even 3-year-old children can systematically distinguish between a photograph of a real and a fake (or pretend) animal.

How should we account for the above developmental findings? We explicitly exclude accounts that equate this early knowledge with innate knowledge. At least in this case, this theoretical move would amount to saying that we are born with an infinitely large list of innate perceptual detectors. Our preference is to postulate a powerful innate engine of learning. The idea is that we benefit from innate first principles that define the domain and drive the learning in the domain. These principles, although skeletal in form, are at least as much conceptual as perceptual. From the outset, the system gathers data that are relevant to pivotal conceptual issues and/or distinctions to which no single class of perceptual factors is an unfailing guide. In the animate–inanimate case these conceptual issues often involve the causes of motion, but they are not restricted to them. Causal principles are often concerned as much with the composition and character-istics of the objects as the energy conditions that underlie their movements.

It follows that our account of the developmental data is that the young children's causal principles serve to encourage attention to, and storage of, relevant information about animate and inanimate objects. Conceptual concerns allow them to reach the point where they already know enough about the kinds of data that tend, on average, to characterize animate and inanimate objects. When they are faced with novel examples, they know enough to make surprisingly accurate guesses on the basis of relevant perceptual features. However, it would be a mistake to conclude from such abilities that perceptual features alone are driving the identification and inference processes. If this were so, the children should not have con-structed non-visible elements when looking at photographs of animals, and they should have mistakenly treated statues as if they were animate things. Further, they should not have been able to distinguish photographs of 'real' animals from photographs of porcelain reproductions.

SUMMARY

Motion is no less ambiguous or indeterminative of ontological category than are static features of objects. Young and mature alike must use addi-tional resources to achieve correct identification of novel cases of animate and inanimate objects and events. A principled concern with the causes, or sources of the movements of separately moveable objects, encourages us to treat as relevant those attributes and conditions that characterize animate and inanimate objects and their kinds of movements. In this way our con-ceptions and perceptions of animate and inanimate objects work together. The more that the input supports the related conceptual structure, the greater is the probability that the attribution will be consistent with the input. However, when data are ambiguous or when there are gaps in the data, we can count on our conceptual structure to assist us.

Machines are a particularly interesting category. Although they appear to move on their own, they are quintessentially ambiguous. They are made of inanimate material and do not exhibit biomechanical motions, nor do they adjust very well to local environmental problems. Robots are not particularly good at adjusting their motions to local perturbations in the environment; in contrast, so predictable is the animate world's ability to deal with unanticipated holes, bodies of water, oil slicks, branches that come below the head, sun in the eyes, weather changes, etc., that we almost forget how remarkable are the action abilities of the animate world. This reflects the fact that machines do not exhibit the kind of action that is controlled by biological mechanisms (e.g. coupled oscillators) — action patterns that are noted by infants (Berthental 1993) and used as cues for animacy (Wilson 1986). Additionally, machines are made of the wrong 'stuff' to be treated as animate. Recall that causal principles yoke information about objects' trajectories and their kind of 'stuff'. If so, machines cannot be classified as examples of one or the other ontological category. Such considerations led us to expect that children and adults would create a new hybrid category for representing machines. All the data presented in this chapter are consistent with this expectation. This is yet another reason to conclude that we cannot assign a novel object to either the animate or inanimate category simply on the basis of information about whether we see that it moves on its own or not.

We have challenged bottom-up models on the grounds that we believe that there is no list of perceptually accessible features that will always tell us what is animate and what is inanimate. The perceptual information, as informative as it might be, is nevertheless usually ambiguous or incomplete. What determines one's categorization of an object is, in the end, conceptual. We have presented data to show that this is true for both adults and young children. Ambiguity is resolved with respect to choices of causes about objects and their motions, given a set of conditions. If, during a trip to the desert, you came upon a round object covered with needle-like protrusions, you probably would call it a 'cactus'. However, should it start to move, you would surely be relieved to find out that it was a non-dangerous echidna and would not insist that it was a cactus because of what it looked like initially. Like our subjects, you might even start to look for its limbs.

ACKNOWLEDGEMENTS

Partial support for the preparation of this chapter as well as some of the research reported here came from grants from the National Science Foundation (BNS 89–16220 and DBS-9209741) and a University of California at Los Angeles (UCLS) Dean's fund to Rochel Gelman. Analyses of the Stewart data and the follow through experiments were accomplished with funds from the same sources as well as graduate student support from the Universities of Pennsylvania and Virginia to Frank Durgin. We gratefully acknowledge the many people who helped us think through and/or code the event analyses of the moving sprite experiments, especially Lisa Becker, Randy Gallistel, Nancy Henley, Betty Meck, and Andy Su. Last and most importantly, we are indebted to Judith Stewart who shared so much with us. We are grateful to Mary McManus for the freehand line drawings in Fig. 6.10.

REFERENCES

Armstrong, S. L., Gleitman, L. R., and Gleitman, H. (1983). What some concepts might not be. *Cognition* **13**, 263–308.

Baillargeon, R. (1987). Young infants' reasoning about the physical and spatial properties of a hidden object. *Cognitive Development* **2**, 179–200.

Baillargeon, R., Spelke, E. S., and Wasserman, S. (1985). Object permanence in 5-month-old infants. *Cognition* **20**, 191–208.

Bassili, J. N. (1976). Temporal and spatial contingencies in the perception of social events. *Journal of Personality and Social Psychology* **33**, 680–5.

Beedham, C. (1987). The English passive as an aspect. *Word* **38**, 1–12.

Berthental, B. I. (1993). Infants' perception of biomechanical motions: instrinsic image and knowledge-based constraints. In *Carnegie Symposium on cognition. Visual perception and cognition in infancy* (ed. C. Granrud). Erlbaum, Hillsdale, NJ.

Carey, S. (1985). *Conceptual change in childhood*. Cambridge University Press.

Cochran, W. G. and Cox, G. M. (1957). *Experimental Designs*. Wiley, New York.

Gallistel, C. R. (1980). From muscles to motivation. *American Scientist* **68**, 398–409.

Gelman, R. (1990). First principles organize attention to and learning about relevant data: number and the animate-inanimate distinction as examples. *Cognitive Science* **14**, 79–106.

Gelman, R. and Brenneman, K. (1993). First principles support universal and culture specific learning about numbers and music. In *Mapping the mind: domains, culture and cognition* (ed. L. Hirschfeld and S. Gelman). Cambridge University Press.

Gleitman, L. R. (1990). The structural source of verb meaning. *Language Acquisition* **1**, 3–55.

Goffman, E. (1974). *Frame analysis*. Harvard University Press, Cambridge, MA.

Golinkoff, R. M. and Harding, C. G. (1980). Infants' expectations of the movement potential of inanimate objects. In *International Conference on Infant Studies, New Haven, CT.*

Heider, F. and Simmel, M. (1944). An experimental study of apparent behavior. *American Journal of Psychology* **57**, 243–59.

Hochberg, J. (1978). *Perception* (3rd edn). Prentice-Hall, Englewood Cliffs, NJ.

Kellman, P. and Spelke, E. (1983). Perception of partly occluded objects in infancy. *Cognitive Psychology* **15**, 483–524.

Kremer, K. (1989). Preschoolers can distinguish between representations of fake and real animals. Unpublished Master's Thesis, University of California at Los Angeles.

Lamb, S. (1991). Acts without agents: an analysis of linguistic avoidance in journal articles on men who batter women. *American Journal of Orthopsychiatry* **61**, 250–7.

Leslie, A. and Keeble, S. (1987). Do six-month-olds perceive causality. *Cognition* **25**, 265–88.

Mandler, J. M. (1992). How to build a baby II. Conceptual primitives. *Psychological Review* **99**, 587–604.

Massey, C. (1988). The development of the animate–inanimate distinction in preschoolers. Unpublished PhD Thesis, University of Pennsylvania.

Massey, C. and Gelman, R. (1988). Preschoolers decide whether pictured unfamiliar objects can move themselves. *Developmental Psychology* **24**, 307-17.

Michotte, A. (1963). *The perception of causality*. Methuen, London.

Murphy, G. L. and Medin, D. L. (1985). The role of theories in conceptual coherence. *Psychological Review* **92**, 289-316.

Pinker, S. (1989). *The learnability of argument structure*. MIT Press, Cambridge, MA.

Poulin-Dubois, D. and Schultz, T. R. (1988). The development of the understanding of human behavior: from agency to intentionality. *Developing theories of mind* (ed. J. W. Astington, P. L. Harris, and S. Warren) Cambridge University Press, Cambridge.

Smith, L. B. Heise, D., and Rivera, S. (in preparation). Surface gradients in 12-month-olds' discrimination of animals versus vehicles. Unpublished MS, Indiana University, Bloomington, IN.

Stanley, J. P. (1975). Passive motivation. *Foundations of Language* **13**, 25-39.

Stewart, J. A. (1982). Perception of animacy. Unpublished Dissertation, University of Pennsylvania.

Stewart, J. (1984). Object motion and the perception of animacy. Presented at the meeting of the Psychonomic Society, San Antonio, TX, November 1984.

Weiner, E. J. and Labov, W. (1983). Constraints on the agentless passive. *Journal of Linguistics* **19**, 29-58.

Wilson, N. J. (1986). An implementation and perceptual test of a principled model of biological motion. Unpublished masters' thesis, University of Pennsylvania.

7

Intention as psychological cause
DAVID PREMACK AND ANN JAMES PREMACK

Domain-specific theory is a major human emergent that evolved specifically for extracting invariances from the world. Most species react to invariances, but humans seek to explain them. The frog, for example, protrudes its tongue when stimulated by objects that move appropriately (Lettvin *et al.* 1959). Humans do not simply react to different kinds of movement, but assign interpretations to them. For example they interpret one kind of movement as causality, and another as intention.

Although precursors of domain-specific theory can be found in other species (Premack 1988*a*, 1993), its development in non-humans is slight. The popular contradictory view that *all* species 'hold theories about the world' and differ only in the nature of the theory that they hold, can be traced to that pillar of ethology, Von Uexküll (1957). He has been read, somewhat mistakenly, as endorsing this view with his example of the tick which does not perceive either cows or horses, only a temperature gradient. However, the difference between a world consisting of objects and temperature values is a difference in perception only. It is not a difference in theory of the world.

Human social competence can be dealt with as a domain-specific theory, i.e. one that accounts for, and seeks to explain, fundamental invariances in the social domain. In this theory, we divide human social competence into three components. The first identifies the class of items to which the theory applies, the second specifies the privileged changes that members of the class undergo, and the third explains the changes.

The first component is a standard peripheral unit, activated by certain perceptual events that it interprets automatically. The second component, an internal unit, is activated by the mental representations from the first, and the third component, another internal unit, is activated by representations from the second.

The perceptual events that activate the first component are self-propelled objects that are goal-directed. These are automatically interpreted as **intentional**. Mental representations of these intentional objects activate the second component, which assigns interpretations to **interactions** between the objects. Finally, mental representations of these interactions activate the third component which seeks to explain them (see Sperber (1993) for a discussion of internal versus external modules).

SELF-PROPELLED AND GOAL-DIRECTED

Infants are aroused by the self-propelled object — the object that appears to move by itself. They expect such an object to engage in goal-directed behaviour and, when it does, they interpret the action as intentional. However, if the apparently self-propelled object does not engage in goal-directed action, the infant inhibits the interpretation. Hence, although potentiated by self-propelled movement, the interpretation of intentional depends ultimately on the combination of self-propelled and goal-directed movement. The first component in the infant's social system therefore outputs the interpretation **intentional**.

What is 'goal-directed movement' in the eyes of an infant? Infants have neither a general formula for goal, nor a motivational theory of which the concept of goal is a part. They do not recognize that actions leading to the attainment of goals are more likely to be repeated than are actions that do not have this outcome, nor do they grasp the role of deprivation–satiation in goal-seeking behaviour. Probably, infants would not even be surprised if an object, after pursuing a goal, failed to accept it when available! In the realm of motivation, we suggest, infants possess no more than the ability to recognize a small number of goals and 'trying'.

'Trying' is exemplified by persistence and vigour — when an intentional object directs a repeated act at a target with greater than baseline intensity. The infant's ability to recognize acts of this kind merely presupposes appropriate default values.

With regard to the goals an infant can recognize, we propose three, although there may well be others: escape from confinement; the responsiveness of another intentional object; overcoming gravity (as in climbing a hill). The latter may seem dubious in view of the contested evidence concerning the infant's recognition of gravity or the need for support (see Chapters 3 and 4), but once the infant masters the need for support, it will entertain this goal. Infants develop motivational theory by discerning what these exemplars have in common, and by working out a theory that will explain their common features.

In addition, what infants accept as proper instances of goal-directed movement will depend in part on the intensity of the action. When an act not only conforms to the exemplar but also exceeds baseline intensity, the infant will be more likely to attribute a goal than when the act does not exceed baseline intensity.

The intentionality judgments of children support these distinctions (King 1971; Berndt and Berndt 1975; Smith 1978). Adults emphatically deny intentionality to certain acts; for instance, acts that are involuntary, accidental, or have unintended effects. Children do not. When shown videotapes of simple actions, four-year-old and, to some extent, five-year-old children called intentional such acts as sneezing, slipping while crossing the floor, and knocking a flower into a basket while reaching for a glass of water. Children denied intention only to those actions that were *not* self-propelled, for instance a seated individual who was moved forcibly by a piece of furniture or the raising of an individual's arm by an umbrella held by another person (Smith 1978). For adults, intention is clearly a mental state; for young children, it is a kind of movement, as it is, we claim, for the infant.

SUMMARY OF INTENTIONAL SYSTEM

The first unit of the three that make up social competence is activated by the combination of self-propelled and goal-directed movement. Objects having these combined properties are interpreted as intentional. We suggest that infants recognize a limited number of goals — escape from confinement, overcoming gravity, and the company (psychological and/or physical) of other intentional objects — and they recognize these cases best when the intensity of action exceeds the baseline. Infants develop motivational theory by discerning what these exemplars have in common, and by working out a theory that will explain their common features.

SOCIAL SYSTEM

We turn now to the second unit in the system making up the infant's social competence which is activated by interactions between intentional objects. Therefore it contrasts with the first unit which is activated by individual objects. Because the social system is activated by mental representations from the first unit, it is an internal module, whereas the first unit, which is activated by perceptual inputs, is a standard peripheral system.

The concept of value is the major tool used in the analysis of the social system, and serves the social unit essentially as **goal** and **intention** serve the intentional unit.

Value theory

The social unit attributes positive or negative value to interactions between intentional objects. In distinguishing positive from negative events, the

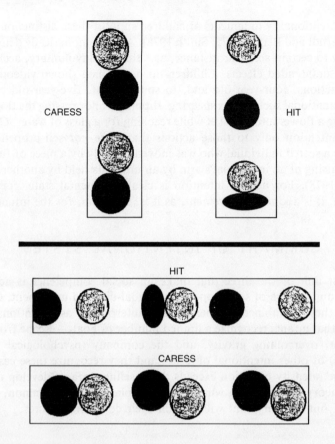

Fig. 7.1. Frames of both 'caress' and 'hit' with motion in both the vertical and horizontal directions. The deformation of the black ball in 'hit' should be noted. (Animations copyrighted 1993 A. J. Premack.)

infant uses two criteria, intensity and sociality. The simpler of these — intensity — consists of hard and soft actions. One object hitting another, a hard action, is coded negative; one object caressing another, a soft action, is coded positive (Fig. 7.1).

In addition to intensity, infants use a criterion of sociality in the attribution of value that is functionally equivalent to the distinction between 'helping' and 'hurting'. Having perceived an intentional object as having a goal, the infant can perceive a second intentional object as either assisting or hindering the first object in realizing the goal. For instance an object that is perceived as trying to escape from confinement can be either 'assisted' or 'hindered' from doing so (Figs 7.2 and 7.3).

Alternative sources of helping and hurting can be found in liberty and aesthetics (Premack 1990). When shown two bouncing objects, one of

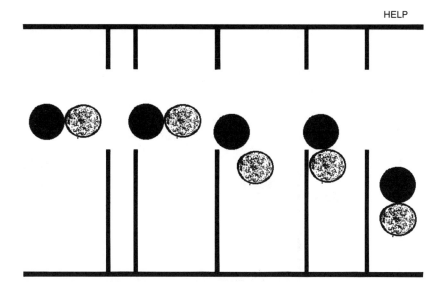

HELP

Fig. 7.2. Five frames of the helping animation. The white ball assists the black ball to escape. Read motion from right to left. (Animations copyrighted 1993 A. J. Premack.)

which becomes trapped in a virtual hole, the infant will interpret the action of a second object that restores the motion of the first as helping and code it positive. While this may seem a simple criterion, it is more complex than first appears for it requires the infant to judge what the first object would have done had it not been trapped.

If an infant is shown that one object stops the motion of another, will it judge this a positive act? If the moving object was on the verge of stopping, the action of the second object would have been an accurate anticipation, and as a form of assistance would be judged positive. However, if the object would have continued its motion, the action of the second object was an interference and would be judged negative. Although deciding whether an act is helpful or hurtful can be complex, complexity can be reduced if an object's routine is simple and well established. In such cases, the infant can 'know' what the object will do if left alone.

The above is an example of 'liberty'; we shall now follow with one on 'aesthetics'. We show an infant two bouncing balls: it prefers, let us say, the one that bounces higher and faster. The preferred ball moves into the vicinity of the other and demonstrates superior bounces several times as though offering an example. It may assist the other directly, placing itself below, lifting the other, and helping the other to bounce higher. The infant

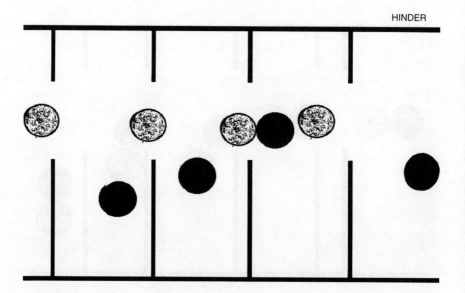

Fig. 7.3. Four frames of the hurting animation. The white ball prevents the escape of the black ball. Read motion from right to left. (Animations copyrighted 1993 A. J. Premack.)

will interpret both actions as helping and therefore positive. In aesthetics, a positive action consists, not in helping an object maintain its liberty, but in assisting the object to reach a preferred state.

Since value is attributed exclusively to the **interaction** between intentional objects and not to the action of an individual, no value is attached to a goal-seeking object that either succeeds or fails to attain its goal. Value is strictly a social property.

It is essential to distinguish value from preference. Value is both principled and domain-specific; preference is neither. Value is domain-specific because it applies exclusively to the interaction between intentional objects, and it is principled because the contrast between positive and negative is based on rules, either of intensity or of sociality.

Preference is neither principled nor domain-specific. One can compare the preference of any item with any other; indefinitely many diverse items can be placed on the same preference continuum. Further, there are no known rules that govern the computation of preference. While we have explicit criteria for computing value, we have none for the computation of preference.

In saying that an infant codes hitting as positive and caressing as negative, we make the following claim. When we show an infant that intentional object A hits intentional object B, the infant will expect B to avoid or withdraw from A on subsequent occasions. Conversely, when we show the infant that A caresses B, the infant will expect B to approach A on subsequent occasions. The same predictions follow, of course, for helping and hurting.

These predictions are independent of the infant's preferences. For instance an infant may prefer to look at cases of hitting; none the less, it will have the same expectations as those described above. When shown object A hitting object B, it will expect B to avoid A on subsequent occasions. This should consolidate the distinction between preference and value that we drew earlier. The principled character of value sets the stage for moral belief, as we have described elsewhere (Premack and Premack 1994).

Intention as internal cause

Although the work of Michotte (1963) concerning the relation between physical objects gives the impression that it is here that the infant is introduced to cause, we suggest that, on the contrary, the infant's earliest encounter with cause is in the psychological domain and occurs the moment that an infant attributes intention to a goal-directed object. **Cause**, or physical cause, is the interpretation given when one object launches another by contacting it; **intention**, or psychological cause, is the interpretation given when one object either moves by itself or affects the movement of another without contacting it. Thus intention is an internal cause, one that comes from *inside* the object rather than from *outside* as in physical cause.

Intention or internal cause differs from external or physical cause in several key respects. While intention can involve contact, as when one individual actually caresses or hits another, it need not. Intentional objects can affect one another without physical contact (impossible for physical objects), as in threat or consolation. Threat and consolation differ from the hitting and caressing we discussed earlier in that threat (e.g. raised fist) is the expression of the intention to hit (rather than actual hitting), and consolation (e.g. smiles and/or appeasing tones) is the expression of the intention to caress (rather than actual caressing). This ability escapes not only spatial limitations but to some extent temporal limitations. For instance the reaction to threat or consolation may follow after some interval rather than immediately, and the reaction will still be recognized. Physical cause requires that objects contact one another and react without delay in order to be recognized.

Although in the cases we have discussed so far the infant has been an observer, attributing intention to other intentional objects, its earliest experience concerns its own intention. This can be its intention to affect others. For example we have observed a 10-month-old infant who, when imitated by an adult, squealed with delight. The infant had been imitating the adult, but did not express pleasure until, when the tables were turned, it realized its intention to affect the adult (Watson 1966).

However, the infant can also recognize the intention of others with respect to itself. For instance, when the infant imitates such movements as tongue protrusion, lip pursing, and the like, it perceives the adult's intentions, recognizing that the goal of the adult's action is to affect it (Meltzoff and Moore 1977, 1983).

Reading intentions produces compliance

How special is imitation? It is special, we suggest, only in the sense that the act of one party matches that of the other; otherwise it is not special at all. On the contrary, it is an example of a general disposition to comply with the intentions of others. When one individual reads the intentions of another, his natural disposition is to comply, to carry out the action that is 'requested' by the other.

This disposition to comply is not confined to infants but is retained by adults even though, of course, adults often do not comply with what they discern to be the intentions of others. However, adults and older children manage to develop complex social interactions only because they have learned to inhibit their natural disposition to comply. Infants have not yet learned to inhibit this disposition and therefore are particularly prone to imitation.

Humans reject demoting cause merely to an antecedent that consistently precedes an 'effect'; they insist that a cause *compels* its effect. It is in part the disposition to comply that prompts this view. Upon reading another's intentions one is caused to comply.

Reciprocation

In reciprocation the action of one intentional object is reciprocated by another, preserving some feature(s) of the original action, either its form or its value or both. If A acts negatively on B and B subsequently acts negatively on A, this constitutes reciprocation with preservation of value.

Is every act reciprocated? Does every reciprocated act preserve value? These are independent questions, for one possibility is that while all acts preserve value only some of them are reciprocated. This seems to be the most likely alternative. Although not all actions are reciprocated, those that are preserve value.

According to the present theory, infants, while expecting a reciprocated act to preserve value, do not expect it to preserve form. Having seen object B caressed by A, the infant will not require B to caress A but will accept that B helps A in any of the many ways which preserve value.

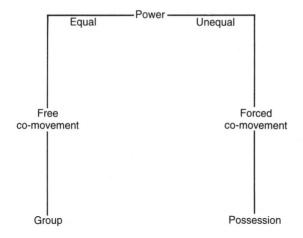

Fig. 7.4. Schematic outline of the effect of power on the infant's attribution of group and possession.

Power: group versus possession

The older infant will notice, although the younger may not, which of two intentional objects controls the other, which is more powerful than the other. It will then use this concept as a basis for distinguishing two major social conditions: possession and group (Fig. 7.4).

Possession

Intentional objects are able to possess, and are seen 'to possess', objects which are 'connected' to them in an appropriate way. The concept of possession is another fundamental component of the present system, and an interpretation made by the infant on the appropriate input.

The input that gives rise to the interpretation of possession is a distinctive kind of co-movement between objects, at least one of which is construed as intentional. The nature of the co-movement is suggested in the work of Kummer and Cords (1991). When an object is both connected to and moves with a monkey, other monkeys refrain from taking the object from the 'owner'. They treat such objects as part of the monkey's body, like the monkey's arm or leg.

These data concern the possession of non-intentional objects, but possession is not restricted to such objects. As the human concept of slavery demonstrates, intentional objects can also be possessed, and the importance of the intentional case is that it demonstrates that possession is not determined by co-movement and connection alone.

When two intentional objects are connected and move together, in order to determine which is the possessor we must consider a third factor, the power relation between the two objects. Possession requires connection, co-movement, and also that one object be more powerful than the other. Size, strength, attractiveness, etc. can serve as indices of power; ultimately, however, it is the ability to *control* movement that counts.

A physical connection between two objects, such as the cord that attached the object to a monkey, may be essential for a monkey to perceive possession, but it is not essential for the infant. What is essential is the difference in power—that one object controls the other. This is the relation that an infant will interpret as possession.

Possession changes the status of non-intentional objects. Ordinarily, infants do not evaluate acts upon such objects. They will not attribute value to the hitting or caressing of non-intentional objects. However, possession changes everything. If the non-intentional object is owned, the infant will attribute value to its being hit or caressed. Further, the infant expects the owner to reciprocate acts upon her possessed objects quite as she reciprocates acts upon herself.

Group

The concept of group, like that of possession, concerns the relation among objects, but differs in that not only are all the objects in a group intentional, but they are also equal in power, i.e. no object controls the movement of any other. While possession is the co-movement of objects of unequal power, group is the co-movement of objects of equal power. Therefore group is a relation among equals.

According to the present theory, the predilection to bring physically similar objects together, found in the 10-month-old child (Sugarman 1983), takes an even earlier form in the infant. The infant expects physically like intentional objects to form groups, and physically unlike ones not to do so. When shown a set of, for instance, white intentional objects, an infant will expect them to cohere and move together; it will have the same expectation for a set of black intentional objects, but not for a mixture of black and white objects.

However, once the infant is shown that the mixture of black and white objects cohere and move together, it will interpret them as a group. Although an infant expects like objects to 'flock together', when shown the uncoerced co-movement of unlike objects, it accepts them as a group to the same degree that it accepts any other. The criterion of uncoerced co-movement takes precedence over physical similarity.

The concept of group generates powerful consequences. First, the infant expects shared reciprocation among group members. For instance, if object C acts positively (negatively) on B, the infant expects not only B, but B's co-group members, to act positively (negatively) on C.

Second, the infant expects like action from group members. Even as the infant expects the same individual to repeat itself, so does it expect one group member to repeat another. Having observed object C act positively (negatively) on B some number of times, the infant expects object C to continue to do so, and extends this assumption to members of the group. Having perceived one group member to act positively on B, it expects other group members to do the same.

Third, the infant expects group members to act positively towards one another. This contrasts with an infant's expectations for interactions between non-group members. Here, the infant has neither positive nor negative expectations.

These three consequences are internal. They concern how a group member perceives another, what one is expected to give another member, and what one expects to receive in return. However, group formation also gives rise to external consequences: how group members perceive *non*members.

A group member both extends prerogatives to members and denies them to non-members. If neither A nor B belongs to a group, the infant is neutral, i.e. does not expect either of them to act positively or negatively towards the other. However, if A belongs to a group and B does not, the infant expects A to act negatively towards B; at least this is the expectation in the male infant, although it is less likely in the female. Hence group membership confers two contrasting properties: the simultaneous expectation of positive action towards members and negative action (primarily in the male infant) towards non-members.

Summary of social system

The social unit is activated by the interaction *between* representations of intentional objects (output by the first unit). Two criteria, intensity and sociality, are the basis for assigning positive and negative value to the interactions. The infant expects value to be reciprocated. Co-movement among objects of unequal power is interpreted as possession, among objects of equal power as group.

THEORY OF MIND (TOM)

Representations of the social system are sent to theory of mind (TOM), the last unit in the module, where interpretation takes a unique form, that of explanation. The output of this unit consist of basic states of mind: **see**, **want** and **belief** (or their variations).

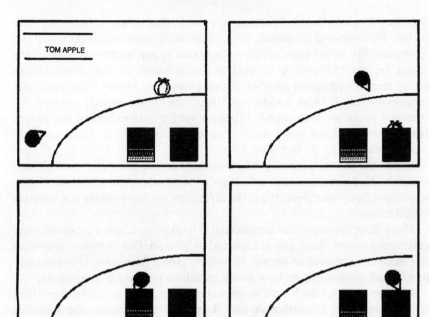

Fig. 7.5. Frames of an animation designed to test infants' theory of mind (TOM). The 'ball' makes several attempts to reach an apple which falls into the black container. It then seeks the apple in either the correct or the incorrect container. (Animations copyrighted 1993 A. P. Premack.)

Four-year-old children attribute states of mind at close to an adult level of competence, passing the so-called false belief test, seen as a kind of rubicon (Wimmer and Perner 1983). Unfortunately, however, whether or not infants attribute states of mind, as the present theory claims, cannot be established for infants have not yet been tested for attribution of mental states.

Moreover, to test infants we can use only implicit procedures – preference or habituation/dishabituation – we cannot ask them, as we can children, to choose between alternatives or to answer questions. There is an advantage in using implicit procedures, however, for they make far weaker test demands than explicit procedures and may therefore disclose capacities obscured by explicit procedures. For example infants who were not able to use the concept of same/different instrumentally proved to possess the concept when judged by habituation/dishabituation data (Premack 1988*b*).

The advantage in testing the infant on TOM would be first to test the possibility that implicit precursors for TOM (not revealed by the explicit tests given children) are present in the infant, and second to test the prediction of the present theory that the infant indeed has TOM.

Using a computer screen, we show the infant an intentional object – a self-propelled 'ball' – which for convenience we will henceforth call 'Jack' (Fig. 7.5). Jack directs his action at an apple perched on top of a hill, 'trying' repeatedly to climb the hill and reach the apple. However, before he can do so, the apple falls, rolling down the hill into one of the two containers at the bottom (the black one and not the white one).

This animation provides the infant with information that any individual who attributes states of mind would need to draw the following conclusion: Jack both *wants* the apple and *knows* where he can get it (he saw where it landed when it fell). An individual who attributed states of mind, given the information above, would be quite clear what Jack will do – he will go to the black container to retrieve the apple.

But what would an infant do? We can answer by showing two groups of infants one or the other of two scenes. In the first, Jack heads for the black container, and in the other he heads for the white. Which group has its expectations denied and therefore looks longer?

If the groups do not differ, we cannot claim that infants attribute states of mind. But if they not only differ but differ in the right direction, i.e. the group looks longer at Jack heading for the white container, there is a basis for the claim. Infants who pass this test can be said to attribute states of mind.

CONCLUSIONS

While the complexity of most species consists in making automatic computations on invariances that they perceive, human complexity consists in having evolved theories that seek to explain such invariances (Fig. 7.6).

Human explanation takes place in the context of 'natural' theories which have three components. One identifies the items to which the theory applies, another specifies the changes to which class members are subject, and a third explains the changes. We have presented a theory of human social competence according to which humans interpret self-propelled objects that pursue goals as having intentions. These intentional objects engage in interactions to which value is attributed; they reciprocate value, join groups, and take possessions. The theory explains these interactions in terms of mental states: **perceive**, **desire**, and **belief**. Human social competence was designed to understand this set of interactions and, we suggest, carries out this objective, using the theory we have described.

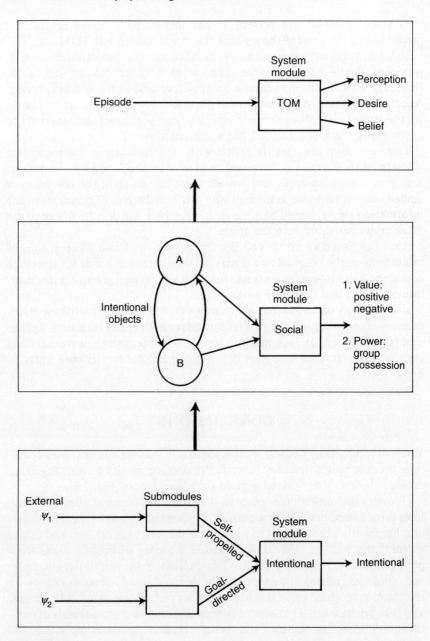

Fig. 7.6. Schematic outline of three interlocking modules that comprise human social competence. The first interprets self-propelled goal–directed objects as intentional, the second attributes properties to the interaction between such objects, and the third explains these properties in terms of states of mind.

REFERENCES

Bernt, T. J. and Bernt, E. G. (1975). Children's use of motives and intentionality in person perception and moral judgment. *Child Development* **46**, 904–12.

King, M. (1971). The development of some intention concepts in young children. *Child Development* **42**, 1145–52.

Kummer, H. and Cords, M. (1991). Cues of ownership in long-tailed macaques, *Macaca fascicularis*. *Animal Behavior* **42**, 529–49.

Lettvin, J. Y., Maturana, R. R., McCulloch, W. S., and Pitts, W. H. (1959). What the frog's eye tells the frog's brain. *Proceedings of the Institute of Radio Engineering* **47**, 1940–51.

Meltzoff, A. N. and Moore, M. K. (1977). Imitation of facial and manual gestures by human neonates. *Science* **198**, 75–78.

Meltzoff, A. N. and Moore, M. K. (1983). Newborn infants imitate adult facial gestures. *Child Development* **54**, 702–9.

Michotte, A. (1963). *The perception of causality*. Meuthen, London.

Premack, D. (1988a). 'Does the chimpanzee have a theory of mind?' revisited. In *Machiavellian intelligence: social expertise and the evolution of intellect in monkeys, apes and humans* (ed. W. Byrne and A. Whiten), pp. 286–322. Oxford University Press.

Premack, D. (1988b). Minds with and without language. In *Thought without language* (ed. L. Weiskrantz). Claredon Press, Oxford.

Premack, D. (1990). The infant's theory of self-propelled objects. *Cognition* **36**, 1–16.

Premack, D. (1993). Prolegomenon to evolution of cognition. In *Exploring brain functions: models in neuroscience* (ed. T. A. Poggio and D. A. Glaser). Wiley, New York.

Premack, D. and Premack, A. J. (1994). Moral belief: form versus content. In *Mapping the mind*, domain specificity in cognition and culture (ed. L. A. Hirschfeld and S. A. Gilman), pp. 149–68. Cambridge University Press, New York.

Smith, M. C. (1978). Cognizing the behavior stream: the recognition of intentional action. *Child Development* **49**, 736–43.

Sperber, D. (1993). The modularity of thought and the epidemiology of representations. In *Mapping the mind: domain specificity in cognition and culture* (ed. L. Hirschfeld and S. Gelman). Cambridge University Press, New York.

Sugarman, S. (1983). *Children's early thought: developments in classification*. Cambridge University Press.

Von Uexküll, J. (1957). A walk through the world of animals and man. In *Instinctive behavior* (ed. C. Schiller). International Universities Press, New York.

Watson, J. S. (1966). The development and generalization of 'contingency awareness' in early infancy: some hypotheses. *Merrill-Palmer Quarterly of Behavior and Development* **12**(2), 123–35.

Wimmer, H. and Perner, J. (1983). Beliefs about beliefs: representation and constraining function of wrong beliefs in young children's understanding of deception. *Cognition* **13**, 103–28.

Part IV

Causal understanding in naïve biology

Causal understanding in naive biology

Foreword to Part IV

A common question unites the papers of Scott Atran, Susan Carey, and Frank Keil: How many innate modules do humans have? All agree that they have modules of physics and psychology. But do they also have a module of biology?. The divergent answers given by these three writers provides a lively and productive debate; among other things, it introduces the question of what is a module.

Carey distinguishes two senses of module: Fodor's input analysers (which require innate domain-specific computation) versus intuitive theories (which, although not necessarily hierarchically innate, specify causal mechanisms and are devices for explanation).

Atran bases his argument for an innate biological domain on three claims: all living things are classified hierarchically, have an essentialist nature, and are explained in teleological terms. These three properties are unique and universal to living kinds.

Teleo-essentialism is the distinctive inference principle that Atran assigns to the domain. Essentialism (the belief that each living kind has an immutable inner nature that ensures the continuity of its identity) and teleological explanation are, he argues, a linked package; an evolutionary scenario separating them is implausible.

Keil asks why we should admit only physical, psychological, and teleological cause, and recommends instead contemplating a far larger number of causal construals, including their combinations. He promotes this liberation on the grounds that construal types and domain types need not be innately or inextricably linked. However, if they are not, how does linkage develop?

Keil's novel answer is that there are general expectations concerning how causal powers of types of properties vary depending on their general category. A new body of research explores this possibility. While exploratory, the results encourage his hypothesis that properties are more significant in one domain than another. For example, he finds shape and size of parts to have greater significance for living kinds than for artefacts or non-living kinds.

Carey, who set the present controversy into action with her well known claims against a naive biology, devotes the bulk of her chapter to sparring with adversaries, each of whom offers another putative example of precocious biological thinking. Some of her sharpest enquiry is focused on Atran's position where she argues that no developmental evidence exists for a biological module. She questions whether hierarchical taxonomy or essentialism are domain-specific since children apply hierarchical naming to non-living things as readily as to living. So, we may add, do chimpanzees, which learn 'toy', 'candy', and 'foodstuff' as readily as 'fruit' and 'animal' (Premack 1976).

Carey links essentialism to language, to the nominal system (which applies, of course, with equal force to both non-living and living things). However, we wonder if essentialism may not be truly domain-general—no more linked to language than, as the chimpanzee data suggest, is hierarchical taxonomy.

Readers will find wide agreement among the writers as to the value of taking a modular approach to naive theories and causal construals, although they will find less than total unanimity in the definition of a module. As to how may modules there are, and even more what their content is, readers should be prepared for open warfare!

REFERENCE

Premack, D. (1976). *Intelligence in ape and man*. Erlbaum Press, Hillsdale, NJ.

D.P.
A.J.P.

8

Causal constraints on categories and categorical constraints on biological reasoning across cultures

SCOTT ATRAN

Aspects of domain-specific thinking, including categorization and causal inferencing from conceptual categories, within and across cultures are considered in this chapter. The focus is on the structure of categories in the domain of biology, such as the organization of taxonomic relations that hold between between CAT and MAMMAL or OAK and TREE. In particular, the extent to which this categorical structure constrains inferences that causally relate biological taxa to one another, and the extent to which (culturally specific) belief systems, or 'theories', are able to modify that structure and hence change the nature of biological reasoning are examined.

FROM FOLK BIOLOGY TO SCIENCE

All human beings, it appears, classify animals and plants into basic groupings that are 'quite as obvious to [the] modern scientist as to a Guaraní Indian' (Simpson 1961, p. 57). This is 'the species of the local naturalist, the species of Ray and Linnaeus' (Mayr 1969, p. 37). It is this common-sense concept that was both the chief inspiration and foil to evolutionary theory (Wallace 1889, p. 1). In addition to the spontaneous arrangement of local fauna and flora into species-like groupings, these basic groupings have 'from the most remote period in . . . history . . . been classed in groups under groups. This classification is not arbitrary like the grouping of stars in constellations' (Darwin 1883, p. 363).

In the anthropological literature, basic folk-biological taxa are commonly referred to as **folk generics** (Berlin 1992), or **speciemes**. (Bulmer 1970). A taxon at this level is immediately recognizable by a distinctive morphological (or morpho-behavioural) pattern, which is easily imaged. It is also readily contrasted and contextualized with respect to all other basic taxa by an obvious ecological proclivity (including habitat and geographical barriers to reproduction). The most phenomenally salient basic taxa often correspond to scientific species (dog, coyote, lemon tree, orange tree). But frequently the locally represented scientific genus is monospecific (bear, redwood), which makes species and genus perceptually coextensive. This occurs regularly with larger vertebrates and trees, and with plants that are especially phylogenetically isolated (e.g. cactus) (Atran 1987a). Invariably, basic-level groupings are mutually exclusive. They also represent virtually exhaustive partitionings of the local fauna and flora in the sense that hitherto unknown or unfamiliar organisms are generally assigned to a basic taxon when attention is directed towards them.

Folk subgenerics, or **specifics** and **varietals**, usually represent strains of domesticated species (collie, retriever; sugar maple, red maple) or species otherwise particularly significant for the culture (noxious, medicinal, etc.). Folk subgenerics are generally polynomial, while basic taxa are usually labelled by a single lexical item. Often, foreign organisms suddenly introduced into a local environment are initially assimilated to basic taxa as subgenerics. For example, the Lowland Maya originally labelled the Spanish horse 'village tapir', just as they termed wheat 'Castillian maize'. Similarly, the Spanish referred to the indigenous pacas and agoutis as 'bastard hares', just as they denoted the Maya breadnut tree 'Indian fig'.

Across all cultures, and probably in all ages, at least two higher-order groups are apparent, the group of non-human animals and the group of plants. It makes no difference whether or not these groups are named. Thus, infants in their first year clearly distinguish plastic representations of animals from plastic representations of all other things (Mandler 1992). English speakers ambiguously use the term 'animal' to refer to at least three distinct classes of living things: non-human animals, animals including humans, and mammals (the prototypical animals). The term 'beast' seems to identify non-human animals in English, but is seldom used today. The English term 'plant' is also ambiguously used to refer to the plant kingdom, or to members of that kingdom that are not trees. Maya languages generally have no name for 'plant' as such, although these languages do permit a clear distinction to be made by other means between plants and all other things (e.g. by assigning a particular numeral classifier to all and only plants). Anthropologists refer to this level of classification as that of **unique beginner** (Berlin et al. 1973) or **folk kingdom** (Berlin 1992).

Very early in life, and probably in every culture, a somewhat lower level of mutually exclusive higher-order groups appears (Stross 1973; Dougherty 1979). Anthropologists call this the **life-form** level (Berlin et al. 1973; Brown 1984). Life-forms represent broad divisions in the 'economy of nature' corresponding to folk terms such as animal (in the sense of mammal or quadruped), bird, fish, insect (bug), tree, vine, grass (herb), mushroom, and so forth (Atran 1985a). Life-forms may differ somewhat from culture to culture. For example some cultures, such as ancient Hebrew or modern Rangi (Tanzania), include the herpetofauna (reptiles and amphibians) with insects, worms and other 'creepy-crawlies' (Kesby 1979). Other cultures, such as the Itza Maya and (until recently) most Western cultures, include the herpetofauna with mammals as 'quadrupeds' (Atran 1994). Some cultures, such as, the Itza Maya, place phenomenally isolated mammals like the bat with birds, just as the Rofaifo (New Guinea) place phenomenally isolated birds like the cassowary with mammals (Dwyer 1976). However, whatever the particular constitution of life-form groupings, or **taxa**, the life-form level, or **rank**, universally partitions the living world into broadly equivalent divisions. These divisions not only share readily perceptible features and functional properties, but also structure inductions about the distribution of underlying properties that presumably relate biology to the local ecology. Other domains have hierarchy, but *none* have rank.

Various intermediate levels also exist between the levels of the folk species and life form. Like folk kingdoms, but unlike folk species, taxa at these levels usually have no explicit name (e.g. rats and mice but no other rodents), although sometimes they may (e.g. equids, legumes). Such taxa, particularly unnamed 'covert' ones, tend to be not as well-delimited as folk species or life-forms, nor does any one intermediate level always constitute a fixed taxonomic rank that partitions the local fauna and flora into a mutually exclusive and virtually exhaustive set of broadly equivalent taxa. None the less, there is a psychologically evident preference for forming intermediate taxa at a level roughly between that of the scientific family (e.g. for the larger, more salient mammals and plants) and order (e.g. for smaller mammals and plants).

In Western science, basic folk taxa eventually 'fissioned' into species (Cesalpino 1583) and genera (Tournefort 1694). The scientifically 'ambivalent' character of basic taxa has led them to be dubbed **generic-speciemes** an admittedly unwieldy term that is replaced here with the less accurate but more convenient notion of **folk species**. As in any folk inventory, ancient Greek and Renaissance herbalists had to contend with only 500 or 600 local species (Raven *et al.* 1971). During the initial stages of Europe's world-wide Age of Exploration, the number of species increased by an order of magnitude. Foreign species were habitually assigned to the most obviously similar European species, i.e. to the generic type, in a 'natural system' (Atran 1987*a*).

A similar 'fissioning' of intermediate folk groupings occurred when the number of species encountered increased by yet another order of magnitude, and a 'natural method' for organizing plants and animals into families (Adanson 1763) and orders (Lamarck 1809) emerged as the foundation of modern systematics (Atran 1983). By looking to other environments to complete local gaps at the intermediate level, naturalists sought to discern a world-wide series that would cover all environments and again reduce the ever-increasing number of discovered species to a mnemonically manageable set—this time to a set of basic family plans. Higher-order vertebrate life-forms provided the initial framework for biological classes, while plant life-forms such as TREE were abandoned as being intuitively and ecologically 'natural' but 'philosophically lubricious' (Linnaeus 1751). Finally, the concept of phylum (or rather the pre-evolutionary notion of **embranchement** that was its precursor) became distinguished once it was realized that there is less internal differentiation between all the vertebrate life-forms taken as a whole than there is within most intermediate groupings of the phenomenally 'residual' animal life-form INSECT (bugs, worms, etc.).

Living kinds exhibit a dual structure that is nowhere apparent in any other cognitive domain (except in easily noticed cases of explicit borrowing), namely that any given organism is associated with one or more hierarchically distinguished ranks and belongs at each rank to one and only one taxon. Ranks are relatively stable sets of sets (e.g. species, class, kingdom) whose elements are taxa (e.g. dog, mammal, animal). Ranks seem to vary little, if at all, across cultures as a function of theories or belief systems (Berlin *et al.* 1973). Taxa are sets whose elements are organisms, and they are identified by clusters of readily perceptible features. These taxonomic clusters of features are maximally covariant, with each such cluster separated from others of its rank by a readily perceptible gap where clusters share few, if any, features (Hunn 1976). In line with these observations, it is suggested that an innate living-kind module, privileges as input all the perceptual information pertaining to the identification of organisms as those things in the world that can be readily assigned a taxonomic description, i.e. assigned to ranked taxa. The living-kind module would thus make identification of an organism contingent upon identification of what *kind* of organism it is in the taxonomic hierarchy.

Essentialism, which appears to be the inferential principle that allows this identification, underlies the stability of taxonomic types (e.g. DOG, FROG), despite obvious token variation among exemplars (e.g. this Chihuahua and that Saint Bernard, this tadpole and that tailless leaper). This stability, in turn, allows for consistent category-based inductions. For example, knowing that a Chihuahua and a Saint Bernard share an internal property is likely to be taken as stronger evidence that all dogs share that property than if only two Chihuahuas are known to share the property.

By recursive application of the perceptual processes and essentialist principles that generate basic taxa, higher-order folk-biological taxa would also be organized on the basis of readily perceptible features that presumably 'go together' because of an underlying essential structure. For example, from the fact that sheep have multichambered stomachs, we can 'safely' infer that deer also have multichambered stomachs. Making inferences from one category to another (from sheep to deer) enables us to set forth assumptions and predictions, and generalize from the known to the unknown (López *et al.* 1992). It is this function of classification that may be considered 'the foundation of the scientific method in biology: To most biologists, the "best" classification must be the one that maximizes the probability that statements known to be true of two organisms are true of all members of the smallest taxon to which they both belong' (Warburton 1967).

A full activation of this principle of category-based induction for all higher-order taxa, and for the whole of the living-kind taxonomy, may require support from a unifying causal theory of the sort that science can provide. For example upon finding that the bacterium *Escherichia coli* shares a hitherto unknown property with turkeys, it may take a Nobel-prize-winning insight and belief in the underlying genetic unity of living kinds to 'safely' make the inference that all creatures belonging to the lowest-ranked taxon that contains both turkeys and *E. coli* also share that property. In this example, the lowest taxon just happens to include all organisms. Of course such predictions lead to errors as well as to new discoveries, thus setting into motion a 'boot-strapping' reorganization of taxa and taxonomic structure, and of the inductions that the taxonomy supports.

This boot-strapping enterprise in Western science began with Aristotle, or at least with the naturalistic tradition in Ancient Greece that he represented (see Chapter 18). For Aristotle, the task was to unite the various foundational forms of the world — each with their own special underlying 'nature' (*phusis* in the implicit everyday sense) — into an overarching system of 'Nature' (*phusis* in an explicitly novel metaphysical sense). In practice, this meant systematically deriving each basic-level folk species (*atomon eidos*) from the causal principles uniting it to other species of its life-form (*megiston genos*). It further implied combining the various life-forms by 'analogy' (*analogian*) into an integrated concept of life. Theophrastus, Aristotle's student and successor at the Lyceum, conceived of botanical classification in much the same way.

Aristotelian life-forms are distinguished and related through possession of analogous organs of the same essential function (locomotion, digestion, reproduction, respiration). For example, bird wings, quadruped feet, and fish fins constitute analogous organs of locomotion. The folk species of each life-form are then differentiated by degrees of 'more or less' with respect to essential organs. Thus all birds have wings for moving about and beaks for obtaining nutriments. But, whereas the predatory eagle is partially diagnosed by long and narrow wings and a sharply hooked beak, the goose, owing to its different mode of life, is partially diagnosed by a lesser and broader wing span and a flatter bill. The principled classification of biological taxa by 'division and assembly' (*diaresis* and *synagoge*) ends when all taxa are defined, i.e. when each species is completely diagnosed with respect to every essential organ (Atran 1985*b*).

This first sustained scientific research programme failed owing to a fundamental antagonism between what were effectively non-phenomenal means and the phenomenal end sought. To explain the visible order of things, Aristotle had recourse to internal functions. However, such functions cannot be properly understood if, as with Aristotle, they are referred primarily to their morphological manifestations. Moreover, like any folk naturalist, he recognized no more than five or six hundred species. Thus he did not foresee that the introduction of exotic forms would undermine his quest for a discovery of the essential structure of all possible kinds.

If different cultures have different theories or belief systems about the relations between biological categories, should there not be clear differences in biological reasoning? Not necessarily. Because there are, intially, universal taxonomic constraints on theories or belief systems about biological categories and their relationships, there should also be some predictible stability and cross-cultural consistency to theory-related inferences. For example, different cultures may have very different beliefs about reproduction, but their judgements about whether or not two species could interbreed may well show the same decreasing function of taxonomic distance.

Thus, for Aristotle, offspring are considered 'unnatural monsters' to the extent that they fail to resemble their fathers and in direct proportion to the number of nodes in the 'common Greek's' taxonomic tree that must be climbed to encounter a likely progenitor. Similarly for the Itza Maya, we found a highly structured taxonomy that enjoys a strong cultural consensus and is strongly correlated with notions about the likelihood of mating between animals that do not normally interbreed (Atran 1994). For example, the jaguar's even-headed temperament, the mountain lion's aggressiveness, and the margay's small size generally disallow mating between these three members of the Itza large-cat taxon *b'alum*. Nevertheless, the Itza are readily inclined to believe that even these matings could occur under certain imaginable situations that accord with their cosmology, and which we experimentally manipulated (e.g. animals that were caged, dwarfed, or drugged). Given Itza explanations of how reproduction works, actual fulfilment of these conditions can never be empirically confirmed or disconfirmed. For Itza believe that offspring are preformed before birth in their same-sex progenitors. Because daughters resemble mothers and sons resemble fathers, there is no empirical counter-evidence to unlikely but imaginable crossings. Aristotle's theory of reproduction and generation is markedly different from the Itza's, but the same sorts of taxonomic constraints operate on both. Indeed, evolutionary theory itself initially had to meet much the same conditions.

Although the development of biological thought in an individual by no means recapitulates its historical emergence, *any* initial elaboration of biological thought is similarly constrained by the living-kind module. The general idea is that initial categories are set up by a universal prototheory; however, both the theories and categories that they pick out may change to some extent. People's initial categories would be organized by an innate predisposition to structure biological kinds along essentialist lines, which can be modified and even replaced by theories that vary across cultures (Atran 1987b; Keil 1989; Medin and Ortony 1989; Gelman and Wellman 1991). Readily perceptible properties of taxa (morpho-types) are generally good predictors of deeper underlying shared properties, and may originally provide the basis for categories. Initially, the underlying essential structures are unknown and merely presumed to cause (teleologically) the observable regularities in biological categories. Attention to this causal link, and a cognitive endeavour to know it better, leads to awareness that this correlation between surface and deep features is not perfect. Added knowledge about these deeper properties may then lead to category modification. For example, most adult Americans categorize whales and bats as mammals despite the many superficial properties shared with fish and birds respectively.

Despite the 'boot-strapping' revision of taxonomy implied in this example, notice how much did not change: neither the abstract hierarchical schema furnished by folk taxonomy, nor, in a crucial sense, even the kinds involved. Bats, whales, mammals, fish, and birds did not simply vanish from common sense to arise anew in science like Athena springing from the head of Zeus. Rather, there was a redistribution of affiliations between antecedently perceived kinds. What had altered was the construal of the underlying natures of those kinds, with a consequent redistribution of kinds and a reappraisal of properties pertinent to reference. In brief, virtually all humans, at all times and in all places, categorize the animals and plants that they readily perceive in a very similar way.

AMERICAN AND MAYA FOLK TAXONOMIES: CATEGORIES AND INFERENCE

Consider some recent experimental findings that Alexander López and I obtained among University of Michigan students raised in rural Michigan and the Itza of Guatemala, the last Maya indians native to the Petén tropical forest. Our working hypothesis was that if the same kinds of folk-biological constraints on taxonomies and inductions describe performances of people in such different cultures, then we have reason to believe that the underlying cognitive processes are part of human nature.

What follows is a brief account of findings with regard to all mammals represented in the local environments of the Itza and Michigan groups respectively. For the Itza we included bats, although they do not consider them mammals. For the students we included the emblematic wolverine, although it is now extinct in Michigan. Each group was tested in its native language (Itza and English), and included six men and six women. No statistically significant differences beween men and women were found.

To compare the structure and content of folk-biological taxonomies with one another, and with evolutionary taxonomy, we first obtained an overall folk taxonomy for each group by aggregating individual judgments of similarity between animals (Atran 1994, in press). Each group's folk taxonomy was then correlated with an evolutionary taxonomy of the local fauna. This was calculated by counting the nodes that must be ascended in an evolutionary tree to arrive at a node that includes all specimens covered by both folk taxa in any given cell of the off-diagonal pairwise similarity matrix of folk taxa (Boster *et al.* 1986). Correlating folk with scientific taxonomies measures *topological agreement* in the structure of their respective taxonomic trees (Farris 1973).

The overall (Pearson) correlations were quite high both between evolutionary taxonomy and Itza taxonomy ($r = 0.81$, $p < 0.000$), and between science and the folk taxonomy of Michigan students ($r = 0.75$, $p < 0.000$). Somewhat surprisingly, the Itza come even closer to a scientific appreciation of the local mammal fauna than do the Michigan students. A comparison of higher-order taxa only (i.e. excluding folk species) still shows a strong correlation for both Itza ($r = 0.51$, $p < 0.000$) and Michigan subjects ($r = 0.48$, $p < 0.000$) (cf. Johnson *et al.* 1992). Although most of the variance must be explained by cognitive factors different from those that target scientific taxa, the topologies of Itza and Michigan folk taxonomic trees at these higher levels compare favourably both with each other and with science in terms of the number of nodes and the levels at which nodes are formed (Figs 8.1 and 8.2). Correlations between the higher-order folk taxonomies and science are maximized at the level of the scientific suborder (i.e. the level between family and order) for both Itza ($r = 0.54$, $p < 0.000$) and Michigan ($r = 0.51$, $p < 0.000$) subjects, with partial correlations for the other levels (genus, family, order, subclass) accounting for less than 10 per cent of the variance.

The correlations indicate that there are at least some universal cognitive factors at work in folk-biological classification that are mitigated or ignored by science. For example, certain groupings, such as felines plus canines, are common to both Itza and Michigan students, although felines and canines are phylogenetically further from one another than canines are from the

Average linkage method
Tree diagram

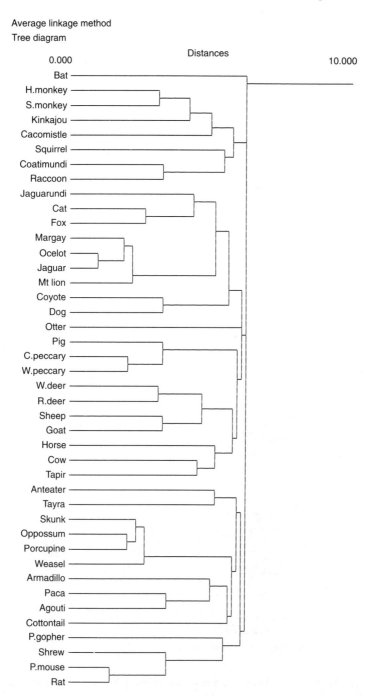

Fig. 8.1. Itza mammal taxonomy (cluster analysis of aggregated individual trees).

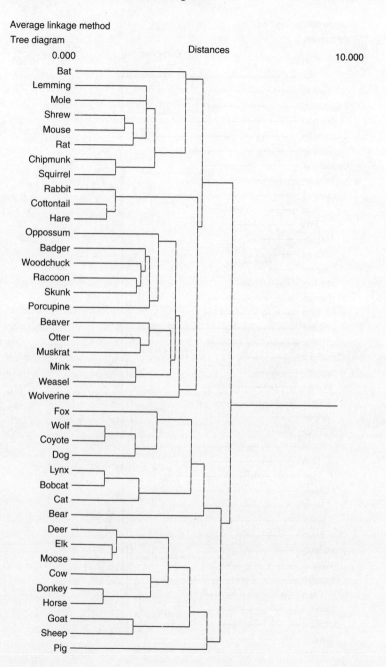

Fig. 8.2. Michigan students' mammal taxonomy (cluster analysis of aggregated individual trees).

other carnivore families (e.g. mustelids, procyonids, etc.). One interpretation of a multidimensional scaling of taxonomies for each cultural group suggests that animals are arrayed along dimensions of size and ferocity (Henley 1969; Rips *et al.* 1973) that a corresponding scientific classification of the local fauna does not exhibit.

Other factors in the divergence between folk taxonomies and science are related both to science's incorporation of a world-wide perspective in classifying local biota, and to its reliance on biologically 'deep' and theoretically weighted properties of internal anatomy and physiology. For example, the oppossum is the only marsupial present in North and Central America. Both Itza and students relate the oppossum to skunks and porcupines because it shares with them numerous readily perceptible features of morphology and behaviour. From a scientific vantage, however, the oppossum is taxonomically isolated from all the other locally represented mammals in a subclass of its own. Thus, if we exclude the oppossum from the comparison between the folk taxonomies and science, the correlation rises notably for both Itza (from $r = 0.51$ to $r = 0.60$) and students (from $r = 0.48$ to $r = 0.55$).

One factor mitigating the ability of the Itza or the Michigan students to appreciate the oppossum in the same way as scientists is the absence of any other local marsupials to which the oppossum can be related. As a result, the most readily perceptible morpho-behavioural difference between the oppossum and other local mammals — carrying its young in a pouch — cannot be linked to perceptible differences that would connect the oppossum to other marsupials and help to differentiate them from non-marsupials. The oppossum's pouch appears as just another characteristic morpho-behavioural feature, like the porcupine's quills or the skunk's smell. Both Michigan students and Itza are apparently unaware of the deeper biological significance of the oppossum's lack of a placenta.

Of course, the best candidate for the cultural influence of theory in American folk biology is science, yet the exposure of Michigan students to science education has little apparent effect on their folk taxonomy. From a scientific view, the students taxonomize no better than do the Itza. Science's influence is at best marginal. For example, science may peripherally bear on the differences in the way that the Itza and the Michigan students categorize bats. Itza consider bats to be birds (*ch'iich'*), not mammals (*b'a'al˜che'*). Like Michigan students, Itza acknowledge in interviews that there is a resemblance between bats and small rodents and insectivores. However, because Itza classify bats with birds, they consider the resemblance to be only superficial and not indicative of a taxonomic relationship. In contrast, Michigan students 'know' from schooling that bats are mammals. However, this knowledge can hardly be taken as evidence for the influence of scientific *theory* on folk taxonomy. Despite learning that bats are mammals, the students go on to relate to mice and shrews just as the Itza might if they did not already 'know' that bats are birds. From a scientific stand, however, bats are taxonomically no closer to shrews and mice than to any other local mammals. The students, it seems, pay little or no attention to the deeper causal relationships that science reveals.

The influence of science education on folk induction may also reflect *less actual knowledge* of theory *than willing belief* that there is a scientific theory that supports folk taxonomy. The high concordance between folk taxonomy and science, particularly at the level of the folk species, provides Michigan students with prima facie support for believing that their folk taxonomy is more or less on a scientific track. Given their belief that science has a causal story to tell, they assume that the same story holds in much the same way for their folk taxonomy. This belief steers them into inductive errors but also to the realization that eliminating such errors leads to a closer accord with science, albeit a modest one.

For example, given that a skunk and oppossum share a deep biological property, Michigan students are less likely to conclude that all mammals share the property than if it were shared by a skunk and a bear (Osherson *et al.* 1990). From a scientific standpoint, the students are using the right reasoning strategy (i.e. inference from the most taxonomically inclusive sample) but reaching the wrong conclusion because of a faulty taxonomy (i.e. the belief that skunks are taxonomically further from bears than from oppossums). However, the students are *told* that oppossums are phylo-genetically more distant from skunks than bears are, they readily revise their taxonomy to make the correct inference. Still, it would be misleading to claim that the students thereby use theory to revise their taxonomy, although revision occurs *in accordance with* scientific theory.

THE LIVING-KIND MODULE

The meaning of domain-specific, or modularized, conceptualization is outlined briefly in this section. The framework was initially developed some time ago (Atran 1981), but has been much influenced and altered by the work of Fodor (1983) and particularly Sperber (1985). Of course, Noam Chomsky is the spirit behind all such contemporary speculation that humans are endowed with a number of distinct knowledge systems, such as language, which are the various products of hominid evolution.

Over the last decade, work in cognitive anthropology and psychology has garnered evidence for a restricted number of 'core domains' at the conceptual level (Atran and Sperber 1991; Wellman and Gelman 1992). Promising candidates include modularized conceptual systems that universally make possible children's understanding of people's belief–desire psychology (see

Chapter 5) the basic physics governing movement of rigid bodies (see Chapter 3), and the biological autonomy of animals and plants (see Chapter 9). The idea is not that these domain-specific conceptual faculties mimic the hermetically closed nature of perceptual modules (Fodor 1983), but that they have 'privileged [rather than exclusive] access to the mental representations that [perceptual] input systems compute' (Atran 1990, p. 285).

For example, a specialized living-kind module would privilege as input whatever outputs from the various perceptual modules it takes to identify something as an organism. Presumably, the specialized folk psychology and basic physics modules would privilege other sets of information produced by the perceptual modules. None the less, there would also be considerable overlap, for instance in representations of object boundaries that help to identify both rigid bodies and living kinds, and in representations of spontaneous movement or heterogeneous arrangement of parts that help to identify both living kinds and persons.

An implicit assumption in much of the work on domain-specificity is that each core domain is the naturally selected product of a distinct set of evolutionary factors (see Tooby and Cosmides (1992) for a rare explicit accounting). If this assumption is correct, then there is no reason to expect that the same kind of reasoning processes are associated with each domain. For example, although scientists and philosophers of science today generally follow Descartes' (1681) proposition that a single set of causal principles pervades the universe, there is prima facie evidence against assuming that people spontaneously 'cognize' the natural world in terms of a uniform notion of causality. Indeed, as Geoffrey Lloyd suggests in Chapter 17, the unitary notion of 'cause' in Western science, like that of 'nature', may have no directly corresponding notion in other historical traditions and thus is an unlikely concept of some universal common sense.

Kant (1790) would have us believe that whether or not the universe is really only extension and mechanics may have no bearing on the fact that people cannot help but think of one another and of the living things they see in non-mechanical terms. In fact, there is experimental evidence for different patterns of inference pertaining not only to mechanical causality relating push and pull on inert bodies to their contingent movements, but also to intentional causality relating beliefs and desires to actions, as well as to teleological causality relating biological parts (e.g. organs) and processes (e.g. growth) to their functional ends (e.g. the homeostasis of a mature organism). These are good candidates for what Hume (1758) would call 'that original stock of ideas' that we are never free of.

Although postulation of core domains might help to account for the (ontogenetically) rapid and (cross-culturally) pervasive learning of 'naive' psychology, physics, and biology, the overall cognitive pay-off appears dubious at first glance. For example, how would conceptual modularity allow for, much less encourage, evident human propensities to conceptual integration, change, and diversity? If not all conceptual domains are modular, as science and religion surely are not, then how would non-modular domains compete with modular domains for input, and how would the adequacy of competing outputs, i.e. claims to knowledge, be assessed, for example between naive physics or biology and scientific physics or biology?

One step towards integration might involve access by one conceptual module to the outputs of another. Although evolution may have privileged a core domain's access to the outputs of the perceptual modules, as a response to the phenomenal salience of environmental factors, exchanges of information between conceptual modules might also have been selected for, or at least not selected against. For example, drawing on information about the structure of an organism from the naive biology module, the naive physics module would represent those objects, and the contingent causal sequences impacting upon them, differently than if that information were not available. Inferences to conclusions in either domain could involve premises from both.

Such forms of integration are probably shared by some non-human animals, assuming that they also have modularized conceptual systems, however rudimentary. But the information that non-human animals generate and use is quite restricted in comparison with humans, who can produce and vary information at will. Human conceptual abilities are con-siderably amplified by the presence of cultural representations. These are public expressions that are causally linked to mental representations through the act of communication. Language (as spoken or written discourse) is the most powerful medium of public expression, but by no means the only one (e.g. painting, dance, etc.).

Public expression allows mental representations to be stored, accumu-lated, ordered, and transmitted via cultural institutions which are the repositories of public representations. The larger and more complex are these repositories of cultural information, the greater is the social division of labour involved in the causal patterning that links public to mental representations. Accordingly, in some cases only some people (e.g. scien-tists, priests) have access to the relevant information that enables them to internalize a public message fully, or at least internalize enough of it to ensure its effective communication. Either by social design (e.g. the struc-tured cells of a Maoist guerilla movement) or because of the cognitive com-plexity and load (e.g. physics), no one person may have the ability to instantiate mentally a full set of institutionalized representations, much less all the messages of the culture's media.

The transmission of public messages through the minds of a culture's population leads, in turn, to further transformations, variations, and innovations in the culture's inventory of shared conceptual representations. In fact, Sperber (1994) argues that, 'all such causally linked, widely distributed representations are what we mean by culture'. What does this imply for the modularized mind? Consider the following:

A module stimulates in every culture the production and distribution of a wide array of information that meets its input conditions. This information, being artifactually produced or organized by the people themselves, is from the start conceptualized and therefore belongs to the conceptual domains that I propose to call the module's *cultural domain(s)*. In other terms, cultural transmision causes, in the actual domain of a cognitive module, a proliferation of parasitic information that mimics the module's proper domain. (Sperber 1994)

This needs some unpacking. By 'proper domain', Sperber means all information in the organism's environment that has been naturally selected for processing by the module's evolutionary history. The 'actual domain' of a module is all the information that just happens to satisfy the module's input conditions. Thus information pertaining to catching and eating flies may constitute the proper domain of the frog's visual system, but information pertaining to the movement of black dots across a screen may be an actual domain of the frog's visual system. For humans, a probable candidate for the proper domain of the living-kind module is information that pertains to phenomenally apparent organisms. Actual (sub)domains for the living-kind module might include culturally mediated information pertaining to phenomena with the presumed aetiology of organisms (e.g. diseases), imperceptible organisms (e.g. bacteria) or extinct organisms (e.g. dinosaurs, giant ferns).

By manipulating input conditions to mimic or evoke the living-kind module's proper domain, humans create a cultural domain of living kinds that extends knowledge over proper and actual domains. Cultural activation of the living-kind module is involved whenever people learn about plants and animals through instruction, as in books. In fact, the module may be triggered simply by appropriate cultural labelling. For example, it suffices to tell a child that a dodo or an emu is a bird for the child to construct 'automatically' some (initially incomplete) representation of the dodo or emu as a kind of bird on a par with other seen or learned kinds of birds (Gelman and Coley 1990).

The living-kind module, when applied to both its proper domain of readily visible organisms and its actual, or extended, domain of culturally represented organisms, involves a domain-specific sort of causal reasoning, which we call 'teleo-essentialist'. The idea is that innate principles lead children to believe that the visible morpho-typical patterns of each readily identifiable biological species are causally produced by an underlying essence (Atran 1987b). The nature of this essence is initally unknown, but presumed. The child must discover how essences govern the teleological relations between visible parts, and how they causally link initially ill-perceived inheritable parts to morpho-typical parts through irreversible patterns of growth (see Chapter 9). Virtually all people, in all cultures, cannot help but follow through this innately driven 'research program' which compels them to deepen and extend the domain of information relevant to living kinds into an all-embracing taxonomy (Atran 1990).

Keil (1994; Chapter 9 this volume), takes a somewhat different position. He suggests that essentialism and teleology are separate 'modes of construal' for organizing and performing computations on information. The teleological and essentialist modes, together with the intentional and mechanical modes (and perhaps a few more), form 'a small but diverse set of fundamental modes of construal'. Collectively, these fundamental modes ensure that 'concepts [are] always embedded in theory-like structures'. On the face of it, Keil's view of modes of construal agrees well with the account of conceptual modularity presented so far. But he notes that children's early awareness of artifacts as having functions, accord just as much with a teleological, or 'design', stance as do living kinds. Similarly, children's tendencies to construe substances and naturally occuring events (e.g. thunderstorms, earthquakes) as 'natural kinds' with presumed underlying natures suggests that inert substances and naturally occurring events may be as much a proper domain of the essentialist mode as are living kinds.

There are two principal reservations about Keil's proposal, which are interconnected. First, it is not at all clear how separately operating teleological and essentialist modes would 'automatically' lock onto one another and to living kinds *independently of any apparent cultural prodding*. In contrast, cultural prodding is obviously involved in the teleological attribution of functions to artefacts and in the essentialist attribution of underlying natures to inert substances. Second, from an evolutionary vantage, it is not easy to imagine what the respective proper domains of teleology and essentialism might be. What *separate* phylogenetic histories might teleology and essentialism have?

A possible scenario is that teleology evolved to deal with artefacts, essentialism evolved to deal with natural substances, and that living kinds just happened to fit the input conditions of both. In other words, artefacts and natural substances would constitute the proper domains of teleology and essentialism respectively, whereas living kinds would comprise only an actual domain for both. This scenario is implausible for reasons that should become clear. In the case of living kinds, teleology and essentialism work as one to provide a domain-specific perception of species of living kinds that is remarkably stable across minds, cultures, and historic traditions. There is no comparable stability in the functional perception of artefacts or in an essentialist perception of inert substances.

One reason that there is no comparable consistency in the functional perception of artefacts across individuals, much less cultures, is because the function of an artefact is assigned to it by an external human agent. An artefact's function is not exclusively assigned to it by its intrinsic structure, as it is in the case of living kinds. This external assignation is to a large extent a matter of cultural convention, and to some extent an idiosyncratic matter of individual preference. For example, whether or not an object is considered to be a solid waste-paper basket or a stool depends on what function the perceiver thinks it has or should have. Perceptual cues may indicate intended function (a waste-paper basket oriented with the open surface up), but may override these cues (an upside-down stool).

In the case of inert substances, there is no body of cross-cultural evidence that people perceive the same kinds of natural substances to be natural kinds across cultures, although there may be some recurrent notions of substance such as METAL (Brown 1992). Earth, air, fire, and water may have been basic natural kinds for Ancient Greeks, but not for us or the Maya. As for naturally occurring events, attributions of essences or underlying natures to them are even more sporadic across cultures. Furthermore, findings by Keil (1986, p. 146), Gelman (1988, p. 93), and Smith *et al.* (1985) indicate that a rich causal understanding of the underlying similarities and differences between kinds of substances develops later and at a slower pace than essentialist knowledge of living kinds. Attribution of essential kindhood to natural substances may indeed involving learning how to embed those substances in theory-like structures. However, people everywhere simply *presume* that organisms belongs to essential kinds, and they tend to perceive kinds that correspond to locally apparent biological species.

In the history of science, the research programme attributing essential kindhood to substances that was first introduced by the Greeks was a derivative of the research programme in biology (Atran 1990). The modern idea of a scientific universe parsed into enduring 'natural kinds' was apparently introduced by Mill (1843) in an attempt to provide science with a unitary structure of natural laws (whose predicates would be natural kinds). Ironically, contemporary science retains the concept of 'essential or natural kind' for substances, but not for living kinds. Nevertheless, it seems that only living kinds may be spontaneously and universally thought of as essential kinds at all ages and in all cultures.

The upshot is that neither artefacts nor natural substances are plausible candidates for the proper domains of teleology and essentialism respectively. In contrast, the obvious evolutionary advantage of acquiring 'automatic' competency in recognition and understanding of living species, coupled with ontogenetic precociousness and cross-cultural robustness of this competency, argue for living kinds as the proper domain of a teleo-essentialist conceptual module. Teleology and essentialism would not, then, be separate modes of construal but aspects of a single basic module that may be variously developed and elaborated in the process of forming new cultural domains, such as the domain of artefacts and the domain of natural kinds.

A similar argument to that presented above holds for Hirschfeld's claim (Hirschfeld 1993; Chapter 11 of this volume) that the specific construal of racial categories and other aspects of social identity constitutes yet another basic conceptual domain that is processed (at least in part) by an essentialist module. In arguing for a domain-specific competence for racial classification distinct from either naive psychology or naive biology, Hirschfeld examines two supposedly alternative interpretations of the relation between biology and psychology. He calls the first 'the naturalization model', which he attributes to me (among others): 'Children might initially borrow from presumptions of the underlying natures of living things in order to better organize their knowledge of HUMANS and merge this knowledge with that of other LIVING THINGS' (Atran 1990, p. 74). Presumably one of the grounds for rejecting this view is the fact that application of the essentialist module in the social domain, unlike in the living-kind domain, does not initially involve the processing of clearly identifiable patterns of perceptual inputs.

He then goes on to examine 'the personification model', which he attributes to Carey (among others). Carey's (1985) idea is that children do not initally have a domain of LIVING KIND. Rather, they have a domain of ANIMATE BEING, including humans and animals, which is initially organized solely on the basis of naive psychology. At first, biological understanding of animals is understood and expressed exclusively in terms of wants and beliefs (e.g. dogs bark because they want to eat, and they want to eat because they believe that by eating they will no longer be hungry). Only later do children come to realize that biological processes may not be psychologically driven, which then allows them to extend their de-psychologized biological understanding to plants. Hirschfeld seems to reject this alternative on the grounds that it provides no understanding of how *classes* of beings are formed, whether human, animal, or plant, nor how it invariably comes about that such classes are essentialistically construed.

Hirschfeld's preferred strategy is to follow what he calls 'the societal model', which he brings in from a bygone era of anthropology. Citing Durkheim and Mauss (1903), he suggests that essential categories may have been initially formed as social categories for people and then applied to animals and plants: 'Moeties were the first genera; clans, the first species' (cf. Dwyer 1976). He points to Lévi-Strauss's (1966) analysis of totemism — the identification of social categories, such as kinship categories, with categories of plants and animals — as an example of how 'the *tension* between aggregate and individual phenomena' can be resolved for understanding humans, and perhaps animals and plants as well.

Let us begin with Hirschfeld's rejection of the naturalization model. The story he tells speaks only to half of it. The unmentioned half is directed to an alternative account of Carey's findings.

Because HUMANS and ANIMALS are adjacent ontological domains, as it were, then one might expect children to initially borrow from their knowledge of HUMANS to begin to organize and merge their knowledge of ANIMALS and PLANTS. So, although children may initially entertain presumptions, rather than knowledge, of the underlying natures of animals and plants, they could use their knowledge of human biology (cum psychology) to begin organizing and merging their knowledge of animal and plant natures. (Atran 1990, p. 74)

Recent work by Keil and his associates (Springer and Keil 1991) and by Gelman and her associates (Gelman 1988; Gelman and Wellman 1991) provides considerable evidence that young children (aged 3 and 4) essentialistically construe categories of animal and plant species. The children further attribute to the essential natures of those categories causal powers (of inheritance, reproduction, growth, interrelation of functional parts, etc.) that show no influence from belief–desire psychology.

Any importation of naive psychology into the living-kind domain is just that: importation. In many cultures, including our own, most importation of this ilk remains figurative (i.e. metarepresentational, see below). This is because such imported information ultimately fails to assimilate readily with information deemed specific to the importing domain. Figurative construal of imported information does not mean it becomes culturally unimportant. Indeed for a time in Ancient Greece animals were put on trial, with all the official ceremony due to humans, to answer for the socially unacceptable aspects of their putative belief–desire psychology. Similarly, totemic relationships to animals and plants (e.g. imputation of animal and plant traits to people and to lineages that bear the names of those plants and animals) may determine all matters of love and war in a society. Whatever such figurative construals of the relations between people and non-human living kinds, the living-kind module can, and does, function properly without them. Totems invariably mate, but species do not.

As for the suggestion that living-kind categories somehow depend on social categorization, this is implausible in the extreme. Species *are* universally perceived living kinds; clans are *not* universally social kinds. Not all people can sensibly ask and expect a response to. 'What clan do you belong to?' But all people can sensibly ask and expect a response to: 'What (species) kind does this readily perceptible organism belong to?' Not only do the contents of social categories vary greatly across ages and cultures (variously including or excluding skin color, language, apparel, etc.), but there is no cross-culturally stable system of social ranks. Kings, dukes, and counts may have a precise ranking in countries of the former Holy Roman Empire, but these rankings bear little relation to those of the true man (*jalach winik*), commander (*nokom*) or axe Wielder (*b'atab'*) of the Precolumbian Maya sociopolitical order. Neither are the racial classifications of Nazi Germany, Louisiana, and South Africa directly comparable in content or rank. In contrast, the English (European and American) categories DOG, FISH, and TREE correspond to the same respective taxa and ranks as the Maya categories *pek'*, *käy*, and *che'*.

If racial categories do not comprise (part of) a basic conceptual domain, what accounts for their persistence and their near universality across cultures in one form or another, as Hirschfeld convincingly argues? Recall the claim that humans and animals are closely related ontological domains (Keil 1979), such that the output from one is easily rendered by the culture as input to the other. By publicly representing this input and directing its transmission, cultural institutions see to it that children come to acquire the 'right' notion of race, despite the fact that children may have no prior basic cognitive disposition to favour, say, clothing over skin colour as an external mark of underlying essence. The result is an essential construal of races (or totems) in terms of readily visible features that may be associated with readily understandable psychological proclivities. Such information is culturally widespread and abiding to the extent that it conforms to basic cognitive dispositions. In other words, racial categories, like totemic categories, are, to paraphrase an idea from Lévi-Strauss (1966), 'easy to think' given prior abilties to understand the core domains of biology and psychology and given the institutional support for having the cultural input mimic the proper input of the core domain.

What makes racial categories even more cognitively contagious (hence culturally more widespread) than totemic categories is that racial categories require only that humans be conceived of as living kinds generally, rather than as particular animals or plants. Any direct equation of humans with particular animals or plants dramatically contradicts some basic core-driven beliefs about their prima facie differences. This non-random inconsistency with basic factual beliefs also ensures their cultural viability, because dramatic contradictions make such beliefs attention-arresting and memorable. However, they cannot become fully assimilated to basic knowledge. Like other mythico-religious beliefs, they retain an element of mystery and open texture. That is, they remain forever figurative to a significant degree, whereas racial beliefs tend to become (wrongly) factual. Similarly, the transfer of essences to substances tends to become (rightly) factual. However, all such developmentals are 'atrogenic', i.e. inadvertent products of our cognitive evolution that were not directly selected for.

So far we have spoken only of the localized 'transfer' of information between core domains and the cultural mediation of this transfer. However, such localized transfer of information could hardly account for religion's poetic license, science's 'isotropy' (e.g. the exploration of any imaginable cross-discipline analogy), or the historically compelling affects of thinking about yin and yang or the original formulation of the complementarity principle in quantum physics (Holton 1973). One solution further extends and elaborates the modularity of mind to a still higher mode of conceptualization, that of 'meta-representation':

> The meta-representational module is a special conceptual module, however, a second-order one so to speak. Whereas other conceptual modules process concepts and representations of things, typically of things perceived, the meta-representational module processes concepts of concepts and representations of representations. (Sperber 1994)

The ability of the meta-representational module to take as input the output of other conceptual modules allows for wide-ranging conceptual integration and production of new knowledge, but it does so along lines that may be somewhat predictable and in a manner that to some extent preserves the distinctive knowledge produced by more basic conceptual modules. Consider the following.

Suppose, as Spelke and Carey claim, that naive physics constitutes a distinct core domain. Suppose further, as Gelman (1980) suggests, that number constitutes another core domain that defines the countable relations among sets of discrete abstract objects, or perhaps, as Chomsky (1988) suggests, numbers and the logic governing them are just restricted products of the language faculty. Suppose, finally, that some enterprising ancient hit upon the idea of meta-representing the output of the naive physics module with the output of the number module. Then Archimedes' statics, Newton's mechanics, and much of ensuing 'hard science' would become conceivable.

Obviously the story is more complicated in a number of important ways. Once (meta-representational) rules of correspondence link object schemata to number schemata, there is no a priori reason why such mathematized objects could not themselves become inputs to the naive (but now slightly more sophisticated) physics module, *provided that they can be readily integrated with prior common-sense notions*. For example, even young children in our society appear to comprehend contemporary Western notions of the earth and other heavenly objects as sphere-like objects (Vosniadou and Brewer 1987), although they are not likely to be aware that such notions were the result of laborious scientific discoveries involving mathematics. Similarly, our children may readily comprehend whales and bats as mammals, despite having only the vaguest awareness of the anatomical insights that made these identifications possible (Medin 1989).

Thus, even when there *are* demonstrable and pervasive affects of meta-cognitive (e.g. scientific) reasoning on basic conceptualization, the effects are not likely to be uniform or to allow common-sense structures to be wholly replaced by new structures (e.g. theories).

Wholesale replacement of common-sense knowledge by meta-representational knowledge may even be impossible in certain cases. There may be (innately determined) limits on the extent to which the domain of a basic conceptual module can be extended to include meta-representational information. Such natural limits on assimilation of new knowledge to basic domains may occur when no phenomenal intuition, commensurate with the core domain, can be given. Thus it is doubtful that any complete physical interpretation, much less phenomenal intuition, can be given to the equations of quantum mechanics. In a crucial sense this is unlike the case for classical mechanics — understanding quantum mechanics is just understanding the mathematics. There is little doubt that people, even quantum physicists, understand and negotiate their interactions with everyday physical objects without ever using, or being able to use, concepts derived from quantum equations.

In biology, modern genetics and evolutionary theory tell us that there are no ontological kinds corresponding to common-sense (pre-Darwinian) conceptions of species. From an evolutionary standpoint, species taxa represent somewhat arbitrary pieces of a geneaological nexus. From a logical standpoint, the members of species taxa are parts (segments) of an individual (lineage) rather than elements of a class. From an epistemological standpoint, species taxa are not natural kinds in the sense of having genetically specifiable constitutions that function with lawful regularity in evolution.

In certain respects, evolutionary understanding of species is as counterintuitive, and as difficult to teach and understand, as quantum mechanics (Hull 1991). Nevertheless, many philosophers and scientists continue to discuss species taxa as if they were enduring natural kinds. Indeed, some take the notion of species as a natural kind as a scientific given, and purport to show from this that there is not only a progressive continuity between common sense and science, but that this 'scientific' notion of species as a natural kind is the ultimate reference for the common-sense meaning of living-kind terms (Putnam 1975; Schwartz 1979). If anything, modern science shows just as much the reverse: there is a marked discontinuity between evolutionary and pre-evolutionary conceptions of species, while the lingering notion of the species as a natural kind in science indicates that certain basic notions in science are more hostage to the dictates of common sense than the other way around.

This suggests that the common-sense knowledge underscored by basic cognitive dispositions remains somewhat separate from more sophisticated, originally meta-representational conceptions, despite the subtle and pervasive interactions between the two kinds of knowledge (Dupré 1981). Thus, such basic 'common-sense' may remain valid for everyday understanding of the world, but perhaps not for either the vastly extended or reduced dimensions of modern science. New meta-representationally created knowledge can filter back into basic conceptual modules and alter their data base, but within limits. These innately determined limits may be such as to preserve enough of the 'default' ontology and structure of the core domain to make the notion of **domain-specific cross-cultural universals** meaningful. This leads to a strong expectation that core principles guide learning in much the same way across cultures.

In the case of symbolic cognitions, such as those involved in religion and belief in the supernatural, concepts are studiously structured so as to *disallow* any fixed intuitions to be associated with them, and thus to preclude them from supplanting, or being fully assimilated to, core beliefs. In multiplying senses and metaphors (e.g. God as father, son, and earth mother) symbolism allows endless interpretation and exegesis. In suspending basic factual beliefs (e.g. animate beings without bodily substance, animals that reincarnate people, blood that transmutes into wine, plants that desire revenge, etc.) symbolism guarantees that no such interpretation will ever be empirically confirmed or disconfirmed. Ever since Kant (1790, section 59), philosophers have emphasized what anthropologists have repeatedly shown, namely that any genuinely symbolic concept is at best 'quasi-schematized' and designed to remain an open-textured meta-representation of whatever other conceptual interpretations or facts are brought to bear.

However, religious beliefs are not unconnected to common-sense knowledge. They are generally inconsistent with common-sense knowledge, but not in random fashion. Rather, by flatly contradicting basic common-sense knowledge about physical, biological, and psychological phenomena, symbolic beliefs become particularly attention-arresting and memorable. As a result, these beliefs are more likely to be retained and transmitted in a human group than are random departures from common sense, and thus to become part of a group's culture. To the extent that basic conceptual modules are interrelated, and perhaps even somewhat hierarchichally structured (Keil 1979), it may even be possible to predict some general tendencies in systems of symbolic beliefs across culture. Thus, within a given religious test or tradition, 'one might predict that the likelihood of a transformation from one thing to another should decrease as the distance . . . between the [basic ontological] categories of these two things increases' (Kelly and Keil 1985). For instance, the metamorphosis of humans into animals and animals into plants may be more common than that of humans into artefacts. To the extent that such violations of category distinctions shake basic notions of ontology, they are attention-arresting and hence memorable (Sperber 1985; Boyer 1990). But only to the degree that the resultant impossible worlds remain bridged to the everyday world, can information about them be stored and evoked in plausible grades (Atran 1990; Chapter 21 of this volume).

HOLY THEORIES VERSUS KNOWLEDGE IN PIECES

Understanding the actual domains of symbolism allows us to cut through some of the vagueness and ambiguity that has attended recent uses of the notion of 'theory' in cognitive psychology and anthropology. A common assumption is that folk theories are like scientific theories in that they provide an explanatory framework of the causal principles which determine the ontology and inferential structure of a domain. However, they may differ in other ways from scientific theories in being more 'rudimentary' or 'incomplete', and in the form of 'cosmologies' they may apply weaker criteria for assessing correspondence between beliefs and evidence (Horton 1967; Murphy and Medin 1985). For example, Keil (1986; cf. Chapter 10 of this volume), citing the work of his student, Sheila Jeyifous (1985), notes that American children and Yoruba (Nigeria) children both come to understand that animal kinds have essences deeper than visible bodily structure. However, the children elaborate different 'theories' to attain this knowledge. In the American case, the theory learned presumably involves some rudimentary scientific knowledge (perhaps acquired in school, from nature programmes on television, etc.), whereas in the Yoruba case 'cosmological' theory involving the supernatural seems to be required.

Without denying the important insights of Keil and Jeyifous (now Walker) regarding children's early understanding of biological essence, it is unlikely that any sense can be made of the claim that cosmological theory fixes the factual beliefs of Yoruba children. Cosmological notions of the supernatural can no more fix factual beliefs about biological kinds among Yoruba children than ideas about Santa Claus can fix American children's factual beliefs about the mechanics of sleigh riding or gravity, for these are non-propositional representations that allow for no consistent appreciation of their logical entailments nor, therefore, for any definite empirical confirmation or disconfirmation. This seriously undermines Carey and Spelke's (1994) claim that 'Yoruba biology differs greatly from the intuitive American biology' with respect to concepts of biological kindhood or essence. No 'theory difference' has been shown for the two cultures because no 'theory' at all has been demonstrated for the Yoruba. Moreover, the 'folk theory' imputed to American children to account for their developing notions of biological essence hardly represents a fully coherent or all-encompassing explanatory framework, as Keil himself notes. Given comparable performances by American and Yoruba children, a plausible interpretation of the data may be that a maturing notion of biological essence develops that does not require, but may be partly supported and justified by, American children's piecemeal theoretical knowledge.

In brief, while the influence of science on American folk is palpable, it is by no means all-embracing. Neither is the affect of science necessarily in the direction of theory development and deep conceptual change. Similarly, there is no overarching cultural cosmology for Itza Maya that uniformly affects folk biology. Rather, for both groups it appears that impinging cultural factors produce what is more like a theoretical 'knowledge in pieces' (diSessa 1988). Thus, whereas scientists, American folk, and Itza are all disposed to build higher categories that capture readily perceptible clusters of morphological features, biological theory (anatomy) enables science to override such obvious features as size and degree of ferocity or remoteness from humans. In contrast, both American folk and Itza consider these broad dimensions as fundamental (e.g. horses and tapirs go with sheep and deer), even though American folk are probably culturally sensitized by science to ignore or downplay singularly striking morphological contrasts (e.g. Itza class bats with birds, while American folk may class them close to rodents).

A science of living kinds, first as natural history and then biology, developed in order to comprehend better what could not be so easily grasped at a glance. The vast numbers of new species exposed during Europe's Age of Exploration stretched common-sense ways of thinking to the limits. More recently discovered aeons, with their indeterminately many fossilized forms, finally caused an epistemological rupture between science and common sense. This rupture is not between what is 'true' or 'false'. Rather, it is between how the world (ideally) is in itself, independent of human observers, versus how it must appear to people, whatever science holds to be reality. A research task of 'the anthropology of science' is to explore and understand the emergence of this division of cognitive labour between science and common sense — to find the bounds within which commonsense thinking stands up and to show where our ready perceptions no longer hold the promise of truth.

In sum, our modularized common-sense conception of living kinds consitutes everyday knowledge of nature, while also serving as a psychologically natural heuristic for regulating our scientific dealings with the world. Why is this common-sense construal of the world, which is arguably determined by a living-kind module, so remarkably robust? Plausibly, it is because this module was the naturally selected product of hominid phylogenetic history. Its ability to generate taxa within a taxonomic structure that supports indefinitely many category-based inductions represents one of the most powerful and readily accessible devices available to human beings for understanding the world that they see around them. Additional (meta-cognitive) human abilities enable us to seek out, manipulate, revise, test, and interpret anew the information that the module produces. This can lead to (scientific) theories that causally unify, simplify, and extend the organization of biological categories (and the inferences that this organization supports) to 'endless forms most beautiful and most wonderful' (Darwin 1883, p. 429).

REFERENCES

Adanson, M. (1763). *Familles des plantes*. Vincent, Paris.

Atran, S. (1981). Natural classification. *Social Science Information* **20**, 37–91.

Atran, S. (1983). Covert fragmenta and the origins of the botanical family. *Man* **18**, 51–71.

Atran, S. (1985*a*). The nature of folkbotanical life-forms. *American Anthropologist* **87**, 298–315.

Atran, S. (1985*b*). Pre-theoretical aspects of Aristotelian definition and classification of animals. *Studies in History and Philosophy of Science* **16**, 113–63.

Atran, S. (1987*a*). Origins of the species and genus concepts. *Journal of the History of Biology* **20**, 195–279.

Atran, S. (1987*b*). Constraints on the ordinary semantics of living kinds. *Mind and Language* **2**, 27–63.

Atran, S. (1990). *Cognitive foundations of natural history: towards an anthropology of science*. Cambridge University Press.

Atran, S. (1994) Core domains versus scientific theories. In *Mapping the mind: domain specificity in cognition and culture* (ed. L. Hirschfeld and S. Gelman), Cambridge University Press, New York.

Atran, S. (In press). Classifying nature across cultures. In *Invitation to cognitive science*, vol. 3, *Thinking* (ed. D. Osherson and E. Smith). MIT Press, Cambridge, MA.

Atran, S. and Sperber, D. (1991). Learning without teaching: its place in culture. In *Culture, schooling and psychological development* (ed. L. Tolchinsky-handsmann). Ablex, Norwood, NJ.

Berlin, B. (1992). *Ethnobiological classification: principles of categorization of plants and animals in traditional societies*. Princeton University Press.

Berlin, B., Breedlove, D. and Raven, P. (1973). General principles of classification and nomenclature in folk biology. *American Anthropologist* **74**, 214–42.

Boster, J., Berlin, B. and O'Neill, J. (1986). The correspondence of Jivaroan to scientific ornithology. *American Anthropologist* **88**, 569–83.

Boyer, P. (1990). *Tradition as truth and communication*. Cambridge University Press.

Brown, C. (1984). *Language and living things: uniformities in folk classification and naming*. Rutgers University Press, New Brunswick, NJ.

Brown, C. (1992). Cognition and common sense. *American Ethnologist* **19**, 367–74.

Bulmer, R. (1970). Which came first, the chicken or the egg-head? In *Echanges et communications: mélanges offerts à Claude Lévi-Strauss* (ed. J. Pouillon and P. Maranda). Mouton, The Hague.

Carey, S. (1985). *Conceptual change in childhood*. MIT Press, Cambridge, MA.

Carey, S. and Spelke, E. (1994). Domain specific knowledge and conceptual change. In *Mapping the mind* (ed. L. Hirschfeld and S. Gelman). Cambridge University Press, New York.

Cesalpino, A. (1583). *De plantis libri XVI*. Marescot, Florence.

Chomsky, N. (1988). Language and problems of knowledge. MIT Press, Cambridge, MA.

Darwin, C. [1872] (1883). *On the origins of species by natural selection* (6th edn). Appleton, New York.

Descartes, R. (1681). *Les principes de la philosophie*. Gerard, Paris.

diSessa, A. (1988). Knowledge in pieces. In *Constructivism in the computer age* (ed. G. Forman and P. Pufall). Erlbaum, Hillsdale, NJ.

Dougherty, J. (1979). Learning names for plants and plants for names. *Anthropological Linguistics* **21**, 298–315.

Dupré, J. (1981). Natural kinds and biological taxa. *Philosophical Review* **90**, 66–90.

Durkheim, E. and Mauss, M. [1903] (1963). *Primitive classification*. University of Chicago Press.

Dwyer, P. (1976). An analysis of Rofaifo mammal taxonomy. *American Ethnologist* **3**, 425–45.

Farris, J. (1973). On comparing the shapes of taxonomic trees. *Systematic Zoology* **22**, 50–4.

Fodor J. (1983). *The modularity of mind*. MIT Press, Cambridge, MA.

Gelman, R. (1980). What young children know about numbers. *Educational Psychologist* **15**, 54–68.

Gelman, S. (1988). The development of induction within natural kind and artifact categories. *Cognitive Psychology* **20**, 65–95.

Gelman, S. and Coley, J. (1990). The importance of knowing a dodo is a bird: categories and inferences in two-year-olds. *Developmental Psychology* **26**, 796–804.

Gelman, S. and Wellman, H. (1991). Insides and essences: early understanding of the non-obvious. *Cognition* **38**, 214–44.

Henley, N. (1969). A psychological study of the semantics of animal terms. *Journal of Verbal Learning and Verbal Behavior* **8**, 176–84.

Hirschfeld, L. (1993). Discovering social difference: the role of appearance in racial awareness. *Cognitive Psychology* **25**, 317–50.

Holton, G. (1973). *Thematic origins of scientific thought: Kepler to Einstein*. Harvard University Press, Cambridge, MA.

Horton, R. (1967). African thought and Western science. *Africa* **37**, 50–71, 159–87.

Hull, D. (1991). Common sense and science. *Biology and Philosophy* **6**, 467–79.

Hume, D. [1758] (1955). *An inquiry concerning human understanding*. Bobbs-Merrill, New York.

Hunn, E. (1976). Toward a perceptual model of folk biological classification. *American Ethnologist* **3**, 508–24.

Jeyifous, S. (1985). Atimodemo: semantic conceptual development among the Yoruba. Ph.D. Dissertation, Cornell University.

Johnson, K., Mervis, C. and Boster, J. (1992). Developmental changes within the structure of the mammal domain. *Developmental Psychology* **28**, 74–83.

Kant, I. [1790] (1951). *Critique of judgement*. Hafner Press, New York.

Keil, F. (1979). *Semantic and conceptual development: an ontological perspective*. Harvard University Press, Cambridge, MA.

Keil, F. (1986). The acquisition of natural kind and artefact terms. In *Conceptual change* (ed. A. Marrar and W. Demopoulos). Ablex, Norwood, NJ.

Keil, F. (1989). *Concepts, kinds, and cognitive development*. MIT Press, Cambridge, MA.

Keil, F. (1994). The birth and nuturance of concepts by domains. In *Mapping the mind: domain specificity in cognition and culture* (ed. L. Hirschfeld and S. Gelman). Cambridge University Press, New York.

Kelly, M. and Keil, F. (1985). The more things . . . Metamorphoses and conceptual development. *Cognitive Science* **9**, 403–16.

Kesby, J. (1979). The Rangi classification of animals and plants. In *Classifications in their social contexts* (ed. R. Reason and D. Ellen). Academic Press, New York.

Lamarck, J. (1809). *Philosophie zoologique*. Dentu, Paris.

Lévi-Straus, C. (1966). *The savage mind*. University of Chicago Press.

Linnaeus, C. (1751). *Philosophia botanica*. G. Kiesewetter, Stockholm.

López, A., Gelman, S., Gutheil, G. and Smith, E. (1992). The development of category-based induction. *Child Development* **63**, 1070–90.

Mandler, J. (1992). How to build a baby: II, Conceptual primitives. *Psychological Review* **99**, 587–604.

Mayr, E. (1969). *Principles of systematic zoology*. McGraw-Hill, New York.

Medin, D. (1989). Concepts and conceptual structure. *American Psychologist* **44**, 1469–81.

Medin, D. and Ortony, A. (1989). Psydhological essentialism. In *Similarity and analogical reasoning* (ed. S. Vosniadou and A. Ortony). Cambridge University Press, New York.

Mill, J. S. (1843). *A system of logic*. Longmans Green, London.

Murphy, G. and Medin, D. (1985). The role of theories in conceptual coherence. *Psychological Review* **92**, 289–316.

Osherson, D., Smith, E., Wilkie, O., López, A. and Shafir, E. (1990). Category-based induction. *Psychological Review* **97**, 185–200.

Putnam, H. (1975). The meaning of 'meaning'. In *Language, mind and knowledge* (ed. K. Gunderson). University of Minnesota Press, Minneapolis, MN.

Raven, P., Berlin, B. and Breedlove, D. (1971). The origins of taxonomy. *Science* **174**, 1210–13.

Rips, L., Shoben, E. and Smith, E. (1973). Semantic distance and the verification of semantic relations. *Journal of Verbal Learning and Verbal Behavior* **12**, 1–20.

Romney, A. K., Weller, S. and Batchelder, W. (1986). Culture as consensus: a theory of culture and informant accuracy. *American Anthropologist* **88**, 313–38.

Schwartz, S. (1979). Natural kind terms. *Cognition* **7**, 301–15.

Simpson, G. (1961). *Principles of animal taxonomy*. Columbia University Press, New York.

Smith, C., Carey, S. and Wiser, M. (1985). On differentiation: a case study of the development of concepts of size, weight, and density. *Cognition* **21**, 177–237.

Sperber, D. (1985). Anthropology and psychology: towards an epidemiology of representations. *Man* **20**, 73–89.

Sperber, D. (1994). The modularity of thought and the epidemiology of representations. In Mapping the mind: domain specificity in cognition and culture (ed. L. Hirschfeld and S. Gelman). Cambridge University Press, New York.

Springer, K. and Keil, F. (1991). Early differentiation of causal mechanisms appropriate to biological and nonbiological kinds. *Child Development* **60**, 637–48.

Stross, B. (1973). Acquisition of botanical terminology by Tzeltal children. In *Meaning in Mayan languages* (ed. M. Edmonson). Mouten, The Hague.

Tooby, J. and Cosmides, L. (1992). The psychological foundations of culture. In *The adapted mind: evolutionary psychology and the generation of culture* (ed. J. Barkow, L. Cosmides, and J. Tooby). Oxford University Press, New York.

Tournefort, J. (1694). *Elémens de botanique*. Imprimerie Royale, Paris.

Vosniadou, S. and Brewer, W. (1987). Theories of knowledge restructuring in development. *Review of Educational Research* **57**, 51–67.

Wallace, A. (1889). *Darwinism: an explanation of the theory of natural selection with some of its implications*. Macmillan, London.

Warburton, F. (1967). The purposes of classification. *Systematic Zoology* **16**, 241–5.

Wellman, H. and Gelman, S. (1992). Cognitive development: foundational theories of core domains. *Annual Review of Psychology* **43**, 337–75.

9

The growth of causal understandings of natural kinds

FRANK C. KEIL

Although we all know that things are not always as they seem, confusions between appearance and reality have caused many problems in the cognitive sciences, particularly in models of concepts and concept structure (Rey 1983). However, even though metaphysics and epistemology must be distinguished, theories of knowledge cannot avoid making some commitments about the nature of the world itself. General principles concerning the representation and acquisition of concepts and the larger causal belief systems in which those concepts are embedded may depend critically on assumptions about what the causal patterns in the world are really like. For that reason, this discussion of causal understandings of one type of natural kind — living things — starts with some assumptions about natural kinds themselves.

WHAT NATURAL KINDS ARE NOT

To some, 'natural kind' is simply a technical term used in philosophical discourse, but that discourse carries with it a number of implicit assumptions that demarcate a set of distinct kinds of much broader interest. Here, I shall ask whether those sorts of kinds might be ones for which we are particularly predisposed to develop certain types of causal understandings. As is usually the case in attempts to classify, it is easier to state what natural kinds are *not* than what they are. However, such negative characterizations may point to more positive proposals. In that spirit, consider four sorts of things that natural kinds are not.

First, natural kinds are not things sharing singly necessary and jointly sufficient features. Despite widespread intuitions that fixed inalienable essences exist, they seem to evaporate when considered as necessary and sufficient features. Many non-controversial instances of natural kinds, such as tigers, do not have strict essences. Tiger DNA will not suffice since no fixed sequence of nucleotides is shared by all tigers.

Second, natural kinds are not merely all naturally occurring classes of things. After all, things heavier than 100 pounds, things at temperatures above 60°F on 8 January 1993, and even red things describe naturally occurring classes, but if our intuitions have any merit at all, they recoil at the prospect of such classes being natural kinds. Moreover, it cannot simply be that natural kinds are those things that allow us to make successful inductions based on their properties. There are many reliable inductions that follow from a thing's mass, colour, or even temperature on a certain date, and these inductions can be more reliable and stable than some for natural kinds. Natural kinds may well foster more intricate patterns of inductions that have unique signatures associated with natural kinds, but the ability to support induction *per se* is not enough to set natural kinds apart.

Third, not only are many naturally occurring classes not natural kinds but, even worse, not all natural kinds may actually exist. A class of things might follow directly from a set of natural laws and have a rich predictable property cluster, but be sufficiently rare as to have not yet occurred or perhaps be prevented from occurring. Astronomers might be convinced that a particular kind of neutron star must occur, but perhaps stellar evolution must continue for a few more million years before one actually exists. Similarly, elements at the uppermost end of the periodic table might still be considered natural kinds, even though some of them have not yet occurred and may never occur. None the less they are natural kinds because the set of laws responsible for the patterns in the periodic table fully predict the property clusters, given their existence.

Finally, natural kinds are not simply bounded physical objects. They can obviously be substances and liquids, such as gold and water, two of the most frequently cited examples (Putnam 1975). In addition, they can be events, such as tornadoes, earthquakes, and measles.

Contrasts with artefacts are often said to highlight the special features of natural kinds. Pencils, chairs, and hammers are artefacts not only because they do not occur naturally, but also because they do not have essences (whatever essences end up being), they do not have sciences centred around them, they require reference to human intention, and they do not have unique paths of origin. However, these contrasts with natural kinds turn out to be more like rough rules of thumb than strict criteria. Artefacts and natural kinds appear to be arrayed along several related continua rather than in sharply contrasting bins, as is seen with more complex artefacts, such as televisions, cars, and computers, and with designed living kinds, such as plants and animals subject to intensive breeding.

WHAT NATURAL KINDS MIGHT BE

More positive proposals of what natural kinds are usually rely on notions of causal structure and the causal powers of properties. One model involves property homeostasis (R. Boyd, unpublished manuscript). Natural kinds may cohere as meaningful classes of things just because they reflect mutually supportive networks of causal relations among their properties. Properties are highly intercorrelated because, either directly or indirectly through a causal chain, they tend to support the presence of each other. In the case of living kinds, many of their salient properties tend to help increase the likelihood of others being present. One common way is for each property to increase the odds of the organism's survival and hence the likelihood of all other properties through survival. More specific links between properties are also frequent. Consider a giraffe for example. Its long neck enables it to eat vegetation that no other animals can reach, special valves in its neck prevent excess cranial blood pressure when it bends down to eat vegetation from the ground, thereby enabling it to have a long neck and also to eat from the ground. Its social habits are also related to the long neck which enables it to see predators in ways different from other species. Its long legs and neck interact causally so that neither is so long as to be impractical.

There are many other properties of giraffes that also causally interact with these gross anatomical features. The properties of giraffes cluster as a stable kind over time just because of these patterns of homeostasis. Examples of this type could be generated in much more detail for a great many plants and animals, and such descriptions are readily available in many detailed functional treaments of species and their physiologies and anatomies. The patterns are not fixed in an inviolate manner, hence allowing evolutionary change, but they are sufficiently stable to give rise to an enduring kind over substantial time intervals.

Several different possible structural configurations are homeostatic, and we may be able to grasp some of these cognitively more easily than others. In addition, the different patterns might lead us to infer fundamentally different kinds of things in the world, i.e. different ontological kinds. Thus, if a sampling of a few properties and their relations suggests a certain kind of causal patterning responsible for stability of that kind, we might use that pattern as the basis for a number of abstract inferences about its general nature. Figure 9.1 illustrates some possible alternative configurations of causal relations that might result in stable configurations of properties but which are, none the less, sufficiently distinct to allow for the possibility of different psychological interpretations.

In this view, natural kinds would correspond to highly correlated clusters of properties, but these clusters would in turn reflect the actions of inter-related sets of causal relations. Properties need not be necessary since the

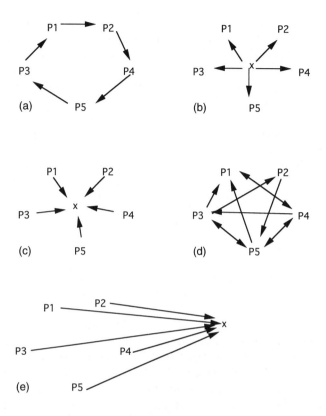

Fig. 9.1. Five different possible sorts of causal interactions among properties resulting in stable kinds. (a) systems where each property supports the others in a circular chain; (b) some non-living natural kinds and a genetic view of living kinds; (c) living kinds where properties are seen as serving internal purposes of an organism possessing them (X); (d) a property homeostasis view of living kinds; (e) simple artefacts where properties all serve the purposes of an external agent.

core of a kind may be a particular configuration of causal relations, each of which could be probabilistically associated with members of the kind. (Moreover, not only can the presence of the properties be probabilistic, but so could the causal links between them, i.e. the presence of a causal rule can be probabilistic, but once it is present it could necessarily have effects x, y, and z on other properties if they are in turn present, or the causal rule itself could act in a probabilistic manner.) Correlated properties that are not part of the core are those without direct causal connections to that central set of links (such as hair length with sex).

Overall causal patterning and homeostasis may be what gives rise to intuitions of essence. Things greater than 30 pounds would be excluded because they do not cohere as a result of a network of homeostatic clustered properties. Having a weight of 30 pounds does have potential causal links to an indefinitely large number of other entities and properties, but no set of links clusters around 30 poundedness; they might cluster around notions of weight and density, but other properties of a physical kind do not seem to reinforce each other mutually by virtue of having a specific weight. There is no converging set of causal dependencies. Similarly, the particular inductions we see for natural kinds might well be linked to the richness of those causal links. If a natural kind represents a 'gold mine of inductions' (Pierce 1931–1935), it may be largely a consequence of such highly stable and reliable clusters. Finally, we can see how artefacts might have homeostatic clusters to different degrees, and that when a sufficiently dense cluster is present and appreciated, they may not seem to be importantly different from natural kinds.

PROMISCUOUS REALISM—THE PROLIFERATION PROBLEM

For all its appeals, the homeostasis model of natural kinds has a proliferation problem. Many cite biological taxonomic categories as model natural kinds from the level of subspecies to orders and classes. However, there is also the folk-biological concept of 'tree'. People in many cultures refer to trees as an apparent natural kind. Yet trees are composed of two very taxonomically distant groups of vascular plants; conifers (such as pines, firs, and redwoods) and angiosperms (such as oaks, elms, and birches), which apparently diverged long ago in the middle Palaeozoic period. Taxonomically an oak has more similarities with a daisy or a tulip than with a redwood.

Perhaps these cases could be multiplied endlessly such that there are as many natural kinds as there are ways of classifying naturally occurring things—what Dupré (1981) has called a promiscuous realism. However, such an inference does not follow from the example with trees. That example merely serves to show that the same entities can be part of more than one homeostatic property cluster. There is clearly a homeostatic cluster that explains the detailed and often very subtle properties of angiosperms, and there is another cluster for conifers. However, another cluster applies more neatly just to trees—a cluster that arises out of ecological models rather than from micro-anatomical and genetic laws of descent, but a cluster none the less. In fact, this cluster is apparent in some simulations of plant evolution that ask what happens structurally when a variety of different plants are selected for increasing size. When competition for light and nutrients and consideration of structural-mechanical constraints are added to the model, such simulations continually yield tree-like shapes across a wide range of inputs. Stiff trunks, bark, branches with multiple green surfaces, and a relatively small set of overall tree shapes emerge as the favoured solutions (Niklas 1992).

Therefore, there is no simple one-to-one mapping of natural kinds to classes of objects. Homeostatic clusters can overlap in complex ways on common properties and entities, but there is no reason to think of those clusters as essentially unbounded and at the mercy of human imagination. They exist in the real world, are easily distinguished, and are the causes of natural kinds. Therefore natural kinds do not proliferate endlessly and they do represent real structure and information for us potentially to learn. It is difficult even to formulate another view of natural kinds that would still allow learning and induction to succeed as well as they do. This last point about learning and induction leads to the central issue of this paper — how we come to represent concepts for such kinds and understand their properties.

CAUSAL BELIEFS AND CORE PROPERTIES

The organization of natural kinds around causal homeostatic property clusters dovetails nicely with one current view of how we might come to acquire and represent concepts of natural kinds: the 'concepts in theories' view. The evidence for this view has been diverse and robust. One source derives from demonstrations of illusory correlations showing that people will see non-existing feature correlations as occurring when they follow from prior sets of beliefs and further reinforce the coherence of those beliefs (Chapman and Chapman 1969; Medin and Wattenmaker 1987). Simple tabulations of feature frequencies and co-occurrences in the world are not enough. Moreover, the acquisition of concepts also shows that they emerge in ways that cannot be explained by mere shifting of either feature frequencies or correlational weights. Thus developmental shifts in what are regarded as legitimate members of a natural kind, such as being a tiger, cannot be plausibly modelled by simply shifting probabilistic weights on features or changing global criteria of what frequencies are to count as important; some modelling of changes in relevant explanatory beliefs is also needed (Keil 1989).

Further support comes from adult processing studies, such as demonstrations that two concepts for which the same feature is equally typical might none the less place very different values on those features because one plays a more central role in patterns of causal explanation. Thus bananas and boomerangs are judged to be equally typically curved, but straight bananas are judged to be a much better new member of the class of bananas than straight boomerangs of the class of boomerangs (Medin and Shoben 1988). Therefore this particular shape change seems to be influencing what it means to be a boomerang to a much greater degree than what it means to be a banana. We all teach our students that correlation does not mean causation, yet it is surprising how many older models of concepts assumed that an account of supposedly objective correlational structure was a complete basis for specifying concept structure.

Therefore patterns of causal–explanatory understanding strongly influence similarity relations, perceived correlations and properties, and hence categories and concepts. The structure of concepts themselves is assumed to depend on characterizations of their relations to those patterns of explanation. Clusters of causal–explanatory beliefs are often said to form coherent intuitive theories in which concepts dwell parasitically (Murphy and Medin 1985).

It seems natural to refer to the patterns of explanation as clusters of beliefs, and that usage will initially be adopted here. However, there may be alternative ways of representing tendencies to adopt certain patterns of causal explanation, tendencies that themselves are not true theories. Many of the patterns discussed so far do not depend crucially on the presence of beliefs *per se*, a point that may be particularly critical in our models of how infants come to understand events. Some speculations on such alternatives are offered later in this chapter in the discussion of perceived causal powers.

ASSOCIATION AND AUGMENTATION

Even as the importance of sets of causal explanation in restructuring similarity and concepts has emerged, there has simultaneously developed a stronger appreciation of the need for a rich associative-like structure to explain much of what we do with concepts. For all but the most contrived cases, it seems that concepts are intrinsic mixes not only of clusters of theory-like explanations but also of atheoretic tabulations of properties.

A personal anecdote may help to illustrate the pervasive need for both associative and theory-driven components. One of my children recently chose to assemble an enormous shell collection for a school science project. As the different types of shells began to proliferate on our dining room table, I realized that I had only *one* causally relevant way of organizing the shell — whether they were univalves (a single shell unit) or bivalves (two opposing halves). Some hypotheses about this contrast and how it might relate to other properties allowed me to interpret several properties that seemed to co-occur among the two types. It was also obvious that there were hundreds of distinct shell types within each of these two categories, and as my son sorted them accordingly, I found myself able to classify items into some of the subgroups as well.

However, this secondary classification was based solely on prototype-like tabulations of visible properties of the shells and without any further reference to causal–explanatory relations (except, of course, that I did have explanation-driven broad hunches about the general relevance of some properties even for the prototype abstraction process, i.e. I did not tabulate information on how many sand grains were left in a shell, or whether the shell had a small chip or its surface.) In fact, the associative tabulations of perceptual properties were vital to the shell project. They provided a critical data set for my son as he read more about shells and learned new causally related principles for the properties of subtypes. They even guided his reading when the prototypes suggested two different categories, and he looked further for information that would provide a reason. Thus the associatively stored information serves as a data base that supports further theory building and concept elaboration, even as the earliest stages of the theory provided hunches about what sorts of properties were likely to be relevant. (It may be that the early theories say less about probable correlations between properties and more about what properties are likely to be important, a point considered again later in this paper.)

The reason for resorting to feature tabulations is simple. No set of explanatory beliefs can ever hope to explain fully all the reasons why categories and subcategories have distinctive features. Eventually all theories fail to provide further explanation for consistent differences in the social and physical worlds. When this happens, we have to fall back on the less efficient but more universal default mechanism of tabulating feature frequencies. We need such tabulations to help us store information as data for further theory development, unless we wish to have no information whatsoever stored that is not fully understood by current theories, a pattern that is neither efficient nor fits with our intuitions.

One might try to exclude the frequency and correlation information from the concept proper, and say that it is only part of the identification procedure; however, I cannot see any basis for such a move because our beliefs are often directed specifically towards explaining those correlations. They form an integral part of the system. Only in special cases, where we have conventionally defined concepts with accidentally correlated features, such as the concept odd number, do the two aspects become fully separate. Although correlation may not mean causation, we are powerfully compelled by most correlations to look for a causal basis. There must not only be belief-like structures that narrow down an indefinitely large number of features and feature relations to a manageable number, but also mechanisms for storing information that is outside the ken of present beliefs. Perhaps most importantly, there must also be a mechanism for linking together our explanatory structures with the tabulations of feature frequencies and correlations, i.e. the theory with the data. Of course, the theory tells one what sort of data to look for, but never so exhaustively as to stipulate all frequencies and correlations. Each side would seem to work through a series of successive approximations supported by changes in the other. The details of such an interaction have been sadly neglected in current models of concepts, but will be central to a full account.

In my own research over the years, it took some time to appreciate fully both facets of concept structure. Some of my earlier studies of concept growth seemed to suggest a shift from young children organizing natural-kind concepts primarily in terms of an associative structure and then shifting to a more principled structure consisting of a set of core-theoretical beliefs. For example young children asserted that zebras who were surgically transformed to look and act like horses were no longer zebras and were truly horses. Older children declared the animal still to be a zebra, suggesting a developmental shift from a phenomenal similarity space to a theoretically driven space. In fact this seems to be precisely the pattern described by Quine (1977) in his classic essay on natural kinds.

However, after many follow-up studies conducted by both my research group and others, a more intricate description has emerged (Keil 1989). Even the youngest children never seem to be total phenomenalists helplessly buffeted about by correlations and frequencies among perceptually salient properties. There invariably seems to be an understanding of deeper relations that allows them to go beyond phenomenal similarity. Thus, even for 3-year-old children, tigers can only be changed into lions if the mechanism of change is plausibly related to being a member of the two kinds. Younger children's beliefs about such mechanisms may differ, but they have them none the less and will use them to override surface similarity information.

At any age, most natural concepts always seem to have a mix of associationistic tabulated information and coherent sets of beliefs for interpreting, explaining, and guiding the acquisition of that information. There can be dramatic developmental change, but not from one kind of representational system to a completely different one. Instead, the predominant change may be in how extensively beliefs are able to interpret and explain the raw data of association. As those beliefs become more and more elaborated over time, the child has to fall back less and less on the associative component to make judgements.

For example, suppose that a child's initial understanding of birds only involved notions of what properties supported flight, and thereby understood clusters of features corresponding to flightless versus flying birds, but did not understand how to organize the features that clustered around predator versus prey. Some more general principles about animals may bias the child to store associatively frequencies and correlation concerning features such as foot shape, beak shape, eye location in head, and typical diet, but these properties may be stored largely in terms of associative relations until the predator–prey insight comes to organize those features dramatically and to shift similarities accordingly.

DUALISM AND DEVELOPMENT

The Quinean version of how we come to understand natural kinds not only seems to conflict with available data, but is also challenged by the failure of attempts to model the emergence of beliefs, causal explanations, and theories out of a network of associations operating on simple primitives. Instead, from the start, the child seems to be endowed with causal-explanatory biases that constrain concept growth. A central question to much of this volume asks how many of these initial biases there might be and what their format could be, i.e. as theories with clusters of beliefs or in a form that would precede such a proposition-like structure but still effectively constrain it.

At this point, the evidence, much of it presented in this book, strongly points to at least two sets of explanatory biases corresponding to two conceptual domains: a physical–mechanical domain that helps explain the properties of kinds subject to mechanical causality, and a folk psychological domain that helps explain the properties of kinds subject to belief–desire accounts of causation. These are radically different ways of construing the world that result in sharply contrasting assumptions about how to relate properties and understand their causal powers.

Carey (1985) was one of the first to postulate the early influences of an intuitive physics and psychology, and, as seen in this volume, the subsequent evidence for the early and universal appearance of these two domains is now robust and diverse. Infants have clear and systematic intuitions about the mechanics of physical objects, and there is increasing evidence for predispositions that lead to a folk psychology and to its disruption in autistic children. There remains much controversy about how intuitive mechanics and psychology should be represented and how they should relate to adult verbalizable intuitions, but beyond those debates there is a consensus that the mental capacities responsible for such intuitive systems do not seem to arise from a single general learning device that has no constraints tailored for each of these two kinds of information. Even the latest connectionist accounts have started to suggest that sets of contrasting biases might favour acquisition of knowledge diverging on two different paths. However, such accounts try to reduce the biases to exceedingly basic non-cognitive primitives, as in attempts to make the 'what' and 'where' centres of the brain be solely a consequence of networks with response rates that are slow versus fast (J. McClelland, forthcoming). Models based solely on such low level biases must face some particularly awkward facts, such as that infants quickly grasp solidity and continuity but take much longer to understand gravity, even though gravity would seem to be just as salient to a general learning device subject only to low level constraints. What sort of 'subsymbolic' bias could lead to such different rates of learning? (However, recent accounts of the more gradual incremental nature of the acquisition of knowledge of physical mechanics open the door for more general learning accounts (Slater 1993; Chapter 4 of this volume).

The early emergence of intuitive psychology and physics raises the interesting possibility that initially, the child has only these two modes of explanation. If so, most concepts must be assimilated into one of these two ways of understanding the world to access any causal–explanatory insight. Such assimilations would result in powerful predictions about the nature of early concepts. If a child is presented with partial information about a novel kind, she will try to decide whether its known and future properties are to be interpreted in belief–desire terms or in physical–mechanical terms, and ensuing inductions about properties will vary accordingly. According to some accounts, even by 6 years of age, children can only causally understand natural kind in physical–mechanical or psychological terms, or else they fall back on more brute-force associative inferences.

It has been speculated that biological kinds and their properties are first interpreted solely in behavioural terms, and in some tasks young children do appear to attribute properties such as eating and sleeping only to those animals that are sufficiently psychologically similar to humans so as to have the behavioural and belief–desire correlates of sleeping and eating. If an animal is seen as having the psychological capacities to feel tired, desire sleep, and behave in a fatigued manner, it sleeps. Similarly, if an animal can feel hungry, know that it wants food, and can enjoy consuming it, it eats (Carey 1985). An appreciation of biological kinds as such would emerge only at a later period in development, causing a profound restructuring of how categories are understood and used. In the course of development there would be a radical shift in how concepts for roughly the same class of entities are understood, such that very different patterns of induction concerning novel properties are licensed. In a related, but more moderate view, younger children would have a greater tendency to make such behavioural interpretations for biological phenomena. That tendency might reflect a less well-developed set of biological explanations, but it does not rule out the ability to entertain such explanations altogether.

PRIMAL PLURALISM: THE CASE OF TELEOLOGICAL EXPLANATION

There is wide agreement that the two primal conceptual domains of physics and psychology (but not a fully fledged theory of mind) are prelinguistic, if not outright innate. However, with only two initial domains, much of conceptual development would have to consist of the distortion of all concepts to fit into this initial state, which would then have to be followed by radical restructurings as new domains, such as biology, arise. Two domains may grossly underestimate the extent to which even the very young child can use different explanatory systems to make sense of the world. It may not be enough to grant the young child theory-like beliefs about only physical objects and psychological beings.

Early thought about living things may not be so neatly subsumed under the psychological heading after all, although fallbacks on this mode may be more common. A larger set of early modes of construal may be needed to model even the earliest stages of conceptual development. In fact, if one grants just six such modes, one is led to a radically different model of the origins of causal understandings, particularly given the combinatorial powers among even such a small number of modes. Just two modes can allow only one possible combination, but among six modes there are hundreds of different possible combinations of different subsets of those six elements. Here, the case of biological thought is explored as part of the more general question of how we might decide about other domains, kinds of understandings, and their emergence. We start with a possible mode of construal concerning functional things, or those whose properties have purposes.

Historically there have been many arguments for a 'design' stance, which can include teleological interpretations and tool construction and use (Dennett 1987). Notions of functional architecture are among the most cognitively compelling ways of approaching the biological world and much of the artificial world as well, and indeed both Mayr and Gould have frequently lamented excessive zeal in using teleological–adaptive explanations for living things (Gould and Lewontin 1978; Mayr 1982). As that theme is covered in much more detail elsewhere (Keil 1992; Keil 1994), in this account we briefly mention some relevant empirical demonstrations in elementary school and pre-school children, and then turn to the question of how the earliest modes of construal might be set up and linked to kinds.

One line of work shows that preschool children prefer teleological explanations as *fitting* better with living than with non-living things. Thus they come to understand that it makes sense to ask what a green colour 'does for' a plant or an animal, but not what it does for a naturally occurring crystal or liquid. Properties have purposes for living things and artefacts

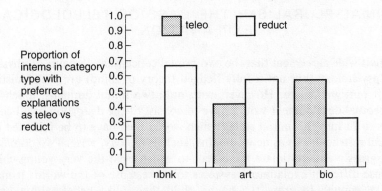

Fig. 9.2. Results of a study asking 5-year-old children to match explanations with either a teleological or reductionist structure to non-living natural kinds (nlnk), artefacts (art), or living natural kinds (bio).

in ways that they do not for other sorts of things. One such pattern of results with a group of 5-year-old children is shown in Fig. 9.2. Bland reductionist explanations for a property are preferred for non-living natural kinds, whereas teleological explanations are preferred for living kinds even though reductionist explanations could work as well; with artefacts, the two kinds of explanations are chosen equally.

However, this research has its limits. Despite occasional spontaneous utterances in much younger children suggesting some linking of the stance to living things, we have found over a large series of laborious studies that children younger than 5 years tend to become confused by the complex locutions of such tasks. They have difficulty in evaluating competing explanations when presented in such a form, raising questions about whether the earliest versions of this stance are fully explicit beliefs. Secondly, these methods force us to use the same properties for all sorts of kinds when, as seen shortly, their importance may vary greatly as a function of the type of kind.

BEHAVIOUR VERSUS BIOLOGY

The 'design' stance leads to different understandings of why properties exist and to different inductions about other properties. Moreover, it can easily be separated from psychological causes, even though some have cast teleological thought in terms of attributing intentions to a causal system with 'goals'. We have explored this issue by looking at many aspects of living things, in each case asking, how well behavioural explanations and mechanisms can be distinguished from biological–functional ones. For example, pre-school children see behavioural–mental anomalies as being transmitted to others in a manner that is profoundly different from physiological–functional anomalies. Although social attributes such as laughter, sadness, and general excitement are certainly transmitted across individuals as well, children understand that the conditions of transmission of such social properties involve fundamentally different mechanisms not implicated by the normal use of 'catching' something (Keil 1994).

What is the basis for this distinction? What are young children picking up in these afflictions that make them so clearly non-contagious, even when there can be clear physiological consequences much like those of known contagious diseases? We have looked more closely at contagion as a function of more subtle degrees of involvement of mental and behavioural states. For example, one can envisage afflictions varying along the following continuum: deviant beliefs, intact beliefs but deviant mental operations (e.g. memory or attention deficits), intact beliefs and mental operations but deviant behaviour (such as facial tics and other involuntary body movements), and finally physiological ailments akin to normal diseases. If children held that contagious things were only those that kept beliefs intact, we might expect only the first to be non-contagious. If they held that clear mental states were not contagious, we might expect the second. If they thought that no behaviour was contagious, they might have also ruled out the third case.

A full exploration of these differences will require several studies, but one initial foray has involved asking children to decide which of two afflictions one is more likely to 'catch' when one has been in close physical proximity and had ample opportunity for touching, food sharing, and the like. As pragmatic factors ruled out running all possible pairs of affliction types, a range of contrasts was studied as a way of beginning to explore the underlying basis for the judgements. The design pitted physiological against behavioural afflictions, behavioural against mental afflictions, mental against false belief afflictions, and false belief against physiological afflictions. We suspected that physiological properties would be clearly distinct from the most belief-laden properties, but were less sure about the other two types of behavioural property.

In general, pre-school children saw the physiological afflictions as more contagious than all the behavioural afflictions, with no clear distinctions among the behavioural types. Apparently they did not rely on beliefs or attitudes, and broader notions of behaviour were sufficient to highlight an important contrast. The other contrasts were not different from each other, suggesting that they were all regarded as equally non-contagious. As the children grow older, the false belief-physiological contrast appears to become more salient relative to the others, suggesting a shift in how mental states are being interpreted. The precise relations among these different sorts of behavioural afflictions and their causal involvement in biological contagion await several further studies, but the findings so far do not support a possible continuum from false belief being least contagious through intact beliefs with defective mental procedures to aberrant behaviour being most contagious. Instead, the findings suggest more of an early dichotomy between all behavioural and all physiological afflictions. Other recent studies also support the pattern that pre-school children might lump together a wide range of psychological and behavioural patterns in their reasoning about causal interactions and see them as distinct group from physiological patterns (Solomon and Johnson 1993; Zaitchik 1993).

A functional mode of construal may be far more basic than these sorts of studies suggest. Even before the first year of life, infants will relate things on the basis of functional similarity, such as being a container, rather than on similarity of overall shape when the function is seen as important and enduring (V. Kolstad and R. Baillargeon, under review). This finding raises the question of whether understanding simple objects in functional terms in infancy might be a precursor of what becomes the teleological stance later on. Seeing things as if their properties have purposes may be essential to any understanding of tool use, design, or modification, and such abilities may have clear origins in infancy. However, the container studies alone do not demonstrate a design stance, as a sensitivity to functional attributes may substantially precede any sort of notion that properties tend to have purposes much more for some kinds of things than for others.

These and other studies suggest that perceiving some things in functional terms, and looking at their properties as if they have purposes, is a powerful way of organizing them and understanding their properties. Moreover, some sorts of properties may do more work for functional stances than for physical or intentional stances, and vice versa. Thus the shape of physical parts may be critically important for a functional stance, whereas weight may be more critical for the physical–mechanical stance. Weight is a critical relation in guiding inferences about the billiard ball mechanics of physical objects, but often plays a more indirect role in our understandings of most living things and artefacts (e.g. weight is only weakly correlated at the extremes with sucessful function as a chair or a television set).

ASSESSING ARTEFACTS

The teleological–design stance alone would not segregate the class of living things. After all, the properties of artefacts also have purposes, and according to at least some accounts psychological kinds might have properties that serve purposes as well (but perhaps only in the sociobiological sense).

We might thus conjecture that young children see the living and the artefactual in the same way, but that they can easily distinguish between these two kinds. The question is how and on what basis, ranging from simple perceptual routines to abstract conceptual relations.

One key difference in the conceptual realm concerns how causal patterns cluster and converge. Even though artefacts and natural kinds both have many salient properties with purposes, the purposes themselves and the causal relations that they enter into may have inportant differences. With simple artefacts in particular, most salient properties serve the goals and purposes of another entity, usually intentional agents that use the artefact. Barbed wire has thorns not to help itself, but to serve the needs of others. Roses are thought to have thorns to help themselves. Pliers have a part that squeezes not to enable the pliers but to enable those using the pliers, while lobsters have comparable structures to help themselves. The difference is captured roughly in Fig. 9.1, where the networks of causal relations converge in the artefact case to serve the needs of an external individual but converge inwardly in the biological case to serve the needs of a plant or animal. (Other possible ways of understanding living kinds may be associated with different patterns in Fig. 9.1.)

Of course, there are exceptions. As artefacts become more complex, they develop increasingly homeostatic mechanisms that, in a local sense, serve the needs of the artefact itself, whether they are the cooling fans in a computer, a governor in an engine, or one of many safeguards in a nuclear reactor. Even in these cases, however, the causal chain is rarely more than one or two steps away from those of an external agent. A computer has a fan to keep it from overheating, so that it can be used at any time and for as long as required. An engine has a governer to prevent it from running too fast and breaking down, so that it can no longer carry out the function desired by the user. Such short steps to the goals of an outside intentional agent do not usually exist for plants and animals. Of course, almost all properties of animals and plants are closely linked to their environmental niches, but an understanding of both the purposes that they serve in real time and the causal forces behind their emergence tend to converge back inside the organism itself, whereas comparable accounts for the real-time purposes and causal origins of artefact properties invariably lead outside the artefact. A related difference involves how we conceive of the historical contexts relevant to understanding the properties of artefacts and living things. Much longer and more intricate historical chains can be assumed for living things (from a talk delivered at Cornell University, November 1992 by R. Milliken).

The lines will become increasingly blurred as domestication of plants and animals becomes ever more sophisticated through genetic engineering. Many properties of dog species or apples are present largely because they were heavily selected for by breeders who needed those properties for their own ends, and these influences are clearly increasing. Even with these exceptions, however, it seems likely that our first notions of the living and artificial worlds are profoundly different because of how we view the patterns of causal convergence. Indeed, these differences may well be related to the notions that living things have essences and/or vital forces while artefacts do not—notions which appear to be universally robust (Atran 1990; Hatano *et al.* 1993). Notions of essence, perhaps even in their less mechanical vitalist forms, may spring from a more correct understanding of how causal relations link properties together and explain their presence.

Young children also seem to be sensitive to these differences in causal direction. One study in progress explores these issues with five animal–artefact pairs and five plant–artefact pairs. In all cases not only were the parts perceptually similar, but they also served a similar purpose; the difference lies in where that purpose is ultimately directed and in understanding why the entity possessed it. The same immediate purpose was described for both members of each pair, with no mention made of the ultimate direction. Children were then asked about the direction. For example, one pair involved a section of barbed wire and a rose, and the thorn-like parts on each. The thorns were described as sharp and painful to any humans or animals that touched them. Unfamilar objects were also used, such as a digging tool and a sloth, both of which possess similarly shaped parts that pull small objects out of the earth. Children were shown these diagrams and asked which of the two had the property for itself rather than for others. A study in progress suggests that this difference in purpose may be understood by children as young as 3 years. If children are asked about the consequences of a property 'becoming absent', they similarly seem to understand that the patterns of consequences are different for living kinds compared with artefacts.

A related study has been conducted based on the notion that asking questions about the purpose of an entire entity makes good sense for artefacts but is confusing for living kinds, whereas questions about the purposes of properties make sense for both. It appears that preschool children give different patterns of answers to these questions when asked about artefacts compared with living kinds, such as giving more immediate and elaborate answers for artefacts when asked about the function of the artefact as a whole (Bloom and Kelleman, personal communication). When a reply is given for living kinds, it is likely to involve a reinterpretation of the question in a way that is related to its own functions (e.g. 'What is an oak tree for?' 'For growing').

CHARACTERIZING CONSTRUALS

What are the consequences of a view that stresses a greater pluralism in early modes of construal, such that we might have as many as a dozen or so instead of just two? One key consequence is that most of the developmental changes in how concepts are represented and used may not reflect the emergence of radically different modes of explanation as much as a shift between uses of modes that are already present. Even the youngest child may possess a wide array of explanatory systems, but may have different defaults and/or biases concerning when to use them in given contexts, and perhaps simply cannot use them at all in some cases early on. This possibility does not disallow theory change or local conceptual revolution, but it does ask if there might not be a small set of explanatory frameworks within which the tempests of theory change may occur while still obeying the constraints of those frameworks.

Therefore young children may have a diverse yet manageable array of modes of construal. These can create an early ontology that highlights such categories as simple solid objects, intentional beings, functional kinds, and perhaps half a dozen more (others might include fluids, morally evaluable acts, and social exchanges). Cases of apparently dramatic change may reflect more the finding of a different resonance with the basic grab-bag of fundamental modes of construal—resonances with real-world patterns of homeostasis. Many far more fine-grained theories and subtheories will also develop, but the basic modes of explanation may be more constant over the course of development. Distinguishing these modes from local theories is a central problem which is discussed later in this paper. Of course we can never fully apprehend these real-world patterns as individuals in a naive untutored way, and perhaps not even in the most sophisticated scientific communities, but we do partially resonate—hence our inductive successes. It has been argued for centuries that one can never fully know the 'real' essence (or presumably the full set of core causal relations) for natural kinds (Locke 1690). The complexity and interconnectedness of these relations may be too complex for us to grasp fully, but at the same time we must remember how well our inductions actually work in the real world.

These early modes of construal still need to be characterized in a way that not only effectively guides and channels theory construction, but which also conforms with the most reasonable statements of what young children and infants actually know. It is tempting to look for perceptual cues and biases that might set off a chain of events leading to different theories, but these invariably seem to end by being too impoverished to act as the flexible and powerful guides of theory development that we need. One example is the discussion of the inabilities of even complex configural perceptual laws to explain infants' understanding of physical objects (Spelke *et al.* 1992).

Instead, early biases may be linked to how the perceived causal powers of properties vary as a function of the kind of thing involved. Therefore pretheoretical biases might include notions of what properties and relations are central to organizing such things as functional/designed entities compared with mere substances. Such biases are one step down from those inherent in patterns of predicability, where kinds of properties cannot even be ascribed to kinds of things, such as colour or shape to an idea (Keil 1979). At this level, of all the properties that an entity can possess, only some types are likely to be causally potent or central to explanation. One might have strong beliefs about what sorts of properties are central, while having has *no* idea about the specific causal relations involved.

The possibility that causal powers of properties vary across types of things points to an intrinsic limitation in the teleological inference studies mentioned earlier. That method required the same property to be used across all types, with only the explanation for the property varying; however, if the properties themselves are seen as having different causal roles as a function of the type involved, those differences would work against any effects. For example, if colour is seen as causally irrelevant for most artefacts, then choosing among reasons for the presence of a particular colour on artefacts will be less meaningful than comparable choices for plants. Similarly, if shape is more important for living kinds than for substances, asking about the purpose of a shape for both is not a sensitive measure. Thus it makes sense to look more directly at notions of how property types might organize different kinds and to ask how such relations might be related to early causal understandings.

PROPERTIES, POWERS, AND KINDS

If the perceived causal powers of properties vary across type of kind, the empirical support of such perceived variations might be linked to the general modes of construal, where different property type clusters are associated with different modes. My colleagues and I have been conducting a series of studies with both children and adults to try to understand better how basic modes of construal might interact with interpretations of the importance of properties.

One set of studies has focused on adult intuitions concerning the importance of properties to category and lexical assignment (G. Gruberth and F. C. Keil, in preparation). The experimental paradigm involves describing counterfactual changes in types of properties of typical members of familiar categories and then asking about the effects of these changes on category membership, labelling, and ability to function as a member of that kind. Four changes in property types have been used: colour, size, shape (as specified by a tripling of width and a one-third reduction of height), and surface pattern. These changes were described for randomly selected members of four categories: animals, plants, artefacts, and non-living natural kinds such as rocks. For example, some subjects might be told that an artefact is exactly like an ordinary chair in every way except that it is uniformly bright pink, and would then be asked if the item could still be called a chair. They might be told about rocks that are just like gold except that they are uniformly bright pink, and asked if they could be called gold.

We have found a strong relation between kind of property and kind of thing. Thus overall shape and size changes had profound impacts on the functional roles of artefacts as well as on their names. In contrast, colour and surface patternings were deemed almost completely irrelevant for all artefacts. The effects were roughly reversed for non-living natural kinds, with colour and patterning seen as essential to the judgements, and shape and size as largely irrelevant. For both plants and animals the results were again distinct, suggesting a set of expectations about the category of living things in general. Thus the profile is different from both non-living natural kinds and artefacts. More subtle patterns are suggested by other judgements. Thus, while shape change is seen as having a dramatic functional consequence for both artefacts and living things, comparable size changes are seen as much more a causally potent factor for artefacts than for living things.

One final measurement adds an important twist. After all the initial ratings were completed, subjects were asked to consider ordinary exemplars of each of the categories judged and to rate how much those items normally vary with respect to overall shape, size, colour, or patterning. Thus a subject might be asked to judge how much ordinary chairs or humpback whales vary in colour. These questions were designed to address an important issue: how much the natural variability of features in a category could cause the discounting or emphasis of the importance of features. Subjects in prior studies have judged a 2 inch disc as more likely to be a pizza than a quarter, even though it is more similar to the quarter in physical size. The minimal variability of currency disallows even modest size changes, whereas the larger variability of size for pizzas allows for a very small, albeit implausible, pizza (Rips 1989).

In our studies, the effects have not been reducible to variability. Although variability judgements show considerable intersubject reliability across kinds and properties, when they are factored out of the analysis most of the patterns remain as before, although they are sometimes diminished. Subjects appear to be well aware of variability and sometimes use causal beliefs to try to understand it, but it is not the direct source of those beliefs.

These patterns, including the modest influence of variability, have been fully replicated with different properties and instances of category members. Thus the same general biases about causal roles of properties emerge across a wide range of instances. The small variability effect points towards a highly abstract model of how properties are causally central to kinds—a model that is relatively impervious to information about local instances. We are now extending the study to pictorial stimuli with novel animals and plants where variability is not known. Thus it will be possible to make direct comparisons of cases with *no* variability information against familar instances where clear intuitions of property variability can exist.

Therefore these studies reveal three key points about adult concepts.

1. The perceived importance of properties to kinds varies dramatically as a function of the type of kind.

2. The changing patterns across kinds cannot be explained by the degree of variability of those properties in a category, nor by their typicality in the category (this last finding should gain additional support from a current study using visual depictions of unfamiliar objects).

3. The category level at which property–kind interactions occur is abstract and high level, and seems to be divorced from the effects of local knowledge.

Even if adults are strongly influenced by abstract explanatory systems in their interpretations of the importance of properties for things, such systems might not be present early in life. Perhaps sets of general theoretical biases precede beliefs about causal roles of particular properties, arising only later as the theories become implemented. Alternatively, such views about properties may help to guide the nascent theories themselves. We have begun a series of studies addressing these two alternatives by looking at developmental patterns in pre-school and elementary school children (F. C. Keil, C. Gochicoa, and D. Sebba, in preparation).

One set of studies uses triads of pictures in which an unfamiliar item with a novel name is shown followed by an object that varies in the shapes of the most salient parts but which preserves colour and surface patterning, and another object that preserves all shapes but varies in colours and surface patterning. Therefore two different kinds of properties are manipulated. The children are then asked which of the two altered cases is more likely to be of the same kind as the original. In each case the novel item and name are clearly depicted as being from one of four categories: artefact, plant, animal, or non-living natural kind. Moreover, the verbal descriptions do not differentiate between count and mass nouns (e.g 'this is an animal that is in the hyrax group', and 'this is a rock that is in the malachite group' or 'this is my hyrax ... it is a kind of animal' and 'this is my malachite ... it is a kind of rock' ... 'which of these is also my hyrax?').

The studies are still underway but some patterns are robust and replicate those found in pilot studies. For non-living natural kinds, it is more common to ignore shape in deciding which of the other pictures indicates the entity that shares the same label. For the living kinds and the artefacts, shape differences, as depicted by different parts, are much more important. Moreover, there is a further suggestion that colour and texture also play a role for living things but not for artefacts where, with few exceptions, they may apparently be understood as purely conventional. This insight may become stronger as the children grow older and enter elementary school, a pattern that is now under study.

Perhaps the changes for the non-living kinds were less dramatic because of the difficulty of quantifying degree of shape change and thereby equating it across stimulus groups. The much smaller generalization by shape for non-living natural kinds could reflect smaller real changes of shape for those stimuli. Adult intuitions about these triad pictures argue against such a possibility, but a more convincing reply uses ambiguous displays where exactly the same set of triads is labelled in one case as a kind of animal and in the other case as a kind of non-living natural kind.

In these cases, with precisely the same display, generalizations might differ depending on whether the depicted entity is construed as a living versus a non-living kind. Our results so far suggest that the same pattern is occurring. When a rock–frog entity is labelled a frog, shape rather than colour and surface markings determines choice, but when it is labelled a rock, colour and surface markings become more important. No simple set of perceptual features drives these notions of what properties are most causally potent. Instead, these properties have to be understood in the context of the kind of thing involved. This pattern argues against any sort of global shape bias in early categorization.

Patterns of overall shape changes may be far too crude to capture the full spectrum of young children's causal expectations. One case might involve a special importance of perceived parts. Again and again, it seems that teleological explanations are particularly prominent in explanations of distinct parts as opposed to the more global properties of an object. There have been several studies suggesting a link between perceived parts of objects and functions, as well as with the basic level of categorization where specific functional relations are supposed to be particularly distinctive (Tversky and Hemenway 1984; Murphy 1992). The question here is whether attention to part-like properties becomes particularly strong and compelling when they are understood to belong to a living thing.

One way of assessing such differences involved changes of an object's overall shape that kept local parts and their relative relations generally intact, as opposed to changes that modified local parts but kept overall

Fig. 9.3. Examples of some stimuli used in a current study of the relative importance of overall shape versus local parts for different kinds of objects.

shape and patterning intact. Stimuli of this sort can be created by graphics programs that allow each member of a set of images to be distorted in precisely the same way. Consider the examples shown in Fig. 9.3 where both artefacts and living kinds are distorted by a 'twirling' algorithm that moves pixel clusters according to a function starting from the centre of the object.

The parts changes are more difficult to quantify and equate across items, but one check requires that part alterations did not change the overall shape when blurred. Thus these changes depicted clear changes in local parts and not in overall shape. In addition, some of the parts changes suggested breakdown of local function, making any tests of a difference very conservative. If a child still chose the artefact with the same overall shape, but part changes which destroy function, over its opposite, the artefact–living kind difference might be particularly dramatic. The results for adults are clear: overall shape changes matter very little for animal and plant membership judgements in comparison with local part changes. For artefacts, the overall shape changes impact more on function, and hence on category type, and subjects showed more equal choices between the two.

A study exploring the same contrast with children ranging from pre-school to middle elementary school age is now under way. At this point, the configuration of local parts seem to be more important for living things, and overall shape seems to be more important for the artefacts. In addition, a set of ambiguous displays described as either artefacts versus plants or artefacts versus animals have been created and children have been asked which sorts of changes have the largest effect. With such displays, parts changes are deemed more important for the living things than for the artefacts, whereas overall shape changes have the opposite effect.

These early studies are just beginning to uncover the details of how and at what levels of abstraction property types interact with categories. The examples offered here raise the possibility that when an item is represented, both patterns of change in that representation and patterns of initial acquisition may flow mostly from our beliefs about the basic kinds of things there are, and what sorts of properties and relations are most explanatorily central to those kinds. Shape, like any other property, may be theory dependent for its perceived causal powers and central organizing role in a category. The preliminary pre-school studies conducted so far offer evidence that young children have sets of strong expectations about the probable causal powers of different properties in organizing categories at a high level of abstraction, such as living thing and artefact. When we look at individual items, the influence does not vary much across items within these larger categories, arguing against the simple storage of concrete exemplars and comparison with those instances.

The specificity problem

These patterns of judgement about causal powers of properties are more interesting if there is a distinctive level corresponding to the general modes of construal which is different from all the local clusters of beliefs and theories that we are constantly acquiring about specific phenomena. Several strands of empirical evidence converge to support such a distinctive level, but a more direct assessment is needed. Do property–category interaction effects lose their strength across subject consistency when examined at finer levels of categoiization? Pre-experimental intuitions may be revealing. Consider, for example, the possibility of property – category interactions for fish versus mammals. Any properties selected must be applicable to both typical fish and typical mammals and must also be negatable. One cannot have the property 'breathes underwater', since that property only applies to normal fish. Instead, the closest appropriate property would be described by phrases such as 'breathes in only one fluid medium'. The negation of the property would then be something like 'consider this new animal that is just like other fish (or other animal type) in every way except that it breathes in a different fluid medium'. Such a fish would seem to be as different from the typical fish as would a mammal that had its fluid medium of breathing changed. Similarly, if properties of life-span or growth rate are changed (e.g. x is like y in every way except that it grows into adult form five times as fast), the changes do not seem to discriminate different subclasses of living things neatly. There may be local differences across individuals, but no generalizations for sets of subclasses seem to emerge.

If broader properties are considered, such as shape, material composition, and colour, the property-by-category effect seems to be largest at the level consisting of modes of construal, and not at lower or more abstract levels. Thus, counterfactuals may be most distinctive across categories at the level of modes of construal. More generally, the kinds of properties that seem to have the largest effects also seem primarily to have systematic effects with categories at the very broad levels correlated with modes of construal.

GLOBAL VERSUS LOCAL EXPLANATIONS

Throughout this paper it has been argued that no adequate model of concepts (or how we use them in induction, in conceptual combinations, or in inferences) can avoid reference to causal explanation, and both adult and developmental data support this conclusion. Moreover, it has been common, at least in adults, to refer to these patterns of explanation as intuitive theories that are clustered in domains. Almost everyone would agree that our beliefs about causal laws are unevenly distributed. They cluster in ways that suggest domains of explanation, which is why we talk about distinct theories even when they have links to other domains. Of course, this notion follows from the causal homeostasis model. Moreover, it seems that we rarely mix broad theories. We have general laws relating beliefs and desires, and laws relating solidity and mass, but few laws apply across these two domains, for example linking desire and solidity.

However, there is a problem. I have suggested that there might be only a handful of fundamental explanatory modes of construal, yet in one sense they would appear to be unlimited. There are explanatory networks for steam heating systems known only by plumbers, with many unique terms that are functionally defined in terms of other terms unique to boilers, such as the Hartford loop which is a special convolution of pipe designed for certain pressure gradients. Cardiologists have similar clusters of terms and laws for hearts, as do a host of other professionals and experts. In most of these cases some terms can only be understood by knowing how they are embedded in the larger system of causal relations of that domain. This is true for terms ranging from 'gene' to 'leveraged buy-out' to 'black hole'. Are these thousands of areas of expertise to be considered on the same terms as a naive psychology, physics, or biology? An enormous number of stable patterns of regularities in the world are relatively circumscribed and could spawn a separate 'theoretical' domain. Most, if not all, of these would presumably be learned through a general learning procedure, since the possibility of a priori dispositions to learn about steam heating systems or hearts or money supply are remote. To the extent that these domains of explanation seem the same as the very young child's modes of construal, we are inclined to see all these forms of understanding as acquired through a single general learning system.

An alternative model would maintain that the handful of fundamental modes of construal has a distinct status that makes these importantly different from local areas of expertise. These fundamental modes may yield notions of ontological kinds in ways not done by local expertise, and they may always be present as a kind of background skeleton when even the most local systems of explanation are also invoked. The plumber's expertise sits inside a more basic framework of causal understandings involving fluids and containers which must be presupposed for the more specific beliefs to be meaningful. The critical question asks whether the most basic forms of understanding are all present from the start, or whether some can emerge through conceptual change and yet still be different from local expertise. When a child comes to learn the difference between weight and density, is that insight part of a fundamental mode of construal or is it a local area of expertise? Can the skeletons themselves gradually be changed through conceptual change such that, even if constraints are needed at the start, nothing of the original remains after enough time has elapsed? Therefore we can envisage two very different accounts of how the basic modes can be involved in cognitive development.

To date, the evidence is still consistent with the notion that much of development and much of our adult intellectual adventures involve trying to see which mode of construal best fits a phenomenon, sometimes trying several different ones, such as thinking of a computer in anthropomorphic 'folk-psychology' terms, in fluid dynamic terms, or in physical–mechanical terms. In some cases, such as the computer, each of these can provide its own insights and distortions. Support for this view will require evidence from many diverse sources, some of which may lie in extensions of the work described here. Thus, if counterfactual statements about properties seem to have only systematic effects at very broad levels of categorization, a small number of basic domains corresponding to those broad levels of explanation might come to have a special status. If patterns of development suggest certain invariant skeletal influences with subtle but powerful effects in adults, such as the suggestions by Spelke *et al.* (1992) regarding misconceptions of physics in adults, the same view is again supported. If the patterns do not show such effects, the challenge is to explain how the acquisition of new modes of understanding and new appreciations of kinds of causal patterning emerge solely by means of general learning principles.

CONCLUSIONS

In sum, three themes have been considered here.

1. One cannot build a coherent account of our concepts of the natural world without some hypotheses about how that world is really structured. This does not mean that we merely reflect that structure or ever fully know it, but it does ask if we can be fully non-committal about metaphysics when trying to understand how we represent concepts.

2. Both empirical studies and some more principled arguments suggest that the property homeostasis view of natural kinds fits very nicely with a psychological model of concepts as always embedded in theory-like structures which owe their origins to a small but diverse set of fundamental modes of construal – a model that posits a specific view of conceptual change.

3. Finally, one key part of these early modes of construal, which may precede the appearance of fully fledged theories, may be more general expectations about how the causal powers of types of properties, such as colours versus shapes, vary strongly as a function of these general

categories and not at more fine-grained levels. These expectations might exist before any specific explanation or detailed intuitive theory, and thus indicate kinds of explanations rather than any particular explanation.

Ultimately, expectations about causal powers may have a special status that is independent of local kinds and categories, and which suggests higher-order regularities in how we come to structure causal understandings. A key question is how far these expectations can carry us.

ACKNOWLEDGEMENTS

The preparation of this paper and much of the research described herein was supported by National Institutes of Health grant R01-HD23922.

REFERENCES

Atran, S. (1990). *Cognitive foundations of natural history: towards an anthropology of science.* Cambridge University Press.

Cannon, W. B. (1932). *The wisdom of the body.* Norton, New York.

Carey, S. (1985). *Conceptual change in childhood.* MIT Press, Cambridge, MA.

Chapman, L. J. and Chapman, J. P. (1969). Illusory correlation as an obstacle to the use of valid psychodiagnostic signs. *Journal of Abnormal Psychology* **74**, 272–80.

Dennett, D. C. (1987). *The intentional stance.* MIT Press, Cambridge, MA.

Dupré, J. (1981). Biological taxa as natural kinds. *Philosophical Review* **90**, 66–90.

Gould, S. J. and Lewontin, R. C. (1978). The spandrels of San Marco and the Panglossian paradigm. *Proceedings of the Royal Society of London* **205**, 581–98.

Hatano, G., Siegler, R. S., Inagaki, K., Stavy, R. and Wax, N. (1993). The development of Biological knowledge: a multi-national Study. *Cognitive Development.*

Keil, F. C. (1979). *Semantic and conceptual development: an ontological perspective.* Harvard University Press, Cambridge, MA.

Keil, F. C. (1989). *Concepts, kinds and cognitive development.* Bradford Books of MIT Press.

Keil, F. C. (1992). The origins of an autonomous biology. In *Minnesota Symposium on Child Psychology* (ed. M. R. Gunnar and M. Maratsos), pp. 103–38. Erlbaum, Hillsdale, NJ.

Keil, F. C. (1994). The birth and nurturance of concepts by domains: the origins of concepts of living things. In *Mapping the mind*: domain specificity in cognition and culture (ed. L. Hirschfeld and S. Gelman), pp. 234–54. Cambridge University Press, New York.

Locke, J. [1690] (1964). *An essay concerning human understanding* (ed. A. D. Woozley). Meridian, New York.

McClelland, J. (paper on connectionism and cognitive development)

Mayr, E. (1982). *The growth of biological thought*. Harvard University Press, Cambridge, MA.

Medin, D. L. and Shoben, E. J. (1988). Context and structure in conceptual combination. *Cognitive Psychology* **20**, 158–90.

Medin, D. L. and Wattenmaker, W. D. (1987). Category cohesiveness, theories, and cognitive archeology. In *Concepts and conceptual development: ecological and intellectual factors in categorization* (ed. V. Neisser), pp. 25–62. Cambridge University Press, New York.

Murphy, G. L. and Medin, D. (1985). The role of theories in conceptual coherence. *Psychological Review* **92**, 289–316.

Niklas, K. J. (1992) *Plant biomechanics: an engineering approach to plant form and function*. University of Chicago Press.

Pierce, C. S. (1931–1935). *Collected papers of Charles Sanders Pierce*. Harvard University Press, Cambridge, MA.

Putnam, H. (1975). The meaning of meaning. In *Mind, language and reality* (ed. H. Putnam). Cambridge University Press, London.

Quine, W. V. O. (1977). Natural kinds. In *Naming, necessity, and natural kinds* (ed. S. P. Schwartz), pp. 155–75. Cornell University Press, Ithaca, NY.

Rey, G. (1983). Concepts and stereotypes. *Cognition* **15**, 237–62.

Rips, L. J. (1989). Similarity, typicality, and categorization. In *Similarity and anological reasoning* (ed. S. Vosnaidu and A. Ortony). Cambridge University Press, New York.

Solomon, G. A. and Johnson, S. C. (1993). Children's intuitive conceptions of inheritance. Presented at the Meeting of the Society for Research in Child Development, New Orleans, LA.

Slater, A. (1993). Comments on symposium on infant cognition. Presented at the Meeting of the Society for Research in Child Development, New Orleans, LA.

Spelke, E., Breinlinger, K., Macomber, J., and Jacobson, K. (1992). Origins of knowledge. *Psychological Review* **95**, 605–632.

Tversky, B. and Hemenway, K. (1984). Objects, parts, and categories. *Journal of Experimental Psychology: General* **113**(2), 169–93.

Zaitchik, D. (1993). Development of the child's theories of mind and biology. Presented at the Meeting of the Society for Research in Child Development, New Orleans, LA.

DISCUSSION

Participants: D. Andler, S. Atran, S. Carey, R. Gelman

Andler: 'Homeostasis' struck me as odd and misleading with reference to a cluster of causal factors which tend to go together and conspire to create conditions characteristic of a given natural kind, particularly if it is a living kind. That is because homeostasis implies a mechanism whereby deviation from equilibrium is corrected. In the present context, where is the equilibrium and sameness through change?

Keil: The notion of causal property homeostasis is different from the sense originally coined by Walter B. Cannon in his classic *The wisdom of the body* (Cannon 1932), which was in turn heavily inspired by Claude Bernard's observations of internal self-regulatory mechanisms in mammals. None the less I still agree with Boyd's use of the term in this context because several important parallels remain. The equilibrium in these cases involves a stable cluster of properties such that, if enough of those properties are present, they will form a stable entity that persists as such over time just because of causal interactions among those properties. Since each property supports several others, entities that tend to 'deviate' by having fewer in the cluster are more likely to disappear, and in doing so 'restore' the membership in the category, and the category as a whole, to a standard pattern. The category of birds maintains a kind of equilibrium because instances that lose too many of the bird-like properties either tend to cease to exist or change into something quite different that has its own stability. Therefore these local equilibria represent stable dynamic interaction patterns that are homestatic because deviations in the form of highly atypical property clusters tend not to be stable and go out of existence.

Atran: It is unclear whether the teleological mode (and perhaps the other modes) is initially a cross-domain way of thinking about the world that tends to become localized to one or more domains by trial and error (fitting the mode of construal to an object domain and finding that it readily gives a coherent causal story that unifies the domain), or whether this mode is originally bound to a specific domain (say, living kinds) used to elaborate that domain causally and then generalized (perhaps meta-cognitively) where possible to other domains once it is fully worked out for the case for which it was naturally selected. Either way you obtain the conceptual flexibility that you think so fundamental to human conceptualization of the world. You incline to the first story: a generalized, or at least unlocalized, teleological mode that appears to lie in an evolutionary nether world between Piagetian or Skinnerian general learning mechanisms and Chomskyan innate givens.

There are problems with the first story. If, as you suggest, we start with an unlocalized mode of construal and an object domain vaguely perceived as a Quinean similarity space, then how do we initiate the process of fixing the mode of construal to the specific object domain that it comes to organize? It is this problem that seems to be the basis for the fairly recent postulation and work on domain specificity in the first place. How does the child come to understand what goes inside the domain and what goes outside?

If, as you claim, living kinds and artefacts are initially susceptible to teleological construal, then how do the two domains come to be reconstructed in the radically different ways you describe so well? How is it that the teleological mode is converted to, or conjoined with, a conception of essence as 'the driving causal nexus' that links together the very peculiar set of perceptual properties that carry 'casual loads' for living kinds, unless we were cognitively predisposed to make the connection in the first place?

Is essentialism a by-product of teleology applied to these properties weighted to comprehending living kinds? If so, how did these properties come to be weighted in the first place? Children seem to target certain perceptual properties of living kinds as teleologically bound, precisely because they seem to be 'good' candidates for an essentialist story. That story, in turn, seems to presuppose understanding that the relevant perceptual properties are precisely those indicative of the peculiar natural growth, development, and functioning of living kinds and their parts.

Therefore the difficulty that your 'middle position' between domain-specificity and generalized learning mechanisms seems to entwine us in is this: to make these cross-domain, but not completely general, modes of construal actually work for a specific domain, you are eventually compelled to introduce some *ad hoc* mechanisms that link or trigger the operation of that mode over just the relevant properties of a specific domain. Instead of just intrinsically organized specific domains, you begin with essentially unorganized object domains, unreferred modes of construal, and unspecified linking mechanisms.

From an evolutionary standpoint, would it not be more plausible that a teleological–essentialist construal evolved that was specifically attuned to living kinds, arguably the most important environmental feature of our own natural selection, rather than for some amorphous object-world including artefacts, a domain perhaps only marginally pertinent to the natural (versus cultural) selection of human cognition?

Keil: It is indeed critical to understand better how modes of construal come to be connected to coherent domains of real-world phenomena, and several models are possible. However, I am not sure that an innate linkage of a teleological mode to living kinds makes the developmental story any easier. Even if an innate linkage were to be shown as preferred, the linkage might be with functional kinds rather than with living things. The mode of construal could achieve this linkage either through a lower-level percep-tual or cognitive triggering, or through attempting applications with a variety of entities and noting the success of those applications. Although artefacts and living things are starkly distinct in many perceptual ways, they share higher-order perceptual properties associated with having distinct parts. Unlike non-living natural kinds, most artefacts and living kinds have neatly separable parts. Non-living natural kinds might have protuberances and other three-dimensional variations on their surfaces, but the patterns of convexity and concavity do not tend to indicate parts in the same way that is apparent for artefacts and living things (Murphy 1992). In addition, artefacts and living things often have a part reproduced several times in a similar format (such as legs on an animal or wheels on a vehicle). The psychological effectiveness of such cues remains to be seen, but in principle at least there are ways in which a larger domain of functional/designed things might be linked a priori to a teleological mode of construal through relatively simple 'triggers'.

However, such a pre-determined linkage between a domain of real-world entities and a mode of construal may not be necessary or even advisable, and the notion of a fully formed domain of explanation may not be the most appealing. If the total number of modes of construal is indeed relatively modest, such as half a dozen, it is possible to apply several such models to instances and then note their successes. Of course, for any suc-cesses to generalize to new instances, some sort of similarity gradient must be set up so that those instances can be identified. Such similarities might initially be on lower-level perceptual grounds and then become more finely tuned and conceptually driven with experience.

The account offered here could be modified in the way that you suggest and still offer a related class of developmental explanations involving shif-ting modes of construal away from an initially prepared linkage to living things. At this point, however, I have no evidence for such a pattern, and see the more neutral and conservative proposal of having the mode as a form of explanation somewhat distinct from local content domains. In the end, as we discover the details of what those modes of explanation must look like in order to function in a developmentally appropriate way, it may turn out that expressing those forms of explanation in terms of specific content domains may be essential. For now, however, the notion of beliefs about causal powers of properties does not seem to force such a conclusion.

Carey: You seem to be suggesting that new modes of construal will arise from the combination of a small set of early developing (innate?) modes of construal. But does not conceptual change (sometimes) involve genuinely new modes of construal, not derivable from the combination of these basic modes? For example, natural selection seems to be a mode of explanation that is not derivable by combination of *any* set of innate modes of construal (although it may incorporate some of them).

Keil: There is no doubt that natural selection is an explanatory account of the origins of species that is unavailable to most pre-school children. It usually emerges in late childhood or adulthood, if at all. Moreover, it provides new insights into how organisms come to have their properties. This pattern is also undoubtedly seen for explanations arising from positive–negative feedback models, regression towards the mean models, and many other forms of explanation that provide important new insights into domains. The critical question asks what is new when such an account emerges. Certainly a central part of a theory of natural selection — functional adaptation — is millennia old, universal, and easily grasped by young pre-school children, whereas natural selection seems to have emerged only when Darwin and Wallace abandoned strongly held ideas of species having essences. Therefore it may be that natural selection relies strongly on a teleological mode of construal, but also needs a component concerning notions of probabilistic distributions which is acquired through general learning procedures, and only when appropriate information is presented to work against essentialist tendencies.

More generally, surely new forms of explanation are not to be found in the simple shifting of a basic mode of construal to a different domain, or the combination of more than one mode; new patterns can be learned through more general means that come to figure prominently in explanations. However, in such cases the basic modes may still be central to organizing explanation, and may indeed be where clear notions of causal force most squarely reside. Thus, in the case of natural selection, any accounts of how change is caused may rely most strongly on teleological notions, while the probabilistic notions of species then allow an appropriate target of those causal forces. Therefore most intuitive theories, and even many that are explicitly taught, might still spring largely from a small number of basic modes of construal and their combinations.

Gelman: Very young children are remarkably good at shifting the definition of relevance depending on what conceptual work they are engaged in.

Keil: It is precisely this sort of shifting of relevance that may enable the young child suddenly to show new explanatory insights.

10

On the origin of causal understanding
SUSAN CAREY

In psychology, discussions of an organism's representation of causality fall into two fairly distinct traditions. The logical tradition analyses causal understanding in terms of modal notions such as necessity and sufficiency, or in terms of statistical relations among variables, and seeks to understand the algorithms that organisms use to establish causal connections between events, particularly events that are only probabilistically related. The explanation–mechanism tradition analyses causal understanding in terms of representations of mechanisms that explain how one event (the cause) brings about another (the effect), with the explanation being couched in terms of theories (intuitive or scientific). The two traditions differ in their commitment to domain-specificity of causal analysis. The logical tradition seeks a domain-general understanding of causality; the statistical relations among variables that provide evidence for causal relations do so no matter whether the variables are physical, biological, chemical, or psychological. The explanation–mechanism tradition, in contrast, stops short of a domain-general understanding of causality. Causal mechanisms differ from domain to domain. Our understanding of why John went to the store is grounded in want–belief explanation, and our understanding of why elephants have long trunks is grounded in functional–evolutionary explanation.

The two traditions are ultimately related, and their relations are the focus of considerable philosophical work on causality. Such questions as whether the notion of causal mechanism is reducible to logical–statistical notions of causality are discussed in that literature. My own view is that such a reduction is not possible (Salmon 1984) but, whether or not this position is correct, I believe that psychological research on causal reasoning must include studies that characterize the basic causal mechanisms in terms of which people explain the world around them. It is the origins of this type of causal understanding that I seek.

COGNITIVE DOMAINS

In order to appreciate the reasons for a commitment to domain-specific analyses of causal understanding, a few words are in order concerning the very notion of a cognitive domain. One impetus for the interest in cognitive domains was Fodor's landmark monograph *Modularity of mind* (Fodor 1983), which argued that an understanding of the human conceptual system (the central processor) is, in principle, outside the reach of cognitive science. He argued that the central theory building system is holistic. By this he meant that there are no ultimate constraints on what sort of evidence can bear on theory choice—for example facts about the orbit of Pluto may ultimately decide between two fundamentally different hypotheses in biology. Another reflection of holism is that the inferential roles of concepts are ultimately all interrelated. Modular input analysers, in contrast, have privileged input and are not subject to second guessing due to the influence from information in other parts of the system. This modularity makes the input analysers fast and efficient, and also amenable to scientific study—they can be isolated.*

Many critics of Fodor's pessimistic view of the possibility of a science of cognition, while accepting his characterization of the central cognitive system as ultimately holistic, have replied that the conceptual system is characterized by a limited type of modularity (Glymour 1985; Sperber 1994). These critics have argued for a variety of domain-specific cognitive modules (see, for example, the papers in Carey and Gelman (1991) and in Hirschfeld and Gelman (1994). Two quite distinct views of cognitive modules emerge in this literature: first they are seen as analogous to Fodorian input modules, and second they are seen as intuitive theories.

COGNITIVE MODULE AS ANALOGOUS TO AN INPUT MODULE

Sperber (1994) distinguishes perceptual processes from conceptual processes:

Perceptual processes have, as input, information provided by sensory receptors, and as output, a conceptual representation categorizing the object perceived. Conceptual processes have conceptual representations both as input and output.

---

* Whether perceptual processes are as modular as Fodor's analysis suggested is a matter of debate (Rhodes and Tremewan 1993). For present purposes, I accept Fodor's characterization of the input analysers and am concerned with its implications for the scientific study of the central processor.

In Sperber's view, cognitive modules share much with Fodor's input (perceptual) modules. They are evolutionarily adapted for, and thus innately specified. They are triggered by privileged input, and they emerge in development without the aid of central theory building machinery. They differ from input modules in that processes of demodularization, resulting from interactions with changing environment and (in humans) the deployment of meta-representational capacities, allow changes in the initial domain and integration of information across domains.

In Sperber's view, the mind has three tiers: a single thick layer of input modules, a complex network of first-order conceptual modules, and then a second order meta-representational module. Initially, this meta-representational module is not very different from the other conceptual modules, but it allows the development of communication and the cultural construction of knowledge, including theoretical knowledge.

Sperber's 'cognitive domain' is a semantic notion. A domain is the extension of a cognitive module, the set of entities in the world that have been evolutionarily selected to trigger the module (the proper domain) or that have come to trigger the module (the actual domain). Sperber insists that the domain of a module is not a property of its internal structure. Sperber states '*all* the internal structure provides is a mode of construal' (of the entities in the domain, emphasis added).

Examples that Sperber offers for first-order conceptual modules include a meta-representational module (whose domain includes people and their minds), a physical object module (whose domain includes objects and the physical relations among them), and a folk biology (whose domain includes animals and plants, particularly their physical appearance). In my view, there is conclusive evidence for the first two as first-order cognitive modules that emerge during the first 2 years of an infant's life (Carey and Spelke 1994; Leslie 1994; Chapters 3, 4, 5, and 7 of this volume). Another first-order cognitive module for which there is conclusive evidence is number (Gallistel and Gelman 1992; Wynn 1992). The evidence for these as first-order modules comes from empirical studies of infants engaged in physical reasoning tasks, in reasoning about people and their behaviour, in learning to talk (which requires understanding the communicative intent of others and hence the meta-representational module), and in counting and adding. The evidence that Sperber offers for folk biology as a first-order cognitive module is of a totally different flavour: an evolutionary plausibility argument plus (following Atran (1990)) cross-cultural universality in some aspects of human conceptions of animals and plants.

Like Sperber, Atran adopts a semantic–extensionalist view of a cognitive domain. He argues, on the basis of a cross-cultural universality in aspects of folk taxonomies of animals and plants, that folk biology is a core domain of human cognition.* Like Sperber, Atran considers representations of core domains to be innately determined, to develop without exploiting the theory building that human meta-representational capacities make possible. He views folk biology as pre-theoretical and constraining, making possible explicit biological theory.

COGNITIVE DOMAINS VERSUS CROSS–CULTURAL UNIVERSALS

The book edited by Hirschfeld and Gelman (1994), like the present volume, brings together philosophers, anthropologists, and psychologists to explore the implications of the existence of cognitive modules for cross-cultural cognitive universals. As Sperber (1994) points out, the fact of great cultural variation in belief systems is often taken as prima facie evidence against the existence of cognitive modules, but this conclusion, he claims, is not warranted since forces of demodularization can lead to culturally diverse actual domains. Carey and Spelke (1994) develop a related argument that the existence of innate cognitive modules does not preclude great cultural variation in belief systems.

But what of the converse argument? Is cross-cultural universality a warrant for an innate domain-specific cognitive module? Both Sperber (1994) and Atran (1994) point to the cross-cultural similarities in living kind classification schemes as evidence for a first order cognitive module with living kinds as its domain. While cross-cultural universality is certainly consistent with the existence of such a first-order module, it does not by any means provide conclusive evidence for it. Since the universality is seen in adults, it could result from theory-building capacities applied to a world that provides massive consistent evidence across cultures. It could also result from domain-general concept-formation capabilities (e.g. pattern formation or correlation–detection computational devices). What is needed to establish folk biology as a first-order module is empirical study of its origin along the lines of the research that has established physical reasoning and meta-representational reasoning as core modules.

Before considering the evidence currently available as to the ontogenesis of folk biology, a second view of cognitive modules is introduced— cognitive modules as intuitive theories.

---

* Here the locutions 'first-order cognitive module' and 'core module' are used more or less interchangeably; the module is the mental representation of the domain. First-order or cognitive modules are those cognitive modules that are innately specified, and core domains are those entities in the world in the extension of core modules.

COGNITIVE MODULES AS INTUITIVE THEORIES

Some of Fodor's critics maintained that intuitive theories provide a limited type of modularity within the central cognitive system (Glymour 1985). Others argue that it is fundamentally misleading to construe cognitive modules as theories. For example, Atran (1994) excoriates those philosophers (e.g. Quine, Putnam, etc.) who see ordinary cognition as continuous with scientific thought, claiming that such a view would seem ludicrous to any anthropologist.

Before this issue can be joined, some agreement on what a theory is must be reached, as well as some agreement on which aspects of scientific theories are being claimed for intuitive theories. Scientific theories are often formalized, and are always the result of institutionalized self-aware cognitive activity. These aspects of scientific theories are not presumed to characterize intuitive theories (hence **intuitive**), but it is not these aspects that make a scientific theory a **theory** either. Philosophers differ in their rational reconstruction of the concept **theory**,* but the analysis offered by those cognitive scientists who believe that intuitive theories provide one type of cognitive modularity is that which sees theories as **explanatory** structures. Theories are those cognitive structures that characterize the causal mechanisms at work in the world, and which therefore provide fodder for explanation (see Salmon (1989) for a review of the considerations in favour of viewing explanation in terms of providing causal mechanisms that account for why the explanandum came to pass). This characterization is true of both scientific and intuitive theories, and distinguishes theories from other cognitive structures (e.g. scripts (Schank and Abelson 1977) or pattern abstraction mechanisms (Posner and Keele 1968)).

Wellman (1990) makes an important distinction between framework theories (or foundational theories (Wellman and S. Gelman 1992) and specific theories. Framework theories are those that determine the basic ontology to which a person is committed and the most general explanatory notions that a person represents. The 4-year-old child's theory of mind is an example of a framework theory; their theories of belief fixation and morality are specific theories constrained by their framework theory. Behaviourism is an example of a framework theory; the behaviourist account of language acquisition is a specific theory. All theories (specific and framework) determine a domain of phenomena involving a theory-specific ontology and articulate causal mechanisms at work in the domain.

---

* For example, theories can be analysed as sets of sentences from which predictions can be logically derived and then tested against empirical data. Relatedly, it has been proposed that scientific explanation can be rationally reconstructed as a process of deductive argument which yield the explanans from premises that include laws (Hempel and Oppenheim, 1948). Neither of these views of theories is that adopted here.

Wellman (1990) convincingly argues that when cognitive scientists write about intuitive theories (e.g. Carey, 1985), they usually mean framework theories.

In this chapter 'intuitive theory' is defined as a cognitive structure that embodies a person's ontological commitments (i.e. specifies the basic kinds of things that there *are* in the world) and provide modes of explanation for the phenomena in its domain. The notion of a 'domain', on this view, is a domain of phenomena involving the entities recognized by the theory; the central components of an intuitive theory are its ontology and the causal mechanisms that it exploits in explanation (see Carey (1985), Murphy and Medin (1985), Keil (1989), Wellman (1990), Wellman and Gelman (1992)), and Gopnik and Wellman, (1994) for related characterizations of intuitive theories and the role that they play in conceptual structure). Intuitive theories determine a limited sense of privileged input, constraining the data relevant to the evaluation of hypotheses licensed by the theory and determining the domain of phenomena explained by the theory, which is how they (as do Sperber's cognitive modules) provide an answer to Fodor's scepticism about isolating any aspect of the central processor for scientific study.

Examples in the literature of intuitive framework theories include the 4-year-old child's theory of mind (Wellman 1990; Perner 1991), the 10-year-old child's theory of matter (Piaget and Inhelder 1941; Smith *et al.* 1985; Carey 1991), the infant's theory of physical bodies and their interactions (Chapters 3, 4, and 5 of this volume), the high school student's intuitive mechanics (Clement 1982; McCloskey 1983), an intuitive cosmology constructed in the early elementary school years (Vosniadou and Brewer 1992), and an intuitive biology constructed by age 7–10 (Carey 1985) or even earlier (Keil 1992, in press; Wellman and Gelman 1992; Inagaki and Hatano 1993). In each case, attribution of an intuitive theory to the child requires establishing that the child distinguishes entities in the domain of the theory from those not in its domain, and appeals to theory-specific causal mechanisms to explain the interactions among the entities in the domain.

It is not clear what Atran is denying when he denies that ordinary cognition relies upon theory-like representational structures. If he denies that ordinary folk formalize their knowledge, or explicitly marshal evidence for it, or are part of the institutions that construct Western scientific and technological knowledge, nobody would quarrel. Nor would anybody quarrel with his speculation that 'the structures of ordinary conceptual domains may strongly constrain, and thereby render possible, the initial elaboration of corresponding scientific fields'. Indeed, those who believe that scientific thought is continuous with everyday cognition see that speculation as one way of *stating* the continuity hypothesis. The ontological commitments of ordinary folk—the phenomena that they represent—are part of the starting points for institutionalized science, as is their causal understanding and their intuitive theories.* To make the debate between Atran and those who hold the continuity hypothesis substantive (as opposed to mere semantic quibbling over the term 'theory'), his denial will be taken to be that core modules need not include any explicit causal understanding, and that folk biology, in particular, does not include any such understanding.

RELATIONS BETWEEN THE TWO VIEWS OF COGNITIVE MODULES

On both views, cognitive modules pick out a set of entities in the world and are responsible for processing privileged sorts of information about those entities. The two views are further confused by the fact that both claim the young child's intuitive theories of mind and of bodies as examples of cognitive modules. None the less, the two conceptions of cognitive modules are genuinely different. The intuitive theory view does not take **innateness** as a necessary property of a cognitive module; intuitive theories can function as cognitive modules even if they are constructed during the course of development. Conversely, the first-order module view does not take causal-explanatory structure as a necessary property of cognitive modules; folk biology, for example, is posited by Atran to be a pre-theoretical cognitive module. In sum, the intuitive theory view claims young children's theories of bodies and mind as cognitive modules because they meet the criteria for intuitive theories; it is accidental that they may also be innate. In contrast, Sperber's view of cognitive modules, by analogy with input modules, claims these domains because they meet the criteria for innate domain-specific reasoning; it is accidental that they also embody causal mechanisms.

BIOLOGY AS A COGNITIVE DOMAIN

The differences between the two views become focused in discussions of intuitive biology, or folk biology, as a cognitive domain. Atran views folk biology as an innate core module that is not theory like even among adults in most cultures. Among those who look upon biology as an intuitive theory, there is controversy as to when it first emerges. Carey (1985, 1988) claims that biology does not emerge as an autonomous domain until the end

* There are several case studies of lay intuitive theories in which it has been found that these are largely the *same* as the first theories developed by institutionalized science that are close to the phenomena: for thermal phenomena see Wiser and Carey (1983) and Wiser (1987), for intuitive mechanics see McCloskey (1983), for matter see Carey (1991), and for folk biology see Inagaki and Hatano (1993).

of the first decade of life; others (Inagaki and Hatano 1993; Keil 1992, 1994) argue that pre-school children have constructed an autonomous intuitive biological theory. Wellman and Gelman (1992) are agnostic as to whether pre-school children have constructed biology as an intuitive theory; they argue that pre-school children certainly recognize animals, and perhaps plants, as ontologically distinct from other entities in the world, but that it is unclear whether they understand any biology-specific causal mechanisms.

Thus the literature raises several possibilities as to the status of intuitive biology as a cognitive module.

1. Folk biology is an innate core module and is not theory-like (Atran in press; Sperber in press).
2. Folk biology is an innate core module and, like intuitive mechanics, is an intuitive theory from the beginning (Keil 1992, in press).
3. An intuitive theory of biology is constructed during the first decade of life, at least in contemporary American culture (Carey 1985).

If the third possibility is correct, there are several options as to the source of an intuitive biology. First, the first and third possibilities could *both* be correct. As Atran suggests, the innate core folk biology may constrain and make possible the construction of explicit causal biological theories. Alternatively, there may be no innate core folk biology, but a different module may determine the ontological type animal — namely an innate folk psychology. The emergence of an autonomous folk biology would then require conceptual change in the innate concept **animal** (Carey 1985, 1988). Finally, there may be no innate core folk biology, and the emergence of an autonomous biology may exploit only domain-general concept formation and explanation-building capacities.

In order to evaluate these alternatives, we must look at how folk biology has been characterized by its adherents, and at the evidence that has been offered for each alternative.

CRITIQUE OF THE SPERBER–ATRAN VIEW

The cross-cultural universality that Atran and Sperber offer as evidence that folk biology is a core-cognitive domain has two components: universality in taxonomic organization of categories of animals and plants,*

---

* Particularly animals; in one of the cultures that Atran has studied, the Itza Maya, fungi and lichens are not considered alive (Atran 1994). An interesting issue is the theoretical significance of such examples of *lack* of cross-cultural universality. Do Itza Maya have different criteria for life, or do they simply lack evidence that fungi and lichens meet their criteria for life? For the present purposes, Atran's point that folk taxonomies are largely universal is accepted.

and an essentialist view of why animals and plants have certain of their properties.

Atran has shown that all cultures divide the living world into two kingdoms (animals and plants), that each of these is taxonomically sub-divided into major life forms (e.g. fish, bird, mammal), and that these are further subdivided into (sometimes unnamed) subcategories (e.g. ungulates, rodents). Finally, the taxonomy bottoms out in all cultures at the level of primary taxa (species/genus, e.g. mouse, dog, wolf, deer). Furthermore, Atran claims: 'Invariably, humans presume each primary taxon to uniquely possess an inherent physical nature or underlying essence, which determines the kind's teleological growth, its characteristic behaviour, morphology and ecological proclivity'.

The Sperber–Atran position has the following empirical and conceptual problems: first, those aspects of folk biology (as they characterize it) which emerge early in childhood are most probably not domain-specific; second, those aspects of folk biology (as they characterize it) that are domain-specific are probably not innate, nor are they theory-neutral; third, Sperber and Atran fail to confront what Carey and Spelke (1994) call 'the problem of perception'; fourth, Sperber and Atran run into what I shall call 'the problem of theory-laden attribution'.

Taxonomic organization and essentialism: plausibly innate but probably not specific to folk-biological classification

Taxonomic organization is a property of the conceptual–linguistic system in general, particularly the nominal system, both in the adult final state and early in development. I believe that this is also true of essentialism, although the argument in the latter case is harder to make.

Natural language nominal systems are built on the backbone of an ontological hierarchy (Sommers 1963; Keil 1979), of which biological classification is just a small part. Furthermore, children set up hierarchical relations among categories very early in cognitive development (see Waxman (1992) for 12-month-old infants, and Smith (1979) and Markman (1989) for 2- to 3-year-old children), and do so equally within categories of animals and within categories of artefacts and food. The earliest lexicalized hierarchies include the following (Markman 1989): animal/dog, cat, bird, etc.; toy/doll, car, block, etc.; food/biscuits, cereal, apple, etc. Each of these hierarchies include intermediate levels that are not lex-icalized by the child (e.g. toy/*building toy*/Lego, blocks, Lincoln Logs, etc.; animal/*mammal*/dog, cat, bird, etc.), a feature that is also universal in folk-biological taxonomies (Atran 1994).

Essentialism, like taxonomic structure, derives from the logical work done by nouns. The child has a default assumption that count nouns are substance sortals, i.e. naming concepts that provide conditions of identity during the maximal lifetime of an entity (see Wiggins (1980), Hirsch (1982), and Macnamara (1986) for related characterizations of substance sortals; see Hall and Waxman (1993) for evidence that young children expect count nouns to be substance sortals). Indeed, every count noun provides identity criteria that distinguish the property changes that signal that the entity ceases to exist from those changes that leave the entity in existence, i.e. the application of every count noun carries with it the idea that the identity of the entity picked out by the noun is unchanged in the face of surface changes. I submit that biological essentialism is the theoretical elaboration of the logical — linguistic concept, substance sortal.

The mutual exclusivity assumption (Markman 1989) that very young children make concerning *all* count nouns (not just animal terms) can be seen as reflecting this basic essentialism. Young children assume that every entity is a member of just one kind, and will have just one kind label*, i.e. at the outset of language learning children assume that each entity can have only one essence, only one criterion for identity.

Finally, at least some experimental demonstrations that very young children have essentialist expectations about living kinds have also shown that they have essentialist expectations about other kinds. For example, Gelman and Markman (1986) showed that 4-year-old children expect shared kind membership, rather than shared appearances, to determine unobservable properties, i.e. a bird that looks like a bat will have unobservable properties of other birds rather than unobservable properties of bats. However, they found this to be equally true of substance kinds; gold that looks like silver will have unobservable properties of gold, not of silver.

Atran (1994) argues convincingly that the commitments of folk biology to taxonomy and essentialism go deeper than in any other cognitive domain. This I freely grant. However, these are characteristics of the adult system. According to the view being developed there, these aspects of universal folk biology are due to a match between the world and important domain-general constraints on the nominal system that are exploited and developed in the course of universal theory-building in this domain. The empirical evidence is that, in development, the roots of these aspects of folk biology are not initially tied to children's expectations about animals and/or plants.

* Of course, establishing a hierarchy of kinds entails violating the mutual exclusivity assumption. My point here is that the mutual exclusivity assumption applies equally to biological and non-biological kinds, as does the ability to overcome this assumption and set up hierarchies.

Aspects of Atran's folk biology that are domain-specific but probably neither innate nor theory-neutral

When Atran characterizes the cross-culturally universal essentialist expectation concerning biological taxa, he characterizes the underlying essence as determining characteristic morphology and behaviour, teleological growth, and characteristic ecology. Characteristic morphology and behaviour are not domain-specific notions. Other natural kinds such as oceans, rivers, and celestial objects have characteristic morphology and behaviour. However, teleological growth and characteristic ecologies are certainly domain-specific properties; only living kinds have these.* But it is doubtful that knowledge of the growth and ecology of animals are part of an innate concept of animal (see below, and also Carey (1985) and Keil (1989) for review of evidence that pre-school children fail to understand people's growth, and that coming to understand patterns of teleological growth as a core property of animal kind reflects theoretical elaboration of the concept of animal during years 6 to 10, and beyond).

The perception problem

Sperber's three-tier view of cognitive architecture includes input modules which take spatio-temporal information and output a categorized entity (as it were, 'animal'), which is the input to a first-order cognitive module (as it were, folk biology) which processes information relative to it. This view raises what Carey and Spelke (1994) call 'the problem of perception'. The issue is: On what basis does the input module categorize entities as animals? The folk-biology module will be useless unless the cognitive system can identify the animals in the world.

Carey and Spelke (1994) distinguish two general ways in which the tasks of apprehending the entities in the domain and reasoning about them could be related. Consider, for example, the domain of reasoning about human action and experience, which requires the identification of people in the environment. It is possible that perceivers single out human beings by virtue of a face-recognizer, a voice-recognizer, a gait-recognizer, and the like (all exploiting spatio-temporal information). Whenever the perceiver is confronted by eyes, hair, and other features in the proper configuration,

---

* This depends, of course, on what is meant by 'ecology'. If a kind's characteristic ecology includes only where it is typically found — fish in rivers and lakes, moose in forests, buffalo on plains — then other kinds have characteristic ecologies as well. Celestial objects are found in the heavens, rivers and lakes on the surface of the earth, furniture in houses, etc. But if 'ecology' includes more biology-relevant information — how animals shelter themselves from the cold, how they protect their young, what they eat etc.- — then these properties are domain-specific. However, they are not theory-neutral, at least in the adult's conceptual system.

her face-recognizer would signal the presence of a person. This signal would then trigger the operation of the first-order theory of mind module, whereby the actions of the person are understood in terms of the person's choices, belief, and desires. Alternatively, perceivers may single out persons by analysing the behaviour of entities, asking which entity's behaviour appears to be directed to some goal, to be guided by perceptions or beliefs about its environment, to be coloured by emotions, and the like. On the second account, processes of perceiving and reasoning about psychological beings are intimately connected: they are guided by the same system of knowledge.

Carey and Spelke (1994) reviewed the evidence concerning the solution to the perception problem in each of the well-established first-order cognitive modules: physical reasoning, reasoning about people, and number. In each case, the weight of evidence favours the second possibility, that perception and reasoning are guided by a single knowledge system. To continue with the example of person perception: infants use contingent response as a way of identifying the people in their environment. For example, infants attempt to interact socially with a mobile that moves in response to a leg kick (Watson 1979).

If the cognitive architecture of first-order modules always has this property, then folk biology as characterized by Atran and Sperber cannot be a first-order module. This is because having an essential nature or being part of a taxonomic structure, the key features of the folk biology that Atran has identified, are not identifiable from spatiotemporal analysis. The only solution to the perception problem for folk biology would be the first type—animals identified on the basis of some properties unrelated to the information that guides reasoning about them.

A plausible solution to the perception problem is that animals are identified by the module that picks out beings with intentional states, i.e. beings capable of attention to the environment and of goal-directed activity. However, these are the features that identify entities in the meta-representational–theory-of-mind module. This line of argument suggests that animals are initially in the domain of a first-order module that is not a folk biology but rather a folk psychology (Carey 1985).

The problem of theory-laden attribution

In describing the cross-cultural universality in taxonomic organization of living kinds, Atran sometimes uses the term 'folk taxonomy', sometimes the term 'folk biology'. These are very different. The term 'folk taxonomy' makes no commitment as to how the entities in taxonomy are construed, but 'folk biology' does. Indeed, the very characterization of the taxonomy as one of **living kinds** also presupposes a concept of 'living', a concept that must go beyond having an essential nature and being part of a hierarchy. Gold has an essential nature and is part of a hierarchy: gold/precious metal/metal/element/substance. In addition, as pointed out above, Atran includes biology-specific features in his characterization of the domain. For example he includes an understanding that a kind's essential nature determines patterns of teleological growth and characteristic ecology as part of universal folk biology. The problem here is wanting it both ways — wanting folk*biology* to be both biology and pre-theoretical.

Sperber's explicity extensionalist view of the domain of a cognitive module contains the same tension. Sperber explicity denies that the internal structure of a module is its core; *all* the internal structure provides is a mode of construal. But it is the mode of construal that makes the module a 'biology'.* Without a biological mode of construal (i.e. specifically biological causal mechanisms explaining biological phenomena), the entities in the extension of the concept 'animal' may not be part of a biology at all. This is not merely a logical point; as already mentioned, there is ample empirical evidence for a first-order cognitive module with animals in its domain that is not a biology but rather is a psychology (a theory of mind, Sperber's meta-cognitive module).

The problem of theory-laden attribution is ubiquitous in hermaneutic disciplines such as anthropology, developmental psychology, and history of science. In developmental psychology, we find evidence that children represent a concept whose extension largely overlaps some adult concept. To communicate that concept, we must use some word in our lexicon, but that word names a concept that plays some particular inferential role in our conceptual system. We must be very careful not to attribute our concept to the child unless we provide positive evidence that the child's concept plays largely the same inferential role within his or her conceptual system. Otherwise, the *problem* of theory-laden attribution becomes the *fallacy* of theory-laden attribution.

BIOLOGY AS A FRAMEWORK THEORY

I have argued against the Sperber–Atran vision of folk biology as a first-order cognitive module as being both innate and not theory-like. The question then arises as to whether folk biology is a cognitive module in the sense of a framework theory, and, if so, when children first construct it during their development.

A framework theory is characterized by ontological commitments, a set of phenomena in its domain, and causal mechanisms that explain these

* Or 'zoology', as Sperber also characterizes the domain.

phenomena. Carey (1985), Keil (1992, 1994), and Wellman and Gelman (1992) all offer related analyses of biology as a framework theory and marshal evidence that bears on the question of when children first represent an intuitive biology. Keil argues that pre-school children can do this, and speculates that biology may be an innate cognitive module. Wellman and Gelman argue that pre-school children certainly make the ontological distinction between animals and inanimate objects, and thus have a separate ontology of biological kinds. They further argue that, while it is unclear whether pre-school children understand any biology-specific causal mechanisms, the weight of evidence suggests that they do. Carey (1985) argued that a first intuitive biology is not constructed by American children until about age 10.

Wellman and Gelman (1992) raise the possibility that pre-school children may draw the ontological distinction between animate and inanimate entities while not representing any biology-specific causal mechanisms. This possibility embodies the fallacy of theory-laden attribution, i.e. evidence that children represent a concept of animal that is distinct from other concepts is not tantamount to evidence for an ontological commitment *by the child* (Keil 1979; Carey 1985). To join this issue, we need an analysis of ontological concepts and some hint of the kind of evidence we could draw on to assess whether some concept of the child has this status.

Keil's analysis of ontological commitments draws on the distinction between predictability and truth. It is a category mistake to assert 'The rock is hungry', whereas it is merely false to assert 'Grass is red'. A rough and ready test of the ontological distinctions that a person draws is provided by their judgements of category mistakes; the categorical distinctions across which we judge category mistakes to occur reflect our ontological commitment (Sommers 1963; Keil 1979). Unfortunately, children aged less than about 5 cannot be probed for judgements of category mistakes (Keil 1979), and so we must appeal to other types of evidence to judge whether a conceptual distinction made by younger children is an ontological distinction for them. Carey (1985) argued that ontological concepts are simply those that are the core concepts in framework theories—those that articulate our most basic modes of construal and explanation. If we accept this analysis, then the question of whether a concept represented by a child is an ontological concept becomes the same question as whether the concept is central to a framework theory.

There are at least two ways in which children could represent a distinction between animals and non-animals without having that distinction constitute an ontological distinction between biological and non-biological entities. First, the distinction could result from domain-general concept-formation capacities, reflecting domain-general similarity computations, and thus could fail to be an ontological distinction at all. Domain-general prototype abstraction mechanisms have been documented in adults (Posner and Keele

1968), young children (Diamond and Carey 1990), and infants (Cohen and Younger 1983). Infants who have been trained to distinguish one random pattern from another would not be credited with an *ontological* distinction between the two patterns. Second, the distinction might be an ontological distinction, but the framework theory in which the concept **animal** is embedded might be an intuitive psychology and not an intuitive biology. The distinction could be one between entities with intentional states and entities without intentional states (agents and non-agents in Leslie's terminology (see Chapter 5)). As argued above, I favour the second possibility, i.e. I believe that the distinction between animals and non-animals is an ontological distinction for babies, but I see no evidence that it is a biological distinction. An example of the fallacy of theory-laden attribution in action is as follows: Wellman and Gelman (1992) point to the fact that infants communicate with humans and not inanimate objects as evidence against a 'domain general understanding of the *biological* world' (emphasis added).

DOES FOLK BIOLOGY EMERGE FROM FOLK PSYCHOLOGY?

Carey's (1985) claim that an intuitive biology emerges ontogenetically from an intuitive psychology has been the subject of voluminous critical commentary (Wellman and Gelman 1992; Inagaki and Hatano 1993; Atran 1994; Keil 1994). Resolving this controversy requires a clearer formulation than that provided by Carey (1985) of what the growth of folk biology from folk psychology might mean.

The claim that an intuitive biology emerges from an intuitive psychology admits of three interpretations, graded from weak to strong.

1. Weak: **animal**, as an ontological kind, is originally part of an intuitive psychology. Animals are behaving beings or agents (see Chapter 5). On the weak interpretation, any properties of animals that the child *can* explain fall in the domain of a theory of mind. Other properties of animals that the child represents are simply unexplained in that region 'where explanation runs dry' (Keil 1989, 1992), and are learned by domain-general mechanisms.

2. Medium-strong: **animal**, as an ontological kind, is originally part of a framework theory that is undifferentiated from intuitive psychology and intuitive biology, i.e. the framework theory's core explanatory principles are undifferentiated with respect to the modes of construal of animal action and the properties of animal bodies. The undifferentiated concept **animal** and the undifferentiated modes of construal are incommen-

surable with the distinct psychological and biological concepts that are constructed when the two framework theories become differentiated (Carey 1988). The initial framework theory is *neither* folk psychology nor folk biology.

3. Strong: **animal**, as an ontological kind, is originally part of an intuitive psychology and the child attempts to explain *all* properties of animals in terms of intentional causation (Keil (1994) renders this interpretation as 'Knowledge of animals is distorted to fit the mold of an intuitive psychology').

Carey (1985) presented some evidence for the strong and medium-strong interpretations, arguing that certain phenomena that are central to adult intuitive biology, such as death and parentage, are initially interpreted by the child in the context of intuitive psychology. Most of the evidence that has been marshalled against the idea that folk biology emerges from folk psychology bear only on the strong version, and I accept that the strong version of the claim is wrong.

In what follows, I begin by giving a flavour of the evidence against the strong version of the claim. This consists of demonstrations that pre-school children know about phenomena involving animals and people that *cannot* be explained in terms of intentional causation. It is argued that these demonstrations leave the weakest version intact, because they provide no positive demonstration of specifically biological explanatory schema. This is followed by a critique of several proposals in the literature for specifically biological modes of construal on the part of 4-year-old children. Of course, evidence for specifically biological modes of construal on the part of pre-school children would license the search for such understanding at an even earlier age, and would be consistent with the view that folk biology is distinct from folk psychology from the beginning. Finally, two promising related proposals for characterizing the preschool child's construals of animals (Keil 1992, 1994; Inagaki and Hatano 1993) are presented and it is argued that these proposals actually support the claim that folk biology emerges from intuitive psychology.

Bodily processes outside intentional control

Many demonstrations that pre-school children represent a domain of bodily phenomena for which psychological causation is irrelevant have emerged from the laboratories of Inagaki and Hatano, Keil, and S. Gelman. Of course, the existence of such a domain does not constitute evidence for an intuitive biology without *positive* evidence that the child represents specifically biological causal mechanisms underlying some of these bodily phenomena (or some other biological phenomena), i.e. the phenomena and properties known to be outside the realm of psychological causation may be unexplained properties of animals, not encompassed within the mode of construal of any framework theory.

The most extensive series of studies demonstrating that pre-school children understand that there are bodily processes and properties outside the realm of intentional causation has been performed by Inagaki and Hatano. They probed whether children think that weight gain, heart beat, sleep, digestion, and other bodily processes are under a person's intentional control. For example, children might be asked whether a boy who has eaten a full main course can make his stomach digest the food faster so that he will have appetite for dessert. Pre-school children are clear that such processes are not subject to the person's desires (Inagaki and Hatano 1993). They are also clear that a person's desires cannot affect the growth of other animals, i.e. a person cannot keep an attractive kitten small for ever however much he may want to do so (Inagaki and Hatano 1987). Gelman and Kremer (1991) have reported a related finding that pre-school children know that human action (and thus human intention) is not involved in the processes by which leaves turn colour in the autumn. Springer and Keil (1991) have provided evidence that children aged as young as 5 years know that human intention is not involved in the processes by which plants and animals acquire their colouring. Thus the pre-school child (or at least the older pre-school child) does not attempt to assimilate all causal processes involving animals and plants into an intentional mode of construal (counter to Piaget's claims of the pre-school child's artificialism, and counter to the strong interpretation of the claim that intuitive biology emerges from intuitive psychology).

Although most of these studies were intended to show merely that children know that there are bodily properties and processes that are not under human intentional control, some children seem to have demonstrated some knowledge of biological causation. For example, Inagaki and Hatano (1993) asked which of a pair of twins would become fat, one who wanted desperately to become fat but who did not eat very much or one who wanted to stay thin but who ate lots of cake and sweets. Pre-school children judged that the latter would be more likely to grow fat. The question has become whether knowledge that eating sweets leads to fatness consists of knowledge of a biology-specific causal mechanism, or whether this is simply one of many facts that the child has learned about people and for which he or she has no explanation. Carey (1985) argues that the latter interpretation is correct. Until the child has constructed an intuitive theory of how bodily processes mediate between eating and growth, or eating and becoming fat, knowledge of mere 'input–output' relations does not constitute causal understanding. Carey (1985) further reviews the huge literature on the construction of a theory of bodily processes mediating such input–output relations in American children aged from about 7 years to about 10 years.

In sum, these findings show that the child knows that there are bodily functions and properties outside the control of human intentional causation. However, the studies reviewed above provide no evidence for any knowledge of biology-specific causal mechanisms. Even knowledge of input–output regularities, such as that eating too much leads to becoming fat, are probably in the realm of knowledge about animals where interpretation has run dry (Keil 1989, 1992). It is unlikely that the pre-school child knows of any biology-specific causal mechanisms relevant to bodily phenomena; these may just be facts that the child has observed about his and others' bodies. Animals and people grow, the heart beats, we become sleepy even if we want very much to stay awake, etc. In sum, such demonstrations defeat the strong interpretation of the claim that folk biology emerges from folk psychology, but leave the weak interpretation unscathed.

Other evidence that pre-schoolers draw a body–mind distinction

There is a second type of evidence that pre-school children have separated the bodily from the mental. A large set of studies from Keil's laboratory shows that the child expects bodily and mental properties to adopt different patterns as they interact with other processes concerning animals. For example Keil (1992, 1994) showed that pre-school children expect people to be able to catch bodily symptoms (e.g. rashes, watery eyes), but not behavioural abnormalities (e.g. excessive hand washing), from other people who have them. Similarly, Springer (1992) showed that pre-school children expect children to resemble their parents in bodily properties (e.g. a baby horse will resemble its mother in having hair in its ears), but not in social or behaviour properties (e.g. in having scuffed knees from playing in a brier patch).

Again, these expectations may reflect theory-neutral knowledge (e.g. correlation of features regarding diseases or experience-based expectations that children will look like their parents). We still seek positive evidence that the child knows any *specific* biological causal processes involving bodily phenomena.

The search for the pre-shool child's biology — some false starts

Welman and Gelman, Keil, and Inagaki and Hatano all maintain that pre-school children have constructed an intuitive biology. The characterization that each one gives of the pre-school child's intuitive biology differs. Welman and Gelman, and Keil, concur with Atran and Sperber in attributing an essentialist understanding of animals to children of these ages, but, as argued above, an essentialist understanding of animals does not, by itself, constitute a biological understanding of animals. More is needed.

Wellman and Gelman (1992) suggest, as does Keil (1994), that pre-school children have a knowledge of at least three specifically biological causal mechanisms: maturational growth, inheritance of physical properties, and disease transmission and contagion. Let us examine each in turn.

Maturational growth

Rosengren *et al.* (1991) showed that pre-school children understand that growth is unidirectional (i.e. animals and plants increase rather than decrease in size), and that growth is a property of animals and plants but not of artefacts. Pre-school children also know that growth is inevitable and is not subject to a person's desires (Inagaki and Hartano 1987). Finally, pre-school children understand that a baby pig will become an adult pig, rather than a cow, even if raised by a cow mother together with other of the cow mother's (cow) babies (Gelman and Wellman (1991) refer to this as knowledge of 'innate potential'). Similarly, Hirschfeld (Chapter 11 of this volume) shows that pre-school children know that a black baby will grow into a black adult, even if adopted by white parents and raised in a family with white children.

That pre-school children have such knowledge about growth is part of the evidence that they have an essentialist understanding of animals and plants — an entity's being an animal or plant means that it is inevitable that it starts out small and becomes larger, and its kind determines the properties that it will have as an adult (i.e. determines the outcome of the growth process). It is also part of the evidence that they distinguish bodily phenomena (such as growth, heart beat, breathing, sleeping, bodily symptoms of illness) from other phenomena involving humans and animals as not subject to intentional causation. However, such knowledge does *not* constitute evidence of knowledge of biology-specific causal mechanisms.

What do pre-school children think is the cause of growth? Two things: birthdays and food. One 3-year-old child combined these ideas into the theory that birthday cake is essential for growth (Carey 1985). Focus on birthdays reflects confusion between 'getting older' and 'getting bigger'.*

But does not knowledge about the relation between eating and growth constitute evidence of knowledge of a biology-specific causal mechanism?

---

* The same child believed that on her mother's birthday, her mother (a few months older than her father) would become taller than her father because her mother would be 38 while her father would only be 37.

As argued above, this may be mere knowledge of an input–output relation, such as knowledge that turning on a light switch causes a light to go on. Such knowledge is probably acquired through being told about input–output relations explicitly ('If you don't eat your vegetables, you won't grow into a big strong girl . . .'). The pre-school child has no clue as to any bodily mechanism which mediates between eating and growing.

Finally, Keil's transformation studies show that pre-school children do *not* consider it essential for an animal to obtain its properties through a process of natural growth, whereas by the age of 9 or 10 years children have constructed this understanding. Pre-school children believe that a skunk can be turned into a raccoon through surgery; by age 9 (and in some studies by age 7 or 8), children believe that the animal which results from such a transformation is still a skunk that just *looks* like a raccoon (Keil 1989). It is not the case, however, that preschool children think that anything that looks like a raccoon is a raccoon: a skunk in a raccoon costume, looking exactly like raccoon, is still judged to be a skunk (Keil, 1989); a dog with all its insides removed (the blood and bones and stuff like that) is judged not to be a dog anymore (Gelman and Wellman 1991). These data suggest that, to pre-school children, the core of the notion of animal kind includes bodily structure—the body must have the right structure, including internal structure, in order for the entity to be an animal, or a particular kind of animal. It is not enough just to look like an animal (as in a stuffed dog) or a particular kind of animal (as in a raccoon-costumed skunk). However, these data also show that 10-year-olds children have constructed a deeper notion of how that bodily structure must be formed: for children aged 4–6 years, surgery is sufficient; for 10-year-old children, it must be a natural growth process. This developmental difference between 4- and 9-year-old children reflects changes in the principles that determine the entities in the domain; by age 9, aspects of the life-cycle have become part of the core principles.*

In sum, there is excellent evidence that by the age of 10 American children have constructed a construal of animals whereby their kind-determining bodily properties are achieved through a process of maturational growth, a construal that Atran claims is an important aspect of universal folk biology. Further, Jeyifous (1986), using Keil's tasks to study the develop-ment of understanding of biological kinds, found the same developmental pattern at roughly the same ages among rural unschooled Yoruba in Nigeria. These data support Atran's claims that this understanding is part

---

* This deepening continues beyond the age of 10 years: 10-year-old children judge that a skunk, accidentally given an injection of a chemical shortly after birth that caused it to grow into an animal that looks just like a raccoon, has indeed become a raccoon; adults judge it still to be a skunk (Keil 1989).

of universal folk taxonomy, but conflict with his vision that this understanding is part of an innate cognitive module. For the pre-school child, knowledge that animals (and plants) grow appears to be one fact among many that they have acquired, probably through domain-general learning mechanisms. Only later (by age 10 in rural Nigeria and the rural United States) does this fact become incorporated into an intuitive biology.

Inheritance of properties

In American folk biology, the explanation of how an animal acquires its bodily properties is pushed deeper still. If an animal's essence determines properties by guiding a process of maturational growth, the question of the origin of that essence then arises. In American folk biology, an appeal is made to the biological inheritance of properties from an animal's parents. Understanding of biological inheritance is the second specifically biological causal process that some have suggested that pre-school children understand. Both Springer and Keil (1989) and Gelman and Wellman (1991) claim that pre-school children understand that babies (including animal babies) inherit an innate potential from their biological parents to develop certain traits rather than others. However, the data presented by each group establish considerably less than this, and the data of Springer and Keil actually provide strong evidence that such understanding is constructed only at about age 7.

An understanding of inheritance of properties is taken to include, at a minimum, two essential components: (1) family resemblance and (2) reproduction. With respect to variations among individuals of the same species, children resemble their parents, i.e. black parents tend to have black children, blue-eyed parents are more likely to have blue-eyed children than are brown-eyed parents, etc. Also, with respect to variations among species, children resemble their parents, i.e. dogs have baby dogs and not baby cats. The mechanism underlying this resemblance crucially involves birth. There are many ways in which children may come to resemble their parents: curly-haired parents may have curly-haired children because they give them permanent waves; prejudiced parents may have prejudiced children because they taught them to be so. Such mechanisms are not part of a biological process of inheritance of properties. To be credited with a biological concept of inheritance, children need not understand anything like a genetic mechanism, but they must distinguish the process underlying family resemblance from such learning or mechanical processes. At the minimum, they should realize that the process through which an animal originates — birth — is crucially involved in the process through which animals come to have their specific characteristics.

Without doubt, pre-school children understand that offspring resemble their parents. Springer (1992) told 4- to 8-year-old children that an animal in a picture had an unusual property, e.g. 'This horse has hair inside its ears'. He probed for projection of the property to a physically similar horse, described as a friend who is unrelated to the target, and to a physically dissimilar horse, described as the target's baby. At all ages, the property was projected more to the baby than to the friend. This important result confirms the mounting evidence that pre-school children are not appearance-bound (Gelman and Coley 1991), and establishes the family-resemblance component of a belief in inheritance of properties. However, since it does not probe the mechanism responsible for inheritance, it cannot provide information on the second component. Springer distinguishes what he considers a biological relationship (parentage) from a social relationship (friendship), but, as Carey (1985, 1988) points out, parentage is also a social relationship. At a minimum, one would like to see biological parentage distinguished from adoptive parentage.

The same issue arises with respect to the data of Springer and Keil (1989). Children aged from 4 to 7 years and adults were told that both parents had a particular atypical property (e.g. pink rather than the usual red hearts) and asked whether an offspring would have that property. They manipulated further information about the unusual property (how the parents acquired it (at birth or in an accident), whether it is internal or external to the body, and whether it had 'biological' functional consequences.* Two important results emerged. First, only the adults based their judgements solely on the information of how the parents acquired the property, i.e. only adults related birth to inheritance. In one study, 7-year-old children were beginning to take this variable into account. Second, even pre-school children make systematic judgments: they were influenced by whether the property was described as having 'biological' consequences or not. From this result, Springer and Keil concluded that pre-school children do have a biological concept of inheritance, but that it is different from the adult concept. Actually, they show only an understanding of family resemblance. Again, a comparison between natural parentage and adoptive parentage is necessary.

Gelman and Wellman (1991) specifically contrasted nature and nurture. For example, they asked whether a cow, Edith, who had been separated from other cows at birth and raised with pigs, would moo or oink or would have a straight tail or a curly tail. Even 4-year-old children judged that Edith would moo and have a straight tail. However, the story asserts that Edith is a cow, despite having been raised in the company of pigs, i.e. it prejudges the question of interest. There is a wealth of evidence, much of

---

* Springer and Keil (1989) offer no analysis of what constitutes a 'biological' functional consequence, and include such as examples as 'has stretched out eyes which make it easier to see their enemies'.

it from Gelman herself (Gelman and Markman 1986), that pre-schoolers children take category membership as predictive of category-relevant properties, even in the face of conflicting information. Further, the task does not stress that the baby cow is raised in a pig family, a child among other children who are pigs. Gelman and Wellman were aware of this problem, but their attempt to test whether category information is driving the inference fails. They posed a story about an apple seed planted in a flower pot and found that, by the age of 5, children judged that it would come up as an apple rather than a flower. Once again they are contrasting environment (in the company of flowers) with parentage (seed from an apple), i.e. these data confirm Springer's (1992) finding that it is *family* resemblance that is crucial but do not provide a test of the distinction between biological and adoptive parentage.

Solomon *et al.* (in press) have carried out two studies contrasting adoptive parentage with biological parentage. For example, children are told a story about a shepherd whose son is taken at birth to be adopted by a king and brought up as a prince. The child is then posed questions such as the following. The shepherd has blue eyes but the king has brown eyes – when the boy grows up, do you think that he will have blue eyes like the shepherd or brown eyes like the king? The shepherd believes that lions have 32 teeth but the king believes that they have 36 teeth – when the boy grows up, do you think that he will believe that lions have 36 teeth, like the king, or will he believe that lions have 32 teeth, like the shepherd? Adults project physical properties such eye colour on the basis of biological parentage and beliefs on the basis of family of rearing. This pattern is not seen, and then only weakly, until age 7, the age at which Springer and Keil (1989) began to see the effect of information as to whether the property of the parent was inborn or acquired. As of now, there is no evidence that pre-school children have a concept of biological inheritance that goes beyond expectations of resemblance between parents and their offspring, i.e. they do not distinguish between different kinds of mechanisms by which such resemblance comes into being.

Thus, just as in the case of their knowledge of growth, pre-school children's knowledge of family resemblance appears to be an unexplained fact about animals that they have acquired, presumably through domain-general learning mechanisms. Callanan and Oakes (1992) provide an amusing anecdote illustrating that the pre-school child's understanding of family resemblance is unexplained.

Child: Why does Daddy, James (big brother), and me have blue eyes and you have green eyes?

Parent: (Told her she got her eyes from Daddy. Then said good night and left the room).

Child: (Calls mother back 5 minutes later). I like Pee Wee Herman and I have blue eyes. Daddy likes Pee Wee Herman and he has blue eyes. James like Pee Wee Herman and he has blue eyes. If you liked Pee Wee Herman you could get blue eyes too.

Parent: (I told her it would take more than my liking Pee Wee Herman to make my eyes blue. I realized that she didn't understand me, so I explained that God gave me this color and that they couldn't be changed).

Child: Could you try to like Pee Wee Herman so we could see if your eyes turn blue?

These data are consistent with those reviewed by Carey (1985) indicating changes in children's understanding of reproduction during these years, such that the pre-school child does not take reproduction as one of the core principles defining animals and governing inferences about them. By the age of 10 (beginning by the age of 7 or 8), knowledge of reproduction begins to organize children's understanding of animals, as reflected both in the beginning understanding of inheritance and in judgements of what makes a skunk a skunk (Keil 1989). This change is part of the construction of the new ontological category, living thing, in the years before the age of 10, that includes plants as well as animals (Carey 1985). New core principles, and new modes of construals of entities, are the hallmarks of the construction of a new framework theory.

Contagion and disease

Knowledge of the causes of contagious disease is the third biology-specific causal mechanism that Wellman and Gelman (1992) claim pre-school children understand. They argue that children's knowledge of disease is domain-specific in three senses: they know that only biological entities become ill, they know that only certain bodily illnesses are contagious, and they know that illnesses are spread by biological means and cannot be explained by appeal to other causal domains (e.g. immanent justice).

Knowing that animals are the only kinds of things that become ill is not the same as knowing that only biological entities become ill. This is the theory-laden attribution error: we know that children have the concept **animal**; what is at issue is whether animal is a biological concept. Similarly, knowledge that only bodily illnesses are contagious is not evidence for knowledge of a causal mechanism underlying contagion. Such knowledge is part of the evidence that children distinguish the bodily from the psychological. As reviewed above, Keil has shown that pre-school children think that one person can 'catch' such symptoms as rashes and watery eyes through physical contact with a person who has them, but not weird beliefs or behaviours. This I grant; the question is whether the child has any knowledge of any biological mechanism underlying such 'catching'.

Several studies have shown that children appeal to germs in explaining contagion. For example, Kalish (1993) showed that pre-school children judge that a person will become ill as a result of eating a piece of apple with germs on it, but not a piece of apple taken from the garbage that does not have germs on it. This shows that pre-school children have learned that 'germs' are a cause of disease, but we do not know whether this knowledge goes beyond naming 'germs' as the cause of disease. Pre-school children also think that eating dirt will make you ill, and that eating poison will make you ill. Such knowledge may simply be a learned input–output relation, such as that eating good foods keeps you healthy and makes you grow, and may not constitute knowledge of any mechanism.

Keil (1992, 1994) argues that pre-school children understand germs as biological entities that make you ill by getting inside you and using part of your body. He showed that if young children are told that germs worked that way, they drew the conclusion that germs are animal-like. This interesting demonstration further supports the view that pre-school children think that animals are the kinds of things that have goals and can use other things, not that they have any antecedent understanding of germs causing disease via such a mechanism.

One method for addressing this issue would be to explore whether children distinguish different types of mechanisms causing disease, particularly with respect to whether the disease is contagious. The logic here is parallel to that of the exploration by Solomon *et al.* (in press) of when children distinguish adoptive and biological parentage in predicting family resemblance in different types of properties. Solomon *et al.* (in preparation) are exploring whether children understand germs to underlie contagion, in contrast with other causes of diseases (such as poisons). Pre-school children demonstrate no such understanding.

In sum, pre-school children's understanding of disease, like their understanding of children's resemblance to their parents and their understanding of growth and bodily processes, is limited to knowledge of input–output relations—dirt, poisons, going outside with no coat on, and germs cause disease. Diseases can be caught from other people. Such knowledge can serve as the input to constructing a first genuine biology (as Atran (1994) suggests), but there is no evidence in this literature that pre-school children have yet constructed any understanding of biologically specific causal mechanisms related to these phenomena.

Preschool children's intuitive biology: two promising proposals

Teleological—functional mode of construal (Keil)

Keil (1992, 1994) argues that a universal component of adult folk biology is a teleological—functional mode of construal. An animal's or a plant's properties are explained (at least in part) in terms of what they are for. For example, a satisfactory answer to the question of why giraffes have long necks is that they need them to eat the leaves from tall trees. Such an explanation is functional because it appeals to the purpose of the property/part. Teleological explanation, in which a present process is explained by a future state, is related — when the future state can be conceptualized as a goal. For example, appeals to equilibrium mechanisms in biology are both teleological (the organism seeks certain balances) and functional (those balances serve some function for the organism).

This basic mode of construing animals becomes culturally elaborated in different ways. In modern biology, evolutionary theory is one elaboration of a teleological–functional mode of construing animals. In other cultures, the argument from design becomes a motivation for the existence of God or gods (Keil (1994), quoting Dawkins, (1986)). Keil (1992, 1994) makes two further claims: (1) the teleological–functional mode of construal is the first specifically biological explanatory schema in a preschool child's biology; (2) this mode of construal constitutes the roots of a biology separate from psychology and mechanics. Let us consider each of these claims.

A series of elegant studies from Keil's laboratory (see Keil (1992, 1994) for summaries) shows that pre-school children (and children in their early elementary years) apply functional explanations to animals and plants, and that animals and plants are differentiated from inanimate natural kinds and even artefacts in this regard. For example, Keil offered children two possible answers to questions such as 'Why are plants green?' and 'Why are emeralds green?' The answers were (a) 'Being green is good for plants (emeralds), it helps there be more plants (emeralds)', and (b) 'There are tiny plant (emerald) parts, which, when mixed together, give them their green color'. Keil found that 5- to 7-year-old children preferred answers of type (a) when the property was a property of animals or plants by a ratio 2.5:1, and that they preferred answers of type (b) when the property was a property of inanimate natural kinds by a ratio of 5:1. In a similar demonstration, he showed children a picture of a prickly plant and a prickly mineral, and pointed out that both were prickly. He then told them that only one of these was prickly because being prickly was good for it, and asked them to choose. By the age of 5, children reliably choose the plant over the mineral. Finally, Keil (1994) showed 3-year-old children pictures of the barbs on barbed wire and the thorns on roses. Both these parts serve functions, but only the thorn on the rose is for the good of the rose. Three-year-old children make the adult choice when presented pairs such as these and asked which has the part for the good of itself and which has the part for the good of others.

Before we accept that these demonstrations show that pre-school children (or at least children aged 5–7) have constructed an intuitive biology, we must guard against the fallacy of theory-laden attribution. A functional analysis lays out some aspect of the role that a property, part, or process plays in achieving some goal, and in order for the functional analysis to be part of a biology, the goal must be a *biological* goal. No doubt these children are construing animal and plant properties in terms of functions, but are they biological functions? This is a serious worry. For example, Springer and Keil (1989) offer as an example of a biological function, 'being able to see one's enemies better in the dark'. I would guess that, for children, *seeing* and *enemy* are more fundamentally psychological than biological concepts.

In some of Keil's demonstrations, the nature of the function–goal is unspecified — 'good for it, good for itself'. None the less, it does seem clear that the child conceives of animals and plants in terms of at least some biological functions. 'Helps there to be more plants', seems a biological function as opposed to a behavioural goal. That these demonstrations include plants as well as animals, itself reinforces this point, for plants are not in the domain of a folk psychology. Therefore Keil has demonstrated a specifically biological mode of construal of animals and plants by 5-year-old children, and perhaps by even younger children. None the less, this demonstration would be much strengthened by an analysis of the *biological* goals and functions that the pre-school child knows about.

Turning to Keil's second claim, I would counter that these demonstrations of a biological mode of construal among 5- to 7-year-old children (and even perhaps 3-year-old childen) do *not* constitute evidence that biology has roots independent of intuitive psychology. It is not that the construal is functional–teleological that makes it biology, it is that some function–goal is *biological* that makes it biology. As Leslie (Chapter 5) points out, the infant's conception of agents involves construing agents' behaviour in terms of goals. If infants analyse their own and others' behaviour in terms of the roles that they play in reaching goals, this is probably the earliest functional analysis, which is thereby part of the child's initial intuitive theory of mind or folk psychology. Certainly, the earliest form of teleological reasoning in which the child engages is in understanding the behaviour of others in terms of their goals, which is also part of folk psychology. My own guess is that the first extension of functional–teleological analysis (beyond this initial psychology) is into an understanding of tools and artefacts. Only then does the child construct a functional–teleological understanding of the parts and properties of animals and plants. Some of this understanding will still sit in an intuitive psychology, i.e. an understanding of the parts that make certain behaviour possible (like seeing in the dark). This developmental sequence is one way in which the child's early intuitive biology emerges from an intuitive psychology.

Vitalist biology (Inagaki and Hatano)

To what biological goals might the pre-school child's functional-teleological mode of explanation apply? The most fundamental biological goal is life itself — maintaining life and avoiding death. Maintaining health and avoiding sickness is another fundamental biological goal. Reproducing the species is another fundamental biological goal (Keil's 'helps there to be more plants'). Might the pre-school child's functional–teleological explanation serve to account for how organisms meet goals such as these?

Evidence that it might comes from classic studies of children's explanation of bodily processes. When asked why we eat, pre-school children often answer in terms of health (as well as growth); when asked what would happen if we do not eat, they answer that we would die. When asked what would happen if we did not breathe, have a heart, have blood, drink water, etc., the modal answer for preschool children is 'we would die' (Nagy 1953; Gellert 1962; Crider 1981). Of course, such statements on the part of the child support the attribution of basic biological goals to preschool children only in so far as they have a biological understanding of life and death, and the evidence reviewed by Carey (1985, 1988), that even by the age of 4 or 5 pre-school children have not constructed an autonomous biological understanding of death (and thus life), still stands.

However, Inagaki and Hatano (1993) present evidence that by the age of 6 the child (at least the modern Japanese child) has constructed an autonomous biology surrounding such goals — a vitalist biology. See Hatano and Inagaki (1994) for an overview. Vitalist biologies have been independently constructed in many different cultures, including some in the West (Toulmin and Goodfield 1962). Since Inagaki and Hatano are studying Japanese children, they place their studies in the context of Japanese vitalism, which is built around the concept of *ki* or life force. *Ki* is roughly analogous to the concept of 'entelechy' or vital force in Western biology prior to the late nineteenth century — the extra something that a body must have to be alive. When an animal or person dies, the vital force leaves the body. In Western vitalism, this was often conceptualized as the vital force (soul) leaving with the last breath. Also common to both Japanese and Western vitalism is the idea that the air is one source of vital energy, and that breathing is in the service of replenishing and sustaining life through obtaining vital energy from the air. Another aspect of vitalism is a 'balance' theory of disease — diseases result from separate components of the life force (humours, yin–yang) becoming out of balance. Japanese vitalism elaborates a theory of the workings of internal organs, whereby they are endowed with agency and work to maintain bodily function by playing a role in the transmission and exchange of vital force. This vital force *ki* is undifferentiated (from modern science's point of view) between a substance, energy, and information.

Inagaki and Hatano present two sorts of evidence that Japanese children have constructed a vitalist biology by the age of 6. First, in free explanations of bodily phenomena, children of this age (or aged 7–8) sometimes elaborated vitalist ideas. For example, when asked what would happen to one's hands if blood circulation were to stop, one child said 'If blood does not come to the hands, they will die, because the blood does not carry energies to them' (Inagaki and Hatano 1993.) In a similar vein, Crider (1981) documented the 'container theory' of the workings of the human body constructed by American children between the ages of 8 and 10, whereby the stomach and lungs are conceptualized as containers for vital substances that are obtained from the outside, and the role of the blood is to transport these vital substances all over the body. Most probably, the vital substances in the American child's container theory are similarly undifferentiated between substance, energy, and information.

Inagaki and Hatano (1993) suspected that free explanation tasks, such as those on which Crider based her characterization, and those that yielded the relatively small number of vitalist explanations from their own subjects, may underestimate the attractiveness of a vitalist construal of animals for young children. Therefore they devised an explanation preference task, the second source of evidence for their claim. Subjects (6- and 8-year-old children, as well as adults) were asked to choose which of three explanations for each of a variety of phenomena they preferred. For example, the question might be 'Why do we eat food every day', and the three explanations offered might be as follows.

1. (Intentional) Because we want to eat tasty food.
2. (Vitalistic) Because our stomach takes in vital power from the food.
3. (Mechanistic) Because we take the food into our body after its form is changed in the stomach and bowels.

Inagaki and Hatano found the 6-year-old children preferred the vitalistic explanations (54 per cent of choices), followed by the intentional explanations (25 per cent of choices). Eight-year-old children preferred the mechanistic explanations (62 per cent of choices), but also showed a substantial preference for vitalistic explanations (34 per cent). Adults overwhelmingly preferred mechanistic explanations (96 per cent).

The data obtained by Inagaki and Hatano provided interesting evidence that a vitalistic construal of bodily processes is psychologically intermediate between an intentional construal and a mechanistic construal. They showed that 6-year-old children confused the vitalistic and intentional explanations, and virtually never confused either with the mechanistic explanations, whereas the 8-year-old children confused the vitalistic and mechanistic explanations, and virtually never confused either with the intentional explanations.

The data in support of Inagaki and Hatano's conjecture that a vitalistic biology is the first autonomous biology constructed by young children, and that it is constructed by the age of 6, is suggestive but not conclusive. The main problems are that only a few children spontaneously produce vitalist explanations, and the choices in the explanation choice task are confounded. For example, the intentional explanations in the study are often little more than tautologies, as in 'We eat food each day because we want to eat tasty food'. More informative intentional choices could have been provided, such as 'We eat food every day because we become hungry and eating gets rid of the feeling of hunger'. The mechanistic explanations often included detailed information and vocabulary that 6-year-old children were unlikely to know, such as that people take in air because the lungs take in oxygen and change it into useless carbon dioxide.* My point here is that such explanation choice tasks are very difficult to carry out; making different explanation types comparable with respect to the informativeness of the explanation and familiarity with the information it contains is no easy matter.

Inagaki and Hatano's conjecture is plausible and should be followed up in several ways. Scholarly work is needed to establish whether vastly different cultures have indeed independently constructed vitalist biologies, and whether vitalist ideas are of the sorts that spread from culture to culture, i.e. we need an analysis of the epidemiology of vitalist representations (Sperber 1985). A more thorough study of vitalist biologies would yield an analysis of what they have in common—the core principles of vitalism. If such core principles are forthcoming, and if research with children in different cultures reveals that young children universally construct a biology that embodies some (all) of these core principles, then we should conclude that vitalist biologies are closely related to construals of the world embodied in first-order cognitive modules.

Such a state of affairs would not establish that a vitalist biology is itself a first-order cognitive module, for all the reasons already outlined in this chapter. Inagaki and Hatano's evidence is that a vitalist biology is constructed by the age of 6, and there is still good reason to deny an autonomous biology to children age 4 or less. Specifically, 4-year-old children cannot have constructed a vitalist biology, for they have not constructed the concept of life (Carey 1985; Carey 1988; Carey and Spelke 1994). So what are the roots of the child's vitalistic construal of animals?

I submit that a vitalist construal of animals is built on the first-order construal of animals as agents (see Chapter 5). As Gelman (1990) has also stressed, one of the core principles that guides identification of, and reasoning about, animals is that they have an internal source of movement (she

* This explanation is also defective as a functional explanation. Why would the body want to change air into something useless.?

denotes this 'the innards principle'). This internal causal power makes animals capable of action, and evidence of an internal source of action is one of the fundamental ways that we differentiate animals from non-animals (see Chapter 7). Initially, the internal causal power is a source of action, not of life.

I propose that the child constructs the concept of life from two sources. First, the child learns a vast array of facts about animals — they (and in some cases plants) grow, become ill, die, reproduce. Initially, these facts are interpreted only within intuitive psychology or are simply unexplained — explanation has to stop somewhere. However, they are interrelated, coherent, and mutually constraining. This systematicity cries out for explanation. There must be some cause of these regularities. The child borrows the innards principle as a place-holder for this cause — just as there is something within the animal that is the source of action, there is something within the animals that is the source of growth and health, and the absence of which constitutes sickness and death. This idea then becomes elaborated into the vitalism of Inagaki and Hatano (1993) or the container theory of the body (Crider 1991). In this way folk biology emerges from folk psychology.

The final question is which version of the claim that folk biology emerges from folk psychology is true — the weak version or the medium-strong version? The answer is — both. Initially, the ontological status of the infant's concept **animal** derives entirely from its place in a first-order theory of mind module (as in the weak version). The young child has no explanation for an animal's bodily properties and processes; knowledge of these is in a region of knowledge where explanation has been exhausted. But, by the age of 3-4, the child has begun to construct explanations for bodily processes, and these explanations are initially undifferentiated between the psychological and the biological (as in the medium-strong version). Carey (1985, 1988) characterizes these undifferentiated concepts, which are incommensurable with those in our adult folk biology. They include an undifferentiated concept **dead/inanimate**, and the undifferentiated (with respect to biology and psychology) concepts **parent** and **family** (see also above). Also reflecting the differentiation of the biological and the psychological over the first decade of life is the change of status of people as animals; for 4-year-old children, people are the prototypical animals and animals are defective people, whereas by the age of 10, people are simply one animal among many (Carey 1885, 1988). Also part of this differentiation is the coalescence of the concepts **animal** and **plant** into a new concept, **living thing**.

CONCLUSIONS—THE ORIGIN OF CAUSAL/ EXPLANATORY NOTIONS IN FOLK BIOLOGY

I have attempted to synthesize the insights of all of the thinkers whose work I have discussed in this chapter. Like Atran (1994), I believe that children's early knowledge of animals does not include explicit biological causal principles and is therefore pre-theoretical (in the sense of pre-*biological* theory.) Also like Atran, I believe that this early knowledge is the input to the construction of a first intuitive biology. Like Wellman and Gelman (1991), Keil (1992, 1994), and Inagaki and Hatano (1993), I agree that Carey (1985, 1988) underestimated the age at which children construct their first autonomous biology (but not by much — I would lower the age from 10 to 6-7). Additionally, I have attempted to sketch the truly important progress that Keil (1992, 1994) and Inagaki and Hatano (1993) have made in characterizing that first biology. Inagaki and Hatano's vitalism and Keil's functional–teleological mode of construal are complementary aspects of the same biology — bodily properties and functions are understood in terms of the function that they play in maintaining life. Finally, I have argued that both aspects of this first biology emerge from a first-order cognitive module that is an intuitive psychology.

REFERENCES

Atran, S. (1990). *Cognitive foundations of natural history*. Cambridge University Press.

Atran, S. (1994). Core domains versus scientific theories: evidence from systematics and Itzaj-Maya folk biology. In *Domain specificity in cognition and culture* (ed. L. A. Hirschfeld and S. A. Gelman), pp. 316-40. Cambridge University Press, New York.

Callanan, M. A. and Oakes, L. M. (1992). Preschooler's questions and parents' explanations: Causal thinking in everyday activity. *Cognitive Development* 7, 213-33.

Carey, S. (1985). *Conceptual change in childhood*. Bradford/MIT Press, Cambridge, MA.

Carey, S. (1988). Conceptual differences between children and adults. *Mind and Language* 3, 167-81.

Carey, S. (1991). Knowledge acquisition: enrichment or conceptual change? In *Epigenesis of mind: studies in biology and cognition* (ed. S. Carey and R. Gelman). Erlbaum, Hillsdale, NJ.

Carey, S. and Spelke, E. (1994). Domain specific knowledge and conceptual, change. *Domain specificity in cognition and culture* (ed. L. A. Hirschfield and S. A. Gelman), pp. 169-200. Cambridge University Press, New York.

Clement, J. (1982). Students' preconceptions in introductory mechanics. *American Journal of Physics* 50(1), 66-1.

Cohen, L. B. and Younger, B. A. (1983). Perceptual categorization in the infant. In *New trends in conceptual representation* (ed. G. K. Scholnick), pp. 197–200. Erlbaum. Hillsdale, NJ.

Crider, C. (1981). Children's conceptions of the body interior. In *Children's conceptions of health, illness and bodily functions* (ed. R.Bibace and M. Walsh). Jossey-Bass, San Francisco, CA.

Dawkins, R. (1986). *The blind watchmaker*. Norton, New York.

Diamond, R. and Carey, S. (1990). On the acquisition of pattern encoding skills. *Cognitive Development* 5(4), 345–68.

Fodor, J. A. (1983). *The modularity of mind*. MIT Press, Cambridge, MA.

Gallistel, C. R. and Gelman, R. (1992). Preverbal and verbal counting and computation. *Cognition* 44(1–2), 43–74.

Gellert, E. (1962). Children's conceptions of the content and functions of the human body. *Genetic Psychology Monographs Monographs* 65, 291–411.

Gelman, R. (1990). First principles organize attention to and learning about relevant data: number and the animate–inanimate distinction as examples. *Cognitive Science* 14, 79–106.

Gelman, S. A. and Coley, J. D. (1991). Language and categorization: the acquisition of natural kind terms. In *Perspectives on language and thought: interrelations in development* (ed. S. A. Gelman and J.P. Byrnes). Cambridge University Press.

Gelman, S. A. and Kremer, K. E. (1991). Understanding natural cause: Children's explanations of how objects and their properties originate. *Child Development* 62, 396–414.

Gelman, S. A. and Markman, E. M. (1986). Categories and induction in young children. *Cognition* 38, 213–44.

Gelman, S. A. and Wellman, H. M. (1991). Insides and essences: early understandings of the nonobvious. *Cognition* 38, 213–44.

Glymour, C. (1985). Fodor's holism. *Behavioural and Brain Sciences* 8, 15–16.

Gopnik, A. and Wellman, H. M. (1994). The theory theory. In *Domain specificity in culture and cognition* (ed. L. A. Hirschfeld and S. A. Gelman), pp. 257–93. Cambridge University Press, New York.

Hall, D. G. and Waxman, S. R. (1993). Assumptions about word meanings: individuation and basic-level kinds. *Child Development* 64, 1550–70.

Hatano, G. and Inagaki, K. (1994). Young children's naive theory of biology. *Cognition* 56, 171–88.

Hempel, C. G. and Oppenheim, P. (1948). Studies in the logic of explanation. *Philosophy of Science* 15, 135–75.

Hirsch, E. (1982). *The concept of identity*. Oxford University Press, New York.

Hirschfeld, L. A. and Gelman, S. A. (ed) (1994). *Domain specificity in cognition and culture*. Cambridge University Press, New York.

Inagaki, K. and Hatano, G. (1987). Young children's spontaneous personification as analogy. *Child Development* 58, 1013–20.

Inagaki, K. and Hatano, G. (1993). Young children's understanding of the mind-body distinction. *Child Development* 64, 1534–49.

Jeyifous, S. (1986). Atimodemo: semantic conceptual development among the Yoruba. Doctoral Dissertation, Cornell University.

Kalish, C. (1993). Preschoolers understanding of germs as causes of illness. Presented at the Society for Research in Child Development, New Orleans, LA.

Keil, F. C. (1979). *Semantic and conceptual development: an ontological perspective*. Harvard University Press, Cambridge, MA.

Keil, F. C. (1989). *Concepts, kind, and cognitive development*. MIT Press, Cambridge, MA.

Keil, F. C. (1992). The origins of an autonomous biology. In *Modularity and Constraints in Language and Cognition. The Minnesota Symposium on Child Psychology*, Vol. 25 (ed. M. R. Gunnar and M. Marstsos), pp. 103–37. Erlbaum, Hillsdale, NJ.

Keil, F. (1994). The birth and nurturance of concepts by domains. In *Domain specificity in cognition and culture* (ed. L. A. Hirschfeld and S. A. Gelman), pp. 234–54. Cambridge University Press, New York.

McCloskey, M. (1983). Naive theories of motion. In *Mental models* (ed. D. Gentner and A. Stevens). Erlbaum, Hillsdale, NJ.

Macnamara, J. (1986). *Border dispute: the place of logic in psychology*. MIT Press, Cambridge, MA.

Markman, E. M. (1989). *Categorization and naming in children: problems of induction*. MIT Press, Cambridge, MA.

Murphy, G. L. and Medin, D. (1985). The role of theories in conceptual coherence. *Psychological Review* **92**, 289–316.

Nagy, M. H. (1953). Children's conceptions of some bodily functions. *Journal of Genetic Psychology* **83**, 199–216.

Perner, J. (1991). *Understanding the representational mind*. Bradford/MIT Press, Cambridge, MA.

Piaget, J. and Inhelder, B. (1941). *Le development des quantities chez l'enfant*. Delchaux et Niestle, Neufchatel.

Posner, M. I. and Keele, S. W. (1968). On the genesis of abstract ideas. *Journal of Experimental Psychology* **77**, 353–63.

Rhodes, G. and Tremewan, T. (1993). The Simon and Garfunkel effect: semantic priming, sensitivity and modularity of face recognition. *Cognitive Psychology* **25**, 147–87.

Rosengren, K. S., Gelman, S. A., Kalish, C. W. and McCormick, M. (1991). As time goes by: children's early understanding of growth in animals. *Child Development* **62**, 1302–20.

Salmon, W. -C. (1984). *Scientific explanation and the causal structure of the world*. Princeton University Press.

Salmon, W. C. (1989). *Four decades of scientific explanation*. University of Minnesota Press, Minneapolis.

Schank, R. C. and Abelson, R. (1977). *Scripts, plans, goals, and understanding*. Erlbaum, Hillsdale, NJ.

Smith, C. L. (1979). Children's understanding of natural language hierarchies. *Journal of Experimental Child Psychology* **27**, 437–58.

Smith, C., Carey, S. and Wiser, M. (1985). On differentiation: a case. study of the development of the concepts of size, weight, and density. *Cognition* **21**, 177–237.

Solomon, G., Johnson, S., Zaitchik, D. and Carey, S. (in press). Like father, like son: young children's understanding of how and who offspring resemble their parents.

Solomon, G., Zaitchik, D. and Cassimatis (in preparation).

Sommers, F. (1963). Types and ontology. *Philosophical Review* **72**, 327–63.

Sperber, D. (1985). Anthropology and psychology: towards and epidemiology of representations (the Malinowski Memorial Lecture 1984). *Man* (NS), **20**, 73–89.

Sperber, D. (1994). The modularity of thought and the epidemiology of representations. In *Domain specificity in cognition and culture* (ed. L. A. Hirschfeld and S. A. Gelman), pp. 39–67. Cambridge University Press, New York.

Springer, K. (1992). Children's beliefs about the biological implications of kinship. *Child Development* **60**, 637–48.

Springer, K. and Keil, F. C. (1989). On the development of biologically specific beliefs: the case of inheritance. *Child Development* **60**, 637–48.

Springer, K. and Keil, F. C. (1991). Early differentiation of causal mechanisms appropriate to biological and nonbiological kinds. *Child Development* **60**, 637–48.

Toulmin, S. and Goodfield, J. (1962). *The architecture of matter*. University of Chicago Press.

Vosniadou, S. and Brewer, W. F. (1992). Mental models of the earth: A study of conceptual change in childhood. *Cognitive Psychology* **24**(4), 535–85.

Watson, J. (1979). Perception of contingency as a determinant of social responsiveness. In *The origins of social responsiveness* (ed. E. Tohman), pp. 33–64. Erlbaum, Hillsdale, NJ.

Waxman, S. R. (1994). Linguistic and conceptual organization. *Lingua* **92**, 229–57.

Wellman, H. M. (1990) *The child's theory of mind*. MIT Press, Cambridge, MA.

Wellman, H. M. and Gelman, S. A. (1992). Cognitive development: foundational theories of core domains. *Annual Review of Psychology* **43**, 337–75.

Wiggins, D. (1980). *Sameness and substance*. Basil Blackwell, Oxford.

Wiser, M. (1987). Novice and historical thermal theories. In *Ontogeny, phylogeny, and the history of science* (ed. S. Straus). Ablex, Norwood, NJ.

Wiser, M. and Carey, S. (1983). When heat and temperature were one. In *Mental modes* (ed. D. Gentner and A. Stevens), pp. 267–97. Erlbaum, Hillsdale, NJ.

Wynn, K. (1992). Addition and subtraction by human infants. *Nature, London* **358**, 749–50.

DISCUSSION

Questions for and answers from Carey

1. Question from Hinde

A question that may seem irrelevant to many here, but important to me because I come from a discipline that fought a long battle for precision in the use of the term 'innate', a battle we thought we had won thirty years ago. By 'innate domains' do you mean that the distinctions between them are hard-wired and independent of experience, or produced by experiences more or less common to all children, or that you do not know? Geneticists apply 'innate' only to differences, not to characters. Its use here blocks the investigation of the possibility of the importance of interaction, gives a (probably false) picture that development involves stages rather than being continuous.

Answer from Carey

The notion of innate domain being appealed to is spelled out most clearly by Chomsky (see Carey and Spelke, 1994, for an analysis of how Chomsky's notion applies to cognitive domains). Several comments about this notion: first, it is sharply distinguished from that of 'highly heritable', the population geneticists' concept that applies to individual differences. Heritability is the proportion of variance among individuals that is due to genetic variation. The heritability of language is near 0 (variation in languages among individuals is almost entirely due to environmental factors), yet language is an innate domain. Second, innate domains are learning mechanisms (e.g. universal grammar is part of an innate language acquisition mechanism), and so positing them requires no commitment whatsoever to the idea that experience is not important to knowledge acquisition. Quite the contrary, to characterize an innate domain one must characterize how learning takes place; one must characterize the precise role of experience in determining the adult state. Third, the learning mechanism for any given innate domain may or may not yield stage like learning. For example, there are domain-specific learning mechanisms for diet selection in rats, and these operate in a continuous manner. There are domain specific learning mechanisms for bird song in sparrows, and these yield stage like learning (there are critical periods). Finally, differences among domains are hard wired, or emerge through mechanisms that are not *learning* mechanisms.

2. Question from Boyer

You said that some aspects of what is often described as 'biological knowledge' in the pre-schooler are not the effect of a domain-specific conceptual structure, but are 'associative residue'. Could you specify the organizational properties and inferential potential, of such an 'associative residue?' If it is highly structured in terms of intuitive expectations, would it not constitute what is usually expected from a domain-specific structure?

Answer from Carey

My chapter is an extended answer to this question, but let me attempt a short one. Clearly, I can't specify the organizational properties and inferential potential of the preschools' concept *animal* in a short answer — my whole 1985 book attempted to do so, and there has been volumes of further work since then. Part of the organizational properties of this structure are similarity based, prototype derived. Prototype abstraction is a domain general associative mechanism. Some are script-like. Both types of conceptual structures are common among children and adults, and are not what is expected from domain-specific structures that are intuitive theories. Finally, some of the inferential potential of preschoolers' reasoning about animals derives from animals being in the domain of intuitive folk psychology.

The question then becomes whether there is any 'biological knowledge' of preschoolers that goes beyond these three types of structures. As I review in my chapter, there is unequivocal evidence for such biological knowledge by all normal children of ages 6 or 7, but not before. Some preschoolers of ages 4 or 5 have certainly constructed a folk biology as well. The theoretically important point (as far as folk biology being an innate domain on a par with folk psychology and folk mechanics) is that most preschoolers have not yet constructed a folk biology.

3. Question from Keil

I grant that there is conceptual change *and* that it is *not* only the product of 'high' culture. But why should that entail that the conceptual change is so unbounded that there is no common framework across cultures?

Answer from Carey

There is no 'should' about it. My point simply is that it is an *empirical* question as to which aspects of the structure of innate domains (if any) are preserved in cross-culturally universal explanatory frameworks.

4.   Question from Keil

The family resemblance argument cannot explain many of the inheritance phenomena. A key subcomponent is that expectations are about only biological features, not about social features. No global family resemblance notion can work.

Answer from Carey

I have two responses. First, calling any given feature a 'biological feature' begs the question. What is at issue between us is whether *any* features, are, for *preschool* children, biological features. Calling a feature such as 'being able to see one's enemies in the dark' a biological feature, as you do, does not make it so.

Still, I agree that preschool children distinguish bodily from social features and that they distinguish bodily from mental features. However, preschool children, for the most part, do not distinguish *adoptive* from *biological* families with respect to projection of these features from parents to children. This is why we deny that the studies to date reveal any causal understanding of biological inheritance.

5.   Question from Nisbett

Does your position imply that the only place to look for universals is among very young children? Is that the only place where they will be found or rather the only place that it would count as theoretically significant if they were to be found?

Answer from Carey

My argument is that the existence of innate cognitive domains guarantees cognitive universals only among very young children. Cross-cultural cognitive universals among adults are certainly theoretically significant, but we need studies of development to ascertain whether they reflect (a) innate domain-specific constraints on knowledge acquisition or (b) common experiences that have led to parallel theory construction across different cultures.

6.   Question from Spelke

I agree that the question of the existence and nature of cross-cultural universals is empirical, but I do not agree that there is no reason to think 'yes'. Here's what gives us reasons to expect cross-cultural universals:

1. Whenever we find concepts in infancy, we also find these concepts in adult common sense.
2. These tend to be represented in early systematic science.
3. When these are given up by developed science, this is only with great difficulty and is very striking when it occurs.

There is no evidence for conceptual change involving these early notions, and there are reasons to think you *won't* get it. First, the early beliefs are (should be) *true*. Second, the early beliefs determine the entities in the domain, so the entities picked out will accord with them.

Answer from Carey

Your question has several parts, some of which contradict each other. You say that the cases in which developed science has overturned core notions are striking (point 3 above), but you also say that core notions are, or should be, true. Of course, when developed science overturns a core notion, it is because it is deemed *not* to be true. And the fact that core notions determine the entities in a domain is what makes any case of conceptual change difficult, so if you grant the possibility of conceptual change at all, your last argument comes to the point that conceptual change is hard, not that it is unlikely. Whether it is unlikely or not depends upon the likelihood that evolution settled on core notions that are useful in getting learning off the ground as opposed to the likelihood that evolution settled on core notions that are true.

Still, I agree that there are empirical reasons to believe that early developing core notions will be preserved in adult common sense in most (all) cultures. These include several mentioned by you. First, they are preserved in *our* culture, which has been maximally influenced by developed science. Second, core notions have been evolutionarily selected for because they are useful, either because they are true, or because they provide explanatory coherence to widely available data. Thus, they will likely become entrenched rather than overthrown. Thus I agree with you that we should expect cross-cultural cognitive universals. My point simply is merely that the existence of conceptual change means that there is no a priori argument from innate domain specific knowledge to such universals.

7. Question from Atran

Susan, I have trouble with your idea of explanatory purpose, what other people call 'theory' (ugh!). I think I know what you want the idea to do — to restrict conceptual interrelations of the referents of the concepts into a tight cognitive 'domain'. But, first, there seems to be a great difference between metacognitive 'theories' which allow for conceptual change of the kind you're describing and modular 'theories' of the kind Spelke describes which do not allow transfer of information across domains: to call both 'theories' seems to fail to capture the fundamental distinction between what you and Spelke are talking about.

Answer from Carey

I consider the question of the relation between explicit statable, beliefs and the modular systems that Spelke, Leslie, and Baillargeon provide evidence for in infancy one of the central issues in developmental psychology. It is very possible that the phenomena in infancy reflect complex perceptual processes which are indeed modular, and which provide input to belief systems. If so, I would agree with you that we would not want to call these structures 'theories'. However, the 4-year-old's theory of mind, or the 7-year-old's intuitive biology are not such systems. These are explicitly statable belief systems, some of whose explanatory principles can be articulated by their adherents.

8. Question from Atran

But, at the metacognitive level, your use of theory in the sense of Frank Keil or Susan Gelman, or Henry Wellman's 'framework theory', fails to distinguish religion, myth, magic, and other traditional 'cosmological' or symbolic systems from truth-preserving metacognitive representation. Not that truth *is* necessarily preserved in specific theories or paradigm frameworks, but there is the *intention* of using them to preserve truth. So that the same initial metacognitive conception — for example, relating the concept of one domain to that of another (e.g. the plant as an upturned person) is treated differently depending upon whether one is interested in preserving truth while extending logically coherent and empirically plausible principles across domains. Symbolic processing aims to keep the metaphor or analogy open, impoverishing logical inference to local coherence and making crucial aspects empirically inscrutable. Truth-preserving 'theoretical' processing ultimately aims to kill the metaphor or analogy by making the logical and empirical relations between the terms of the analogy transparent. So 'theory' seems to confound some of the fundamental cognitive distinction we are all interested in.

Answer from Carey

As I say in my chapter, part of the differences you and I have are merely semantic — concerning the use of the term 'theory'. I would not object to dropping the term — in favour of 'truth preserving explanatory structure' or some such. I think your distinction between truth preserving use of analogy and symbolic use of analogy is insightful, and is one I have not thought about before. Would you argue that there are cultures that do not make the distinction? That there may be a point in development where children do not make the distinction? If not, then translate my use of 'theory' to 'truth preserving explanatory cognitive structures'.

I certainly agree with the thrust of your question. We want to distinguish a variety of cognitive/symbolic structures in our attempts to characterize the architecture of the mind. They include:

1. modular input systems
2. scripts
3. prototype/similarity based associative structures
4. explicitly held, causal-explanatory belief systems

You point out that the last category should be subdivided into two — truth preserving explanatory systems and symbolic systems such as myth, magic, and religion which are not truth preserving. A point well taken.

Part V

Understanding social causality

Part V

Understanding social causality

Foreword to Part V

In the three previous sections, we have seen powerful evidence and arguments suggesting that humans have innately determined dispositions to expect certain types of causal processes in the physical domain, other types of causal processes in the psychological domain, and (more controversially) yet other types in the biological domain. Humans are social animals. What kind of causal expectations do they have when it comes to social interaction? Is there a domain-specific form of understanding for the social domain? Much of social interaction can be understood as being governed by psychological processes, and thus psychological understanding, and at least some aspects of social understanding, can be seen as continuous, as suggested by Premack and Premack (Chapter 7).

Still, causal understanding in the social sphere seems to involve more than one mode of classification and more than one type of causation. Both Lawrence Hirschfeld and Ian Hacking explore this diversity. However, they do so in very different ways. Hirschfeld's approach is in the spirit of much current developmental psychology, with its emphasis on domain-specific innate mechanisms. Hacking, in contrast, challenges more radically than any other participant of our meeting (with the possible exception of Geoffrey Lloyd) the naturalistic cognitive approach favoured by most of the contributors.

In Chapter 11 Hirschfeld discusses the variety of causal factors appealed to in social understanding. He focuses on traits and dispositions that are attributed to people by virtue of the social categories or groups to which they are assumed to belong. Some of these groupings, such as sex or 'race', are construed in an essentialist manner. Others, such as occupation, are construed functionally. Drawing on new experimental findings, Hirschfeld challenges the dominant view according to which early social categorization is wholly based on superficial cues such as bodily appearance or dress. He argues that children have an innate disposition to construct both essentialistic and functional social categories, and do so before they have much relevant evidence for such categorization. He discusses how causal understanding in the social sphere relates to understanding in the psychological and biological domains.

In Chapter 12 Hacking argues that today's understanding of causal processes in human affairs relies crucially on concepts of 'human kinds' which are a product of the modern social sciences, with their concern for classification, quantification, and intervention. 'Child abuse', 'homosexuality', 'teenage pregnancy', and 'multiple personality' are examples of such recently established human kinds. What distinguishes human kinds from 'natural kinds', Hacking argues, is that they have specific 'looping effects'. By coming into existence through social scientists' classifications, human kinds change the people thus classified. From this perspective, it is not hard to see cognitive psychologists as producers of yet more human kinds, which they mistake for natural kinds. Even more than the written discussion at the end of Hacking's chapter can show, many participants at the meeting felt challenged by his views, and challenged them in turn.

D.S.

11

Anthropology, psychology, and the meanings of social causality
LAWRENCE A. HIRSCHFELD

It is hardly controversial to claim that the social environment shapes human behaviour and that humans everywhere recognize this to be so. Still, considerable cultural variation exists, for example, in the extent to which parents attempt to shape their children's development by 'managing' the social milieu in which child-rearing occurs. There is also considerable variation in how members of different cultures talk about this social environment, variation in the social entities that members recognize, and variation in the social consequences that members expect such entities to have. Further, how children come to acquire knowledge in, how they begin to grasp the meaning of, the social environment—in short, how they come to understand social causality—is crucial to children's explanations of human action. These are some of the issues that will be explored in this chapter.

By drawing insights from both anthropology (on the nature of the social arena) and psychology (on how understanding is represented), this exploration will yield a more comprehensive description of social causality. Anthropologists and psychologists frequently invoke the concept of social causality (typically treated under models of causal attribution in psychology). Despite the apparent (and unusual) shared analytic commitment to this notion, it will be argued that they use it to refer to quite different things. Just as England and America are often said to be divided by a common language, psychology and anthropology may well be separated by a common mode of explanation.

SOCIAL CAUSALITIES

It is widely accepted in psychology that common sense distinguishes between physical and social causes of events. Physical causes involve the transmission of energy and typically have an external origin. Social causes involve the enactment of intentions, and are usually internal (Shultz 1982).

Two aspects of this kind of causal taxonomy stand out. First, the same event can always be analyzed from both perspectives: kicking a can has both internal and external causal sequences, and so does committing suicide by leaping off the Golden Gate Bridge. Thus, understanding the meaning of physical and non-physical causality is not derived from a categorization of either objects or actions in themselves, but from an understanding of the notion of *distinct* causalities. Second, and more germane, a more prudent way of naming this contrast would be to distinguish physical from *mental* rather than social events. Thus the principal aim of this chapter will be to demonstrate that mental and social causalities are distinct, in terms of both mental representation and course of development.

An appreciation of physical and mental causalities emerges early and is quite robust (Michotte 1963). Expectations about complex (and contingent) physical relations appear to be in place virtually at birth (Spelke 1991). Similarly, infants seem to monitor care-givers' reactions to unfamiliar events in determining their own interpretations (Campos and Sternberg 1981). A considerable body of research on the pre-school child's emerging theory of mind has persuasively demonstrated that by the second year children understand the notions of pretend desires and goals (Dunn 1988; Leslie 1988), and that by the end of the third year children possess a rich cognizance of other people's mental states (Astington *et al.* 1988; Wellman 1990).*

Later, children come to interpret their own behaviour and that of others not simply in terms of transitory mental states such as beliefs and desires, but in terms of the enduring and stable mental states of **traits** and **dispositions**. Controversy exists concerning the age at which children begin to understand themselves and others in such terms. While earlier accounts suggest this understanding does not develop until middle childhood (Rhodes and Ruble 1984), Eder (1990) offers evidence that by 3½ years of age, children possess rudimentary dispositional concepts. In a review of existing studies, Yuill (1992) concludes that, although preschool children appeal to traits in interpreting behaviour, such traits are construed more as behavioural regularities than as explanatory constructs. Only later, perhaps in middle childhood, do children begin to interpret traits as *causal* factors in promoting desires and actions 'in the sense that they imply a unified set of goals that produce superficially diverse actions' (Yuill 1992, pp. 270–1). Importantly, even if their construal of traits and dispositions is not *fully* causal, young children appear to distinguish 'trait–disposition' interpretations from 'belief–desire' explanations. Psychological and character

---

* 'Theory of mind' is meant to capture a mentalistic construal of the world, including the notion that beliefs about things are distinct from the things themselves, and that mental states like belief and desire play a role in shaping behaviour.

explanations are thus seen as potentially *competing* (or alternative) accounts of behaviour. As Eder (1989) argues, young children recognize that some types of behaviour and emotion are consistent with a given dispositional self-construal while others are not.

As will become clear, the recognition that trait–disposition interpretations differ from those of belief–desire is an important issue. Adults readily recognize that people behave in certain ways in virtue of the kinds of people that they are. Kindhood, of course, is a broad concept. In one sense the kinds of people there are can be interpreted in terms of the sorts of human groups to which an individual belongs. Some of these involve intrinsic qualities, such as gender or race. Others involve extrinsic qualities, such as occupation. Another type of kindhood prevails in the models that underlie most psychological research. For instance, researchers in social causality frequently sort people analytically into person categories based on the traits or dispositions that dominate an individual's personality. These categories specify the kinds of people that there are in terms of a model seemingly derived from mentalistic or belief–desire reasoning. Thus, for example, a common strategy in social psychology contrasts people with high versus low self-esteem, high versus low self-monitors, depressed versus non-depressed individuals, etc. in terms of the outcome of interest.

From an ethnographic perspective, this often produces culture-bound research. In many, perhaps most, cultures there is a marked absence of discourse that explains human behaviour in terms of trans-situationally stable motivational (or intentional) properties captured by explanations of trait and disposition (Geertz 1973; Lutz 1988). Anthropologists and a number of psychologists have recently pointed out that standard treatments of self- and other-construals in social psychology may describe only a small percentage of people, not only in traditional societies studied by anthropologists but also in modern secular ones (Triandis 1989; Markus and Kitiyama 1991). However, these scholars often underestimate the implications of the observation. Rather than seek an explanation for collectivist self-construals among (most) non-Westerners, (many) women, and (members of most) ethnic minorities in America, it may make more sense to understand why it is that Northern Euro-American males have a strong preference for explaining human behaviour in terms of trans-situationally stable traits and dispositions.

THEORY AND FOLK THEORY

Scientific theories, as Hacking (Chapter 12) persuasively argues, are not immune to the context in which they emerge—there is a social causality of science as well as a science of social causality. Thus it is of interest to explore the possibility that the psychologist's focus on trait–disposition explanations may be part of a particular folk tradition. One way of examining this question is to consider what psychologists have proposed as the derivation of such explanations. At least two developmental origins have been suggested.

Wellman (1990) and Bartsch and Wellman (1989) argue that traits derive from the system of belief–desire reasoning. There are clear parallels between the belief–desire and trait–disposition systems of reasoning—for example, both provide a framework for understanding single actions. However, as Yuill (1992) notes, many traits, such as 'lazy' or 'arrogant', are difficult to link directly to beliefs and desires. Gelman (1992) suggests an alternative source for trait–disposition reasoning that may be more ethnographically sound. She notes that causal interpretations of traits have many parallels with young children's beliefs about essences. Recalling Medin's (1989) notion of psychological essence (i.e. that which makes something the sort of thing it is), Gelman notes that traits share many of the qualities of underlying essences—both explain a phenomenon by appealing to a hidden and non-obvious quality. The principle difference is that essences cause objects (or creatures) to be the sorts of things they *are*, while traits are thought to cause creatures to demonstrate certain characteristic *behaviour* (see also Chapter 19). On the face of it, cultural evidence appears to do little to resolve the question of the source of trait–desire reasoning in that both proposed derivations (theory of mind, on the one hand, and essentialist reasoning, on the other) are apparently universal (for theory of mind see Avis and Harris (1991); for essentialist reasoning see Atran (1990)), while the derived state (trait–disposition explanation) is not.

Recall that we are probing the origin of a system of *social causal* attribution. Traditional treatments have typically identified social causality with trait and disposition explanations. Does this make sense? From an ethnographic point of view, it may not. Cross-cultural evidence prompts us to broaden the notion of social causality away from the purely mentalistic. Although cross-cultural studies support the conclusion that 'theory of mind' is universal, there is a good deal of cultural evidence that a mentalistic construal of behaviour is not part of a universal discourse. While theory of mind may be universal, an ethnotheory of mind may not be. In contrast, there is compelling evidence that a (social) category–identity construal of behaviour *is* part of a universal discourse or ethnotheory (van den Berghe 1981; Hirschfeld 1988). Thus, in exploring social causality it may be more profitable to focus on a **theory of society** (and a societal module) than on a **theory of mind** (and a psychological module).*

* My point here is similar to that of Jackendoff (1992) in his discussion of the relationship of the faculty of social cognition to folk theory of mind.

Physical and mental causalities are often contrasted in the psychological literature (Shultz 1982, Chapter 20 of this volume). From an anthropological perspective, however, this seems peculiar. While anthropologists would not be uncomfortable with the notion that social and non-social causality are distinct, most would be surprised to identify *social* causality with *psychological* (or mental) causality. It is a truism of the ethnological literature that social identity shapes behaviour, but 'social identity' is understood in the sense of *social category identity* (for a psychological model of identity more in accord with anthropological theory, see Tajfel (1981)). Across a range of otherwise conflicting anthropological theories runs a common concern with the way in which social life promotes *corporate* (or collective) identities that constrain and compel behaviour.

Euro-American folk theory tends to obscure the societal and corporate aspects of identity and behaviour that anthropological accounts (of traditional society) emphasize, preferring instead to conceptualize identity and the causes of behaviour in terms of a radical individuality (Geertz 1973; Bellah *et al.* 1985; Cushman 1990). Central to most Western psychological accounts is a notion of the masterful, bounded, and individuated self, characterized by a core personality that transcends situations and contexts. While this view can be interpreted as a scientific theory about mentation, it is also possible to interpret such descriptions as part of Euro-American folk theory. Perhaps paradoxically, such an ethnotheory would be a theory of society (or sociality) that ignores situational constraints, contextual variables, and other aspects of societal and cultural environment. None the less it is a theory of society. Accordingly, the evocation of a mentalistic logic in the psychologist's discourse on trait–disposition reasoning might be described as a particular cultural construction of category identity (one in which category identity is largely effaced and individualized). Again, considerable literature on intellectual history supports the notion that the modern Euro-American emphasis on individualism is a relatively recent development (Mauss 1938; Dumont 1985).*

Social causality and Euro-American common sense

Although modern secular folk theory effaces most collectivist aspects of identity, this does not necessarily mean that *all* aspects of human category identity reasoning are absent from Euro-American thinking. One hallmark of reasoning about the identity of natural kinds is the notion of 'by nature.'

---

* There is now a considerable literature in cultural studies interpreting formal scientific theories of behaviour as ethnotheories. Foucault's work, with its sustained treatments of theories of sexuality (Foucault 1978), the human and natural sciences (Foucault 1970), psychiatry (Foucault 1965), and medicine (Foucault 1973), is perhaps the most comprehensive elaboration of this insight.

Unlike mentalistic attributions, in which behaviour results from intentions and desires, natural kind category identity attributions often leave part of the causal mechanism unspecified. Dogs bark, not because they want, yearn, or mean to bark, but because it is in their *nature* to bark. However, the nature of this nature is often only vaguely understood, if at all (Medin 1989; Atran 1990). Rather, there is an expectation that the underlying essence captures both the substance and process through which a creature's nature unfolds.

Social categories in many traditional societies involve elaborate essentialist reasoning that parallels the attribution of natural kind identity. One of the most familiar cases is the Hindu notion of caste, or *jati*, a term that also means 'species'. However, the essentialist construal in Indian social life is much deeper than this classificatory parallel. As Daniel (1985) has shown, the notion of underlying and non-obvious essence (what he calls a 'fluid sign') is central to Tamil thought, animating a comprehensive system of beliefs that link humans and their essences not only with other humans, plants, and animals, but also with geographic place and physical abode. Boyer (1990) suggests that many traditional societies naturalize social categories, a position that Rothbart and Taylor (1990) extend to Euro-American society.

Despite this, modern secular societies tend to find the essentialist interpretation of social phenomena 'dissonant'. Unlike the Tamil case examined by Daniel (1985), where essentialized social categories are part of *accepted* common sense, Rozin and his collaborators have shown that most elaborations of essentialist thinking in Euro-American culture fall under the rubric of superstition and hence are viewed as marginal or suspect causal reasoning (Rozin *et al*. 1989). However, this is not true of all appeals to essentialized social nature in non-traditional cultures. Consider race, which is possibly the predominant essentialized social category in any culture. Race is seen as a biological phenomenon—immutable, heritable, and linked to an individual's underlying nature.* Thus, from the adult perspective at least, a strong parallel exists between the way one reasons about racial and non-human living-kind categories: there are limited varieties of non-human living things typified in terms of shared essences, and there are limited varieties of humans typified by shared underlying essences (Mauss 1947; Allport 1954; Atran 1990; Hirschfeld 1993). Just as there are apples and oranges, there are Japanese and Javanese. Just as all apples share an under-

---

* We are concerned here with the common-sense notion that racial categories reflect non-random heritable biological differences between human populations otherwise defined socially; a notion that appears to be a cultural universal (van den Berghe 1981). However, biologists and anthropologist have long argued that such groupings of humans do not pick out biologically interesting or uniform populations, and thus do not reflect biologically relevant entities (Brace 1964; Gould 1983).

lying essence that causes apple blossoms (specifically apple ovaries) to become apples (and not oranges), so do all Japanese share an underlying essence that causes infant Japanese to become adult Japanese (and not Javanese).

One characteristic of living-kind categories is their rich inferential potential — knowing category membership allows one to reason beyond the information given. Racial category identity also involves inferential potential in that such membership underwrites **stereotypes** — expectations about enduring behaviours and potential. If, as history too readily documents, we know the (minority) racial identity of a person, we know how that person will behave across similar situations (whether it be with greed, cowardice, or malice); such things are, it is too often said, in their nature. While the sorts of prejudices projected about members of minority races (e.g. low intellectual but high athletic potential if a black) may differ in valence from the sorts of properties projected over members of non-human animal kind (e.g. barks if a dog), the underlying conceptual structure appears to be similar (Rothbart and Taylor 1990).

YOUNG CHILDREN'S UNDERSTANDING OF SOCIAL CAUSALITY

The young child's enriched understanding of how internal psychological states shape subsequent behaviour emerges between 3 and 5 years of age (Astington *et al.* 1988). During this period children begin to categorize themselves (and others) in terms of stable states closely resembling traits and dispositions (Eder 1989, 1990). The young child's repertoire of societal categories (such as gender, kinship, and race) also undergoes marked development during this time, suggesting that as a theory of mind emerges so does a theory of society. In fact, societal terms are among the first words that young children acquire (Hirschfeld 1989*a*, *b*, 1994*a*). By early preschool age, children readily categorize themselves and others in terms of race (Hirschfeld 1988, 1993), occupation (Blaske 1984; Garrett *et al.* 1977), and body build (Lerner 1973).

Racial, occupational, and body-build categories each have distinct implications for identity. For adults, each is associated with a specific causal account of the behaviour of members of each category. Most important, all function to interpret behaviour without reference to specific mental states. While occupational categories, for example, are conceptualized in terms of behavioural regularities (Hirschfeld 1994*b*), these regularities are not envisaged in terms of underlying causation. Rather, they involve functional (goal-oriented) relations: understanding 'plumber' means understanding that plumbers unplug sinks, install lavatories, repair washing machines, etc. Like racial categories, occupational categories bear inferential potential, figuring in what are often invidious comparisons, for example used car salesmen are untrustworthy or plumbers overcharge. However, such generalizations appear to be empirical summaries rather than explanations. Other lexicalized social identity categories may be intermediate between the functional and the essentialized status. Types of body build, such as 'fat', are linked to a physical or corporeal quality, although not necessarily an essence (and many occupations are linked to body builds, so that basketball players are tall, football players are muscular, etc.). Like both occupational and racial category identities, body builds are associated with behaviour that does not evidently follow from the category itself (e.g. fat people are jolly, or short people are insecure). One way of unpacking the relationship between these various causal principles is by exploring the development of the meaning of category membership in children. How do young children conceptualize social concepts, particularly in the context of making judgements of identity? In examining such conceptualizations, we gain insight into the importance that these categories have for causal understanding.

Racial categories

Race is by far the most extensively researched social category. It is generally thought that young children do not reason deeply about race. Thus, although adults typically believe that race is closely tied to notions of underlying essence, young children are thought not to be capable of interpreting racial categories in terms of such abstract criteria (Aboud 1988). Most accounts of racial thinking indicate that pre-school children focus exclusively on *conspicuous features* of appearance, without any appreciation of the putative biological implications of race (Clark *et al.* 1980; Katz 1982; Vaughan 1987; Aboud 1988). Moreover, while older children and adults view humans as 'one mammal among many' (Carey 1985, p. 94), young children appear to hold humans apart from other biological species, treating them as a taxonomic (Carey 1985; Inagaki 1990; Johnson *et al.* 1992) and ontological (Keil 1979) isolate.

It is not coincidental that changes in children's understanding of humans as animals, on the one hand, and racial variation as implicating differences in essence, on the other, occur during the same period. According to the common-sense adult view, race is a biological phenomenon spanning both the animal and human domains (van den Berghe 1981). Only by biologizing *both* race and humans could this expectation emerge. As just noted, the standard view in the identity literature is that young children do not conceive of social difference in biological terms; although young children can readily categorize people by race and ethnicity, a number of studies suggest that, prior to 8 years of age, children do not understand that a person's race or ethnicity is immutable (Semaj 1980; Aboud 1987, 1988).

They fail to understand this, Aboud (1988) argues, because they are aware only of the obvious features of race and ethnicity, and not that race and ethnicity are derived from family background (Alejandro-Wright 1985). In one study, Aboud and Skerry (1983) found that most children under 8 years of age believed that their own ethnicity changed when shown a picture of themselves dressed in clothing associated with another ethnic group. This over-reliance on physical appearance in identity judgments may be quite general. Studies by Keil (1989) indicate that 4-year-old children fail to grasp identity constancy in the face of changes in outward appearance of animals. Similarly, a number of studies suggest the same for human gender (Kohlberg 1966; Slaby and Frey 1975; Emmerich *et al.* 1977; Carey, 1985; Gelman *et al.* 1986).

However, this conclusion contrasts with recent work challenging the view that, at least for non-human living things, young children believe that *outer* appearances determine relevant aspects of a creature's *inner* nature. Pre-school children appear to have a more adult-like grasp of causality (Massey and Gelman 1988; Gelman and Kremer 1991) and are considerably less reliant on appearances when deciding whether a living kind has a non-obvious property (Gelman and Markman 1986) or underlying essence (Gelman and Wellman 1991) than the externalist model implies (see also Carey 1985; Brown 1989). In the light of these results, it is intriguing that identity studies find young children to have so little appreciation of the biological importance of gender, race, and other social properties.

Identity, growth, and inheritance

In order to explore the meaning that different social identities might have for pre-school children, and in particular to assess the degree to which children naturalize such categories, a series of studies was conducted to probe children's expectations about possible and impossible identity-relevant changes within the context of normal growth and inheritance. Does an individual change identity when gaining or losing a feature? Is such a change conceivable at all? For adult common sense, change of dress is not a change of identity but change of sex is. Change of race, in contrast, is not conceived of as a genuine possibility. Would children use their know-ledge of social categories — particularly their understanding of body build and skin colour, on the one hand, and categories such as occupation and clothing, on the other — in making judgements about preserved identity?

Children aged 3, 4, and 7 were shown a series of pictures, each portraying an adult of a specific race and body build, and wearing occupationally rele-vant apparel (e.g. a stout black police officer, or a heavy Hispanic nurse).

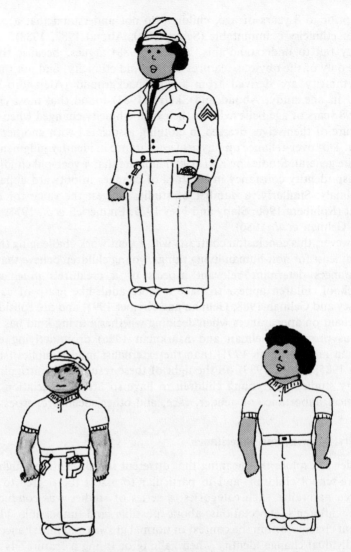

Fig. 11.1. Sample items: male set.

The children were then shown a series of paired pictures, portraying two children, each of whom shared two of the three social features (body build, race, and occupation) of the target picture. Each pair contrasted with the target picture on one social dimension (e.g. one pair consisted of a thin black child wearing a police hat, a toy gun, and a whistle, and a plump white child wearing a police hat, a toy gun, and a whistle), so that all possible contrasts were presented across the three pairs. Figure 11.1 illustrates

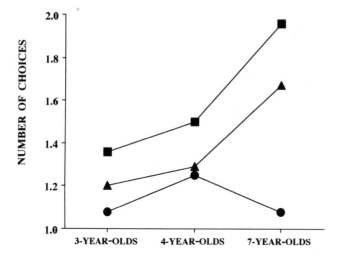

Fig. 11.2. Mean number of choices by age and type of comparison (maximum score, 2): ■, race over body build; ▲, race over occupation; ●, occupation over body build.

one set of items. Two conditions were used, an inheritance condition and a growth condition. In the inheritance condition children were asked which of the contrast pair was the child of the target adult; in the growth condition children were asked which of the contrast pair was a picture of the target adult as a child (see Hirschfeld (in press) for a detailed description of this study).

Children's responses varied as a function of both age (i.e. older versus younger subjects) and the type of comparison that children were asked to make (i.e. whether the contrast was between race and occupation, occupation and body build, or race and body build). Children chose race over body build significantly more than race over occupation, both of which were chosen significantly more often than occupation over body build. When each age group is considered separately, for the youngest children, only race over body build choices were significantly above chance; for the 4-year-old children, all three contrasts differed from chance; for the oldest subjects, race over body build choices and race over occupation choices were also reliably above chance. Figure 11.2 summarizes these findings.

Previous work suggested that social cues are salient to young children as a function of their conspicuousness in determining outward appearances (Kosslyn and Kagan 1981; Flavell 1985; Aboud 1988). One prediction of this work is that pre-school children should not distinguish between the contribution of either corporeal features (like skin colour) or non-corporeal features (like clothing) to identity. Springer and Keil (1989) propose a more moderate version of this hypothesis, i.e. that some, but not all, conceptually enriched distinctions might be drawn (for example social and behavioural properties would be jointly contrasted with physical and biological properties). Thus, on their view, finer-grained conceptually enriched contrasts (say, between qualities that are relevant to collectivities versus those not relevant to collectivities) would not influence young children's judgements of identity. In contrast with both these views, the data from the study indicate that young children show considerably more nuances in the distinctions that they draw among social dimensions.

Strikingly, there was no difference in children's judgements about growth and about inheritance. It is worth considering the implication of this finding. Most studies of identity constancy ask children to assess the possibility or consequences of changes in characteristic but non-essential cues (dress) versus changes in characteristic but essential features (skin colour). Implicit in such contrasts is the notion that inessential features are non-corporeal, while essential features are literally embodied. Although these tasks all use familiar properties, they do not all involve familiar *transformations*. Children (or adults presumably) typically do not witness abrupt and major changes in a person's intrinsic physical state or presentation of self. Accordingly, asking children to determine whether someone's identity remains the same under several different *meaningful* but unfamiliar changes in appearance may confuse young subjects since it is not clear whether the pre-transformed and post-transformed individuals are supposed to be (as opposed to could be) the same individual (Bem 1989).

However, children do have considerable experience with, and knowledge of, natural transformations whose scope is as dramatic as those used in most identity studies: children are familiar with major physical and behavioural changes occurring *across the life-span* (i.e. in the context of growth) and *across generations* (i.e. in the context of inheritance). Young children appear to understand that these natural transformations are both lawful and non-random, and this understanding apparently involves domain-specific knowledge (Keil 1989; Springer and Keil 1989; Rosengren *et al.* 1991). For adults, these two sorts of resemblance (or canonical change) follow from the same processes, i.e. biological relatedness. However, there is no a priori reason to assume that young children's inductions have the same basis. The finding from this study—that children do identify the preservation of features in growth with the preservation of features across generations—suggests that children view this preserved identity in both circumstances as resulting from the person's intrinsic nature, in that by definition it is *this* intrinsic quality that is constant over both growth and inheritance. Thus, young children appear to have a biological understanding of these social properties.

In short, and in contrast with previous studies, it was found that children do not consider all physical properties of a person to be equally informative of their identity and, by extension, equally resistant to modification. If children were focusing only on changes in corporeal appearance when making judgements about identity, they should find modifications in skin colour as likely as changes in body build to signal a change in identity. Clearly this is not the case. It is important to keep in mind that body build *is* informative of individual identity, particularly in racial affiliation (Molnar 1992). Moreover, variation in body build is attention-demanding for young children and has inferential potential in the sense that stereotyping is predicated on it (Lerner 1973). In short, body build is not a superficial property to either the biologist or the child. Yet it is consistently seen as irrelevant to *identity* even by 3-year old children. These findings are also inconsistent with the view that a clear appreciation of the biological nature of race emerges only in middle childhood. In contrast with earlier reports, by 4 years of age children find race to be more critical to identity than either occupation or body build. Moreover, the congruence in performance in the growth and inheritance conditions points to a general biological understanding of essential traits.

Carey (Chapter 10 of this volume) and Carey and Spelke (1994) caution that these, and the results of a study of inheritance by Springer and Keil (1989), do not mean that young children have an adult-like appreciation of the biological relevance of physical features. They argue that pre-school children expect parents and their offspring to resemble each other, but they may attribute this resemblance to social rather than biological causes. Carey and Spelke (1994) cite a set of studies (Solomon *et al.* 1993) showing that pre-school children do *not* project physical properties like height on the basis of biological parentage. Two points can be raised regarding their concerns. First, pre-school children do not believe that all physical properties are equally relevant—skin colour and even occupation are better predictors than body build (the feature that most closely parallels stature). Thus their results do not establish that pre-school children deny the biological (as opposed to social) implications of physical properties; rather they indicate that pre-school children do not view *some* physical properties as biologically caused. Other physical features may well be conceived by pre-school children as having biological implications. I have argued that skin colour is one of these. Second, results of a subsequent study (Hirschfeld, in press) strongly suggest that pre-school children *do* expect skin colour to be determined by birth, not experience (thus involving biological not social causality). Pre-school children and children aged 7 and 10 were shown a picture story in which infants were switched at birth in hospital. They were then shown pictures of school-age children, and asked to identify the picture of the child corresponding to each of the infants. Subjects in all three groups performed well above chance: almost 80 per cent of the pre-school children, 80 per cent of the 7-year-old children, and all the 10-year old children expected children to have a skin colour that matched that of their birth rather than that of their adoptive parents.

Person identity and strategies for social reasoning

One particular result of the identity studies needs further comment. Three-year-old children expect skin colour to be more important to identity than body build. However, they do not seem to believe that skin colour is more important than apparel. This is puzzling. Clothing, except in the case of ethnic costume, is much less related to a person's intrinsic nature than, say, body build. Previous research has indicated that, relative to skin colour and gender, young children do not find clothing an important dimension on which to sort persons (Davey 1983). One explanation for the difference in results may be that, in the task presented in this study, children may not have been reasoning about clothing but about occupation, a social category for which clothing is diagnostic.

To test this possibility, children in the same age groups were asked to look at a target picture depicting a child wearing clothes of a certain colour and with certain occupation emblems. They were then shown two comparison pictures of an adult version of the child portrayed in the target picture: one wore clothes of the same colour but without the occupational emblems, and the other wore different coloured clothing but with the same occupational emblems. Subjects were asked to identify which of these was the child portrayed in the target picture after he or she had grown up. Two sets of pictures were used – a male set depicting a fire fighter, and a female set depicting a waitress.

When the results from the two sets of items were combined, children's judgements were at chance, suggesting that they believed that occupation was no more important than shared clothing to preserved identity. However, a second analysis, contrasting children's inferences about male and female item sets, showed that children reliably believed that occupation preserves male but *not* female identity, i.e. children inferred that occupation is crucial to male but not female, identity. Thus performance in the first study – in which 3-year-old children showed evidence of believing that both occupation and race are diagnostic of identity – cannot be attributed to children's inferences about clothing *per se*, but (for the male items) reflect an expectation about occupation (for which apparel is emblematic). Children expect sartorial cues associated with occupation to be more meaningful and conceptually suggestive than shared apparel.

Why is this? Elsewhere it has been shown that young children attend closely to goal-directed and functional categories like occupation. In fact, when the task involves parsing a social environment (as opposed to making inductions about intrinsic identity, as in the present studies), occupation is the *most* salient social category relative to race, gender, activity engaged in, and body build (Hirschfeld 1993). These findings support the claim that children are concerned about the kinds of social beings there are, and that their curiosity about human variation goes beyond attention to superficial aspects of activities or appearance. However, this curiosity is not uniform. Young children explore the biological nature of human variation (in race) as well as its functional architecture (in goal-directed activities like occupation). In both cases, the child is concerned to define social groups and not psychological properties.

Taken together, these data suggest that young children reason deeply about intrinsic properties, like skin colour, and extrinsic properties, like occupation. Acquiring knowledge of social category identity turns on assigning social categories to the appropriate domain. Domain assignment occurs by virtue of the child's ontological commitment to social *groups*, embedded in a theory of society, rather than psychological properties, embedded in a theory of mind (Hirschfeld 1993, 1994*a*). Whether young children are concerned with elaborating a social ontology because they are concerned with finding plausible explanations of behaviour remains an open question. What does seem clear is that the causal repertoire of even the young child includes physical, psychological, *and* social (or societal) causal principles. Keil (Chapter 9) suggests that there are a number of modes of construal available to the child — a 'plurality of biases' that may underwrite conceptual change. A theory of society, or societal mode of construal, comprised of intrinsic expectations about sociality may well be one of these. Interestingly, in the social domain the child may recognize causal relations that are both essentialist, those associated with a biological mode of construal, and non-essentialist, those linked to a teleological mode of construal.

Innate potential and social categories

Not all aspects of the adult model of social categorical reasoning are evident in the causal attributions of the young child; some areas of social causal reasoning emerge later. One less precocious reasoning structure involves the elaboration of the notion of 'innate potential' that is at the root of children's expectations about non-human living kinds. Gelman and Wellman (1991) present evidence that young children expect living kinds to have an innate potential which causes them to develop in a given way regardless of environment and initial state. Tigers grow to be large, fierce, and capable of growling even though as cubs they are small, helpless, and purring. Children also expect tiger cubs to grow into tigers even if they are reared by lions. Adults explain this continuity across changes in behaviour and appearance by appeal to the tiger's underlying essence.

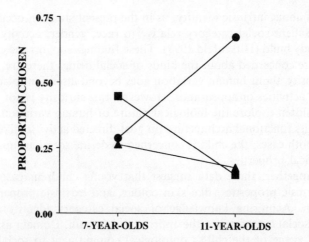

Fig. 11.3. Mean proportion of black (●), white (■), and intermediate (▲) infants chosen by age group.

Recently, Rothbart and Taylor (1990) and Boyer (1990) have argued that many social categories are similarly essentialized. The results of the switched-at-birth study, described earlier, confirm that even pre-school children expect race to be governed by innate potential, in that it is birth, not life experiences, that fix racial features. In a recent study, I explored one aspect of essentialist thinking that is unique to social categories; namely the notion that different races have distinct innate potentials. Adults expect some races to have greater innate potential than others in the sense that they expect some races to contribute 'more' identity to future generations than others. Such folk notions are codified in the laws about racial status in many states in the USA. In Louisiana, for example, a person is black if one of his (or her) great grandparents were classified as black. Thus, one-sixteenth black 'blood' has more innate potential than fifteen-sixteenths white 'blood' ('What makes you black? Vague definition of race is the basis for court battles', *Ebony*, January 1983).

Children's expectations about the offspring of racially mixed couples were assessed by showing two groups of children, aged 7 and 11, pictures of four couples, one at a time: a black couple, a white couple, a black male and a white female, and a white male and a black female. Each couple were holding an infant whose face was obscured. Each child was then shown pictures of three infants (a black infant, a white infant, and an infant with intermediate skin tone and hair colour and texture), and asked which infant was the child of the target couple.

As Fig. 11.3 shows, younger children displayed no preference, believing that it was equally likely that the offspring of a racially mixed couple would have black, white, or intermediate coloured skin. Older children, in contrast, overwhelmingly chose the black baby. In short, by the age of 11 children expect the offspring of a mixed-race union to be black. One explanation of these findings is that, by the age of 11, children have developed a general expectation about how physical properties are inherited such that a darker coloured property prevails. This would be consistent with the common-sense adult belief that is expressed in legal traditions like that described for Louisiana. It is worth bearing in mind that this is not a marginal classificatory strategy; it is applied by the United States Census Bureau when it assigns children of mixed-race couples to the minority parent's race (Molnar 1992). However, children may be making categorical judgments specifically about race, rather than about physical properties generally.

To test this possibility, a parallel task involving hair colour was conducted, in which children were shown pictures of couples whose hair colour was either the same or different (blond mother and father, brunette mother and father, blond mother and brunette father, and brunette mother and blond father). Subjects were asked which of three infants (a blond, a brunette, and an infant with red hair) was the child of each pair. Both 7- and 11-year-old children chose at chance, expecting parents with different hair colour to be as likely to have blond, brunette, or red-headed children. To see whether children believed that hair colour was more likely to 'mix' than race, the numbers of intermediate value choices (red for the hair colour task; intermediate for the racial task) were compared. Children selected the intermediate value considerably more often in the hair colour task than in the race task. (Interestingly, these expectations cannot be attributed to inferences from direct observation since they do not correspond to biological regularities: there is no genetic dominance for skin colour (Bodmer and Cavalli-Sforza 1976), while for the inheritance of hair colour, darker tends to be dominant over lighter (Robins 1991).)

In sum, these results suggest that during the late elementary school years children come to believe that a child of one black parent will be black, i.e. they expect different races to have distinct innate potentials. This notion is specific to beliefs about race and does not reflect a general strategy for understanding the inheritance of colour-related physical properties. Moreover, this expectation — a subtle but important aspect of racism — developed in a liberal college community where children may well not have been directly taught how to calculate the innate potential of various races. Rather, it may be a spontaneous induction, surely facilitated by a pervasive racist climate in the USA but made plausible by an early-emerging biologicalization or naturalization of human variation.

FOLK BIOLOGY, FOLK PSYCHOLOGY, AND FOLK SOCIOLOGY

I have tried to show that if we conceive of human causality simply as a type of psychological causality, we may fail to appreciate how rich are our expectations of social category identity. Human behaviour is interpreted in terms of causalities to behave in a certain way and to become a certain sort of thing. While this contrast is useful, it should not be overemphasized. There is considerable overlap in causal principles generally (Shultz 1982). By proposing to distinguish attributions of category identity from both psychological (belief–desire) and personality (trait–disposition) attributions, I do not assume them to be completely *distinct* types.

How then does the child sort them out, particularly in modern Euro-American society, where verbal descriptions of societal entities (typified by a causality *to be*) are indistinguishable from psychological phenomena (typified by a causality *to behave*)? The task is not easy. Language provides some hints. The syntax of many languages distinguishes between the incidental features, functional roles, and intrinsic properties of persons. Combinations involving incidental and identity features for example, are constrained in English. One can say 'the tall black police officer' or 'the friendly black police officer', but not 'the black tall police officer' or 'the black friendly police officer' or 'the tall police-being black'. This rule of conceptual combinations picks out an expression like 'black police officer' as a *kind* that cannot be separated. French makes a similar, but more pronounced, move: 'le grand facteur noir', but not 'le grand noir facteur' or 'le noir facteur grand'.* Other languages, such as Indonesian, employ counters for many objects including humans so that language is structured to inform the hearer when the speaker is mentioning the *kind* of person someone is (i.e. the tribe or ethnicity to which he or she belongs), for example 'orang Perancis yang tinggi' (person-counter French who is tall) but not 'orang tinggi yang Perancis'.

A more subtle but equally informative cue is the tendency to apply different kinds of social causality to different domains of the world. Psychological and personality attributions tend to be applied to the human domain; category identity attributions tend to be applied to the non-human living-kind domain. For adults in modern secular societies, attributions of causality *to be* a certain sort of thing within the human domain generally involve the biologicalization of humans. It is not coincidental that gender and race, pre-eminent types of humans (as opposed to the types of activities

---

* Waugh (1977) argues that an adjective in French is pre-posed when it is defined in relation to the noun it modifies and post-posed when it is not dependent on the meaning of the noun. Thus nationality and colour are typically, but not always, post-posed.

humans may engage in), are essentialized in folk thinking. By conceiving of such differences as deriving from biological structure (which may be trivially true in the case of gender, but not in the case of race) 'biological' reasoning about race and gender appears to be an 'appropriate' import from the domain of non-human living kinds to humans (Atran 1990; Boyer 1990).

The non-figurative identification of human with the animal domain is relatively infrequent in modern industrial societies. In contrast, in the types of societies commonly studied by anthropologists, it is easy to find extensive elaborations of the putative parallel between the two realms. Since cognitive scientists and anthropologists have long assumed that we can distinguish between the system of human difference (consisting of social and psychological categories) and the system of natural difference (consisting of species categories), the apparent common conflation of the two systems demands explanation. Indeed, a persistent discussion in anthropology has explored the meaning of one instance of this confluence of human and natural differences, namely totemism. Totemic beliefs involve the identification of membership of a particular social category (such as a kin network) with membership of a particular plant or animal category. As many have observed, such identifications and associations are quite attractive cognitively, as witnessed, if nothing else, by the prevalence of animal names for sports teams. Early accounts suggested that totemic associations reflected beliefs about identity, such that members of the social category *were* members of the animal or plant category (Crocker 1977; Turner 1989). Subsequent research tempered the way that this association was interpreted. For example, Mauss (1947) suggested that members of the linked animal and human categories were believed to share an underlying essence (a 'kinship of substance'), a view developed in greater detail by Hallowell (1976). Contemporary treatments concur with the views of Boas (1916) and Radcliffe-Brown (1922) that totemic claims are evidence for symbolic figurative associations (Lévi-Strauss 1962; Tambiah 1969; Rosaldo 1972; Crocker 1977; Turner 1989).

The naturalization model

Recently, cognitive scientists from within and without anthropology have proposed an alternative model. According to this argument, the natural order impinges onto our organization of the human world through knowledge transfer, rather than through symbolic or figurative association. Atran (1990), Boyer (1990), and Rothbart and Taylor (1990) have independently argued that the natural and human orders converge when social categories are 'naturalized'. Here, naturalization involves a process whereby principles derived from the understanding of biological variation come to govern understanding of social difference. What is imported to the target (social) domain, according to all three proposals, is a belief that members of a category share an essence which gives rise to the surface similarities supposedly shared by members of the category. The naturalization of social categories proposal (hereafter, the **naturalization model**) has developmental consequences as well: children naturalize social differences by using their enriched knowledge of biological variation to structure their emergent understandings of the social world. 'Children might initially borrow from their presumptions of the underlying natures of living things in order to better organize their knowledge of HUMANS and merge this knowledge with that of other LIVING THINGS' (Atran 1990, p. 74).

Atran (1990) and Boyer (1990) have separately argued that this borrowing is well motivated and follows from a confluence of conceptual similarity and cognitive need—much the same impetuses that Boas (1916) and Radcliffe-Brown (1922) appealed to in their early speculations on the cultural origin of totemic beliefs. However, the argument about individual representations is framed epistemologically: children readily transfer principles organizing biological concepts to social concepts because of the ontological proximity of the two domains—the fact that humans and animals 'are adjacent ontological domains, as it were' (Atran 1990, p. 74) (see also Greeno 1983; Spiro *et al.* 1989). At the same time, the projection of biological principles to the social domain meets demands for cognitive economy (Spiro *et al.* 1989; Vosniadou 1989; Boyer 1990) (cf. Inagaki and Hatano 1987; Inagaki and Sugiyama 1988): such transfers import constraints on social categories which the semantics of these social categories do not themselves afford.

The personification model

A somewhat different perspective on the relation between the human and natural orders has recently been proposed by developmentalists. Carey (1985) and Inagaki and colleagues (Inagaki and Hatano 1987; Inagaki and Sugiyama 1988, Inagaki 1990) also contend that the biological and human domains are closely linked. However, unlike Atran (1990), Boyer (1990) and Rothbart and Taylor (1990), rather than exploring how biological principles are elaborated in social understanding, they suggest that young children use their extensive appreciation of people to enrich an emerging naive biology.

The theory from which an intuitive theory of biology emerges is an intuitive theory of behavior, I call it a 'naive psychology' because it mainly concerns human behavior, and because it explains behavior in terms of wants and beliefs. Though based on human behavior, it also concerns animal behavior, since animals are also seen as behaving beings. Many phenomena fall under both a theory of behavior and a theory of biology—that is, the two domains overlap. (Carey 1985, p. 188)

Thus, according to this view (hereafter, the **personification model**), young children use humans as the standard (and psychology as the model) for reasoning about natural non-psychological, but human and familiar, biological properties (ranging from hunger to growth and sleeping to kinship). The projection of biological properties, then, is both graded and asymmetrical. It is asymmetrical in that, while 4-year-old children will readily project novel biological properties from humans to dogs, they are less likely to project such properties from dogs to humans, and it is graded in the sense that they are more likely to project a property from human to dog than from human to bee (Carey 1985; cf. Osherson *et al*. 1990). Both these features of the relationship follow from young children's privileging of the human domain — their intrinsic anthrocentrism.

The differences between naturalization and personification views of causality should not be overstressed, for the causalities implicit in the naturalization model, on the one hand, and the personification model, on the other, are not unrelated. This is particularly evident if we consider the projection of properties from humans to artefacts rather than from humans to non-human creatures (or vice versa). Young children generally honour an animate–inanimate distinction (Meck 1932; Gelman *et al*. 1983; Bullock 1985; Massey and Gelman 1988). However, several studies have found that young children also project properties of animate creatures on to inanimate objects, and that they tend to do so more frequently when the inanimate objects bear a resemblance to those that are animate (Bullock 1985; Carey 1985; Inagaki and Hatano 1987).

For instance, Carey (1985) found that 4-year-old children (but not older children) were as likely to project biological properties (eats, sleeps, has bones) onto a mechanical monkey as onto a fish. This finding has been interpreted as evidence that children are using a reasoning strategy that relies on person analogy, i.e. the attribution of properties appears to follow a judgement of the similarity of the target object to the source domain (persons) (Carey 1985; Inagaki and Sugiyama 1988). The critical inheritance, then, involves a causality based on appearance and the relationship of appearance to what the object is. Thus Carey (1985) argues that 4-year-old children are confused by the discrepancy between a similarity in appearance (a mechanical monkey that resembles a person) and a dissimilarity in terms of kind (animate versus inanimate) when making attributions about non-obvious properties. The causal principle involved is a causality '*to be*' (a certain sort of thing).

However, the perceived similarity between some artefacts and living kinds (that warrants the projection of animate properties onto inanimate objects) is also predicated on *behavioural* similarities. Objects which are interactively associated with animacy, even if they are not themselves animate, tend to be attributed with animate properties. For example, Dolgin and

Behrend (1984) found that 3-year-old children were more likely to attribute animate properties to dolls than to dead animals. These data are consistent with a person-analogy argument, but not one based exclusively on physical similarity. Young children's property projections are also shaped by person analogies derived from beliefs about the sorts of interactions that humans have with objects. In other words, objects which are seen as interactively like persons – as participating in behaviour that appears to be motivated by belief–desire psychology – *are* in some respects conceived of as essentially similar to persons.

Vosniadou (1989) observes that, while very young children do *not* believe that astral bodies physically resemble people, they nevertheless give psychological explanations (e.g. in terms of intentionality) to the sun's movements. In this case, young children are using their knowledge of intentional systems, best articulated and developed for humans, to explain by analogy the behaviour of seemingly self-propelled objects (Premack 1990). In projecting animate qualities to inanimate objects, young children appear to be concerned, as Massey and Gelman (1988) suggest, with the causal mechanisms governing an object's behaviour. Objects for which intentional movement is possible are likely to be attributed with other animate qualities (Inagaki and Sugiyama 1988). Adults also tend to personify those artefacts which perform complex tasks (Scheibe and Erwin 1979). In fact, as Dennett (1976) notes, it is *best* to treat some inanimate objects (e.g. a chess-playing computer) as if they were animate in many circumstances (e.g. if you want to win).

The societal model

Elsewhere, it has been suggested that an additional perspective on the relationship of the natural and human realms is possible and has developmental implications (Hirschfeld 1989b, 1993). The suggestion borrows from a much earlier evolutionary, rather than developmental, account first proposed by Durkheim and Mauss (1903) (see Dwyer (1976) for a more recent version of this model):

... the first logical categories were social categories; the first classes of things were classes of men, into which these things were integrated. It was because men were grouped, and thought of themselves in the form of groups, that in their ideas they grouped other things, and in the beginning the two modes of grouping were merged to the point of being indistinct. Moieties were the first genera; clans, the first species. (Durkheim and Mauss 1963, pp. 82–3)

The relation that Durkheim and Mauss describe (hereafter, the **societal model**) involves a transfer from the human to the animal orders, and thus follows the trajectory suggested by Carey and Inagaki. However,

Durkheim and Mauss also contend that the relation involves the transfer of principles for reasoning about human societal variation (as opposed to human psychology) to animal variation. Hence, the link establishes a parallel between *categories* of people and *categories* of animals in the sense described by Atran and Boyer.

Durkheim and Mauss's claim for a social origin for natural and other categories has few remaining champions, largely because there are few committed to the social ontology that they proposed (Hirschfeld *et al.* 1982). However, their position is of interest with respect to the naturalization versus personification contrast since a societal model shares aspects of each. Durkheim and Mauss proposed that the inheritance of knowledge runs from humans to animals, but they also saw the objects of that inheritance as collectivities rather than individuals. They saw these two aspects as uncontroversial. Lévi-Strauss was perhaps the first to observe that the totemic relationship implicates a *tension* between aggregate and individual phenomena, not only on the level of discipline of the analyst, but on the mode of thinking of the native. It is 'the direct perception of the *class*, through individuals, which characterizes the relation between man and the animal or plant, and it is this also which helps us to understand totemism' (Lévi-Strauss 1962, p. 93).

The issue can readily be put in cognitive terms as well. Adapting the categories that Sperber (1990) uses to characterize patterns of knowledge distribution, the different ways of co-ordinating knowledge across domains can be described in terms of (i) those that involve spontaneous, widespread, and highly shared parallels (as is apparently the case with the personification of a certain class of inanimate things, notably those apparently capable of spontaneous movement), (ii) those that involve highly shared but institutionally contingent transfers (naturalization of Fang religious categories (Boyer 1990) or reductive analogies in medicine (Spiro *et al.* 1989), and (iii) those that involve spontaneous, widespread, but highly idiosyncratic analogies (e.g. variation in explanatory analogies for evaporation (Collins and Gentner 1987) or the operation of a thermostat (Kempton 1987)).

I wish to argue that co-ordinations of the first sort — spontaneous, widespread, and highly shared — may entail rendering causal principles accessible across domains by making the commonalities in objects to which they apply more apparent. This is what I have proposed for the extension of the causality across the biological and human realms. However, like Lévi-Strauss's realization that accomplishing this on the level of shared belief involves a commitment to a cultural order, I propose that accomplishing this on a cognitive level (i.e. achieving the naturalization of the social and the personification of the natural) involves the recognition that these causalities apply to a single class of objects, namely humans.

One highly shared, spontaneous, and widespread belief is that humans

Naive Biology

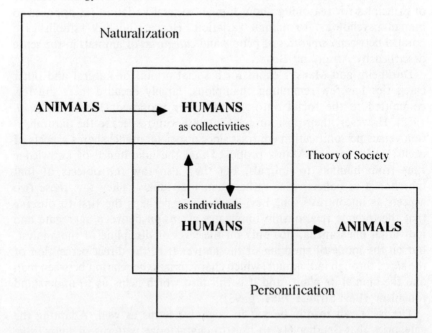

Fig. 11.4. Relationship between naive biology, theory of mind, and theory of society.

have societal identities. It is a belief that young children understand. They do not come to this understanding by opening their eyes and looking. Nor do they come to it by 'opening' their psychology and 'extending it', as it were. Rather, they are prepared to see humans as members of collectivities, and they construe behaviour in terms of such membership. In part, this construal consists of exploring the nature of human collectivities as well as their boundaries. Thus, despite the discursive overlap between them, common-sense psychology, biology, and sociality *explain* different things, appeal to different aspects of the world, and activate different sorts of data and relations between entities. Racial thinking is the cognitive space—provides the cognitive task—for working out expectations about collectivities. Race, in short, serves as a sort of 'laboratory' of causality, as the context in which the child comes to decide on the natures of social objects and how to predict their actions. Humans are perceived both as objects of causal attributions (in which psychological and interpersonal information is used to make causal judgments) and societal attributions (in which collective information is used to make causal judgments). Figure 11.4 illustrates the relationship between these various causal models.

The claim that common-sense biology, psychology, and sociality explain different aspects of the world and underwrite generalizations about specific relations between entities is not the same as the claim that naive biology, psychology, and sociality span different objects of the world (say, living things, thinking things, and social things). However, Atran's (1990) account of the relationship between racial thinking and naive biology can be interpreted as making this claim. He suggests that racial thinking is parasitical on common-sense biology in virtue of biological causality being applied by analogy to human variation. Yet data from ethnobiology itself indicate that this may not always be the case. It is precisely where the discourse of naive biology fails, unnamed intermediate taxa, that principles of social classification become crucial for describing (if not perceiving) biological phenomena. In Chapter 8, Atran shows how strikingly difficult it is to engage unschooled Itza informants in a classification task involving covert taxa without appeal to instructions using kinship and other social terms. Bulmer (1974) and Berlin (1992) note that this is a general phenomenon: traditional peoples in MesoAmerica, Africa, and Melanesia have been found to talk about covert and other higher ethnobiological groupings using terms borrowed from the realm of human societal relations. While the relationship marked by such imported social terms (which pick out groups of related but distinct sorts of creatures) is central to common-sense biology, nonetheless some aspect of the underlying causality may be derived from a theory of society.

Atran (Chapter 8) calls this possibility 'implausible in the extreme'. He reasons that because there is obvious evolutionary advantage to acquiring the notion of species, and that this acquisition is both precocious and cross-culturally robust, it *must* represent a core competency. Indeed, this may be true. However, it does not follow, as he further contends, that *essentialism* is derived from the way that plants and animals are conceptually organized. Clearly, evolutionary considerations do not decide the case. The plausibility of an evolutionary advantage for humans to possess a nuanced understanding of the social world is as compelling as an advantage for such an understanding of the natural world (Cosmides and Tooby 1994). Developmental evidence does not resolve the issue because, as Atran himself notes, essentialistic construals of plants and animals appear to be no more precocious than essentialistic construals of race.

By the same token, there is no greater evidence for cross-cultural robustness in natural kind classification than in social classification. Atran's argument to the contrary takes the following form.

Species are universally perceived living kinds, clans are not universally social kinds. Not all people can sensibly ask and expect a response to: 'What clan do you belong to?' But all people can sensibly ask and expect a response to: 'What (species) kind does this readily perceptible organism belong to?'

I am not sure who proposed that *clan* is a universal concept; certainly I did not. Rather, I have proposed that kinship is a universal kind for humans (Hirschfeld 1986, 1989*a*), as is race (Hirschfeld 1988, 1993) and gender. The question 'What species is this?' is not the same as the question 'What gender (race) (kinship relation) is that person?' If it were, then there would be no reason to explore how social and natural knowledge articulate; they would be the same sort of thing. However, it is not the case that the answers to the latter question are more *conceptually* variable than are answers to the former. Essentialist construals of social phenomena allow the racial classifications in Nazi Germany, Louisana, and South Africa to differ, just as they allow three-legged albino tigers to be easily categorized with the sorts of beast that we encounter in circuses. Essentialism disengages conceptual structure from the physical structure of the world. This is no less true of non-human living kinds than of races.

Finally, Atran never engages the central problem that I raise with his claim about essentialism in race. He argues that essentialist construals of race are made 'in terms of readily visible features'. Yet, my research strongly suggests that essentialist construals of race emerge *before* the child closely attends to the physical correlates of race. These studies assessed the conceptual saliency of race and other social categories to pre-school children using both verbal and visual stimuli. The crucial finding is that race, unlike other common social categories, has strikingly low salience when the stimulus materials are *visual*, but moderate to high salience when the stimulus is *verbal* (Hirschfeld 1993). In short, children acquire knowledge of race before they know much about its physical correlates. This is not consistent with Atran's contention that race is essentialized because physical discontinuities in the human array are seen as analogues to phenotypic gaps between non-human living kinds. Young children (who otherwise do essentialize race) simply do not attend to these physical discontinuities.

The personification model, in turn, implies that children do not need a cognitive laboratory in that the language of naive psychology does not seem to contain the sorts of gaps found in the covert categories of naive biology. This may follow from the usefulness of psychological understanding; it makes good sense evolutionarily to expect that all creatures capable of spontaneous movement are motivated to action by a belief–desire psychology. What this good sense does not capture is the graded and asymmetrical nature of the intentional stance. Why are humans the quintessential psychologically motivated creature if personification is not an extension of a *human* capacity? If it is an extension, the principle of extension offered thus far (similarity in appearance) makes little sense given the experimental and anthropological evidence reviewed earlier. If it is not an extension of principles from a human-based naive psychology to other domains, but the application of a principle of psychological causation to multiple domains, then some account of the *variation* in that application is also needed. A societal model allows us to begin providing that account.

ACKNOWLEDGEMENTS

The research reviewed in this chapter was supported by grants from the National Science Foundation (INT 8814397 and RCD 8751136), the Fondation Fyssen, and the Office of the Vice President for Research, University of Michigan. I am grateful to Susan Carey, Dan Sperber, Ann Stoler, and Bob Zajonc for their comments on earlier drafts of the chapter.

REFERENCES

Aboud, F. (1987). The development of ethnic self-identification and attitudes. In *Children's ethnic socialization: pluralism and development* (ed. J. S. Phinney and M. J. Rotheram), pp. 32–55. Sage, Beverly Hills, CA.

Aboud, F. (1988). *Children and prejudice*. Basil Blackwell, New York.

Aboud, F. E. and Skerry, A. (1983). Self and ethnic concepts in relation to ethnic constancy. *Canadian Journal of Behavioural Science* **15**, 14–26.

Alejandro-Wright, M. (1985). The child's conception of racial classification: a socio-cognitive developmental model. In *Beginnings: the social and affective development of Black children* (ed. M. B. Spencer, G. K. Brookins, and W. R. Allen), pp. 185–201. Erlbaum, Hillsdale, NJ.

Allport, G. (1954). *The nature of prejudice*. Addison-Wesley, Reading, MA.

Astington, J., Harris, P. and Olson, D. (1988). *Developing theories of mind*. Cambridge University Press, New York.

Atran, S. (1990). *Cognitive foundations of natural history*. Cambridge University Press, New York.

Avis, J. and Harris, P. (1991). Belief–desire reasoning among Baka children: evidence for a universal conception of mind. *Child Development* **62**, 460–7.

Bartsch, K. and Wellman, H. (1989). Young children's attribution of action to beliefs and desires. *Child Development* **60**, 946–64.

Bellah, R., Madsen, R., Sullivan, W., Swindler, A. and Tipton, S. (1985). *Habits of the heart*. University of California Press, Berkeley, CA.

Bem, S. (1989). Genital knowledge and gender constancy in preschool children. *Child Development* **60**, 649–62.

Berlin, B. (1992). *Ethnobiological classification*. Princeton University Press.

Blaske, D. (1984). Occupational sex-typing by kindergarten and fourth-grade children. *Psychological Reports* **53**, 795–801.

Boas, F. (1916). The origin of totemism. *American Anthropologist* **18**, 319–26.

Bodmer, W. and Cavalli-Sforza, L. (1976). *Genetics, evolution, and man.* W. H. Freeman, San Francisco, CA.

Boyer, P. (1990). *Tradition as truth and communication.* Cambridge University Press, New York.

Brace, L. (1964). A non-racial approach toward the understanding of human diversity. In *The concept of race* (ed. A. Montagu). University of Nebraska Press, Lincoln, NB.

Brown, A. (1989). Analogical learning and transfer: what develops? In *Similarity and analogical reasoning* (ed. S. Vosniadou and A. Ortony). Cambridge University Press, New York.

Bullock, M. (1985). Animism in childhood thinking: a new look at an old question. *Developmental Psychology* **21**, 217-25.

Bulmer, R. (1974). Memoirs of a small game hunter: on the track of unknown animal categories in New Guinea. *Journal d'Agriculture Tropicale et Botanique Appliquée* **21**, 79-99.

Campos, J. and Sternberg, C. (1981). Perception, appraisal, and emotion: the onset of social referencing. In *Infants' social cognition: empirical and social considerations* (ed. M. Lamb and L. Sherrod). Erlbaum, Hillsdale, NJ.

Carey, S. (1985). *Conceptual development in childhood.* MIT Press, Cambridge, MA.

Carey, S. and Spelke, E. (1994). Domain specific knowledge and conceptual change. In *Mapping the mind: domain specificity in cognition and culture,* (ed. L. A. Hirschfeld and S. A. Gelman), pp. 169-200. Cambridge University Press, New York.

Clark, A., Hocevar, D. and Dembo, M. (1980). The role of cognitive development in children's explanations and preferences for skin colour. *Developmental Psychology* **16**, 332-9.

Collins, A. and Gentner, D. (1987). How people construct mental models. In *Cultural models in language and thought* (ed. D. Holland and N. Quinn). Cambridge University Press.

Cosmides, L. and Tooby, J. (1994). Origins of domain-specificity: the evolution of functional organization. In *Mapping the mind: domain specificity in cognition and culture* (ed. L. A. Hirschfeld and S. A. Gelman), pp. 85-116. Cambridge University Press, New York.

Crocker, J. (1977). My brother the parrot. In *The social use of metaphor: essays on the anthropology of rhetoric* (ed. J. Sapir and J. Crocker), pp. 164-92. University of Pennsylvania Press, Philadelphia, PA.

Cushman, P. (1990). Why the self is empty: toward a historically situated psychology. *American Psychologist* **45**, 599-611.

Daniel, E. (1985). *Fluid signs: being a person the Tamil way.* University of California Press, Berkeley, CA.

Davey, A. (1983). *Learning to be prejudiced: growing up in multi-ethnic Britain.* Edward Arnold, London.

Dennett, D. (1976). Conditions on personhood. In *The identities of persons* (ed. A. Rorty), pp. 175-96. University of California Press, Los Angeles, CA.

Dolgin, K. and Behrend, D. (1984). Children's knowledge about animates and inanimates. *Child Development* **55**, 1646-50.

Dumont, L. (1985). A modified view of our origins: the Christian beginnings of modern individualism. In *The category of person* (ed. M. Carrithers, S. Collins, and S. Lukes). Cambridge University Press, New York.

Dunn, J. (1988). *The beginnings of social understanding*. Basil Blackwell, New York.

Durkheim, E. and Mauss, M. [1903] (1963). *Primitive classification*. University of Chicago Press.

Dwyer, P. (1976). An analysis of Rogaifo mammal taxonomy. *American Ethnologist* **3**(3), 425–45.

Eder, R. (1989). The emergent personologist: the structure and content of 3 1/2, 5 1/2, and 7 1/2 year-olds' concepts of themselves and other persons. *Child Development* **60**, 1218–28.

Eder, R. (1990). Uncovering young children's psychological selves: individual and developmental differences. *Child Development* **61**, 849–63.

Emmerich, W., Goldman, K., Kirsch, B. and Sharabany, R. (1977). Evidence for a transitional phase in the development of gender constancy. *Child Development* **48**, 930–6.

Flavell, J. (1985). *Cognitive development*. Prentice-Hall, Englewood Cliffs, NJ.

Foucault, M. (1965). *Madness and civilization: a history of insanity in the age of reason*. Vintage Books, New York.

Foucault, M. (1970). *The order of things: an archaeology of the human sciences*. Vintage Books, New York.

Foucault, M. (1973). *The birth of the clinic: an archaeology of medical perception*. Vintage Books, New York.

Foucault, M. (1978). *The history of sexuality. I: An introduction*. Pantheon, New York.

Garret, C., Ein, P. and Tremaine, L. (1977). The development of gender stereotyping of adult occupation in elementary school children. *Child Development* **48**, 507–12.

Geertz, C. (1973). *Interpretation of cultures*. Basic Books, New York.

Gelman, R., Spelke, E. and Meck, E. (1983). What preschoolers know about animate and inanimate objects. In *The development of symbolic thought* (ed. D. Rogers). Plenum, New York.

Gelman, S. (1992). Commentary. *Human Development* **35**, 280–5.

Gelman, S. and Kremer, K. (1991). Understanding natural cause: children's explanations of how objects and their properties originate. *Child Development* **62**, 396–414.

Gelman, S. and Markman, E. (1986). Categories and induction in young children. *Cognition* **23**, 183–209.

Gelman, S. and Wellman, H. (1991). Insides and essences: early understandings of the non-obvious. *Cognition* **48**, 213–44.

Gelman, S., Collman, P. and Maccoby, E. (1986). Inferring properties from categories versus inferring categories from properties: the case of gender. *Child Development* **57**, 396–404.

Gould, S. (1983). *The mismeasure of man*. W. W. Norton, New York.

Greeno, J. 1983. Conceptual entities. In *Mental models* (ed. D. Gentner and A. Stevens). Erlbaum, Hillsdale, NJ.

Hallowell, A. (1976). *Contributions to anthropology: selected papers of A. Irving Hallowell*. University of Chicago Press.

Hirschfeld, L. (1986). Kinship and cognition: genealogy and the meaning of kinship terms. *Current Anthropology* **27**, 217–42.

Hirschfeld, L. (1988). On acquiring social categories: cognitive development and anthropological wisdom. *Man* **23**, 611–38.

Hirschfeld, L. (1989*a*). Rethinking the acquisition of kinship terms. *International Journal of Behavioral Development* **12**(4), 541–68.

Hirschfeld, L. (1989*b*). Discovering linguistic differences: domain specificity and the young child's awareness of multiple languages. *Human Development* **32**, 223–36.

Hirschfeld, L. (1993). Discovering social difference: the role of appearance in the development of racial awareness. *Cognitive Psychology* **25**, 317–50.

Hirschfeld, L. (1994*a*). The child's representation of human groups. In *The psychology of learning and motivation: advances in research and theory*, Vol. 31 (ed. D. Medin) pp. 133–85. Academic Press, San Diego, CA.

Hirschfeld, L. (1994*b*). Is the acquisition of social categories based on domain-specific competence or knowledge transfer? In *Mapping the mind: domain specificity in cognition and culture* (ed. L. A. Hirschfeld and S. A. Gelman), pp. 201–33. Cambridge University Press, New York.

Hirschfeld, L. (in press). Do children have a theory of race? *Cognition.*

Hirschfeld, L. A. and Gelman, S. A. (ed) (1994). *Mapping the mind: domain specificity in cognition and culture*. Cambridge University Press, New York.

Hirschfeld, L., Atran, S. and Yengoyan, A. (1982). Theories of knowledge and culture. *Social Science Information* **21**, 161–89.

Inagaki, K. (1990). Young children's everyday biology as the basis for learning school biology. *Bulletin of the Faculty of Education, Chiba University* **38**, 177–84.

Inagaki, K. and Hatano, G. (1987). Young children's spontaneous personification and analogy. *Child Development* **58**, 1013–20.

Inagaki, K. and Sugiyama, K. (1988). Attributing human characteristics: developmental changes in over- and underattribution. *Cognitive Development* **3**, 55–70.

Jackendoff, R. (1992). *Language of the mind: essays on mental representation*. MIT Press, Cambridge, MA.

Johnson, K., Mervis, C. and Boster, J. (1992). Developmental changes within the structure of the mammal domain. *Developmental Psychology* **28**, 74–83.

Katz, P. (1982). Development of children's racial awareness and intergroup attitudes. In *Current topics in early childhood education*, Vol. 4 (ed. L. G. Katz). Ablex, Norwood.

Keil, F. (1979). *Semantic and conceptual development: an ontological perspective*. Harvard University Press, Cambridge, MA.

Keil, F. (1989). *Concepts, kinds, and cognitive development*. MIT Press, Cambridge, MA.

Kempton, M. (1987). Two theories of home heat control. In *Cultural models in language and thought* (ed. D. Holland and N. Quinn). Cambridge University Press, New York.

Kohlberg, L. (1966). A cognitive-developmental analysis of children's sex-role concepts and attitudes. In *The development of sex differences* (ed. E. Maccoby). Stanford University Press.

Kosslyn, S. and Kagan, J. (1981). 'Concrete thinking' and the development of social cognition. In *Social cognitive development: frontiers and possible futures* (ed. J. Flavell and L. Ross). Cambridge University Press, New York.

Lerner, R. (1973). The development of personal space schemata toward body build. *Journal of Psychology* **84**, 229–35.

Leslie, A. (1988). Some implications of pretense for mechanisms underlying the child's theory of mind. In *Developing theories of mind* (ed. J. Astington, P. Harris, and D. Olson). Cambridge University Press, New York.

Lévi-Strauss, C. (1962). *Totemism*. Beacon Press, Boston, MA.

Lutz, C. (1988). *Unnatural emotions: everyday sentiments on a Micronesian atoll and their challenge to Western theory*. University of Chicago Press.

Markus, H. and Kitiyama, S. (1991). Culture and self: implications for cognition, emotion, and motivation. *Psychological Review* **98**, 224–53.

Massey, C. and Gelman, R. (1988). Preschoolers decide whether pictured unfamiliar objects can move themselves. *Developmental Psychology* **24**, 307–17.

Mauss, M. (1947). *Manuel d'ethnographie*. Payot, Paris.

Mauss, M. [1938] (1985). A category of the human mind: the notion of person; the notion of self. In *The category of person* (ed. M. Carrithers, S. Collins, and S. Lukes). Cambridge University Press, New York.

Mead, M. (1932). An investigation of the thought of primitive children with special reference to animism. *Journal of the Royal Anthropological Institute* **62**, 173–90.

Medin, D. (1989). Concepts and conceptual structure. *American Psychologist* **44**, 1469–81.

Michotte, A. (1963). *The perception of causality*. Basic Books, New York.

Molnar, S. (1992). *Human variation: races, types, and ethnic groups*. Prentice-Hall, Englewood Cliffs, NJ.

Osherson, D., Smith, E., Wilkie, O., Lopez, A. and Shafir, E. (1990). Category-based induction. *Psychological Review* **90**, 339–63.

Premack, D. (1990). The infant's theory of self-propelled objects. *Cognition* **36**, 1–16.

Radcliffe-Brown, A. (1922). *The Andaman Islanders*. Cambridge University Press.

Rhodes, E. and Ruble, D. (1984). Children's understanding of dispositional characteristics of others. *Child Development* **55**, 550–60.

Robins, A. (1991). *Biological perspectives on human pigmentation*. Cambridge University Press, New York.

Rosaldo, M. (1972). Metaphor and folk classification. *Southwestern Journal of Anthropology* **28**, 83–99.

Rosengren, K., Gelman, S., Kalish, C. and McCormick, M. (1991). As time goes by: children's early understanding of growth in animals. *Child Development* **62**, 1302–20.

Rothbart, M. and Taylor, M. (1990). Category labels and social reality: do we view social categories as natural kinds? In *Language and social cognition* (ed. G. Semin and K. Fiedler). Sage, London.

Rozin, P., Nemeroff, C., Wane, M. and Sherrod, A. (1989). Operation of the sympathetic magical law of contagion in interpersonal attitudes among Americans. *Bulletin of the Psychonomic Society* **27**, 367–70.

Scheibe, K. and Erwin, M. (1979). The computer as alter. *Journal of Social Psychology* **108**, 103–9.

Semaj, L. (1980). The development of racial evaluation and preference: a cognitive approach. *Journal of Black Psychology* **6**, 59–79.

Shultz, T. (1982). Causal reasoning in the social and nonsocial realms. *Canadian Journal of Behavioral Sciences* **14**, 307–22.

Slaby, R. and Frey, K. (1975). Development of gender constancy and selective attention to same-sex models. *Child Development* **46**, 849–56.

Solomon, G., Johnson, S., Zaitchik, D. and Carey, S. (1993). *The young child's conception of inheritance*. Presented at the Society for Research on Child Development, New Orleans, LA, April 1993.

Spelke, E. (1991). Physical knowledge in infancy: reflections on Piaget's theory. In *The epigenesis of mind: essays on biology and cognition* (ed. S. Carey and R. Gelman). Erlbaum, Hillsdale, NJ.

Sperber, D. (1990). The epidemiology of belief. In *The social psychological study of widespread belief*. (ed. C. Fraser and G. Gaskel). Clarendon Press, Oxford.

Spiro, R., Feltovich, P., Coulson, R. and Anderson, D. (1989). Multiple analogies for complex concepts: antidotes for analogy-induced misconception on advanced knowledge acquisition. In *Similarity and analogical reasoning* (ed. Vosniadou and A. Ortony). Cambridge University Press, New York.

Springer, K. and Keil, F. (1989). On the development of biologically specific beliefs: the case of inheritance. *Child Development* **60**, 637–48.

Tajfel, H. (1981). *Human groups and social categories*. Cambridge University Press.

Tambiah, S. (1969). Animals are good to think and good to prohibit. *Ethnology* **8**(4), 422–59.

Triandis, H. (1989). The self and social behaviour in differing cultural contexts. *Psychological Review* **96**, 506–20.

Turner, T. (1989). 'We are parrots', 'Twins are bird': play of tropes as operational structure. In *Beyond metaphor: the theory of tropes in anthropology* (ed. J. Fernandez). Stanford University Press.

van den Berghe, P. (1981). *The ethnic phenomenon*. Elsevier, New York.

Vaughan, G. (1987). A social psychological model of ethnic identity. In *Children's ethnic socialization: pluralism and development* (ed. J. Phinney and M. Rotheram). Sage, Beverly Hills, CA.

Vosniadou, S. (1989). Analogical reasoning as a mechanism in knowledge acquisition: a developmental perspective. In *Similarity and analogical reasoning* (ed. S. Vosniadou and A. Ortony). Cambridge University Press, New York.

Waugh, L. (1977). *A semantic analysis of word order: position of the adjective in French*. E. J. Brill, Leiden.

Wellman, H. (1990). *The child's theory of mind*. MIT Press, Cambridge, MA.

Yuill, N. (1992). Children's conception of personality traits. *Human Development* **35**, 265–79.

DISCUSSION

Participants: P. Boyer, F. Keil, G. Lewis

Lewis: The characteristics which come under your heading of 'biological' or 'essentialist' are likely to be continuously present and visible, but those which are 'behavioural' are more transient and are shown intermittently. Would that difference help to explain why 'biological' rather than 'behavioural' traits seem to be paid more attention?

Boyer: The 'societal' model is strongly supported by your data on kinship categories and their acquisition. However, your work on racial categories is of course consistent with the societal model, but does not entail that model. For instance, the data would be compatible with an essentialist interpretation. One reason for choosing the societal interpretation in this domain as well is that it seems more parsimonious to have a single type of intuitive domain-specific structure for social categories in general. Obviously, this may beg the question, in that it presupposes that there is a proper cognitive domain here. There may be different cognitive domains involved in the acquisition and representation of social categories. Moreover, the 'essentialist' interpretation does not require that the child projects biological expectations onto social categories. It only requires that he or she project the essentialist construal that underlies these biological presumptions.

Keil: Your adoption and inheritance studies seem to converge in powerful ways, suggesting that the same sorts of properties are being distinguished and judged differently. There seem to be three such kinds of properties: essential social properties, biological properties, and transient properties. Are these three sorts of properties showing different patterns of judgements? That is, are they kept distinct in the mind of the young child?

Do you see an understanding of people as goal-directed but not having a theory of mind, as compatible with the proposals by Leslie and Premack in this workshop? If not, what is your version of having a goal-directed representation?

How is the essentialist construal of social groups set up and maintained? One possibility is that one uses and maintains a mode of understanding to the extent that it is successful in guiding one's inductions and other reasoning about the relevant phenomena. In the case of essentialist beliefs about social groups, this possibility leads to the conclusion that such essentialist beliefs have some predictive value for those who hold them. In view of the more odious essentialist beliefs about groups, this is a depressing conclusion. To what extent is it warranted and what are the alternative possibilities?

Hirschfeld: Lewis cautions that I may have underestimated the contribution made by frequency in encounter. However, it should be recalled that children in the identity task did not find all continuously present and visible cues equally attention-demanding. Race preserved identity over time and generations, but body build did not. Moreover, the importance that children place on social cues does not reflect a general preference, but is specific to the task that they are performing. In another set of studies (Hirschfeld 1993), I presented pre-school children with either a visual or a verbal tableau depicting common social contexts. As in the identity studies, the participants' race, occupation, and physique (among other social cues) were marked in each tableau. I then asked the children to recall what they had seen (in the case of the visual narrative) or heard (in the case of the verbal narrative). In contrast with the identity task, children in the social context study did not find race or physique attention-demanding at all, and focused on occupation more than on any other social cue. Thus it is not the case that young children's attention to corporeal features like skin colour in the identity studies represents a bias towards more continuously present and visible cues; rather, it reflects the meaning with which they invest race.

Boyer also brings up an important issue, and of course it is correct that an appeal to domain parsimony would beg the question here, if for no other reason than that we do not yet have a good description of 'proper cognitive domain' (Hirschfeld and Gelman 1994). It is also correct that there may be more than one domain involved in the acquisition and representation of social categories: multiple domains are involved in the acquisition and representation of *any* sort of category. Knowing about plants means knowing about taxonomic structure and underlying essence, but it also means knowing about edible versus inedible, cultivated versus wild, etc. These artefact categories are no less part of our ethnobotanical knowledge for being artefact categories. Clearly, they figure in how we reason about exemplars. This is why attempts to define domains in terms of objects in the world is a perilous enterprise.

Why then worry about domains at all? Perhaps it is sufficient just to describe modes of understanding—in this case, an essentialist one which just happens to span *all* biological kinds, *some* societal kinds, and *some* supenatural entities. The problem is that essentialist understanding is constrained, and the trick is to discover what those constraints are. It is not self-evident that all cases of essentialist understanding need to have a single source, any more than that all causal explanations must have a single derivation. However, it may be that there is a single essentialist mode of understanding that underlies biological presumptions, societal presumptions, and so forth. Again, the question is why this particular set of presumptions and not others? The notion of a societal construal or societal model does not *compete* with that of an essentialist construal; rather, it defines a universe of non-obvious entities (human and other collectivities) over which an essentialist interpretation might span. Essentialism provides a rationale for ontology; it does not specify one. In contrast, an impulse to interpret humans as societal beings implies an ontology, but does not explain that ontology.

Keil interprets my argument as distinguishing social organizing properties—biological properties—from transient properties. I am not sure that this distinction is the same as the one that I propose. Skin colour is a corporeal (and thus biological) property that is social organizing; body build is a corporeal (and thus biological) property that is not social organizing; occupation is social organizing but not biological (yet it is presumed to be heritable by pre-school children). I believe, but the data are only suggestive here, that each of these types of property is associated with a distinct pattern of judgement. The results of the identity constancy study could be interpreted as indicating that younger children rely on race and occupation in almost equal measure, suggesting a single pattern of judgement. However, in another set of analyses (Hirschfeld 1994*a*) I show that, when making judgements of identity, children rely on *either* race *or* occupation. In other words, children make use of alternative strategies for reasoning about social difference, each representing a distinct way of organizing social experience. Given adult racial thinking, it makes sense to think about those children who opt for a racial solution as using a biological or biology-like reasoning strategy. What of the children who rely on occupation? At this point I can only speculate. We know that children focus on occupation because it is meaningful in some way beyond similarity in apparel. It is plausible that this meaning, as I suggested in the chapter, implicates the notion of goal-directed. As Keil has shown, children of this age have a rich and subtle understanding of function. Crediting them with using this in the social realm does not seem implausible. However, it is important to bear in mind that, here, goal-directed probably does not necessarily involve a notion of mental goal but rather a social goal. To the extent that Leslie and Premack derive the notion of goal-directedness strictly from mental goals, there would be some incompatibility between our positions. However, I see no reason why they would want to. In fact, Premack's model, based on perceptual primitives, does not seem to at all. He has collapsed social relations and mental intentions, but apparently only because this is what psychologists usually do and not because the model requires it.

A more interesting link between the model that I propose and theory of mind involves the theory-of-mind impairment that Leslie and others have documented for autistics. The explanation of this impairment as damage to a module that functions to form meta-representations makes sense in terms of false beliefs, where autistics appear to have difficulty in forming a representation of another's mental representation. But I have proposed that societal beliefs, possibly including such seemingly mentalistic representations as traits and dispositions, may not be derived from belief–desire reasoning and thus do not involve ascriptions of mental states. If this is the case, autistics may well not show impaired performance in social reasoning that parallels their deficits in psychological reasoning.

With respect to Keil's question about how essentialist understanding is established and maintained, it is easier to say what the derivation of the essentialist understanding of social groups is *not* than to answer his query. There are a number of reasons for rejecting the claim that it is set up and maintained by analogy with biological reasoning. Analogic transfer from biology assumes that there is a perception of parallel variation in the way that different human groups (namely races) differ physically and the way that animal groups (namely folk species) differ physically. First, it is not universally the case that stipulated racial differences correlate with conspicuous physical variation. van den Berghe (1981) points out that different racial groups have been marked by distinct physical (as opposed to cultural) features only recently in human history, subsequent to long-distance colonial exploration. Prior to that, adjacent groups tended to resemble each other, via interbreeding, rather than to differ markedly. Second, as I pointed out in the chapter, the expectations of school-age children (and adults) about the contribution that race makes to the appearance of future generations does not reflect the actual pattern of inheritance of racial features such as skin colour.

Keil suggests an alternative route for the emergence of an essentialist bias about social groups, namely that it is successful in guiding children's inductions about the relevant phenomena. On the face of it, this is both plausible and, as he points out, discouraging. However, I am persuaded that it is not the case. The problem is that it is not clear what the criteria of success might be. Typically, success is understood in terms of some behavioural outcome related to the prediction. That is, an essentialist construal encouraging pervasive racism might be considered successful to the extent that it prompted children to make the 'right' sorts of racial judgements. However, 'right sorts of racial judgements' must be understood in terms of behaviour rather than mentation.

There are two reasons for this. First, it is likely, although as far as I know unexplored, that adults are less concerned about what their children say about social interaction and are more concerned about what they do. Even if this does not turn out to be the case, we know that young children talk very little about race and rarely use racial terms (Hirschfeld 1988). It is not a discourse into which young children readily enter (an informal search of the CHILDES natural language data base for ethnic, national, and racial terms yielded virtually nothing except an occasional reference to 'Chinese dolls' and similar terms, i.e. nothing that would suggest that pre-school children are talking about the race of others). It should be recalled that it is precisely during this age period that the essentialist understanding of social groups is emerging.

Second, even if the measure of success is strictly behavioural, the possibilities are limited. Behaviour that would provide feedback about an appropriate mental representation of social groups would be behaviour that sets certain social groups apart from others. We know that young children do treat social groups differently: gender and relative age are powerful predictors of pre-school children's social interactions. Strikingly, however, race is not. It is not a significant factor in pre-school chilren's choice of playmates *unless* ethnicity is also combined with language differences (see Hirschfeld (1993) for a review of the relevant studies).

In fact, research on young children's racial attitudes contains a paradox in that the presence of racial prejudice is easily established in experimental settings but not in normative settings. This is paradoxical *only* if it is assumed that children see the same things in experimental tasks that they see in natural settings. Specifically, it is assumed that when children are (i) presented with a pair of stimuli which contrast in race, (ii) asked to choose the one they prefer, think is prettier, would like to have as a friend, etc., and (iii) select the majority race stimulus over the minority race stimulus, these data should be interpreted as evidence for racial prejudice. However, this interpretation assumes that children are conceptualizing the contrast between majority and minority race in the same way as the experimenter.

I have shown that pre-school children attend very little to the physical features of race when parsing a social context; early racial categories appear to contain little visual information (Hirschfeld 1993). When experimenters contrive social contexts in which only one contrast is available, children attend to that contrast. But when the social context is more complex, as normative social contexts invariably are, they do not attend closely to the physical aspects of race. Why? Because they are more concerned with understanding the racial ontology, the ambient social system, than with specifying the physical features diagnostic of that system; pre-school children devote more effort to elaborating a social ontology than to picking out the features that instantiate it. Contrary to previous accounts, fleshing out the physical meaning of race appears to develop later, during the school years. Again it should be recalled that children first show evidence of an essentialist understanding of race during the pre-school years. In short, this understanding emerges before any actions that would allow such cognitions to be behaviourally assessed in normative contexts. Thus it is not plausible to attribute such cognitions to their 'success'.

What are the alternatives? Frankly we do not know. I have suggested that one alternative is that children spontaneously seek to understand humans as members of social groups. Membership in collectivities is predicated on a number of different possibilities: functional role (like occupation), psychological predilection (like disposition), or intrinsic quality (like race). A fairly rich body of literature now suggests that children possess rich reasoning skills related to each of these modes. How they are distributed across things in the world, or things in the world in certain contexts, is the question facing all of us.

12

The looping effects of human kinds
IAN HACKING

My topic is at some distance from others in this book. This is not because I am a philosopher given to abstraction and high generality. Many of my examples are all too reminiscent of sensationalist popular journalism. My causal understandings are complex and shady, my cognition is controversial applied knowledge, and my culture is our culture and none other.

Culture I am addressing not a human universal but ways of classifying that became possible only in industrial bureaucracies. Today their most salient features are the result of a recent democratization of some social sciences.

Cognition The classifications that I call human kinds make sense only within a peculiar conception of knowing and finding out.

Causality Human kinds are formulated in the hope of immediate or future interventions in the lives of individual human beings. If we change the background conditions we can improve the person, if only we can understand what kind of person we are dealing with. The causal understanding (or aspiration to understand) is practical.

None the less my theme is obsessively philosophical, for it is about self-reflection. It is about how a causal understanding, if known by those who are understood, can change their character, can change the kind of people that they are. That can lead to a change in the causal understanding itself. This chapter is about feedback effects in cognition and culture, and is a contribution to the study of what I call 'making up people' (Hacking 1986).

WHAT ARE HUMAN KINDS?

'Human kinds' is such an ugly turn of phrase that, as Auguste Comte said of *sociologie*, no one else would ever want to use it. I do not intend to pick out a definite and clearly bounded class of classifications. I mean to indicate kinds of people, their behaviour, their condition, kinds of action, kinds of temperament or tendency, kinds of emotion, and kinds of experience. I use the term 'human kinds' to emphasize kinds – the systems of classification – rather than people and their feelings. Although I intend human kinds to include kinds of behaviour, act, or temperament, it is kinds of people that concern me. That is, kinds of behaviour, act, or temperament are what I call human kinds if we take them to characterize kinds of people.

However, I do not mean any kinds of people. I choose the label 'human kinds' for its inhumane ring, and mean the kinds that are studied in the marginal, insecure, but enormously powerful human and social sciences. An operational definition of an insecure science is: a science whose leaders say they are in quest of a paradigm, or have just found a paradigm. Insecurity is consistent with immense power. Thus, to turn to a natural science, Walter Gilbert, tsar of the best-funded non-military research programme in the world, the $300 million human genome project, responded to criticism with an article entitled 'Towards a paradigm shift in biology' (Gilbert 1991).

By human kinds I mean kinds about which we would like to have systematic, general, and accurate knowledge; classifications that could be used to formulate general truths about people; generalizations sufficiently strong that they seem like laws about people, their actions, or their sentiments. We want laws precise enough to predict what individuals will do, or how they will respond to attempts to help them or to modify their behaviour. The model is that of the natural sciences. Only one kind of causality is deemed relevant: efficient causation. One event brings about another, although the causal laws may be only probabilistic laws of tendency.

The term 'human kind' is patterned after the philosopher's 'natural kind', and so I have to make some disclaimers. It is hard to believe that a philosopher could be so mealy-mouthed about natural kinds. I have no doubt that nature has kinds which we distinguish. Some seem fairly cosmic: quarks, probably genes, possibly cystic fibrosis. Others are mundane: mud, the common cold, headlands, sunsets. The common cold is as real as cystic fibrosis, and sunsets are as real as quarks. More law-like regularities are known about mud than quarks – known to youths who play football, parents who do the family laundry, and to mud engineers on oil rig sites. The regularities about mud do not have profound consequences for theoreticians. That does not make mud any the less a natural kind of stuff. In the domain of living things, Atran's speciemes – trees, vines, grasses – are kinds that we find in nature; so are the species of today's systematics.

Nelson Goodman has used the happy phrase 'relevant kinds' in which he includes 'such artificial kinds as musical works, psychological experiments and types of machinery'. As far as I am concerned, natural kinds are relevant kinds that we find in nature. Are the varieties of plants and animals that we owe to horticulturalists and stock breeders 'natural' by now? For me, plutonium is a natural kind, even though humans made it. There are many distinctions to be made among the natural kinds, including historical ones. Psycholinguists debate whether children innately distinguish the artefactual from the natural, or the mechanical from the living. On a quite different level there is undoubtedly a sense in which some kinds are more cosmic (the word is Quine's) than others. Perhaps nature and its laws are such that some kinds are more truly fundamental than others. Graceless philosophers repeat Plato's words out of context and talk of carving nature at her joints. Does nature have ultimate joints? For present purposes I am indifferent to all such questions—metaphysical, psycholinguistic, or historical. This is because they do not matter to the distinctions that I do wish to notice between human kinds and natural kinds.

Since I am so tolerant about natural kinds, should I not count human kinds among the natural kinds? For a certain convenience I shall restrict human kinds to kinds that are, at least at first sight, peculiar to people in a social setting. I do not deny that people are natural or that human societies are part of nature. For convenience, I follow the custom of calling something natural only when it is not peculiar to people in their communities. A great many types of attributes of people apply in the world at large or at least to other living beings: mass, longevity, distribution of digestive organs, the pancreatic enzymes such as amylopsin, trypsin, and steapsin, or the structure of the genome. Many items that occur in the scientific study of human beings present no significant contrast with other kinds that we find in nature. There is a proper tension here, because one thrust of research into human kinds is to biologize them. Drunkards form a human kind; according to one school of thought, apparently favoured by the editor of *Science*, alcoholism is carried by a gene. Five years ago I copied from a doctor's office the statement 'We have learned more about this illness in the past five years than in the past five hundred years and it is now evident that alcoholism and other drug additions are truly psychosocial biogenetic diseases'. Suicide is a kind of human behaviour; it was proposed late in 1990 that it too has a genetic component. These are instances not so much of what Imre Lakatos called research programmes as of what Gerald Holton called themata. Holton gives atomism in its successive manifestations (Leucippus, Lucretius, Boyle, Dalton, and onwards) as an example of a thema. Equally old and powerful is the idea that we acquire knowledge of humanity by replacing human kinds by physiological or mechanical or neuroelectrical or biochemical ones. This is not just a tradition of research, but also represents a metaphysics. In Chapter 13 Philip Pettit discusses how we can have real causation in psychology. One solution is to make psychology, and all else that is human or social, into biology. That is, a built-in metaphysical motivation for biologizing human kinds.

There are many more tensions—some in the philosophy of the natural and some in the methodology of the biological. Yet I think that there is little difficulty in picking out characteristic human kinds. When I speak of human kinds, I mean (i) kinds that are relevant to some of us, (ii) kinds that primarily sort people, their actions, and behaviour, and (iii) kinds that are studied in the human and social sciences, i.e. kinds about which we hope to have knowledge. I add (iv) that kinds of people are paramount; I want to include kinds of human behaviour, action, tendency, etc. only when they are projected to form the idea of a kind of person. Homosexuality provides us with a perhaps all too familiar example. It is quite widely asserted that, although same-sex acts are common in most human societies, the idea of 'the homosexual' as a kind of person came into being only late in the nineteenth century as homosexual behaviour became an object of scientific scrutiny. If this were correct, then homosexual behaviour would be what I am calling here a 'human kind' only late in the nineteenth century, even though there has been plenty of pederasty, for example, at all times and places, for only at that time was this kind of behaviour taken as an indication of a kind of person.

In important personal relationships we seldom think or feel directly in terms of human kinds. In friendship, love, and animosity we care about all that is particular, unusual, intimate, and circumstantial, all that is glimpsed or shared or felt glancingly—in short, all that is caught in the nuance of the novel rather than the classifications of the scientist. One person is trusting, another gentle, a third selfish and arrogant. One, who although forgetful is responsive and enthusiastic, has a friend who is an insensitive busybody. We know a great deal about such kinds of people, but we do not profess scientific knowledge about them. We neither make surveys that count their proportions in a given population, nor subject them to factor analysis. Yet these are the kinds that matter to us—the kinds we use to organize our thoughts about our companions, friends, and loved ones, not to mention those whom we try to avoid. Since they also matter to employers, teachers, and the military, psychologists devise tests that use questions often recalling these familiar traits. The results are tabulated or summarized to form 'profiles' or 'personal inventories' that then become human kinds. They are digests of what matters in intimacy, but they acquire the abstraction of the sciences or impersonal management.

Yet human kinds are not so irrelevant to us as people. Straightforward and well-established human kinds studied in the social sciences *do* affect intensely personal concerns. If you see someone whom you love (or see yourself) as of a kind, that may change your entire set of perceptions. Human kinds usually present themselves as scientific and hence as value-free, but they have often been brought into being by judgements of good and evil. Sociology of the numerical sort began by measuring the incidence of behaviour such as suicide. Durkheim's classic and originating work *Suicide* could draw upon 80 years of studies. Suicide was tabulated because it was a Bad Act, perhaps the very worst, beyond the possibility of repentance and even forgiveness. A body of knowledge about suicide changed beliefs about what kind of deed it was, and hence its moral evaluation: 'an attempted suicide is a cry for help'. Your attitude to a friend who attempts suicide will be different from that which your great-grandparents would have had. Suicides in novels today are not what they were at the time of young Werther or Heinrich Kleist, partly because science has made suicide into a human kind.

Human kinds are of many categories. I use the word 'category' in an old fashioned way, which is also the colloquial way. A category is a tree of classifications, or else the most general classification at the top of such a tree. Many authorities, ranging from cognitive scientists to psycholinguists, now use 'category' as a synonym for 'class' as in George Lakoff's title, *Women, fire and dangerous things: What categories show about the human mind*. Women-fire-and-dangerous-things is a class, or kind, distinguished by an Australian people, but Lakoff calls it a category. I do not. Race, gender, native language, nationality, type of employment, and age cohort are all what I call categories. The experts most versed in these categories work out of census bureaux, institutions whose modern form is coeval with quantitative social science. Indeed I willingly extend my grouping, human kinds, to include any of the kinds enumerated by the census, or at least those kinds when endowed with their social connotations. Say, to abbreviate too much, that gender is the social meaning of sex — the category of sex not being peculiar to human beings, but the category of gender being peculiar to humans in a society. I follow tradition surprisingly closely in all this. Philosophers took 'natural kind' as a term of art after J. S. Mill. As soon as he had introduced his idea of a *real Kind*, he asked whether the sexes and races were real Kinds. (He hoped not. His programme was anti-sexist and anti-racist). These two human categories, race and gender, have been obsessively discussed of late. Our thoughts about them are so redolent of ideology that I shall leave them on one side. Conclusions about human kinds are indeed relevant to those categories, but we would be misled about human kinds if we followed Mill and used race and gender as our core examples. The very relationship between science, and race or gender, is unclear. I have defined human kinds as the objects of the insecure sciences, as the kinds about which we would like to have knowledge. I took for granted that those sciences are modelled on natural science, particularly in their conception of causality. That was what Mill was talking about. However, there is a strong present prejudice against making race the object of science. A few forthright spokesmen like Michael Dummett make plain that we do not want the knowledge that we might find out. The more familiar pusillanimous complaint is that race science is bad science. In the case of gender, many outspoken feminists claim knowledge, but reject a knowledge patterned on causal natural science. These important issues would take us aside from my main topic.

I have mentioned kinds 'with their social meaning'—an obscure phrase. To illustrate, take teen-age pregnancy. That is as determinate a classification as could be. You are teen-aged, female, pregnant, and (unwritten premise) unmarried. There is a rigorous definition, then, with succinct chronological, physiological and legal clauses. If we make 'teen-age' precise and adapt 'unmarried', then this concept can be applied in many cultures unlike our own. However, it became a relevant kind only at a certain moment in American history. After 1967 it was the subject of interminable sociological study and debate. Recently the cultural meaning of the term has switched sufficiently that a euphemism has been introduced by sociologists: early parenting. Teen-age pregnancy—the word, and also the idea with a certain set of implications—reared its ugly head in the white American suburbs of the 1960s. Early parenting connotes black urban ghettos of the 1990s. Thus far we have an idea and no knowledge, but once the idea was in motion experts arrived to determine a knowledge and to transform it. The classification 'teen-age pregnancy' or 'early parenting' is completely grounded in nature, but is a human kind—and is the subject of social science—only in a certain social context. There is a similarity to and a difference from another human kind of person—the adolescent. Adolescence cannot be fully grounded in nature. Even if we define it as beginning with first menarche/ejaculation, there is nothing in nature beyond a social context that signals its end. Anna Freud said that we owe the discovery of adolescence to psychoanalysis. Historians of developmental psychology locate its discovery elsewhere. Nevertheless there is a remarkable agreement that whatever grander social changes made adolescence possible, the adolescent exists as a kind of person thanks to the social sciences. The first major work on adolescence was the two volume treatise by G. Stanley Hall (1904), the man who is commonly called the founder of American experimental psychology. He called it *Adolescence: its psychology and its relations to physioloqy, anthropology, sociology, sex, crime, religion and education.* You might think that this title is exhaustive, but it is not quite. After over 1200 pages we reach a long final chapter, 'Ethnic psychology and pedagogy, or adolescent races and their treatment'. We find that one third of the human race are 'adolescents of adult size'. Even lineages which are by now regarded as 'decadent', 'often exemplify the symptom of *dementia praecox* magnified to macrobiotic proportions' (Hall 1904, Vol. II, p. 649).

Those were the bad old days, of course. To fix ideas further, I shall take two up-to-date human kinds and a recently proposed causal law that connects them. Child abuse is a kind of human behaviour. It breaks up into several kinds, including sexual abuse, physical abuse, neglect, and, a current topic of fierce controversy in North America, sadistic cult abuse (read Satanic rituals). Child abuse is a kind that has been remarkably malleable. It has connections with cruelty to children, a classic kind of behaviour brought to the fore in Europe and America about 120 years ago. But the present classification, child abuse, began exactly 30 years ago with battered baby syndrome, took incest and sexual abuse under its wing 18 years ago, and picked up cruel ritual cult abuse 5 years ago. The recent trajectory is primarily American with European classifications following loosely in step (Hacking 1991, 1992c).

Child abuse certainly fits my rough and ready criteria for being a human kind.

1. In many quarters today, it is a highly relevant kind.

2. It is peculiar to people, even when we draw some analogies to some sorts of primate behaviour.

3. It is a kind of behaviour about which we would like to have knowledge, for example to prevent child abuse and to help abused children.

4. We have an inclination to project the kind of behaviour to the person, i.e., we think that there are child abusers, that abusive parents may be a type of parent.

We can make an even stronger statement about child abuse. The Center for Advanced Study in the Behavioral Sciences at Stanford University liked, and perhaps still likes, to use the epithet 'cutting edge' for work conducted under its auspices. An operational definition of a cutting-edge human kind would be: there is at least one professional society of experts dedicated to studying it; there are regular conferences, one of which is major and a number of which are more specialized; there is at least one recently established professional journal to which the authorities contribute (and which helps define who the authorities are). We have the International Society for the Prevention of Child Abuse and Neglect, a great many conferences, and the journal *Child Abuse and Neglect*, among others. Child abuse is a cutting-edge human kind.

Child abusers are all too common. A much rarer kind of person is the one suffering from what is now called multiple personality disorder (Hacking 1992b). These people used to be very rare indeed, and they usually suffered from two, or perhaps three or four, alternative personalities; one personality was usually amnesic for another. There has been an epidemic of multiple personalities in North America, starting in the early 1970s; the 9th International Conference on the topic was attended by 800 professionals (psychiatrists, psychologists, social workers), many of whom have case loads of over 40 multiples a year. The face of multiplicity has changed a great deal in the past 20 years. It is now commonplace for clinicians to have patients with 25 alter personalities. This whole discourse takes place under a larger rubric of 'dissociative behaviour'. Dissociation was first named by Pierre Janet during the French wave of multiples that started in Bordeaux in 1875, but has been retrieved only recently. In the inner circles of dissociation experts, Janet is revered while Freud is cast out.

Many psychiatrists, particularly those with a medical/biochemical/ neurological approach to mental illness, are dubious or even cynical about multiple personality. They argue that multiples are a cultural artefact. Now, if I had said (as so many philosophers do say) that human kinds must in some sense be indubitably 'real', and perhaps even cross-culturally cosmic, I should have been obliged to discuss this opposition. Instead, I made some disclaimers not only about the human but also about the natural. I do believe that some psychiatrists, the media, a wing of the women's movement, concern about sexual abuse of children, and much else have brought about the present prevalence of multiple personality disorder. That does not make the malady any less real. It is a condition with associated behaviour that afflicts a significant number of people who at present are crying out for help. It is a human kind, and a cutting-edge human kind to boot. There is the International Society for the Study of Multiple Personality and Dissociation. There is an annual international conference and many regional conferences. The journal *Dissociation* is about to enter its fifth year of publication.

I stated that we want knowledge about human kinds. There has been a remarkable breakthrough in thinking about multiple personality. The cause of this disorder is now known to people who work in the field. Multiple personality is the consequence of repeated trauma early in childhood, almost always involving sexual abuse. This fact is so accepted among workers in the field that many regard it as almost definitional. This causal knowledge is deeply incorporated into theories of the disorder. The various alters represent dissociated ways of coping with particular experienced trauma. This in turn has had a great impact on methods of treatment, which now focus on abreaction of the trauma through the voices of the various alters which may in time become co-conscious, collaborative, and finally integrated. Thanks to media exposure, particularly on afternoon television talk shows that appeal to lower-class women who empathize with the oppressed and the bizarre, this scientific knowledge is very widely disseminated in the USA. The details are the property of experts, but the general structure is remarkably common knowledge.

My example is sensational but serves to fix ideas. Despite its role in social rhetoric and politics of numerous stripes, child abuse was first presented and is still intended to be a 'scientific' concept. Of course, there are demarcation disputes. Which science? Medicine, psychiatry, sociology, psychology, social work, jurisprudence, or self-help? Whatever the standpoint, there are plenty of authorities firmly convinced that there are important truths about child abuse, for example 'most abusers were abused as children'. Research and experiment should reveal them. We hope that cause and effect are relevant, that we can find predictors of future abuse, that we can explain it, that we can prevent it, and that we can determine its consequences and counteract them. For example, it is held that abusive mothers have often not bonded adequately to their children, and that premature babies in incubators are at risk of inadequate bonding. This causal hypothesis leads authorities to establish elaborate bonding rituals in maternity hospitals.

It might be thought that child abuse is such a complex concept that questions of developmental psychology or the theory of cognition could not arise. We are considering how a social organization makes and moulds an idea, not about concept acquisition in children. Quite the contrary. In Chapter 11 Lawrence Hirschfeld discusses the early stage at which American children acquire concepts of race. A parallel issue has been debated, with very practical consequences, in connection with child abuse. Many American jurisdictions introduced early training to enable children to recognize and report incipient abuse. Two years ago California rescinded these laws, on the basis of declarations by expert witnesses, based on Piagetian grounds, that children could not understand these ideas. There is now a back-backlash contesting this cognitive claim.

On the score of being scientific, a different type of issue emerges. Perhaps we fail to help children (some say) because all our endeavours assume that we are dealing with a scientific kind? This worry has been expressed in terms of the 'medicalization' of child abuse. Child abuse is not for the doctors, even if paediatricians did first sound the alert with battered baby syndrome. Thus far, the complaint is only about the type of expert, not about the very possibility of expertise. In general, the anti-experts usually claim that they are the true experts: the social workers defy the police, the psychologists confront the judiciary, etc. Multiple personality is a case of yet another type of concern about scientism. Some critics contend that there is no such thing as multiple personality disorder (I have heard it called 'the UFO of psychiatry') and that multiple behaviour results from interaction with doctors or, more recently, from sensationalist reports in the media. Nevertheless the debate is left to experts. This or that group claims to have knowledge about what really ails the troubled patients and how they could be treated better.

Thus what I call human kinds begin in the hands of scientists of various stripes. Human kinds live there for a while. A while? My example of the homosexual foreshadows something to be discussed later. People of the kind may rise up against the experts. The known may overpower the knowers.

I have stated that *we* want laws precise enough to predict what individuals will do. Or *we* want to know how people of a kind will respond to attempts to help them or to modify their behaviour. I have stated 'we' would like all this, typically in order to help 'them'. I made these statements because that is what the social sciences have been up to since their inception. The search for human kinds that conform to psychological or social laws is inextricably intertwined with prediction and reform. These aims can be perverted, but they have generally been well-intentioned when seen from the vantage point of the reformers. Groups of experts now collaborate and say that together they are members of the 'helping professions': social workers, therapists, parole officers, policemen, judges, psychiatrists, teachers, 'Ph.D. psychologists', paediatricians. They try to distinguish kinds of people or behaviour that are deviant. They invite more theoretical and foundational studies on which to base their practical work. Sociologists and statisticians form and test law-like conjectures about people of those kinds. Such knowledge enables the front line to interfere and intervene so as to help more effectively and predictably. Or so the sciences present themselves: cynics suspect that there is no knowledge to be had, and that these forms of knowledge legitimate the use of power.

Why are my examples so unattractive? I seem to have in mind a rather shady bunch of kinds, marginal human kinds, kinds about which we claim or hope to have systematic knowledge, kinds that are, loosely, topics for actual or prospective sciences. But not real social science! I could develop the argument that what I call human kinds are at the historical root of sociology—the science of normality and deviance. Even if I am correct, should not 'human kinds' by now serve as the generic name for the classifications used in the social sciences—the *sciences humaines*, or perhaps even *Geisteswissenschaften*? What then of the classifications made in anthropology, linguistics, economics, and history? Why lay such emphasis on the sciences of deviancy, social pathology, healing, and control?

In the context of this book I shall evade the question (and the historical or archaeological response) by saying that I am choosing my own type of causal understanding to think about. I fix on a certain type of practical causality. By human kinds I mean kinds of people and their behaviour which (it is hoped) can enter into practical laws—laws that if we knew them we would use to change present conditions, and predict what would ensue. We want the right classification—the correct sorting of child abuse or teen-age pregnancy—so that confronted by abusive parents or pregnant teenagers we can embark on a course of action that will change them for the better and will prevent others from joining their ranks. We do not want to know the 'structure' of teen-age pregnancy in the fascinating but abstract way in which we want to know the structure of kinship among a certain people, or the structure of the modal auxiliaries in their language. We want principles according to which we can interfere, intervene, help, and improve. The closest comparison within the social sciences would be with economics. The applied economists say that they want to make things better, but their kinds are not usually what I call human kinds. Most of them are at least one remove from individual people and their actions. The bank rate and the money supply depend upon what some people do, but they are not kinds of people.

I have been trying to make vivid the concept of a human kind. There is one last general point to make. Which comes first, the classification or the causal connections between kinds? There are two coarse pictures of concept formation. In one, people first make certain distinctions and then learn the properties and causal relationships between distinguished classes. In another, causal relationships are recognized between individuals, and these relationships are used to distinguish classes. I believe that my fellow philosophers are the chief sinners in cleaving to one or other of these extreme pictures. Whatever conclusion be urged about infant cognition, it is plain that in later life recognition and expectation are of a piece. Or, to put it linguistically, to acquire and use a name for any kind is, among other things, to be willing to make generalizations and form expectations about things of that kind. We should take for granted that guessing at causes goes hand in hand with increasingly precise definition.

To take two examples which are unfavourable to this theme, suicide and teen-age pregnancy have been with us always, and with many another society. Hence one might have the picture of first there being the kind of human behaviour or condition, and then the knowledge. That is not the case. The kind and the knowledge grow together. At the beginning of the nineteenth century people were still debating the noble suicide of Cato the Elder, but soon suicide was to be defined as 'a kind of madness' with numerous subkinds, all tended over by the right sort of medical man. Suicides were sorted by their conjectured causes. When we turn to child abuse, it sounds as if it were a classification of behaviour preceding any knowledge. But this is not the case. It emerged in 1961–1962 in company with a quite specific body of knowledge — paediatric X-rays (which showed unexpected healed fractures of babies' arms and legs). The technology of the rapidly declining profession of infant radiology was revived to define 'battered baby syndrome', and doctors asserted in powerful public statements that they were in control of the treatment and prevention of abusive behaviour. Cause, classification, and intervention were of a piece.

WHAT'S SO SPECIAL ABOUT HUMAN KINDS?

My phrase 'human kind' is patterned after 'natural kind'. Evidently I think that human kinds are importantly different from natural kinds. In this section I shall do three things.

1. I shall sympathetically state the idea to which I am opposed: that human kinds are, at worst, messy natural kinds.
2. I shall make plain that I am not arguing anything remotely like *either* a *Verstehen or* a constructionist position. Yes, I think that the human differs from the natural, but not because what I call human kinds are to be understood hermeneutically rather than explained by causal principles. Yes, I think that the human differs from the natural, but not because human kinds are social constructions while natural kinds are discovered in nature.
3. I shall state the difference between natural and human kinds that interests me. I do not argue that it is the only difference. Perhaps the *Verstehen* and the construction distinctions are both right, but they are not mine. They are deep. Mine is shallow.

Natural and human

The modern phrase 'natural kind' resonates with antique controversies. Does nature have kinds, or are they of our making? If nature has kinds, do those kinds themselves have natures (essences)? Whatever stance we take on these issues, another arises. Given the aspirations of those sciences that investigate human kinds, will not something be a 'real', or at any rate a useful human kind, only if it is a natural kind?

The positivist version of this idea proceeds roughly as follows. If we want to obtain knowledge about people and their behaviour, we have to make correct distinctions. Only if we sort correctly will we be able to formulate descriptive law-like statements. But that fact is not peculiar to the human sciences. In any science we must discover what the natural kinds are. That involves rigorous exploration, experimentation, conjecture, and refutation. As we hone our causal hypotheses, we sharpen our classifications, and approach closer and closer to the kinds that are found in nature. The chief difference between natural and human kinds is that the human kinds often make sense only within a certain social context. But even there we constantly strive to go behind the phenomena. Where once we had descriptive criminology, now we have genes for violence and we are working on the genetic component of suicide.

The positivist supposes that the idea of a natural kind is clear and timeless. Here is a historicist version of the view that the human must be the natural. The idea of a natural kind (it is proposed) is not timeless but has evolved during the history of Western science. Long before the advent of the natural sciences, kinds played a major role in the development of early technological civilizations. Sowing and reaping, breeding and baking, mining and melting have all needed an ability to pick out the right kinds. The kinds of animals, vegetables, and minerals that came to be named, cultivated, and created are the very kinds that philosophers came to call natural kinds. Some features of them have been invaluable as we have learned how to alter, improve, control, or guard against nature. The different theories about these kinds, whether in Aristotle, Locke, Mill, or Hilary Putnam, are owl-of-Minerva state of the art. That is, they effectively correspond to the level of technological expertise and scientific mastery current at the time that they were proposed. Each author thought that he was giving a timeless account of universals, or sorts (Locke), or real Kinds (Mill), or kind terms (Putnam). But each obediently represented a particular state of mastery of the non-human world, so that when we read these authors, we read a précis that could have been headed 'natural kinds as we know them today'. The chief source of the differences among these canonical writings is that they represent different stages in the growth of Western knowledge. The concept 'natural kind' (by whatever name) is not impugned. We are reminded only that this idea is (like everything else) historical and evolving.

The history of human kinds will prove (continues the historicist) to be similar and indeed part of the story. We find attention to suicide, incest, cruelty to children, and even teen-age pregnancy in many places and times. Some scholars urge that demonic possession, trance states, and shamanism are 'the same kind of condition' as multiple personality disorder, perhaps even deploying distinct sites in the brain. Human kinds require a fairly specific social organization for their existence. Teen-age pregnancy cannot exist until unmarried teen-age girls form a distinct group who are not supposed to be pregnant. The idea of juvenile delinquency depends partly on the family, on views of dependency, and on how age cohorts are structured. Nevertheless, there may be some human kinds that are of more general application than others.

We have (the historicist concludes) slowly come to a correct understanding of the idea of a law of nature—we have passed from Aristotelian essences through positivist instrumentalism, and to some extent back again to universal laws of causation and symmetry. In much the same way we will come to a correct understanding of laws of human beings. We could only do so, perhaps, when our idea of law had passed from the deterministic to the probabilistic, when we had created a new type of science geared to normalcy and deviation from the norm, when (just as essences gave way to law-like natural kinds) the idea of human nature had been displaced by the idea of normal people (Hacking 1990). The right laws about human beings have been slow in coming, and we have only just begun to come to grips with human kinds that will prove to be useful. But human kinds will in the end be a subclass of natural kinds. That will not leave things the same. The inclusion of human kinds within natural kinds will be one further step in the evolution of our causal understanding of nature.

You will have expected, from my early profession of indifference to any particular theory about natural kinds, that I do not want to conduct a stale argument with the positivist view, that all good human science is natural science, and that all good human kinds will be made into natural kinds. I take issue with the far more sensitive historicist view. It is the right view about philosophies of natural kinds, but it is wrong about the end of the story.

Understanding, construction

I am liable to be misunderstood. I shall be thought to be arguing for old theses, not for a new one. I have to make plain that whatever cleavage may result from my analysis, it is not one that has been much discussed. I do not argue for or imply either of two extremely important-sounding theses. I do not contend that the natural sciences want explanation while the human sciences demand understanding. I do not urge that human kinds are constructed while natural kinds are not.

The *Verstehen* dispute has partly to do with methodology, a subject that I abhor. There is an immense body of argument to the effect that quite distinct methods befit the natural and the human sciences, the one aiming at explanation and the other at understanding. I believe that there are some deep insights on the *Verstehen* side of the argument, but here they are irrelevant. That is because I have defined human kinds as finding their place in bodies of knowledge patterned after the efficient causation of the natural sciences. I am not about to say that human kinds are a horrible mistake — the error of striving for control rather than understanding.

We do not have the choice not to use human kinds, and human kinds (as I have defined the idea) are causal and instrumental. We are stuck with human kinds that demand causal analysis rather than *Verstehen* or meanings. They are part of what we mean by knowledge about people. It may be a pleasant romantic fantasy to think of abandoning or replacing the instrumental human sciences, but that is not possible. They are not just part of our system of knowledge; they are part of what we take knowledge to be. They are also our system of government, our way of organizing ourselves; they have become the great stabilizers of the Western post-manufacturing welfare state that thrives on service industries. The methodology of making 'studies' to detect law-like regularities and tendencies is not just our way of finding out what's what; 'studies' generate consensus, acceptance, and intervention. The one great argument for Durkheimian functionalism is weirdly self-reflexive: although the conscious aims of the social sciences are knowledge and helping, the function served is that of preserving and adapting the status quo. This fits Douglas's (1986) 'feedback' gloss on functionalism in her lectures *How institutions think*. The more the status quo is dissatisfied with itself, the more social science studies are in demand, and the greater the reliance on their results as definitive. As questioning is put aside, stability tends to ensue.

I now turn to the other way in which I might be understood. I do not claim that human kinds are somehow constructed while natural kinds are somehow given. Here I try to take absolutely no view on the constructionist controversies that swirl around us. I cannot exactly take no notice, because I have found that the anti-constructionist ('realist', for short) says that all good human kinds are (real) natural kinds, while the social constructionist says that everything is social and so the natural is social. (In a discussion some years ago of an article of mine on child abuse, James Bogen said the former and Bruno Latour said the latter).

I take courage from the fact that the most compelling social constructionist arguments about kinds are about high class 'high tech' natural kinds. I think of Latour's first book (with Steven Woolgar), *Laboratory life: the (social) construction of a scientific fact* — the word 'social' was in the 1979 edition but deleted from the 1986 edition on the ground that everything is social. The book is about the discovery of the chemical structure of a tripeptide important to the hypothalamus, to metabolism, and to maturation. Or I think of Andy Pickering's *Constructing quarks*. These authors contend, among many other things, that it is misleading to talk of scientific discoveries. The facts in question were constructed by a microsociological process, and in an important sense did not exist before the incidents described.

My strategy is willingly to swerve to the left and side with the constructionists. Yes, facts are socially constructed, and so are the kinds about which there are facts. But within the domain of social constructions, I can still claim that there is an important difference between quarks and tripeptides on the one hand, and what I call human kinds on the other. Hearing an uproar to my right I then turn to the realists and willingly agree that multiple personality disorder and adolescence are just as real as electricity and sulphuric acid; Anna Freud claims the discovery of adolescence for psychoanalysis, and the discovery of the phenomenon of dissociation is claimed for Pierre Janet. Who am I to resist such claims to fame, except on petty points that perhaps somebody else made the discovery?

Hence for present purposes I operate as if there were no vital contradiction between realism and constructionism. Teen-age pregnancy is as 'real' as could be, with rigorous defining characteristics. It is also aptly described as socially constructed as a human kind at a certain point in American history. Likewise, children were abused before 'child abuse'. The history of the concept in the past three decades displays social making and moulding if anything could. This example has the fortuitous advantage that some of the more vociferous social constructionists, who urge that almost anything is a social construction, say (without noticing the switch) exactly the opposite about child abuse. It is, they rightly say, a real evil that the family and the state covered up. Our discovery of the prevalence of child abuse is a powerful step forward in Western awareness, they say. I agree. Child abuse is a real evil, and it was so before being socially constructed as a human kind. Neither reality nor construction should be in question.

I do not mean to imply that no construction–realism issues are important for human kinds. They do matter, but only in a specific context. Their significance is independent of inflated all-purpose general philosophical themes. The most carefully worked-out example, i.e. what has been called the social constructionist controversy about homosexuality, has mattered deeply to the people who were classified. It was important to one party to maintain that 'the homosexual' as a 'kind of person' is a social construct, chiefly of psychiatry and jurisprudence. It was important for others to insist that some people in every era have been sexually and emotionally attracted chiefly to people of their own sex. There are endless variants on these themes. Stein (1992) (in an essay in his collection *Forms of desire*) has made the appropriate conceptual distinctions, and thereby established several ways in which essentialist and constructionist attitudes are not only compatible but also mutually supporting.

Looping

How then may natural kinds differ from what I call human kinds? I do accept, but wish to downplay, one fundamental difference. Human kinds are laden with values. Caked mud and polarized electrons may be good or bad depending on what you want to do with them, but child abuse is bad and multiple personality is a disorder to be healed.

It is the shibboleth of science that it is value-neutral. Throughout the history of the social sciences there has been a strident insistence on the distinction between fact and value. That is a give-away, for the natural sciences have seldom had to insist upon this distinction. On the contrary, elderly natural scientists regularly regret that there are not more values to be found in the natural sciences. Should we not argue that we are moving closer to the mind of God, and therefore to the Good? In social science things go differently. There is the clarion call for facts, facts, and more facts. Only with facts, and generalizations inferred therefrom, can the social scientist serve the apparatus of our civilization. The social sciences deliver the raw facts and we, the people, are then able to make rational choices depending on the facts and our values.

There has been much cynical backbiting about the valiant claim to value neutrality. It is said that the professed knowledge serves certain interests, and so is value-laden. That is controversial, and I have little use for what has been called interest theory—the sweeping attribution of interests to all sorts of knowledge. Instead, I dwell on the less controversial observation that the classes I call human kinds are themselves laden with value. In sociology they have typically been classes of deviants, to which have been opposed normal children, normal behaviour, normal development, normal reactions, and normal feelings, and the deviations are usually bad. Of course, normal distributions in statistics have two tails, idiots on one side of normal intelligence, and geniuses on the other, with (as Francis Galton put it) mediocrity in between. Value-free? I am not implying that there need be evaluation in the causal laws about characteristic human kinds. The discoveries need serve no interest and the facts discovered may be value-free. I am drawing attention to the presuppositions of enquiries: we investigate human kinds that are loaded with values.

There is a regular attempt to strip human kinds of their moral content by biologizing or medicalizing them. Child abusers are not bad; they are sick and need help! Their crimes are not their fault. They were abused as children, and that is why they abuse their own children. We must not make pregnant teen-age girls feel guilty. The world would be a better place if there were no single parents / child abusers / suicides / multiple personalities / vagrants / prostitutes / juvenile delinquents / recidivists / bulimics / alcoholics / homosexuals / paedophiles / chronic unemployed / homeless / runaways, etc. But let us not blame them, let us medicalize them. This fits well with the metaphysical thrust that I mentioned earlier, that somehow causal connections between kinds are more intelligible if they operate at a biological rather than a psychological or social level.

I do not propose to discuss the intense moral content of human kinds. I am not interested in the moral overtones of human kinds as a way of challenging the fact–value distinction, or as a way of challenging sociology's claim to be above (or underneath) the level of evaluation. I mention it because it is relevant to another difference between the human and the natural. Human kinds are kinds that people may want to be or not to be, not in order to attain some end but because the human kinds have intrinsic moral value.

If N is a natural kind and Z is N, it makes no direct difference to Z, if it is called N. It makes no direct difference to either mud or a mud puddle to call it 'mud'. It makes no direct difference to thyrotropin-releasing hormone or to a bottle of TRH to call it TRH. Of course seeing that the Z is N, we may do something to it in order to melt it or mould it, cook it or drown it, breed it or barter it. If there is mud on my child's T-shirt I use ordinary detergent to remove it, not the enzyme-activated product that I would use for a grass stain or blood. Because a particular liquid is a thyrotropin-releasing factor, an experimenter may see what happens if it is injected into sex-starved frogs or sleeping alligators, or given in megadoses to suicidal women (true stories all). But calling Z N, or seeing that Z is N, does not, in itself, make any difference to Z.

If H is a human kind and A is a person, then calling A H may make us treat A differently, just as calling Z N may make us do something to Z. We may reward or jail, instruct or abduct. But it also makes a difference to A to know that A is an H, precisely because there is so often a moral connotation to a human kind. Perhaps A does not want to be H! Thinking of me as an H changes how I think of me. Well, perhaps I could do things a little differently from now on. Not just to escape opprobrium (I have survived unscathed so far) but because I do not want to be that kind of person. Even if it does not make a difference to A it makes a difference to how people feel about A—how they relate to A—so that A's social ambience changes. I discuss this second-hand effect below in connection with children who cannot in any direct sense understand how they are classified and treated, for example autistic children.

It is a common theme in the theory of human action that to perform an intentional act is to do something 'under a description'. As human kinds are made and moulded, the field of descriptions changes and so do the actions that I can perform, i.e. the field of human kinds affects the field of possible intentional actions. Yet intentional action falls short of the mark. There are more possible ways to see oneself, more roles to adopt. I do not believe that multiple personalities intentionally choose their disorder, or that they are trained by their therapists. However, if this way of being were not available at the moment, hardly anyone would be that way. It is a way for troubled people to express their difficulties; the role is one of many that awaits, and some are chosen for it, often by a new way of describing their own past.

Human kinds have (what could be presented as) an even more amazing power than that of opening possibilities for future action. They enable us to redescribe our past to the extent that people can come to experience *new* pasts. A striking number of adults come to see themselves as having been abused as children. There has recently been a fashion of saying that we define ourselves by our biographies, by our personal narratives. Well, if there are new story lines, there can be new stories. To take an extreme example, some people come to see themselves as incest survivors, which in turn changes their lives and their relationships to their families. This is no mere matter of recovering forgotten trauma; it is a matter of there being new descriptions available, connected in law-like ways to other new descriptions, explanations, and expectations. One of the more powerful words in this group of examples is 'trauma' itself, naming a relatively new kind of human experience. The word used to denote physical wounds, injuries, or lesions, but now it denotes a kind of mental event in the lives of people—the psychic wound, forgotten but ever active. We did not know that we had them until recently—or, more paradoxical but more true, they were not a possible kind of experience to have had. But surely trauma, in its present sense of psychic wound, has been a permanent fixture in human life? Only in the past century has it been a human kind, i.e. a kind of experience about which scientific knowledge is claimed. Only recently has it become a self-evident link between rape, infant seduction, shell-shock, and being held hostage by terrorists, as in Judith Herman's powerful study, *Trauma and recovery* (1992).

Thus one way in which some human kinds differ from some kinds of thing is that classifying people works on people, changes them, and can even change their past. The process does not stop there. The people of a kind themselves are changed. Hence 'we', the experts, are forced to rethink our classifications. Moreover, causal relationships between kinds are changed. Sometimes they are confirmed to the point of becoming essential definitional connections. It becomes part of the *essence* of multiple personality that it is caused by repeated childhood trauma. This is not because we have found out more about the natural disorder, but because people who see themselves as having this human disorder now find in themselves memories of trauma, often traumas of a kind that they could not even have conceptualized 20 years ago. (This can be illustrated by astonishing empirical facts, for example hundreds of people with memories of grotesque sadistic ritual cult abuse appeared in American clinics 6 years ago; much of what they remember under these descriptions they could not have thought of 12 years ago.).

To create new ways of classifying people is also to change how we can think of ourselves, to change our sense of self-worth, even how we remember our own past. This in turn generates a looping effect, because people of the kind behave differently and so are different. That is to say the kind changes, and so there is new causal knowledge to be gained and perhaps, old causal knowledge to be jettisoned.

Here I should both acknowledge labelling theory and distance myself from it. It was once argued that calling a person a juvenile delinquent (etc.), and institutionally confirming that label, made the person adopt certain stereotypical patterns of behaviour. When a youth was labelled as J, he assumed more and more of the characteristic features of J. That is a claim about labelling *individuals*. I am sure that there is some truth in it for some individuals. I go two steps further. I assert that there are changes in individuals of that kind, which means that the kind itself becomes different (possibly confirmed in its stereotype but, as I go on to urge, quite the opposite may happen). Next, because the kind changes, there is new knowledge to be had about the kind. But that new knowledge in turn becomes part of what is to be known about members of the kind, who change again. This is what I call the looping effect for human kinds.

The greater the moral connotations of a human kind, the greater the potential for the looping effect. Although I shall not develop the theme here, we find similar effects in the relatively value-neutral kinds counted by the national census and similar government agencies. These effects have been investigated with remarkable results by a number of researchers such as Desrosières (1993). That is a piece of self-reflection in itself—the bureau that includes the French census looking at what past censuses have done to the very people who have been enumerated. Each decade the census draws up a new classification of the population, a classification that then becomes experienced as the structure of the society for the next decade or more. Similarly, Americans know that 'Hispanic' is an ethnic kind invented by the Bureau of the Census, with some effect on many people who now think of themselves as Hispanic and with rather more effect on their non-Hispanic neighbours, but see below in the discussion of administrative and self-ascriptive kinds. I have myself asserted, with too little argument, that the endless reports and tabulations prepared by countless British government functionaries, and so carefully scrutinized by Karl Marx, had more to do than Marx himself with the formation of class consciousness.

Responses of people to attempts to be understood or altered are different from the responses of things. This trite fact is at the core of one difference between the natural and human sciences, and it works at the level of kinds. There is a looping or feedback effect involving the introduction of classifications of people. New sorting and theorizing induces changes in self-conception and in behaviour of the people classified. Those changes demand revisions of the classification and theories, the causal connections, and the expectations. Kinds are modified, revised classifications are formed, and the classified change again, loop upon loop.

MORE KINDS

Two distinct objections arise. First, it will be objected that I choose some examples that may be favourable to the looping-effect thesis, and that even in those cases the evidence is skimpy. I cannot reply to that objection here because I require detailed observation, history, and to some extent 'archaeology' (in the sense of Michel Foucault). I list some of my recent homework in the references at the end of this paper.

Secondly, it will be objected that my thesis rests on special pleading, on an all too judicious choice of examples. I sympathize completely. My reply is slightly circuitous. The objection may suggest that there are really core, 'prototypical', kinds studied in the human and social sciences, and that these are different in many respects from my overly sensational and problematic examples. In my opinion there are many more types of human kinds than I have discussed—thus far I agree with the objection—but I do not think that there is any core. Therefore I shall suggest a number of types of kinds in the region of the social and human sciences. I should have liked to provide a taxonomy of these, but I do not believe that there is a structure to be had. Hence I offer only a motley collection governed by very rough headings such as second-order kind, biologized kinds, inaccessible kinds, administrative kinds, and self-ascriptive kinds. These are neither exhaustive nor mutually exclusive. I intend to diminish the appeal of any one fixed idea of what human kinds are like by drawing attention to many facets of human kinds that people tend not to think about. I want to transform the second objection from 'You have missed the most central examples of human kinds' into Wittgenstein's warning, 'You have too slender a diet of examples'. My response is to agree, and then to vary the diet.

Second-order kinds

For well over a hundred years the most powerful second-order kind used in connection with people has been normalcy. We owe to Georges Canguilhem the recognition of the normal as a key organizing concept for medicine. Michel Foucault took over the idea when he described the nineteenth-century clinic as a site that focused not on health but on normalcy. Normal–pathological cast its net far beyond the medical domain. Auguste Comte readily adapted it to the political sphere. It was given a statistician's formulation by Adolphe Quetelet, Francis Galton, and Karl Pearson (who in the 1890s renamed the Gaussian bell-shaped curve 'the normal distribution').

I call normalcy second-order for much the same reason that one might (after Kant) call existence a second-order predicate or (after Frege) call number a second-order concept. Nothing is just two (or for that matter one): there are two apples or two heroes or two sources of infection. You have to say two *what*. Likewise nothing is just normal. You have to say normal *what*: a normal child, normal idiosyncrasies, normal speech patterns, or normal development. Normalcy provides a remarkable all-purpose vehicle for characterizing new human kinds as deviations from the norm.

Typically, the human kinds that involve normalcy are defined in terms of abnormality. The *Journal of Abnormal Psychology*, founded in 1906, was once a cutting-edge organization of kinds. It was in the business of carving out human kinds with, as it happens, a particular emphasis on multiple personality. 'Ortho', which is Greek for normal, is also for kind-forming. The American Orthopsychiatric Association was formed in 1924 by the child guidance clinicians; the *Journal of Orthopsychiatry* followed soon after. It may sound as if the object of study was the normal, but this was not the case. The aims were to recognize, classify, guide, and heal deviant children. They were to be transformed so that they could develop as normally as possible.

Normalcy is not restricted to the human. Its origin is in physiology (normal and pathological physiology), and it readily adapts to much that is biological and beyond. We can have abnormal quasi-stellar objects — even pathological ones. The adjectives are not used to indicate that the quasar is sick, but that there is something quite out of the ordinary about it which astrophysics and cosmology cannot quite understand yet.

The normal can be anywhere, but its home is human. The idea of the normal is partly responsible for the moral overtones of so many human kinds. Deep in the root of the words, the Latin 'norm' and the Greek 'ortho' bridge the fact–value distinction. Even in geometry a line normal to another, orthogonal, is at a right angle, an angle of 90 ° (descriptive). It is also a 'right' angle, good for carpenters and surveyors (evaluative). Orthopsychiatry is the study of the normal and abnormal development of individual children, noting how some deviate and how they can be put right. Any human kind explained in terms of deviation from the normal is partly descriptive — the kind differs from the usual. However, it is also partly evaluative: the kind differs from what is right; it is worse, or in the case of Galton's deviation from mediocrity, possibly better.

Biologized kinds

I have mentioned the thrust of human kinds towards the biological. Biological is my shorthand for biochemical, neurological, electrical, mechanical, or whatever is the preferred model of efficient causation in a given scientific community or era. This thrust is one of the more powerful themata in scientific thought. Its very success has made us swell with optimism. We have an immense confidence in its potential and plenty of proven examples. I have no quarrel with biological research programmes into human behaviour. However, I do want to note that biologizing human kinds does not thereby make them immune to looping effects.

One effect is obvious. At present we tend to hold that we are not responsible for our biological attributes, except such as we can change by regimens, namely abstinence and spiritual or physical exercises. Of course biology is not a foolproof excuse; Susan Sontag has written about how people are made to feel as morally involved in their cancers as others once were in their tuberculosis. Then the claim is that the disease is not purely biological, but also has a psychic component. The disorders of women have been particularly ambivalent in this respect. However, by and large, biology is exculpating.

Thus alcoholism has plausibly been regarded as a moral failing. It is regarded as such by the most successful widespread programme to counteract it, namely Alcoholics Anonymous. It evolved a form of meeting patterned on both chapel and confessional, in which resort is made to a higher power 'as each individual understands that term'. The alternative view, favoured by many treatment programmes patterned after hospitalization, is biological, biochemical and even genetic. In this view the alcoholic has a disease for which he is not responsible, and is required to follow a regimen chiefly in the way in which someone with high blood pressure follows a regimen. The scientific (biological) knowledge about alcoholics produces a different kind of person. Results about this are masked because both the scientist and the moralist compete for control over all alcoholics, as a kind, and will not acknowledge that the persons under their sway tend to have projections, expectations, and (probabilistic) law-like regularities different from those of the other lot. Sometimes this comes out at a straightforward level. Thus the Alcohol Research Foundation in my city, a very powerful medical institution, claims to have identified a class of alcoholics who can return to very moderate social drinking; Alcoholics Anonymous denies that there is such a human kind.

Until recently, i.e. until the surge of self-ascriptive kinds discussed below, Alcoholics Anonymous and kindred anti-addiction groups have been anomalously moralistic. Few others have fought the demoralizing impact of biologization. We are exposed to enthusiastic programmes every day. Partly because they tend to be programmes rather than conclusions, they are involved in the looping dynamics of human kinds. Today (as I write) happens to be 13 November 1992. This morning's *New York Times* has on the front page an article headed 'Study cites biology's role in violent behavior'. It begins:

In a sharp departure from traditional criminology, the [U.S.] National Research Council has found that biological and genetic factors should be considered along with environmental factors such as poverty in efforts to understand the causes of violence.

In case we are in doubt as to the authority of the National Research Council, the next sentence reminds us that the Council is 'the research arm of the [U.S.] National Academy of Sciences'. One of the general messages is that 'instead of relying on more prisons and longer sentences, America needs more flexible more pragmatic and less ideological approaches'. After all, if the violence is partly genetic and biological, people are not usefully put in penitentiaries and reformatories to repent and reform. Is this a 'sharp departure from traditional criminology'? What is described is in outline similar to the criminal anthropology of Cesare Lombroso and many others. It flourished a century ago; its heyday in Italy was 1875–1895. Those are Bad Guys, refuted to the point of ridicule in many a wise volume, of which Gould's (1981) *The mismeasure of man* is the best known. Yet the programme of the criminal anthropologists was parallel to that of the most recent report of the National Research Council, right down to its mixture of biology, inheritance, prison reform, and exculpation.

Violence in not a human kind according to my criteria (i)–(iv). However, criminology is a social science. Institutionally, it is descended from criminal anthropology, i.e. the first criminology departments had Lombrosian aspirations. 'Criminal', like 'suicide', has been used by professionals as a grouping of human kinds. The concluding sentence of the *New York Times* story reads:

'The most significant accomplishment of the [National Research Council] panel is the integration of biological and social science data to develop a new conceptual framework', said Klaus Miczek, a professor of psychology at Tufts University and director of the psychopharmacological laboratory.

A 'new conceptual framework' is in part a new sorting, a new taxonomy, a new array of human kinds, or a reorganization of old ones.

Reorganization is critical. Very seldom do we devise a wholly new human kind. Rather, as in all our endeavours, we build on old ones. Child abuse inherits a good deal from cruelty to children. What we do not notice is the extraordinary amount of not merely making and moulding of kinds that occurs, but also of what is best described as wandering. The wandering is partly the result of the way in which a human kind, once biologized, reacts to the way in which the people who fall under the kinds themselves react to being treated in the way that science dictates.

Inaccessible kinds

I have laid great emphasis on the ways in which people of a kind can become self-conscious about that kind. What about human kinds in which the people classified cannot take in how they are classified? Call those inaccessible kinds. Human beings who cannot understand, such as infants, provide obvious examples. There cannot be self-conscious feedback. However, there can be looping that involves a larger human unit, for example the family. I was brought up by a generation of parents who accepted, as scientific knowledge about infants, that babies must be nursed at set times, regardless of how much they might fuss and scream for more food. Current science holds that the psyches of my age cohort are irrevocably damaged.

My own children grew up at the end of an era when science taught feeding on demand, as counselled by the best-selling American paediatrician Dr. Spock. Spock's science, believed by parents, is held to have created a generation of flower children and peaceniks. We can see this series of episodes as a feedback cycle, but I shall not pursue such specious claims. Consider instead a much more localized human kind that is inaccessible to people of that kind, namely autism. Many aspects of this story will be well known to some readers.

The dictionary defines **autism** as 'abnormal self-absorption, usually affecting children, characterized by lack of response to people and actions and limited ability to communicate; children suffering from autism often do not learn to speak'.* We seem to owe the word to Bleuler's description of the self-absorption and 'separation of thought from logic and reality' in schizophrenics, an idea proposed in his profoundly influential book of 1911, *Dementia praecox oder die Gruppe der Schizophrenien*. We now apply the term primarily to children, or to adults who were autistic children and remain abnormal.

By my criteria, 'the autistic child' is a human kind. It became a cutting-edge kind in the 1970s. The *Journal of Autism and Childhood Schizophrenia* was founded in 1971, and was renamed the *Journal of Autism and Developmental Disorders* in 1979. We are strongly inclined to say that autistic children form a definite class that could, in principle, have been picked out in many populations at many times. We say this because we take it to result from a biological rather than a social deficit. In fact, autism was first characterized by Leo Kanner on the of basis children he noticed in 1938. He thought that they would previously have been called

---

* The *Diagnostic and statistical manual* (DSM-III(R)) of the American Psychiatric Association (1987) begins its diagnostic criteria for **Autistic Disorder with the** *Note* 'Consider a criterion to be met *only* if the behavior is abnormal for the person's development level'. It gives three groups of criteria, 16 in all, and requires that a person has two items from (A), one from (B), and one from (C): (A) qualitative impairment of reciprocal social interaction; (B) qualitative impairment in verbal and non-verbal communication; and in imaginative activity; (C) markedly restricted repertoire of activities and interests. For example, (A) is manifested by 'marked lack of awareness of the existence of feelings of others; no or abnormal seeking of comfort at times of distress', (B) is manifested by 'no mode of communication, such as communicative babbling, facial expression, gesture or spoken language; markedly abnormal nonverbal communication, as in the use of eye-to-eye gaze', and (C) is manifested by 'marked distress over changes in trivial aspects of the environment'. The *International classification of diseases* (ICD-10) published by the World Health Organization (1992) has somewhat different emphases but agrees on large issues: 'no prior period of unequivocally normal development', 'inadequate appreciation of socio-emotional cues', 'qualitative impairments in communication are universal', 'impaired use of variations in cadence or emphasis to reflect communicative modulation', 'restricted, repetitive, and stereotyped patterns of behaviour, interests and activities', 'attachment to unusual, typically non-soft objects'. ICD-10 mentions sleeping and eating disorders, temper tantrums, phobias, and self-injury such as wrist-biting as being common.

born-deaf or feeble-minded. He described them in print (Kanner 1943) in *The Nervous Child*, a cutting-edge journal then entering its second year of publication.

The criteria for identification, let alone theories about what autism 'is', have changed a good deal since 1938. The optimistic scientific view is that we are establishing a better and better understanding of autism, refining our definition of this natural kind of behaviour and discovering its cause and its essence. The outside observer may be less sanguine. I think that no one now doubts that many children, diagnosed as autistic, are suffering from some distinct biological (biochemical or neurological) impairment. This must, we feel, be a human kind (or several kinds) that will yield to biology! At the time of writing there is no known brain pathology, and various optimistic correlates (PET scans etc.) do not seem to replicate. We should also note that autism is regularly defined in contrast with the 'normal' development of a child, as in the DSM-III(R) definition cited in the footnote to p. 375.

Kanner reported 11 children who were 'self-absorbed' almost from birth. They adopted abnormal postures when picked up. They did not connect a part of another person's body with the person. Normal children, when annoyed by an interruption, look at the face of the intruder; Kanner's children struck out at the foreign hand or other body part that was disturbing them. The children had remarkable rote memory. They did not learn to communicate, but many echoed what other people said. There was an obsessive desire to keep everything 'the same', and every arrangement of objects or pattern of behaviour was obsessively repeated. There were serious feeding problems; whereas children with lack of affect tend to overeat when given the chance, Kanner's children ate little and stayed away from anything living, but were fascinated by objects. Their toys of choice were inanimate, or sometimes mechanical, rather than cuddly. They had a rigorous compulsion to preserve objects in 'the same' geometrical arrangements.

Kanner's children, drawn from a Johns Hopkins clinic, had very successful workholic parents. Autism was soon taken to be an innate inability to relate to people, exacerbated by parents who were not very good at that either. In those days children at public schools in North America had their report cards graded according to their ability to 'relate to' children of their own age and to 'relate to' their teachers. Low grades in relationships had heavy loads of guilt laid on them, as I can assure you from personal experience as a 7-year-old in 1943 in the backwoods of a Canadian province a long way from the heartland of such doctrines.

Kanner came to emphasize lack of relatedness and wrote of parents who reared their children in 'emotional refrigerators'. By 1955 this was understood as the primary cause of autism: it was the parents' fault. Parents of these abnormal children were advised to undergo years of intensive therapy. Over 20 years later Bruno Bettelheim (1967) was still urging exactly that concept of autism. Notice the moral shift. Kanner's children would once have been dismissed as stupid, feeble-minded (therefore feeble, bad), or deaf (therefore dumb, stupid). Now they are liberated. It is not their fault. The parents are emotional refrigerators and that, the whole period 1938–1967, is *bad*.

Autism moved around a good deal. Authors ceased to mention the unusual postures of infants. Feeding had virtually disappeared as a stated problem by 1955 (but see ICD-10 in 1992 (footnote to p. 375)). After that the disorder was increasingly described as 'psychobiological'. The 1968 *Diagnostic and statistical manual* (DSM-II) did not distinguish autism from a kind of schizophrenia. Here there was a certain loyalty to Bleuler, but also a strong resistance to recognizing autistic children as a distinct kind at all. Note the change in title, mentioned above, in the premier journal for autism: from *Autism and Childhood Schizophrenia* (1971) to *Autism and Developmental Disorders* (1979). That was the decade in which autism was separated from schizophrenia, for example by epidemiology: 75 per cent of autistic children are male and the onset is in early childhood; the disproportion is not nearly so great for schizophrenia and the onset is in adolescence. This is an example of the characteristic self-sealing argument we find in debates about human kinds. On the basis of our diagnoses, we find measurable (here chronological) differences between two populations; therefore our distinctions and diagnoses are sound. By 1980 the *Diagnostic and statistical manual* (DSM-III) gave a separate definition of 'infantile autism' that was nevertheless rejected by people working with these children. The definition in the 1987 DSM-III(R), referred to in the footnote to p. 375, is more acceptable but is much altered in the proposals for the next edition.

A standard survey article (Sevin *et al.* 1991) lists five fairly distinct systems for diagnosing autism. There is much emphasis on social problems, lack of play with other children, lack of imaginative play with objects, lack of empathy, and inability to perceive other people's emotions. Half the children do not develop useful speech. The clinical descriptions are rather different from those of non-parents who have to work closely with autistic children. Workers with sufficient time and a small case-load often develop close emotional bonds; the more commonly overworked and underpaid staff quickly lapse into discussions of how hard it is to 'handle' these children. We have a kind, doubtless biological, that nevertherless has been wandering. An authoritative article by Steffenburg and Gillberg (1989, p. 75) states that:

It is high time that autism be regarded as an administrative rather than specific disease label. Autism, like mental retardation, is not a disease, but an umbrella term, covering a variety of disease entities with certain common behavioural features.

This remark can usefully contribute to the typology of human kinds; autism is an *administrative* kind about which I say a little more below.

Under what sciences should autism be investigated? One contender is cognitive science. Many readers will be familiar with the following sequence of events. Premack and Woodruff (1978) introduced criteria for saying that 'an individual has a theory of mind'. They meant 'that the individual imputes mental states to himself and others' (Premack and Woodruff 1978, p. 515). Philosophers commenting on the paper (Jonathan Bennett, Daniel Dennett, and Gilbert Harman) all referred to an idea apparently first described by Lewis (1969). Two subjects observe a state of affairs. One leaves and the state of affairs is changed; the other sees this. Does the second subject subsequently act as if the other still believes (falsely) that the old state of affairs obtains? For example children are shown a sweet package and shown that it does contain sweets. Some children leave and a plastic alligator is put in the sweet box in front of remaining children; do these expect the other children, on returning, to be surprised by the contents of the package? If so, they impute beliefs to others and have the kernel of a theory of mind.

In the early 1980s numerous experiments in developmental psychology were published to discover the point at which young children acquired a theory of mind, attributing belief systems to others (Wimmer and Perner 1983; Perner and Wimmer 1985; Perner *et al.* 1989). The definitive application to autistic children was made by Baron-Cohen *et al.* (1985). Children with Down's syndrome and autism were compared. The researchers found striking contrasts in the experimental ability to impute beliefs to others: 'our results strongly support the hypothesis that autistic children as a group fail to employ a theory of mind'. These conclusions have been corroborated a number of times by more sophisticated experiments. There turns out to be a residual class of autistic children (one in five) who do 'impute intentionality'. Children in this class tend to be better at language in general. That fits well with Paul Grice's idea, elaborated by Sperber and Wilson (1986) and by Dennett (1987), that linguistic communication demands attributions of intentions. This research has stabilized in a body of thinking represented in the papers collected by Baron-Cohen *et al.* (1991).

However, cognitive scientists do not own autism outright. From the antipodes comes a rehabilitation worker, Rosemary Crossley, who started 'facilitated communication' about 20 years ago. She had begun with cerebral palsy patients, helping them to have control over their movements. The facilitator holds the hand, shoulder, or finger of an autistic person who presses keys on a keyboard—primarily, it is said, to stop the autist from repeatedly pressing the same key (controlling the fixation on 'sameness').

The result is vastly more ability to express understanding of other people than cognitive science allows for. But was not this all the work of the facilitator choosing the keys? (The Supreme Court of Victoria ruled that it was not, siding with a cerebral palsy victim who, working with a facilitator, had communicated a desire to be deinstitutionalized.) The procedure has stood up to fairly rigorous testing to exclude overenthusiastic facilitation. The facilitator is blind to events observed by the autist and then reported by the keyboard. The method has been exported from Australia with a vengeance: for highbrow professional audiences, in the *Harvard Educational Review* (Biklen 1991); for middlebrow audiences where I live, in a five-part series run by the Canadian Broadcasting Corporation in 1991, and in more popular media. It has had a great impact on pressure and self-help activist groups such as (again where I live) the Autism Society of Canada. Not for them the theory that autistic children lack a theory of mind. They lack facilitators. There are all sorts of forces at work. For example, Crossley's star autist is taking a university degree. Autistic children are not stupid, not retarded, and not feeble-minded, but suffer from an unknown disadvantage. There is no stigma attached to autism, and so there is much urgency to have children with difficulties classified as autistic. The cognitive science approach is disliked, for if there were children who did not think that other people have minds, they themselves would thereby be inhuman. But is there not a truth of the matter? Is there not a real kind (or kinds) of children out there that in the end we will know something about? That is by no means clear to me. The looping effect works on the kind and its auxiliaries—family and remedial workers—and of course on the success stories who simply deny the no-theory-of-mind approach.

I should conclude this section with the latest radical twist. Adult autism had for long been diagnosed simply as communication impairment among adults who had been autistic as children. Adult autists were grown-up child autists who had not outgrown their difficulties. But yet another notion is now being discussed: there are adults who are apparently normal, yet suffer from an inability to talk about certain general domains of experience. These would formerly have been regard as suffering from a psychological disorder, and perhaps have been subject to psychoanalysis to remove repression. But a current theory, developed from workers with an analytic training, holds that these adults suffer from 'specific autisms'. Thus the stigma of being psychologically disordered (crazy) is replaced by something less diminishing of the patient's stature.*

---

* Many thanks to Malcolm MacIver for far more work on autism than I have used here.

Administrative kinds

It was suggested that autism is an 'administrative' entity. When we reflect on the origins of the social sciences, this becomes a rather compelling concept. Obviously it fits census classifications. Naturally an administrative kind can have quite unexpected effects, as when 'Hispanic' becomes a tool of political unity. Another example is 'Lithuanian language', in part a product of emigrés in Pittsburgh and the US Census (Peterson 1986). The idea of an administrative kind equally fits many social kinds if, as I claim, the social sciences arose together with the bureaucratic imperative to distinguish, enumerate, control, and improve deviants. In the beginning and in the end the deviants would be an administrative problem. In our day the 'administrative' tag is used negatively by those who want a biological kind of which there is biological knowledge. Thus the urge to say both that autism is administrative and that there are several kinds of disorder which we shall find out about. Exactly the same thing has been said about child abuse. The idea of an administrative kind reminds us that there may be rivalry between administrators, battles for territory. Those have been very evident in the child abuse field from the beginning, and at present there is plenty of more muted dispute about who owns autism.

The idea of an administrative kind enables us to bring together a number of different types of objections to my looping thesis. Of course, it will be said, there may be looping effects on administrative kinds. The administered react to their administration! Administrative kinds probably cover a number of different natural kinds, for which there is no feedback effect, and which have real causal, perhaps biological, relationships between them. Except on the point of brevity, I will not be accused of understating the force of this objection. What I deny is that there is a sharp distinction, within the human kinds, between what is given by nature and what is administrative. I deny this in part because of characteristics that I take to be essential to the social sciences and the kinds with which they deal. Doubtless, we shall debate this. Having set the terms of a debate, I wish to conclude with a further, and very recent, feature of human kinds.

Self-ascriptive kinds

Human kinds, I claim, are the product of a particular vision of the sciences of Man. They were formed on two axes. The one is that of the natural sciences. After 1815 the moral sciences were to be patterned on the quantitative natural sciences — sciences that themselves took a notable leap forward as new types of physical phenomena were made the target of measurement. In particular, their conception of causality was made identical to that of the physical sciences, a move abetted by the positivist movement from the 1820s which interpreted causation as regularity. Their other axis was bureaucratic–statistical, which allowed both the counting and tabulation of kinds of people – the analysis of statistical regularity as cause. I single out these two axes as dominant, without wishing to downplay the importance of the anti-statistical backlash, and the insistence, above all in the medico-forensic domains so important to the social sciences, that the individual, rather than the group, is the object of enquiry.

Within these two axes (and also when the third axis, individualism, is added to the display) there is knowledge and the known. 'We' know about 'them'. There are plenty of looping effects, but the known are passive and do not take charge of knowledge of themselves. The second half of the twentieth century has seen the introduction of a radically new axis. Gay liberation provides the classic example.

I have mentioned one official story about homosexuality – that the homosexual as a kind of person emerges in medico-forensic discouse late in the nineteenth century, with instant dispersion. (A colleague in Montreal, an emigré Chinese psychiatrist, noted in a paper that although there were numerous stories and colourful terms in Chinese literature, there was no word meaning 'homosexual' until 1887 or 1888. I had to tell him that was about 2 months or one boat trip after it was confirmed in Europe.) To simplify overly much, the label 'homosexual' was a term in its original sites applied by the knowers to the known. However, it was quickly taken up by the known, and gay liberation was the natural upshot. One of the first features of gay liberation was gay pride and coming out of the closet. It became a moral imperative for people of the kind to identify themselves, to ascribe a chosen kind-term to themselves. That way they also became the knowers, even if not the only people authorized to have knowledge.

There are plenty of obvious relations to other categories, such as race and gender, black pride and women's liberation. That is only the beginning. A very general process of self-ascription of kinds has arisen, which I believe will go on affecting human kinds in ways that we cannot foresee. It is no accident that the USA is in the forefront of this movement (just as post-revolutionary post-*empire* bureaucratized France was the original site of human kinds). There are two reasons. One is the far greater role of rights in American social consciousness than is found anywhere else. People of a human kind demand their rights, or people associated with that kind demand rights for members of that kind. The other is that the USA is a uniquely democratic society (with most of the properties that Plato abhorred in the *demos*) which is also predicated on freedom of speech and information flow. (Do not misunderstand me, I am not praising or envying; my own national ethos sides with Plato on such matters.)

There has been a bizarre proliferation of self-help groups of late. Their core feature has been self-ascription; their rhetoric is that of taking control of themselves. New categories emerge. One of the most powerful has been that of the 'handicapped'. This is, like so many matters pertaining to the human, an administrative category. It groups a subclass of those who do not have 'normal' abilities in this or that respect. The label originated during the Second World War, with procedures enabling people with various kinds of disabilities to work in understaffed industries. There were many jobs that people with different disadvantages could perform perfectly well. Subsequently, interest groups arose urging the rights of people with a variety of handicaps. The old pejorative labels — cripples, dumb, retarded, feeble-minded — were replaced. People gladly took the new labels on themselves and became members of pressure groups — or else their friends or family members did it for them.

There is little end to this process of self-ascription, or even ascription and then rejection: witness the current rejection of Hispanic by some of those for whom the term was invented, and replacement by Latino and other self-avowed subgroups. I have mentioned autistic support societies which include activist groups, self-help groups for families with autistic children, and groups whose direct members are autistic individuals in several age groups. A decade ago I injudiciously made a point sharply by contrasting multiple personality and homosexuality as human kinds. There would, I said, never be any split bars for people with multiple personality disorder. Well there are now multiple personality social groups, and I am told that there is indeed a multiple personality bar in Denver (There is some New Age input into all this as well, and so the maxim is Denver today, Memphis tomorrow, Lyon next week?) Self-help groups tend to remoralize a human kind. Some are even patterned after Alcoholics Anonymous, developing their own twelve-step variations.

This is the right place to conclude a discussion introducing the looping effects of human kinds. We are experiencing a wholly new type of looping effect, when so many of the kinds claim rights to their own knowledges.

REFERENCES

American Psychiatric Association (1987). *Diagnostic and statistical manual* III (Revised). American Psychiatric Association, Washington, DC.

Baron-Cohen S., Leslie, A. M. and Frith, U. (1985). Does the autistic child have a 'theory of mind'? *Cognition* **21**, 37–46.

Baron-Cohen, S., Tager-Flusberg, H., Cohen, D. and Volmar, F. (ed) (1991). *Understanding other minds: perspectives from autism.* Oxford University Press.

Bettelheim, B. (1967). *The empty fortress: infantile autism and the birth of the self.* MacMillan, London.

Biklen, D. (1990). Communication unbound: autism and praxis. *Harvard Educational Review* **60**, 291–314.

Desrosières, A. (1993). *La Politique des grands nombres.* Découverte, Paris.

Dennett, D. C. (1987). *The intentional stance*. MIT Press, Cambridge, MA.

Douglas, M. (1986). *How institutions think*. Syracuse University Press.

Gilbert, W. (1991). Towards a paradigm shift in biology. *Nature* **349**, 99.

Gould, S. J. (1981). *The mismeasure of man*, Norton, New York.

Hacking, I. (1986). Making up people. In *Reconstructing individualism* (ed P. Heller, Sosna, M., and Wellberry, D.), pp. 222-36. Stanford University Press.

Hacking, I. (1990). The normal state. *The taming of chance*, Chapter 19, pp. 160-9, see also pp. 178 ff. Cambridge University Press.

Hacking, I. (1991). The making and molding of child abuse, *Critical Inquiry* **17**, 235-58.

Hacking, I. (1992*a*). 'Style' for historians and philosophers. *Studies in the History and Philosophy of Science* **22**, 1-20.

Hacking, I. (1992*b*). Multiple personality disorder and its hosts. *History of the Human Sciences* **5**(2), 3-31.

Hacking, I. (1992*c*). World-making by kind-making: child abuse for example. In *How classification works* (ed M. Douglas and D. Hull), pp. 180-238, Edinburgh University Press.

Hall, G. (1904). *Adolescence. Its psychology and its relation to physiology, anthropology, sociology, sex, crime, religion and education*. Appleton, New York.

Herman, J. L. (1992). *Trauma and recovery*, Basic Books, New York.

Kanner, L. (1943). Autistic disturbances of affective contact. *Nervous Child* **2**, 217-50.

Lewis, D. (1969). *Convention: a philosophical study*. Harvard University Press, Cambridge, MA.

Perner, J. and Wimmer, H. (1985). 'John *thinks* that Mary *thinks* that . . .' Attributions of second-order beliefs by 5- and 10-year old children. *Journal of Experimental Child Psychology* **9**, 315-60.

Perner, J., Leekham, S. R. and Wimmer, H. (1989). Exploration of the autistic child's theory of mind: knowledge, belief and communication. *Child Development* **60**, 689-700.

Petersen, W. (1986). Politics and the measurement of ethnicity. In *The politics of numbers* (ed W. Alonso and P. Starr, pp. 187-233. Sage, New York.

Premack, D. and Woodruff, G. (1978). Does the chimpanzee have a theory of mind? *Behavioral and Brain Sciences* **4**, 515-26.

Sevin, J. A., Matson, J. L., Coe, D. A., Fee, V. E., and Sevin, B. M. (1991). A comparison of three commonly used autism scales. *Journal of Autism and Developmental Disorders* **21**, 417-32.

Sperber, D. and Wilson, D. (1986). *Relevance: communication and cognition*. Blackwell, Oxford.

Steffenburg, S. and Gillberg, C. (1989). The etiology of autism. In *Diagnosis and treatment of autism* (ed C. Gillberg). Plenum, New York.

Stein, E. (1992). The essentials of constructionism and the construction of essentialism. In *Forms of desire* (ed. E. Stein), pp. 295-325. Routledge, New York.

Wimmer, H. and Perner, J. (1983). Beliefs about beliefs: representation and constraining function of wrong beliefs in young children's understanding of deception. *Cognition* **13**, 103-28.

World Health Organization (1992). *The ICD-10 classification of mental and behavioural disorders. Clinical descriptions and diagnostic guidelines*. World Health Organization, Geneva.

DISCUSSION

Participants: S. Atran, S. Carey, D. Hilton, P. Jacob, F. Keil, A. Leslie, M. Morris

Hacking: Thank you very much for the generous and serious questions. I have stopped at each question mark to answer in a word: yes or no. Some qualification then follows. One seldom means simply yes or no, but I think that it is clearer to have the short answer first, followed by back-tracking.

Keil: Counting and classifying people into kinds certainly predates the last 100 years or so. Class structures and associated attributions about their members have been around for centuries. As an explicit science, however, practice is of course much more recent. Is the shift to being a formal science that which results in the desire to see human kinds as things to be changed and controlled?

Hacking: Yes. I would not speak of a shift to a formal science. There was a break with what Enlightenment authors called moral science. That was reflective, rational, what we would call a priori – and very formal. Then came what was still called moral science, but based on counting. It relied at first on the huge bureaucracies brought into being during the Napoleonic Wars. As ever, war was the mother of the new science.

'Counting and classifying people predates the last 100 years': one can be more exact. *Classifying* is part of human speech. It has long been self-conscious: I like to quote from the translation of inscriptions at Persepolis: 'I am Xerxes, the great King, King of Kings . . . King of the countries containing many kinds of people . . .'. As for *counting*, central events in Jewish and Christian history are about counting. David made a census of Judah and Israel; God waxed furious; David began building the temple in order to mollify Him. (2 Sam. 24:1; 1 Chr. 21:1). Mary and Joseph were on their way to Bethlehem to be taxed, a process that included enumeration. Nevertheless, until what I call the avalanche of printed numbers in the 1820s, counting was for the purposes of taxation, military recruitment, or to determine the power of the kingdom. Its results were usually kept privy just because they were instruments of power. Only enumerations of births, marriages and deaths had been public. It was in that decade, the 1820s, that social science was invented.

Keil: Much of cognitive science is concerned with the intensive study of humans, but in terms of universals and not individual differences. Do you mean that your views should be restricted to those views that study individual differences?

Hacking: No. Since my paper was about kinds of people and their behaviour, it is about differences and not about universals. Hence in the paper I argue only for theses about differences between people. I happen to be cautious about the enthusiasm for universals, best exemplified by Chomsky, who introduced one of the most exciting research programmes of all time. Here is an example of a thesis about universals looping back on people. American Sign Language (ASL) is a language, and so it must have the same underlying grammar as spoken language. I have iconoclastically suggested (*London Review of Books* 5 April 1990) that this is causing the grammar of ASL to be moulded to fit a current view about spoken language. ASL itself will change in consequence, and so will the deaf conception of language.

At this meeting, universal equals Chomsky. There are many other universalists. Think of Jung and the archetypes. Think of Freud and the Oedipus complex, presented as a universal feature of the life of the human infant. The looping effect of that great universalist, Freud, is the story of twentieth century sensibilities. We do not even dream in the same way as people did a century ago!

Keil: It does not always seem that, by classifying and counting humans, we seek or are compelled to change them. In many cases just the opposite seems to be at work, when those in positions to influence will often embrace a label, such as a minimal brain dysfunction, or impulsive personality, as the basis for abdication of responsibility for positive change. The members of that kind can be shown to have a fundamental property; there is no need to change them. Do you mean instead that classifying and counting is a way of deciding whether or not one wishes to change?

Hacking: No. Obviously I base much of my approach on Michel Foucault. One has to emphasize over and over again that his ideas about power–knowledge are not about control exercised by those in power over those about whom they have knowledge. It is a reciprocal relationship in which all parties participate. (Non-reciprocal control is violence.) The new kind of knowledge undoubtedly came into being as part of a vision of bureaucratic administration. However, it became public knowledge, with innumerable unpredicted developments, including the ways in which people classified have taken charge of their own kind (gay rights) or more generally the phenomenon of self-ascriptive kinds that I discuss at the end of the chapter. Keil rightly points to *one* use of kinds. In his words, from a handwritten note, 'suggesting that by counting and classifying human beings we can thereby change them may be just the opposite of why parents, teachers embrace labels like "develop", "disabled", "brain damage", just because they enable them to abdicate responsibility'. Exactly so. That is *one* use of human kinds, one which certainly has effects on the people who are classified.

Carey: Are you arguing that the very notion of a human kind is a twentieth-century Western construction, made possible because of the invention of statistical reasoning?

Hacking: There are two parts to the question.

Is the notion a twentieth-century (and 19th-century!) Western construction? Yes. That is because of my condition (iii) in my opening section headed 'What are human kinds?' — 'kinds that are studied in the human and social sciences, kinds about which we hope to have knowledge'. The human and social sciences begin in the nineteenth century.

Is the notion made possible because of the invention of statistical reasoning? Perhaps. I prefer a weaker formulation. I do claim that some social sciences came into being at the time of the 'avalanche of printed numbers' during the 1820s. Because of that event, people began to think statistically and to think about empirical statistical laws of society. It is less clear that the social sciences could have arisen only in conjunction with statistical thought. Comte coined the word *sociologie* precisely to name a non-statistical social science. Notice that the human kinds that I discuss in the chapter (multiple personality, child abuse, autism) are not subject to peculiarly statistical laws.

Carey: Is it not equally likely that there is a universal tendency to apply natural kind reasoning to types of human beings (e.g. ethnic differences), but that this universal tendency has taken a different form through the twentieth-century convergence of statistical reasoning and the 'helping professions'?

Hacking: Once again two questions are implied. Has the form of reasoning about human kinds been affected by the twentieth-century convergence of statistical reasoning and the helping professions? Yes. But I would describe the background presupposition differently. I do not see a growing convergence between statistics and the helping professions; I argue that they came into being together quite early in the nineteenth century. The point of collecting all that early data about suicide, prostitutes, madness, crime, vagrancy, and so forth, was to help. I believe that this theme has always been present, as long as there have been human kinds. However, that assertion should be qualified, as I do in my response to Leslie below.

Carey: Is it not equally likely that there is a universal tendency to apply natural kind reasoning to types of human beings (e.g. ethnic differences)?

Hacking: Yes, but a very qualified yes. I shall conclude this answer with a statement that we could both fully assent to.

Kinds of people, particularly including ethnic kinds, appear to be practically primaeval—see the reference to Xerxes in my reply to Keil for a technologically advanced example of self-conscious ethnic classification. Xerxes had his statement inscribed in three languages in three alphabets, and had carved on a staircase the stereotype of each kind of people over whom he held dominion. However, I do not think of Xerxes as applying natural kind reasoning to his tributary peoples. I am much taken with an idea emanating from the cultural anthropologist Mary Douglas, with antecedents at least as far back as Durkheim. Human groups or societies need to have practices that bind them together and to exclude others; otherwise there are no groups, clans, peoples, or whatever. Human beings do this by a widespread and perhaps universal set of practices for inclusion and exclusion. These are, to use Douglas's, words, practices of purity (for inclusion) and danger (for exclusion). These are not particularly ethnic in the modern American race-conscious sense of that word, although usually some sort of extended kinship relation is at work. It is intimately connected with practices which, if they are not ours, we call rituals. Because they involve emotions of love, tenderness, fear, and loathing, one would conjecture that such distinctions are among the earliest ones that children pick up from their community. That is how I interpret the results reported by Hirschfield (Chapter 11)—and hence doubtless have an underlying difference in analysis from Carey. However, this thought does connect with the second part of her question. Those very classes—the suicides, the murderers, the prostitutes, the vagrants, the mad—that I have mentioned were the pollutants of the new industrializing nations that gave birth to the social sciences. The dangerous classes! It is astonishing how often Douglas's insight fits in quite unexpected places.

I am resisting Carey's 'natural kind reasoning'. I think that the properties of the other, the polluters, are only incidentally 'natural'. I also resist taking the idea of a natural kind as something transparent and transcultural. The idea of a natural kind is, I state in the paper, just as historical as that of a human kind. It is a product of the natural sciences. Our visions of what a natural kind is, have changed with our vision of the sciences. I would not put what is universal in terms of natural kinds. There is a universal tendency to talk among human beings. Talking involves distinguishing various kinds of items in ways that are relevant to the speakers: Nelson Goodman's relevant kinds. In fact, I really disagree with Carey at a point that arises long before her question is asked!

Could we compromise on the following statement, a rewriting of her question? 'There is a universal tendency to distinguish relevant kinds of human beings, particularly those that mark out communities or group membership (including what we now call ethnic differences). This universal tendency has taken new forms through the nineteenth- and twentieth-century evolution of social science, statistical reasoning, and the helping professions.'

Morris: When accused witches in Salem, Massachusetts, confessed and began behaving erratically, this was a looping effect from what might be termed a 'supernatural kind'. 'Supernatural kinds' share many qualities of 'human kinds', for example they are not value-neutral. Perhaps the novelty of 'human kinds' is the use of probability to define classes of normal and abnormal and to propose causal relationships that are non-deterministic. How are the looping effects from 'human kinds' different from other looping effects?

Hacking: The essential difference is that people are aware of what they are called, adapt accordingly, and so change, leading to revisions in facts and then knowledge about them. We are familiar with so many types of feedback that I do not imagine that there is any other difference in general.

Is the novelty about human kinds a matter of normal–abnormal or of probability? No. Only some human kinds are novel in that way. Many of the human kinds that I mentioned are ones where the normal–abnormal or normal–pathological distinctions come into play. Many, but by no means all, of these are statistical. There is no relevant probabilistic measure of autism, child abuse, multiple personality, or handicap (as opposed to measures of the incidence of various conditions).

I do not think of witchcraft as a supernatural kind. A witch was a kind of person within a framework of knowledge different in type from ours, but no less rigorous. Salem is a curious freak in American history, but fifteenth-century witch-hunts are an integral part of European history, with perhaps a million people accused over the course of a century. In the four-teenth century you could bring suit against a person for exercising the power of a witch and thereby infringing your civil rights. If one were to extend my notion of human kind to apply to a classification within a system of knowledge for which there are sharp criteria—procedures of accountability, canons of evidence, and so forth—then in Europe 'witch' was a human kind.

Morris: Is the cognition of a 'looping' person different when the 'kind' has a probabilistic nature?

Hacking: No. Perhaps the word 'cognition' confuses me; also I am not sure how to use the phrase ' "looping" person'. The question seems to concern how a person feels about, and reacts to, being labelled. I do not think that it makes much difference whether the kind is intrinsically probabilistic. For example it does not seem to matter much to the rhetoric of excuse. Child abuse in one's own past is at best statistically correlated with adult bad behaviour. However, plenty of malefactors plead their abuse as children as an extenuating or mitigating circumstance, as if they could not help doing what they did, given their childhood. People in therapy find the revelation of their early abuse as convincing an explication of their present distress as any universal causation. Perhaps they should not do this, but you asked about the 'cognition' of the classified person.

Jacob: I want to disagree with the historical sketch of the background to present cognitive science which you have presented. You insist on the role of statistics and counting in the social sciences and in psychology. Rochel Gelman has made the point that, although statistical and probabilistic reasoning are useful tools for experimental psychologists, they are just tools and do not define the enterprise of either Freud or Piaget. I would like to refer to the importance of Chomsky's work in linguistics in shaping the present state of cognitive science. Now, on the one hand, it does not seem to me that counting and statistics play a central role in Chomsky's project. On the other hand, it seems to me that Chomsky's project, in effect, rehabilitates in psychology traditional issues from philosophy, such as the problem of *induction* raised by Hume (and revived by Nelson Goodman). It seems to me that Chomsky tried to turn philosophical perplexities about inductive acquisition of language into an empirical investigation. Therefore, on my view, cognitive science is closer to seventeenth- and eighteenth-century philosophy than to the nineteenth-century statistical revolution.

Hacking: Jacob is here commenting on my intemperate spoken presentation, in which I extended written remarks to themes closer to this conference—to developmental psychology and cognitive science.

Yes. Cognitive science began with Chomsky and his companions—the 'cognitive revolution'. It was self-consciously seventeenth-century in alignment. One of the reasons I have always resisted it is the way in which Cartesian and Lockeite ideas resurfaced as representations. I am now a born-again neural network person. The disappearance of a need for internal representations gratifies my Wittgensteinian sensibilities.

Yes. Probability and statistics are excluded by Chomsky, Freud, and Piaget; Rochel Gelman uses them only as handy tools for communication among scientists. I think that their role in developmental psychology is deeper than appears in the work of our colleagues at this conference, but I leave that as a promissory note. The connection between counting and my looping-effect thesis was limited. There is very little about counting in the written paper except in so far as that has to do with the origins of social science. I mentioned one looping effect of universal grammar in my response to Keil—American Sign Language. I argue case by case by case, because there is so little that is universal to be said about human kinds except the looping-effect phenomenon. Therefore I pass from example to example. Pierre Jacob next mentions Piaget. I referred to the following example in the paper: it was recently argued in a California court that early child abuse classes were to be dropped from the curriculum because Piaget had shown that children did not have the requisite concepts at the early age in question. Some critics have argued that this decision will predictably have an effect on children. The critics are more confident of their anti-Piagetian knowledge than I am. However, my point is that the children's development will be affected no matter what action is taken, and subsequent research on Californian children will be on children whose concepts have been formed in that way rather than another. As for Jacob's third example, Freud, I have already said enough about the king of the loopers.

Jacob: My third point is about your view about what distinguishes *human* kinds from *natural* kinds. In the written chapter you argue that the *only* interesting difference between distinctly human and non-human natural kinds is that, unlike the latter, the former have what you call looping effects on individuals who instantiate them. Therefore I took your written paper to reject strongly a dichotomy view according to which *realism* would be an appropriate attitude towards natural kinds and not towards human kinds. However, in some of your responses to questions, you seem to revert to such a dualistic view.

Hacking: Yes, I reject the dichotomy. I know of no general distinction between natural and human kinds except the feedback phenomenon. It has no consequences for philosophical realism or anti-realism about any relevant kinds.

Am I a backslider about this? I do not intend to be. We must distinguish philosophical scepticism, such as Hume's, from practical scepticism about this or that claim to knowledge. Hume was not a philosophical sceptic about miracles; he thought that, by the ordinary practical standards of evidence, we never have grounds for believing testimony about miracles. Unlike Hume, I try never to say never. I am sceptical, in a practical way, about much of our supposed knowledge about kinds of people. I am sceptical that there is any knowledge, in developmental psychology, that either corroborates or refutes the claim about school-teachers giving child abuse instruction to young children—even if there were, it would become invalidated almost at once by what that very education does to the conceptual potential of those very children. Nelson Goodman speaks of his 'sceptical, analytical and irrealist' orientation, an orientation which I admire and to which I aspire. The irrealism is in part a discounting of realist–anti-realist debates. We sceptics should be more analytical than I was in distinguishing philosophical from practical scepticism.

Incidentally, I do not agree with Jacob that Goodman revived Hume's philosophical problem about induction. I argue at great length elsewhere that Goodman's new riddle of induction is entirely distinct from any problem known to Hume. This is not irrelevant to our discussions here because Goodman's riddle is about kinds, not the future.

Hilton: Are you saying that the notion of childhood was created by statistics in the late nineteenth century?

Hacking: No. I tend to agree with Philippe Ariès' famous thesis about the discovery of childhood in modern times, but statistics had little to do with that. I do believe that the notion of child development is a work of the late nineteenth century. Statistical studies had something to do with that, but the example of Piaget suffices to show that statistics may be irrelevant to developmental studies.

Hilton: What about Romanticism in the early (e.g. Elizabethan) studies of child 'instruction'? Are you not being a bit strong?

Hacking: Yes. I do not know the Elizabethan studies, but of course Ariès built his original case around Louis XIII, born just before Elizabeth I died. Romanticism as more commonly understood—early nineteenth century and German—is closely connected with the kindergarten and like movements. However, the practice of monitoring a child for its passage through a series of stages emerged in the late nineteenth century.

Hilton: Regarding the co-emergence of statistical and experimental reasoning, what about Roger Bacon, Francis Bacon, and J. S. Mill (all concerned with administration and political change) who identified the experimental method well ahead of the development of statistics?

Hacking: Sorry. I keep the experimental and statistical in separate boxes. I have distinguished what I call the laboratory style of reasoning as a more precise sense of 'experimental'—part of the laboratory style is the construction of instruments and apparatus to produce phenomena (Hacking 1992a). Francis Bacon foresaw it; Robert Boyle established it. Another style of reasoning, exploratory and observational, is much earlier, and I would put Roger Bacon into that category, although history is always more complex than boxes. Statistical reasoning was not used at all in the natural sciences—as opposed to astronomy, photometry, geodesy, and the like—until the present century (1895 is a good starting date). The fact that the remarkable philosophers of the sciences were administrators is striking. I add William Whewell to the list.

Leslie: The exercise of power in wanting to help or change etc. what you say about social science may well be right. Perhaps the notion of 'person' belongs to social science. However, rightly or wrongly, I do not regard what I do as part of social science. What I do is part of cognitive science. This is the study of subpersonal properties, for example the computational properties of a bodily organ, a brain. Therefore I do not want to sort persons. I want to sort cognitive architectures. I do not want to help autistic children or to change them. I am sometimes criticized by people for exactly that – for not wanting to help or to change autistic children. This follows from the subtle distinctions between the neuropsychological and the clinical approaches.

Now we are not taking anything for granted with respect to human nature or with respect to whether there is a human nature at the subpersonal cognitive level. What we are doing is empirically investigating these questions under certain assumptions. These are empirical assumptions which are investigated by pursuing a certain enterprise.

Now history has not stopped (and incidentally to show the historical origins of an idea while interesting in no way bears on whether the idea is valid or true). Given that history has not stopped, it will be left to future generations to evaluate the enterprise that we are undertaking now. Beyond this, all your problems stem from being 'an extreme nominalist' as you say in your opening remarks!

Hacking: That was a very interesting remark. I have really learned a great deal about what people are doing from this conference, and from further reading to which I have been directed. As I write my replies I am just concluding a seminar in which we have been studying the work of many of the participants at this conference. I shall make just two comments, one about helping and one about history.

When I emphasized helping, to make clear that I have no use for simplistic power-and-control ideas now fashionable in some other quarters in Paris and elsewhere, I did not mean that every practitioner of a human science wants to help. Leslie is not a social scientist. I take the point about subpersonal properties, but I also notice that people who work with autistic children listen very seriously to theories about parts of the brain and adapt them, albeit uncritically, to working with autistic children. Leslie may make models of the brain, but those models will have enormous consequences for how people think about themselves. His work may be much closer to the ways in which we think about, classify, and interact with people than he admits. That is just another way in which no pure research, in our technoscientific and informatic society, is an island.

About history: 'the historical origins of an idea in no way bears on whether it is valid or true'. I agree. I do not study history. I abuse the past by considering how we came to take for granted that something is true or false. We evolve the criteria of truth or falsehood for what we are saying.

Historical events help to show that there is nothing inevitable in our thinking of some facts as candidates for facticity. Notice, by the way, that although I do have views about the connections between statistics and the social sciences forged in the 1820s, the examples in my paper are up to date. I follow how facts and people are being made up right now before our very eyes. We are the agents of that. Nor does one ever escape agency. Someone who, like me, emphasizes making up people is automatically part of the problem. Looping feeds back on those who notice loops.

Atran: You seem to be saying that the natural sciences and the social or behavioural sciences are both committed to probing a possibly nonsensical question: What is there? More to your point, the specific questions of the social and behavioural sciences deal with illusions — What kinds of people are there? What kinds of thoughts are there? What is the stuff of society and mind? — because framing the question literally makes them stuff. But are you telling us that this quest for the Grail is at best amoral and at worst immoral?

Hacking: No. The explicit claims in my paper are epistemological, not moral. Grail is Atran's word, not mine! I do not deny my moralistic overtones, but I did not say that the social and behavioural sciences deal with illusions. Even if framing questions literally makes stuff, the result would not be a case of illusion. Once something is identified as a candidate for truth or falsehood (see my reply to Hilton), we well know the conditions for sorting out illusions from truth.

Atran: Let us consider two aspects of the social and behavioural sciences, the one dealing with humankind and the other dealing with human kinds. Could not we distinguish these aspects, reserving claims of scientific objectivity (in the sense reserved for the natural sciences) for the former and informed subjectivity for the latter?

Hacking: No. I disagree in three different ways. Note that I did not speak of objectivity or subjectivity in my paper. Moreover, Jacob's comment above was correct, that I do not urge a dichotomy between a realist approach to natural sciences and an anti-realist approach to human sciences. In more detail I disagree with Atran's suggestion in four distinct ways.

1. I do not think that there is anything particularly subjective about the study of individual people, for we bring into being the standard of objectivity there as elsewhere — after which there is perfectly good ordinary truth, falsehood, or confusion.

2. It is misleading to think of the natural sciences as satisfying some pre-existing criteria of objectivity. We owe our present idea of objectivity in part to the natural sciences, and also in part to the social sciences.

What could be more objective than performing 'studies' subject to precise statistical analysis? That is how we settle questions nowadays.

3. I have spoken earlier in this discussion about the suggestion that the universal involves no looping effects.

4. Finally, I conclude with a touch of moralizing: I do not trust humankind studies. They are far more likely to try to remake the other in our image than any ordinary imperialism which at least tries to keep the other other. The more well-meaning one is, the greater, in my opinion, is the danger. That is a penalty that Atran knows, and bears, better (perhaps) than anyone else at this conference. I respect him immensely for his candour and self-awareness.

Atran: Granting that the pretence to an objective science of human kinds is no more than a pretence, what of the claim after an objective science of humankind: — What is an inextricable (and therefore basically uncorrectable) part of any person, such as the ability to perceive objects and other species, or the capacity to learn a language and tell a story?

Hacking: You will see that I do not grant that knowledge of human kinds is only a pretence. There is much objectivity. I did not say of any science that it is not objective, for what we call sciences set the standards of objectivity in their domain. Like everyone else, I believe that talking is part of what it is to be human. Like everyone else I am curious about it, but I am not confident that the notions of 'a language' or 'perceiving objects' are transparent.

Atran: Concerning human kinds, what if we *become* aware of the looping effect you describe, knowing full well that we cannot control it? Could not such awareness provide at least a necessary condition for making the quest a moral one for the betterment of humankind — less suffering and misery — to be negotiated as all of social life must be, but in a more overt and informed way, creating institutional mechanisms for rooting out covert agendas and tracking the inevitable skewing of information?

Hacking: Yes. This is the expression of a noble hope. Note by the way that the looping effect is not necessarily a bad thing. Liberation movements of which many of us approve are part of the game.

Atran: If so, do you think that statistics and experiments are less liable to advance this [the aim summarized in the last question] than novels, politics, and paintings?

Hacking: No.

Part VI

The legitimacy of domain-specific causal understandings: philosophical considerations

Foreword to Part VI

The existence, character, and epistemological relevance of causality have been debated by modern philosophers since Hume and Kant (not to mention the ancient philosophers—see Chapter 18 in Part VIII). However, the conference was not about causality itself, but about the ways in which it is mentally represented. Of course, it would have been of great interest to evaluate representations of causality in the light of a generally accepted picture of causality itself. However, there is no consensus on causality among philosophers. Indeed, there are few domains in philosophy where differences of opinions are so radical, many-faceted, and enduring.

One issue in the philosophy of causality, though, was of special relevance to the conference. Many participants were stressing the domain-specific character of much of causal cognition. Physical causation, biological causation, intentional causation, and social causation are represented, it was argued, by means of different mental devices, each using proprietary conceptual resources. The legitimacy of such domain- or level-specific approaches to causality has been a topic of discussion in both the philosophy of science and the philosophy of mind. The two chapters in this section are representative of these discussions.

Pettit's 'Causality at higher levels' revolves around a dilemma in philosophy of science. Modern science—including cognitive science—adopts a physicalist point of view, according to which anything that has causal powers has them by virtue of its microphysical properties. But if causal powers are microphysical powers, are there any causal facts left to be uncovered by the special sciences at higher levels of reality? What is the value of common-sense causal claims, which all concern levels well above the microphysical? Pettit analyses various types of causal relationships and argues for the legitimacy of causal claims at higher levels. His discussion ends with a favourable evaluation of common-sense understanding. It thus contrasts with Jacob's discussion of causal claims in psychological matters, which does not have a similarly optimistic conclusion.

The problem of higher-level causality raised by Pettit is particularly difficult at the psychological level. Common sense explains behaviour by invoking beliefs and desires. More specifically, it sees the *content* of an agent's mental states as causing his or her behaviour. However, content does not fit easily in a physicalist view of the world. Jacob, in 'The role of content in the explanation of behaviour', reviews the main proposals developed in contemporary philosophy of mind regarding the causal role of content. He shows that all these proposals have deep problems. A clear implication of Jacob's discussions is that we do not really know to what extent and by what means common-sense psychological understanding ('theory of mind') succeeds in being genuine understanding.

D.S.

13

Causality at higher levels
PHILIP PETTIT

There are two different problems to which causality gives rise from the point of view of the psychological and social sciences, and indeed from the point of view of common sense — from the point of view, for example, of the commonplace psychology and sociology that we practise in everyday life. One is the epistemological problem as to how causality is understood and detected within these higher-level forms of inquiry. The other is the more fundamental ontological problem as to whether there is really anything there at all for these forms of research to unearth — whether there is really such a thing as higher-level causality. This chapter deals with the ontological issue and bears only indirectly on the epistemological question.

The ontological problem of concern is not motivated by a general scepticism about causality — by a scepticism about whether there are causal relations to be uncovered by any sciences, natural or psychological or social. Rather, it is motivated by a physicalist outlook on the world. Suppose that we are physicalists and believe that the empirical world moves to a causal rhythm that physics is in the best position to identify.* Does that mean that we have to condemn the psychological and social sciences, and indeed natural sciences like chemistry and biology, to a secondary role? Does it mean that such special sciences, as they are sometimes called, are not in a position to identify any causal dynamics in the empirical world? Does it mean that the factors that they identify are only of ephiphenomenal significance? (See Block (1990), Blackburn (1991), Jacob (1991-2), Macdonald (1992), Pettit (1992), and Yablo (1992).) That is the question that is addressed in this chapter.

The chapter is in three sections. The first formulates the physicalist

---

* It should be noticed that the physicalist may believe this even if he thinks, as many do, that the category of causality is not strictly needed in physics. Whatever the provenance of this category, it is assumed here that the physicalist will think that it applies in the microphysical realm, if he thinks that it applies anywhere. Certainly, it would seem to be applicable with entities at the level of electrons and protons.

doctrine against the background of which the question arises.* The architecture of instrumental control — control at different levels — that this physicalism allows is discussed in the second section. The third section examines how far this architecture of control is mirrored in an architecture of causality: how far causality, like control, can be found at higher levels. It is argued that we can reasonably countenance higher-level as well as lower-level causality and that the special sciences are not at any particular disadvantage in the exploration of causal matters.

PHYSICALISM

There are two pairs of claims that the physicalist envisaged will make. They give expression, respectively, to the following two ideas: first, the empirical world is constituted out of materials that physics is in the best position to identify; second, the empirical world is governed by forces or regularites that physics is best equipped to describe. The two pairs of claims articulate a picture of the world as at once physically constituted and physically governed (cf. Crane and Mellor 1989).

Claim 1. There are microphysical entities

A. There is an empirical world of the sort that physics posits.

B. Different kinds of thing in the empirical world share (subatomic) levels of composition of the kind that physics — specifically, microphysics — posits: there is a realm of smaller and simpler, microphysical entities.

The first part of this claim gives expression to a realist view of physics, under which the physicist is in the business of telling us about an objective world and the business is a potentially successful enterprise — there really is a world there for the physicist to chart. The second part of the claim directs us to the fact that physics, unlike the other sciences, has comprehensive as well as realist ambitions (on this matter see Papineau (1990) and Crane (1991)). In the world that physics posits, things of different kinds — things of all kinds, if the next claim is sound — share certain (subatomic) levels of composition, and microphysics is identified as the discipline that covers everything in that realm, at whatever level of composition. Physics, then, is potentially more encompassing than the other sciences. It does not confine itself to particular ranges of empirical reality, unlike psychology or biology, nor does it confine itself, in the manner of chemistry, to the study of empirical reality above a certain (atomic) level of complexity.

---

* This section reproduces material in Pettit (1993b). See also Pettit (forthcoming).

In endorsing this first claim, the physicalist can remain relatively uncommitted on a variety of troublesome issues.

1. He may be more or less sanguine about the accuracy of actual physics, or even about the propriety of its methods; he may be more or less optimistic about how far actual physics is on the right track. He has to suppose that microphysics is directed at a real target — a realm of smaller and simpler entities — for the discipline is identified by this orientation (rather than by its claims or methods). But he need not think that its sights are well set or that it has achieved any particular degree of accuracy in hitting that target; he can even admit that microphysics may be forced to countenance entities that by present intuitions are not of an intuitively 'physical' character.

2. He can remain neutral on the proper way to formulate the claims of physics, in particular microphysics: he may think of it as the study of small particles, for example, or he may endorse a field-style formulation, under which small particles correspond to property-instances with thin world-lines.

3. Since he understands microphysics as the physics of the subatomic (or whatever) realm, he can leave open the matter of how small or how simple microphysical entities become at lower levels of composition within that realm; he can leave open, as some physicists wish to do, even the question as to whether there is any bottom level of smallest or simplest grain.

4. Consistently with defending a certain 'non-emergentist' view on the relationship between the microphysical realm and other levels — such a non-emergentism is defined in the further claims below — he may think of the microphysical realm in a non-atomist way. He may believe that certain relational microphysical properties — apart from spatiotemporal properties — are in some way fundamental.*

5. Consistently with defending such a non-emergentist view of the relationship between the microphysical realm and other levels, he may even concede that that view need not hold of the relationship between

---

* This microphysical non-atomism is inconsistent with the 'Humean' picture that attracts Lewis (1986, pp. ix-x): 'We have geometry: a system of external relations of spatiotemporal distance between points. Maybe points of spacetime itself, maybe point-sized bits of matter or aether or fields, maybe both. And at those points we have local qualities: perfectly natural intrinsic properties which need nothing bigger than a point at which to be instantiated. For short: we have an arrangement of qualities. And that is all'. Lewis articulates the view that all that there is apart from this Humean configuration supervenes on that configuration; this amounts to a microphysicalism akin to the sort defined here. The present point, roughly, is that the microphysicalist can keep the supervenience aspect of Lewis's picture — can maintain his microphysicalism — while dropping the Humean one.

different levels, assuming that there are some, within the microphysical realm.

Claim 2. Microphysical entities constitute everything

A. Everything in the empirical world is composed in some way — composed without remainder — out of (subatomic) entities of the kind that microphysics posits, or is itself uncomposed and microphysical.

B. The composition involved is conservative or non-creative in this sense: absent the introduction of a new source of higher-level laws or forces, two microphysically composed entities cannot differ intrinsically without some difference of a microphysical kind — without some difference in the character or configuration of their microphysical components.*

Part A of the claim is left indeterminate to the extent that no specification is offered of the sort of composition required. The mode of composition may involve any of a variety of relationships, and any of a number of mixes among those varieties: for example it may involve the relationships of identity, member to set, part to whole, token to type, realizer to role, and so on. Part B offers the one constraint that the composition must satisfy. It must be the case, under the proviso about novel laws and forces, that if there is an intrinsic difference between two things, or between the same thing at different times, then there is a microphysical difference between them. There is no macrophysical difference without a microphysical difference. As it is often put, the macrophysical supervenes on the microphysical, or at least it does so subject to the proviso given.

The supervenience claim leaves a number of matters indeterminate, but that is not relevant for our purposes. The point is that the physicalist must believe in a conservative sort of microphysical composition that makes any failure of supervenience problematic — a conservative sort of composition that will force us to explain any failure of supervenience by reference to an independent source of novel laws or forces. We shall be returning to the possibility that composition is attended by the appearance of such novel laws or forces in discussing the second pair of claims associated with physicalism.

The main object of this chapter is to define physicalism, not to defend it. But it may be worthwhile asking who is likely to reject this second claim: who, that is, apart from those who interpret physics in such a non-realist way that they cannot endorse any variant of the first claim. One opponent will be the dualist who thinks that there are things in the empirical world, say Cartesian minds, that are not in any way composed out of

---

* My thanks to Peter Smith for a helpful exchange on the content of this clause.

microphysical entities. Another will be the person, perhaps difficult to imagine, who accepts microphysical composition but thinks that the composition involved is not necessarily conservative; it allows, without further need of explanation, that two entities that are composed in the same way, and of the same materials, may yet different intrinsically from one another.

Claim 3. There are microphysical regularities

A. Microphysical entities are subject to certain law-like regularities by virtue of their microphysical properties and relations.

B. The laws at work in the microphysical realm do not obtain because they are required to obtain by the obtaining of certain laws at a macrolevel — perhaps the same laws (e.g. the same conservation laws), perhaps different ones. The microphysical laws, as we may say, are primitive.

Part A is not as strong as it may at first seem. It is silent on exactly how laws should be understood and on whether they may be probabilistic as well as deterministic. It allows that certain microphysical laws may ultimately apply by virtue of certain relations among microphysical entities, not by virtue of their atomistic properties. It states not that the behaviour of microphysical entities is governed entirely by microphysical laws, but only that there are some microphysical laws that play a governing part. Finally, part A does not say that the microphysical laws all bear on entities of the same grain; the laws involved may include laws that apply, as it were, at different levels of grain, provided that those levels are all subatomic. Part B gives some edge to the claim. The laws envisaged in the microphysical realm obtain for independent reasons, whatever those may be, not because they are necessary for the operation of macrolevel laws. There is no top-down push at the origin of the laws; they are as primitive as laws can be.

Who might reject this third claim? The rejection of part A involves the denial that there are laws in operation in the microphysical realm. Someone may deny that there are microphysical laws on the ground that there are no laws whatsoever; this would undermine physicalism in the precise sense defined here, but it would be consistent with a variant formulation that refers to forces or whatever in place of laws. Alternatively, someone may deny that there are microphysical laws while asserting that there are laws of a macrolevel kind; this will constitute a much more challenging attack on physicalism in my sense. The rejection of part B would go to matters of deeper metaphysics. Someone who thinks that there are microphysical laws but who holds that they are not primitive is going to have to tell a story whereby macrolevel regularities propagate their requirements downwards and establish an order of microphysical law. This is not a common picture but, presumably, is a possible one.

Claim 4. Microphysical regularities govern everything

If there are macrolevel laws, as there surely are, then the following holds.

A. They do not complement microlevel laws, taking up some degree of slack left by those laws.

B. They are not independent of microlevel laws; they do not have the potential to conflict with them and they do not serve to reinforce them, representing an extra booster for sequences of events that are established in accordance with those laws.

This fourth claim is relevant in the debate between physicalists and anti-physicalists, because if there are any macrolaws, then those laws must ultimately put constraints on the behaviour of microphysical entities.* They govern things that are composed out of microphysical entities and, if they are to dictate what happens to such things, they must impose constraints on what happens to the microphysical components of those things. However, if macrolaws constrain the behaviour of microphysical entities, then there is a question about how they relate to the microphysical laws which, by claim 3, are relevant to the behaviour of those entities. That is the question addressed in claim 4.

One sort of physicalist may deny that there are any macrolevel laws — that there are any laws, for example, that apply by virtue of the satisfaction of certain chemical or biological, psychological, or social conditions. This line is not going to be attractive to many, at least not under a generous conception of laws. The more usual sort of physicalist will admit that there are macrolevel laws, as there are laws in the microphysical realm, but will argue, by defending claim 4, that those laws do not represent a regime that is independent of the microphysical order. The macrolaws do not complement microphysical laws, filling in gaps which those laws leave, and the macrolaws do not obtain on an independent basis. The satisfaction of a macro-antecedent cannot require a result that conflicts with microphysical laws. If the satisfaction of a macro-antecedent requires a result that is already guaranteed by microphysical laws, it does not represent an extra determinant of that result. Macrolevel regularities, however objective and however worthy of notice, are fixed in place by the regime which the microphysical laws establish.†

---

* Crane and Mellor (1989, p. 190) illustrate the point nicely with reference to Boyle's (macrolevel) law. Suppose that the volume of a gas sample is suddenly halved. 'If the gas is ideal', they say, 'Boyle's law entails that when its pressure settles down again it will be twice what it was. That law does not dictate all the interim behaviour of the sample's molecules — except that it must be such as will eventually double the sample's pressure'.

† The point applies to the case where the same law, for example the same conservation law, is involved, now at a microlevel, now at a macrolevel. The point then is that that law will not have to do double duty.

This physicalist denies that the laws that appear at the macrolevel are of the novel kind, or are associated with the novel forces mentioned in the proviso governing the second claim. He holds that in worlds like ours that proviso is fulfilled, as a contingent matter (Lewis 1983), and so he defends a non-provisional but contingent supervenience of the macrophysical on the microphysical.* His overall position can be expressed as follows: once the microphysical conditions and the microphysical laws have been fixed, then all the crucial features of a world like ours will have been fixed, namely all the other laws that obtain at the world, all the conditions — all the initial conditions — that engage those laws, and all the things that happen in accordance with the laws. The position on laws is put in place by claim 4, where the position on initial conditions is entailed by claim 2. The position on laws amounts to a sort of nomological fundamentalism. Not only is the empirical world microphysically constituted, the empirical world is also microphysically governed.

Why should we be disposed to take the physicalism defined by our four claims as a backgound for discussion? There are three points that should be made. One is the familiar consideration that, even if it offends against democratic instincts, the sort of doctrine in question displays an attractive economy and simplicity (Pettit 1993a, Chapter 3). For example the doctrine explains why laws at different levels work so smoothly and systematically in tandem; it does not have to appeal to any happy coincidence of effect or any pre-established harmony (Pettit forthcoming). The second and third considerations are not so commonly mentioned.

The second is that the physicalism defined here is a concrete but fairly cautious version of an abstract and plausible claim (cf. Lewis, forthcoming). The abstract claim is that the various kinds of things in the world are composed of less varied items, that this composition establishes a hierarchy of different levels of thing, and that there is some less-than-highest level of composition such that if we fix how things are governed from there down, then we shall have fixed how things at every level are governed. This claim is concretized in the physicalism defined here. The composing items are said to be the kinds of thing that microphysics aspires to identify and the level at which we go to microphysics — the subatomic level — is said to be one such that if we fix how things are governed from

---

* Crane and Mellor (1989, p. 205) offer an argument against supervenience, with reference to the psychological and the physical, but one that leaves me unmoved. They admit that 'token thoughts and sensations are only supposed to supervene on simultaneous tokens of non-mental properties' but maintain, none the less, that this supervenience conflicts with the possibility of non-mental indeterministic causation of mental events, in particular, the causation by the same non-mental antecedents of these mental events here and of those, different, mental events there. I see no difficulty. Past non-mental causes can give rise indeterministically to different mental events, consistently with supervenience, provided that they do so, as all physicalists will surely say, through giving rise indeterministically to different non-mental subveners.

there down, then we will have fixed how everything is governed. Both these claims are cautious, abstracting as they do from microphysical detail, and to that extent they should not be found excessively controversial (cf. Smart 1978; Smith 1992, pp. 25–6).

The third point is of a different and perhaps more compelling character. Many philosophical projects attempt to vindicate commonplace discourses about colour or value or mentality or, as in the present case, the causality countenanced in common sense and in the special sciences. It is good practice with such projects to try to vindicate the target discourse under hard rather than easy assumptions—under assumptions that would make vindication more rather than less difficult. The assumptions associated with physicalism, as it is defined here, satisfy that desideratum. They represent a worst-case, or at least quite a bad-case, scenario from the point of view of relevant discourse-saving projects. It is going to be extremely difficult to argue for the reality of higher-level causality if this sort of physicalism holds and, equally, it is going to be really difficult to deal with a large range of philosophical questions, for example with questions bearing on the standing of secondary and evaluative properties, on the reality of mind, and on the validity of modal claims. Of course, the fact that the physicalist picture is a worst-case scenario does not give us reason to believe it, but it may give us reason to carry on as if it were sound; it may give us reason to treat physicalism as a standard working hypothesis.

PHYSICALISM AND THE ARCHITECTURE OF CONTROL

Let us say that a property or a group of properties represents an instrumental control for some type of event or condition just in case it would make sense, in principle, to realize that property or group of properties with a view to realizing the result-type in question. Let us also say that a given instance of a property was a control for some instance of a result-type just in case it would have made sense, in principle, to have put it in place in order to promote that result. The control represents a way in which the associated event or condition can be promoted or could have been promoted. At one limit, it may necessitate the occurrence of the result; at another, it may facilitate the occurrence in some minimal measure. (See Menzies and Price (1993) for the development of such ideas.)

The notion of an instrumental control is weaker than the notion of a causal control. Any cause will represent a control for the sort of event that it generates, but factors that are not causally operative may also represent instrumental controls. For example a standby cause that does not actually do any causal work in generating the relevant effect represents a control for that result: it is the sort of thing that one may put in place with a view, as we say, to promoting the likelihood of the result. A non-causal factor that could not possibly do any causal work may also represent a control for a certain event or condition: in the old example, Socrates' dying is a control for Xanthippe's becoming a widow, although it does not cause her to become a widow. The notion of a control is introduced before coming to causes proper, as it may enable us to gain a perspective on the issue that causes raise within a physicalist picture. In this section we consider how far physicalism allows for higher-level controls, and in the next section we go on to see how far it allows for higher-level causes.

The notion of a control connects intimately with the notion of something that makes a certain event or condition more probable or, at the least, that is fitted by its intrinsic character to make it more probable; it need not make it more probable in the actual world, where another factor may already have raised the probability beyond improvement (in the limit, raised it to unity), but it is, roughly, of a sort that raises the probability of such a result in various other surroundings, whether in the actual world or in worlds like the actual world (cf. Lewis 1986, pp. 206 ff). The control of any result is, as we may put it, a *pro tanto* probabilifier of that result. However, if we describe controls as *pro tanto* probabilifiers we should be careful to note that they are not probabilifiers of just any old kind; they are probabilifiers that represent potential means for promoting the associated type of result. Something may probabilify a result, say because it represents evidence that the result has ensued, without being a potential means for promoting the result (Menzies and Price 1993).

It is assumed that the definition of a control means that generally, when we have a law that relates the satisfaction of some antecedent to the satisfaction of a consequent, the antecedent-property is a control for the consequent.* Under the physicalist picture described in the previous section there are laws that govern the world at different levels. There are laws that relate microphysical conditions to microphysical results, and there are laws that relate conditions involving macrophysical configurations — chemical or biological, psychological or social-scientific — to macrophysical results. This implies that there are controls — controlling properties — to be found at different levels in the empirical world: there are micro-controls and, at different levels of composition, there are a variety of macro-controls.

However, the physicalist picture does not allow us to think of these controls as governing different areas. It does not allow us, for example, to think that the microcontrols rule in the microdomain and that, quite independently, the different macrocontrols rule in the different domains

---

* I am grateful to Frank Döring for drawing my attention to an incautious formulation of this point.

to which they are relevant; it does not even allow us to think that macro-controls complement their microphysical counterparts, taking up some slack that they leave. Every consequent that is governed by any macro-control involves a configuration of microentities which subveniently fixes the intrinsic character of the consequent. Every such consequent is controlled in the maximum measure available by the microproperties that relate to the configuration in question; it is controlled by the micro-antecedents whose satisfaction leads, by microphysical laws, to the appearance of the configuration.

The fact that everything falls under microphysical control may seem to raise a problem. Under the physicalist picture the microphysical laws, and therefore the microphysical controls, are primitive. Again, under the physicalist picture macrophysical laws, and therefore macrophysical controls, are not independent of their microphysical counterparts; they do not represent potentially conflicting or actually reinforcing influences. However, if everything that is controlled for by macroproperties is also controlled for by microproperties, and if the control of the microproperties is more primitively sourced, does not this mean that there really are not any macrophysical controls at all? Does it not mean that the microphysical properties have a monopoly in the control of what happens in the empirical world?

Not at all. To control a type of result is just to be a factor that might in principle be manipulated with a view to promoting it or to be a factor that might have been manipulated with a view to promoting it in some instance. There is no problem with the idea that one and the same instance of a result-type may be subject simultaneously to many different controls. That is just to say that a number of different factors might in principle have been manipulated with a view to promoting the result-type in that instance. There is no more difficulty in this idea than there is in the notion that a number of different factors may each have served to raise the probability of a certain event's occurring. In principle, then, there is nothing incoherent in the thought that microproperties and macroproperties may serve simultaneously as controls of a given event. But can we go further than defending the coherence in principle of the idea? Can we show, more concretely, how such multiple control can obtain in a world that satisfies the physicalist picture?

In explaining how factors at different levels can be causally relevant to one and the same event, Jackson and Pettit (1988, 1990) have introduced what is described as the program model of multiple relevance; we return to this in the next section. A simple analogue of that model serves to provide an account of how micro- and macroproperties can simultaneously enjoy a controlling role in relation to a given type of event. It suggests an architecture under which such simultaneous control is unproblematic.

The physicalist has no problem with the idea that certain microproperties control for a given event-type E. Suppose then that such an event comes about and comes about, as we may say, under the control of a microproperty or group of properties. How can a macroproperty H (for higher-level) serve at the same time in the role of control for E? The program model suguests that it will do so only in the case when the following three conditions are realized.

1. The realization of H involves the realization of certain microlevel properties — perhaps these, perhaps those.
2. However H is realized at the microlevel more or less, the realizing properties serve as controls for an E-type event.
3. H is realized and E occurs.

The best way to make the projected architecture vivid may be by the use of an analogy. Suppose that we are dealing with a toy world in which certain small balls correspond to microphysical entities and in which macrophysical properties are represented by the shapes which various sets of these balls are capable of assuming on a flat surface. Take the shape-property of being triangular. There will be many different ways in which a set of balls may assume a triangular shape: different numbers of balls may be involved, different sets of balls may be involved, and the same set of balls may be distributed over different places. Suppose now that no matter how a triangular shape is realized, the balls which realize it remain in position for a characteristic period; whatever the mechanics involved, the ball-level laws which apply in each of these cases ensure a certain stability. The toy world envisaged presents itself like a randomly shifting kaleidoscope except in the event that certain of the balls assume a triangular shape; in that event, we find that the balls come to display a certain temporary stability.

Consider now what we should say about the factors that control for the appearance of a period of stability. We may certainly say that that phenomenon is controlled for by the simultaneous satisfaction at a certain time of the relevant ball-level laws — by the satisfaction on the part of the balls involved of certain ball-level properties, intrinsic or relational. But we can also say in such a case that the phenomenon is controlled for by the satisfaction of the triangular property on the part of the aggregate of balls. We can do so, because the program architecture applies. The realization of the triangular property involves the realization of certain ball-level properties. No matter how the ball-level properties realize the triangular property, the realizing configuration of properties controls for a certain temporary stability, in the manner appropriate to a potential means; in fact, by the story we have told, it makes a certain temporary stability certain.

The lesson of the analogy should be clear. Even if we go along with the physicalist picture of the last section, we can think of the history of the empirical world as unfolding under the simultaneous control of microphysical and macrophysical properties. The microphysical properties may represent more basic controls — they are presupposed by their higher-level counterparts and they are more primitively sourced — but they do not deprive macrophysical properties of the capacity to serve a similar controlling role.

There is an objection. Is the scenario of multiple-level control consistent with the supervenience which the physicalist picture asserts? This supervenience means that if we have put all microphysical controls into place, then we will also have fixed all macrophysical controls in position. At first that may seem to suggest that the only controls that really exist are the microphysical ones. But the suggestion does not survive reflection. Supervenience is a relationship in the same family as entailment; it directs us to what must also be realized, give or take certain constraints, in the event of realizing a certain condition. It is clear that if one state of affairs obtains and if it entails another, then the other also obtains. It should be clear, in parallel, that if certain microphysical controls exist and if they superveniently underpin certain other macrophysical controls, then the macrophysical controls exist also. Supervenience of the kind envisaged is not an eliminativist relationship; it serves to conserve that which it supports, not to subvert it.

PHYSICALISM AND THE ARCHITECTURE OF CAUSALITY

The fact that the physicalist world allows an architecture of lower- and higher-level controls should not really be surprising. The notion of a control carries no explicit ontological burden; it does not explicitly require the presence of any particular sort of substantive relationship. There is nothing astounding in the claim that, though the world is microphysically constituted and governed, we can still identify macrophysical conditions that serve as potential means for realizing various sorts of results.

Controls are ontologically light to the extent that they do not necessarily count as causes. A control is required only to make something instrumentally more probable, in the *pro tanto* sense, than it would otherwise have been. That condition can be satisfied, as we mentioned, by factors that have no causal effect. Consider the standby cause of something: the factor that does not itself cause the event but that is there to play a causal role if the actual cause fails. Consider, for example, the cancer which ensures that someone who has been killed in a car accident would have died before the year's end. Such a standby cause can count, by our definition, as a control for the event, since it represents a means of promoting the person's death before the end of the year; yet, by hypothesis, the control is not itself causally active in generating the event — it represents an inert control, as we might put it.*

Again, consider the sort of factor that instrumentally facilitates or necessitates something but which does so in what our intuitions represent as an essentially non-causal way. This factor is not contingently inert, in the manner of a standby cause, it is necessarily of this inert character. The presence of antibodies in John's bloodstream ensures that he is immune. Mary's attendance ensures that there will be someone at the lecture. John's death ensures that Jane has become a widow. In each of these cases we find a controlling property but we do not find anything that looks intuitively like a causal connection. The controlling property constitutes, or helps to constitute, the type of result in question; it does not lead to that result via a causal process.

The contrast between controls and causes leads us to ask whether the physicalist world of the first section is compatible, not just with an architecture involving lower- and higher-level controls, but also with an architecture that allows lower- and higher-level causal, i.e. causally active, controls. Can we believe that the world is microphysically constituted and microphysically governed and still hold that there are macrophysical as well as microphysical causes? In particular, can we hold that causally active controls are to be found equally at microphysical and macrophysical levels?

If a controlling property is to be causally relevant to the event that it controls, then what extra condition must it satisfy? The property must not be a standby factor, in the manner of the cancer. Equally, it must not be the sort of non-causal constitutive factor that appears in our other examples. But what sort of condition must it satisfy on the positive side if it is to count as causally relevant to the result for which it controls? The controlling property, or rather the relevant instance of the controlling property, must relate to the event in question in the manner illustrated when I push this table and it moves, when the wind bends this branch and it breaks, or when the fire touches this paper and it burns. But what manner of connection do these paradigms illustrate?

Philosophers divide, notoriously, on this question. We can distinguish three broadly different approaches. Some philosophers think that it is possible to give an account of the connection in more or less formal mode — in terms of laws or conditions or counterfactuals or the like. Others go to the opposite material-mode extreme and hold that the connection

---

* Notice in this connection that, though the criminal law is introduced as a control on deviancy, it is commonly recognized that most individuals are going to conform for reasons that have nothing to do with the law.

should be taken as a primitive irreducible exercise of power on the part of certain property-instances – as the display of a productive 'oomph' or 'bif', whether as a singular or a systematic matter, on the part of those properties.* Others again assume an intermediate position, maintaining that the causal connection should be identified, not by immediate reference to the material mode, but by reference just to certain paradigms – by reference to that relationship which those paradigms are taken to exemplify. This third approach may take the relationship in question to be of a more or less immediately salient kind. Or it may allow that the relationship is to be illuminated in science, in the way in which science illuminates the kind – H_2O – that samples of water exemplify; thus it may allow the possibility that the relationship in question boils down to the sort of energy transfer that is sometimes taken to be involved in paradigm causal connections.

However the causal connection is to be understood, the question before us is whether we can countenance a scenario under which causal controls are to be found at higher as well as lower levels. Causal controls are motor controls, as we may put it – motor controls as distinct from the inert controls represented by standby causes and by essentially non-causal factors. They are properties which control for the types of event to which they are relevant and they are properties whose instances relate to the events on which they bear in the productive manner in which my pushing relates to the movement of the table.[†]

The problem that we face may be usefully presented with the help of a tree diagram. We have seen that controls are a species of *pro tanto* probabilifiers, and that causal or motor controls are a species of controls. The question before us is whether motor controls can be found at higher levels as well as within the microphysical domain.

---

* If a certain property-type displays the required efficacy as a singular matter – if singularism holds – then that means that it is a primitive fact about each instance of the property – a fact not replicated necessarily in otherwise indiscernible worlds – that the instance is efficacious. It will not be because it is an instance of that property – of that property rather than of any of the apparently irrelevant properties that it co-instantiates – that it is efficacious; its being efficacious is an independent fact.

[†] In focusing the discussion on motor controls, I seek to bypass a question that interests some philosophers. This, in our jargon, is the question of whether the word 'cause' refers to any property-instance that plays a motor role or whether it only properly refers to a property-instance that satisfies a double condition: the instance plays a motor role and, moreoever, the property plays a controlling role. Suppose that two properties, F and G, are co-instantiated and that their co-instance is causally relevant to some result, E. Suppose further that the F-property controls for that result and the G-property does not. The G-property may be wholly irrelevant to the type of result in question; it may even be the property of being reported in yesterday's newspaper. Is it reasonable to describe the G as the cause of E? Or should we reserve that description only for the F? I avoid this question, while making it clear that I am only interested in properties like the F-property – in properties thai are at once controls and, in their instances, motors.

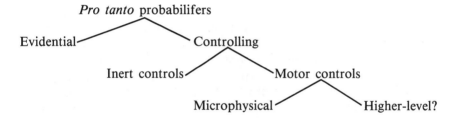

How do we approach our problem? We know from the previous section that there is no difficulty in countenancing higher-level properties as controls, even in a physicalist world. We shall identify conditions under which such higher-level controls will certainly count as 'programmers' of events that are microphysically produced; this is done by reference to the program model. Then we shall explore two questions: Does the enjoyment of such a programming status mean that the controls involved are more than inert controls? In particular, does it mean that they are motor controls in the same sense as microphysical antecedents?

We assume that the physicalist, whatever his conception of the causal connection, will have no hesitation in taking some microphysical properties as motor controls. The program model mentioned earlier identifies conditions under which it is appropriate to say that a higher-level property 'programs' for a result that issues at the same time from a microphysical motor control or, more generally, from any lower-level motor control. A higher-level property H will program for a microphysically produced result E just in case the following three conditions are fulfilled (the last two conditions are stronger than those involved in the architecture of control, because of the difference made by the motor requirement).

1. The realization of H involves the realization of certain microlevel properties, perhaps these, perhaps those.

2. However H is realized at the microlevel — more or less — the realizing properties are apt to be motor controls responsible for an E-type event.

3. The microlevel properties that actually realize H are motor controls that are responsible for E in the manner envisaged in condition 2.*

These conditions can be illustrated by reference back to the example from the toy world. Suppose that the ball-level properties that engage with the relevant laws count in any instance as motor controls of the stability that follows on their realization. The triangular shape must be said to

---

* The phrase 'in the manner envisaged in condition 2' is necessary to avoid certain deviant chain cases where roughly speaking, the realizing properties are responsible for the right sort of event but in the wrong sort of manner. I am grateful for a discussion on this point with Daniel Andler, Jean-Pierre Dupuy, Pierre Jacob, and Francois Recanati.

program for the appearance of that stability on any occasion where it materializes in the appropriate way. It meets the required conditions. First, the realization of the shape always involves the realization of certain ball-level properties. Second, however the shape is realized, the realizing configuration of ball-level properties tends to produce an ensuring period of stability in the motor-control way. Third, the actual configuration that realizes the shape is a motor control of the actual stability that ensues.

The sort of relationship envisaged between macrophysical programmers and microphysical motor controls is a relationship that can obtain between properties at any two levels of composition.* Assume as an illustration that the molecular structure of this eraser is a motor control relevant to the fact that it bends under a certain pressure. The malleability of the eraser programs for that bending because the instantiation of the malleability involves the instantiation of certain molecular-structural properties. The sorts of properties associated with instantiations of malleability are apt to motor-control the sort of bending effect in question. The molecular-structural property associated with the actual instantiation of malleability is a motor control of the bending.†

Other examples of the program model become salient as we recognize suitably corresponding relations across levels in different cases. The square-ness of the peg stops it going into the round hole. The redness of the rag enrages the bull. The rise in unemployment raises the level of crime. The rational appeal of the option leads the agent to select it. In every case the instantiation of the higher-level property involves the instantiation of motor-control properties at the lower level. The squareness of the peg involves the sort of molecular contact which blocks the peg going through the round hole, the redness of the rag involves the sort of physical stimulation which provokes the bull, the rise in unemployment involves a shift in motives and opportunities that is likely to increase aggregate crime, the rationality or perceived rationality of an action involves the sort of neural disposition which produces suitable behaviour, and so on across a great variety of possible cases. The harmony of levels holds for different reasons

---

* If a microphysical property produces something in the manner of a motor control, then, whatever relevance a macrophysical property has to the result, it meets two conditions. First it presupposes the microphysical influence. Second, it is not the relevance of an earlier cause of the microphysical factor or of a cause with which the microphysical factor needs to join forces; the macrophysical property is causally insulated from the microphysical. I assume here that such conditions will be fulfilled by any families of properties that belong, as I put it, at higher and lower levels of composition. Elsewhere I have referred to such conditions in defining what it is for two families of properties to belong to respectively higher and lower levels (Pettit 1992, 1993a, Chapter 3).

† The example is rather trivial because knowledge that the molecular structure combined in the ordinary way with a certain outside pressure to cause the bending yields knowledge that the malleability was also causally relevant. However, not all illustrations of the program model have this feature.

in the different cases, but the fact that it obtains shows how the program model may apply in any of the examples.

Suppose that the program model is satisfied by certain macrophysical controls relative to the microphysical motor controls that are responsible for a given type of event. Does that mean that the macrophysical controls are more than controls in the instrumental sense introduced in the last section? In particular, does it mean that they amount to motor controls of the event in question—to controls of the same causal status, if not of the same hierarchical standing, as the microphysical factors?

First question

The answer to the first question is certainly positive. There is more involved in a higher-level property's programming for an event than there is in its just controlling for it. Take our earlier example of a standby cause. Suppose that someone has cancer and that this higher-level property means that there will be some specific organic failure or vulnerability—perhaps this, perhaps that—which will lead to death, in the motor-control way, within the year. Suppose that the person does indeed die within the year but dies as a result of injury in a car accident. The cancer controlled for that event, but it does not count as a programmer of the event. The reason is that death does not come about at the level of specific organic breakdown in the manner associated with cancer; the breakdown that leads to death would have been just as likely, or so we assume, in the absence of the cancer.

This observation already teaches us an important lesson about higher-level programmers. Whatever views we come to hold about their motor-control status, we must at least recognize that there is more involved in a higher-level property's programming for something than there is in its controlling for it. Even if the programming property is not a motor control, it is a property which is relevant only in the case where the lower-level motor control is of a certain kind. The cancer would count as a programmer of death, not just as a controller, only if death came about in a certain way at the level of organ failure. Whether or not a programming property is to count as a motor control—we come to that question in a moment—it requires the presence of a certain sort of motor control; it puts constraints on the sort of motor control that is in operation. Thus the programming property is not just a control of an inert kind.

Second question

Can higher-level programming properties generally count as motor controls in the full sense? With this question, we come to the heart of the matter that concerns us. It is granted for sure that microphysical properties have a certain hierarchical priority in the motor control of how the world goes. But the question is whether the factors that count as microphysically productive are motor controls in a sense that allows us to think of investigating similar motor controls — similar productive properties — in the special sciences and in common-sense inquiries. Motor controls are full-blooded causes, so we assume, and the issue is whether such investigations can generally aspire to identify full-blooded causes in the same sense.

My answer to the question is that it all depends. It depends, in particular, on how exactly we choose to conceptualize the motor connection that distinguishes motor controls from inert controls: from standby causes, for example, and from controlling factors of a non-causal kind. As mentioned earlier, while everyone agrees that my pushing causally moves this table, and while the wind's blowing causally bends the branch, the connection involved is variously understood. Whether programmers are to be taken as motor controls depends on which construal is adopted.

The first approach to the question about the motor connection assumes that the connection lends itself to a more or less formal-mode analysis, say by reference to laws or counterfactuals. Under this approach there can be no difficulty, in principle, with the idea that higher-level programming properties count as motor controls. For, as it is possible for such properties to do as well as microphysical properties in fulfilling the control conditions, so it is going to be possible for them to fulfill most of the conditions that are likely to be invoked in explicating the motor connection.

The approach that stands at the opposite extreme from this first approach would say that the motor connection is irreducible — that it involves the exercise of a notion of power that we have no independent means of elucidating; it is a connection in which the instantiation of the relevant property contributes an 'oomph' or a 'bif' that gives rise to the event produced. As there is no difficulty in recognizing programming properties as motor controls under the purely formal-mode analysis of the motor connection, so there is no possibility of doing so under this extreme version of the material-mode approach.

A little reflection makes clear why. It is granted under the physicalist picture that everything is governed in a primitive way by microphysical laws. This must mean that the motor controls to which those laws direct us can and do enjoy the irreducible 'oomph' that is characteristic of the motor connection. It is granted equally under the physicalist picture that higher-level laws are not on the same primitive footing as microphysical. This must mean that they do not direct us to rival motor controls. If the higher-level laws did direct us to rival motor controls, then there would be a potential for conflict between the different powers involved and, in cases of harmony, the higher-level powers would have to be seen as reinforcing the microphysical powers.

As an aside, it should be noticed that the fact that higher-level laws do not direct us to independent motor controls need not mean that every particular macrolevel control that we invoke is bound to be something less than a motor control. It may happen in this description that a macrolevel control is just the same particular — the same property-instance — as the corresponding microlevel control. This will mean that it has a dual aspect. As an abstract property it will count as a higher-level control, on a par with other macrophysical factors. As a concrete property-instance it will count as a motor control, on a par with microphysical factors (Macdonald and Macdonald 1986).*

What of the remaining sort of approach to the motor connection — the intermediate approach that directs us to the material mode but in a way that defers to certain paradigms, and perhaps to what science is capable of revealing in those paradigms? This approach may say that the motor connection is that sort of relationship — one that has a natural salience for us and one whose features should be available to reflection — involved in certain paradigms. Or it may say that it is that sort of relationship which science is likely to uncover or define — say, a relationship involving a transfer of energy or, at a certain level, a locality of contact — in those paradigms. The approach assumes that the paradigm cases point us to a definite kind and the connection is picked out rigidly as that relationship which unifies those cases in the actual world.

This intermediate approach points in the same way as the first on the question before us. For all that the approach says on the motor connection, it is possible for higher-level programmers in general to satisfy the connection. It is possible for a higher-level programmer to control for a given event, for example, and to control for it in a manner that involves even something apparently so fitted for microphysical causes as a transfer of energy. It is possible for the redness of the rag to control for the bull's anger in such a manner or for the rise in unemployment to control in that way for an increase in the level of crime. The realization of the higher-level property leads to the event and leads to it in a way that involves a transfer of energy; the realization of the higher-level property does not merely connect with the result in the fashion of an inert control. Therefore when a macrocontrol and a microcontrol relate in the programming way, they can both count as motor controls for the event that ensues. They can each involve a transfer of energy — the same transfer of energy, no doubt — and

---

* Under the singularism mentioned in the footnote to p. 412, the fact that the property-instance is an instance of the higher-level property will be just as relevant — in fact, just as irrelevant — to its efficacy as the fact that it is an instance of a microphysical property or group of properties. But there will still be an asymmetry between microphysical and macrophysical properties, since many macrophysical controllers — those which cannot be co-instantiated with microphysical controls — will be systematically deprived of the status of motor controls.

they can each be hailed, at different levels in the program architecture, as things that served to bring the event about.

It has already been stated that it is possible in principle for either of the first two approaches to the motor connection to allow higher-level programmers as motor controls. Not every version of those approaches will do so, of course, but this is not the place to debate specific proposals; I am content to defend the more abstract point. In conclusion, however, I would like to buttress the abstract point by mentioning some reasons why we should avoid the third approach and go along with one of the first two. For the record, my own preference is for the intermediate approach, but I shall not defend that preference in the present context.*

A first point to notice about the third, irreducibilist, approach is that it is hostage to empirical theory in a way in which the first two are not. Some physicists speculate that there may be no bottom microphysical level, as I mentioned earlier in passing, and it is interesting that this would plausibly mean, on the irreducibilist approach, that there are not really any motor connections to be found in the world. It would seem to be an arbitrary choice on the part of the irreducibilist to pick out one level in an infinitely extended progression of levels downward and to say that there, at that level, is where we find the 'oompz' that is allegedly characteristic of motor connections. The absence of a bottom level would not make any problem, of course, for the first, formal-mode, approach and neither need it cause a difficulty with the intermediate approach; the feature that is characteristic of the motor connection can be quite compatible, for all we know, with an infinite progression downwards.

A second point against the irreducibilist approach is that it would force us to give substantive significance to choices of representation that appear to be more or less arbitrary. Do we say that the malleability of the eraser is just the molecular structure—and ultimately, we presume, the microphysical configuration—that leads to bending under suitable pressure? Or do we say that it is the higher-order state of having such a molecular (and microphysical) structure that leads to bending under that pressure? Intuitively this is a free and arbitrary choice of presentation—a matter of book-keeping, not of discovery. (Jackson and Pettit 1988). However, under the irreducibilist approach it is a matter of the deepest ontological significance. Under the first approach the malleability can count as a motor control, since its instance will just be the same thing as the instance of the microphysical control. Under the second approach it cannot; its instance does not coincide with the instance of the microphysical control.

---

* For the record, I tend to think of motor controls as controls that are analogous to the controls represented by our actions, as when I push and the table moves, or I blow and the candle goes out.

Any approach that gives such significance to ontological book-keeping ought to be suspect.

A third and related point against the irreducibilist approach is that it forces us to recognize a difference where intuitively there is none. Determinable properties are co-instantiated, of necessity, with their more determinate versions: the redness of this rag is co-instantiated with the particular shade of red, and let us suppose with the particular microphysical realizer of that shade, which disturbs the bull. With such a determinable property, then, we must regard it as a motor control of anything for which it programs. But there is no intuitive difference between the way that the redness programs for the bull's reaction and the way that other sorts of property have programming effects — the way that the squareness of the peg programs for its being prevented from going through the round hole or the way that the rise in unemployment programs for the increase in crime. On the third, irreducibility, approach there ought to be a glaring metaphysical chasm dividing these cases. However, there is no obvious gap to be found there.

The upshot of such considerations, then, is that things look good for the special sciences, and indeed for common sense. Under the most pessimistic scenario, that associated with the irreducibilist picture of the causal connection, the special sciences are generally going to identify factors that count as more than just instrumental controls — factors that count as programmers.* Under more likely scenarios the special sciences are going to count as uncovering real full-blooded causes — causes in the same motor sense as that which applies in microphysics. It is true that the causes uncovered in microphysics are going to come lower in the hierarchical programming architecture, and it is true that once the microphysical motor controls are in place, then everything else is in place also. But these considerations are quite compatible with the thought that higher-level controls are real and important and that higher-level controls are of the motor kind.

If there is any lingering resistance to this idea, then I suspect that it will come from the thought that in principle microphysics could do all that the special sciences do in the recognition of higher-level causes: it could, in principle, identify the laws and the controls associated with those sciences by identifying the different ways in which the laws or controls may be instantiated and by recognizing that each mode of instantiation leads to a certain sort of effect. But this possibility is entirely abstract — it supposes an ideal epistemology that we can never approximate — and in any case the

---

* Non-programming controls may also be worth investigating. My picture of rational choice theory (Pettit 1993a, Chapter 5) suggests that outside market-like contexts such theory involves the identification of standby causes that help to stabilize certain patterns of behaviour — that render them resilient — without actually causing people generally to produce the behaviour.

lesson that it teaches sounds a positive note. What it means is that when we involve ourselves in the special sciences then we track the laws and controls—the real and important laws and controls—that an ideal microphysics would address in a different idiom. What it means is that research in the special sciences—research in chemistry and biology, psychology and social science, even research of a common-sense type—can be seen as microphysics by other means.

ACKNOWLEDGEMENTS

This chapter was written during 2 months in Paris, where I held visiting appointments, first at the Ecole des Hautes Etudes en Sciences Sociales (CEMS centre), and then at the Ecole Polytechnique (CREA centre). I am grateful to both institutions for their support. I benefited greatly from the stimulus I received in thinking about the topic of the Chapter from exchanges with a number of colleagues there and from comments on an earlier draft by Pascal Engel, Pierre Jacob, and, especially, Frank Doring. I owe a particular debt of gratitude to John Broome, Frank Jackson, and Peter Menzies for discussions of certain points.

REFERENCES

Blackburn, S. (1991). Losing your mind. In *The future of folk psychology* (ed. J. Greenwood), pp. 196–225. Oxford University Press, New York.

Block, N. (1990). Can the mind change the world? In *Meaning and method: essays in honour of Hilary Putnam* (ed. G. Boolos), pp. 137–70. Cambridge University Press.

Crane, T. (1991). 'Way Indeed? Papineau on supervenience and the completeness of Payous. *Analysis* **50**, 32–7.

Crane, T. and Mellor, D. H. (1989). There is no question of physicalism. *Mind* **99**, 185–206.

Jackson, F. (1994). Armchair metaphysics. In *Philosophy in Mind* (ed. J. O'Leary-Hawthorne and M. Michael). Kluwer, Dordrecht.

Jackson, F. and Pettit, P. (1988). Functionalism and broad content. *Mind* **97**, 381–400.

Jackson, F. and Pettit, P. (1990). Program explanation: a general perspective. *Analysis* **50**, 107–17.

Jacob, P. (1991–2). Externalism and mental causation. Proceedings of the Aristotelian Society **92**, 203–19.

Lewis, D. (1983). New work of a theory of universals, *Australasian Journal of Philosophy* **61**, 343–77.

Lewis, D. (1986). *Philosopical papers*, Vol. 2. Oxford University Press.

Lewis, D. (forthcoming). Reduction of mind. In *A companion to philosophy of mind* (ed. S. Guttenplan). Blackwell, Oxford.

Macdonald, G. (1992). The nature of naturalism. *Proceedings of the Aristotelian Society* (Suppl.), **66**, 225–44.

Macdonald, C. and Macdonald, G. (1986). Mental causes and expl anation of action. *Philosophical Review* **36**, 145–58.

Menzies, P. and Price, H. (1993). Causality as a secondary quality. *British Journal for the Philosophy of Science* **44**, 187–203.

Papineau (1990). Why supervenience? *Analysis* **50**, 66–71.

Pettit, P. (1992). The nature of naturalism. *Proceedings of the Aristotelian Society* (Suppl.), **66**, 245–66.

Pettit, P. (1993*a*). *The common mind: an essay on psychology, society, and politics* Oxford University Press, New York.

Pettit, P. (1993*b*). A definition of physicalism. *Analysis* **53**, 213–33.

Pettit, P. (forthcoming). Microphysicalism without contingent micro–macro laws, *Analysis* **54**.

Smart, J. J. C. (1978). The content of physicalism. *Philosophical Quarterly* **28**, 339–41.

Smith, P. (1992). Modest reductions and the unity of science. In *Reduction, explanation, and realism* (ed. D. Charles and K. Lennon). Oxford University Press.

Yablo, S. (1992). Mental causation. *Philosophical Review* **101**, 245–80.

DISCUSSION

Participants: D. Andler, F. Döring, P. Jacob, M. Kistler, D. Sperber

Andler: The ontology of microphysics, as you see it, seems to include not only microphysical entities, space–time, operators on microphysical entities, and operators on space–time, but also any relation or operator of whatever arity, as well as higher-order relations and operators. For example, when you state that the realization of the triangular property, in your imaginary example, 'involves' the realization of certain ball-level properties, surely you mean to include at least either n-ary relations with unbounded n or higher-order relations, and possibly both. My question then is how to distinguish such a generous microphysical ontology from an ordinary macrophysical one. I have no qualms, for instance, about squareness or roundness when only a (small) number of particles are concerned, but I do worry about round holes and square pegs.

If one allows a broad definition of the microphysical ontology, then one must distinguish it from the proprietary domain of microphysics, which is considerably narrower. As you clearly imply yourself (and contrary to what Putnam suggests when he proposes this example), microphysics has at present nothing at all to say about square pegs not fitting in round holes; moreover, as you also allow, there is not the slightest reason to believe that it will ever have anything to say. But, if that is so, what plausibility remains to the claim (which you do not endorse but do take into consideration) that 'in principle microphysics could do all that the special sciences do in the recognition of higher-level causes'? What more is involved in seeing research in the special sciences as 'microphysics by other means' than disposing with elegant humour of a rather unpromising philosophical speculation?

Pettit: Andler asks whether I am excessively generous in my understanding of the ontology of microphysics. I take this question, specifically, to be the following. Does my admission that certain irreducible relations, besides those of space–time, may play an important role in microphysics involve the admission that microphysical reality, as traditionally conceived, is not all that there is? Does it involve the admission that there may be a macrophysical reality that does not supervene on the microphysical, in a traditional narrow construal, but that emerges as a new realm?

I think not. To believe that there are certain primitive non-local relations that play a microphysical part is to be a non-atomist about the microphysical level. But to believe in such microphysical non-atomism is not necessarily to believe in macrophysical emergentism; it is not necessarily to believe that there is a novel non-supervenient macrophysical realm. Irreducible microphysical relations of the kind envisaged would have as good a claim as any other relations or properties in this area to be regarded as microphysical. Who can be sure that there are no such relations still to be identified?

I have argued elsewhere (Pettit 1993a) that in social ontology it is important to distinguish the question as to whether human beings depend non-causally on their relations with one another for the possession of any fundamental capacities, such as the capacity for thought, and the question as to whether human beings are vulnerable to structural laws or forces which do not supervene on what happens at the level of human psychology but come on stream independently of that psychology and represent novel pressures on human behaviour. The first question bears on whether non-atomism holds, the second on whether some sort of emergentism is in order. I have argued in defence of such non-atomism — such holism — and against such emergentism in the social area. I see no reason why a similar combination — non-atomism and non-emergentism — might not hold at the microphysical level.

Andler also asks whether there is any plausibility to my concession that 'in principle microphysics could do all that the special sciences do in the recognition of higher-level causes'. I think that there is, in the following anaemic sense. Imagine a god-like microphysicist who had a thorough understanding of all microphysical laws, a complete grasp of the microphysical conditions that actually obtain and actually engage those laws, and that might obtain and might engage those laws, a full sense of what will happen under actual conditions and what would happen under counterfactual conditions, and an insight into everything that is entailed by such patterns. Such a subject, I claim, would recognize all the truths which we may have to rely on the special sciences to reveal to us. She would recognize all the laws and predictions of the special sciences, for example, since they would all be entailed, under the supervenience thesis, by the microphysical patterns (Jackson 1994). When I say that the special sciences represent 'microphysics by other means', I intend only to draw attention to this connection between the patterns displayed in the special sciences and the microphysical basis for those patterns.

Döring: I think that I understand your definition of instrumental control, but I worry that this is because I illegitimately translate it into causal or action language, made easy by phrases such as 'it makes sense to', 'with a view to', or 'means–ends'. I find it difficult to square my intuitive understanding with your gloss on probabilities and with some of the examples. You say that instrumental controls are 'probabilifiers'. From your comments I gather that you want to affirm that if C is an instrumental control for an effect E, then $P(E|C) > p(E)$ (or some quantified version of this). Now, surely we never have completely unconditional probabilities. So what we want to say is that $p(E|C.B) > p(E.B)$, for some suitable set of background conditions B. But now we have a problem about how to specify B. If we let B equal all of our background knowledge, then causes will not always be instrumental controls as they should. If we know that John has terminal cancer, then learning that he has a car accident does not increase the probability of his death before the year's end: $p(\text{death}|\text{cancer} + \text{accident}) = p(\text{death}|\text{cancer})$. (The same holds, *mutatis mutandis*, for supervening macro- and subvening micro-causes or controls—unless they are necessarily connected.) In order for cancer to be a probabilifier of death, concurrent and standby causes have to be excluded from B. But using causal notions (or the notion of instrumental control) in order to constrain B (if it could be done, of which I am not sure) would be to move in an explanatory circle. How else can we specify B?

Also, I do not quite understand what it means to say that 'whenever we have a law which relates the satisfaction of some antecedents to the satisfaction of a consequent, then the antecedent-property is a control or controller for the consequent'. Take Boyle's gas law $PV = rT$, which entails conditionals such as 'If the pressure of an ideal gas is raised, then the ratio of temperature to volume increases'. But pressure is not in instrumental control: we cannot change it directly, we can only change it indirectly by changing volume or temperature. Does Boyle's law not count, or is the inferred conditional illegitimate?

Pettit: Döring's question about the connection between the notion of a control and a probabilifier has caused me to make some revisions in my formulations. I had inadvisedly said that a control always serves to make that for which it controls more probable than it would otherwise have been, neglecting the fact, pointed out by Döring, than it will not do this if some other factor has already raised the probability of the controlled event beyond improvement. For example, if someone's having cancer makes it certain that he will die before the year is out, then his being in a fatal car accident does nothing to raise the probability of that event. My response to Döring's challenge is to replace the notion of a probabilifier with that of a *pro tanto* probabilifier—a factor that raises the probability or that is fit to raise the probability, being of a kind that raises it in various other contexts. But he has also led me to downplay probabilistic notions in my exposition of the relationship whereby one factor controls for another. I see now that such notions are as likely to raise dust around the question of what it means for one factor to control for another as they are to throw light on that issue.

There may seem to be another way to answer Döring's challenge: distinguish between raising the probability of a result and reinforcing its probability, where to reinforce its probability is to raise it in some possible world and to do so without lowering it in the actual world. Does a control always raise or reinforce the probability of the controlled event? Unfortunately, no.* A factor may cause something to occur, and therefore control for it, while at the same time putting out of action, not just pre-empting, a potential cause that made the event more probable still. It causes the event, and is therefore a control for it, but nevertheless it lowered the probability that the event would occur.

Jacob: As you yourself clearly acknowledge, your notion of a probabilifying controller-property is much wider than the notion of a property to which you are willing to grant a role in a causal explanation of an event. You can have, as you point out, *inert* controls in the form of what you call *standby* causes and *non-causal* factors. An example of the latter might be that my wife's being married to me is a controller of her becoming a widow, since her eventually becoming a widow is made more probable by her being married to me than it would be were she a spinster. You give a telling example of a standby cause when you mention a person's having cancer and dying of a car accident. Therefore you want to be able to set aside standby causes such as the having-cancer property of a person killed in a car accident. You propose to set aside such standby causes by appeal to your notion of a *programmer* property. I want to pressure you on how appealing to a programmer property (in your sense) will do the job that you want it to do.

You say that although the cancer controlled the person's death 'in the weak sense of making it suitably probable ... still, it does not count as a programmer of the event. The reason is that death does not come about at the level of specific organic breakdown in the manner associated with cancer ...'. Now, your notion of a programmer-property has three conditions, the second and third of which are designed to handle such a case.

2. However H is realized at the microlevel ..., the realizing properties are apt to be motor controls responsible for an E-type event.

---

* I am grateful to Peter Menzies for making this clear to me.

3. The microlevel properties that actually realize H are motor controls that are responsible for E in the manner envisaged in condition 2.'

Thus, on your view, if the E-type event is death from a car accident, then having cancer will not be a programmer-property because it will not program the realizing properties responsible for bringing about death in the right manner, and hence it will not be the right sort of controller for the E-type event.

My worry is that being a programmer-property (and hence a control of the right sort) will then heavily depend on the description used to identify the explanandum (the E-type event). Condition 2 says that 'the realizing properties are apt to be motor controls responsible for an E-type event'. In this formulation I detect a dependence of what may count as a motor control upon the way one identifies the E-type event to be explained. If the E-type event to be explained is the person's death within 2 years or an event of the type 'being reported in the *Times*' obituary section in the year such and such', then, it seems to me, what you want to call a standby cause will turn out to be a programmer-property and hence a control of the right sort. Therefore you must be able to sort out the right descriptions of an explanandum (the E-type event) from the wrong ones before you can distinguish the genuine from the spurious controls. Arguably, however, sorting the relevant descriptions of an explanandum from the irrelevant ones appears to depend on a prior distinction between properties of a causal factor which seem to be genuine motor factors from ones which seem spurious. Thus there seems to be a circularity lurking somewhere.

Pettit: Jacob raises a question that also bears on the example of the cancer victim who dies in a car accident. While the cancer controls for the victim dying within the year — in fact it makes that event inevitable — it does not program for the dying and is not causally relevant to it. Jacob agrees that that indeed is what I should want to say but thinks that I do not have the resources for supporting such a line.

I argue that the cancer does not program for the victim's dying within the year, because the organic way in which the cancer is realized is not causally relevant to the death, and *a fortiori* is not causally relevant to the victim's dying within the year. In order for a factor to program for the occurrence of a certain type of event, the various ways in which it can be realized must be apt to be causally relevant to an event of that type and — this is the crucial condition — the way in which it is actually realized must be causally relevant to the event that actually takes place. The cancer controls for the victim's dying within the year — it necessitates that result — but it does not satisfy this crucial condition for programming and for counting as causally relevant. The organic realizer of the cancer has no causal relevance whatsoever to the victim's dying.

But does not the organic realizer have relevance to the victim's dying within the year and so does not the cancer program for the result under that description? That is Jacob's challenge, as I understand it. In reply, I distinguish. The organic realizer may be relevant to the truth of the following claim: there will be an event — perhaps this, perhaps that — which will involve the victim dying within the year. However, that does not mean that the organic realizer is relevant in a causal way to the actual event that involves the victim's dying within the year. The relevance in question is not a form of causal relevance, only of the relevance associated with necessitation and control. It is not a form of relevance to the actual event that involves the victim's dying within the year, only to the fact that there will be an event of that kind.

Kistler: The 'programme model' was initially intended as a theory of *explanation* at different levels. In your paper, you try to apply it to the *ontological* analysis of causation as well. You suggest that the program model could elucidate the relation between properties of a given event which are causally efficacious at different levels of determination, On your view, a higher-level property could be causally efficacious by way of being a programming (more general, Icss specific) property for one of a set of more determinate microphysical properties (that it programs for).

However, I believe that it is misleading to transfer the model from the theory of explanation to ontology, for the following reason. The scientific investigation of a causal process will, in general, lead to the discovery of *one* definite level of determination which is most appropriate to account for the production of the effect event.

At least that seems to be true for your examples. In the case of the bull's excitation by the redness of the rag, it should be possible to determine a certain definite range of wavelengths to which the receptors and nervous connections of the bull are tuned. It is a perfectly empirical task to find the range of maximum excitability of the bull. Let us assume that it corresponds to the part of the spectrum which we identify as red. This means that it would simply be *wrong on empirical grounds* to move 'upwards' in the scale of abstractness and to hold, say, perception of a warm colour as responsible.

In contrast, to name a property which is too determinate will not be inaccurate, but simply accurate, in describing the causal process in question. In a particular case it may then be correct to say that the rag's being scarlet caused the bull to be excited. But, as a matter of fact, it might have no difference at all to the bull's humour if the rag had been ruby or some other shade of red rather than scarlet. There is exactly one level of determination which is maximally adequate to the process in question. In this case the reason is that (the initial segment of) the event effect (i.e. the perception of red) selects exactly one such level of determination.

In choosing or evaluating an *explanation*, however, we must obey pragmatic criteria. If some auditor is explicitly interested in the specific colour of the rag, it will be appropriate to mention its being scarlet; it may even be appropriate to explain the event by reference to the actual rag's being of a warm colour.

It is the latter case which makes a definite contrast with the ontological question: only with respect to a *representation* of the cause event in question, as it might be used in the context of explanation, is it possible to select a more general, less informative, and more abstract level of determination of the property referred to as causally responsible, i.e. less determinate compared with the level at which it has been identified as efficacious in the production of the event to be explained. In general, it will be misleading to go below that level, although in special cases (see above) it may be appropriate for pragmatic reasons.

The same point can be made with respect to your example of the square peg in the round hole: you best *explain* the event of the peg's staying on the grid with reference to the geometrical facts even if they are not themselves physically efficacious. Explanation is precisely the domain where the programme model works. It is much more economical and parsimonious to leave the mircophysical details of forces between the peg and the grid aside, and to mention only the geometrical constellation which amounts to a quantification over the (large) set of possible realizing atomic (repulsive) interactions. However, from a physical point of view, the geometrical form is simply not causally relevant at all. There are no geometrical interactions.

In that sense it is misleading to use the model to give an account of the relation of different *ontologically relevant levels* of a causal relation; as to the description of the actual causal process, there is one highest level of determinateness which is actually characteristic of the type of causal relation in question. Finding that level is left to empirical inquiry.

Pettit: Kistler raises a number of questions, but the central one is a doubt as to whether I keep ontological and pragmatic matters sufficiently separate in my account of the program model of higher-order causal relevance. His picture is that for any event, taken as of a certain type, there is one privileged level at which we can identify the properties that are causally relevant to its realization and that if we seem to find causally relevant properties at other levels, that is an illusion: Really, what we are finding at other levels are properties that it is pragmatically useful to mention in giving an explanation of the event.

When I describe a property as causally relevant to a certain event, I mean that to have information about the presence of that property is to have information of some relevant kind about the causal genesis of the event in question. It is to have information such that someone who lacked it would not understand some aspect of the genesis of the event. How in this sense can properties at different levels be causally relevant to one and the same event (Pettit 1993*a*, 256-7)? Well, a high-level property may be relevant in the sense that the presence of the property means that at some lower level there will be properties present — properties that realize the higher-level property — sufficient to produce an event of the kind in question. A property at that lower level may be relevant in the sense that it is the presence of that property, rather than the presence of any of the other possible realizers of the higher-level property that actually plays a role in the genesis of the event. Not to have information about the high level property would be to miss the fact that the event in question is not dependent for its realization on the presence of the precise lower-level property that is involved. Not to have information about the lower-level property would be to remain in ignorance about how exactly the event came to be realized at that level.

Having identified the class of causally relevant properties in this manner, I can go on to agree with Kistler that in some explanatory contexts mention of these properties here is pertinent, whereas in others mention of those properties there is more to the point. In other words, I can agree that there are pragmatic criteria of relevance that come into play in determining what sorts of answers should be given to different explanatory questions. But from my point of view, pragmatic criteria of this kind come into play fairly late in the game. In particular, they come into play after the stage at which we have a picture of different levels of causally relevant factors.

An analogy may help to make my perspective more persuasive. Everyone agrees that it is possible to find earlier and later causes for any event, and that at any stage in that diachronic chain of causation it is possible to identify a number of relevant synchronic factors: the striking of the match and the presence of the oxygen are both relevant to combustion. Everyone also agrees that pragmatic criteria come into play after the point at which these distinctions are available and that they indicate which factor at which stage in the chain it is going to be explanatorily pertinent to mention in different contexts. My picture is that things assume a similar profile in regard to the hierarchical dimension of causation — the hierarchical as distinct from the diachronic and synchronic dimensions. We can identify causally relevant factors at different levels, as we can identify different diachronic and synchronic causal factors, and it is only after those distinctions are available that pragmatic criteria come into play and determine which level it is appropriate to focus on in different contexts.

Sperber: One question that may be raised about common-sense representations of causality—the study of which is central to this conference—is the extent to which these representations are compatible with modern physicalists' views of the universe. After all, common sense is not monist, let alone physicalist in a modern sense. It could be that cause–effect relationships, as they are commonsensically understood, do not really exist. It could be that common representations of causality are systematic misrepresentations. You argue that they are not, and you even conclude that common-sense investigation of causal relationships 'can be seen as microphysics by other means'. This is good news to students of causal cognition, but I am not sure of the extent to which you are prepared to vindicate common causal understanding in this way. In particular, there seem to be disjoint forms of causal understanding, most notably push–pull mechanical causation on one side and intentional causation on the other. Do you want to argue that common-sense causal–intentional explanation involves some idea of motor control in the same manner as does common-sense mechanical explanation? Or, to put the question in more general terms: Is there *nothing* seriously wrong with common-sense causal understanding, despite its unacceptable pluralistic ontological foundations?

Pettit: Sperber identifies a crucial issue. He asks how far I am prepared to find that perhaps common sense is in error about causation—perhaps our ordinary causal understanding is misconceived in some serious way. The question is well put, because under the physicalist metaphysic that I adopt, there are higher-level causal linkages of the kind that common sense and the special sciences aspire to track only if the microphysical world obliges—only if it makes available the sorts of motor controls that such linkages presuppose. It ought to be an open possibility that in some cases the microphysical world does not oblige at all and it ought to be an open possibility, as Sperber stresses in particular, that the microphysical world obliges in such diverse ways for different cases of higher-level causation that we cannot continue to think of such causation as a single category. He illustrates this second possibility with reference to the different microphysical ways in which we may assume that higher-level mechanical causation is realized on the one side and higher-level intentional causation on the other.

In my paper I mentioned those philosophical projects, the dominant enterprises in contemporary analytical thought, which attempt to vindicate commonplace discourses under the hardest scientific assumptions—which attempt to reconcile the manifest, commonsense image of things with the scientific image. Such projects explore the possibility of analysing the central concepts of the commonplace discourse—concepts of colour or value or mentality or whatever—in such a way that they retain a reference in the physicalistic world to which science points us. This paper is an attempt, in this vein, to explore the possibility of analysing higher-level causation—the causation of the manifest image—in such a way that we can continue to give it countenance within the naturalistic or physicalistic picture described in the first section.

The paper does not claim to save the full appearances of higher-level causation. It argues that higher-level controlling factors, and higher-level pregamming factors, can be readily admitted within the physicalistic picture. But it acknowledges that whether higher-level programmers are to count as full causal factors, as motor controls of a kind with the motor controls of microphysics, depends on which broad view is adopted about how to distinguish motor controls from inert controls—which of the three views that I described as formal-mode, material-mode, and intermediate-mode. I admit that if the material-mode view is is embraced, i.e. if causation proper is associated with the presence of an irreducible efficacy—an 'oomph' or 'bif'—then higher-level causes must be downgaded by the physicalist from the status that they enjoy within ordinary thinking, and in that sense common sense must be judged to be mistaken. I suggest, however, that that is not an attractive position and that things are still looking good for our everyday understandings of causality.

What of Sperber's suggestion that if microphysics reveals very different mechanisms at work in different instances of higher-level causality, then that shows that really there is not a single category here? I am not inclined to concede on this point. My hunch, as mentioned in the footnote to p. 418 is that we ordinary folk conceive of motor controls—real causes—as controls that are similar in various ways to those controls that we experience as we push tables around and blow out candles. If this is right, then we are not committed to there being any single physical essence, as it were, to causation; for all we know, there may be no single physical basis to the similarity that we find so salient. Causation may be a functional kind that is unified by the role it plays—a role it may play on different bases in different cases—rather than a natural kind that is identified by a single physical nature.

14

The role of content in the explanation of behaviour
PIERRE JACOB

INTRODUCTION

Intentions, beliefs, desires, conjectures, fears, etc. are what philosophers call propositional attitudes. Such mental states are supposed to be internal to a person or an individual, and hence not publicly observable by a third person. They are called propositional attitudes because humans ascribe such states to other members of their species by means of a complex sentence containing a verb expressing the individual's attitude towards the propositional content expressed by the clause embedded under the verb.

Common sense tells us that propositional attitudes have both causal and intentional properties. They are causes and they have content. They have effects and they are semantically evaluable. Beliefs, in particular, can be causes, and they are true or false (correct or incorrect) representations of states of affairs. An organism's perceptual beliefs result from causal interactions between the organism and his or her environment. Beliefs and other propositional attitudes are causes and effects of other mental states; beliefs generate other beliefs. Desires also generate beliefs, as in the case of wishful thinking. Beliefs and desires produce intentional actions or behaviour. My belief that the glass in front of me contains water (together with my desire for a sip of water) causes me to pick up the glass. Here, I shall concentrate on the production of action or behaviour.*

---

* As this paragraph makes clear, I agree with Keil who pointed out in the discussion that of course beliefs do not always lead to behaviour; they also lead to other beliefs and desires. In this paper, however, I concentrate on the contribution of beliefs to intentional actions. But I disagree with Keil when he says that actions can be independent of beliefs 'as in the actions caused by neural stimulation of muscles, in dreams, reflex and startle responses'. We need to distinguish bodily motions, behaviour and actions. Unlike the cause of an individual's bodily motion (which may be external to the individual), the cause of an individual's behaviour has to be internal to the individual. Unlike the cause of an individual's behaviour, the cause of an individual's action must be an intentional state (a propositional attitude) of the individual.

Two common-sense theses of unequal strength on mental causation will be distinguished in this chapter: the weaker thesis is that beliefs are causes, and the stronger thesis is that intentional properties of beliefs are causal properties. In the first three sections, reasons why a physicalist might view the stronger thesis with suspicion are suggested. In the three following sections, three strategies designed to save the stronger thesis are examined and criticized. In the first six sections, it is assumed, with the weaker common-sense thesis, that beliefs *do* cause behaviour. In the final section, a strategy which abandons this assumption is examined.

TOKEN PHYSICALISM

Contemporary philosophers of mind borrow a distinction from philosophers of language which has been made famous (I believe) by Peirce: the distinction between types and tokens. Consider different tokens of the word 'banana'. All such tokens are instances of the same abstract word-type. Each token of the word is a concrete particular physical object. Some tokens are written symbols; others are spoken symbols. Written tokens (inscriptions) have optical properties that can be detected by a camera; spoken tokens (utterances) have acoustic properties that can be detected by a tape-recorder. Distinct inscriptions of the word 'banana' may have distinct optical properties. Distinct utterances of the same word-type may have distinct acoustic properties. However, all these distinct tokens share the same semantic or intentional property; they all denote or refer to members of the class of bananas. Alternatively, they stand for, denote, or refer to the class of bananas, or they express the property of being a banana.*

This is a clear case of multiple realization of a higher-order property — the semantic or intentional property of all tokens of the word 'banana' — by distinct physical properties. Now, symbol tokens typically enter causal interactions in the processes whereby they are detected (or perceived) by physical devices such as a camera, a tape-recorder, or a human eye or ear. Prima facie, such physical devices pick up physical (optical or acoustical) properties, and not semantic or intentional properties, of symbol tokens. Therefore it seems rather natural to assume that symbol tokens enter causal interactions by virtue of their physical (optical or acoustical) properties, not by virtue of their semantic or intentional properties.

On the standard version of token physicalism, the mental relates to the physical as the intentional property of a linguistic symbol relates to its

* I assume that different tokens of a word belong to a type by virtue of their common semantic or (intentional) property. This assumption is made more or less inevitable, I believe, as soon as one says that an inscription and an utterance of a word can be two tokens of one and the same word-type.

physical properties. On this picture, which I find myself driven to adopt, a mental state token – a belief token – is said to be identical to a physical state token (a brain-state token). A mental or intentional property is not assumed to be identical (nor reducible) to a physical property (let alone a physical property of an individual's brain state). None the less it is assumed to be *realized* by, or *supervenient* upon, some physical property.* Clearly, according to this way of thinking, physical properties are more primitive and more fundamental than intentional (or mental) properties. The latter are derivative from or upon the former. If the set of basic physical facts (or states of affairs) in the world is fixed, the intentional or mental facts (or states of affairs) in that world are thereby fixed.

Type physicalists entertain the thought that the genuine nature of each intentional property consists in some (complex) physical property or other (perhaps some complex physical property of an individual's brain). On the type physicalist picture, the identity between a given intentional property and some specific physical property is rather like the chemical identity expressed by 'water = H_2O'. The view is that the physical property that a given intentional property consists in is not stipulated but is a matter for empirical discovery.

However, token physicalists have given up the type identity thesis (the identity between intentional and physical properties). They embrace the view that the instantiation of an intentional property on a given occasion is nothing over and above the instantiation of some physical property on this occasion, even though the instantiation of one and the same intentional property on different occasions is not 'realized' by one and the same physical property on each occasion. Given the physicalistic secondary status of intentional properties, and on the plausible assumption that a disjunctive set of physical properties is not a natural kind of physical property, this comes perilously close to assuming that intentional properties have no nature at all!

In discussing token physicalism, I have focused on the contrast between semantic and physical properties of symbol tokens. Token physicalists assume that an individual's beliefs (and concepts) are brain state tokens of the individual. Admittedly, unlike concepts (and beliefs), tokens of a type of English word are tokens of a non-mental, external, or public representation. Like tokens of linguistic symbols, however, tokens of mental representations presumably have both contents (or intentional properties) and physical properties. Given that the causal properties of symbols seem

---

* A set of properties M is said to supervene on a set of basic (or subvenient) properties P if no M-property would be instantiated unless a P-property were. The instantiation of any pair of distinct higher-level M-properties requires the instantiation of a pair of distinct P-properties. However, two distinct basic P-properties may underlie the instantiation of a single M-property.

to be their physical properties (not their intentional properties), one may well wonder how, in the words of Perry and Israel (1991, p. 166), 'can causal and content properties of tokens mesh'.

COMMON SENSE AND MENTAL CAUSATION

On our common-sense understanding of how beliefs cause actions, content and causal properties seem to go hand in hand. The content of my belief that the glass in front of me contains water seems quite relevant to what I do when I extend my right arm, pick up the glass with my right hand, raise the glass to my lips, tilt my head slightly backwards, and drink water from the glass. My limbs perform these complicated motions because of what I believe. Had I not believed what I believe, I would not have done all this (for an evaluation of the vindication of the causal efficacy of intentional properties of beliefs by such counterfactuals see p. 441). In addition, I have many other beliefs with different contents (different intentional properties). For example, I believe that Bill Clinton is the recently elected President of the USA. However, I did not pick up the glass and drink water from it because I believe that Bill Clinton is the recently elected President of the USA. Therefore, on our common-sense understanding of what I do, the intentional property of my belief — its content — just *seems* to be one of its causal properties.* This should be puzzling on minimal physicalist assumptions.

It is no objection to common sense to point out that my desire for water also plays a causal role in my behaviour. True, had I not experienced a yearning for water, plausibly I would not have picked up the glass and drunk from it. However, it is not part of common sense to assume that behaviour has one, and only one, cause. Rather, it is part of common sense to assume that the intentional property of a mental state (belief and/or desire) is a causal property of the mental state. This thesis will be denoted the causal efficacy of intentional properties (CEIP). CEIP should puzzle a physicalist.

Common sense can afford to be as ontologically profligate as it sees fit. As far as mental causation is concerned, common sense may well be attracted to substance dualism: the famous view held by Descartes, according to which mental causes are made out of a different stuff (unextended thought) than physical causes. Physicalism cannot afford such ontological licence. From the standpoint of token physicalism, which

---

* Other causal properties of a belief might include what makes a belief a belief (as opposed to some other propositional attitude), not to mention the physical properties of the brain state token which, by assumption, the belief is.

I will accept, every token of an individual's propositional attitude is a brain state token of the individual. Since, presumably, brain state tokens can be bona fide causes, so too, if token physicalism is accepted, can tokens of propositional attitudes. Therefore token physicalism vindicates the naive psychological thesis that propositional attitudes can be causes. This thesis will be denoted the minimal causal thesis (MCT).

However, common sense does not merely assume (with MCT) that beliefs are causes; it also assumes CEIP—the thesis that intentional properties of beliefs are causal properties or that beliefs can cause various things to happen by virtue of their intentional properties. In other words, it assumes that intentional properties—contents—of beliefs are causally efficacious. However, unlike type physicalists, token physicalists refrain from embracing the view that intentional properties of mental state tokens are identical (or reducible) to physical properties of an individual's brain state tokens. Hence, from the standpoint of token physicalism, a belief token—being an individual's brain state token—will be held to have a number of properties. It may have various physical (e.g. electrical, chemical, and other such properties) and functional properties, and it may have an intentional property as well, such as the belief that a given glass contains water. As the examples of tokens of word types suggest, physical (optical or acoustical) properties, not semantic properties, are causal properties of symbol tokens.

Dretske (1988*a*, *b*) has supplied a number of examples which should motivate a physicalist's scepticism towards CEIP. Acoustic vibrations in the air may shatter glass; they may also have a meaning, or semantic properties, but it is not the semantics of the acoustic vibrations that is efficacious in the shattering of the glass. In Dennett's (1987) words, 'the brain is a syntactic engine'. Dennett's (1991, p. 119) claim that 'a semantic engine is a mechanistic impossibility—like a perpetual motion machine' seems fairly widely accepted. On this view, a mechanism may move gears and possess intentional or semantic properties, but it cannot move gears by virtue of its semantic or intentional properties. Although there are significant differences between Stich's (1983) syntactic view of the mind and Fodor's (1981) formality condition (or methodological solipsism), they both seem to accept the view that a semantic engine is a physical impossibility.

MERE CAMBRIDGE CHANGES AND PSEUDO-PROCESSES

Assuming the standpoint of token physicalism, I now want to scrutinize CEIP, the thesis that intentional properties of beliefs are causal properties. In order to do so, I shall borrow ideas from the philosophers Peter Geach and Wesley Salmon. Let me try to shake our naive confidence in the commitment of common sense to CEIP.

Geach (1969, pp. 72, 99) has called the change undergone by Socrates when he became shorter than Theaetetus as a result of Theaetetus's physical growth and the change posthumously undergone by Socrates 'every time a fresh schoolboy [comes] to admire him' mere Cambridge changes. Let us assume that Theaetetus's growth is a physical (or biological) process, as a result of which Socrates became shorter than Theaetetus. Let us assume further that each time a boy comes to admire Socrates, some physical process of belief formation occurs in the boy's brain, as a result of which Socrates becomes the object of the boy's admiration.

Now consider the following example of a *genuine* physical process borrowed from Salmon (1984). A pulse of white light travels from a spotlight to a wall. The travelling light pulse is a paradigmatic physical process. A red filter is now placed at some point on the path between the spotlight and the wall. From the instant that the light pulse interacts with the filter, it becomes red and remains so until it reaches the wall. Thus, before interacting with the filter the light pulse is white; after meeting the filter it is red. If the wall is white, the spot of light projected on the wall will be red. On Salmon's view (following the lead of Hans Reichenbach), a genuine physical process is one which can transmit a mark.

A single intervention at one point in the process transforms it in a way that persists from that point on . . . If we do intervene locally at a single place, we can produce a change that is transmitted from the point of intervention onward . . . The light pulse is a causal process whether it is modified or not, since in either case it is capable of transmitting a mark. (Salmon 1984, p. 142)

Therefore a genuine causal process can transmit or preserve a change introduced locally in a single step.

Now, imagine a spotlight attached to the centre of the ceiling of a circular room which is otherwise dark. When the light is turned on for a brief instant, it casts a spot of light on a particular point on the wall. Call this point A. The spotlight is now mounted on a rotating device. If the light is turned on and the rotating device is set in motion, the spot of light which is cast upon the wall will turn in a regular fashion around the wall – or it will be perceived to do so by a human observer at the appropriate speed of rotation. Whereas each emission from the spotlight to a point on the wall is a genuine causal process, the succession of revolving spots of light on the circular wall is what Salmon takes to be a paradigmatic *pseudo-*process. The revolution of the spot of light can be taken to be the product of two genuine processes: the emission of light from the spotlight and the rotation of the spotlight.

We now place a red filter at any point on the path of the light pulse from the spotlight onto the wall. Let the red filter be at A. Then the spot of light on the wall at A will be red. Now, as the spotlight revolves and emits a spot of light onto point B (distinct from A) on the wall, the spot of light on the wall at B will no longer be red. The succession of spots of light on the wall does not preserve the mark locally produced in one step. We could install a red lens in the spotlight, but this would not constitute a local intervention. Placing many different red filters in several different places along the wall, or having a red filter revolve around the wall at the same speed as the spot of light would involve several local interventions at several different points, not a single intervention at a single point in the process.

Now imagine that we extend the radius of the circular room or the distance between the revolving spotlight and the circular wall. If the spotlight rotates at a constant speed, then the revolving spot of light on the wall may well reach a speed greater than the speed of light, contrary to the principle of special relativity. As Salmon (1984, p. 143) says, 'there is no upper limit on the speed of pseudo-processes'.

For another example of a pseudo-process in Salmon's sense, consider a car moving at 150 km/hour. As the car projects a shadow on the side of the road, the shadow moves at the same speed as the car. Unlike the motion of the car, the motion of the shadow is a pseudo-process. If the car, moving at 150 km/hour, collides with a brick wall, it will bear the marks of the collision and carry them along. However, if the shadow collides with a brick wall, it may be temporarily distorted (or vanish) but will then resume its previous shape oblivious of the distortion.

Therefore it is tempting to say that a 'mere' Cambridge change (in Geach's sense) is a pseudo-process (in Salmon's sense). However, this would be misleading. When Socrates became shorter than Theaetetus as a result of Theaetetus's physical growth, Theaetetus changed but Socrates himself did not. Similarly, when Socrates undergoes a posthumous Cambridge change every time a schoolboy comes to admire him, he undergoes no change at all. However, a pseudo-process is a process: when a revolving white spotlight projects a sequence of light spots on a dark wall, there is a sequence of events – a succession of revolving spots of light on the wall. The reason why the revolution of *the* spot of light on the wall is a pseudo-process is that there is no causal relation between the constituent events: no spot of light on the wall causes the occurrence of its successor. The succession of spots of light on the wall is a pseudo-process. When Socrates becomes smaller than Theaetetus or when he is admired by a schoolboy, he undergoes a Cambridge change.

Ordinary human social life abounds in pseudo-processes (if not in Cambridge changes) which, to common sense, may well seem indistinguishable from genuine processes. Xantippe, who was Socrates' wife, became a widow upon his death. Did not Xantippe undergo a genuine change since she turned into a widow? Notice that if such a change occurred, it does not supervene upon any physical property of Xantippe. Xantippe has acquired the property of being a widow, and no underlying or subvening physical property intrinsic to Xantippe subserves her change in legal status. How could Socrates' death cause such a change in Xantippe? How could it cause her to acquire the property of being a widow? Notice that there is no time delay between Socrates' death and the instant at which Xantippe becomes a widow. Could such a causal influence take place instantaneously? Xantippe could be in or out of the Milky Way, as far away from Socrates' body at the time of his death as you please, and still acquire this property upon Socrates' death. Could such a process — such a causal influence — take place at a speed greater than the speed of light?

Xantippe's acquisition of the property of being a widow requires or presupposes the existence of Socrates' death — a genuine physical (or biological) process. The propositions that Socrates and Xantippe were married before t and that Socrates died at t entail the proposition that Xantippe is a widow at t. But what of Xantippe's change from being a married woman to being a widow? Is it a pseudo-process or a mere Cambridge change? I would argue that it is a Cambridge change. There is a single event — Socrates' death — but no process — no sequence of events — involving first Socrates' death and then Xantippe's widowhood. Xantippe's widowhood is conceptually more complex than Socrates' death since the latter, unlike the former, is independent of the legal relation between Socrates and Xantippe. Socrates' death is a constituent of Xantippe's widowhood, but the former does not cause the latter.

We often confuse causal and conceptual relations or dependences. Consider the following example from Menzies (1988, pp. 565–66).

Fred runs 100 meters in a foot-race in 10 seconds and in doing so outruns the competitor on his left, but is outrun by the competitor on his right. Here his outrunning the competitor on his left and his being outrun by the competitor on his right circumstantially supervene on his running the race in 10 seconds in virtue of different circumstantial facts about the running times of the other two competitors. Yet we might say the cause of his losing the race was his being outrun by his competitor on the right, not his outrunning the competitor on his left.

I want to object: Fred's losing the race is *constituted*, not caused, by his being outrun by the competitor on his right. He lost the race by being outrun, and being outrun is part of losing. The relation between being outrun and losing is *conceptual*, not causal.

There is a clear sense in which the common-sense picture of mental causation — encapsulated in CEIP — may be suspected by a physicalist to confuse pseudo-processes and genuine processes. Consider my belief c that the glass contains water. It causes me to extend my right arm, pick up the glass with my right hand, raise it to my lips, and drink water from it. Call my behaviour *e*. Both common sense and token physicalism can grant that *c* causes *e* (this is MCT). But is CEIP true? Does *c* cause *e* by virtue of its intentional property—by virtue of having the content that the glass in front of me contains water? Or does *c* cause *e* by virtue of some of its physical (presumably neurological) properties?

My behaviour is a process, but the suspicion arises that the genuine process whereby my brain state *c* brings about my behaviour *e* is a biological, chemical, and physical process through and through, involving the physical, chemical, and biological properties of *c*, not the intentional property of *c*. The process whereby, as common sense would have it, *c* causes *e* by virtue of its intentional property would be a pseudo-process—a mere shadow of the genuine physical process. It would stand to the genuine physical process as one of the following pseudo-processes stand to the real thing: as the motion of the car's shadow stands to the motion of the car itself, or as the regular revolving spot of light around the wall stands to the combination of the emission of light from the spotlight onto the wall and the rotation of the spotlight. One suspects that the intentional property of *c* is no more efficacious in bringing about *e* than is Xantippe's standing in the marriage relation to Socrates in bringing about her widowhood upon Socrates' death. In a word, the suspicion is that intentional properties of mental states are epiphenomenal—they play no causal role. If intentional properties do turn out to lack causal efficacy, then CEIP and, with it, the common-sense picture of mental causation is rightly in jeopardy.

This is a conclusion explicitly accepted by a number of eliminativist writers such as Stich (1983) and Churchland (1989). A conclusion such as this cannot be entertained lightheartedly. As Fodor (1987, p. xii) has put it with characteristic emphasis:

... if commonsense intentional psychology really were to collapse, that would be, beyond comparison, the greatest intellectual catastrophe in the history of our species; if we're that wrong about the mind, then that's the wrongest we've ever been about anything. The collapse of the supernatural, for example, didn't compare; theism never came close to being as intimately involved in our thought and our practice—especially our practice—as belief/desire explanation is. Nothing, except, perhaps, our commonsense physics—our intuitive commitment to a world of observer-independent, middle-sized objects—comes as near our cognitive core as intentional explanation does. We'll be in deep, deep trouble if we have to give it up.

A number of strategies are open to vindicate the common-sense assumption that intentional properties *are* causal properties.

THE COUNTERFACTUAL STRATEGY

Common sense may derive comfort in its commitment to CEIP from the truth of such counterfactuals as:

(*C*) Had I not believed that the glass contained water, then I would not have picked up the glass and drunk water from it.

The counterfactual strategy expects to offer support for CEIP by deriving a sufficient condition on the causal efficacy of properties from the counterfactual dependence between an effect and a cause, together with the innocuous assumption that, in order to refer to a cause, we need to pick it up (or identify it) via one of its properties. Suppose that c causes e and we refer to c as the event having property M. Suppose furthermore that we agree that if c (so identified) had not occurred, then e would not have occurred either. If the counterfactual holds, are we not justified in assuming that the property of c used in referring to c is indeed causally efficacious?

Although the truth of the singular causal statement 'c caused e' may indeed entail the truth of the counterfactual 'if c had not occurred, e would not have occurred', the truth of the latter can hardly entail the truth of the former. The kind of dependence expressed by counterfactuals is broader than strict causal dependency. In other words, the truth of such counterfactuals may count as a necessary, but hardly as a sufficient, condition for the truth of singular causal statements.

To see this, consider with Kim (1973) the following counterfactuals.

(a) If yesterday had not been Monday, today would not be Tuesday.

(b) If George had not been born in 1950, he would not have reached the age of 21 in 1971.

(c) If I had not written 'r' twice in succession, I would not have written 'Larry'.

(d) If I had not turned the knob, I would not have opened the door.

(e) If my sister had not given birth at t, I would not have become an uncle (at t).

Although the latter depends on the former, the fact that it was Monday yesterday is no cause of the fact that it is Tuesday today. Neither is George's birth in 1950 a cause of his reaching the age of 21 in 1971. Despite one's possible reluctance nowadays to rely on the analytic–synthetic distinction, such dependences may, I believe, plainly be called conceptual, not causal. If they instantiate some regularity, the regularity instantiated is no more a causal regularity than what is expressed by the sentence 'Night follows day' or, for that matter, 'Day follows night'. Days do not cause nights, nor conversely do nights cause days. I wrote 'Larry' by writing 'r' twice in succession. The latter is not a cause but a constituent of the latter. Nor is my turning the knob a cause of my opening the door. Again, my turning the knob is part of my opening the door. What my turning the knob causes is the rotation of the knob. (See my previous remarks about losing and being outrun.) I conclude that the counterfactual strategy is too liberal to vindicate CEIP.

THE NOMIST STRATEGY

An alternative strategy for the vindication of CEIP is to appeal to a nomological view of mental causation, or to the putative existence of covering causal intentional laws. The idea is that a covering causal intentional law is a sufficient condition for the causal efficacy of intentional properties. In other words, if an intentional property is nomic and the law in which it occurs is a causal law, then the property is causally efficacious.

One powerful advocate of the nomist strategy is Fodor (1987, 1990*b*). Fodor has long argued for a picture of scientific psychology in which there are causal intentional laws and non-intentional syntactic mechanisms responsible for the implementation of the intentional laws. Non-intentional syntactic mechanisms stand to causal intentional laws as, for example, biochemical processes stand to Mendel's laws of inheritance of hereditary factors. One ingredient of Fodor's nomist strategy is to argue that, in its quest for intentional causal laws, psychology is in the same boat as any other special science. All special sciences are in the business of supplying causal explanations (explanations backed by causal laws). A special science law is causal if it is implemented by lower-level underlying mechanisms.

Like all causal laws in the special sciences, and unlike laws of basic physics, intentional laws are *ceteris paribus*. Suppose with Fodor (1987, pp. 4–5) that it is a geological law that meandering rivers erode their outside bank. To say that it is a law *ceteris paribus* is to say that it is not a basic law or a law of basic physics. To say that a law is non-basic, or alternatively to say that it is *ceteris paribus*, is to say firstly that it may have exceptions—a river may freeze, or it may dry up, or humans may build a dam—and it is to say secondly that neither the propositions stating the exceptions nor the propositions revealing the underlying mechanisms responsible for the law can be stated in the vocabulary of the special science to which the law belongs. They can only be stated by adverting to the vocabulary of a more basic science, for example we appeal to the vocabulary of chemistry or fluid mechanics to state the mechanisms responsible for a geological law.*

Ceteris paribus laws are non-basic laws. According to Fodor's view, whether we can know them or not, what makes a law basic is that there are no underlying mechanisms responsible for its implementation. As Fodor (1990*b*, p. 144) says:

... a metaphysically interesting difference between basic and nonbasic laws is that, in the case of the latter but not the former, there always has to be a mechanism in virtue of which the satisfaction of its antecedent brings about the satisfaction of its consequent. If 'Fs cause Gs' is basic, then there is no answer to the question how do Fs cause Gs; they just do, and that they do is among the not-to-be-further-explained facts about the way the world is put together. Whereas, if 'Fs cause Gs' is nonbasic, then there is always a story about what goes on when — and in virtue of which — Fs cause Gs.

In the case of intentional laws, Fodor assumes that the mechanisms of implementation are syntactic. In the picture of cognitive science which he assumes, the content of a propositional attitude reduces to the intentional property of a symbol in the language of thought. Along with the computer model of the mind, he assumes that cognitive processes or mechanisms can detect only syntactic (or formal) non-semantic properties of mental symbols. If, as I think is right, not all special science laws are causal laws,[†] is it not circular to try and define causal properties by means of properties occurring in causal laws? I shall not be concerned with this putative circularity which need not be vicious.

Rather, two other potential difficulties for the nomist strategy will be considered. The strategy says that nomicity is sufficient for the causal efficacy of a property. One problem is that many different properties coincidentally co-instantiated with a causally efficacious property may be

---

* For scepticism about the notion of *ceteris paribus* intentional laws, see Schiffer (1991). Max Kistler has raised the question of whether what is distinctive of special science laws is 'the fact that they are 'hedged' by *ceteris paribus* clauses or . . . the fact that . . . they are heteronomic, in the sense that the conditions of their valid application cannot be stated within the vocabulary of the science they belong to'. I am tempted to say that both are distinctive. Furthermore, I would be content to leave it up to physicists to decide what is the appropriate level of basic physics at which to find 'strict' (not *ceteris paribus*) laws. As Kistler points out, it is controversial whether there is any such level of basic physics. However, as Fodor (1990*b*, p. 154) has said: 'Surely this is as should be: strict laws are just the special case of hedged laws where the *ceteris paribus* clauses are discharged *vacuously*; they are hedged laws for which 'all else' is *always* equal'. Now, what is distinctive of *intentional* (*ceteris paribus*) laws is that they are intentional, i.e. they appeal to the *contents* of mental states, whether they make reference to, or quantify over, such contents.

† Many chemical and biological identities might well be laws, but they are not causal laws. For an elaborate defence of this claim, see Cummins (1983).

sufficient for the production of an effect. Not all of them can be causally efficacious. Another problem is whether intentional generalizations of a commonsensical sort are genuine causal laws.

First, we may imagine cases in which two properties F and G are nomically sufficient for some effect e, only one of which, F, is intuitively efficacious in producing e, G being regularly co-instantiated with F because each instantiation of F is correlated with an instantiation of G. This may happen if instantiations of F and G have a common causal source.

Menzies (1988, p. 567) mentions the fact that a piece of metal can be electrically conductive, thermally conductive, and opaque by virtue of having one and the same physical state, namely having a certain kind of cloud of free electrons permeating it: 'the cloud of free electrons occupies the typical causal role associated with a metal's conductivity and opacity'. However, as pointed out by Jackson and Pettit (1990a, p. 204): 'the person who dies because she allows her aluminum ladder to touch power lines does not die because her ladder is a good conductor of heat, or because it is . . . highly opaque; she dies because her ladder is a good electrical conductor'.* In such a case, any of the properties (electrical conductivity, heat conductivity, or opacity) is nomically sufficient for the result (the person's death by electrocution). However, intuitively, only electrical conductivity has contributed to the result. Opacity and thermal conductivity are inert properties of aluminum co-instantiated by the metal's exhibiting electrical conductivity. It is incumbent upon the advocate of the nomist strategy to set aside all such forks of property co-instantiations—not an easy task.

The second objection is that it is questionable whether there are *ceteris paribus* causal laws of the sort required by the nomist strategy. Fodor is emphatically inclined to cite the 'platitudes' expressed by the following sentences as examples of causal intentional laws.

Reasoning according to *modus ponens*: If a person X believes that p and that *if p then q*, then (*ceteris paribus*) he or she will acquire the belief that q.

Practical syllogism: If a person X desires that q and he or she believes that *not q* unless p, then (*ceteris paribus*) he or she will act so as to bring it about that p.

According to Fodor's own view of the matter, such generalizations are respectable causal *ceteris paribus* laws of intentional psychology. They are implemented by non-intentional syntactic mechanisms. Take the case of the law of reasoning according to *modus ponens*: there are in a person's brain computational processors which detect only the syntactic (formal)

---

* Block (1990) offers in effect the same example under the guise of the Wiedemann–Franz law linking thermal and electrical conductivity. In his example, the thermal conductivity of a metal rod is efficacious whereas the electrical conductivity of the rod is not.

properties of the mental symbols sitting in the person's belief-box and standing for (or meaning) p and q.

As a number of philosophers have noticed, the view that such generalizations express analytic or conceptual truths is almost irresistible. It is almost irresistible to suppose that the principle of reasoning according to *modus ponens* is constitutive of what it is to have beliefs, or that the practical syllogism is constitutive of what it is to have beliefs and desires. Here are a few samples.

It is an error to compare a truism like 'If a man wants to eat an acorn omelette, then he generally will if the opportunity exists and no other desire overrides' with a law that says how fast a body will fall in the vacuum. (Davidson 1980, p. 233)

Commenting upon the practical syllogism, Schiffer (1987, p. 148) writes:

What is problematic here is that, first, it is by no means clear that this 'generalization' has any true completion, and second, to the extent that we can fill it out, to that extent it begins to look more and more analytic, more and more expressive of truths constitutive of our propositional-attitude concepts, and thus less and less like a contingent causal law.

In the context of a contrast drawn between what he calls 'regularizing' and 'normalizing' explanations of actions, Pettit (1986, p. 27) writes:

A striking feature of action–explanation is that the covering principles—those conforming to the belief–desire schema—are knowable a priori. One does not have to search around for inductive evidence to learn that if it is desirable that p, and if it happens that not p, and if one can ensure that p by A-ing, then other things being equal one ought to A. Equally, moving to the third person, one does not have to rely on inductive premisses to establish that if someone desires that p, and believes that by A-ing he can ensure that p, then *ceteris paribus* he As. Such a principle gives expression to our conception of what it is to believe and desire things. Understand that conception and you will be in a position to see that the principle is true.

Faced with the general agreement as to the quasi-analytic, conceptual nature, a priori knowability of intentional 'laws', one can, following Fodor (1990a, p. 184), take a hard Quinean line and respond that analyticity here, as with any profound scientific principle, is just an illusion fostered by 'centrality misperceived'. Belief–desire generalizations are so central to our conceptual scheme that we do not know how to give them up. But so are fundamental laws of physics. This does not make them analytic or knowable a priori. I think that the intuition that belief–desire generalizations seem analytic and knowable a priori is robust and cannot be disposed of in this way. They do seem to be analytic and knowable a priori in a way in which the law of universal gravitation does not seem to be. However, I propose to postpone discussion of this problem until I consider the distinction between narrow and broad content.

THE PROGRAM EXPLANATION MODEL

As mentioned already, token physicalists have given up the view that intentional properties are identical with physical properties. One fundamental reason why physicalists are sceptical of the truth of CEIP is that intentional properties are higher-order non-basic physical properties, whose instantiation depends on the instantiation of more basic properties. Suppose, with standard functionalism, that intentional property I is a higher-order physical property of an individual's brain or that intentional property I supervenes upon some physical property P of an individual's brain. Then the question is: Does not the causal efficacy of physical property P of the individual's brain pre-empt or screen off the causal efficacy of the higher-order intentional property I? This is what LePore and Loewer (1987) call the pre-emption threat, and what Kim (1989, 1991) and McLaughlin (1989) call the problem of explanatory exclusion.

In a number of papers, Jackson and Pettit (1988, 1990a,b) have elaborated a view of explanation, which they call the program explanation model, specifically designed to deal with the pre-emption threat. My belief caused my thirst-quenching behaviour. Jackson and Pettit assume that basic physical properties of my brain are efficacious in producing my behaviour. Let us further distinguish the fact that a property of a cause is efficacious in the process whereby the effect is produced by a cause, from the fact that a property of the cause is relevant to the causal explanation of why an effect occurred. If a property is efficacious, then it is relevant. Must it be efficacious to be relevant?

Consider how a higher-order intentional property I stands with respect to a more basic physical property P of an individual's brain, with the assumptions that I supervenes upon P, and that P is efficacious in producing effect e. A physicalist will assume that I is efficacious only if P is, since P realizes I. Given that I is a higher-order property than P, and given that I and P are both properties of one and the same brain state, the instantiation of I does not contribute to bringing about the instantiation of P. The instantiation of I with respect to e is not a sequentially more remote causal factor which produced the instantiation of P which in turn produced e. Nor does the instantiation of I combine with the instantiation of P to produce e collaboratively. Given all these assumptions, how can the instantiation of P be efficacious, and the instantiation of I not be superfluous, in producing e?

Jackson and Pettit's idea is that, although the instantiation of I is inefficacious, none the less it is relevant to explaining the occurrence of e for it programs the existence of a lower-level basic property P which is causally efficacious. It should be noticed that the program relation between the instantiation of I and the instantiation of P is a conceptual or

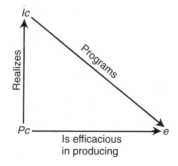

Fig. 14.1.

logical non-causal relation: *I* and *P* are co-instantiated. The instantiation of *I* is evidence that some *P* is thereby co-instantiated.

The model draws on two distinct ideas about how higher-order property instantiation may be realized by lower-order property instantiation. I shall call one intrinsic and the other extrinsic.

The first is the idea that an explanation referring to a higher-order property relates to an explanation referring to a lower-order property, as a proposition involving existential quantification relates to a singular proposition. The former is true by virtue of the latter: this relation is intrinsic to a given process. If *I* is instantiated by some cause *c* in the process whereby *e* is produced, then there is a basic property *P* which is also co-instantiated by *c*. Consider the process of the breaking of a glass. Compare the two following explanations: the glass broke because Tony dropped it (process explanation); the glass broke because somebody dropped it (program explanation). Knowing that somebody dropped the glass is to know something about a class of possible physical processes. What warrants the analogy is that one may think of a reference to the higher-order property as a quantification over a set of lower-order properties. A program explanation stands to a process explanation as an explanation which proceeds by quantifying over a set of causally efficacious properties stands to an explanation which refers to a particular efficacious property.

The reason why the process explanation does not supersede the program explanation is that they do not supply the same information. The former tells us which actual process led to the result; the latter characterizes a class of possible processes leading to the result. The program explanation informs us that had John or Sarah, or whoever else dropped the glass, it would have broken.

The second ingredient of the program explanation model—the fact that a higher-order relation holds between two distinct processes entails the existence of a lower-order property, causally efficacious within each independent process — is more objectionable. Obviously, the higher-order relation is extrinsic to either process since it involves a correlation between two distinct processes.

With Jackson and Pettit (1988, pp. 392–3), consider the following requests for explanation: Why does electron A accelerate at the same rate as electron B? Why was the price of lamb at the Portland auction the same as the price at the Ballarat auction? Why did the Bourbons last longer than the Windsors? Why do trees grow faster in Melbourne than in Canberra? Electrons A and B accelerate at the same rate because the forces acting on A and B have the same magnitude. The price of lamb is the same in both places because the relationship between supply and demand was the same at both places. The Bourbons lasted longer than the Windsors because the former had more offspring than the latter. Trees grow faster in Melbourne than in Canberra because there are fewer frosts in Melbourne than in Canberra. As Jackson and Pettit (1988, p. 393) put it:

the property we cite as explaining the result is the relevant property in common between the various members of the range of possible situations, each member of which would have produced the result and one of which did in fact produce the result. We will describe such a common property as causally programming the result, and call explanations in terms of properties which program without producing, program explanations, as opposed to process explanations which do cite the productive features.

Clearly, the program explanation model is intended to cover both intrinsic and extrinsic realizations of higher-order properties by lower-order properties. I believe that this confusion is a mistake. Consider any of the above explananda. We can assume that electron A gains its acceleration as a result of being acted upon by a given force. On Jackson and Pettit's own assumptions, A's acceleration is a process independent of B's acceleration. We can compare the rates of A's and B's acceleration. We then bring out similarities and differences between two independent processes. We can compute arithmetical equalities and/or inequalities. Granted, comparison and computation are brain processes in their own right — and brain processes are physical processes. However, they are, so to speak, second-order physical processes. In effect, any non-causal explanation (e.g. a mathematical proof) is such a second-order physical brain process.

Jackson and Pettit have collapsed two distinct ways that a non-basic physical property relates to a set of basic physical properties. On the one hand, having a functional higher-order property is definable as having one of a disjunctive set of basic properties. On the other hand, a pair (or n-tuple) of magnitudes may stand in the equality relation by virtue of instantiating many different values. Explaining why some effect occurred as a result of a process by quantifying over a set of causally efficacious properties is one thing. Explaining the similarities and differences between the results of two separate processes is something else. If we assume that the twin accelerations of two independent electrons constitute a complex process, then, in my view, when we compare the accelerations, we provide a conceptual analysis (or decomposition) of a complex process into its conceptual constituents. We do not provide a causal explanation of a further causal process standing above each independent electron's acceleration. I conclude that the program explanation model is too liberal in including extrinsic modes of realization of higher-order relations by lower-order properties.*

NARROW CONTENT AND BROAD CONTENT

As a result of a famous thought experiment devised by Putnam (1975), most contemporary philosophers of mind nowadays subscribe to *externalism*, the view that intentional properties of belief-states do not supervene on physical properties of an individual's brain. I shall take this view for granted.†

Externalism entails that two microphysical twins might have beliefs with different intentional properties. In my view, the threat that externalism raises for mental causation ought to be distinguished from the pre-emption threat. Intentional properties run the risk of being screened off by the causal efficacy of lower-order properties just because they are higher-order properties. However, if in addition externalism is true of intentional properties, then not only are they higher order than basic physical properties of an individual's brain, but they do not even supervene on basic physical properties of an individual's brain. Of course, externalism is no direct threat to physicalism since intentional properties may still supervene on pairs of physical properties — on physical properties of an individual's brain together with physical properties of his or her environment. None the less it remains attractive to physicalists to assume that physical twins must have the same causal properties.‡ Now, if externalism is correct, then, unlike physical properties of an individual's brain,

---

* Having read a previous version of this paper, Philip Pettit has pointed out to me that extrinsic relations like 'the sameness in mass of two objects in the pans of a balance may be causally relevant to the balance being level'. I disagree that sameness in mass is causally efficacious. Sameness in mass is relevant to an interpretive non-causal explanation.

† Externalism can be distinguished from what Burge (1979) calls 'anti-individualism': externalism is the view that an individual's physical environment enters the content of an individual's beliefs. Anti-individualism is the view that what other members of an individual's community believe enters the content of an individual's beliefs.

‡ For an explicit defence of this view, see Fodor (1990b, p. 138).

intentional properties are non-local properties of an individual's brain; their identity depends on the individual's environment.

For physicalists who want to maintain the assumption that the causal properties (or power) of two individuals must supervene upon (or be fixed by) their local physical properties (or the physical properties of their brain), the natural suggestion is to distinguish two notions of content (or intentional property): the *broad* commonsensical notion corresponding to the truth-conditions of a belief and a *narrow* notion. Only the latter would supervene on the physical properties of an individual's brain and would be relevant to the causal explanation of an individual's behaviour. If the physicalist wants to save CEIP, he will have to do two things: construct a revisionist notion of content (or intentional property), i.e. narrow content, and argue that only narrow content (because it supervenes on physical properties of an individual's brain) can causally explain behaviour.

Consider two microphysical twins Bill and Bob. Bill believes that cup c_1 in front of him contains coffee; he wants a sip of coffee. This is why he picks up c_1 with the fingers of his left hand, raises the cup to his lips and drinks coffee from it. Bob believes that cup c_2 in front of him contains coffee; he too wants a sip of coffee. This is why he performs the same bodily motions as Bill. Suppose that cups c_1 and c_2 are perceptually indistinguishable. Now, there is a sense in which Bill and Bob believe different things since Bill's belief is true if and only if c_1, not c_2, contains coffee. Bob's belief is true if and only if c_2, not c_1 contains coffee. Therefore Bill's and Bob's beliefs have distinct broad contents. However, there is a sense in which they believe the same thing: they both believe that the cup in front of them contains coffee. This is the narrow content of their respective belief.

Content-dualism is a natural view to take for physicalists who want to subscribe to the view that microphysical twins share all their causal properties; if two microphysical twins can have beliefs with the same narrow content, and if narrow content can explain behaviour, then causal properties of individuals can be fixed by physical properties of their brains.

Content-dualism has often relied on the argument that causal psychological explanation ought to restrict itself to the explanation of behaviour on a construal of behaviour such that Bill and Bob do the same thing when they both simultaneously pick up the cup in front of them, raise it to their lips, and drink coffee from it.* Narrow content is indeed suited to explain what Bill and Bob do when we think of it as the same thing. Call the explanandum narrow behaviour. The assumption that causal psychological explanation ought to explain narrow behaviour has been questioned by

---

* This is argued by Kim (1982), Stich (1983), and Fodor (1987, 1991).

Evans (1982, pp. 203–4) on the grounds that there is no such thing as narrow behaviour since what Bill does is to pick up cup c_1, not c_2, and what Bob does is to pick up cup c_2, not c_1. It seems to me uncontroversial that we may want to explain why Bill and Bob pick up the cup in front of them* and also why Bill picks up c_1, not c_2, whereas Bob picks up c_2, not c_1. Narrow content will help to explain the former (narrow behaviour); broad content will help to explain the latter (broad behaviour).

Given that two microphysical twins may have beliefs with the same narrow content, not broad content, it is incumbent upon a physicalist content-dualist to argue that only explanation of narrow behaviour by narrow content is genuine causal explanation. Behaviour can be non-intentional, intentional and narrow, or intentional and broad. Narrow content and narrow behaviour involve an existential quantification over cups. Broad content and broad behaviour involve a reference to a particular cup. The explanation of narrow behaviour by narrow content tells us that an agent's behaviour is intentional and not instinctive. An agent's cup-related behaviour counts as intentional behaviour — as behaviour performed for some reason as opposed to instinctive (or reflex) behaviour if the agent has some cup-related internal representation. In contrast, the explanation of instinctive or reflex behaviour does not require the postulation of any such internal representation. The standard argument for the role of mental representation in the explanation of intentional behaviour points out that non-intentionally described physical motions are not amenable to psychological nomological explanation. Content-dualists like to think that this argument is cast at the level of the explanation of narrow intentional behaviour by narrow content. At this level there may, in their view, be species-wide psychological laws, unlike the level of explanation of broad behaviour by broad content.

Logically, broad content and broad behaviour entail narrow content and narrow behaviour, as a singular proposition entails an existentially quantified proposition. We move back from narrow content to broad content by replacing an existentially bound variable by a singular term. In the perceptual process of belief formation, broad content comes first in that the perceptual belief is triggered by the detection of a particular cup. Narrow content is abstracted from broad content.

But now when we explain broad behaviour by broad content, we seem to move away from causal explanation to some kind of conceptual explanation. Is it not analytic that if Bill believes that cup c_1, not c_2, contains coffee, then he will pick up cup c_1, not c_2? Fodor (1991) has even suggested the view that it is analytic, necessary, or non-contingent that if

---

* Where 'the cup in front of them' may be true of either c_1 or c_2.

Bill believes that c_1 contains coffee and he wants some coffee, then he will seize c_1 and not some other cup. The reasoning seems to be this. We start with an explanation of narrow behaviour by narrow content. We assume that such an explanation is a causal explanation of intentional behaviour. We then jointly feed into narrow content and narrow behaviour some contextual item from the environment (reference to a particular cup, for example). We thereby simultaneously turn narrow content into broad content and narrow behaviour into broad behaviour. The same contextual item is required to turn narrow content into broad content and narrow behaviour into broad behaviour. So now when we look at the explanation of broad behaviour by broad content, it seems as if all the causal work is accomplished by narrow content to generate narrow behaviour; the additional relation between what makes content broad and what makes behaviour broad seems causally spurious. Therefore it seems purely conceptual or analytic.*

Indeed, it may seem so; but it is not. We take for granted, as part of our background assumptions, that particular cups do not instantaneously disappear; they do not miraculously come and go. But of course, unnoticed by Bill, c_1 might be replaced by c_2. Therefore Bill might erroneously believe that c_1 contains coffee while gazing at c_2. If he wants coffee, he may well seize c_2 while believing that he is seizing c_1. This is of course conceptually possible, even if physically unlikely. What might be analytic is not the following conditional: if Bill believes that c_1 contains coffee and he wants coffee, then he will seize c_1. What may be analytic is the conditional with the same antecedent and the following consequent: then he *intends* to seize c_1. However, it is not analytic that if he believes c_1 contains coffee and he wants coffee, then he will succeed in seizing c_1. If it is not analytic that if Bill believes that c_1 contains coffee and he wants coffee, then he will seize c_1, then the grounds for thinking that the explanation of broad behaviour by broad content is not causal explanation vanish. It seems to be as much causal explanation as the explanation of narrow behaviour by narrow content, which is just as well since, presumably, narrowness (of mind or behaviour) is a comparative, not a classificatory notion, or rather it is relative to a given broadness.[†]

---

* It might look puzzling that Fodor (1991) argues that the relation between broad content and broad behaviour is analytic whereas he denies that the principles of belief–desire psychology are analytic. I think that the solution to the puzzle is that he is inclined to count as analytic the relation between broad content and broad behaviour, but he thinks that the explanation of narrow behaviour by narrow content is causal and that there is no analytic relation between narrow content and narrow behaviour.

† I agree with the point made by Max Kistler that explanation of broad behaviour by broad content might be less informative than the explanation of narrow behaviour by narrow content. However, on the one hand, this is consistent with the former being as much causal explanation as the latter. On the other hand, I think I disagree with Kistler's further claim

THE COMPONENTIAL CONCEPTION OF BEHAVIOUR

Davidson's (1980) anomalous monism and functionalism are committed to a pair of assumptions, one of which is deeply entrenched in common sense: they assume that beliefs cause behaviour and they assume that behaviour is just physical motion. According to functionalism, behaviour is the observable output of an input–output device. Even though physical (or physiological) predicates may not be appropriate for the description of intentional behaviour, behaviour is still supposed to be nothing but physical motion. In the orthodox conception, my behaviour is the physical motion of my right arm allowing the fingers of my right hand to pick up the cup of coffee and bring it up to my lips. As this chapter illustrates, the hard question faced by the orthodox conception of behaviour is: How can the intentional property of my belief be causally efficacious in producing my behaviour in the presence of the physical properties of my belief (itself a brain state token of mine)? How can the former not be screened off by the latter? How can the intentional property of my belief trigger the propagation of electrical pulses through my nerves and bring about the contraction of my muscles?

I now want to entertain the possibility that both assumptions, that beliefs cause behaviour and that behaviour is physical motion, might be false. Consider first the assumption that behaviour is physical motion. I will draw on ideas derived from Dretske's (1988*b*) impressive treatment of behaviour. I shall call the alternative view of behaviour the *componential* view. In the componential view, the physical motion of my right arm and fingers when I pick up the cup of coffee is not my behaviour — it is a *constituent* of my behaviour. Rather, my behaviour is the extended *process* whereby some internal state of my brain (say my belief) causes or produces the physical motion of my right arm and hand. In general, behaviour is the process of production (or prevention) of physical motion *m* by an internal state *c* of a physical device (a predator's behaviour might involve the retention, not the production, of motion).

On the componential view, two physically indistinguishable motions may be components of two distinct behaviours: my left hand may follow the

---

that 'broad' explanation [of broad behaviour by broad content] would be on the same footing as the explanation of 'the event that turned Xantippe into a widow' by reference to 'Socrates' most morally valuable action', with the latter being an explanation which refers to two events which are causally linked. It is, though, an explanation which names each event by one of its extrinsic properties which plays no role in the production of the effect by its cause'. As should be apparent from the discussion of this very example in the text, I disagree with the assumption that there are two events to be distinguished — Socrates' death and Xantippe becoming a widow — which are linked by a causal relation. In my view, although the latter is conceptually more complex than the former, it is not a distinct event to be causally explained by the former.

same path twice: The first time, it moved as a result of *my* intention to raise it and so it was part of *my* behaviour. The second time, it moved as a result of *your* intention to raise it and so it was part of *your* behaviour. Now, if one accepts the componential view of behaviour, it follows that beliefs do not cause behaviour. My belief c, that the cup contains coffee does not cause my behaviour. Rather, both my belief c and the physical motion m of my right arm and hand are components of my behaviour. What my belief causes is the physical motion of my right arm and hand. The behaviour is the process via which c causes m. In favour of the componential conception, Dretske (1991*a*, p. 199) has argued that it accommodates the autonomy of intentional behaviour better than its orthodox alternative. In the latter view, any cause of c (my belief) is by transitivity of the causal relation, a cause of my behaviour. Therefore intentional behaviour is not autonomous. In the componential conception, the cause of belief c cannot cause behaviour since c does not cause behaviour in the first place.

Under the componential conception, the question is not: Is the intentional property of my belief causally efficacious in the production of behaviour? Since my belief does not cause my behaviour, the question becomes: Can the intentional property of my belief explain why my belief c causes physical motion m? Drawing on the componential conception, we can adopt what Kim (1991) has labelled the 'dual-explanandum strategy', i.e. we can split the neurobiological explanation of motion from the intentional explanation of behaviour. As Dretske (1988*a*, pp. 33–4) has written:

Content certainly does not seem to be a useful, let alone essential, explanatory notion in neurobiology. One doesn't hear anything about beliefs and desires in neurobiological explanation of the origin, pattern or propagation of those electrical pulses that bring about muscle contractions and, hence, finger and arm movements. Hence, if it were muscle contractions, finger and arm movements, we were trying to explain, it would be hard to see from this standpoint, what role content was supposed to play in this explanatory game. Unless, of course, one is prepared to say, as I am not, that neurobiologists systematically overlook an important causal factor in their explanatory efforts.

Thus we can distinguish two explananda: explaining the muscular contraction and the propagation of electrical pulses is one thing; explaining behaviour is something else. Now the vindication of CEIP becomes the task of showing that intentional properties may help explain, not muscular contraction, but the general shape or structure of behaviour. With Dretske, consider a simple artefact like a thermostat. Suppose that it turned the boiler on when the temperature was 16 °C. That is what the thermostat does. Now, within the thermostat is a bimetallic strip, each half of which is made of two distinct metals which have different rates of contraction and dilation. When the temperature changes, one contracts faster than the other and forces the other to bend. The bending then acts as an electrical switch which can turn the electricity on and off. When we look at the bimetallic strip merely as a switch we may forget the historical process whereby the metals contracted and dilated as a response to temperature changes.

When we consider what the thermostat does, namely turn the boiler on, we may ask at least two distinct questions: (i) Why did the thermostat turn the boiler on at t? (ii) Why did the thermostat turn the boiler on rather than something else? Why did it do that rather than something else? In response to the first question, we can say: because the temperature at t was 16 °C. In response to the second question, we can say that an electrician has selected the particular bending c of the bimetallic strip produced by an external temperature of 16 °C and has turned c into an electrical switch in the circuit connecting the thermostat to the furnace so that when the temperature reaches 16 °C, electric current flows through the wires to the boiler. Call m the flow of electric current through the wires. Thus c causes m.

Since the bending of the bimetallic strip c covaries with the temperature, we can say that it indicates (or carries information about) the temperature F. It also indicates many other things. If the change in temperature is correlated with a change in atmospheric pressure, it also indicates the atmospheric pressure. It should be noticed that the fact that c indicates (or carries information) about states of affairs with which it covaries is an objective fact about c − a fact which may hold even though the information carried is never processed.

However, in Dretske's view, c only represents F, the temperature (or perhaps the fact that the temperature is 16 °C), and not some other state of affairs, because it is c's function to indicate the temperature and c represents what it is its function to indicate. How has c acquired such a function? c has been assigned this function by an electrician who recruited c to cause m, the flow of electricity through the wires to the furnace. Of course, the electrician has intentions, beliefs, and desires. Therefore when a state c carries information about a number of states of affairs, it represents the state of affairs which it is its function to indicate. Let us take stock: c carries information about temperature F; it has acquired the function of indicating F; thereby it represents F. Now Dretske's strategy is to argue that the fact that c represents F explains why c causes m when F, along the lines of Fig. 14.2.

Furthermore, Dretske assumes that living organisms − plants and animals − have states which have indicator function as a result of either natural selection or individual learning. In his view, beliefs of the kind that humans harbour result from learning. Hence beliefs are states of the brain with indicator property; they acquire their indicator function by being

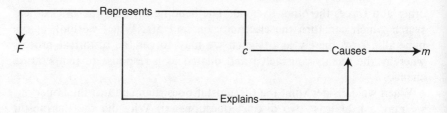

Fig. 14.2.

recruited via a learning process as causes of bodily motion.* Therefore the intentional property of a belief (not merely a neurological property) can help explain why the belief produces a motion. The intentional property of my belief c—the fact that it represents the cup in front of me as containing coffee (F)—explains why c prompts the motion of my right arm when F obtains. It acquired its indicator function by being recruited as a cause of m when F holds. Therefore it seems as if Dretske has succeeded in vindicating CEIP after all.

But as Baker (1991) has pointed out, there seems to be a hidden circularity in Dretske's account of the efficacy of intentional properties: c happens to indicate F but c acquires the function of indicating F only after c has been turned into a cause of m. If c acquires its indicator function—its function of indicating F—by being recruited as a cause of m, then it is circular to rely on c's indicator function to explain why c causes m.

One way out of the circularity (which seems to be adopted by Dretske (1991b) is to weaken the condition of c's acquisition of an indicator function. c would not acquire its function of indicating F by being recruited as a cause of m (with reference to m, a particular motion); it would acquire its function of indicating F by causing some movement or other. In other words, for any indicator c of F, c acquires the function of indicating F if

---

* Anthony Dickinson has raised the following objection to Dretske's teleological conception of representational states: 'by fixing representational properties by reference to some externally defined function . . . or goal . . ., the componential analysis appears to attempt an account of how causal states acquire representational properties for a designer. What is less clear, however, is whether this analysis can also explain how mental states act causally via their representational properties for the *agent*'. The following could be said on behalf of Dretske's teleological view of representations. First, it might be said that an account of what the representational properties of a representational state are *for the agent* properly belongs to a theory of *consciousness*, and not directly to a theory of representations. Secondly, in the view advocated by Dretske, information is just nomic covariation. Representation is information plus function, where function can be natural or artificial. Artificial function presupposes beliefs and intentions of a designer. A natural function can be bestowed on an informational state by natural selection or by learning. Beliefs are representations formed by learning. Plausibly, beliefs do, but innate representational states do not, enter inferential relations. It might well be also that some peculiar phenomenological properties—what the representational properties of a representational state are for the agent—are attached to beliefs (as opposed to other representations).

there is some bodily motion or other which c causes. But there is no particular bodily motion which could confer upon any indicator c its indicator function. There is no circularity any more; no reference to a particular bodily motion m is involved in the condition by which c acquires its indicator function. Thus, the fact that c has the function of indicating F can be exploited in explaining why c causes a particular bodily motion m. Now, the problem faced by such a move is that it is far from clear that the fact that c is recruited to produce some bodily motion or other is sufficiently robust a condition to confer upon c its function of indicating F or its ability to represent F.

ACKNOWLEDGEMENTS

In addition to participants at the Fyssen Symposium, I am grateful to Paul Horwich for his comments and to Philip Pettit for several discussions of the topic of this paper.

REFERENCES

Baker, L. R. (1991) Dretske on the explanatory role of belief. *Philosophical Studies* **63**, 99–111.

Block, N. (1990). Can the mind change the world? In *Meaning and method: essays in honour of Hilary Putnam* (ed. G. Boolos). Cambridge University Press.

Burge, T. (1979) Individualism and the mental. In *Midwest studies in philosophy*, Vol. IV (ed. P. A. French, T. E. Uehling, and H. K. Wettstein). Minnesota University Press, Minneapolis.

Churchland, P. (1989) *A neurocomputational perspective*. MIT Press, Cambridge, MA.

Cummins, R. (1983). *The nature of psychological explanation*. MIT Press, Cambridge, MA.

Davidson, D. (1980). Psychology as philosophy. In *Essays on actions and events* (ed. D. Davidson). Clarendon Press, Oxford.

Dennett, D. (1987). Three kinds of intentional psychology. In *The intentional stance* (ed. D. Dennett). MIT Press, Cambridge, MA.

Dennett, D. (1991) Ways of establishing harmony. In *Dretske and his critics* (ed. B. McLaughlin). Blackwell, Oxford.

Dretske, F. (1988*a*). The explanatory role of content. In *Contents of thought* (ed. R. H. Grimm and D. M. Merrill). University of Arizona Press, Tucson.

Dretske, F. (1988*b*). *Explaining behavior*. MIT Press, Cambridge, MA.

Dretske, F. (1991*a*) Dretske's replies. In *Dretske and his critics* (ed. B. McLaughlin). Blackwell, Oxford.

Dretske, F. (1991*b*). How beliefs explain: reply to Baker. *Philosophical Studies* **63**, 113–17.

Evans, G. (1982). *The varieties of reference*. Clarendon Press, Oxford.

Fodor, J. A. (1981). Methodological solipsism considered as a research strategy in cognitive psychology. In *Representations*. MIT Press, Cambridge, MA.

Fodor, J. A. (1987) *Psychosemantics*. MIT Press, Cambridge, MA.

Fodor, J. A. (1990*a*) Review of Schiffer's *Remnants of meaning*. In A theory of content and other essays. MIT Press, Cambridge, MA.

Fodor, J. A. (1990*b*). Making mind matter more. In *A theory of content and other essays*. MIT Press, Cambridge, MA.

Fodor, J. A. (1991). A modal argument for narrow content. *Journal of Philosophy* **88**(1), 5-26.

Geach, P. (1969). *God and the soul*. Routledge and Kegal Paul. London.

Jackson, F. and Pettit, P. (1988) Functionalism and broad content. *Mind* **97**(387), 381-400.

Jackson, F. and Pettit, P. (1990*a*) Causation in the philosophy of mind. *Philosophy and Phenomenological Research* **50**, 195-214.

Jackson, F. and Pettit, P. (1990*b*). Programme explanation: a general perspective. *Analysis* **50**(2), 107-17.

Kim, J. (1973). Causes and counterfactuals. In *Causation and conditionals* (ed. E. Sosa). Oxford University Press.

Kim, J. (1982). Psychophysical supervenience. *Philosophical Studies* **41**(1), 51-70.

Kim, J. (1989). Mechanism, purpose, and explanatory exclusion. *Philosophical perspectives*, Vol. 3, Philosophy of mind and action theory (ed. J. Tomberlin). Atascadero, Ridgeview.

Kim, J. (1991). Dretske on how reasons explain behaviour. In *Dretske and his critics* (ed. B. McLaughlin). Blackwell, Oxford.

LePore, E. and Loewer, B. (1987). Mind matters. *Journal of Philosophy* **84**(11), 630-42.

McLaughlin, B. (1989). Type epiphenomenalism, type dualism, and the causal priority of the physical. In *Philosophical perspectives*, Vol. 3, *Philosophy of mind and action theory* (ed. J. Tomberlin). Atascadero, Ridgeview.

Menzies, P. (1988). Against causal reductionalism. *Mind* **97**, 551-74.

Perry, J. and Israel, D. (1991) Fodor and psychological explanation. In *Mind and meaning* (ed. B. Loewer and G. Rey). Blackwell, Oxford.

Pettit, P. (1986). Broad-minded explanation and psychology. In *Subject, thought, and context*. (ed. P. Pettit and J. McDowell). Clarendon Press, Oxford.

Putnam, H. (1975). The meaning of 'meaning'. In *Philosophical papers*, Vol. II. Cambridge University Press.

Salmon, W. (1984). *Scientific explanation and the causal structure of the world*. Princeton University Press.

Schiffer, S. (1987). *Remnants of meaning*. MIT Press, Cambridge, MA.

Schiffer, S. (1991). *Ceteris paribus* laws. *Mind* **100**(397), 1-17.

Stich, S. (1983). *From folk psychology to cognitive science*. MIT Press, Cambridge, MA.

Part VII

Domain-general approaches to causal understanding

Foreword to Part VII

Parts II–V illustrated the domain-specific approach to causal understanding. In part VI we saw two philosophers investigating the legitimacy of domain-specific causal understanding. They took for granted, as do most philosophers since Hume, that causation is a unitary phenomenon, whether or not it can legitimately be described in different terms at different levels of reality. Until recently, most psychologists also approached causal understanding in a unitary manner. Formal properties of causal inference have been discussed, in particular in the framework of attribution theory. Under the influence of Fritz Heider and H. H. Kelley, social psychology had been particularly dynamic in studying causal attributions at a time when other branches of psychology showed much less interest in the topic. This work has by no means been made obsolete by the development of domain-specific approaches, as the two chapters in this part testify (see also Chapter 20 in which a synthesis of the domain-general and the domain-specific approaches is suggested).

Two views of causality have long coexisted—smoothly in practice, more problematically in theory. According to the first view, causality is a matter of covariation or conditional dependency. According to the second view, causality is a matter of regularities and mechanisms. The two views can be seen as closely related: a reliable causal mechanism brings about a conditional dependence between a cause and an effect, while a conditional dependence is typically based on the existence of an underlying causal mechanism. But how is knowledge of causal relationships acquired? By identifying mechanisms or by discovering covariations? The problem with the latter view is that mere covariations fail, or so it seems, to distinguish between genuine and spurious causal correlations. Nevertheless, Cheng and Lien argue in 'The role of coherence in differentiating genuine from spurious causes' for a sophisticated probabilistic version of the conditional dependence view. Their model, supported by experimental evidence, solves the usual problems of the covariation view by giving a crucial place to considerations of coherence. It offers an explanation of how knowledge of mechanisms is acquired.

In 'The logic and language of causal explanation', Hilton considers causal explanation as a conversational practice, and draws on H. P. Grice's account of verbal communication in terms of a 'co-operative principle' and of 'maxims of conversation'. Whereas much of the work on causal inference has focused on the problem of 'causal discounting'—sorting real from apparent causes—Hilton focuses on the problem of 'causal backgrounding'—sorting relevant from irrelevant causes. He illustrates his analysis with the case of the explosion of the space shuttle *Challenger* in 1986, showing how consideration of relevance modified over time the kind of explanations favoured, moving from increasingly specific accounts of mechanical failure to discussions of human and social responsibility. The structure of causal explanation is described as governed by domain-independent considerations of conversational relevance, rather than by domain-specific properties of the events explained.

D.S.

15

The role of coherence in differentiating genuine from spurious causes
PATRICIA W. CHENG AND YUNNWEN LIEN

INTRODUCTION

Statistical relevance and causal structure

How do people recover the causal structure of the world? A potential answer is that we do so according to statistical relevance, a concept based on the difference between the probability of an effect given the presence of a potential cause and that probability given its absence (Salmon 1971; Cartwright 1983; Cheng and Novick 1990).* We will refer to this difference as 'contrast', or 'probabilistic contrast', following Cheng and Novick (1990). If the contrast for a potential cause with respect to an effect is noticeably different from zero, then that factor is said to be statistically relevant to the effect or to covary with the effect. One issue that confronts this approach is that not all statistically relevant relations are causal. For example, although total sales of ice cream covary with crime rate, one would not draw the conclusion that ice cream sales causes crime or vice versa. Similarly, although a drop in the barometric reading covaries with storms, one would not think that the drop in the reading causes the storms. These judgements are possible even in the absence of any independent manipulation of the candidate cause. Adopting Suppes' (1970) terminology, we shall call the potential cause in a relevant relation that is intuitively judged to be causal a *genuine* cause, and that judged to be non-causal a *spurious* cause.

To explain this distinction between genuine and spurious causes, one answer within the statistical relevance approach is to base judgements on conditional contrasts (Reichenbach 1956; Suppes 1970; Salmon 1971; Cartwright 1983). A rough characterization of this variant of the approach is that contrast for potential cause C with respect to effect E is computed within subsets of events in which alternative causal factors K_i are kept

---

* The item 'statistical relevance' originates from Salmon (1971).

constant: if $P(E|C.K_1.K_2. \ldots K_n) - P(E|\overline{C}.K_1.K_2. \ldots K_n)$ is noticeably greater than zero, C is inferred to be a facilitatory cause of E. An isolated full point denotes 'and'; each K_i denotes a definite choice between the presence and the absence of the factor. It is assumed that events, causes, and effects can be represented discretely. For the barometer example, when the contrast for a drop in the barometric reading with respect to storms is computed conditional on a genuine cause—a drop in atmospheric pressure in this case—a drop in the reading no longer covaries with storms. It is therefore a spurious cause, 'screened off' from storms by drop in atmospheric pressure. The ideal set of conditionalizing factors would include all and only those that are actually causal. Given the limitations of knowledge, however, the best people could do is to select as conditionalizing factors those that they currently *believe* to be plausible causes. In view of this uncertainty, a conclusion based on conditional contrasts should be particularly compelling when there is independent manipulation of C. Alternative causes are more likely to be kept constant in such cases than in observational cases.

The solution in terms of conditional contrasts has not been directly tested, but it receives indirect empirical support from studies of observations of cue interactions in classical conditioning and human causal induction (Cheng and Holyoak, in press). Rather than assessing the adequacy of this solution, however, we focus here on the situation in which it does not apply but none the less people seem able to form systematic causal judgements. There is not always sufficient information for computing conditional contrasts. One might be unable to do so either because one does not know a plausible cause on which to conditionalize a contrast, or because the genuine cause covaries perfectly with a spurious one. Despite a lack of such critical information, people do differentiate genuine from spurious causes under such circumstances (Bullock *et al.* 1982). Their judgements are no doubt fallible, probably more so than when the critical information is available, but they are systematic and plausible. For example, someone who does not know that a true cause of storms is a drop in atmospheric pressure, and therefore cannot conditionalize the contrast for a drop in the barometer reading on it, might none the less judge that the drop in the barometric reading does not cause the storm. Similarly, someone who has never encountered a defective barometer (and has not been instructed about the cause of storms) would still be likely to form a similar opinion. For this person, because there is always a drop in the barometric reading when there is a drop in atmospheric pressure, the probability of a storm given (a) a drop in atmospheric pressure and (b) no drop in the barometric reading—one of the two quantities required for computing the relevant conditional contrast—is undefined.

An explanation of the power view

An intuitive explanation for the distinction that has been popular in psychology is that when one knows of an underlying causal power or mechanism, one will judge the relevance relation to be causal; otherwise, one will judge it to be non-causal (Bullock *et al.* 1982; Shultz 1982; White 1989). Although we agree with this intuition, we feel that this answer is incomplete in that there is no explicit specification of what this knowledge is and how it is related to the target relevance relation. One aim of this chapter is to provide an explication of the power view, including a partial specification of what is meant by the knowledge of an underlying power and of how such knowledge influences causal judgements. Because the power view assumes the causality of the underlying power, it does not address the problem of why the power in question is understood as causal. However, treating the causal status of the power as a given, this view does provide a top-down solution for when a specific instance would or would not be judged causal. Our aim is to explain this top-down solution, rather than more ambitiously to trace the root of the causality of the power in question. A second goal is to explicate the relationship between the power view and statistical relevance. Proponents of the power view often regard power as a competing alternative to statistical relevance. In contrast, we shall show that the power view makes use of, rather than contradicts, statistical relevance.

At least one type of situation where the power view would apply is that in which there is insufficient information for computing conditional contrasts. We propose that checking for an underlying power means checking for consistency between the target relevance relation and the relatively abstract statistical relevance relations implied by prior causal knowledge. (We use 'abstractness' to refer to the generality or inclusiveness of a concept.) For the storm example, one would check for consistency between (a) the specific relevance relation involving a drop in the baro-metric reading and storms and (b) any more abstract relevance relation implied by prior causal knowledge. For instance, one might see that the target relation is not consistent with one's knowledge about laws of mechanical motion, according to which the small physical movement of a small object (the mercury in the barometer) is not statistically relevant to the movement of large objects (masses of air and rain), nor is it consistent with other causal knowledge regarding the storm encoded at any level of abstraction. When a target relevance relation is consistent with a super-ordinate relevance relation implied by prior causal knowledge, it will probably be judged causal. However, when it is inconsistent with any such relation, it is less likely to be judged causal.

Our example about the laws of mechanical motion involves a single causal relation at the more abstract level. However, we do not imply that all superordinate causal knowledge is of this simple type. Such knowledge could also involve a chain of abstract causal relations. More generally, other things being equal, if a target relevance relation is consistent with a link in a chain of previously acquired superordinate causal relations (a chain trivially could have a single link), it will be judged causal; if it is not consistent with any link in any such chains, it will be less likely to be judged causal.

Coherence plays a critical role in the application of top-down causal knowledge. When a target relevance relation between a potential cause X and an effect is inconsistent with a relevance relation between a superordinate known cause X' and the effect, it is logically possible to create a new rule that consists of (a) a relevance relation between X' and the effect and (b) an exception involving X. Therefore statistical relevance without the constraint of coherence cannot explain why some relevance relations are judged to be non-causal. For the storm example, one might create the following rule: a small mechanical movement in an object causes, upon impact, a small mechanical movement in another object (i.e. it does not cause a large mechanical movement), except when the cause is the fall of mercury in a barometer and the effect is the large movements of air and rain in a storm, in which case the small mechanical movement does cause the large mechanical movement. This complex rule then would receive 'confirmation' at the general level as well as from the exception. However, the high confirmation comes at the cost of increased complexity—a nemesis of coherence. Given a preference for simple rules, then, one might stay with the less confirmed (i.e. sometimes violated) but simpler general relation involving X' alone, treating the relevance relation involving X as spurious. A situation in which this is particularly likely is when the target phenomenon contradicting the general relation is consistent with a known or plausible counteracting cause. Then both the general rule and the exception to it can be maintained with no increase in the complexity of the knowledge system.

In contrast, when the relevance relation involving X is consistent with that for X', then X would be regarded as a genuine cause. Thus, if one obtains higher causal judgements in situations involving *consistent* relevance relations across levels of abstraction than in situations involving inconsistent relations, this result would support the preference for a simple representation of the cause and indicate the influence of coherence in differentiating genuine from spurious causes.

We do not attempt to provide a general theory of the role of coherence in causal judgements. Rather, we merely seek to test what seems to us to be an indisputable component of it—the notion of consistency, with its related notion of simplicity. We assume that two relations that are

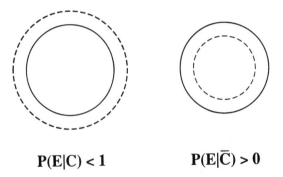

$$P(E|C) < 1 \qquad P(E|\bar{C}) > 0$$

Fig. 15.1. Conditional probabilities of the effect as a function of the level of generality of the cause: —— effect E; ----- potential cause C.

consistent are simpler, and hence more coherent, than two relations that are contradictory.

Our explanation of the distinction hinges on an assumption that there is a particular level of abstraction at which a causal relation is naturally defined. Whether or not a given target relation is consistent with a more abstract relation depends on the level of generality at which the abstract relation is defined. What determines the appropriate level? We argue that for any given type of effect, there is a level of abstraction of its cause at which contrast is at a maximum (Cheng 1993). This level then could provide a criterion for the definitions of both the cause and its contrast with respect to the effect. (Factors that are causally irrelevant to the effect will have relatively low contrasts for all levels of abstraction.) To see why there is a level at which contrast for a potential cause is at a maximum, consider the simple case in which the causal relation is deterministic. The Euler circles in Fig. 15.1 illustrate the situations for this case in which the set of events in which the cause C occurs is 'larger' and 'smaller' respectively than the set of events in which effect E occurs. When set C is larger than set E, $P(E|C)$ is reduced from its optimal value of unity. When set C is smaller than set E, $P(E|\bar{C})$ is increased from its optimal value of zero. However, when set C coincides with set E, $P(E|C) = 1$ and $P(E|\bar{C}) = 0$, giving the maximum contrast. An analogous argument applies to the probabilistic case, in which the sets do not completely coincide. One way of conceptualizing this case is that there is a subset of events in E that never overlaps with C, and conversely there is a subset of events in C that never overlaps with E. Since these subsets are constant, they do not affect the solution. We see that the above argument applies for the rest of the events, including events in E that potentially overlap with C. Therefore, as in the deterministic case, there is a level of abstraction that yields a maximum contrast.

The above criterion for determining the level of abstraction at which a cause is defined requires that there is a predefined effect with a certain level of abstraction. To summarize, for a simple (i.e. coherent) description of a potential factor, its causal status is defined at the level of abstraction for which its contrast is at a maximum.

Causal judgements based on an established power do not involve the discovery of a new cause, as judgements made on the basis of conditional contrasts can. Although both kinds of causal inference require prior causal knowledge, the type and role of such knowledge differ: whereas the top-down inference involving power requires prior causal knowledge concerning the superordinate category of the relation in question, conditional contrasts require prior knowledge of causes *alternative* to the relation in question. For the top-down inference, prior knowledge supplies the candidate cause; for conditional contrasts, such knowledge is used for control — for removing established causes so that the causal status of a candidate factor can be evaluated and potentially discovered. Thus, whereas induction by the assessment of conditional contrasts allows the possibility of a novel type of relation becoming a member of the causal repertoire, induction by knowledge of power involves the recognition that a novel token of a relation is of a type that has already been established as a member of the repertoire.

Relation between power and statistical relevance

Proponents of the power view have presented evidence to refute statistical relevance. We think that although the power view is an alternative to the bottom-up application of statistical relevance, it is consistent with a top-down use of previously acquired causal knowledge that involves relatively abstract relevance relations. For example, saying that a drop in the barometric reading does not cause a storm because there is no mechanism underlying the relation could be regarded as a shorthand for our explanation presented earlier.

Explanations analogous to that for the storm example can be constructed to show that the evidence purported to refute statistical relevance presented by power theorists is actually consistent with it, supporting the role of consistency between relevance relations across levels of abstraction (Cheng 1993). The following interpretation of an experiment by Bullock (Bullock 1979; Bullock *et al.* 1982) illustrates the argument. In this experiment, children judged what caused a Jack-in-the-box to pop up from its box. Before it popped, two identically timed events occurred simultaneously: a ball rolled down a slope towards the box, and a series of lights 'rolled' down a parallel slope towards the box (the lights produce the *phi* phenomenon). Both the ball and the light were occluded from sight for a second before Jack was seen to pop. The above sequence was repeated many times, thus defining identical covariational relations for the rolling of (a) the ball, and (b) the light with respect to Jack's popping.

To manipulate the plausible underlying causal power or mechanism, there were two conditions. In the *standard* condition, the entire apparatus appeared to be in a single box. On the mechanism view, the popping of Jack was consistent with a plausible mechanism involving impact by the ball ('rolling and hitting [by an object with mass] can produce movement in another object through impact' (Bullock *et al.* 1982, p. 225)). In contrast, the travelling series of lights is presumably less consistent with prior knowledge about mechanisms that can produce the movement in another object. Therefore a consideration of plausible mechanisms should lead a subject to attribute the popping to the ball, despite identical covariational relations for the ball and the light. In the *unconnected* condition, there was a 6 in gap between the box containing Jack and the boxes containing the ball and the light. The popping of Jack was thus clearly inconsistent with being hit by the ball. Bullock *et al.* reasoned that for older children who were familiar with electrical phenomena, the light might seem to provide the more plausible mechanism. These children might assume that the light is produced by electricity, which also causes Jack to jump. The results show that 3- to 5-year-old children were more likely to attribute the popping to the ball than to the light in the standard condition. In contrast, except for 3-year-old children, they were more likely to attribute it to the light in the unconnected condition. Bullock *et al.* concluded that the differences obtained in children's causal inferences for situations involving identical statistical relevance relations reflect a use of the principle of mechanism.

Although the rolling of the ball and the light each covaried perfectly with Jack's popping, the results need not contradict the statistical relevance view — subjects might not have restricted their assessment of covariation to the sequences of events presented in the experiment. The rolling of the ball and the series of lights are likely to be represented not only at the specific level used by the researchers in equating covariational information, but also at a more abstract level. The ball is not only a specific ball but also an object with mass; the series of lights is not only a specific series of lights but also an electrical device. Knowledge about causal mechanisms clearly implies knowledge about covariational relations at an abstract level. Having 'mechanistic' knowledge about motion in an object produced by the impact of a moving object implies knowing that when there is impact by a moving object on another object, motion in the latter object is likely, but when there is no such impact, other things being equal, motion in the latter object is unlikely. Therefore consistency between the target statistical relation and a superordinate relevance relation for a simple description of a cause can explain the results.

Doubtless, however, our interpretations of the storm example and of

Bullock's findings are speculative. It is impossible to isolate and examine the abstract causal knowledge used in these particular judgements. Lien and Cheng (1992; Y. Lien and P. W. Cheng, in preparation) therefore conducted an experiment to test the idea that manipulating coherence in terms of consistency between statistical relevance relations for simple descriptions is indeed sufficient to produce the distinction between genuine and spurious causes.

TESTING THE ROLE OF CONSISTENCY BETWEEN STATISTICAL RELEVANCE RELATIONS: AN EXPERIMENT

The primary task in this experiment was to judge whether or not a target relevance relation is causal. Subjects (96 undergraduate students at the University of California at Los Angeles) were shown a relevance relation between a novel of target object and an effect. We created a situation in which conditional contrasts could not be computed. The primary manipulation was the prior knowledge established in the subjects during the learning phase of the experiment. Across two groups of subjects, this knowledge could be either *consistent* or *inconsistent* with the target relevance relation at an abstract level along a causally relevant dimension. For simplicity, we constructed our stimuli in each condition to reflect only one relevance relation in the prior knowledge base. Therefore failing to be consistent with this relation meant failing to be consistent with any superordinate relation.

One criterion for categorizing a novel item (judging it to be causal or non-causal here) is according to some function of cue validity (Reed 1972; Rosch and Mervis 1975) — the probability of being in a category (e.g. the effect's occurring) given a feature of the item (e.g. red). To show that consistency with contrast at an abstract level, rather than cue validity, is what governs causal judgements in this experiment, the cue validity of every feature of the target items was kept constant at every level of abstraction across the consistent and inconsistent conditions.

Our hypothesis predicts that the target relevance relation will be judged differently across the conditions. In the inconsistent condition subjects will reject the target relation as causal, whereas in the consistent condition they will accept it as causal.

Cover story

The experiment was conducted under the following cover story, which was identical across conditions. Subjects were told to assume that they were applying for a job as an assistant to a gardener who was an expert on growing a kind of flowering plant. To select from the many candidates, the gardener gave each applicant a test. He wanted to see if they could discover what caused the plants to bloom. To find out, he asked the applicants to predict accurately whether or not plants fed with various types of substances bloomed. First, he showed them some of his plants. He told them that these plants were seeded in separate pots, and that each plant in a group of 10 was fed with one ounce of a particular type of substance. In addition, there were ten plants that were not fed any substance. All the plants were put in a greenhouse to keep the environmental conditions constant. The information about the growth of each plant at a certain time after feeding was recorded on a card, which indicated the substance fed to a plant and whether or not that plant bloomed. The cards (380 in total) were mounted on a wall in front of the subjects.

Because the cover story supplies a causal context, subjects in our experiment did receive causal information that goes beyond the statistical information that we manipulate. However, because the cover story is held constant across conditions, it cannot account for any difference between conditions in the causal judgements observed.

Design

The target relevance relation presented to each subject concerned five plants that were fed a warm-coloured and irregularly shaped substance, of which four bloomed. In contrast, a much lower proportion of plants that were not fed any substances bloomed — specifically, one out of ten in the consistent condition and two out of ten in the inconsistent condition. (We shall return to this difference between the conditions.) The primary task was to judge whether this substance caused blooming. As mentioned, prior to making this judgement, two groups of subjects received information that was, respectively, consistent and inconsistent with the target relevance relation. Within each group were three subgroups, each of which was presented with the target relevance relation instantiated with a specific variant of warm-coloured and irregularly shaped substances. These three critical test items were constructed to test whether subjects (a) were sensitive to contrast and (b) used contrast at an abstract level, as will be explained. Therefore there were six subgroups with 16 subjects in each.

Stimulus structure

Information about the stimuli — the set of substances fed to the plants — was created to satisfy three constraints. First, the stimuli had to allow encoding at various levels of abstraction. Second, the target relevance relation had to be consistent with the abstract relevance relation for one group but inconsistent with that for the other group. Third, the cue validity of every

Inconsistent (colour-relevant) Condition

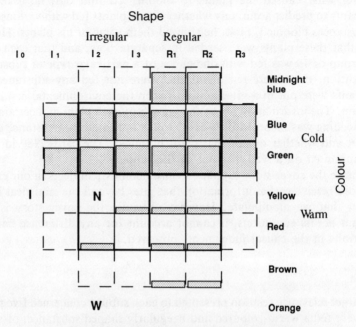

Consistent (shape-relevant) Condition

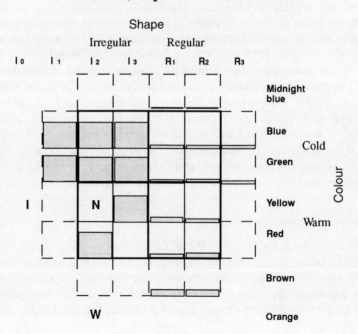

feature of the critical items in the target relation (e.g. the probability of blooming given yellowness) had to be constant across the consistent and inconsistent groups. The second and third constraints allow statistical relevance to be tested against cue validity. By definition, the contrast for a feature (e.g. yellowness) is the difference between its cue validity and the probability of the stimulus item's being in the category (e.g. blooming) given the absence of that feature (e.g absence of yellowness). Therefore varying the contrast for the features of the critical items, while keeping their cue validities constant (i.e. the last two constraints), implies that the relative frequency of blooming given the joint absence of the features of the critical items differed across the consistent and inconsistent conditions.

Consistency

To manipulate consistency between the target relevance relation and previous knowledge, we constructed stimuli that varied along two dimensions — shape and colour. Shape was statistically relevant for the consistent group, and colour was relevant for the inconsistent group. Statistical relevance was defined by the frequencies of blooming for substances of various colour and shapes. The target items have a type of shape that is generally associated with much blooming for the consistent group and a type of colour that is generally associated with little blooming for the inconsistent group.

Figure 15.2 summarizes the frequency structures of the stimuli in the inconsistent and consistent conditions, together with the positions of the critical items in the target relevance relations. The proportion of area that is shaded within each colour × shape cell represents the average proportion of plants that bloomed when fed with a substance of that colour and shape. A solid horizontal line within a cell indicates that *none* of the plants fed with that type of substance bloomed. An empty cell indicates that that type

---

Fig. 15.2. The average proportion of plants that bloomed when fed with substances of various shapes and colours in the inconsistent and consistent conditions. The proportion of area that is shaded within each colour × shape cell represents the average proportion of plants that bloomed when fed with a substance of that colour and shape. The cells in the 4 × 4 region drawn with solid lines in the middle of the diagram for each condition represent the information presented in the first part of the learning phase; the cells in the surrounding regions drawn with broken lines represent information presented only in the second part of the learning phase. A solid horizontal line within a cell indicates that none of the plants fed with that type of substance bloomed. The cells labelled N, W, and I indicate the values of the critical test items. An empty cell indicates that that type of substance was not presented at all during the learning phase. In addition to information represented in this figure, subjects in the inconsistent condition were shown that two out of ten plants that were not fed any substances bloomed, and those in the consistent condition were shown that one out of ten such plants bloomed.

of substance was not presented at all during the learning phase. In addition to the information summarized in this figure, subjects also received information on 10 plants that were not fed any substance.

As can be seen from Fig. 15.2, for the inconsistent condition, most plants fed with cold-coloured substances bloomed (on average nine out of ten); few plants fed with warm-coloured substances did (on average two out of ten). Two of the ten unfed plants bloomed. The frequency information on unfed plants allowed subjects to compute contrast for a substance conditional on the absence of all other substances. Therefore colour is the relevant dimension. In contrast, for the consistent condition, most plants fed with irregularly shaped substances bloomed (on average eight out of ten); few plants fed with regularly shaped substances did (on average one out of ten). One of the ten unfed plants bloomed. Therefore shape is the relevant dimension for this condition.

The cells labelled N, W, and I indicate the values of the three critical test items within the stimulus structures. These were the items in the target relevance relation. They all occupied the lower left quadrant of the stimulus structure (i.e. they were warm and irregular) and they were novel in different ways. The item N had the values I_2 and yellow; it had a *novel combination* of irregularity and warmth. The item W had a *warm* colour (orange) that did not belong to any type of colour (row) presented during the learning phase. The remaining item I had a novel *irregular* shape that did not belong to any type of shape (column) presented during the learning phase. Figure 15.3 shows the actual shapes of these three items and indicates their colour. The bottom diagram in that figure shows the shape of I. To see the novelty of this shape, compare it with the shapes for which subjects were given frequency information on blooming during the learning phase, which are depicted in Fig. 15.4. As can be seen, the shape of I is quite unlike the shapes of any other items.

We defined consistency by the relationship between the target relevance relation presented during the test phase and the frequency information for the various stimuli presented during the learning phase. Recall that the target relevance relation consists of a warm irregular item generally being associated with mostly blooming plants, whereas few plants fed none of the items bloomed. As can be seen in Fig. 15.2, in the colour-relevant condition, contrary to this target relation, warm items, regardless of shape, generally lead to little blooming. However, in the shape-relevant condition, consistent with this target relation, irregular items, regardless of colour, generally lead to much blooming.

The learning phase

The cells in the 4 × 4 region drawn with solid lines in the middle of the diagram for each condition represent the information presented in the first

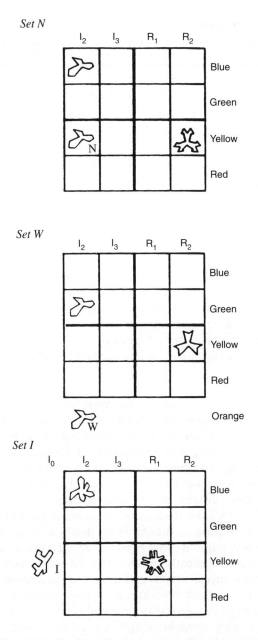

Fig. 15.3. The items in various categorization sets.

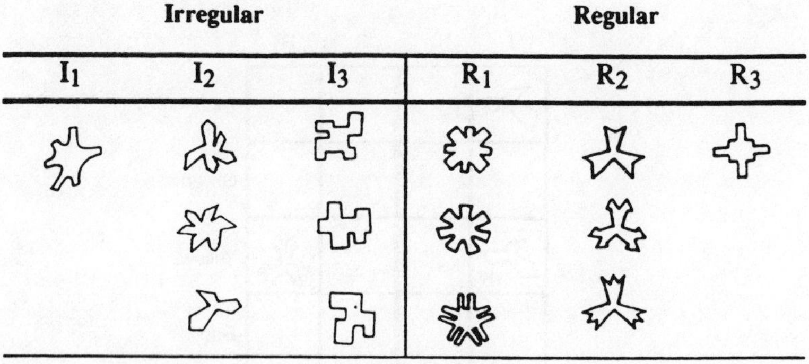

	Irregular			Regular	
I_1	I_2	I_3	R_1	R_2	R_3

Fig. 15.4. The shapes for which subjects received frequency information on blooming during the learning phase.

part of the learning phase; the cells in the surrounding regions drawn with broken lines represent information presented only in the second part of the learning phase. The two phases will be explained later. The items W and I first appeared in the second part of the learning phase; N first appeared in the test phase. No information regarding blooming was given about any of the critical items in any part of the learning phase.

Cue validity

To test cue validity against contrast, we constructed a pattern of blooming rates for each condition such that cue validity for each feature of the critical test items was identical across the two conditions for all levels of abstraction. As explained earlier, varying the contrast for the features of the test items, while keeping their cue validities constant, implies that the relative frequency of blooming given the joint absence of the features of these items (i.e. cold and regular) differed across the colour-relevant and shape-relevant conditions. In Fig. 15.2 this variation can be seen in the large difference in the proportion of shading in the top right quadrant of the stimulus structures of the two conditions: this region is mostly shaded in the colour-relevant condition, and mostly unshaded in the shape-relevant condition. Another large difference between conditions is in the proportion of shading of two cells in the lower left quadrant. Information about some cells in this region was necessary to rule out the possibility of an interaction between shape and colour (e.g. irregular shapes are not associated with blooming unless the colour is cold). Because of the difference in these two cells across the conditions, however, in order to keep the cue validities of the features of the critical items constant, we varied slightly both the average high rate and the average low rate of blooming across conditions. We also varied the number of items across cells within each condition. For example in order to keep the probability of blooming given the feature 'warm' (i.e. the bottom half of the structures) constant across conditions, the rate of blooming given warm and regular (i.e. the lower right quadrant) was slightly higher in the colour-relevant condition than in the shape-relevant condition. For both conditions, there were also many more items per cell in the lower right quadrant than in the lower left quadrant.

Given the patterns of blooming rates in the two conditions, our hypothesis predicts that the test items will be classified as non-causal in the colour-relevant condition and causal in the shape-relevant condition. In contrast, the cue validities of the features of these items predict that these items will not be classified differently across conditions.

Level of abstraction

To allow variation in contrast across levels of abstraction, for each of the dimensions of shape and colour, the stimulus items, which were presented pictorially, had visual features that could be represented at various levels of abstraction. For example the colour of an item can be represented as (a) a particular shade of yellow, (b) yellow, or (c) warm. Analogously for shape, an item can be classified as a particular variant of irregular shape type I_2, irregular, or of any shape. As can be seen, the shapes vary with respect to several features, the most important of which, for the purpose of our design, is regularity. We define a regular shape as one that is constructed by rotating an elemental outline i times (i is an integer greater than 2) around a point, end-to-end each time, until the first and last ends meet.

It can be seen from Fig. 15.2 that the contrast for the relevant feature in each condition is at a maximum at a certain level of abstraction. To see the contrast for a value at a certain level of abstraction on a dimension (e.g. blue), the difference between the average proportion of shading for that value and the average proportion of shading for the rest of the values on that dimension (e.g. all non-blue shades) should be noted. For the inconsistent condition, in which colour is relevant, the level of maximum contrast partitions warm from cold colours. For the consistent condition, in which shape is relevant, this level partitions regular from irregular shapes. The contrasts for values on the irrelevant dimension are low, regardless of the level of abstraction, as can also be seen in Fig. 15.2 by noting differences in the proportion of shading for various partitions. Figure 15.5 is a graph of the contrast values at various levels of abstraction on the relevant dimension in the colour- and shape-relevant conditions.

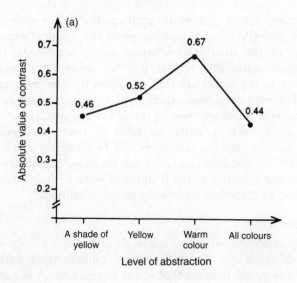

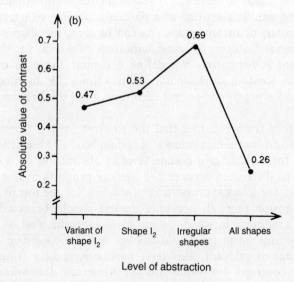

Fig. 15.5. Contrast at various levels of abstraction for (a) the colour-relevant and (b) shape-relevant conditions.

Procedure

During the learning phase, subjects established a knowledge base about the blooming of plants and the features of the substances fed to them. There were two parts to this phase. First, subjects were presented with information about whether plants fed with various types of substances bloomed. For each type of item fed to the plants, subjects recorded the number of plants that bloomed. Second, they were given various old and novel items and asked to predict whether plants fed with each type bloomed. Feedback was given for an item after each prediction, except when the item was one of the critical test items.

Then came the test phase, in which no feedback was given. Subjects were given the first of two sets of categorization tasks. This was followed by the presentation of five plants fed with a target substance. Subjects were asked to give a causal rating of the type of item in the target relation. They were also given a second set of categorization tasks, with the ordering of the causal rating and the second categorization tasks counterbalanced across subjects.

Categorization tasks

Subjects were asked to 'sort' the three items in various sets into, at most, two groups. As part of the test given by the gardener, they were told to base their categorization on the information regarding the substances and blooming. The three sets of concern to this experiment each contain one of the three critical test items N, W, and I. The other two items in each set were related to the critical item as follows: one of them matched the critical item's shape and the other matched that item's colour. The stimulus values of item N and the other two items in that set are shown in the top diagram in Fig. 15.3. The categorization sets for the other two critical items (set W and set I), also shown in Fig. 15.3, were constructed analogously, with the difference that the value along one of the dimensions is shared only at an abstract level. This is also the dimension on which the critical item has a novel value. For example, for the set involving item W, which had the novel colour orange and the old irregular shape I_2, one item was the same shape but green and the other item was yellow with shape R_2, thus sharing the colour value with W only at an abstract level.

One purpose of the categorization tasks was to test whether subjects were sensitive to contrast and therefore categorize items by the causally relevant dimension. If so, subjects in the colour-relevant condition should group the critical item with the colour-matched item, whereas subjects in the shape-relevant condition should group the critical item with the shape-matched item. Another purpose, attempted by the tasks involving items I and W, was to test whether subjects categorized the items by the causally relevant dimension at an abstract level. Thus subjects in the shape-relevant condition should group I with the item that had a different irregular shape, even though the third item was of exactly the same colour as I. Similarly, subjects in the colour-relevant condition should group W, which was orange, with the yellow item, even though the third item had exactly the same shape as W. The subjects were asked to sort these three sets twice, once before they saw the target-relevant relation and once afterwards.

Target relevance relation and causal rating

The target relevance relation for each group was presented under the following cover story. A friend from a distant foreign country visited the gardener and obtained a type of his plant-feeding substance (N, W, or I) together with some seeds of the flowering plant. The friend raised the plants in his own yard upon return to his country, feeding them with the substance, and subjects were shown that four out of five of these plants bloomed. To ensure that subjects observed the target relevance relation, they were asked a set of 'observation' questions. They were asked to refer to the gardener's plants presented in the learning phase and to report the percentage of unfed plants that bloomed. Then they were asked whether a much greater percentage of the plants fed with the novel substance in the friend's yard bloomed. It should be noticed that, although unconditional contrast could be computed, contrast conditional on the new environment — a plausible cause — cannot be computed owing to the lack of information on plants raised in the friend's yard that were not fed the novel substance. It should also be noticed that the new environment supplies a plausible alternative cause. In the inconsistent condition, this cause could be seen as counteracting the effect of colour. In addition to the observation questions, the subjects were asked a counterfactual question: 'Suppose that exactly the same granules were fed to a new group of plants in the gardener's yard. Would most of these plants have bloomed?' They were asked to rate on a scale from -4, which meant that these plants certainly would not have bloomed, to $+4$, which meant that these plants certainly would have bloomed. Zero indicated that the subject had no idea whether these plants would bloom. This counterfactual question aimed at indirectly assessing whether subjects thought that the critical item was a cause of blooming. Our prediction was that, for each of the three target relations, subjects in the consistent (shape-relevant) condition should give a higher causal rating than subjects in the inconsistent (colour-relevant) condition.

Results

First categorization tasks

Performance in the first categorization tasks confirmed that subjects indeed

Table 15.1. *The percentage of subjects who grouped particular target items with the colour-matched item (C-M), the shape-matched item (S-M), or neither in the first categorization task of the colour-relevant and shape-relevant conditions (n = 48 in each)*

	Item type grouped with target		
Condition	C-M item	S-M item	Neither
Target item N (*n* = 48)			
Colour-relevant	73	23	4
Shape-relevant	10	88	2
Target item W (*n* = 48)			
Colour-relevant	56	42	2
Shape-relevant	2	94	4
Target item I (*n* = 48)			
Colour-relevant	88	6	6
Shape-relevant	.25	69	6

categorized according to the statistically relevant dimension. Moreover, they defined statistical relevance at an abstract level. For the first categorization tasks with each of the critical items N, W, and I, Table 15.1 shows the percentage of subjects who grouped the critical item with the colour-matched item, the shape-matched item, or neither in the colour-relevant and shape-relevant conditions. For every categorization set, most subjects in the shape-relevant condition categorized the critical items by shape, whereas most subjects in the colour-relevant condition categorized these items by colour. The difference in categorization performance between conditions is highly significant for each set.

Causal rating task

It should be noted that the target-relevance relation in the colour-relevant condition was inconsistent only if subjects attributed the blooming to the colour of an item. For item W, the attribution has the additional requirement of being at the level of the warmth of the colour. Otherwise, the information on the target relation could be just a piece of information about a new item and would not elicit any conflict. The definition of consistency for the shape condition analogously depends on subjects having learned the relevant dimension at the appropriate level of generality. Therefore, to test our hypothesis about inconsistency, we restricted our analysis of the ratings for each critical item to subjects who correctly categorized that item in the first categorization task.

The causal ratings show that subjects in the inconsistent (colour-relevant)

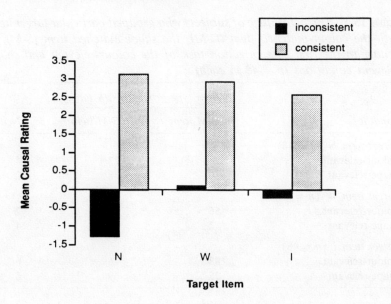

Fig. 15.6. Mean causal rating on the target items in the inconsistent and consistent conditions for subjects who categorized the respective items correctly in the first categorization task.

condition rated the novel items as less causal than subjects in the consistent (shape-relevant) condition. Fig. 15.6 shows the mean causal ratings on each of the critical items (N, W, and I) in the inconsistent and consistent conditions given by subjects who categorized the respective item according to the statistically relevant dimension in the first categorization task. Subjects in the inconsistent condition did not rate the target items as causal, whereas subjects in the consistent condition did. This difference was highly significant for every critical item. In sum, as we predicted, when given a target relevance relation subjects judged it to be more causal when it is consistent than when it is inconsistent with their knowledge about contrast involving the potential cause in question at a level of abstraction that yields maximum contrast.

Second categorization tasks

Performance in the second categorization tasks supports the same conclusion. As a result of the contradictory target relation, a smaller proportion of subjects in the inconsistent condition grouped the critical items with the colour-matched item. None the less, reliably more of them did so than subjects in the consistent condition.

Summary

We manipulated coherence in terms of consistency between a target relevance relation and a statistical relevance relation at a more abstract level implied by prior causal knowledge. We showed that the target relation is accepted as causal when it is consistent with knowledge of a relevance relation at the more abstract level; otherwise, it is not accepted as causal. Moreover, we showed that the cue validities of the features of the test items, which were kept constant across conditions, cannot explain the systematic differences obtained between the inconsistent and consistent conditions.

ASSESSING ALTERNATIVE EXPLANATIONS

Baselines for assessing categorization performance

It might be argued that evidence from the categorization tasks did not show that subjects in the colour-relevant condition — the one critical for demonstrating the role of coherence — acquired contrast at the abstract level of warmth of colour. If so, conflict with a relevance relation at the level of maximum contrast might not be what explains the difference in causal judgements across conditions. The argument might proceed as follows. If one assumes that the subjects are equally likely to group the target item with the colour-matched item as with the shape-matched item when they do not know which dimension is relevant, then there is a 50 per cent chance of either classification and subjects in the colour-relevant condition do not perform significantly differently from this 'chance' level for the comparison involving the critical item W. Adopting this as the chance level might be reasonable because other possible ways of sorting can be excluded: (a) classifying all items into the same category counters one's understanding of 'sorting' as putting into separate groups, even though the instructions allowed it; (b) the third of the three possible pairings — grouping the colour-matched item with the shape-matched item, leaving the target item by itself — can readily be ruled out because two items shared no feature, whereas the target item shared a feature with each of the other two items.

It should be noted that the above argument applies only for classification of item W. Subjects in the colour-relevant condition classified the other items, N and I, according to colour reliably above the chance level. Therefore, by the above criterion they did learn which is the relevant dimension. Similarly, subjects in the shape-relevant condition classified all three critical item according to shape reliably above the chance level, indicating that they induced both relevant dimension and the optimum level of abstraction.

However, a more appropriate baseline for comparison is not chance, but people's spontaneous classification of a set of items given the perceptual similarity among the items. It is possible, for example, that shape is a much more salient dimension than colour, leading most subjects to categorize by shape spontaneously. The categorization performance of subjects in the colour-relevant condition might then reveal a significant influence of the knowledge acquired during the learning phase.

To allow this comparison, we assessed subjects' perceptual similarity judgements outside the context of the knowledge base established in the learning phase. Two groups of subjects were shown a sheet depicting the three items in either categorization set W or set I, and were asked: 'Among the three items, which two do you think look most similar to each other?' In the categorization task described earlier in the consistency experiment, we asked subjects to sort the three items into at most two groups. To equate for the possibility that the items are placed in a single group, we gave subjects the option of judging the three items as equally similar in the perceptual similarity test.

None of the 25 subjects given set W judged item W and the colour-matched item as the most similar pair; 24 indicated that W and the shape-matched item were most similar, and the one remaining subject judged all three to be equally similar. Compared with this baseline, the percentage of subjects in the colour-relevant condition pairing item W with the colour-matched item was reliably higher. This difference indicates that subjects in the colour-relevant condition learnt that the warmth of colour was the critical dimension.

Thirty of the 42 subjects given set I indicated that item I and the shape-matched item were most similar. Compared with this result, the percentage of subjects in the shape-relevant condition who paired item I with the shape-matched item did not reliably increase. However, there was a reliable difference across conditions in how subjects justified their choices. For the 30 subjects in the perceptual similarity condition who paired item I with the shape-matched item, (excluding three who did not give any justification), only 44 per cent referred to regularity in some way. In contrast, for the 34 subjects in the shape-relevant condition who chose the same pair in either categorization task (excluding nine who did not give any justification) 72 per cent mentioned regularity in some form.

In sum, when compared with the corresponding baseline of subjects who made a perceptual similarity judgement on set W and set I, as well as with the baseline of subjects in the shape-relevant condition, the categorization performance of subjects in the colour-relevant condition shows that they did infer the relevant dimension. Moreover, they inferred it at an abstract level of warmth. A directly analogous conclusion can be drawn about the categorization performance of subjects in the shape-relevant condition.

Judging the novel items by consistency with the most similar items

Another counter-argument against our interpretation is that subjects might have simply classified or rated the test items by assuming that they should have effects similar to those of the most perceptually similar items. In particular, the other items in the lower left quadrant of the stimulus structure in Fig. 15.2 were associated with little blooming in the colour-relevant condition and much blooming in the shape-relevant condition. Therefore the amount of blooming in the test items would contradict subjects' expectations based on these adjacent items in the colour-relevant condition, but be consistent with their expectations in the shape-relevant condition.

This argument is not supported by our observations. First, none of the 96 subjects in the experiment justified their performance by similarity to any of the adjacent items in the stimulus. Instead, over 90 per cent of the subjects justified their performance by referring to a feature of either the colour or shape dimension. More importantly, if subjects did base their performance on a comparison with the adjacent items, rather than on a learned dimension, there should be no interaction between the three items and experimental conditions, i.e. the ordering of performance on these items should remain constant across conditions. The test items are a priori just as similar to the adjacent items across the consistent and inconsistent conditions. On the the contrary, subjects in the colour-relevant condition conformed less to our predictions for item W than for the other two test items, and subjects in the shape-relevant condition conformed less to our predictions for item I than for the other two items. For example, for the first set of categorization tasks, consider subjects who classified W, but not I, according to the relevant dimension, and conversely those who classified I, but not W, according to the relevant dimension. For the colour-relevant condition, one and 16 subjects, respectively, fell into these two categories, whereas for the shape-relevant condition, the respective numbers were 13 and one. This interaction follows from the level of generality required for categorizing W and I given colour or given shape as the relevant dimension: for the colour-relevant condition, classifying W according to colour requires the relevance relation to be represented at the higher level of warmth, whereas classifying I according to colour does not. A converse ordering of requirements holds for the shape-relevant condition.

A difference between conditions in effective sample size or in contrast values

It might be argued that the difference between causal judgements across the consistent and inconsistent conditions merely shows that subjects induced the relevant dimension, but does not imply that they induced contrast at the abstract level of regularity or warmth, nor that consistency between the relevance relation at the general level and the target relation at the specific level explains the difference in causal judgements across the conditions. As described earlier, our critical test items W and I were constructed so that there was a novel value along one dimension, and a known value along the other dimension. Consider judgements on item W across the two conditions for subjects who induced the respective relevant dimensions. For the inconsistent (colour-relevant) condition, because W was of a novel colour, the relevance relation involving W could be treated as the only piece of relevance information on this value of colour, if subjects did not generalize the relevant relation to the level of warmth. Therefore the sample size for this relevance relation would be relatively small. For the consistent (shape-relevant) condition, the same item W was of a known shape. Hence there is much more information about that value. Thus, even without generalization to an abstract level, subjects might still rate W less causal in the colour-relevant than the shape-relevant condition, simply as a result of the smaller effective sample size in the colour-relevant condition. (A similar argument can be made about the categorization performance.)

This argument is refuted empirically in two ways. First, if the same argument is applied to item I in the consistent (shape-relevant) condition, it would predict that the causal ratings for I in that condition would be comparable to that for W in the inconsistent condition. Item I has a known colour but a novel irregular shape, and the target relevance relation could be treated as the only piece of relevance information on this value of shape for the shape-relevant condition. Contradicting this prediction, the mean rating given to W by subjects who categorized W correctly in the colour-relevant condition was reliably lower than the mean rating given to I by subjects who categorized I correctly in the shape-relevant condition. This difference follows from the difference in consistency across the two conditions.

Second, the argument that the low ratings for W are due to a smaller effective sample size implies that if subjects are given the target regularity involving W alone, without the knowledge base established in the learning phase, their ratings for W would be comparable to those given by the colour-relevant subjects. We tested subjects in a 'no prior knowledge' condition in which they were given a cover story and a rating task highly similar to those in the consistency experiment, except that the learning phase and the first categorization tasks were omitted. Information regarding blooming identical with that in the colour-relevant condition was given for the plants that were not fed any substances in the gardener's yard and for the plants that were fed the target item in the friend's yard. The mean rating for an item that corresponded to W was reliably higher than the mean rating for W for the colour-relevant condition. This difference indicates that the low ratings for W in the colour-relevant condition cannot be attributed to a small effective sample size, but are due to the inconsistency between the relevance relation involving W and the contrast for the warmth of colour established in the learning phase.

An analogous comparison between the shape-relevant condition and a corresponding 'no prior knowledge' condition shows that the mean rating for item I in the shape-relevant condition is reliably higher than that in the corresponding 'no prior knowledge' condition. The above comparisons indicate that it was the knowledge base established during the learning phase that lowered the causal ratings for subjects in the colour-relevant condition and raised them for subjects in the shape-relevant condition.

Furthermore, these results indicate that the difference in causal ratings between the consistent and inconsistent conditions cannot be due to the small difference in the target relation presented to the two groups. Recall that the contrast values for the two groups were different in the ratio 1:10. The exact same difference was presented to the two groups in the 'no prior knowledge' condition.

Recognizing the novel relation as an instance of a known type

It might be argued that no principle of coherence is involved: the findings can be explained by the categorization of a novel instance of a known type of relevance relation. People judge a target relevance relation to be causal if it is an instance of a superordinate causal category; they judge it non-causal otherwise. We do not disagree that the application of prior causal knowledge may be regarded as a case of recognizing an instance as a member of a causal category. However, we do disagree that this renders coherence irrelevant. On the contrary, we would argue conversely that coherence plays a role in categorization. There is no logical reason why a complex category involving a general rule and an exception case cannot be created. Exemplar models of categorization (Medin and Shaffer 1978), for example, allow the formation or definition of a category consisting of any arbitrary collection of instances. Such models, if extended to the domain of causal reasoning, are unable to explain the distinction between genuine and spurious causes. The categorization explanation above assumes that we do not form a new category consisting of the abstract relevance relation and a conflicting specific relevance relation. Although we some-times form categories that contain exception cases, the very fact that we do not resolve conflicts by indefinitely creating such categories reveals the role of coherence.

In addition to this theoretical argument, some results from our experiment cannot be explained simply by reference to a 'cause' category defined at the abstract level of the dimensions. A pattern of performance in the categorization tasks shows an influence by information at multiple levels of abstraction. Consider how the three groups of subjects in the colour-relevant condition who were given a target relevance relation involving items N, W or I categorized set W in the second categorization task. At the abstract level of warmth of colour, the three groups received identical relevance information. However, at a more specific level, subjects who were shown the target relevance relation for item W, which is orange, received evidence supporting a positive relevance relation between orangeness and blooming. In contrast, the remaining two groups of subjects did not receive any such evidence. The results of the second categorization task show that subjects who were presented the relevance relation for N or I were reliably more likely to categorize W by colour (78 per cent of 18 subjects) than those who were presented the relation for W (33 per cent of nine subjects). Thus, while the differences in categorization and rating performance between the consistent and inconsistent conditions demonstrate the influence of knowledge of relevance at an abstract level, the above difference in categorization performance indicates an influence of knowledge of relevance at a specific level.

DISCUSSION AND CONCLUSION

We illustrated the top-down influence of superordinate causal knowledge, but left unanswered the important question of how that knowledge might have come about. In special cases that knowledge might be innate (Garcia *et al.* 1968; LoLordo 1979; Baillargeon 1986, 1987; Leslie and Keeble 1987; Gelman 1990; LoLordo, 1979), but in most cases it is probably learned. Computing conditional contrasts, which we mentioned at the beginning of this chapter, is one way of learning new causal relations, particularly for situations in which a candidate cause is independently manipulated. However, innate knowledge and conditional contrast cannot fully account for the inception of causal knowledge. An example given by Salmon (1989) illustrates a case that does not involve knowledge of a superordinate cause, is not innate, and does not allow the application of conditional contrasts. Long before the time of Newton, mariners were fully aware of the correlation between the position and phase of the moon and the rise and fall of the tides. However, they did not infer a causal connection between the moon and the tides, and they had no explanation for the ebb and flow of the tides. It was not until Newton furnished his Law of Universal Gravitation that the tides could actually be explained by a causal connection. How did Newton's law make the connection between the moon and the tides causal? Why is Newton's law itself causal? This example seems to point to the role of another aspect of coherence. What Newton's law adds is the subsumption of diverse phenomena — celestial and terrestrial motion — under a single general principle.

To summarize, even when conditional contrasts cannot be computed, people are able to make a systematic distinction between a genuine cause and a spurious cause. According to the power view, a statistical relevance relation is judged as causal if one knows of an underlying power or mechanism. To explicate this view, we propose that an underlying power means a causal relation that implies a relevance relation at a more abstract level than the target relevance relation; when the target relation is consistent with the more abstract contrast it will be accepted as causal, but when it is not consistent with any such contrast it will be less likely to be accepted as causal. Solely by manipulating consistency between a target relevance relation and a more abstract relevance relation inherent in a previously acquired causal relation, we were able to produce the predicted difference in causal judgements. Like the power view, our explanation *assumes* rather than explains the causality of the power in question. However, statistical relevance in terms of conditional contrasts, and coherence in a more general form than consistency alone, may provide an account of the inception of learned causal relations.

ACKNOWLEDGEMENTS

The research reported in this chapter was supported by National Science Foundation grant DBS 9121298. We thank Michael Anderson, Daniel Andler, Bruce Burns, Anthony Dickinson, Keith Holyoak, Frank Keil, Michael Morris, and Dan Sperber for discussion of earlier versions of this paper. Requests for reprints may be sent to Patricia Cheng at the Department of Psychology, Franz Hall, University of California, Los Angeles, CA 90024-1563, USA.

REFERENCES

Baillargeon, R. (1986). Representing the existence and the location of hidden objects: object permanence in 6- and 8-month old infants. *Cognition* **23**, 21–41.

Baillargeon, R. (1987). Young infant's reasoning about the physical and spatial properties of a hidden object. *Cognitive Development* **2**, 179–200.

Bullock, M. (1979). Aspects of the young child's theory of causation. Unpublished Doctoral Dissertation, University of Pennsylvania.

Bullock, M., Gelman, R., and Baillargeon, R. (1982). The development of causal reasoning. In *The developmental psychology of time* (ed. W. J. Friedman). Academic Press, New York.

Cartwright, N. (1983). *How the laws of physics lie.* Clarendon Press, Oxford.

Cheng, P. W. (1993). Separating causal laws from casual facts: pressing the limits of statistical relevance. In *The psychology of learning and motivation*, Vol. 30 (ed. D. L. Medin). Academic Press, New York.

Cheng, P. W. and Holyoak, K. J. (in press). Complex adaptive systems as intuitive statisticians: causality, contingency, and prediction. In *Comparative approaches to cognition* (ed. J. A. Meyer and H. Roitblat). MIT Press, Cambridge, MA.

Cheng, P. W. and Novick, L. R. (1990). A probabilistic contrast model of causal induction. *Journal of Personality and Social Psychology* **58**, 545-67.

Garcia, J., McGowan, B., Ervin, F., and Koelling, R. (1968). Cues: their relative effectiveness as reinforcers. *Science* **160**, 794-5.

Gelman, R. (1990). First principles organize attention to and learning about relevant data: number and the animate-inanimate distinction as examples. *Cognitive Science* **14**, 79-106.

Leslie, A. M. and Keeble, S. (1987). Do six-month-old infants perceive causality? *Cognition* **25**, 265-88.

Lien, Y. and Cheng, P. W. (1992). How do people tell whether a regularity is causal? Presented at the Annual Meeting of the Psychonomics Society, November 1992, St Louis, MO.

LoLordo, V. M. (1979). Selective associations. In *Mechanisms of learning and motivation: a memorial volume to Jerzy Konorski* (ed. A. Dickinson and R. A. Boakes). Erlbaum, Hillsdale, NJ.

Medin, D. L. and Shaffer, M. M. (1978). Context theory of classification learning. *Psychological Review* **85**, 207-38.

Reed, S. K. (1972). Pattern recognition and categorization. *Cognitive Psychology* **3**, 382-407.

Reichenbach, H. (1956). *The direction of time.* University of California Press, Berkeley, CA.

Rosch, E. and Mervis, C. B. (1975). Family resemblances: studies in the internal structure of categories. *Cognitive Psychology* **7**, 573-605.

Salmon, W. C. (1971). Statistical explanation. In *Statistical explanation and statistical relevance* (ed. W. C. Salmon, R. C. Jeffrey, and J. G. Greeno), pp. 29-87. University of Pittsburgh Press.

Salmon, W. C. (1989). Four decades of scientific explanation. In *Scientific explanation: Minnesota studies in the philosophy of science*, vol. 13, (ed. P. Kitcher and W. C. Salmon). Minneapolis: University of Minnesota Press.

Shultz, T. R. (1982). Rules of causal attribution. *Monographs of the Society for Research in Child Development* **47**(1).

Suppes, P. (1970). *A probabilistic theory of causality.* North-Holland, Amsterdam.

White, P. A. (1989). A theory of causal processing. *British Journal of Psychology* **80**, 431-54.

DISCUSSION

Participants: F. Keil, M. Morris

Morris: At first glance, your proposal of general-purpose covariational processes seems to buck the trend of this conference, which is to propose domain-specific modules for causal perception. You exhume Hume instead of dancing on his grave. However, it seems to me that your model is consistent with the view that causal representations are domain-specific. As an example of a superordinate causal relation, you give the 'laws of mechanical motion' (p. 465). It seems reasonable that this would be the natural level of abstraction for a causal relation—it seems to capture a natural kind of causation. If this is the kind of top-down knowledge that guides causal induction, then causal induction would differ across physical, psychological, and social domains. Does the coherence model make different predictions about genuine/spurious cause judgements than modular models?

Cheng and Lien: You are right that, although we regard covariation as a necessary component of normal causal induction, we are not purely Humean. We postulate coherence as another component, and we also allow specific innate constrains, presumably a small set of them. However, these additional assumptions do not turn our approach into a modular one. A major difference concerns the distinction between process on the one hand, and the input and output of a process on the other. We assume that, by modules for mechanical motion and social phenomena, you mean different processes for causal inference in these domains. As you point out, because our hypothesis assumes domain-specific superordinate causal laws, it predicts that causal judgements in different domains will be influenced by different top-down constraints. However, the variation across domains need not reflect the workings of different processes. The superordinate laws, rather than being processes, could be input to a process that is general across causal domains. (We envisage such a process to involve covariation in a more general form than that defined for discrete variables, and coherence in a more general sense than consistency alone.) Moreover, these laws could themselves be the output of such a general process. In terms of our example about the laws of mechanical motion, we allow the possibility that such laws, which serve as the top-down input to a general process involving covariation and coherence, are previously the output of the same general process.

Our predictions, which are based on statistical relevance and consistency, are more specific than those that follow from the modular view. For example, not only do we predict differences across domains when the statistical relevance relations inherent in the superordinate causal relations are different, we also predict that, within a domain, top-down influences would occur in the same way. The top-down influence that we demonstrated in our experiment is the result of differing relevance relations within the same domain.

We do not see our approach as being incompatible with evidence supporting domain-specific constraints. Specific constraints on the perception of mechanical causation that covers phenomena such as launching, for example, is not incompatible with covariation being a general process, as we have argued (Cheng 1993). The specific constraints of this module seem to supplement rather than replace covariation. Our approach and the modularity approach have potentially complementary goals: we seek to understand domain-general aspects of causal inference; modularists seek to understand domain-specific aspects.

Morris: Do you think that coherence supports causal beliefs even when the beliefs are erroneous? A case in point might be paranoid schizophrenics who have extremely coherent systems of causal beliefs that are wildly delusional.

Cheng and Lien: The example you mention certainly suggests so. Gilbert Lewis described a case study in New Guinea of a normal man—the man explaining the pain in his knee—that illustrates the same point. Perhaps covariation and coherence are separable components.

Keil: It would seem that children and even infants can learn that small physical events can have large physical consequences: the key that starts the car moving, or opens a door; the switch that lights up the whole room or starts a large toy train set moving; the tiny nudge that knocks over countless fragile items in a house that have the misfortune of being delicately balanced. Can these sorts of general heuristics really constrain much of our inferences about the natural world, or are much more specific hunches about mechanisms at work, such as not seeing any plausible mechanism linking a rooster to the rising of the sun?

Cheng and Lien: Your examples bring up several important points. First, there are situations in which conditional contrast does apply. In your examples about the keys and the switches, there is independent manipulation of the candidate cause. These cases allow a comparison of the states of the target phenomenon before and after the manipulation, with other factors held constant or very nearly constant. Conditional contrasts can lead to the introduction of novel causal relations. Therefore we would expect that young children and others who do not have any understanding of the superordinate causal laws would still regard such cases as causal.

Second, although some of your examples do not fit the laws of mechanical motion (e.g. turning an electrical key to open a garage door) and some do not concern any mechanical effect (e.g. lighting a room), all of them are consistent with some causal superordinate covariational relation (e.g. electric current producing light and heat in a resistor) or a link in a chain of such relations. The example of delicately balanced objects falling may not involve independent manipulation, but it is consistent with gravity acting on multiple links in a causal chain. People have plenty of experiences involving gravity. Commonsensically, they probably perceive the weights of the objects as the causes, supported by experiences of very light objects such as balloons not falling or falling slowly, and objects beyond some threshold of weight falling or falling at a faster rate unless there is some counteracting cause (e.g. being supported or having flapping wings). We postulate that when conditional contrasts do *not* apply, and when the target relation is inconsistent with any superordinate covariational relation implied by a causal relation, then it is judged as spurious. None of your examples fit both conditions.

Third, one might object that we are simply replacing the term 'mechanism' with 'superordinate causal relation, or chain of such relations, that implies one or more covariational relations' (as indeed we are). By doing so, what might we hope to gain to offset the wretched clumsiness of the new phrase? As we mentioned, the mechanism view is often characterized as an alternative that opposes covariation. It is important to show that they are not opposing alternatives because, although the mechanism view does contribute by pointing out the importance of top-down influences in causal inference, it does not offer any clue as to how knowledge of the mechanisms (e.g. an electrical current brightening a light bulb) is acquired. Unless some other process is proposed to solve the problem, the opposition to covariation leaves the mechanism view at a dead end. Recasting the mechanism view in terms of covariation and coherence not only makes the view more specific and testable, it also allows an extension of the covariation view — based on conditional contrasts, in cases where they apply — to account for the acquisition of mechanisms. We do not object to the postulation of mechanisms, powers, and capacities, either as the output of a causal inference process or as the subsequent top-down input to this process, but we do disagee with their proliferate use as unexplained primitives in a theory of causal induction.

Keil: The demonstration that people will sort elements at high levels of abstraction even in the face of competing lower-level perceptual similarities is extremely important to developing a general model of concept acquisition and change. But it is difficult to know how to follow this up without a better idea of how levels of abstraction are to be understood. Do you mean distance from perceptual primitives, distance from individual instances in a taxonomic hierarchy, distance along an attribute to a relational-based similarity continuum (Dedre Gentner), or some combination of these or yet other senses? It would seem to matter which is meant; if not, perhaps more detail of why not would help.

Cheng and Lien: By abstraction, we mean inclusiveness in a taxonomic hierarchy. We clarified this point in our chapter in the light of your question. Abstractness in Gentner's sense does not seem to work for us. Cheng and Novick (1990) treat causes involving more than one factor as higher-order contrasts (differences between differences in conditional probabilities of the effect for a cause involving two factors). It does not seem intuitive to say that a cause involving more factors is more abstract, even though they involve higher-order relations. For example, the conjunction of watering, exposure to sunlight, and plant food as the cause of a plant's healthy growth feels more complex, but not more abstract, than a push by one child as the cause of another child's falling.

16

Logic and language in causal explanation
DENIS J. HILTON

Wittgenstein once spoke of the need not to confuse the grammar of language with the grammar of reality in the analysis of thought. Descriptions that may superficially sound the same may in fact denote quite different underlying cognitive processes. Thus a 'theory' might refer to a well-supported set of covering laws for a class of events, such as Einstein's Theory of Relativity, or to a tentative supposition about the particular cause of a single event, such as when we say that 'the police are working on the theory that the murder was the work of terrorists'. An 'explanation' might refer to the cause of an event, as when we say 'he died because he was poisoned', or explain how we know that something is the case, as when we say 'I know he is dead because I saw the body'. Seeing a body, unlike poisoning it, does not cause that body's death.

In this chapter I take the position that causal explanation is a speech act, in which *someone* explains *something* to *someone else* (cf. Turnbull 1986; Harré 1988; Turnbull and Slugoski 1988; Hilton 1990, 1991). Causal explanation depends on who is doing the explaining, what is being explained, and what the explainee knows and wants to know. The aims of a causal inquiry thus determine what is at issue and what needs explaining. Therefore a conversational model of causal explanation, which highlights the interpersonal dimension of explaining, is outlined below.

In particular, it is argued that explicit recognition of the interpersonal functions of explanation enables a better understanding of the logic of causal explanation. For example, it helps us to distinguish interpersonal relevance from truth as contributors to the quality of a given explanation, to distinguish the cognitive process of causal scenario generation from the conversational process of interpersonal explanation, to distinguish causal explanation from epistemic justification, and to distinguish the explanation of general and particular events. Such distinctions are not afforded by the various analogies of common sense with scientific explanation (Kelly 1955; Kelly 1967, 1972, 1973; Nisbett and Ross 1980; Read and Marcus-Newhall 1993) which highlight the importance of truth and accuracy but not relevance in causal explanations. In related vein, these 'man the scientist' analogies do not explicate the interpersonal functions of causal explanation, and obscure the divergences between the pragmatic localized concerns of everyday explanation and the quest for generalizations characteristic of scientific explanation.

A CONVERSATIONAL MODEL OF CAUSAL EXPLANATION

The conversational model of causal explanation (Hilton 1990, 1991) highlights the role of counterfactual reasoning, contrast cases, and conversational constraints in causal explanation. Counterfactual reasoning can be used to determine the necessary conditions without which the event would not have occurred (Mackie 1980; Hesslow 1983, 1984, 1985; Hart and Honoré 1985; Hilton 1988; Lipé 1991).

In many cases, there are many necessary conditions without which the target event would not have happened, and which can fairly be considered candidate causes. In the case of the explosion of the *Challenger* space shuttle shortly after lift-off on 26 January 1986, there is indeed a plethora of such conditions that can be identified by counterfactual reasoning. Thus, we might reason that the space shuttle would not have exploded 'if only' the weather had not been so cold at launch time, the seals had functioned properly in cold weather, the wind had not blown cold from the frozen oxygen tank over the adjacent seals making them even colder, there had not been a wind shear shortly after lift-off which unseated the seals, there had not been oxygen in the atmosphere when the hydrogen burst out, the NASA launch team had not ignored the engineers who warned against launching, there had not been pressure for NASA to meet its launch schedule, hydrogen did not explode when mixed with oxygen, and so on (McConnell 1987).

In most ordinary conversation, we select just one or two factors as *the* cause. To do this, we need selection rules. The conversational model proposes that people compare the target case with a contrast case in which the target event did not occur. The selection of the contrast case will be determined by the kind of question at issue. For example, the usual question for the lawyer, historian, and layperson, but not the scientist, is particular rather than general (Hart and Honoré 1985). In the case of *Challenger*, they would ask how and why *this particular* explosion happened when and how it did, not how and why explosions happen *in general*. Hart and Honoré (1985) propose that a usual strategy is to contrast the target case with the case of normal functioning where the disaster did not happen and to select the 'abnormal condition' which differentiates the two. Experimental research has indicated the power of this selection criterion (Hilton and Slugaski 1986; see also McGill, 1989).

The *Challenger* space shuttle was launched in the coldest weather conditions of any of the 25 space shuttle launches up to that point; hence the cold weather would be identified as the abnormal condition without which the disaster would not have happened and thus is defined as *the* cause. Indeed, cold weather figures prominently in the explanation of the space shuttle disaster (McConnell 1987). Other necessary conditions, such as the presence of oxygen in the atmosphere and the disposition of hydrogen to explode when mixed with oxygen, are not cited as causes because they do not differentiate the disaster from normal functioning.

However, just as 'cold weather' is not the only explanation possible for the *Challenger* disaster, so is the normal case not the only possible contrast case (Hesslow 1988). Another possible contrast case is the 'ideal case', as when economists compare a real economy with an ideal economy or doctors compare an actual body with a healthy body and thus identify 'high inflation' or 'high blood pressure' relative to some ideal level as causes of dysfunction. It should be noted that, although high inflation or high blood pressure might be the statistical norm amongst a given reference group of economies (South America) or people (stressed executives), they would still be cited as causes of their ills through reference to the ideal case.

In the case of the *Challenger* explosion, comparison with ideal performance aids identification of malfunctions in both the design of the rocket and the operation of the launch decision-making process. Thus the 'faulty seal' or 'defective O-ring' is regarded as deficient because it lost flexibility at low temperatures, thus failing to meet the engineering ideal of effective sealing at all temperatures (McConnell 1987). Likewise, the failure of NASA decision-makers to follow standard operating procedures (SOPs) in the ill-fated conference on the evening before the launch became identified as one of the contributory causes to the disaster (McConnell 1987). As one participant commented afterwards, he felt that the rules of the game had changed from having to prove that it was safe to fly, which is the norm in aeronautics, to having to prove that it was unsafe to fly.

Hart and Honoré (1985) make a distinction between *explanatory* inquiries, which seek to understand how an event happened, and *attributive* inquiries, which seek to apportion responsibility and blame for an event whose genesis is effectively understood. This distinction implies a difference between *causal* and *responsibility* questions which, as noted above, showed itself clearly in accounts of the *Challenger* disaster. For example Marx *et al.* (1987) suggested that the disaster held as many lessons for American management practices as it did for American engineering. Consistent with the view of Hart and Honoré (1985) that attributive inquiries become relevant *after* an event has been explained, we found that the *New York*

Times tended to pose responsibility questions only after the process of causal explanation had begun to exhaust itself, indicating that the physical mechanisms underlying the disaster had been understood (Hilton *et al.* 1992).

The kind of contrast cases we bring to bear will define what we consider to be normal, and hence which conditions we see as abnormal and thus causes. This may explain why *The Times* of London identified America's pioneer spirit as a cause of the disaster. Whereas nineteenth-century Britain had this spirit, in this journalist's view, this factor now makes the difference between the two countries.

In addition, it is worth noting that events can be explained by reference to hypothetical contrast cases which never occurred, as when we explain President Bush's decision to enter the Gulf War by reference to the counterfactual scenario of what would have happened had he not done so. Thus Bush was able to explain to his troops that Americans were in the Gulf because their cause was just and America's interests were at stake, implying a contrast with a scenario in which international law was ignored and vital oil supplies would be in the hands of a man whom America could not trust. It is not clear how this kind of explanation could be made straightforwardly on the basis of observation of covariation.

Finally, since causal explanation is a form of conversation, it is governed by the rules of conversation. According to this view, explanations are typically guided by co-operative concerns and must satisfy general rules of conversation such as Grice's (1975) maxims of quality, quantity, relation, and manner which would require explanations to be true, informative, relevant, and clear. Causal questions and answers are thus pragmatic phenomena whose interpretation depends on context. The point that explanations have to satisfy relevance as well as truth criteria in order to be felicitous in Austin's (1962) sense will be returned to later.

The above model of common sense causal explanation will be treated a kind of 'prototype'. It incorporates core features (counterfactuals, contrast cases, conversational constraints). It suggests that 'normal' explanations resolve a puzzle as to why a particular event occurred in a target scenario rather than in some contrast scenario. The kind of contrast case brought to bear on a focal scenario may be determined by pragmatic factors such as who is asking the question, what his or her state of knowledge is, and what the aim of the enquiry is. We may assume that the explainer and explainee are 'normal' people, unless we attribute special characteristics to them such as being scientists or children.

According to this point of view, the 'prototypic' explanation is one which focuses on the abnormal rather than the normal case. This is one way in which the present approach goes beyond that of Cheng and Novick (1991) in emphasizing the role of pragmatically defined contrasts in causal explanation. Thus Cheng and Novick (1991, experiment 2) show convincingly that people *can* focus on and explain prevalent events (e.g. why four crops grew whereas one failed by using the same contrastive logic as that adopted to explain rare events (e.g. why one crop grew whereas four failed). However, consistent with the conversational approach, Hilton and Slugoski (1993) showed that subjects found questions that focus on rare rather than prevalent events in Cheng and Novick's scenarios to be more natural. This result suggests that, while people can explain both normal and abnormal events, from a psychological point of view it is more natural in such contexts to focus on *abnormal* events. This position is similar to that of Kahneman and Miller (1986) (see also Kahneman and Tversky 1982) on counterfactual reasoning, who argue that it is easier to imagine the counterfactual of an abnormal rather than a normal event.

CONSTRUCTING CAUSAL SCENARIOS VERSUS GIVING CAUSAL EXPLANATIONS

Causal explanation of particular events seems to involve two main processes. The first consists of building a mental model or causal scenario for an event which represents it in its full complexity. The second consists of selecting a part of that scenario which is worth mentioning in a given explanation. The distinction between causal diagnosis (identifying the probable cause) and causal selection (selecting a cause from a set of necessary conditions) is essentially logical: no causal selection can occur until there is a set of necessary conditions underlying the production of an event to select from.

At this point, a caveat is in order. Although the generation of a scenario is necessary before a given explanation can be furnished, further scenario generation may follow from a given verbal explanation. For example, a physician may be able to determine from a visual and tactile investigation that the swelling of a knee is due to 'soft tissue damage', and give such an explanation to the patient. However, the physician may have to await the results of radiology or arthroscopy before constructing a more elaborate mental model of the trauma causing the swelling, this enabling a more precise explanation referring to 'strained ligaments' or 'torn cartilage'.

In fact, evidence has accumulated that people *do* construct fairly elaborate mental models of the causal networks underlying the production of events. In some settings, such as story comprehension (Trabasso and Sperry 1985; Trabasso and van den Broek 1985) and social judgement (Read and Marcus-Newhall 1993), we may expect the model-construction process to be relatively effortless, automatic, and unconscious in so far as most stories and many social judgement tasks are 'user-friendly', i.e. they are presented in such a way as to aid comprehension. In other settings, such as jury decision-making (Pennington and Hastie 1986; Carlson and Dulany 1988; Bennett 1992) and clinical diagnosis (Elstein *et al.* 1978; Weber *et al.* 1993), the causal connections between events may be initially unclear to the judge, who must therefore carry out more 'detective work', such as searching for more information and trying out various hypotheses, in order to fill in the gaps and construct a coherent causal scenario.

The processes of scenario construction are illustrated below with reference to a study of how the *New York Times* built up an explanation for the *Challenger* space shuttle disaster (Hilton *et al.* 1992). This study has the advantage of showing how a causal scenario is generated to explain a rich natural example. It will be used to illustrate the distinction between causal *diagnosis* and causal *selection* to analyse how contextual information changes the quality of a candidate explanation by affecting either its perceived truth-value or its perceived relevance, leading in the first case to causal discounting and in the second case to causal backgrounding. The field study is complemented by experimental evidence.

The construction of mental models of events: the example of the *Challenger* disaster

The difference between truth conditions and relevance criteria for causal explanations can be illustrated by reference to the example of the *Challenger* space shuttle disaster. The *Challenger* space shuttle blew up 8 miles above the earth about 78 seconds after lift-off on 26 January 1986. The disaster seemed utterly inexplicable at first, prompting an unprecedentedly thorough search for an explanation. This culminated in the report of the Rogers Commission to the President of the United States in May 1986. Tracing the construction of a full explanation for this disaster through months of painstaking investigation enables us to identify different stages of the inquiry process during which different questions are at issue. In particular, the truth of an explanation is at issue during the stage of causal diagnosis, whereas its relevance is at issue during the stage of conversational explanation (Table 16.1).

The first stage of causal diagnosis is initiated by the occurrence of an event that needs explaining, and is characterized by uncertainty as to which of several suspect causes is actually responsible for the event. In this state of uncertainty the best explanation is the most probable. Thus, immediately after the *Challenger* disaster, three hypotheses were generated attempting to explain why disaster occurred. Each corresponded to a major vehicle system: the disaster was due to something involving the booster rockets, the external fuel tank attached to the shuttle, or the shuttle itself. When close study of film of the last few seconds before the explosion of the

Table 16.1. *Features of causal diagnosis and causal explanation*

	Causal diagnosis	*Causal explanation*
Models	Competing models	Single model
Certainty	Judgement under uncertainty	Assumed certainty of model
Alternative explanations	Suggest competing model	Fill out existing model
Judgement task	Selection of most probable model	Selection of causes from conditions
Judgemental criterion	Truth	Relevance

ill-fated shuttle revealed the emission of abnormal smoke from the side of the booster rockets, suspicion naturally concentrated on a fault in this system as being the most probable cause. At this stage of causal diagnosis 'something about the booster rockets' constituted the best explanation because it was judged to be the most probable cause.

The eventual explanation of the *Challenger*'s explosion, as expressed in the report of the Rogers Commission, identified a multitude of necessary conditions for the disaster which, 'if only' they had been different (cf. Kahneman and Tversky 1982; Kahneman and Miller 1986), would have averted the final disaster. These included the faulty O-rings, which lost elasticity in cold weather, and the fact that *Challenger* had been launched in colder conditions than had any other space shuttle. Other factors implicated were the occurrence of a wind shear that placed additional stress on the joints shortly before the catastrophe, contributing to the rupture of the seals. The report might also have mentioned the presence of oxygen in the atmosphere, which in combination with the hydrogen that leaked from the external fuel tank, resulted in the final fireball. Had hydrogen leaked from the external fuel tank in outer space, there might not have been a fire because oxygen would have been absent.

Despite the plethora of necessary conditions that jointly constitute an event's sufficient cause, we typically mention only one, or at most two, of these factors as *the* cause in everyday explanation (Hesslow 1988). Causal scenarios are typically rich interconnected networks of conditional relations (Trabasso *et al.* 1984; Hilton 1985; Trabasso and Sperry 1985; Read 1987; and Abelson and Lalljee 1988) that may occupy many volumes of text when expressed in natural language, for example the report of the Rogers Commission or Tolstoy's *War and Peace*. The selection of one of these conditions as *the* cause from a set of conditions in ordinary explanation is constrained by general relevance criteria, such as the explanation's informativeness and relevance to the question posed—not just whether the condition mentioned is more likely to be true than one which is not mentioned explicitly but is presupposed in the representation of the causal scenario.

Therefore good causal explanations should aim to maximize both truth and relevance. For example the commonly accepted explanation of the *Challenger* explosion, that the O-ring seals were faulty, is very probably, but not certainly, true. We are more certain that the presence of oxygen in the atmosphere was involved in the explosion than the faulty O-rings. However, we select the slightly less probable explanation that the O-rings were involved because it is more relevant. If probability were the only criterion for selecting an explanation, then we would rather explain the explosion by reference to the presence of oxygen. This *reductio ad absurdum* suggests the insufficiency of truth conditions to be complete determinants of good explanations.

When an explanation is discarded at the first stage because it is no longer believed to be true, we speak of causal discounting. In the *Challenger* example, this occurred when the explanation 'Something about the external fuel tank' was discarded in favour of its rival 'something about the booster rockets'. When we discard an explanation because it is no longer relevant, or as relevant as some other cause to mention in an explanation, we speak of causal backgrounding. In the *Challenger* case, this would happen if an explanation had to be given to two different interlocutors, one who knew that the O-rings were faulty, but not that the spacecraft was launched in cold weather, and another who knew that the spacecraft was launched in cold weather, but not that the O-rings were faulty. Felicitous explanations would follow Grice's maxims of quantity in being informative to the respective interlocutors by referring to the cold weather in the first case and the faulty O-rings in the second. It should be noted that, although the relevant verbal explanation changes as a function of the interlocutor, the causal scenario hypothesized to underly the production of the event does not. Although the given explanation changes, this does not reflect any change in the perceived probability of the scenario underlying the truth-value of the explanation.

Probability, relevance, and levels of explanation

Einhorn and Hogarth (1986) and Einhorn (1988) point out that a causal process can be analysed at different levels, much as a scientist can use different levels of magnification of a microscope to focus on molecular or molar issues. Thus they point out that a biochemist may see the link between smoking and cancer as being due to the chemical effects of tar, nicotine, and the like on cell structure, whereas an immunologist might see the causal link as due to the suppression of the immune system in controlling diseases in general. Here, it seems meaningful to speak of changing the 'causal field' (Mackie 1980), since describing the causal process at the immunologist's level seems to presuppose the existence of the kinds of processes studied by the biochemist. It should be noted that simply 'changing the field' does not necessarily weaken the probability that an explanation made at a particular level is true or not. It simply enables the whole causal scenario to be fleshed out further at a richer level of detail.

In fact, Mackie (1980) gives an insightful analysis of what he terms 'the progressive localization of cause', whereby causal inquiries proceed by establishing that one level of explanation is true and then 'dig deeper' by focusing on more specific details. The progressive localization of cause may be used to illustrate the subtle interplay between conversational maxims and explanatory quality. This is illustrated with reference to how the enquiry into the *Challenger* space shuttle explosion proceeded.

At an early stage of the inquiry, it was established that a fault in the booster rockets was probably responsible. However, although 'something about the booster rockets' identifies the probable cause of the *Challenger* disaster, it is still a somewhat vague and unhelpful explanation. In particular, while saying 'something about the booster rockets' refers to a true or probable cause (thus satisfying Grice's maxim of quality), it is not very informative (thus violating Grice's maxim of quantity) and its relation to the inquiry's goals (defined as establishing the cause of the accident and ensuring that appropriate corrective action be taken) is not particularly clear (thus violating Grice's maxim of relation). Consequently, the explanation needs to be expanded in detail so that it becomes informative and relevant as well as probably true.

Having located a fault in one of the booster rockets, the next question was 'Which part of the booster rockets was responsible?'. Since smoke was seen to be emitted near the joints which held the rocket casing together, the explanation became 'something about the joints'. And so on. The part of the joints held responsible for the failure was the seals, and in turn, the parts of the sealing system that were held responsible were the now infamous rubber O-rings.

Producing a good explanation thus requires that a trade-off be made between truth and relevance criteria. In Gricean terms, this represents the tension between the maxims of quantity and quality. Speakers will try to be as informative and relevant as possible without being improbable. Factors which can be presupposed, or are already known to be true, are relegated to the 'causal field' of backgrounded conditions that are necessary for the production of the target event. As the cause becomes progressively localized, there is no gain in the truth-value of the explanation. Indeed, there is some risk of *loss* of truth-value because more specific explanations are easier to falsify. One runs more risk of being wrong by attributing the disaster to 'something about the seals' than to 'something about the booster rockets', since proving the former always proves the latter, whereas falsifying the former may not falsify the latter. However, the full causal account, by becoming more specific, gains the potential of providing more informative and relevant answers to causal questions.

Contextual effects on explanations: Causal discounting versus causal backgrounding

The distinction between causal discounting and causal backgrounding enables clarification of how adding contextual information leads us to change an explanation. Einhorn and Hogarth (1986) argue persuasively that changes in context can cause us to change one target explanation in favour of another. However, they do not clearly distinguish changes in the value of an explanation which are due to changes in its perceived probability as opposed to its perceived relevance.

This can be illustrated with the two examples that Einhorn and Hogarth discuss as reflecting changes in the 'causal field' of background presuppositions for an event (Mackie 1980). In their first example, causal discounting appears to be involved since the contextual information suggests an alternative mental model or causal scenario which could explain the effect in question. Thus the preferred explanation for a worker's cancer, previously thought to be due to working in a factory where there is a high incidence of cancer may be changed when we learn of his heavy smoking and family history of cancer. Here, the new information reduces belief in the original hypothesis by suggesting a rival mechanism which could independently produce the effect in question.

In the second example given by Einhorn and Hogarth (1986) causal backgrounding occurs because the added contextual information refocuses elements of a causal scenario but does not cause an alternative scenario to be generated. Thus when we learn that a hammer strike, which resulted in a watch's shattering, did so in the context of a factory control procedure, we change our explanation of the destruction of the watch from 'because the hammer hit it' to 'because of a fault in the glass'. The hammer strike is still seen as a necessary part of the scenario leading to the watch's destruction, but is normalized by information indicating that this is a routine factory procedure. The hammer strike is thus relegated to the backgrounded 'causal field' of necessary conditions, and the watch's faulty glass is focused as the factor which made the difference between it and other watches which presumably did not shatter. Here, the context changes what is perceived as the 'abnormal condition' in the circumstances (Hilton and

Slugoski 1986) by changing the 'focal set' (Cheng and Novick 1990, 1991), but does not significantly change either the perceived necessity of the hammer strike or its perceived probability.

Although Einhorn and Hogarth (1986) did not make a clear distinction between causal discounting and causal backgrounding, Hilton and Erb (1991) show that people do indeed distinguish the effects of contextual information suggesting alternative explanations in the cancer and watch examples. Thus the additional contextual information that the worker smoked heavily and came from a family with a history of lung cancer led subjects to judge working in the factory as less necessary for cancer to occur, whereas the additional contextual information that the hammer strike happened as part of a routine testing procedure did not change perceptions of the necessity of the hammer strike for the watch to shatter.

Another experiment showed that, while the additional contextual information reduced the quality of the focal explanation in both cases, it did so in the watch example without reducing the perceived probability of the explanation's being true. In the cancer example the contextual information *reduced* the perceived probability of the explanation. Thus the results support the view that contextual information reduced the goodness of the explanation that the worker contracted cancer because he worked in the factory by reducing the perceived truth-value of the explanation, whereas it reduced the goodness of the explanation that the watch broke because the hammer hit it solely by reducing its perceived relevance, not its perceived truth-value.

Probability and relevance of goal-states and preconditions as explanations

The distinction between probability and relevance in causal explanation enables us to adopt a new perspective on some unexplained phenomena and paradoxes in causal explanation. It is shown below how the approach can be used to analyse two different questions. The first is why goal-states make better explanations than script-preconditions (Schank and Abelson 1977), and the second is why conjunctive explanations referring to two or more factors are better than simple explanations referring to one factor. As will be shown below, gaining a satisfactory answer to the first question will help us answer the second.

The story begins with Leddo *et al.* (1984), who initiated the systematic study of conjunctive explanations. They proposed a pattern-matching procedure to explain their results. They suggested that people have knowledge structures with multiple 'slots' to explain an event. Two explanations are better than one if both match slots in the knowledge structure. Leddo *et al.* suggest, for example, that common activities are often explained by goals. If the reasons given for an action (e.g. eating in a restaurant) match the goals commonly associated with that activity (e.g. feeling hungry, wanting to have an evening out), then the conjoint explanation 'She ate in the restaurant because she felt hungry and wanted an evening out' would be judged better than either alone (if both goals matched slots in the knowledge structure associated with eating in restaurants). According to Leddo *et al.*, the more that features of the (conjoint) explanation match 'slots' in the knowledge structure associated with the target activity, the more 'representative' and therefore probable the explanation is perceived to be (Tversky and Kahneman 1983).

Leddo *et al.* found, for example, that goals (e.g. being hungry) were considered more likely than script-preconditions (e.g. having money) as factors influencing a decision (e.g. stopping to eat in a restaurant). They labelled goals and script-preconditions as 'typical' and 'atypical' reasons respectively for an action, and they found that a conjunctive explanation, which combined a goal and a script-precondition, would be judged more probable among the factors influencing a decision than a script-precondition alone, and that a conjunctive explanation combining two plausible goals would be judged more probable than one such goal alone.

Leddo *et al.* also suggested that types of events have different types and numbers of explanatory 'slots' associated with them. In their view, failure of an action is typically explained by one reason only, such as a precondition for the success of an outcome not holding true. This would explain the finding (Leddo *et al.* 1984, experiment 2) that, in attempts to find a reason for the failure of an event to occur, two explanations are worse than one.

Although Leddo *et al.* argue that explanations are generated through calculating representativeness rather than covariation or necessity and sufficiency, they implicitly subscribe to the 'probabilist' view that a good explanation is a probable explanation (Kelley 1967, 1972, 1973; Crocker 1981; Schustack and Sternberg 1981; Alloy and Tabachnik 1984; Downing *et al.* 1985; Shanks and Dickinson 1987, 1988). Thus they asked their subjects to rate the probability of the target explanation's being part of the actual explanation, and assumed that an explanation judged probable is to be considered good. Abelson *et al.* (1987) briefly addressed the possibility that subjects may be considering some other characteristic of explanations in their judgements but did not explore the issue in detail. Finally, Leddo *et al.* (1984) note that conjunctive explanations, which are rated more probable than their conjuncts, seem to violate the conjunction rule which is a fundamental law of probability (Tversky and Kahneman 1983).

However, the findings of Leddo *et al.* (1984) and their interpretation of the results leave an important issue unresolved: they offer no independent grounds for assessing the typicality or atypicality of an explanation.

Claiming that goals make typical explanations for an action and preconditions make atypical explanations runs the risk of being circular. Why should
goals be typical explanations for an action in the first place? The pattern-
matching approach is silent on this issue, despite the priority that the
knowledge structure places on goal-based explanation in both psychology
(Schank and Abelson 1977; Newcombe and Rutter 1982; Lalljee and
Abelson 1983; Hilton 1985; Read 1987, 1988; Hilton and Knibbs 1988) and
artificial intelligence (Lehnert 1978; Carbonell 1979, 1981; Wilensky 1978,
1981, 1983; Pazzani 1985; DeJong and Mooney 1986; Pazzani *et al.* 1986).

The notion that good explanations should be informative, and relevant,
as well as true, could resolve the above issue. Thus the finding that
goal-states are preferred over script-preconditions as causal explanations
(Leddo *et al.* 1984; Abelson *et al.* 1987; McClure *et al.* 1989) may be
attributable to a general tendency to treat goal-states as necessary and
sufficient conditions, whereas script-preconditions are treated as necessary
but not sufficient.

In fact, this prediction can be derived from Heider (1958), who notes that
personal causality, by virtue of its goal-directed nature, has the property
of equifinality which impersonal causality does not. Equifinality implies
that intentional behaviour will be constantly directed to a goal, but will vary
in the means used to obtain it. Thus Heider (1958, p. 102) writes:

> Attribution to personal causality reduces the necessary conditions essentially to one,
> the person with intention, who, within a wide range of environmental vicissitudes,
> has control over the multitude of forces required to create the specific effect.

Therefore personal causes are necessary conditions that are sufficient to
produce the desired effect, since any circumstantial obstacle can normally
be circumvented and another route found to the desired goal.

Thus, if we ask, 'Why did Fred stop to eat at the Italian restaurant?',
we may assume that the facts that Fred was hungry and had money in his
pocket were both equally necessary for the production of the act of dining.
After all, if Fred had not been hungry, or not had money in his pocket,
he would hardly have decided to visit the restaurant for a meal. However,
to say 'Fred was hungry' seems intuitively a better explanation of his
decision to stop and eat at the restaurant than to say 'Fred had money
in his pocket', since it is more likely to be 'sufficient in the circumstances'
(Mackie 1980) for the decision to stop and eat.

Consequently, it should be noted that the two 'explanations' will probably
not make equally informative and relevant contributions to a conversation
about causes. This is because, generally speaking, the mundane fact that
Fred had money in his pocket will be part of the presupposed set of
background necessary but not sufficient conditions included in the 'causal
field' (Mackie 1980) that would typically be shared by the speaker and

hearer involved in such a conversation. To cite the fact that 'Fred had
money in his pocket' would violate Grice's (1975) maxim of quantity which
states, *inter alia*, that speakers should not tell hearers things that they
already know or can presuppose from their own general world knowledge.
In contrast, stating the fact that 'Fred was hungry' would be more likely
to be an informative contribution to the conversation, since hearers would
not be able to presuppose that Fred was hungry from their own world
knowledge. Thus, while 'Fred was hungry' and 'Fred had money' might
both be, from a purely logical point of view, equally *true* as causal
explanations of Fred's decision, only 'Fred was hungry' would be, from a
conversational point of view, more *felicitous* (Austin 1962) or *relevant*
(Sperber and Wilson 1986).

Hilton and Knott (1993) obtained data to support this analysis. Using
the original scenarios designed by Leddo *et al.* (1984), they showed that
subjects judged both goal-state explanations (e.g. 'Fred was hungry') and
script-preconditions (e.g. 'Fred had money in his pocket') to be equally *necessary* for the target event to occur (e.g. Fred stopped at the restaurant to eat)
in a conditional reasoning task. However, they perceived that goal-states
were more likely to be *sufficient* conditions for the target event to occur.

A second experiment showed that goal-states were also perceived as
more informative and relevant as to whether the target event would occur.
This is consistent with the view that goal-states are favoured over script-
preconditions because they have more information value and relevance as
explanations. A final experiment showed that judgements of the informativeness or relevance of explanations predicted the goodness of an
explanation independently of its perceived likelihood. This result confirms
the claim that the goodness of an explanation depends on both its perceived
truth and its informativeness or relevance.

Contrasts and the amount of explanation required

Another problem for the pattern-matching approach of Leddo *et al.* (1984)
is that, although they postulate that failures only 'need' one explanation,
they do not offer independent assessments of how much explanation an
event actually needs. Without some independent definition of how many
'slots' are needed to explain a given event, their theoretical position is in
danger of becoming circular and unfalsifiable (cf. Zuckerman *et al.* 1986).
For example, both McClure *et al.* (1989) and Zuckerman *et al.* (1986) found
substantial conjunction effects with failed actions or non-occurrences. This
appears to invalidate the claim by Leddo *et al.* (1984) that failures 'need'
only one explanation.

However, the conversational model addresses the issue of 'amount of
explanation required' in a way different from knowledge structure theory.

As noted above, conversations about causes are initiated by puzzles (Turnbull 1986; Turnbull and Slugoski 1988), and attributional processes have been shown to be triggered by the occurrence of unanticipated or unwanted events (Hastie 1984; Weiner 1985; Bohner *et al.*, 1988). In this vein, Brown and van Kleeck (1989) have shown that the more cognitively imbalanced an event is (Heider 1958), the more explanation it requires. Hilton and Slugoski (1986) have shown that normal events often do not require explanation. Moreover, using the procedure pioneered by McArthur (1972), conjunctive explanations are more likely when covariation information indicates that the the target event is infrequent, i.e. when there is low consensus, high distinctiveness, and low consistency (Pruitt and Insko 1980; Jaspars 1983; Hewstone and Jaspars 1987; Hilton and Jaspars 1987). Consequently, we can expect conjunctive explanations to be judged better when they are given for rare events (cf. Cunningham and Kelley 1975). Consistent with this, Locksley and Stangor (1984) obtained stronger conjunction effects with a rare event (suicide) than with a common one (marriage). In the same vein, McClure (personal communication) obtained ratings of the prior probabilities of the events used as stimulus material by McClure *et al.* (1989, experiment 2), which were also used by Leddo *et al.* (1984). He found a positive correlation between the *a priori* improbability of an event and conjunction effects, as indexed by the conjunction coefficient of Abelson *et al.* (1987).

In addition, McGill (1991) showed that subjects are more likely to give conjunctive explanations when two relevant causal backgrounds (defining two relevant contrasts) are present than when only one background is present. All these results point to the same conclusion: abnormal and untoward events require more explanation, and conjunctive explanations are likely to be given or judged better in such cases. The exception seems to prove the rule: McClure *et al.*, (1991) found that when extreme events were explained by a single cause, the explanations used referred to high levels of that cause (e.g. brilliance in the case of scientific discovery). Thus subjects were still responding to the extremity of the event in determining the 'amount' of explanation needed.

This prediction — that rare events need more explanation — differs from the suggestion of Leddo *et al.* (1984) that actions activate frames with different numbers of 'slots' from failed actions. The conversational perspective predicts that the amount of explanation required is a function of the gap between what is observed and what is presupposed, independent of the type of event concerned. Thus, while failed actions may often be fairly normal, leading to relatively little need of explanation, this may not always be so. For example, consider the explanation for the '*Challenger*' catastrophe (a highly abnormal failure): the O-rings failed to seal in cold weather, the space shuttle was launched in cold weather against engineers' advice, NASA was under pressure to meet a heavy launch schedule in 1986, NASA had failed to redesign the O-rings despite warnings, and so on (McConnell 1987). Thus while the suggestion by Leddo *et al.* (1984) that failures 'need' only one explanation has some initial plausibility, the amount of explanation needed seems more parsimoniously attributed to degree of abnormality rather than event-type.

Similarly, Leddo *et al.*'s point, that adding a precondition to a goal should clearly increase the probability of an explanation because, strictly speaking, the conjunctive explanation must be more necessary for the event, would be invalidated by the conversational model. Co-opting a redundant and uninformative script-precondition into an explanation (e.g. 'Fred stopped to eat because he was hungry and because he had money in his pocket') may affect neither its necessity nor its sufficiency. However, by including a precondition, such a conjunctive explanation may violate the maxims of quantity and manner in being uninformative and long-winded, and thus be judged as an improbable explanation. This would indeed predict the result that Leddo *et al.* (1984) obtain without implying that necessity does not play an important role in causal explanation.

'Philosophical' and 'conversational' discourse: Implications for judging conjunctive explanations

The conversational model of causal explanation provides a new perspective on a number of problems for attribution theory. On the one hand, a 'good' explanation should be the sum of necessary and sufficient conditions required to produce an event (cf. Jaspars 1983). In particular, Jaspars' (1983) inductive logic model instantiates Mill's (1872) definition of causality, given in his *System of logic* (Book III, Chapter V, Section (iii)), that the true cause 'philosophically speaking' should be 'the assemblage of its conditions', i.e the conjunction of conditions that are individually necessary but only jointly sufficient for the occurrence of the target event. Thus a 'good' explanation 'philosophically speaking' would mean, in the restaurant example, that the correct explanation of Fred's decision to stop and eat would be the conjunctive explanation plus any other necessary conditions that we may care to consider.

The conversational model offers an alternative definition of a 'good' explanation. Although the above explanation that 'Fred was hungry, and had money in his pocket, and the restaurant looked respectable' might seem to be a good explanation because it maximizes sufficiency without losing necessity (Einhorn and Hogarth 1986), it would clearly seem to violate the rules of everyday discourse (Grice 1975). In particular, such a conjunctive explanation might violate Grice's maxims of quantity (forbidding redundancy) and manner (forbidding long-windedness).

As Mill himself noted, citing the complete set of necessary conditions in a causal explanation 'would generally be very prolix' and we often omit conditions 'because some of them will in most cases be understood without being expressed, or because for the purpose in view they may without detriment be overlooked'. Thus Mill gives implicit recognition to the definition of the cause, 'conversationally speaking', as the condition which may not be presupposed from general world or specific context knowledge (Grice 1975), and which is thus 'sufficient in the circumstances' for the effect, (Mackie 1980). Typically, in everyday discourse, we cite one of the necessary conditions as *the* explanation, and the correct explanation is the one that has the most 'explanatory relevance' (Hesslow 1983, 1988). In default of specific context, as in the restaurant example, this would be the goal-state 'Fred is hungry' which is the factor that will make the difference to Fred's decision to stop and eat in the situation under consideration.

Consequently, the subject who is asked to judge the likelihood that a particular condition or conjunction of conditions will be 'part of the actual explanation' in the experiments of Leddo *et al.* (1984) and McClure *et al.* (1989) is in somewhat of a quandary. Does the experimenter intend 'the actual explanation' to mean the cause 'philosophically speaking' (i.e. the complete conjunction of individually necessary but only jointly sufficient conditions), or to mean the cause 'conversationally speaking' (i.e. the most informative relevant condition that is sufficient in the the circumstances)? The procedures used by Leddo *et al.* (1984) and McClure *et al.* (1989) offer no possible way of resolving this question. The present research helps to answer the question by showing that subjects *prefer* explanations which refer to necessary conditions which are 'sufficient in the circumstances'.

McGill (1990) shows how the kind of question asked may determine whether subjects focus on the condition that is 'sufficient in the circumstances' or on the complete set of necessary and sufficient conditions for the occurrence of an event. In the 'explanation mode' subjects were asked to rate the quality of possible explanations for the event. Therefore, in line with our findings, we can expect changes in background to affect the perceived quality of an explanation by affecting its sufficiency in the circumstances, and hence its relevance, i.e. the cause's quality 'conversationally speaking'. This pattern of results is indeed what McGill found. When such a background was present, subjects rated the relevant explanation as much better than the irrelevant one. Moreover, they rated the conjunction of a relevant and an irrelevant explanation as intermediate in quality between the relevant explanation alone and the irrelevant explanation alone. However, when no background was present, both single explanations appeared moderately relevant. In this condition, subjects rated the conjunctive explanation better than either single explanation alone.

McGill also presented the same experimental tasks, but with the rating procedures used by Leddo *et al.* (1984), Locksley and Stangor (1984) and Read (1988). In this 'influence mode', subjects are asked to rate the probability that different factors were among those that influenced the event. This could prompt subjects to consider the whole causal scenario in making their judgement, i.e. Mill's 'true' cause 'philosophically speaking'. Consequently, introducing a causal background should not lead subjects to focus attention on particular aspects of the target scenario, making them seem more relevant than others. McGill predicted, and found, that in this mode subjects were likely to rate the conjunctive explanations more probable than either the 'relevant' or 'irrelevant' explanation alone, regardless of whether the background was present or not. Hence the 'influence' response mode used by Leddo *et al.* (1984), Locksley and Stangor (1984) and Read (1988) predisposes respondents to consider the *full* set of necessary and jointly sufficient conditions, facilitating the production of conjunction effects.

Causal chains, scenarios, and explanatory relevance

An example of a conjunction of causes is a causal chain. Consider the illuminating example of how sunspot activity might be related to stock prices (Einhorn and Hogarth 1986, 1987; Einhorn 1988). If a questioner asks 'Why did the stock market fall this year?' and receives the reply 'Because of the sunspots last year', he may be somewhat puzzled. Consequently, because he considers the explanation to be peculiar, he may consider it unlikely, uninformative, and irrelevant. However, additional information may explain how the putative cause might have led to the effect. Thus the questioner may expand the explanation: 'Because sunspots affect weather, which affects agricultual production, which affects the economy, which affects profits, which affects stock market prices'. By giving the hearer enough information to build a mental scenario which allows him to comprehend how sunspots can affect stock market prices, the speaker follows Grice's maxims of quantity and thus enables the hearer to understand the point of the explanation, thus following Grice's maxim of relation. Consequently, the hearer may consider the fuller explanation to be more likely than the initial one.

Einhorn and Hogarth (1986) note that long scenarios are sometimes judged to be more probable than short ones (Slovic *et al.* 1976) and correctly point out the relevance of this finding to the conjunction fallacy discussed by Tversky and Kahneman (1983). Given that a conjunction cannot be more probable than any one of its conjuncts, it may seem fallacious to judge an explanation with multiple elements to be more probable than any one of its elements. However, distinguishing scenario generation from explanation tuning can resolve the paradox if we assume that subjects are not judging the probability of the explanations *per se* but the probability of the causal scenarios implied by those explanations. Thus subjects may be judging the probability of two causal scenarios that connect a cause (e.g. sunspots) to an effect (e.g. stock market prices). In one case, the 'slots' in the causal scenario are filled with features that make it collectively plausible, in which each provides evidence for the existence of a causal scenario which would make the hypothesis (that sunspots cause stock market fluctuations) true. However, in the second case the slots are unspecified, giving no evidence for a causal scenario that would make such a connection true. By assuming that it is the mental models of causal scenarios that constitute the units of belief, not the individual elements that make up those scenarios, the issue is reframed in terms of whether a plausible scenario, for which we have evidence, is more probable than an implausible scenario, for which we have none. According to this interpretation, it would be quite rational to judge 'conjunctive explanations' as more probable, since they describe only one underlying hypothesis.

In addition, it should be noted that adding more explanations in the sunspot example does not seem to reduce the necessity of the focal explanation(s). Indeed, by making the causal scenario more probable by showing how sunspot activity may be connected to stock market fluctuations, sunspot activity may be seen as even *more* likely to be a necessary condition for stock market fluctuations. Consequently, conjunctive explanations may be perceived as more necessary than single explanations.

Finally, Einhorn and Hogarth (1986) use the example of 'domino chain' to illustrate the case where all the links in a causal chain are (almost) certainly true. Their example reads as follows:

Mrs. Jones, a middle-aged lady, was looking for her seat at a football game. While trying to ease past some other spectators on a steep staircase, she lost her balance and fell over. She hit another spectator, who was also off balance. This person, in turn, fell on someone else who unwittingly pushed Mr. Smith, a 70-year-old man, against some iron railings. Mr. Smith broke a leg in the incident. How likely did Mrs. Jones' fall cause Mr. Smith to break his leg? (Einhorn and Hogarth 1986, p. 12).

Clearly, Mrs Jones's fall almost certainly caused Mr Smith to break his leg. Indeed, when reading stories such as these, we take everything that is said in them as if they were guaranteed by Grice's maxim of quality, and therefore true, even when they are patently invented examples. However, it should be noted that there are several events that are equally probable causes of Mr Smith's breaking his leg, such as the second spectator's being off balance, his falling on someone else, the pushing of Mr Smith, and Mr Smith's position by the iron railings. Although Mrs Jones's fall is a *conditio sine qua non* without which Mr Smith's leg would not have been broken (Hart and Honoré 1985), it may not be the most relevant explanation. In a legal inquiry, the most relevant explanation would refer to the most blameworthy feature of the situation. For example, were the stairs dangerously steep and therefore badly designed? Was Mrs Jones negligent in not being careful while climbing the staircase? Was the other person who was off balance negligent? Although the whole causal chain may answer an 'explanatory' inquiry as to how the event happened, it may not be focused enough to answer an 'attributive' inquiry which seeks to fix blame (Hart and Honoré 1985).

PARTICULAR AND GENERAL EXPLANATION

It has been commonplace to compare the layperson's causal inference with that of a scientist, whether that scientist be a hypothesis-tester (Kelly 1955), a bottom-up inductive statistician (Heider 1958; Kelley 1967) or a top-down consistency seeker (Read and Marcus-Newhall 1993). Whatever use is made of these analogies, it is important to note that scientists generally have a different causal question in mind than does the layperson (Hart and Honoré 1985). Scientists typically ask why normal events occur: Why does the sun rise every day? Why do apples fall downwards? Why is grass green? Why does smoking cause cancer? In each case, the question invites a response that explains *how* two regularly covarying events are *connected* to each other, for example referring to mediating entities and mechanisms such as planets and rotation, mass and gravity, chlorophyll and photosynthesis, and so on. The layperson, like the lawyer and the historian, typically asks why a particular event happened when and how it did.

Thus rephrasing general scientific questions as particular, localized questions gives rise to a sense of anomaly, and hence attempts to redefine their sense: Why did the sun rise today? Why did the apple fall downward just now? Why is the grass outside this building green today? Why did Joe's smoking cause him to get cancer last month?

The kind of person who makes such remarks may seem to us to be in some way irrational. A person who wonders why the sun rose or why the grass is green today may be considered 'odd'. All things being equal, the sun rises every day, apples always fall downwards, and all grass is green. Only a person who does not know or understand these basic generalizations about the nature of our world would ask such foolish questions. As the exception that proves the rule, note that it is sensible to ask why a friend has cancer, for some, but not all, people who smoke contract cancer. Therefore an implicit contrast can be made between our friend who did contract cancer and other people who did not. This results from the *gappiness* (Mackie 1980) of the supporting generalization that can be expressed as 'some smokers get cancer', or modally as 'smoking may cause cancer'.

One kind of person who often asks why apples fall downwards and suchlike, is of course the child, who lacks an understanding of the basic mechanisms of our world. Therefore, the child needs to *acquire* knowledge of the normal functioning of objects before he or she can focus on abnormalities. Consistent with this view, Spelke and colleagues (Chapter 3) note that younger children focus more on the normal behaviour of physical objects, such as objects falling on to a surface and then coming to rest, whereas the attention of older children is more attracted by abnormal behaviour, such as that of objects appearing to fall but then hanging in mid-air. In the social domain, younger children are more likely than older children to seek consensus information about what other people would do in similar circumstances when asked to explain someone's behaviour (see Hilton (1990) for a review).

From an evolutionary perspective, there are obvious advantages in automating the processing of predictable information in order to free resources to process new information indicating changes in the environment (Kahneman and Miller 1986). The adaptivity of human beings to various physical and cultural environments attests to the usefulness of childhood as a period in which to discover how a complex world works (Bruner 1972).

Indeed, the difference between expectancies about how the world generally works and deviations from those expectancies throws into relief the complementary relationship between categorization and explanation. Categorization tells us what typically goes with what in the world: all birds fly; people in restaurants always ask for the menu. Category members which are exceptions to these rules are often recognized as being 'special' rather than 'poor' members of the category. Thus restaurants in which people do not ask for menus tend to fall into special categories or 'tracks' (Schank and Abelson 1977; Bower *et al.* 1979), such as fast-food restaurants' where a special property (speed) 'explains' the 'aberrant' feature (paying for food at the counter).

Categories and scripts define expectancies which, when violated, trigger causal attribution processes (Lalljee *et al.* 1982; Hastie 1984; Brown and van Kleeck 1989). Children have to acquire these categories and scripts before they are endowed with the kind of world-knowledge that will enable them to recognize exceptions that provide puzzles to be explained. Adults will have pre-computed knowledge-structures that 'explain' tipping in a restaurant because it is already part of a restaurant script; they will recognize such behaviour as a token of a known type. However, children will need post-computed explanations to make sense of this behaviour.

'Theories' and 'causes'

The *Challenger* example can illustrate the distinction between 'theories' and 'causes', where the former are understood as the underlying mechanisms connecting a series of events, and the latter as particular factors selected as having 'made the difference' in the outcome of the target event when contrasted with a comparison case. One of the early hypotheses about the cause of the disaster involved the cold weather. In this scenario the effect of the cold was mediated through the formation of icicles on the launch parapet which, when blasted onto the fragile skin of the orbiter led to the disaster. Although this hypothesis was discarded, the cold weather reappeared later as a cause of the O-ring scenario, which was of course accepted.

This raises some interesting issues about the claim that cold weather caused the disaster. When interpreted in the context of the blasted ice scenario, the claim was rejected as false. However, when interpreted in terms of the O-ring scenario, it was accepted as true. The observation remains true, even if we note that in both cases the causal claim would be supported by the counterfactual observation that the accident would not have happened if the weather had not been so cold. Clearly, counterfactual support is not a sufficient condition for the attribution of causality.

In fact, on the day following the accident, the *New York Times* actively scanned for differences between the *Challenger* launch and successful launches. One graphic example of this strategy is in the production of a diagram comparing *Challenger*'s launch path with that of a normal launch. Cold weather soon emerged as one of the differences between the *Challenger* launch and normal launches. The example illustrates how the method of difference can be used in a blind bottom-up way to aid the discovery of causal relationships. This 'empty inductivist' use of the method of difference seems to be the one contrasted by some critics of the ANOVA model (Kelley 1967) with top-down 'hypothesis-testing' models of causal explanation (Lalljee and Abelson 1983; Lalljee *et al.* 1984).

While critics who propose that supporters of the ANOVA analogy conceive of it as a model of bottom-up causal induction are probably right, they would be wrong if they attributed such a position to Mill. Mill was perfectly aware of the difference between what has come to be called the 'context of discovery', and the 'context of justification'. He made it quite clear that his methods of induction were methods of *proof* of the inductions made. The top-down use of the method of difference can be quite clearly seen in the tests performed to verify the O-ring theory *after* it had been generated. Thus the difference between O-ring burns in cold and warm weather launches was compared, revealing significantly more burn-through during cold launches. Another example is of the vivid demonstration by one of the members of the Rogers Commission, Nobel-prize-winning physicist Richard Feynman, of what happens to the flexibility of rubber when it is dipped in cold water.

For Mill, the issue of how people arrive at inductions was quite another matter from their process of checking them (as his two books on *Operations subsidiary to induction* in his *System of logic* testify). For Mill, operations subsidiary to induction include categorization and analogy, which are precisely those cognitive activities which his critics most often say are left out of a Millian account. Harré (1988), for example, takes issue with Mill on such grounds, and then uses Darwin's analogy of natural and artificial selection as the prototype of non-Millian theory-making. The injustice of this criticism can be gauged by noting that Mill added an extensive footnote to his *System of logic*, commending Darwin's analogy as a means of scientific discovery just 3 years after the publication of the *Origin of Species* in 1859. Mill noted that Darwin himself had never claimed that his hypothesis was *proved*, but his perspicacity in choosing this example can be judged by the amount of fruitful research that, as Mill predicted, it went on to generate.

Why and how questions

In the paradigm of experiments devised by McArthur (1972) to test the ANOVA model of causal attribution (Kelley 1967) there is not much of a puzzle about *how* a hypothesized characteristic, such as kindness, might lead to helping behaviour. It seems nonsensical to ask 'Why did Paul's kindness cause him to help Linda?'. But this transparency is not always evident. However, in the *Challenger* space-shuttle disaster it is less clear how the seal failure led to the final fireball, and it would be reasonable to ask 'Why did the seal failure cause the explosion?'.

In the case of the *Challenger* disaster, the mechanism connecting cause and effect is complex and will be puzzling to those lacking the appropriate background knowledge. Hence the puzzle about why the cause led to the effect. Here the 'why' question solicits an answer about the mechanism *connecting* the cause to the effect, rather than *selecting* a cause from a set of conditions that are equally necessary for the effect to happen. A more precise probe for causal connection would have been to ask a 'how' question: 'How did the seal failure lead to the explosion?'.

'How' questions are more specific than 'why' questions in that they always probe the connections leading from a cause to an effect. 'Why' questions are ambiguous since they can probe either the connection between a cause and an effect or the factor that made the difference to an effect's occurrence. Graesser *et al.* (1980, 1981) found that 'why' questions caused story-readers to chain backwards from an event to its causes, whereas 'how' questions caused readers to chain forwards to its consequences. Thus the question 'Why did they cross the stream?' would receive a reply in terms of a motivating goal such as 'Because they wanted to get to the giant's castle', whereas 'How did they cross the stream?' would be answered through means such as 'By getting their horses to swim over'.

The distinction between explanations that identify the selected cause as opposed to the connecting mechanism may help illuminate questions about the rationality of children's answers to causal questions. Bullock *et al.* (1982) report an experiment where children were tricked as to the mechanism which mediated one of their actions to a certain effect. Children's claims that their action caused the target event to happen were correct since, if they did not perform the action, the effect in question (a toy falling into a basket) would not happen. Their only 'mistake' was to identify the physical workings of the apparatus that they were shown as the mediating mechanism; in fact, the mediating mechanism was the hidden intervention of the experimenter. Actually, the child's action *did* cause the target effect to happen by prompting the experimenter to act in secret to bring about the effect.

CAUSAL EXPLANATION AND EPISTEMIC JUSTIFICATION

I wish to conclude by differentiating causal 'why' questions, and 'because' statements from a non-causal variety, which I shall call epistemic justifications. Causal 'why' questions and answers imply explanations of causal relationships, whereas epistemic justifications simply back a claim by explaining how someone came to know something along the lines of 'It was Monday because I put the washing out' (cf. Davies 1979; Hilton 1990; Antaki and Leudar 1992). The distinction between explanation of general patterns and particular events will be discussed below, but it is already helpful in establishing a typology of 'why' questions and 'because' statements. Thus Table 16.2 classifies 'why' questions in terms of their speech act function (puzzle resolution or claim-backing) and their content (causal explanation or categorization).

Imagine an aeroplane disaster due to an explosion caused by a bird flying into the jet engine during take-off. Several questions might be posed in such a case. In the prototype case of causal explanation we would say that 'the plane exploded because a bird flew into the engine'. However, we might be asked to back such a claim when asked 'Why was it a bird?' or 'How do you know it was a bird?'. Here we would refer to a consequence of the accident, by alluding to feathers recovered from the foreign object in the engine, and say 'It was a bird because there were feathers in the engine'.

Table 16.2. *Classification of 'why' questions by speech–act function and content*

	Speech act function	
	Explanation	Justification
Content type	(puzzle resolution)	(claim-backing)
Causal explanation	Why did it explode?	Why was it a bird?
Categorization	Why does it explode?	Why is it a bird?

Distinguishing causal from epistemic justification explanations helps to avoid confusion over the meaning of 'because' statements. Trabasso *et al.* (1981) convincingly argue that failure to do so led Piaget to the mistaken claim that young children cannot distinguish causes from consequences. They present data supporting their claim that children do indeed report *causes* when they understand a 'why' question to be seeking a causal explanation, but report *consequences* when they understand a 'why' question to be seeking support for a claim.

A detailed explanation of the aeroplane disaster example given above might describe how the irruption of the bird into engine caused aviation fuel to be set alight by a spark. At this point a child might well ask why fuel explodes. This question would not probe why *this particular* fuel exploded (we already know that it was caused by a spark) but why fuel explodes *in general*. An appropriate answer to this 'science' question would refer to the laws of combustion and the particular properties of the fuel.

Finally, a question about how we know that something belongs to a category ('Why is it a bird?' or 'How do you know that it is a bird') would simply appeal to general knowledge of class characteristics such as 'Because birds have feathers' or 'Because it has feathers'. The use of 'because' simply identifies how we know that an object belongs to a class.

However, it should be noted that only one of the verbal statements justifying a classification would felicitously substitute for the explanation given to justify how we know that a bird got into the engine. We *could* felicitously answer the question 'Why was it a bird?' by saying 'Because it (the object we found) has feathers' but *not* by saying 'Because birds have feathers'. The second explanation does not allow us to identify directly the object found in the engine as a bird. One useful point about this example is that it shows how the same answer 'because we saw its feathers' to the questions 'Why was it a bird' or 'Why is it a bird?' can have the different functions of justifying either a causal explanation or a classification depending on the context. This emphasizes the importance of context in interpreting the deep meaning of explanations.

Nevertheless, each explanation follows a kind of counterfactual logic. We can say that if the bird had not flown into the engine, it would not have exploded, that if fuel did not have combustible qualities it would not explode, that if we had not found feathers in the engine we would not have said that it was a bird, and that if an object does not have feathers we would not call it a bird. Thus, while the logic underpinning each of these 'why' questions and 'because' statements is counterfactual, the content of their predicates changes.

CONCLUSIONS

A conversational model of causal explanation based on counterfactual reasoning, contrast cases, and conversational constraints has been presented in this chapter. This model argues that prototypic cases of causal explanation resolve puzzles as to why an event occurs in a target case, rather than in a given contrast case. Thus, although causal questions may vary, the counterfactual logic of explanation remains the same. Causal explanation is a form of conversation, and as such follows the rules of conversation and thus should satisfy requirements of truth and conversational relevance.

Other sorts of causal question exist which may be posed and answered by 'why' and 'because' statements, such as backing claims, explicating the mechanism which connects two events and so on. Thus, in examining any given act of explanation, we should always ask: What is the puzzle at issue here? To what question should a good explanation be relevant? Is it why a particular event *unexpectedly* occurred, or why a kind of event *typically* occurs? Does the question attempt to *select* the factor that 'made the difference' between the occurrence and non-occurrence of the event in question, or does it focus on how the factor is *connected* to the outcome? Is the relevant contrast between what actually occurred and what normally occurs, as in causal questions, or is it between what occurred and what should have occurred, as in responsibility questions? Does an explanation resolve the puzzle as to *why* an event happened, or account for *how* the explainer knows that something was the case? I have argued that, although all these cases involve explanation, they address different kinds of questions, not all of them causal. Moreover, I have argued that in answering these diverse kinds of questions felicitously, good explanations need to do more than simply be perceived as true. Recognizing the different kinds of causal questions at issue can prevent misunderstanding of causal statements, whether they are made by children or adults in either natural and experimental settings, and help to recognize their rationality.

REFERENCES

Abelson, R. P. and Lalljee, M. G. (1988). Knowledge structures and causal explanation. In *Contemporary science and natural explanation: commonsense conceptions of causality* (ed. D. J. Hilton), pp. 175–203. Harvester Press, Brighton and New York University Press.

Abelson, R. P., Laddo, J., and Gross, P. H. (1987). The strength of conjunctive explanations. *Personality and Social Psychology Bulletin* **13**, 141–55.

Alloy, L. B. and Tabachnik, N. (1984). Assessment of covariation by humans and animals: the joint influence of prior expectations and current situational information. *Psychological Review* **91**, 112–49.

Antaki, C. and Leudar, I. (1992). Explaining in conversation: towards an argument model. *European Journal of Social Psychology* **22**, 181–94.

Austin, J. L. (1962). *How to do things with words*. Clarendon Press, Oxford.

Bennett, L. (1992). Legal fictions: telling stories and doing justice. In *Explaining one's self to others: reason-giving in a social context* (ed. M. L. McLaughlin, M. J. Cody and S. J. Read). Erlbaum, Hillsdale, NJ.

Bohner, G., Bless, H., Schwarz, N. and Strack, F. (1988). What triggers causal attributions? The impact of valence and subjective probability. *European Journal of Social Psychology* **18**, 335–45.

Bower, G. H., Black, J. B. and Turner, T. J. (1979). Scripts in memory for text. *Cognitive Psychology* **11**, 177–220.

Brown, R. and van Kleeck, R. (1989). Enough said; three principles of explanation. *Journal of Personality and Social Psychology* **57**, 590–604.

Brown, R. and Yule, G. (1983). *Discourse analysis*. Cambridge University Press, Cambridge.

Bruner, J. S. (1972). Nature and uses of immaturity. *American Psychologist* **27**, 687–716.

Bullock, M., Gelman, R. and Baillargeon, R. (1982). The development of causal reasoning. In *The developmental psychology of time* (ed W. Friedman), pp. 209–54. Academic Press, New York.

Carbonell, J. (1979). *Subjective understanding: computer models of belief systems*. Report 150, Yale University Department of Computer Science Research.

Carbonell, J. (1981). Politics. In *Inside computer understanding: five programs plus miniatures* (ed R. C. Schank and C. K. Riesbeck). Erlbaum, Hillsdale, NJ.

Carlson, R. A. and Dulany, D. E. (1988). Diagnostic reasoning with circumstantial evidence. *Cognitive Psychology* **20**, 463–92.

Cheng, P. W. and Novick, L. R. (1990). A probabilistic contrast model of causal induction. *Journal of Personality and Social Psychology* **58**, 545–67.

Cheng, P. W. and Novick, L. R. (1991). Causes versus enabling conditions. *Cognition* **40**, 83–120.

Crocker, J. (1981). Judgment of covariation by social perceivers. *Psychological Bulletin* **90**, 272–92.

Cunningham, J. D. and Kelley, H. H. (1975). Causal attributions for interpersonal events of varying magnitude. *Journal of Personality* **43**, 74–93.

Davies, E. C. (1979). *On the semantics of syntax: mood and condition in English*. Croom Helm, London.

DeJong, G. and Mooney, R. (1986). Explanation-based learning: an alternative view. *Machine Learning* **1**, 145–76.

Downing, C. J., Sternberg, R. J. and Ross, B. H. (1985). Multicausal inference;

evaluation of evidence in causally complex situations. *Journal of Experimental Psychology: General* **114**, 239–63.

Einhorn, H. J. (1988). Diagnosis and causality in clinical and statistical prediction. In *Reasoning, inference and judgement in clinical psychology* (ed D. C. Turk and P. Salovey). Collier Macmillan, London.

Einhorn, H. J. and Hogarth, R. M. (1982). Prediction, diagnosis, and causal thinking in forecasting. *Journal of Forecasting* **1**, 23–36.

Einhorn, H. J. and Hogarth, R. M. (1986). Judging probable cause. *Psychological Bulletin* **99**, 1–19.

Einhorn, H. J. and Hogarth, R. M. (1987). Decision-making: going forward in reverse. *Harvard Business Review* **65**, 66–70.

Elstein, A. S., Shulman, L. S. and Sprafka, S. A. (1978). *Medical problem solving*. MIT Press, Cambridge, MA.

Försterling, F. (1989). Models of covariation and attribution: how do they relate to the analogy of analysis of variance. *Journal of Personality and Social Psychology* **57**, 615–26.

Graesser, A. C., Robertson, S. P., Lovelace, E. R., and Swinehart, D. M. (1980). Answers to why-questions expose the organisation of story-plot and predict recall behaviors. *Journal of Verbal Learning and Verbal Behavior* **19**, 110–19.

Graesser, A. C., Robertson, S. P., and Anderson, P. A. (1981). Incorporating inferences in cognitive representations: a study of how and why. *Cognitive Psychology* **13**, 1–26.

Grice, H. P. (1975). Logic and conversation. In *Syntax and semantics 3: Speech acts* (ed P. Cole and J. L. Morgan), pp. 41–58. Academic Press, London.

Grice, H. P. (1989). *Studies in the way of words*. Harvard University Press, Cambridge, MA.

Harré, R. (1988). Modes of explanation. In *Contemporary science and natural explanation: Commensense conceptions of causality* (ed D. J. Hilton). Harvester Press, Brighton, and New York University Press.

Hart, H. L. A. and Honoré, T. (1985). *Causation in the law* (2nd edn). Clarendon Press, Oxford.

Hastie, R. (1984). Causes and effects of causal attribution. *Journal of Personality and Social Paychology* **46**, 44–56.

Heider, F. (1958). *The psychology of interpersonal relations*. Wiley, New York.

Hesslow, G. (1983). Explaining differences and weighting causes. *Theoria* **49**, 87–111.

Hesslow, G. (1984). What is a genetic disease? On the relative importance of causes. In *Health, disease and causal explanations in medicine* (ed L. Nordenfelt and B. I. B. Lindahl). Reidel, Dordrecht.

Hesslow, G. (1988). The problem of causal selection. In *Contemporary science and natural explanation: commonsense conceptions of causality* (ed D. J. Hilton), pp. 11–32. Harvester Press, Brighton, and New York University Press.

Hewstone, M. R. C. and Jaspars, J. M. F. (1987). Covariation and causal attribution: a logical model of the intuitive analysis of variance. *Journal of Personality and Social Psychology* **53**, 663–72.

Hilton, D. J. (1985). Causal beliefs: from attribution theory to cognitive science. In *Foregrounding background* (ed J. Allwood and E. Hjelmquist). *Foregrounding background*. Boksforlaget, Lund.

Hilton, D. J. (1988). Logic and causal attribution. In *Contemporary science and natural explanation: commonsense conceptions of causality* (ed D. J. Hilton), pp. 33–65. Harvester Press, Brighton, and New York University Press.

Hilton, D. J. (1990). Conversational processes and causal explanation. *Psychological Bulletin* **107**, 65–81.

Hilton, D. J. (1991). A conversational model of causal explanation. *European Review of Social Psychology* **2**, 51–81.

Hilton, D. J. and Erb, H. P. (1991). Mental models and causal explanation: judging probable cause and explanatory relevance. Presented at the Subjective Probability, Utility and Decision Making conference, Fribourg.

Hilton, D. J. and Jaspars, J. M. F. (1987). The explanation of occurrences and non-occurrences: a test of the inductive logic model of causal attribution. *British Journal of Social Psychology* **26**, 189–201.

Hilton, D. J. and Knibbs, C. S. (1988). The knowledge-structure and inductivist strategies in causal attribution: a direct comparison *European Journal of Social Psychology* **18**, 79–92.

Hilton, D. J. and Knott, I. C. (1993). Explanatory relevance: pragmatic constraints on the selection of causes from conditions. Unpublished manuscript.

Hilton, D. J. and Slugoski, B. R. (1986). Knowledge-based causal attribution: the abnormal conditions focus model. *Psychological Review* **93**, 75–88.

Hilton, D. J. and Slugoski, B. R. (1993). Perceptions of normal and abnormal questioners and questions. In preparation.

Hilton, D. J., Mathes, R. H. and Trabasso, T. R. (1992). The study of causal explanation in natural language: analyzing reports of the Challenger disaster in the *New York Times*. In *Explaining one's self to others: reason-giving in a social context* (ed M. L. McLaughlin, M. J. Cody and S. J. Read). Erlbaum, Hillsdale, NJ.

Jaspars, J. M. F. (1983). The process of attribution in common-sense. In *Attribution theory: social and functional extensions* (ed M. R. C. Hewstone). Blackwell, Oxford.

Kahneman, D. A. and Miller, D. T. (1986). Norm theory: Comparing reality to its alternatives. *Psychological Review* **93**, 136–53.

Kahneman, D. A. and Tversky, A. (1982). The simulation heuristic. In *Judgement under uncertainty: heuristics and biases* (ed D. Kahneman, P. Slovic and A. Tversky). Cambridge University Press.

Kelley, H. H. (1967). Attribution theory in social psychology. In *Nebraska Symposium on Motivation*, Vol. 15 (ed D. Levine), pp. 192–241.

Kelley, H. H. (1972). Causal schemata and the attribution process. In *Attribution: perceiving the causes of behavior* (ed E. E. Jones, D. E. Kanouse, H. H. Kelley, R. E. Nisbett, S. Valine and B. Weiner). General Learning Press, Morristown, NJ.

Kelley, H. H. (1973). The process of causal attribution. *American Psychologist* **28**, 103–28.

Kelly, G. A. (1955). *The psychology of personal constructs.* Norton, New York.

Lalljee, M. G. and Abelson, R. P. (1983). The organization of explanations. In *Attribution theory: social and functional extensions* (ed M. R. C. Hewstone), pp. 65–80. Blackwell, Oxford.

Lalljee, M. G., Watson, M. and White, P. (1982). Explanations, attributions and the social context of unexpected behaviour. *European Journal of Social Psychology* **12**, 17–29.

Lalljee, M. G., Lamb, R., Furnham, A. and Jaspars, J. M. F. (1984). Explanations and information search: inductive and hypothesis-testing approaches in arriving at an explanation. *British Journal of Social Psychology* **23**, 201–12.

Leddo, J., Abelson, R. P. and Gross, P. H. (1984). Conjunctive explanations: when two reasons are better than one. *Journal of Personality and Social Psychology* **47**, 933–43.

Lehnert, W. G. (1978). *The process of question-answering*. Erlbaum, Hillsdale, NJ.

Lipé, M. G. (1991). Counterfactual reasoning as a framework for attribution theories. *Psychological Bulletin* **109**, 456–71.

Locksley, A. and Stangor, C. (1984). Why versus how often: causal reasoning and the incidence of judgmental bias. *Journal of Experimental Social Psychology* **20**, 470–83.

Mackie, J. L. (1980). *The cement of the universe*. Oxford University Press.

McArthur, L. A. (1972). The how and what of why: some determinants and consequences of causal attributions: *Journal of Personality and Social Psychology* **22**, 171–93.

McClure, J. L., Lalljee, M. G., Jaspars, J. M. F., and Abelson, R. (1989). Conjunctive explanations of success and failure: the effects of different types of causes. *Journal of Personality and Social Psychology* **56**, 19–26.

McClure, J. L., Lalljee, M. G. and Jaspars, J. M. F. (1991). Explanations of extreme and moderate events. *Journal of Personality* **25**, 146–66.

McConnell, M. (1987). *Challenger: a major malfunction*. Doubleday, New York.

McGill, A. L. (1989). Context effects on causal judgment. *Journal of Personality and Social Psychology* **57**, 189–200.

McGill, A. L. (1990). Conjunctive explanations: the effect of comparison of the target episode to a contrasting background instance. *Social Cognition* **8**, 362–382.

McGill, A. L. (1991). Conjunctive explanations: accounting for events that differ from several norms. *Journal of Experimental Social Psychology* **27**, 527–49.

Mandler, J. M. and Johnson, N. S. (1977). Remembrance of things parsed: story structure and recall. *Cognitive Psychology* **9**, 111–51.

Marx, R., Stubbart, C., Traub, V., and Cavanaugh, M. (1987). The NASA space shuttle disaster: a case study. *Journal of Management Case Studies* **3**, 300–18.

Mill, J. S. [1872] (1973). *A system of logic* (8th edn). In *Collected works of John Stuart Mill*, Vols. 7 and 8 (ed J. M. Robson). University of Toronto Press.

Newcombe, R. and Rutter, D. R. (1982). Ten reasons why ANOVA theory and research fail to explain attribution processes: 1. Conceptual problems. *Current Psychological Reviews* **2**, 95–108.

Nisbett, R. E. and Ross, L. (1980). *Human inference: strategies and shortcomings of social judgment*. Prentice Hall, Englewood Cliffs, NJ.

Pazzani, M. J. (1985). Explanation and generalization based memory. *Proceedings of the 7th Annual Conference of the Cognitive Science Society, Irvine, CA*, pp. 323–28.

Pazzani, M. J., Dyer, M. and Flowers, M. (1986). The prior theories in generalization. *Proceedings of the National Conference on Artificial Intelligence, Philadelphia, PA*, pp. 545–50.

Pennington, N. S. and Hastie, R. (1986). Evidence in complex decision making. *Journal of Personality and Social Psychology* **51**, 242–58.

Pruitt, D. G. and Insko, C. A. (1980). Extension of the Kelley attribution model: The role of comparison-object consensus, target-object consensus and consistency. *Journal of Personality and Social Psychology* **39**, 39–58.

Read, S. J. (1987). Constructing causal scenarios: a knowledge structure approach to causal reasoning. *Journal of Personality and Social Psychology* **52**, 288–302.

Read, S. J. (1988). Conjunctive explanations: the effect of a comparison between a chosen and a nonchosen alternative. *Journal of Experimental Social Psychology* **24**, 146–62.

Read, S. J. and Marcus-Newhall, A. (1993). Explanatory coherence in social explanations: a parallel distributed processing account. *Journal of Personality and Social Psychology* **65**, 429-47.

Schank, R. C. and Abelson, R. P. (1977). *Scripts, plans, goals and understanding: an enquiry into human knowledge structures.* Erlbaum, Hillsdale, NJ.

Schustack, M. W. and Sternberg, R. J. (1981). Evaluation of evidence in causal inference. *Journal of Experimental Psychology (General)*, **110**, 101-20.

Shanks, D. R. and Dickinson, A. (1987). Associative accounts of causality judgement. In *The Psychology of Learning and Motivation*, Vol. 21 (ed G. H. Bower). Academic Press, New York.

Shanks, D. R. and Dickinson, A. (1988). The role of selective attribution in causality judgment. In *Contemporary science and natural explanation: commonsense conceptions of causality* (ed D. J. Hilton). Harvester Press, Brighton and New York University Press.

Slovic, P., Fischhoff. B., and Lichtenstein, S. (1976). Cognitive processes and societal risk taking. In *Cognition and social behavior* (ed. J. S. Carroll and J. W. Payne). Erlbaum, Hillsdale, NJ.

Sperber, D. and Wilson, D. (1986). *Relevance: communication and cognition.* Blackwell, Oxford.

Thorndyke, P. W. (1977). Cognitive structures in comprehension and memory of narrative discourse. *Cognitive Psychology* **9**, 77-110.

Trabasso, T. and Sperry, L. L. (1985). The causal basis for deciding importance of story events. *Journal of Memory and Language* **24**, 595-611.

Trabasso, T. and van den Broek, P. (1985). Causal thinking and story comprehension. *Journal of Memory and Language* **24**, 612-30.

Trabasso, T., Stein, N. L. and Johnson, N. L. (1981). Children's knowledge of events: a causal analysis of story structure. In *The psychology of learning and motivation* (ed G. H. Bower), pp. 237-82. Academic Press, New York.

Trabasso, T., Secco, T. and van den Broek, P. (1984). Causal cohesion and story coherence. *Learning and the comprehension of discourse* (ed H. Mandl, N. L. Stein, and T. Trabasso), Erlbaum, Hillsdale, NJ.

Turnbull, W. M. (1986). Everyday explanation: the pragmatics of puzzle resolution. *Journal for the Theory of Social Behaviour* **16**, 141-60.

Turnbull, W. M. and Slugoski, B. (1988). Conversational and linguistic processes in causal attribution, In *Contemporary science and natural explanation: commonsense conceptions of causality* (ed D. J. Hilton). Harvester Press, Brighton, and New York University Press.

Tversky, A. and Kahneman, D. (1983). Extensional versus intuitive reasoning: The conjunction fallacy in probability judgment. *Psychological Review* **90**, 293-315.

Weber, E. U., Böckenholt, U., Hilton, D. J. and Wallace, B. (1993). Determinants of diagostic hypothesis generation: Effects of information, base-rates and experience. *Journal of Experimental Psychology: Learning, Memory and Cognition* **19**, 1151-64.

Weiner, B. (1985). 'Spontaneous' causal thinking. *Psychological Bulletin* **97**, 74-84.

Wilensky, R. (1978). Why John married Mary: understanding stories involving recurring goals. *Cognitive Science* **2**, 236-66.

Wilensky, R. (1981). PAM. In *Inside computer understanding: five programs plus miniatures* (ed R. C. Schank and C. K. Riesbeck). Erlbaum, Hillsdale, NJ.

Wilensky, R. (1983). *Planning and understanding: a computational approach to human reasoning.* Addison-Wesley, Reading, MA.

Zuckerman, M., Eghrari, H. and Lambrecht, M. R. (1986). Attributions as inferences and explanations: Conjunction effects. *Journal of Personality and Social Psychology* **51**, 1144-53.

DISCUSSION

Participants: D. Andler, R. Gelman, P. Jacob, F. Keil, L. Talmy

Jacob: 'You seem to assume that *relevance* is an alternative *goal* in explanation to *truth*. In other words, you seem to assume that sometimes we prefer *relevant* explanations over true explanations. However, it seems to me that *relevance* is a higher *property* of truths. Some truths are, and some truths are not, relevant. We prefer *relevant true explanations* over irrelevant true explanations. But this does not make relevance an alternative to truth as a property we want explanation to have.

Hilton: It is certainly true that my research started off with the working assumption that truth and relevance could be treated as independent characteristics of explanation. This is because I sought to apply Grice's (1975) model of conversation to causal explanation, which would assume that truth, informativeness, and relevance are independent properties of contributions to conversation, including causal explanation. It so happens that Grice has since accepted that his maxims of conversation may not be completely independent, in that the maxims of quality are more basic than the maxims of quantity, relation, and manner. As he writes: 'False information is not an inferior kind of information; it is just not information' (Grice 1989, p. 371). When applied to causal explanation, this would imply that a causal explanation that is perceived as false cannot a priori be perceived as being informative and relevant. In fact, as cited in the paper, the data of Hilton and Erb (1991) tend to support this view. When contextual information reduced belief in the probability of a hypothesis in the cancer example, this also caused reductions in perceived truth and relevance. However, it was still possible for the context in the watch example to reduce the informativeness and relevance of an explanation without reducing its perceived probability.

As a general rule then, it may seem that we should generate a set of the most probably 'true explanations' and then select the most relevant from that set. However, it is worth remembering that there may be exceptions to this rule, as when we prefer specific to general explanations, although the former must be less probably true than the latter. Presumably, we are willing to trade off probability against relevance in specifying explanations when the losses of probability are sufficiently small.

Gelman: It is not clear that all causal questions focus on making sense of the 'abnormal'. Both adults and children (whom I do not think of as abnormal) frequently engage in thought experiments. As Kuhn says, thought experiments offer us one way to learn.

Andler: You may want to use, instead of a normal/abnormal dichotomy, a distinction between transparently used tools and breakdown. In the transparent situation, certain questions may be asked, even by children: Why is grass green? Why does the hammer drive the nail?. In another kind of situation, another kind of question is called for, quite unconnected to the first despite surface resemblance: Why is grass yellow? Why does the hammer fail to drive the nail? This distinction is similar to Hubert Dreyfus's critique of artificial intelligence and cognitivism inspired by Heidegger and Merleau-Ponty.

Hilton: Your questions make the point that questions about normalities and abnormalities, or 'transparent' and 'breakdown' questions, are quite general in nature and can be found in both child and scientific discourse. However, I would hypothesize that we would expect 'transparent' questions to indicate that the inquirer is more interested in 'how the world works in general' than 'why event x in particular happened', and that such inquiries tend to be conducted by children or scientists. Children and scientists are particular kinds of human being, and are not prototypic in a Roschian sense. If I told you 'I saw somebody go up the stairs just now', would a child or a scientist be the first kind of person to come to your mind? I think not. I suspect that you would think of an unidentified adult.

The distinction between 'transparent' and 'breakdown' questions is similar to one I make in the second half of the paper, and extends it to areas that I have not considered. I would note that we seem to agree that the difference between these two types of causal explanation resides not so much in different reasoning processes as in the same kind of reasoning process applied to different kinds of question. Some commentators appear to take a different view, for example Lalljee and Abelson (1983) who make a similar distinction between 'contrastive' and 'constructive' explanation, but address this distinction in information-processing terms. A related problem of talking about 'breakdown' types of situation is that it can lead to the hypothesis that certain types of explanation are required by this category, as when Leddo *et al*. (1984) posit that failures 'require' only one explanation. However, as noted above, this does not seem to be the case. 'Amount of explanation required' seems to be better predicted by the number or degree of gaps between the target event and relevant contrast cases.

Keil: The ways in which relevance can shift preferred explanations raises questions about how flexible such shifts might be and the dynamics of the relevance assumptions. Do current theories of relevance give you a clearer model of how relevance assumptions might change in the course of conversation? For example are they constantly shifting with every new utterance, or are there larger temporal intervals or 'episodes' over which the relevant is held relatively constant to provide a kind of bounded event unit in which to make inferences and assumptions over a fixed set of relevance assumptions?

Hilton: The research that I have described clearly focuses on what might be called 'local explanation' puzzles, i.e. why a particular event occurred when and how it did, or why a certain kind of object exhibits a certain kind of property. In discourse we would generally expect such explanations to be associated with their focal events at the sentence level, such as when we say 'President Bush lost the election because of his poor economic record'.

However, 'aboutness' can exist at different levels in discourse. A medical consultation may be about why a patient is ill, and then branch down to specific questions about why he feels dizzy or has pains in his stomach etc. Similarly, larger units of explanation can exist, such as when the 'moral' of a folk tale can illustrate/explain why a characteristic may lead to an outcome, as when tenacity in the face of a series of reverses eventually leads to a happy ending. Such an explanation must, in some sense, be held in attention over a number of episodes within the story. Thus the answer to this question will probably be found through understanding what determines 'aboutness' in discourse. There are a number of overlapping terms such as 'theme', 'rheme', and 'focus' (Brown and Yule 1983) which will need to be clearly distinguished. The solution will probably be found through an understanding of the hierarchical chunking of discourse in memory (Mandler and Johnson 1977; Thorndyke 1977).

Talmy: One commonality that seems to run through the examples of causal description that you cited for the *Challenger* case, which did not come out in your description, is that they were all intended to ascribe responsibility or blame to some particular sanctioned individual or group, rather than mere physical causes or physical interactions. For example, no one cited the physical principles of the universe, under which rubber molecules contract in cold, as a cause of the O-ring's failure, but rather blamed those engineers who chose and decided to use contractive material for such O-rings. Comparably, no one cited the cold weather alone as a cause of the disaster, but rather the selection and decision of those who gave the go-ahead to launch despite the cold weather. Likewise, in a case of a rail accident, no one cites the physics of metal fatigue or of train weight in explaining it but rather seeks to ascribe blame to those who fail to inspect the rails or consider the consequences of a train of a certain weight on rails of a certain condition.

To be sure, there are cases where what people cite in their causal explanations are indeed physical interactions. The question must then be addressed as to when exactly such physical causes are adduced, and when, instead, people seek to assign responsibility or blame to the sentient individuals or groups for their decisions involving acts of commission or omission, or responsibility for ignorance that should not have existed.

Hilton: It should be noted that here we are generally talking about causal chains in which we trace through physical causes to an antecedent human action. Thus we trace a train accident through a bent rail to negligence, and we trace the *Challenger* disaster through the physics of contractive material in cold weather, to the faulty design of the O-rings decided on by the engineers. Physical causes are adduced at lower ends of the chain, as when we explain that the seals failed because they contracted, and that they contracted because rubber contracts in cold weather. When we reach a human action, we tend to stop tracing further back.

One reason that we may stop when we reach human actions is that these provide maximum explanatory power or relevance in the sense of maximum number of new implications for minimum processing effort suggested by Sperber and Wilson (1986). If we know that the engineers chose rubber, we can predict that this causes the seal to contract in cold weather, which caused the accident. Generally, human actions provide a point of high variability in a chain since freedom of choice enables us to generate many counterfactual alternatives (they could have chosen plastic, or used bolts, to make the seals etc). Thus knowing what in fact the choice was offers high inferential power since it excludes many possibilities and allows many deductions.

Gelman: 'But for' causal arguments are legal arguments used to go backwards in time and ask 'What change would make a difference such that (a) the presently observed case would not have occurred, and (b) there was intention to do harm'. It is a technical term for this class of causal reasoning. Think of the Jewish mother syndrome: 'Oi, if you only had listened to me and not done that ...'! This can be contrasted with causal arguments involving making predictions about the future.

Hilton: Counterfactual reasoning is often triggered by the occurrence of harm making us wonder how it could have been 'undone' (Kahneman and Tversky 1982). This thinking, like causal explanation, is retrospective. In causal explanation, we always seek to explain an event by reference to a previously occurring one through backward chaining. As you correctly say, this does not exhaust all forms of causal reasoning, as when we use forward chaining to assess the consequences of an event. For example, Hilton *et al.* (1992) distinguish reasoning about the causes of events (backward chaining) from reasoning about their consequences (forward chaining) in their codebook for the *Challenger* disaster.

Part VIII

Causal understanding in cross-cultural perspective

Foreword to Part VIII

Psychologists study *mental* representations using experimental data and techniques. Historians and anthropologists study *cultural* representations using as their data texts and records of interactions, and as their methods various interpretive techniques ranging from philology to reflective hermeneutics. Historians and anthropologists invest years of scholarship in order to gain a familiarity with alien ways of thought. The reports that they produce are in many ways much richer and more subtle than those of experimental psychologists. At the same time, they are harder to evaluate, and much harder to use as evidence for or against precise theoretical claims. Are the cognitive scientist's and the social scientist's approaches to causal thinking mutually relevant, and, if so, how? This was hotly debated at the symposium (see also Chapter 12).

Another closely related issue also debated at the symposium was the degree to which different cultures differ in their understanding of causal relationships. Social scientists show greater awareness of cultural differences and often question the relevance of the cognitive scientists' universalistic approach. However, the dividing line on this issue was not the traditional one with all the social scientists on a more cultural-relativist side, and all the cognitive scientists on a more universalistic side. In Section III we saw the psychologist Carey give a greater role than the anthropologist Atran to cultural factors in causal cognition. In this section, the first two chapters (Lloyd and Lewis) are by a historian and a social scientist expressing doubts about cognitive universalism, but the third chapter (Morris, Nisbett, and Peng) is by psychologists focusing on cultural differences, and the fourth (Boyer) is by an anthropologist who adopts an universalistic stance (as does another anthropologist, Hirschfeld, in Section V).

In 'Ancient Greek concepts of causation in comparativist perspective', Geoffrey Lloyd illustrates the wealth and exigency of an interpretive historical approach. He disentangles the legal, philosophical, and scientific sources of Greek ideas of causation, and their evolution from the pre-Socratics to the Stoics and Epicureans. He then compares

Greek and classical Chinese ideas of causation. While Greek ideas are focused on natural regularities, Chinese ideas are focused on exceptional occurrences (a contrast also discussed by Hilton in Section III). Lloyd argues that modern concepts of causation cannot be appropriately used to render either the Greek or Chinese views. He questions the relevance to the historian's task of the kind of cognitive approach illustrated in most contributions to this volume. Historians must explain variations, and that cannot be done, he argues, by appealing to underlying commonalities.

In 'The articulation of circumstance and causal understanding', Gilbert Lewis illustrates the complexity of the anthropological approach and data. He discusses causal accounts of illness given by the Gnau of Papua New Guinea. Where he, as a Western-trained medical doctor, would be more concerned with the process and mechanism of illness, the Gnau seemed more concerned with agency and intention. This led Lewis, in typical anthropological fashion, to pay greater attention to *interpretations* of illness in terms of supernatural agencies than to other Gnau accounts that he saw as mere *descriptions* of events. However, at the same time, he was systematic in his recordings and reflective in his practice. He acknowledges that what he classified as descriptions were often causal explanations of a trivial and mundane kind. He records that more than half the episodes of illness he encountered were explained, if at all, in such mundane 'descriptive' rather than 'interpretative' terms. But does this suffice to make the Gnau case less challenging to cognitive scientists than the Greek and Chinese cases discussed by Lloyd? The Gnau case suggests, at least, that understanding of disease need not be grounded in a domain-specific naïve biology.

Chapter 19 on 'Causal attribution across domains and culture' shows how many social psychologists, in their study of causal representations, are moving beyond standard 'attribution theory' (see also Section VIII). They enrich their recognized competence in the domain by paying greater attention to the developmental and cultural dimensions of causal attributions. Morris, Nisbett, and Peng propose that causal attributions are guided by implicit theories, and that these theories vary in generality across both cognitive domains and culture. Specifically, they argue that there are relatively abstract domain- and culture-general features of causal understanding, that understanding of internally and externally caused motion is domain-specific but not culture-specific, and that understanding of social causation is both domain- and culture-specific. They discuss both the mental and the public representations of causal relationships. They use both cross-cultural experimental data and cultural data as evidence for their claims.

In 'Causal understandings in cultural representations', Pascal Boyer asks whether concepts of causation are culture-specific and answers in the negative. He uses as a test case causal representations in religion and magic which, being unconstrained by objective facts, seem to exhibit maximal cultural diversity. Despite this, domain-specific cognitive dispositions are at work and, even in the religious domain, favour an understanding of causation that is generally trivial, intuitive, and not culture-specific. A few striking counter-intuitive assumptions do mark off the religious domain, but Boyer argues that these too are predictable, given an appropriate universal model of human cognition.

D.S.

17

Ancient Greek concepts of causation in comparativist perspective
GEOFFREY LLOYD

Even a cursory familiarity with ancient Greek thought brings to light a recurrent preoccupation with notions of causation and explanation. This applies to their philosophy, their science, their historical writing, and much of their poetry, including particularly both epic and drama. Not only is the interpretation of these ancient Greek ideas complex and disputed, but the issue of the idiosyncracy of their preoccupations is also worth pursuing. A comparison with ancient China of the Warring States, Qin, and Han periods can be used to suggest marked differences between these two ancient civilisations, both in the *level* of concern with causation, and in the *forms* of that concern. My primary task here will be to identify and interpret key features of ancient Greek ideas on the subject. However, some very preliminary observations on the Chinese material will also be offered.

In approaching the ancient Greek concern with causes, a difficulty lies in the potential for muddle in our own philosophical or lay concepts — relations between causes, motives, reasons, explanations, and so on — muddles that have often been diagnosed as the source of considerable misinterpretations of ancient Greek ideas. Our best tactic is to revert to the Greeks' own terminology, and if that gives our discussion an air of unfamiliarity, there may be advantages as well as disadvantages in this.

Their primary terms in this area include *aition*, *aitia*, and *prophasis*. The first two cover what is 'responsible', or what is 'to blame', and the cognate masculine *aitios* can be used of the guilty party. The third term, *prophasis* is more complex and disputed. It can be used of an excuse or pretext, or offered as a justification for certain behaviour, although it has been suggested (Rawlings 1975) that in medical texts of the fifth century BC the term is used as the precondition of disease, useful to the doctor for prediction. In that context it is close to *sēmeion* (sign) and contrasted with the necessary or primary cause (*aition*). However, both in other classical medical texts and elsewhere, *prophasis* is often used as a synonym for *aition*, as cause (Rawlings 1975; Lloyd 1979, pp. 53 ff.).

One point that is immediately striking in both fifth century BC and later Greek literature is the prominence of this whole nexus of ideas. The historians of the fifth century BC, for instance, are concerned to identify the real causes of historical events, as opposed to what the parties involved may have claimed — as famously in Thucydides' discussion of the true causes of the Peloponnesian War (I 23). Contemporary medical writers are frequently exercised over the distinction between the causes of an illness and mere concomitant factors. Thus the author of *On regimen* III remarks that 'the sufferer always lays blame on the thing he may happen to do at the time of the illness, even though this is not responsible (*aition*)' (*On regimen III* ch. 70), and the writer of *On ancient medicine* also observes that doctors as well as lay people tend to assign the cause of a disease to something unusual that the patient has done near the onset of the complaint (such as 'taking a bath or going for a walk or eating something different') (*On ancient medicine* ch. 21).

Similar preoccupations continue, and with a richer conceptual framework to talk about them, in Plato and Aristotle, and beyond to Hellenistic philosophy and medicine. The centrality of this concern is not simply that much attention is paid to aetiologizing, i.e. to giving substantive answers to substantive questions about the cause of different types of things or events. It is also evident in the effort that went into clarifying the notion of *aition* itself, or rather of justifying one interpretation against others — one framework for the aetiologies against rival frameworks.

Among the areas of ancient Greek dispute that complicate our task of matching their concepts against our notions of either causation or explanation are the following (cf. Frede 1980). Should we think of an *aition*, or again of an *aitia*, as an entity, substance, body, or whatever? Or are they events? Or are they predicates? Or do they correspond to statements, propositional items? Some ancient writers appear to use the two terms more or less interchangeably, but Chrysippus, for instance, is reported (by Stobaeus I. 139) to have distinguished an *aitia* as the statement (*logos*) of an *aition*. That view tends to make *aitia* approximate to 'explanation' and *aition* to 'cause'.

Again, are the effects activities, or events, or objects, or the bringing about of a certain change in the *being* of a thing? There is a distinction, in some of our sources, between an Aristotelian view, where the effect is described by a noun (e.g. a ship, a liquefaction), and a Stoic view, where a cause is that of a predicate's being true of something expressed by a verb (e.g. something's coming to be a ship, or of being liquefied). Sextus Empiricus reports these views in order to cast doubt on both of them from his own sceptical position (*Pyrrhonian Hypotyposeis* (PH) III 14), and a quotation from Clement's *Miscellanies* (VIII 9 26) will give some idea both of the sophistication of some Greek discussions and of how far they are from certain of our own supposedly basic intuitions.

Hence becoming, and being cut — that of which the cause is a cause — since they are activities, are incorporeal. It can be said, to make the same point, that causes are causes of predicates, or, as some say, of sayables (*lekta*) — for Cleanthes and Archedemus [two Stoics of the late third and second centuries BC respectively] call predicates 'sayables'. Or else, and preferably, that some are causes of predicates, for example of 'is cut', whose case [i.e. substantival form] is 'being cut', but others of propositions, for example of 'a ship is built', whose case this time is 'a ship's being built'. (Translation from Long and Sedley 1987, Vol. 1, Sect. 55 C; pp. 333 f.)

Thus there was controversy both about what an *aition* is, and about what would count as an *aition*, howsoever construed.

What types of a *aition/aitia* are to be sought or investigated? Aristotle arrived at his systematic and would-be comprehensive analysis of the four types (material, formal, final, and efficient) by claiming that they subsume, and go beyond, all his predecessors' thinking on the subject.* The **matter** corresponds to what a thing is made of, the **form** to the characteristic features that make it the thing it is, the **final** cause is its function or the good it serves, and the **efficient** selects what brings it about. Thus in the case of an object such as a table, its matter may be wood, say, its form characterizes what makes it a table (rather than some other wooden object, say a chair), its final cause corresponds to the function of a table, and the efficient cause is the craftsman who made it. But Aristotle would offer the same type of analysis not just of objects, but also of events.

It is clear that of these four, only the efficient cause looks like a *cause* in any ordinary English sense — even though the convention to speak of all four as causes is still deeply rooted in those who specialize in ancient Greek philosophy. Aristotle maintains, however, that all four correspond to different, but equally valid, questions asking, in relation to things or events, 'because of what?' (*dia ti*). The answers to all four may tell us something relevant to the full account of what the 'thing' or 'event' is. However, it is not the case that all four types of question will be given positive answers in every case. In particular, not everything has a final cause. Thus, residues in the body serve no good and are just the end-products of natural processes; the residues themselves have no final cause, though the natural processes (e.g. digestion) certainly do (*On the parts of animals* 677 a11 ff.). Again, having eyes of a particular colour serves no purpose, but *having* eyes certainly does (*On the generation of animals* 778 b16 ff.).

Moreover, Aristotle also insists that in any type of inquiry there is a distinction between an account merely of the fact and an account that gives the explanation (reasoned fact). To take one of his examples, one can conclude that planets are near because they do not twinkle, but a proper

---

* Some of the problematic features of Aristotle's theory of causes are discussed by Moravcsik (1974), Sorabji (1980), and Waterlow (1982).

demonstration proceeds via a middle term that sets out the cause, i.e. it concludes that they do not twinkle because they are near. This means that there is no mere constant conjunction between causes and effects, but an important *asymmetry* (*Posterior analytics II* ch. 16, 98 a35 ff.).

In this area the Hellenistic philosophers went far beyond Aristotle, offering a variety of overlapping and competing schemata, with Stoic views being particularly influential (Frede 1980; Barnes 1983). How far they were originally reacting directly to Aristotle is not clear; the treatises by which we know him were not generally available in Athens in the generations immediately following his death. However, our chief sources for the Stoic view, such as Galen, Alexander, Clement, and Stobaeus, were all aware of the broad contrasts between the Aristotelian and Stoic taxonomies of causation.

For one of the fuller accounts we may refer, again, to Clement's *Miscellanies* (VIII 9 33).

When preliminary (*procatarctic*) causes are removed the effect remains, whereas a sustaining (*synectic*) cause is one during whose presence the effect remains and on whose removal the effect is removed. The sustaining cause is called synonymously the complete (*autoteles*) cause, since it is self-sufficiently productive of the effect.

This makes the *synectic/autoteles* cause a sufficient condition, but then Clement proceeds to other types of cause, auxiliary (*synergon*) and joint (*synaition*).

The difference between the joint cause and the auxiliary cause lies in the fact that the joint cause produces the effect along with another cause which is not independently producing it, whereas the auxiliary cause, in creating the effect not independently but by accruing to another, is acting as an auxiliary to the very cause which is independently creating the effect, so that the effect is intensified. (Translations from Long and Sedley, Vol. 1, Sect. 55I, p. 336)

Athough Clement does not elaborate on preliminary (*procatarctic*) causes, we find a further distinction between them and antecedent (*proēgoumenon*) causes attributed by Galen to a Stoic-influenced medical theorist called Athenaeus. On this view, preliminary causes are external factors whose function is to produce some change in the body, whatever this change may be.

If what is thus produced in the body belongs to the class of what causes disease, then, while it has not yet actually given rise to the disease, it is known as an antecedent cause ... Often, he says, the sustaining cause is produced directly from the preliminary cause without an intermediary, though sometimes it comes through the medium of the antecedent cause (Galen, *On sustaining causes* 1–2; translation from Long and Sedley 1987, Vol. 1, Sect. 55F, pp. 334 ff.)*

---

* For Galen on antecedent causes, see Hankinson (forthcoming).

We do not know how far this view was shared by other Stoics, and elsewhere we find other uses of the term translated here as 'antecedent'. But we can see the relevance, in medical theory, of the distinction between external factors and the alterations that they produce in the body. We shall be considering other more general contexts in which the internal–external contrast is crucial later.

Three general remarks can be made at this stage. First, in the Hellenistic period the idea that an *aition* is *active* gained ground. We can see this, for instance, in Sextus's general characterization (*PH* III 14) that 'in the broad sense cause is that by whose activity the effect comes about'. Therefore it would appear that Aristotelian 'efficient causes' looked to *them* more like *aitia*, just as to us they look more like 'causes' (Frede 1980, p. 218).

Second, two of the major philosophical debates between Stoics and Epicureans relate (a) to whether 'final causes' form any part of the valid explanation of things and events – the problems of teleology and providence, asserted by the Stoics, but just as emphatically denied by the Epicureans – and (b) to fate and determinism – is everything determined, and if so in what sense? According to some reports Chrysippus made fate a preliminary, not a complete, cause, although anti-Stoic commentators, such as Plutarch (*On stoic self-contradictions* 1056b), replied that that made him inconsistent. But if the Stoics were certainly determinists in some sense, the Epicureans defended free will with the notorious postulate of the swerve, a minimal deviation in the trajectory of an atom that is, by definition, *un*caused.*

Third, in connection with the determinism issue, the distinction between internal and external factors comes to the fore and the relative importance of each is fiercely disputed. Our principal sources, Cicero and Gellius, attribute to Chrysippus a famous analogy between human action and the rolling of a cylinder. A cylinder does not move without being pushed, but once pushed, the way that the cylinder rolls is due to its own *nature* (*sic*). So in human agency we can distinguish between two factors. An 'assent' does not occur unless prompted by an 'impression'. But

just as the person who pushed the cylinder gave it its beginning of motion but not its capacity for rolling, likewise, although the impression encountered will print . . . its appearance on the mind, assent will be in our power. And assent, just as we said in the case of the cylinder, although prompted from outside, will thereafter move through its own force and nature[†] (Cicero, *On Fate* 43; translation from Long and Sedley 1987, Vol. 1, sect. 62C, pp. 386 ff.)

Of course, there are many problems connected with the details of the taxonomies offered – with what they owe to different thinkers from

---

* Much of the ancient evidence for these debates is assembled by Long and Sedley (1987, Vol. 1, Sects. 20, 55, 62, pp. 102 ff., 333 ff., 386 ff.).

[†] *Suapte vi et natura*, cf. *suapte natura*, 42.

philosophy or from medicine, and with the shifts in emphasis that occurred between the classical and the Hellenistic periods — none of which can be broached, however cursorily, here. But enough has perhaps been said to enable two central and overlapping questions to be identified, although both will involve a good deal of speculation in attempting an answer.

What sustains all this concerted interest, in ancient Greece, in *aitia*? What are the principal models or paradigms that the Greeks appealed to: in other words, can we identify the chief sources of *their* primary intuitions in this area? I shall try to use the study of the latter question to help answer the former.

The first and fundamental point is simple. As I have already intimated, and as has often been remarked, the original connotations of the terms *aition*, *aitia*, and their cognates connect them firmly not just with the domain of human behaviour in general, but with what we may call, broadly, the 'legal' context in particular. *Aition* selects what is 'responsible' for something. *Aitios*, in the masculine, is used of the 'guilty party'. *Aitia* is 'blame' or 'guilt' or the apportioning of such or an accusation imputing blame. These terms come from the 'legal' domain, and , I shall claim, the original associations with responsibility *stay* with them to a remarkable degree.

True, other paradigms are also influential. Aristotle routinely illustrates his fourfold schema with examples drawn from (1) the arts and (2) nature (Lloyd 1966, pp. 287 ff.). Ideas drawn from crafts are very common in a wide variety of contexts of particular physical explanation, not just in Aristotle, and they are particularly prominent in support of 'final causes' to illustrate the way that nature acts intelligently. But without any clear idea of final causes, the pre-Socratic philosopher Empedocles had already compared the workings of his cosmic principle *philia* (love) with metal-working, wood-working, and even baking. Equally, the growth and reproduction of living creatures are often prime explananda, and the explanations given of them provide models for other explanations. Thirdly, the broadly political notions of ruling, controlling, and having authority over provide a further important set of models for use also in other fields.

Some of the uses of these models relate purely to a pair of domains, as in the frequent analogies between nature and the arts, between the arts and politics, and between nature and politics. Thus we find Aristotle both comparing the body with a well-ordered state, and comparing the state with the body. It took some 80 pages in *Polarity and analogy* (Lloyd 1966, ch. 5) to run through just the major examples of such comparisons in particular explanatory accounts in Greek philosophy and science of the fifth and fourth centuries BC.

Sometimes the models in question are the sources of general cosmological theories — representations of the world as a unity and as a whole (Lloyd 1966, ch. 4). Several of the pre-Socratic philosophers had already pictured the cosmos as a political state, although they diverged on its type. Some (such as Anaximander as early as the sixth century BC) saw it in terms of a balance between opposed equal powers, and Empedocles represented the relations between his equal cosmic principles as being governed by a 'broad oath', i.e. a kind of contract between them. Yet others (Xenophanes, Anaxagoras, Plato, and Aristotle) saw the cosmos as a monarchy under a single divine ruler, while Heraclitus saw the cosmos as strife or anarchy. As for technological and vitalist images of the cosmos, Plato represents the divine ruler as a craftsman and speaks of the world itself as a living creature. All three ideas—the world as state, as artefact and as living creature—can be found combined in various Stoic thinkers. (e.g. Diogenes Laertius VII 137–43).

This cosmological application of these types of models shows how ready the ancient Greeks were to attempt *unified* explanatory accounts that *start* with causal ideas that may appear domain-specific to us, but that *end* with grand generalizations in which the cosmic order as a whole is apprehended on the basis of one or more domain-derived ideas.

The examples considered so far do not exhaust all the types of models used in ancient Greek causal explanations. Some complicating factors are summarized below.

1. In his analysis of movement, ('locomotion'), Aristotle operates not so much with a nature versus craft dichotomy, as with natural versus 'forced' motion, where the latter requires a push, i.e. an external efficient cause, and the former does not, since nature is (by definition) a source of motion and rest in itself.

2. Similarly, in various versions of atomism, the changes for which the atoms are responsible are construed in what we may call mechanical terms, although some of the associations of that term should not mislead us. The most complex machines that the ancient Greeks knew were the compound pulley, the screw press, the corn mill, and the ballista. The interactions of atoms are typically a result of their colliding, pushing, rebounding, and interlocking. That was the way that every atom behaved, including the spherical atoms with which soul was identified. Psychological properties, like all other secondary phenomena, have their ultimate ground in the *only* real existents—atoms and the void.

3. Again, there are various cases of what has been called (somewhat anachronistically) 'action at a distance' which illustrate the Stoic doctrine of 'sympathy'. From the time of Posidonius (first century BC), at least, the lunar cycle and the tides were known to be linked, and although for the Stoics everything is connected with everything else, there was, for them (as earlier for Aristotle), an important asymmetry between causes and effects. This emerges, for instance, in the debate on the status of

signs of different types – by doctors as well as philosophers – where, in both the Stoic and the 'dogmatist' medical view, there are so-called indicative signs which reveal the hidden causes of diseases or the bodily condition generally.* There is much learned discussion, in this connection, of the relationship between lactation and pregnancy and also between smoke and fire, and day and light.

Although generalizing across all the controversies concerned must be considered rash, nevertheless let me try to illustrate some of the contexts in which the notion of *responsibility* remains at, or near, the centre of preoccupation. First, it is evident that it is *the* key question in the debate between free will and determinism – an argument which revolved, precisely, around what *we* can be held responsible for, what is 'up to us' (*eph' hēmin*), and in *what* sense it is up to us.

That is only to be expected, no doubt, given that free will versus determinism is primarily an ethical – moral debate. But the distinctions between external and internal factors, between 'preliminary', 'antecedent', and 'sustaining'/'complete' causes, are not limited to what can be called narrowly moral questions. The rolling of Chrysippus' cylinder may be an analogue for human behaviour, but it is an analysand in its own right! The interest in drawing the distinction between the role of the push and the role of the nature of the cylinder itself remains, to some extent at least, an interest in apportioning divided, if impersonal, responsibilities, i.e. their relative importance in bringing about the effect produced.

Equally, when doctors deployed the same general distinction, they were intent on identifying the factors that needed countering. They interrogated the individual case (or the general epidemic) to try to find out what was principally to blame (although of course medical aetiology is not always a matter of apportioning *blame*, since some of the effects investigated are desirable). True, sometimes an *external* cause was perceived as primarily responsible, but it was often assumed that it operated via the production of some change in the *internal* condition or state of the patient. Although doctors sometimes concentrated on removing external causes (when these were not irremediably past or otherwise beyond control), they were more often concerned with trying to induce the opposite *internal* condition in the patient i.e. to return to *nature*.

The Stoic and the medical uses of the contrast between external and internal causes are not the only contexts in which causation and nature are deeply intertwined, but I had better preface my remarks on that topic with a warning that there was nothing natural, in the sense of given, about the Greeks' conception of nature. Rather, that concept was deployed – or as I

---

* On the medical debate on the types of signs that can, or cannot, be admitted see, for example, Hankinson (1987, 1991, pp. xxviii ff.).

have recently referred to it, invented (Lloyd 1991, ch. 18) — in the context of a hard-hitting polemic between rival claimants to knowledge and prestige. It was *the* concept that both so-called 'natural philosophers' and medical theorists invoked to identify a domain of the investigable — their area of expertise. The contrast was with the miraculous, the magical — with, precisely, the 'supernatural'. Yet what nature was to include was, and remained, intensely controversial, as Aristotle's twin claims — that humans are by nature city-state-dwelling, animals and that slavery is a 'natural' institution — illustrate very eloquently.

Thus, long before the Stoics and Hellenistic doctors, there is no doubt of Aristotle's preoccupation with the natures of things and their essences (what makes them the things they are, as opposed to their accidental characteristics) in his 'causal' schemata. Of course 'natural' locomotion is contrasted with 'forced', but the natural is primary — it alone can be continuous — and the forced is secondary and subordinate to it. Again, nature is often contrasted with art and craft, but here too nature is, from many points of view and the most important one, the *primary* domain. Aristotle even says that art imitates nature (e.g. *Physics* 194a21f, 199al6f), doing so indeed in the context of final causes, where *we* might have thought (but we would be wrong) that they are better observed in art where they correspond to intentions and purposes on the part of human agents. It is clear that, for Aristotle, the final cause does *not* depend on intentions; rather, it is the good served.

Moreover, in Aristotle and others, nature is all the *aition* that is needed, and that can tell us much about 'nature' and perhaps even more about *aition*. Once some effect has been successfully traced back to an origin in the nature of the thing in question (for some philosophers, its essence) that is all the explanation that is required, indeed all that can be given; the inquiry is at an end. Thus, whereas in some of our modern intuitions about causation, causes can be tracked back indefinitely — if A is caused by B, we can ask what B in turn is caused by — that is importantly not true of much Greek thinking about *aitia*. Conversely, objections that were later raised about the circularity of explaining the effect of opium in terms of a *vis dormitiva* do not bother an Aristotle or a Galen at all. They were confident, after all, that there *are* natures and essences, however difficult they may be for *us* to ascertain correctly. And these natures and essences are the *aitia* of the effects that we observe, whether or not we have independent evidence relating to those essences over and above the very effects themselves.

At this point it might be objected that, whatever may be said on behalf of the thesis of the ongoing connections between the notions of responsibility, cause, and nature, the thesis runs into two major difficulties. The first is that in the legal context the notion of *aition* is often, although of course not exclusively, used in apportioning blame, often by way of a distinction between the voluntary and the involuntary. But *aition* in Greek physics is even-handed, and, in the teleologists, weighted in favour of a focus on the good produced. As just noted, for Aristotle, the good is not a matter of intentions.

The second and more fundamental objection might proceed as follows. Granted that the natural philosophers are interested in giving causal accounts, is it not the case that their accounts differ, precisely at the point at issue, from those that carry the associations of blame and personal responsibility that are central to the legal context? Was it not by offering a quite new idea about *im*personal causation that they developed the new inquiry into nature?

Both points have some validity, but the thesis should be refined and not abandoned. It is true and significant that the vocabulary of *aitios* and *aitia* antedates the development of the inquiry into nature and is indeed shared by the naturalists and their opponents. Thus the author of the Hippocratic work *On the sacred disease* sets out to refute the 'purifiers', whose accounts of the different types of 'sacred disease' refer these to various gods as the responsible agents or *aitioi* (the term repeatedly used in this connection in chh. 2f). Against them, the Hippocratic writer insists that the disease, like all others, is natural and has a natural cause (where he uses *aitios*, *aitiē* along with *prophasis* and *phusis* (nature) for his *own* view) (Lloyd 1979, ch. 1).

It is not that, in the naturalists' view, *all* causes are natural, of course. We have noted that Aristotle has a category of forced motion opposed to the natural. Nor are all *regular* causes natural (the view of the opponents of *On the sacred disease* might well be that Poseidon is regularly responsible for cases of the disease where the patient 'snorts like a horse'; he is usually also responsible for earthquakes). However, the claim was that where natures have been identified as causes, they are the ones that count.

Thus the naturalists did not invent an entirely new custom-built vocabulary to apply to causation specifically in the physical domain. Rather, they adapted the terminology that had applied, and that continued to apply, primarily to human behaviour. However, this use of a shared terminology makes the competition between alternative accounts, the naturalists' and the traditional, far sharper. The effect of this is to enable the naturalists not just to claim that their accounts are superior, but to *exclude* alternatives. 'What is responsible' must now be located *not* in the domain of personal agency, but in that of species-specific essences.

Therefore the naturalists' idea of what counted as causal did indeed differ from many traditional stories, in that the factors to be invoked are not personal. Nature is certainly not wilful, and the vocabulary of blame is inappropriate (although the *praise* of nature is, in fact, common in the teleologists* and we should not imagine that the study of nature is entirely value-free even for the non-teleologists). But they thereby secured an area to be investigated and at the same time prescribed the manner of its investigation. In this programme natures are the goals of inquiry, yet the idea of responsibility is still present for this is now the area over which, in a sense, nature itself is responsible. In addition, it shared with the original contexts of responsibility that, once what counts as such has been identified, the inquiry is at an end.

We may now bring to bear other related aspects of Greek thought that are relevant to emerging philosophy and science. It has often been remarked that much of the well-developed and extensively deployed vocabulary for evidence, testing, and proof stems from or owes much to, the legal sphere. (Some of the principal evidence is set out in Lloyd (1979, pp. 252 ff.)). Thus two of the principal general terms for evidence, namely *tekmērion* and *marturion* relate primarily to witnessing. Similarly, some of the standard terms used in philosophy and elsewhere for the testing or evaluating of ideas or theories come from the examination of witnesses. Thus, in principle, slave witnesses could only give evidence under torture, and the word for this, *basanizein* (originally associated with the touchstone, *basanos*) is one of the words used of scientific testing or experimenting. For sure, the proofs that the scientists offer are sometimes defined *by contrast* with the proofs 'beyond reasonable doubt' claimed by the orators in courts of law. Both Plato and Aristotle insisted that *their* proofs were of a totally different kind from the speciously persuasive exercises of the orators and politicians, for their own proofs were secure, indeed incorrigible and incontrovertible. However, it must be emphasized that the *vocabulary* of proof is the *same*. The word that Aristotle uses of the arguments that proceed via valid deductions from self-evident non-demonstrable primary premisses, to demonstrate their conclusions, is the same word, *apodeixis*, that the orators had used and continued to use along with a number of other cognate terms for their proofs.

To repeat, nature is interrogated neither as a potentially guilty party nor as an intentional agent. Yet even in the study of nature, the framework within which much causal explanation is cast is drawn from the broadly legal domain. Ancient Greek causation is typically a matter of assigning responsibility, and that applies well beyond the original context of human behaviour.

What can the foregoing analysis tell us about the second of my two initial interrelated questions: *why* does there appear to be such a concerted interest in causation in ancient Greece? Evidently, to suggest an answer here we must be a good deal more speculative than we have been so far.

---

* Galen's *On the Use of Parts* is devoted to this theme and waxes eloquent on the subject.

Certainly, traditional lines of interpretation should not be lost from view. Aristotle himself spoke of curiosity and wonder as the primary sources of philosophizing—not the same thing, to be sure, as an interest in causation, but for him, closely related to it. However, this suggestion is not as helpful as might appear, since curiosity and wonder may be as much part of the explananda as part of the explanations.

Greek legal experience may not help us much either, but it may be relevant in two separate ways—the first associated with the types of philosophical and scientific discussion that were so prevalent in ancient Greece, and the second associated with the models that the law provided for causal inquiry.

Concerning the first I can be brief. Following a familiar line of argument, I have recently discussed (Lloyd 1990) how much the adversarial patterns of debate that are such a feature of early philosophy and science in Greece owe to models of legal speech and counter-speech, and to the general experience of many Greek citizens of debate in the lawcourts and in political assemblies. It is there, principally, that the audiences that the philosophers and scientists addressed gained experience in testing arguments, in evaluating evidence, and particularly in assessing one point of view in relation to its rivals. Even beyond the literal audiences that the philosophers and scientists addressed in their exhibition speeches, the point about the relevance of the law still holds for the imaginary audiences who were addressed in many literary works, since they are often thought of as familiar with legal argument. Moreover, the way in which the philosophers and scientists debated with one another and with other claimants to intellectual leadership exhibits this further feature of the lawcourt scenario, that the arguments developed were often directed at defeating opponents rather than simply at securing the truth—a feature which Aristotle explicity recognizes to be a general tendency among his fellow Greeks. The development of the new styles of wisdom owed much to the contests of argument in which the principals engaged in their bids for leadership.

However, the second aspect is the one that emerges from my earlier analyses of what the notion of causation itself may owe to the legal domain. Certainly, there is no doubt that the forensic orators were keenly alert not just to questions of personal motives and deliberate intentions, but also to those of assigning responsibility and cause more generally. Take a case described by the fifth century BC orator Antiphon. A javelin thrower was practising in the gymnasium and a boy ran in front of the target just as the javelin was thrown. The boy was killed. Who was the cause of death: the boy or the javelin thrower? This example comes in one of the *Tetralogies* composed by Antiphon as models for lawcourt rhetoric. In each case, they comprise two speeches for the prosecution and two for the defence, arguing antiphonally on either side of the case.

The considerable *direct* experience of the law that many Greeks (male citizens) must have had in the classical period is worth emphasizing. The case of Athens is no doubt extreme, for the Athenians were notoriously litigious, but their experience was mirrored, if to a lesser extent, elsewhere. Apart from direct involvement in private law suits as prosecutor or defendant or witness, many would have had extensive experience as so-called dicasts. The dicasts acted as both judge and jury, and from the time of Pericles (middle of the fifth century BC) they received regular pay. In ancient Greece, there was no question of a lay jury merely having to decide questions of guilt and innocence. The dicasts, instructed by no judge, settled matters of law, passed sentences, and gave verdicts. In Athens they could number as many as 5001 individuals in a single court, and even if that was very exceptional, they regularly numbered more than a hundred. The chance that a citizen might be involved as a dicast in any year, let alone in a life time, was high (Lloyd 1992, pp. 42 ff.).

Thus, in addition to the adversarial framework within which much Greek speculative thought was cast, the investigation of cause, in science and philosophy, could be considered a natural extension of the inquiry into responsibilities familiar to many Greeks from the lawcourts to a degree that is quite without parallel in our own societies, unless we happen to be judges or magistrates ourselves, and, mercifully, there are not many of them. We can see the general Greek preoccupation with causation in a new light if we take into account that the lawcourts provided a deeply formative experience for many Greeks.

In any writing of tragedies we expect conflict between individuals, but the style of accusation and counter-accusation in Greek tragic drama often undoubtedly echoes the antiphony of forensic debate. Opposing speakers were allotted the same number of lines to state their point of view, just as the speeches in civil cases were timed by a water-clock.

Again, a historian wishes to give not just a narrative of events, but also to discuss why they occurred. Yet Greek historical writing seems exceptional in the way that a Herodotus or a Thucydides records and investigates differing versions of events presented by different actors or observers, and their different assignations of responsibilities (Hartog 1988).

It would be absurd to suggest that Greek philosophers and scientists directly or indirectly reflected Greek experience of the law in *all* their interests in causation; we have seen how multifaceted those interests were. However, that experience certainly appears to be one factor in the cultural background. A way of testing that is to turn briefly to some of the Chinese evidence relevant to our hypotheses.

Trying to generalize about classical Chinese thought may be as foolhardy as generalizing about Greek thought. There are important differences between both different periods and different fields of inquiry on issues that are relevant to our study. The inappropriateness of using our modern concepts of causation in relation to ancient Greek thought is even more applicable in the Chinese case. This is because there is a relative lack of explicit discussion of what we may take to be among the more important terms in question, notably 故 (*gu*) and 使 (*shi*).

This lack of explicit discussion points to one immediate difference. Where the Greeks develop elaborate taxonomies of *aitia*, the classical Chinese analyses consist mainly of some elliptical passages in the Mohist canon now dated between the late fourth and the late third centuries BC. There, *gu* is said to be what something must get before it will come about, and this is followed by two explanations. In Graham's translations, 'minor reason: having this, it will not necessarily be so: lacking this, necessarily it will not be so', (Graham 1978, p. 161), and 'major reason: having this, it will necessarily be so, lacking this, necessarily it will not be·so', which Graham himself glosses 'the minor reason is the necessary condition, the major the necessary and sufficient condition'. For *shi* we are given two 'definitions' — 'to tell' and 'a reason' — with the explanations 'to give orders is to tell: the thing does not necessarily come about. Dampness is a reason: it necessarily depends on what is done coming about' (Graham 1978, p. 162).

Now, the Mohists were not exactly in the mainstream of Chinese philosophy, and their influence after the end of the Warring States period was negligible. Just how far their views on *gu* and *shi* correspond to general Chinese perceptions is doubtful. Graham himself remarked of *gu* that it is 'in the first place what is at the origin of something; the word can also be used of a thing in its original state or of the fact behind a statement', and of *shi* that it is used primarily of employing a person — which corresponds to the first of the two explanations, to give orders. But we can see that in both cases the human domain provides one of the sources for Chinese thinking about reasons and causes. However, the points taken from that domain relate, in the case of *gu*, to the fact underlying a statement, and, in the case of *shi*, to the context of commanding. In neither case do they relate to the context of legal responsibilities.

However, there is a fundamental difference in the actual experience of the law between ancient China and Greece. First and foremost, far from delighting in private litigation, as the Athenians did, the Chinese generally considered any case that came to law as a failure, a breach of good order (Hulsewé 1986). In any event, practically speaking there was no civil law. Differences between individuals or groups that might well have been the subject of appeal to litigation in Greece were generally settled by discussion, by arbitration, or by the decision of the responsible officials. The Chinese had no experience that remotely corresponded to that of the Greek dicasts or to the Greeks' open debate of political issues in the assemblies.

But how far do such differences account for differences in type or emphasis in thought about *aitia*, *gu*, and *shi*? One of the two effects that I suggested might have stemmed from the experience of law in Greece concerned the adversarial framework within which much philosophical and scientific debate was cast, and here some points appear reasonably clear and uncontroversial. First, despite the title of a recent book by Graham, *Disputers of the Tao*, the rivalry between schools and individuals was appreciably less confrontational in China than in ancient Greece (Graham 1989; cf. Sivin 1992). In philosophy, in medicine, and elsewhere there is criticism of other points of view, including those expressed by reputable authorities such as Confucius himself. But the Chinese generally conceded far more readily than did the Greeks, that other opinions had something to be said for them, even when they did not capture the whole of the *dao* (Sima Qian ch. 130 and Zhuang Zi ch. 33 would be cases in point). Second, and correspondingly, there is little to compare with the Greek idea that victory in such confrontations would go to the individual or group mustering superior arguments. Far more readily than the Greeks, the Chinese recognized that silence may be superior to words, that the real sage does *not* talk, that the *dao*, as the first stanza of Lao Zi already had it, is ineffable. Third, while persuasion was practised in many different spheres — political, moral, cosmological, medical — the emphasis was more often on the *psychology* of persuasion (as for example in the *shuo nan* chapter of Han Fei Zi) than on the arguments to be used. Moreover, the context of persuasion was not the citizen body gathered in the lawcourts or assemblies. The principal target of Chinese persuasion was the emperor, whose sole opinion was decisive. The memorial to the throne was the preferred format of persuasion. This was often a text actually presented to the emperor in person, but, even when that was not the case, the composition was often cast into the form of such a presentation according to a well-established literary convention.

The second effect of Greek legal experience that I proposed related to the models that it provided for causal thinking more generally, and here we come to the nub of the issue. Much of Graham's discussion is directed to establishing that the classical Chinese favoured *correlative* as opposed to *causal* thinking (Graham 1986, 1989). But to take these as exclusive alternatives clearly will not do. It will not do as far as the ancient Greek evidence is concerned, for the interest in constructing general schemata of analogies or correspondences can be seen in much Greek cosmology alongside considerable attention to the question of causal explanations. The point remains valid even if the Greeks never managed any quite such grand schema as that provided, eventually (although perhaps not before the Han), by *yin*, *yang*, and the five phases — a conceptual framework within which heaven, earth, the seasons, the state, the emperor, the body, and everything else could be comprehended.*

A general fondness for systems of correspondences does not discriminate ancient Greece from ancient China; neither does the fact that in both cultures cosmological inquiry was certainly not value-free, but rather a resource for moral, even political, recommendations and particularly the lauding of order. It is in the intensity of the further interest in causal relations, and in the nature of that interest, that differences may still have to be acknowledged.

Caution, as always, must be the watchword. Of course there is much more to Chinese reflections on *gu* and *shi* than those Mohist texts suggest of themselves. Other terms, such as 原 *yuan* (source) and 因 *yin* (the operative factor, or the one you rely on), would also have to be taken into account in any even moderately full survey. As can be seen in Sima Qian's *Shi Ji* (c. 100 BC), Chinese historical texts explain the events that they record, often commenting on the moral factors involved in the successes or failures of individuals, rulers, or dynasties. Again, medical treatises, such as the *Huang Di Nei Jing* (first century BC), often offer accounts of the origin of diseases, in both general and particular cases, distinguishing particularly between internal and external factors (*yin*) (Sivin 1987, pp. 100 ff.).

Yet it is noticeable that in many contexts the Chinese interest is in the exceptional, the particular, the breaches of regularity, the failure of order. The regular itself may be and is *described*, but it stands in need of no *explanation*, no invocation of a particular cause. This applies to the ordinary processes within the body and to many other examples of the correct balance of *yin* and *yang* or of the orderly sequence of the five phases. The difference here is that the Greeks *did* attempt causal explanations of the natural, invoking natures themselves as those causes!! Thus, what marks the contrast in the causal patterns in the two cultures corresponds, at least in part, to the Greek preoccupation with the investigation of the domain of the responsibilities of nature.

The Chinese exception who may prove the rule is the philosopher Hui Shi (fourth century BC), generally characterized in Western writings as a sophist or a logician, although neither label is particularly apposite. But it is clear that, like the later Mohists, he too was out of the mainstream of philosophizing. Here, for once, was a Chinese thinker who did pursue explanations almost in the Greek manner — only to evoke some sardonic comments from Zhuang Zi.

---

* On the development and systematisation of *yin*, *yang*, and the five phases, see Sivin (forthcoming).

There was a strange man of the south called Huang Liao, who asked why heaven did not collapse or earth subside, and the reasons (*gu*) for wind, rain and thunder. Hui Shi answered without hesitation, replied without thinking, had explanations for all the myriad things, never stopped explaining, said more and more and still thought he had not said enough, had some marvel to add. (Graham 1989, p. 77)

What, then, can a discussion of causation in ancient societies contribute to a general analysis of the topic? I am struck by the differences in the working assumptions made by those who approach the subject from the different perspectives represented in this book. Those who study cognitive development in infants and young children assume that they are dealing with cross-cultural universals. Some anthropologists too are convinced that there are 'common-sense' conceptions that underlie the diverse systems of belief reported from around the world, including beliefs relating to what we call causation.

First, we need to be clear on the differences between the domains of evidence with which we have to deal. As a historian of ancient Greece, I am concerned neither with what ancient Greeks might have revealed if, as infants, they had been exposed to the experimental situations described by Baillargeon, Spelke, Carey, Gelman, and others, nor with how they would have responded to the type of questions that Atran puts to his Maya, including, incidentally, questions that presuppose some familiarity with microscopes. Questioning ancient Greeks, as babies or as adults, is not possible, and it is pure conjecture what their answers would be. What Francesca Bray and I are concerned with is, rather, the actual ideas expressed — with greater or less clarity and explicitness, certainly — in the actual extant sources available to us.

The key message that I wish to convey is that there is great diversity on the subject of causation both within Greek thought and between Greek and Chinese thought. That diversity cannot be dismissed. It is our problem *as historians*. It would clearly be no explanation of that diversity to appeal to postulated underlying common conceptions for these are, *ex hypothesi*, *common* and so can do nothing to help explain the differences that we find, for instance, between Aristotle and the Stoics, or between the writer of *On the Sacred Disease* and the purifiers he attacks, or between a given Greek thinker and Mo Zi, or Zhuang Zi, or Hui Shi.

For the historian, problems arise from the divergences both between *different* ancient conceptions and between ancient and modern conceptions, not that we all have a transparent and agreed notion of causation ourselves.

On the Greek side I have offered suggestions concerning (1) the differences between their ideas and ours, (2) the features of their experience that their ideas reflect, (3) the motivations that they had for developing their ideas, and (4) the issues that were at stake when they entered into explicit debates on these problems. The data on the Chinese side are just as rich, just as complex, and just as strange, as Francesca Bray's work confirms.*

One lesson that can be learnt from this type of historical investigation is that the distinctions that we often take to be basic are anything but, in the sense that people have managed very well *without* them. This is not just a matter that they did not have explicit concepts for implicit ideas, for, as we all know, we can use prose without having that concept. Rather, it is that the explicit ideas are different — one of the lessons that I learned from my original study of the introduction of the category of nature, or rather *phusis*, in ancient Greece. It did not simply *label* what had all along been recognized quite happily without the label; it *transformed* the perceptions of those who did the introducing. It had a very definite role to play in marking out *one* view of what is worth investigating from competing views. The absence of any single notion that corresponds to Greek *phusis* in China is connected with their very different construals of what is problematic, what is investigable. Their concerns in this area relate to the different nexus of issues selected by their concepts of (1) 天 *tian* (heaven), (2) 理 *li* (pattern), (3) 物 *wu* (things), (4) 道 *dao* (the way), and (5) 自然 *zi ran* (spontaneity, literally 'self so').

Of course, I am not suggesting that those Greek and Chinese ideas are so different from our own that we simply have no access to an understanding of them. The strong notion of incommensurability prevents all historical investigation. My own position is very different. After all, my discussion is full of *judgements* about what I think the authors in question are discussing. But it is not as if I believe that we can go to that investigation armed with a map of the terrain that *they* were trying to chart. Rather, we have to try to start further back and see what they needed their ideas *for*, and that is never likely to be a question with a simple answer. To judge from the Greek material, the answers often include a fair element of polemic along with attempts at ordering different aspects of experience.

But, it will be objected, is it clear that there are such great differences between the conceptual frameworks of the ancient Greeks, the ancient Chinese, and ourselves? Is it not possible that all this diversity is superficial and that the ideas expressed are, essentially, all compatible with underlying common-sense conceptions, indeed with cross-cultural universals? To that it has to be replied, first, that the ancient Greeks did not see it like that. *They* thought that their ideas offered different *rival* accounts of the *same* problem, not merely different aspects of a common core of shared underlying assumptions.

---

* Unfortunately, Francesca Bray's paper and presentation to the symposium are not available for publication in this volume. However, I refer to her contribution to a forthcoming volume to be edited by Don Bates for a perceptive exploration of notions of causality in Chinese medical theory and practice in particular (Bray, forthcoming).

Of course, it could be argued that the source of much causal thinking — for us, for the ancient Greeks, and for the ancient Chinese — is one or other of three principal domains: (1) that of the artificial, art or artefacts (or what are construed as such); (2) that of the natural (howsoever construed); (3) that of the social–political–legal (again, however they are construed). 'Causal thinking' here can cover thought about causes, reasons, motives, responsibilities, explanations — once again, however these are construed. Furthermore, additional special points of contact are not hard to suggest. I argued, for instance, that systems of correspondences, or 'correlative thinking', are a concern for both the ancient Greeks and the ancient Chinese.

That much *can* be granted, but it is not sufficient to generate much confidence that basic cross-cultural models are at work or that such an assumption is useful to the historian. First, those who argue for this are not satisfied with the type of disjunctive proposition that sets out three possibilities, introduced by either ... or ... or ..., such as is implied by my distinction between the three general domains. Second, the whole problem arises with those provisos that I introduced under the rubric 'however construed', for the appearance of correspondence begins to fade very rapidly as soon as we press particular points.

Do we think that cylinders have a nature? That humans are by nature social animals? That slavery is a natural institution? How are we to explain that, in ancient Greece, the notion of a cause as *active* gained ground in the Hellenistic period? Was that just philosophers coming to their senses? Why had a different view been taken before? What about the dispute over causes of things versus causes of predicates, about effects being incorporeal? It is not enough for us merely to intervene and adjudicate that *some* or most of these ideas are wrong factually, morally, or whatever. We have to work harder and see what notions of nature, what notions of cause, are in play for those ideas to be expressible — which still does not mean, of course, that we have to agree with them.

We can indeed express our preferences for some philosophical solutions to difficulties, for some proposed clarifications of obscurities or confusions, over others, expressing indeed and inevitably value judgements on the matter. But the risk that we face, as historians, is of *underestimating* the reasons that there were, within the different conceptual frameworks in question, for expressing what seem to us such strange ideas in the first place.

On finding such differences, the universalist may be tempted to legislate and exclude them as *not* a matter of cause, *not* a matter of nature, but something else. But the alternative is not relativism, let alone a conceptual free-for-all. It is not as if everyone can invent their own ideas and none is intertranslatable into anyone else's, as between ancients and moderns or between one modern and another. No: the alternative is pluralism, the recognition that we are dealing with complex theoretical constructs used, to be sure, to arrive at some understanding of aspects of human experience, but where, if we bear in mind the diversity that may exist within what human experience may cover, we should be prepared also to recognize the diversity of the understandings arrived at. Investigation of the different notions of causation developed in different contexts, at different junctures, by different individuals or groups, is the historical task that we have undertaken. But *why* these issues came to be a matter of explicit concern when they did, in the way they did, and to the people they did, is not a matter of some of those people being clever enough to anticipate us, but rather has, in each case, its own historical, social, and intellectual dynamic.

ACKNOWLEDGEMENTS

I should like to thank all those who contributed to the discussion of the presentations by Francesca Bray and myself at the symposium, and particularly to Scott Atran and Gilbert Lewis for written comments and queries, which I hope have enabled me to see more clearly where misunderstandings may arise and where ongoing areas of disagreement persist. I also wish to express my gratitude to the organizers of the symposium and to the Fyssen Foundation for their courage in attempting an interdisciplinary workshop and for their generous hospitality.

REFERENCES

Barnes, J. (1983). Ancient skepticism and causation. In *The skeptical tradition* (ed. M. Burnyeat), pp. 149–203, University of California Press.

Bray, F. (1995). A deathly disorder: understanding women's health in late Imperial China. In *Knowledge and the scholarly medical traditions*, (ed. D. Bates), pp. 235–50, Cambridge University Press.

Frede, M. (1980). The original notion of cause. In *Doubt and dogmatism*, (ed. M. Schofield, M. Burnyeat and J. Barnes), pp. 217–49. Oxford University Press.

Graham, A. C. (1978). *Later Mohist logic, ethics and science*. School of Oriental and African Studies, London.

Graham, A. C. (1986). *Yin-yang and the nature of correlative thinking*. Institute of East Asian Philosophies, Singapore.

Graham, A. C. (1989). *Disputers of the Tao*. Open Court, La Salle, IL.

Hankinson, R. J. (1987). Causes and empiricism. *Phronesis* **32**, 329–48.

Hankinson, R. J. (1991). *Galen On the therapeutic method, Books I and II*. Oxford University Press.

Hankinson, R. J. (forthcoming). *Galen On antecedent causes*. Cambridge University Press.

Hartog, F. (1988). *The mirror of Herodotus* (transl. J. Lloyd). University of California Press.

Hulsewé, A. F. P. (1986). Ch'in and Han law. In *The Cambridge history of China*, Vol. 1, (ed. D. Twitchett and M. A. N. Loewe), ch. 9, pp. 520–45. Cambridge University Press.

Lloyd, G. E. R. (1966). *Polarity and analogy*. Cambridge University Press.

Lloyd, G. E. R. (1979). *Magic, reason and experience*. Cambridge University Press.

Lloyd, G. E. R. (1990). *Demystifying mentalities*. Cambridge University Press.

Lloyd, G. E. R. (1991). *Methods and problems in Greek science*. Cambridge University Press.

Lloyd, G. E. R. (1992). Democracy, philosophy and science in ancient Greece. In *Democracy, the unfinished journey* (ed. J. Dunn), pp. 41–56. Oxford University Press.

Long, A. A. and Sedley, D. N. (1987). *The Hellenistic philosophers*. Cambridge University Press.

Moravcsik, J. M. E. (1974). Aristotle on adequate explanations. *Synthese* **28**, 3–17.

Rawlings, H. R. (1975). A semantic study of PROPHASIS to 400 BC. Hermes Einzelschriften 33, Wiesbaden.

Sivin, N. (1987). Traditional medicine in contemporary China. *Science, Medicine and Technology in East Asia* **2**.

Sivin, N. (1992). Review of 'Disputers of the Tao'. *Philosophy East and West* **42**, 21–9.

Sivin, N. (forthcoming). Yin-yang and five phases.

Sorabji, R. (1980). *Necessity, cause and blame*. Duckworth, London.

Waterlow, S. (1982). *Nature, change, and agency in Aristotle's physics*. Oxford University Press.

18

The articulation of circumstance and causal understandings

GILBERT LEWIS

The subject of this chapter is the causal understanding of illness. The data come mainly from work in Papua New Guinea, and the discussion is concerned with what people do in naturally occurring circumstances. It is about reasoning in practice by adults who come from a culture which maintains belief in the presence in nature of powers and spirits that can respond to human behaviour. These ideas lie behind various rules for the conduct of daily life. Illness may provoke special attention to them, in that a description of circumstances can imply a possible interpretation of cause. The shift in thought from description to interpretation may be left unstated. But relevance requires recognition. To leave the conclusion implicit protects it from challenge and refutation; it also prevents debate of the ideas and the development of theories.

THE DIRECTION OF EXPLANATORY EFFORT

Many of the processes to which we attribute illness are invisible to the naked eye. With which of the senses can we grasp the facts: sight, touch, hearing, smell? How much of our understanding depends on seeing and direct experience? How much is a matter of interpreting relationships of contiguity, timing, sequence, probability, and possibility? In biomedicine, knowledge of disease depends on years of special training and on having the means to see (e.g. microscopes, chemical tests, electrocardiograms). People who have none of this technology look at illness in other ways. Their frames of understanding are different. Ideas about what goes on inside the body, the hidden processes of disease, are inevitably speculations about what cannot be seen. I shall discuss a society in which people tend to consider things *outside* rather than *inside* the body to explain illness.

Any social event can be seen to have multiple causes. There are biological, psychological, and social aspects of illness, although more attention is paid to some aspects than to others. The kind of attention that is paid depends on our perception of the problem. People in African or New Guinean societies do not always rush to explain an ailment by witch-craft or some other mystical cause. They respond to illness in a variety of ways. Little has been written about their practical responses to trivial ailments, such as coughs, cuts, etc. Their reactions depend on the severity or threat that an illness seems to pose, and on whether they see the illness primarily as a social or a medical or some other sort of problem. There are cultural assumptions about the appropriate questions to ask. The assumptions imply views about nature and normality, about cause and effect, and about what it is possible to know. In the same way as the title of a painting can suggest how the painting is to be viewed, the initial identification or labelling of a problem may be crucial, for example 'he's not wicked, he's mad'. A classification which 'medicalizes' can shift a problem from the non-medical into the medical domain. The identifica-tion sets up a potential field of relevance and relevant questions. Percep-tions of illness are influenced by people's cultural assumptions about what to look for: they contribute to a 'social construction of reality' (Berger and Luckmann 1967), to a 'cultural construction of clinical reality' (Kleinman 1980). Therefore classification may be a critical step, orientating the search to understand.

An example of this sharp difference in approach was one I experienced repeatedly among the Gnau in the West Sepik Province of Papua New Guinea when I attempted to treat them for illness. I wanted to carry out a clinical examination, but in their view my whole approach—questions about symptoms, examination of the body signs—was not the way to deter-mine the cause of the illness or to establish its treatment. The word for 'he examines something', *nitemangupa*, which they used for what I did (and would normally apply to such actions as identifying the marks on an arrow, or tracks in the mud) was not one that they would use for their procedure with a sick person. I thought that I could extract information about the kind of illness, its cause, and how to treat it from the clinical or body signs and symptoms; they did not. In general, they paid them casual attention. We had different views about how to identify the cause. I had ideas about *processs* and *mechanism*; they were more concerned with *agent* and *intention*.

Evans Pritchard's famous study of Zande witchcraft (1937) showed how, in the case of that Sudanese society, the causes of many misfortunes—particularly illness—could be explained at more than one level. His own attention was selective. He was interested in their ideas about witchcraft more than in their knowledge of the empirical processes or mechanisms of illness (Gillies 1976). However, he made it clear that although they might say that the cause of an illness was witchcraft, this did not mean that they failed to see the observable circumstances or processes by which the illness was brought about (e.g. a bite, an injury, a swelling).

The world known to the senses is just as real to them as it is to us. We must not be deceived by their way of expressing causation and imagine that because they say a man was killed by witchcraft, they entirely neglect the secondary causes that, as we judge them, were the true causes of his death. They are foreshortening the chain of events and in a particular social situation are selecting the cause that is socially relevant and neglecting the rest. Belief in death from natural cause and belief in death from witchcraft are not mutually exclusive. On the contrary, they supplement one another, the one accounting for what the other does not account for. Besides death is not only a natural fact but also a social fact. (Evans Pritchard 1937, p. 73)

Zande attention was also selective. Their interests reflected cultural assumptions as well as personal involvement. Azande recognize a plurality of causes; the social situation indicates the relevant focus. A Zande cannot plead that witchcraft made him steal or commit adultery as a means of escaping responsibility for his action and punishment.

Evans Pritchard's analysis dispelled any idea that reasoning was simply vague, weak, or confused. It alerted anthropologists who followed to notice distinctions in other people's thinking about causation—distinctions between questions of process or mechanism (how something happened?), questions of agency (who or what made it happen?), questions of origin, reason, or motive (why did it happen?) (Zempléni 1985).

Evans Pritchard identified links of reasoning and thought which were implicit or unspoken. His style was to challenge Azande to make their thinking plain.

He declared that witchcraft had made him knock his foot against the stump. I always argued with Azande and criticized their statements, and I did so on this occasion. I told the boy that he had knocked his foot against the stump because he had been careless and that witchcraft had not placed it in the path, for it had grown there naturally. He agreed that witchcraft had nothing to do with the stump of wood being in his path but added that he had kept his eyes open for stumps, as indeed every Zande does most carefully, and that if he had not been bewitched he would have seen the stump. (Evans Pritchard 1937, p. 66)

Such questioning gives us the sense of insight into their thinking, but it also directs a respondent to explain himself in a particular way—perhaps with finer distinctions, exposure of contradictions, etc. Socrates asked questions to make his interlocutors see the confusions in their thought. His method of question and answer might give unwonted clarity and direction to the representation of causal understanding in another culture. The solution is not easy since thought is internal and silent. The anthropologist's dilemma is the choice between being too active or too passive. How does one encourage people to express thoughts, which are silent or implicit, without distorting them with a foreign style of questioning? Of course much thought is asserted publicly. The advantage of illness as a subject for exploring causal understanding is that it provokes discussion.

Intrinsic features of an illness (such as severity or pain) may push people to persist with questions, although not necessarily about cause. An urgent wish to act (because of pain, fear, uncertainty) can lead people to disregard questions of cause. They think that there is no time to wait for an answer; they must act immediately. Or the answer may be important, more as a justification for action than as a statement of belief. Freidson (1970, pp. 163, 169) noted this as a characteristic of the practice of medicine. There are two additional features to note: the timing of causal explanation (was it put forward at the time or later?) and its relation to practical action. The first can bring out contrasts between prospective and retrospective views, between deliberation and contemplation; the second contrasts theory and practice.

Prediction, prognosis, and plans to treat all have forward-looking aspects which link present state or action and future effect. Sindzingre and Zempléni (1982) note the contrast between prospective and retrospective causal understanding in illness, and between theory and practice. Thinking can be assertive and speculative; it can be focused on making a decision, i.e. deliberative. Fears which may look ridiculous after the event need not have seemed so before it. Retrospective explanation is not subject to the same pressures or the same risks of being exposed as wrong. A theory that fire will not burn is hard to maintain. The implications of this can be emphasized to stress the difference between causal understandings in which there is no possibility of knowing whether they are true (e.g. myths about the origin of the incest taboo) and interpretations of cause which can be immediately put to test (my hand hurts because I am touching a hot frying pan). Between immediacy and impossibility of testing come all shades of possibility. There are obvious implications in this for the survival of suggested causal explanations, and for how people respond to causal explanations when they are put forward.

The contrast between theory and practice lies behind a sense of misconception that other anthropologists may also have experienced when they compared their understanding of ideas derived from discussing them in theory, with their subsequent understanding of the same ideas after seeing them in practice.

In the village in the Sepik where I was working, a man had a sudden pain in his knee. A few hours after its onset, while he lay inside his house, a cricket jumped out of the thatch onto his painful leg. A few minutes earlier, a girl from the hamlet above had walked past. She was the 'grandchild' of a man who had died with a painful bad leg caused, it was said, by a certain spirit. The villager thought the 'shade' (spirit) of the dead man must have followed the girl, entered the cricket, jumped onto his knee, and alerted the spirit; his knee became more painful. He voiced his fears, his wife relayed them, and his kin discussed them. (In fact he had tried to catch the cricket to kill it but had failed.)

This speculation was plausible given the Sepik people's assumptions about 'shades'; their presence and interest in their descendants, and their ability to activate other spirits. The pain heightened the man's perception of events that he would scarcely have noticed otherwise. 'Coincidence' requires special attention. It is not very rare for an insect to jump from the thatch, but it jumped onto his bad leg, when he was in pain, and just after the girl had gone past. The events could be connected even though the girl had passed and the cricket jumped *after* the pain had started. Illness had singled them out, prompting the man to see them as significant. He remembered a death and used an idea about something invisible (the spirit of the dead man) as a theory to link together the other perceptible elements (the cricket, his knee, the girl) into a causal hypothesis (the spirit had followed the girl and entered the cricket, which had jumped down from the thatch onto his bad leg). He, and others with him, chose what they considered relevant: the range of time and distance, and the connections to accept. The range of time or distance might vary greatly; could even alter the size of the frame within which an illness was seen. In this case it was the focus on his painful knee, the concatenation of elements, and the near coincidence that made him discern the links.

Horton (1967) has suggested that traditional African thought (such as ideas about spirits of the dead) can be compared to causal theories or hypotheses in Western science on the grounds that both make a jump to theory from the limited vision of natural causes provided by simple observation and common sense. They both start from the world of everyday things and people, and go beyond these to causes which are outside the grasp of simple or unaided perception; they widen the context in which a particular event is seen to link it to a more general explanatory theory. One of the difficulties in listening to Gnau accounts of illness and the circumstances surrounding it was to decide when those jumps were being made.

The episode described above was easy to remember; it was obviously 'their' reasoning, not mine. It did have some consequences: it precipitated the girl's departure from the sick man's hamlet. She had been staying in his wife's house, hesitant, waiting, about to marry one of his brother's sons, but she left, (her guardian urged her to return). After an appeal to the spirit of the dead man, people lost interest in that particular explanation for the sick man's pain as matters became worse and other explanations were developed.

CAUSE BY DESCRIPTION OR BY INTERPRETATION

Most people expect exotic examples of causation from an anthropologist – a spirit entering a cricket – rather than accounts of trivial cuts and scratches. However, I remember the Gnau's account of the circumstances of Maluna's scalded leg (he had been pouring boiling water to make sago jelly in a camp while hunting) because they laughed so much at his ineptitude – a man doing a woman's task – not because it was a clear example of causal explanation focused on mechanism, on how the harm was caused. They looked no further to explain it. I tended to think of it (and shelved it in my mind) as description rather than causal explanation or interpretation. This indicates my simple bias to think that causes should *make* things happen. Their accounts of process and mechanism were at risk of being passed over as mere description because I looked for agency and intention (answers to the question 'why?') before I registered them as 'causal explanations'.

I have noted (Lewis 1975, pp. 197-8) the Gnau explanation of breast abscesses because it was not what I expected. In fact it belongs with many unsurprising instances of explanation in which observation and description of the circumstances of things like a cut, a sore, or an injury constitute sufficient explanation – the description explains the cause in terms of what happened or how it happened. It stays in the world of everyday things. The breast abscess explanation also clearly implies recognition on their part of similar cases – the linking of the particular with the general, recognition of regularity in nature. They said that abscesses sometimes happen if a child dies in early infancy so that the milk swells the breast, is blocked inside, and changes into pus.

I recorded this natural explanation after trying to treat a young woman with a large suppurating breast abscess. I was told this much detail because I persisted with questions, being surprised, given the death of her baby, her pain, and what I knew by then about their ideas, that no one referred to spirits or sorcery as possible causes. She accepted the abscess as a misfortune of ordinary life that did not require a more particular causal explanation. The positive acceptance of the physical explanation as sufficient explanation was striking, as was the fine detail which agreed so well with what I believed. The breast abscess was certainly abnormal (very unpleasant and painful for the young woman), but she took it as a natural sequence. In Gnau (her language) she said that it just happened – *wap diyi*, 'it was without purpose' – there was no agency or intention behind it – *wewup gipi'i*, literally 'it came up nothingly'. She was making distinctions both between the normal and the abnormal (the abscess was abnormal as only some women suffered from such a condition after the death of their baby) and between the natural and the 'super-natural' or 'intended' (the abscess was a natural misfortune, and there was no invisible spirit or malevolent agency behind it).

The idea of agency or intention appeals to the Gnau imagination (and to ours) and may dominate in some contexts, particularly perhaps in illness and misfortune. It focuses attention on purpose and agent rather than mechanism — on 'who' and 'why?' rather than 'how?' — on interpretation rather than description. There may be more than one reason for this: that the basic notion of cause derives from subjective experiences of making something move or change and implies power and volition, or that suffering and pain make sense as threat, punishment, or attack, and provoke explanations in terms of responsibility or blame. However, the phrase 'make sense' begs the question about what constitutes adequate or sufficient explanation in causal terms. I used a double standard for 'explanation' when I compared Gnau theory and practice in the Sepik. If they identified the cause in terms of some agency or actor, I placed their explanation in the category of 'explained' illness, but not if they just described how it happened.

In attempting to compare what the Gnau said in theory with their actual practice, I noted the illnesses that occurred in the population (355 people) of one of their villages over a period of 23 months (Lewis 1975). I learned about the causes of illness including several kinds of destructive magic and sorcery, many spirits, and elaborate prohibitions about food and action. However, despite many causes 'in theory', in more than half (57 per cent) of the 274 episodes of illness recorded, I heard no explanation that went beyond mere acknowledgement of the disorder, or a matter-of-fact description of the circumstances in which it occurred. Of course, during this study there were changes on my side of insight, familiarity, and language-grasp, and on theirs of trust. I did not include trivial cuts, skin sores, and infected scabies in this count of 'illness', and I have discussed elsewhere the question of the match and discrepancies between Gnau views and mine (Lewis 1975, pp. 95–153, 229–46). In another area of New Guinea, among the Huli of the Southern Highlands, Frankel (1986, pp. 72–4, 175–80) rather similarly found that 81 per cent of Huli diagnoses were concerned largely with the nature of the lesion, rather than its causation (he included all episodes of illness, however trivial, recorded over 6 months from a sample of 417 respondents living in one parish (552 episodes)). In other words, they noted the illness but offered no complex interpretations of it in terms of its social or spiritual significance.

Many anthropological studies or comments on illness have been primarily concerned with its social and spiritual significance, with diagnoses of the 'why?' sort. Medical diagnosis, which we may tend to think of as the identification of *what* is wrong, often entails an interpretation of cause (e.g. in diagnosis of fevers, and biomedical differentiations between infectious, metabolic, traumatic, and neoplastic diseases). The diagnostic labels identify the cause as well as indicating what signs to expect. However, some Gnau diagnostic categories were simply identifications of the cause; 'labelling' was by cause. In those cases, the diagnosis was an aetiological interpretation, not an identification or clinical description of the manner in which someone would be ill. It did not specify the bodily signs or symptoms to look for. In contrast, we generally expect to be able to tell something about the manner of a person's illness from a biomedical diagnosis. (This is not always so; for example, the label 'AIDS' or 'diabetes' may be precise on cause, but give no help on the signs that a patient will show.)

SHIFTS OF ATTENTION

There are three factors to consider in analysing causal understanding: (1) the intrinsic or distinctive features of the problem; (2) the interests of the people involved; (3) their cultural assumptions. Cultural assumptions alert people to the features of a situation thought to be relevant for understanding and responding to it. They include ideas about what it is possible to know and how to find this out, and they influence people's perception of the event or situation.

Evans Pritchard's (1937) analysis of witchcraft gave a convincing account of the social construction of what was, in effect, a different clinical reality. It has been quoted as an illustration of the cultural relativity of understanding and truth, the acceptance of different criteria of evidence and proof (Winch 1970). Witchcraft explained unfortunate events and was a key explanatory theme in Zande life, although not the only level of understanding (Gillies 1976). Other ethnographies could be used to illustrate different aetiological themes which seem to dominate the causal understanding of illness in a culture: e.g. Fore concepts of sorcery during the period when they were devastated by the disease kuru (Lindenbaum 1982); the peculiar Huli theory of injury and delayed illness, associated with litigation for compensation (Frankel 1986, pp. 124–36); the surrealist theory of powers described by Augé (1975) as the explanatory *idéo-logique* of the Alladian peoples of the Côte d'Ivoire; theories relating illness to the emotions — *susto*, fright (Rubel 1964) and *popokl*, pity and unrequited exchange expectations (Strathern 1968) — to the hot and cold properties of foods (Anderson 1987), to pollution (Douglas 1966; Frankel 1986, pp. 100–23), to spirits (Lewis 1972), and to sin or destiny (Fortes 1959). Analyses of these have served as keys to distinctive aspects of different cultures. Although a monograph may focus on the dominant idea, most also refer to other socially accepted ways to explain illnesses. To have only one explanation for all illness would be unlikely. Given the variety and vagaries of illness, rigidity in causal understanding would be unbearable. In practice, people need to leave some room for development — to be able to change their expectations or their explanations.

Mechanical, teleological, and intentional explanations of cause focus on different kinds of question. Culture and professional training alter the frameworks, the assumptions, and the apparent validity of questions. People have different views on what to ask and on what it is possible to discover. The Gnau examined the circumstances of an illness. They might be content with simply describing them, or they might see something special in them to suggest some agency, motive, or intention at work.

On a few occasions, I observed the shift in attention as a sharp change. A clear example of this was after the death by drowning of a girl aged 12 years old. She was known to have seizures in which her face went blank, and she jerked and fell unconscious, sometimes being incontinent at the same time. Early one morning she was sent to fetch water, but did not return. The villagers looked for her, and her father found her head downward in the pool. He pulled her out by the legs. I heard a sudden burst of crying from her hamlet. People rushed there. In front of her mother's house her body was laid out, her father squatting by it. Women wept and wailed. Her father said what he had seen and done. He said that Sunikel (his daughter) must have had a fit and fallen into the pool. Others said that it was wrong to have sent her alone; he knew she had fits, and he had other children who could have been sent. People gathered from all the hamlets. Her father, after weeping for an hour, got up to clear the ground to make a grave. Her body was taken into her mother's house to prepare it for burial. Her father's younger brother went to the water hole and measured its depth with a bamboo pole which he notched; it was about three and half feet deep. On return, he stood it against a child younger than Sunikel to compare the depth and the child's height. Some men sitting near me began to discuss *sanguma* sorcery (*langasutap*) and to agree with each other that it must have been *langasutap* for her to fall and drown in such shallow water. They began to discuss what paths the men with *langasutap* could have taken. It was by now about two hours after the body had first been laid out in the village. The theme of sorcery was taken up. By the afternoon it had been decided to fetch a clan relative from another village to perform a particular kind of divination. It was carried out at night two days later. Her spirit, by entering a special pole, answered their questions in beats on the *garamut*, slit-gong (Lewis 1975, pp. 259–63).

The shifts in discussion and comment were noticeable: the statement of what happened; the reproaches for sending her unaccompanied; the measuring of the depth of the pool; a crucial point made by setting the notched bamboo against the height of a younger child; the shift to suspicion of sorcery; a new set of issues; the question of divination to find out. The heat of discussion grew as people gathered. In most cases people take note of the circumstances and often, no doubt, various possibilities cross their minds without being voiced. The father's younger brother went to measure the depth because he suspected something; he set the notched pole against the child to make a dramatic point—a visually telling point. It orientated subsequent discussion more effectively than simple assertion.

Gnau people often speak at the same time and the effect can be cumulative. They do not have recognized authorities for deciding between alternative explanations in such situations. Debate is open, although women rarely speak out unless closely involved. The men are assertive in public. Despite the loud and ready voicing of different opinions, they do not argue them through. Certainly the talk can lead to treatment; but it is unpredictable. Everyone has the right to speak; age and experience carry some weight but no conclusive authority. Arguments are not teased apart, nor are debates engaged between experts with reputations to make or lose. There may come a point when talking has to stop and the people have to act. A state of continuing or worsening illness is likely to influence this. Reflection back on past illness does not have decision and urgency to contend with.

In discussing the social background to the emergence of critical thought and science in ancient Greece, Lloyd (1979, pp. 226–67) has suggested that the duty of all free men to take part in public debate as equals sharpened their attention to skill in rhetoric and to questions of logic and evidence in argument. At Gnau gatherings, there is free speech among equals but little procedural formality; they do not take turns to speak, and often they hardly seem to 'listen to' each other. The volume rises, punctuated by shouts that people should not speak at once. (Is this an absurd comparison? What about literacy, population size, and political variety? New Guinea abounds in tiny independent egalitarian communities—a few thousand people at most making up each independent political unit. Is the scale so different from that of the ancient Greek polities?) During illness, Gnau people come to show concern; the gatherings produce discussion. The talk may lead to treatment without necessarily resolving discrepancies between explanations or deciding between them. Divinatory procedures are occasionally used, but typically not until after a death. Otherwise, when the illness is over, people tend to lose interest in the question of what caused it. But in present illness, if it is seen as serious, people recount the circumstances surrounding it because these may contain the clues for understanding what caused it.

In the case of the drowned girl, the shift between description of the circumstances and interpretation was sharp. The shift was from the question of 'how?' to questions of 'what?' and 'why?' The talk went from discussion of process to issues of sorcery—the perpetrators and the possible motives or reasons behind it. In English we may use 'how?' and 'why?' to ask different kinds of question. The contrast is most obvious with intentional human actions in which choice, responsibility, and blame become matters of interest. In many empirical or scientific contexts it makes little difference whether we say 'We don't know "how" something (e.g. aspirin) works' or 'We don't know "why" it (aspirin) works', but with human actions it does matter: 'how he did it' does not answer the question of 'why he did it' (Edwards 1967). The difference at issue is partly like that between description and interpretation. Lyons (1977, pp. 443–5, 493) notes a distinction between 'causes' as second-order entities, which are observable processes, events, or states of affairs, and third-order entities, or 'reasons', which are propositional in nature: 'unobservable and cannot be said to occur or to be located in space or time. Third-order entities are such that "true" rather than "real" is more naturally predicated of them' (Lyons 1977, p. 445). This is an aspect of the difference between interpretation (the propositional) and description (the observable).

Quite often in illness, as pointed out earlier, it may be impossible for people to see or know about disease processes hidden inside the body; comment on the processes must be speculative. In contrast, people's social relations are observed—their hopes or fears and their intentions are relatively intelligible or possible to guess. Therefore the intrinsic difficulties of providing 'how?' compared with 'why?' explanations of cause appear in different lights. The question of agency and intention is highly significant in many African and New Guinean contexts. From fresh research among Zande in the République Centrafricaine, Buckner (1985) has shown that the two levels (or registers) of causation analysed by Evans Pritchard (1937) correspond to two Zande terms for 'cause': the first *sa*, which also literally means 'tail', refers to a mechanical cause, something empirical or observable, or an event from which an effect follows, while the second term *ndu*, also meaning 'leg, foot', refers to a motive, a reason, or a final cause. She analyses how *sa* and *ndu* fit Evans Pritchard's distinction between the 'perceptible causes' and the 'mystical causes' (such as witchcraft, magic, or breach of prohibition), and Lyons's contrast between 'cause' (observable) and 'reason' (propositional). *Ndu* explanations for why an illness occurred may be used to impute responsibility. To know why it happened does not necessarily entail knowing how.

THE RECOGNITION OF IMPLICIT RELEVANCE

Although I have described Sunikel's death in which the shift between description and interpretation was noticeable, the distinction was often hard to make when listening to Gnau accounts of illness. So much stayed implicit. A seemingly simple descriptive statement might have a deeper meaning; indeed it might ring with significance to them yet mean nothing much to an outsider. People would describe the circumstances surrounding someone's illness without comment. They left implications implicit, or, with the hindsight of illness, what had been merely experienced before could take on fresh significance. It was a matter of context and alerting. Things could be left unsaid because people shared the same presuppositions—the same cultural style and assumptions. One of their narrative devices was to use simple description of a movement or a gesture to convey someone's response or feeling: for example, 'I asked him to eat. He sat'. In this context 'he sat' meant 'he refused my offer'. I sometimes failed to see implications because I lacked the same knowledge or the assumptions. For example, I heard a particular myth several times uncomprehendingly until someone explained a meaning that was obvious to them: three times in the narrative the hero set out from the old woman's house and got just so far away; then he stopped and turned back. That was all they said: what I did not guess but what Gnau listeners realized, given the context, was that the old woman was pulling night down, bringing darkness, and that was why he turned back. It was not said explicitly, yet it revealed the old woman to be a demon spirit.

This was a problem of recognition: I had missed seeing what the story was 'about'. The general issues that this raises are those of presupposition, context, and the perception of relevance—the degree to which a listener can fill in the background to make sense of what is said or interpret gaps or incoherences (Johnson-Laird 1983, pp. 63–6; Levinson 1983, pp. 167–225). To 'make sense' of an illness and the events surrounding it, Gnau people must have ideas about what is possible and what to expect. These imply some recognition of regularity or uniformity in nature and behaviour. If people share similar assumptions about causal relationships, they can construe them for themselves. There is less need to explain them. We all more or less unconsciously do something similar as we assess the scenes before our eyes for anything odd or special to notice or react to.

A Gnau narrative of events must involve selection and simplification: things are taken for granted because they are obvious, or they may be left out because they are irrelevant or too time-consuming to describe. Only a fraction of all the facts are included. From the narrator's point of view, the narrative requires selection and ordering. The narrator's theories about causation influence the facts that he sees as relevant—how they are put forward, their order and priority—a reciprocity at work between fact and theory. The mental picture formed from a verbal description does not impose a conclusion. A larger frame might have included more, or events that happened earlier or at a different place, and suggested different conclusions. In narrative accounts people can add details, or introduce or emphasize different events. This happens in the repetitions and discussions of the circumstances surrounding illness, or as the illness changes. It has the merit of flexibility and the weakness of being inconclusive.

The Gnau use description to put forward or hint at a causal interpretation. The recognition of regularities in life is essential in adjusting to any social and physical environment. Reactions and interpretations depend on assessment of what is ordinary or likely and what seems unusual, uncanny, or contrived. Gnau people approach causal understanding in the case of serious illness rather as we might approach the explanation of a traffic accident, considering the likelihood of the occurrence given the time, the place, and the actions going on. They may identify certain components of the situation because of risks associated with them or because something is unusual. The explanatory approach is similar to ours with accidents, but the components and assumptions differ. In a car accident, the explanation might be focused on the car and the driving, the place where it occurred (a dangerous crossroads), and the time (night). In a Gnau woman's illness, an explanation might be focused on the place (a garden), the timing, and her action (walking through it when it was newly planted). The place is significant for identifying who should treat her, as lineage spirits would have been invoked by the planter to watch over the garden and strike down trespassers; the timing is significant because it is believed to be dangerous to pass through a garden in the days just after planting.

The explanation rests on the intersection of certain components in the circumstances. It is a deduction from straightforward observation and is dependent on their assumptions. I analysed the explanations that I heard for all the illnesses in a village over 23 months. It emerged from this (Lewis 1975, pp. 229–330) that they used a rather restricted range of actions to explain illness. The range reflected their perceptions of different risks, their salience, and how often they were exposed to them. The salience of something as cause might be suggested by the long gap between when it happened and referring back to it to explain current illness, for example someone bringing up a quarrel that had flared up long before. But, surprisingly, many things that they did were rarely (e.g. hunting) or not at all (e.g. cards and gambling) related by them to illness. In over half the explanations which clearly involved actions (apart from eating), the actions had to do with some aspect of gardening or subsistence work such as planting, cutting things down, or harvesting a crop. The implication was that spirits were annoyed at injury to their things or people taking them away; they referred to ideas of spirit presence, localization, or concentration at places, their attachment to crops and interest in them, and their possessiveness. The power of spirits is ambivalent—they bring benefits and abundant food as well as ills. Illness acted as a reminder of their power and presence; it provoked thought. If the cause of an illness was attributed to some agent, it was more likely to be a spirit (81 per cent of the 117 cases in my sample were attributed to conscious agents) rather than a human agent (19 per cent including cases attributed to breaking a taboo as well as to acts of sorcery and magic).

The evidence for what they understood about spirits as causes of illness comes from their behaviour (precautions, avoidances, gestures in treatment, etc.) and from what they said. In treatments and ceremonies they would make direct speeches to spirits, addressing them in a loud voice, stating what they wished or hoped for or what they feared. They addressed them as persons. In ordinary talk about illness, their choice of words implied much. I shall mention the verbal imagery that they used but I cannot go into the even more basic matter of the grammar and logical connectives which is a minefield of practical questions—translation, an unwritten non-Austronesian Papuan language, and the nuances and the linguistic and philosophical difficulties of positing equivalents in their forms for the parts of speech and the little words which are important in conveying our ideas of cause, consequence, and intention (questions of word order, mood, 'because', 'so that', 'in order to', 'and so', 'if . . . then', 'therefore', 'thus', etc.).

But the verbs that they used exhibit an imagery suggesting kinds of causation including ideas of mechanical cause, intention, and function. The verbs have evocative everyday meanings: ideas of contact or entry expressed as the spirit 'strikes', 'shoots', 'stays in', 'goes down into' someone or some part of him; ideas of constraint expressed by verbs meaning to 'crush', 'tie up', 'pull', 'hold tight'; concepts of localization involved in a spirit 'staying', 'watching over', 'looking after', 'departing'; verbs expressing the spirit's attention to a person it afflicts—it 'sees', 'knows', 'recognizes', 'smells' someone; expressing an intention as when the spirit is 'cross about its things', 'grieves for', 'intends to harm', etc. Wind, like scent and sound, offers an experience of invisible non-material presence and plays a part in the imagery of spirit presence and of power at a distance.

How many metres would someone have to move to escape from a spirit's presence? This is practical question for the Gnau. The problem for us as outsiders, of course, is to tell how far their different verbal expressions were literally understood, or purely metaphoric, or dead metaphors. Many of their actions and the gestures of treatment might imply literal understanding because they are logical consequences of the implied causal mechanism— removal, blows, flames or nasty smells to make the spirit leave, or sucking out 'arrows' shot invisibly. Alternatively they might be viewed as symbolic actions. When someone says that his illness results from eating the fruit of a plant whose roots bind him down and his brothers go to the garden where the plant stands and dig it up, roots and all, to release him, should one call this evidence of literal or symbolic understanding? The answer might be mixed: the sense of binding and constraint is perhaps literal and the releasing action at a distance is symbolic. Almost everywhere adult language is full of imagery and metaphor that seems to make nature animate, responsive, and purposive. How far the phrases represent living or discarded theories, mere words and conventional imagery, or relics of once vivid childish thought may be unclear or the answer may be mixed. For instance, when in English we hear someone say 'I caught 'flu', or 'he gave it her', referring to infection, there can be similar uncertainty or ambivalence over how to take the metaphor, or how dead it is. The situation and personal involvement can alter whether someone sees a meaning in literal or symbolic terms.

Spirits watch over food and food enters the body. It is a possible vehicle of entry for illness. This was a clear idea when food was associated with some forms of sorcery and made its use seem conceptually close to poisoning. But it was not so clear in the diagnosis of spirits. Eating might single someone out and make a spirit attend to him. In theory a spirit might strike someone with illness in reaction to some fault like greed or negligence, but in practice the wrong actions were not often identified even though the food was. If certain foods were conspicuously associated with dangers from spirits, we might expect to find the foods singled out in explanation long after eating them, but the identifications were nearly all of food eaten recently at ordinary daily meals, not feasts or special food received in ceremonial exchanges. Instead, it seemed that ordinary food led to illness because spirits occasionally chose to strike, but why was not made clear. No specific motive was given. The kind of food was important in diagnosis because of associations between particular spirits and certain vegetable foods.

The ideas which connect food, actions, and spirits provided some principles of explanation. They helped to provide answers to the typical diagnostic questions asked by the Gnau: 'What is this' (*Meni eita*?), 'What have you done to get ill?' (*Gagai meni wa dji wola*?), 'What have you eaten to get ill?' (*Ganu meni wa dji wola*?). Gnau rules of behaviour and their warnings about actions that might give offence to other people or to spirit are intended among other things to give them guidance and protection against illness. Everyday life would be impossible without assuming that there is some regularity in nature, and that human behaviour has causes that are in principle ascertainable (Carr 1964, p. 94). However, people are not sure of understanding spirit agents and their purposes or intentions. They may speak of them as causing illness and be aware of those whom they afflict, but they do not blame them as they would a human agent.

If the wind causes damage to someone but no one supposes that it has aims or motives, it cannot be blamed as a moral agent. The effects that it produces cannot be given a meaning in the same moral terms as the actions of a human agent. The difference in understanding spirits is suggested by the different quality of emotion shown, — sometimes far more intense, when human rather than spirit agents are blamed for causing illness. Although conscious of not really understanding them, the Gnau attributed awareness and intention to spirits present in nature. With spirits as the explanatory middle term, they could represent nature as responsive to human action in moral as well as physical terms. Spirits in nature had volition; they could *make* things happen. They were treated as agents and that made their effects different from the effects of breaking taboos. The Gnau had a forest of rules about prohibitions in which the consequence of the forbidden action was supposed to be inherent or automatic. The difference appeared also in phrasing: they used the connective *wa* ('then', a marker of sequence, consequence, e.g. you do X *wa*—then—Y occurs) for taboos but they did not use, as they would with people or spirits, the connective *∧la* indicating purpose, intended consequence ('in order to', e.g. it struck *∧la*—in order to—crush him). The taboos identify dangers as regularities of nature, almost like natural laws or properties of things, which are innate sometimes to the material, the place, the time, sometimes the person, the action, the relationship, and the conjunction—particularly the conjunction. The dangers might strike specifically ego or alter or object or process. But at the same time people knew that their neighbours had other rules and suffered no harm, and that the prohibitions could change with situation or as someone grew mature or achieved a certain social status; they also knew that people made mistakes and nothing happened, and that some did not bother to obey them.

In his chapter on causation in history, Carr (1964, Chapter 4) discusses how the historian selects the facts which are significant for an explanation. He is concerned with distinguishing between what he calls rational and accidental causes in history (Carr 1964, p. 107). The rational causes serve some purpose; they are potentially applicable to other cases, they lead to fruitful generalizations, and lessons can be learned from them. Accidental causes teach no lessons and lead to no conclusions. The historian must select from a multiplicity of sequences of cause and effect.

It is true that Cleopatra's nose, or Bajazet's gout, or Alexander's pet monkey-bite, or Lenin's death, or Robinson's cigarette-smoking, had results. But it makes no sense as a general proposition to say that generals lose battles because they are infatuated with beautiful queens, or that wars occur because kings keep pet monkeys, or that people get run over and killed on the roads because they smoke cigarettes. If on the other hand you tell the ordinary man that Robinson was killed because the driver was drunk, or because the brakes did not work, or because there was a blind corner on the road, this will seem to him a perfectly sensible and rational explanation; if he chooses to discriminate, he may even say that this, and not Robinson's desire for cigarettes, was the 'real' cause of Robinson's death. (Carr 1964, pp. 105–6)

For the ordinary man or woman, the relevance and adequacy of an explanation will depend on particular assumptions and values. Despite all that the Gnau had to say about spirits, they could not fully predict or control them; illness revealed that. Dangers often showed up only in retrospect. Predictability is a matter of degree.

The mixture of their ideas about spirits and their capriciousness, the rules of behaviour to follow in dealing with them, and the prohibitions allowed illness to seem at times like retribution, at times the result of someone's own fault or folly, but most often there was no final verdict. The lack of a separate focus may be a factor in this. Their ideas were not organized systematically around the subject of disease as a field of knowledge. Instead, things relevant for understanding illness belonged primarily to other domains of major interest to them (e.g. gardening or hunting). They gardened and hunted on a regular and frequent basis. They could plan the activities and turn to a body of relatively coherent and systematic knowledge about them. Illness, in contrast, was an unwanted and unexpected intervention in people's lives. It came at a tangent to their plans; they were not in control. Illness had some of the qualities of accident. There was no special branch for medicine and healing in their division of cognitive labour, no category of specialist to elaborate ideas and practice or make them more coherent. Instead, individuals were free to put their own views forward. Possibilities were left open. Different people might intervene in treatment. No authority issued a conclusion. That was generally left to experience or uncertainty.

REFERENCES

Anderson, E. (1987). Why is humoral medicine so popular? *Social Science and Medicine* **25**, 331–9.

Augé, M. (1975). *Théorie des pouvoirs et idéologie*. Hermann, Paris.

Berger, P. and Luckmann, T. (1967). *The social construction of reality*. Doubleday, New York.

Buckner, M. (1985). Reflexions sur l'étiologie zande. *Ethnographie* **81**, 65–80.

Carr, E. H. (1964). *What is history?* Penguin, Harmondsworth.

Douglas, M. (1966). *Purity and pollution*. Routledge and Kegan Paul, London.

Edwards, P. (1967). Why. In *The Encyclopedia of philosophy*, Vol. 8 (ed. P. Edwards), pp. 296–302. Macmillan and Free Press, New York.

Evans Pritchard, E. E. (1937). *Witchcraft oracles and magic among the Azande*. Clarendon Press, Oxford.

Frankel, S. (1986). *The Huli response to illness*. Cambridge University Press.

Fortes, M. (1959). *Oedipus and Job in West African religion*. Cambridge University Press.

Freidson, E. (1970). *Profession of medicine*. Dodd, Mead, New York.

Gillies, E. (1976). Causal criteria in African classifications of disease. In *Social anthropology and medicine* (ed. J. Loudon), pp. 358–95. Academic Press, London.

Horton, R. (1967). African traditional thought and Western science. *Africa* **37**, 50–71, 155–187.

Johnson-Laird, P. (1983). *Mental models*. Cambridge University Press.

Kleinman, A. (1980). *Patients and healers in the context of culture*. University of California Press, Berkeley, CA.

Levinson, S. (1983). *Pragmatics*. Cambridge University Press.

Lewis, I. M. (1972). *Ecstatic religion*. Penguin, Harmondsworth.

Lewis, G. (1975). *Knowledge of illness in a Sepik society*. Athlone Press, London.

Lindenbaum, S. (1982). *Kuru sorcery*. Mayfield,

Lloyd, G. E. R. (1979). *Magic, reason and experience*. Cambridge University Press.

Lyons, J. (1977). *Semantics*, Vol. ii. Cambridge University Press.

Rubel, A. (1964). The epidemiology of a folk illness: susto in Hispanic America. *Ethnology* **3**, 268–83.

Strathern, M. (1968). Popokl — the question of morality. *Mankind* **6**, 553–62.

Sindzingre, N. and Zempléni, A. (1981). Modèles et pragmatique, activation et répétition: reflexions sur la causalité de la maladie chez les Senoufo de Côte d'Ivoire. *Social Science and Medicine* **15**, 279–94.

Winch, P. (1970). Understanding a primitive society. In *Rationality* (ed. B. Wilson), pp. 78–111. Blackwell, Oxford.

Zempléni, A. (985). La maladie et ses causes. *Ethnograpie* **81**, 31–44.

DISCUSSION

Participants: P. Jacob, F. Keil

Keil: Could you interpret your report as suggesting that, in fact, different sorts of beliefs are kept quite distinct in explanatory accounts, such that one might not rely on evidence while the other will? Moreover, could such difference be accounted for by assuming that some explanations that are more intentional/social in nature are of the no-evidence sort, while those of the biological/functional type are viewed as needing evidence?

G. Lewis: I do not think that the different sorts of belief were really kept quite distinct. Some of their descriptions of the events surrounding an illness could be taken either way—they might be interpreted as an explanation for why the person had been made ill, or they might be heard simply as an account of how and when that person came to be ill. People differed in what significance they saw. Questions or argument might provoke someone to find or point out some interpretation; on other occasions no one bothered. In some ways their descriptions were analogues of clinical case histories, with information possibly relevant, possibly containing clues or evidence, for either intentional/social explanations or biological/functional explanations. Sometimes I noticed a sharp shift of explanatory focus, as in the case of the girl who drowned; sometimes I could not tell whether I was listening to an explanation of motive or a simple report of events. The question of what they counted as evidence is interesting. Often they had only circumstantial evidence, but sometimes they picked on something that they had noticed (e.g. remains of food spotted by a fire, footprints); in claims for compensation, occasionally they brought with them the material evidence of damage caused (half-eaten crops, damaged fencing). However, it would be hard to segregate the use of evidence according to type of explanation. When a man was thought to be ill because he had eaten a particular lizard, taboo to him because he knew a certain magical technique, those who believed this said (out of earshot) who it was that had seen remains of the lizard by a fire he had made. This was enough to account for his illness by the danger inherent for him in that food (the particular kind of lizard). In Gnau terms it was a 'biological/functional' understanding according to their views on how taboo violations worked, but it also contained the highly discreditable implication, which they explained to me with some sniggering, that he was guilty of greed and foolishness, eating in secret what he knew he should not. The need for evidence, what would count as evidence, and whether it is possible to provide it all play a part. I am not sure whether you would regard the findings of divination as evidence confirming a suspicion of sorcery or spirit attack, but they did. In that sense they looked in a variety of ways to find evidence in support of suggested explanations that were 'intentional/social' in nature. They included techniques of divination, spirit possession, dreams, and special signs or omens.

Jacob: My question is about the man with the pain in his knee, and it has three related parts. First, do you have any conjecture as to why the man felt compelled to bring together two independent events like the cricket falling on his knee and the girl walking by? Second, do you think that the very fact that the man was feeling pain is a relevant causal factor in his compulsion to bring the two events together? Do you think that his wife, who was not feeling his pain simultaneously, would have provided the same explanation of the pain? Third, how stable or robust in the man's community would such an explanation be?

Lewis: I think that the pain, coupled to the closeness in the timing of the cricket's jump onto his knee and the girl's passing by, made him think of the connection. I would not have said that he was compelled to think of it. If he had had no pain, I do not suppose that it would have crossed his mind. One great function of pain is to alert not only the sufferer, in an immediate sense, but also others. The expression of pain alerts them, and its expression is often strongly influenced by who is present and by culture. As to his wife, she could not have provided the same explanation unless she had had the same knowledge of the man's death in the past to link it with the girl who walked by. Of course she could not feel her husband's pain, except perhaps in a literal sense of sympathy, but her attention to events concerning him was certainly greatly heightened by his evident distress. Therefore she might have tried to find explanatory connections as well. In fact, his illness went on for a long time and I was able to follow very closely how the explanations changed. This particular explanation did not last long, for other new speculations and new features of his illness caught people's attention. Long serious illnesses were likely to give rise to shifting and multiple explanations as people tried to find a remedy. One social factor contributing to the instability of explanations was the absence of people specialized as authorities in the diagnosis and treatment of illness. No one was recognized as the authority for confirming or legitimating a particular explanation.

19

Causal attribution across domains and cultures

MICHAEL W, MORRIS, RICHARD E. NISBETT, AND KAIPING PENG

Contemporary cognitive scientists agree with Hume (1734) that human knowledge of the universe is held together by inferences of cause and effect relations—that causation is for us the 'cement of the universe'. Cognitive, developmental, and social psychologists, as well as anthropologists, have described basic processes through which people attribute events to causes in order to make sense of experience and to construct mental models of the environment. Researchers have identified patterns in people's causal attributions and have explained these patterns by proposing underlying cognitive mechanisms for attribution. Yet perhaps because they have focused on different kinds of people (social behaviour, physical events, etc.) and kinds of people (American students, Hindu villagers, British infants, etc.) researchers have not agreed about the nature of the mechanisms. Theoretical proposals about underlying mechanisms have been numerous and disparate (world views, theories, concepts, *Gestalten*, heuristics, modules, etc.). In particular, researchers have disagreed about the generality of attributional mechanisms—about whether the same 'mental cement' used to connect physical events is used to connect social events, and about whether people in one culture use the same mental cement as those in another culture.

Two questions of generality face any proposed attributional mechanism: (1) How broad is its scope (across kinds and domains of events)? (2) How widely is it distributed (across individuals and societies)? Our view is that these two questions are intertwined. Proposals about the domain-generality of a cognitive mechanism ultimately must commit themselves on the issue of cross-cultural generality, and vice versa. In this chapter, we review proposals about attributional patterns and mechanisms from various disciplines with attention to questions of generality. Attribution research can be divided into studies of **verbal explanation** of causality, which we will cover in the first part, and of **visual perception** of causality, which we cover in the second part. In the first part we review attribution theory in social psychology and examine evidence from ethnographic and cross-cultural studies that question the universal validity of the theory. Then we present a proposal about the cross-domain and cross-cultural generality of attributional mechanisms. We describe two studies of causal explanation that support the hypothesis that Americans and Chinese tend to attribute social behaviour to different types of causes. In the second part we review early research by *Gestalt* theorists and recent research by modular theorists about mechanisms for visual perception of causality. We refine the proposal about domain-specific and culturally specific mechanisms. Then we describe two studies of causal perception which support the hypothesis that social events but not physical events are attributed differently. We also describe some findings that are consistent with proposals about culturally general mechanisms for causal perception.

The dimension of causal attribution that is discussed in this chapter was perhaps first articulated in Lewin's (1935) essay on modes of explanation for behaviour that drew an analogy to modes of explanation for physical events:

[In the Aristotelian theory of dynamics, the forces which cause] an object's movements are completely determined by the object. That is, they do not depend upon the relation of the object to the environment, and they belong to that object once for all, irrespective of its surroundings at any given time. The tendency of light objects to go up resided in the bodies themselves; the downward tendency of heavy objects was seated in those objects. In modern physics, on the contrary, not only is the upward tendency of a lighter body derived from the relation of this body to its environment, but the weight itself of the body depends upon such a relation. . . . This view of dynamics does not mean that the nature of the object becomes insignificant. The properties and structure of the object involved remain important also for the Galileian theory of dynamics. But the situation assumes as much importance as the object. (Lewin 1935, pp. 28–9)

Lewin distinguished attributions to internal dispositional forces from those to external situational forces. He identified a tendency toward internal dispositional attributions in early scientific explanations for physical events (e.g. wood floats because of its 'levity') and social events (e.g. a man kills because of his 'hostility'). A similar tendency has been identified by subsequent researchers who have studied lay people's explanations for physical (McCloskey 1983) and social (Ross 1977) events. As we shall see, psychologists have proposed various mechanisms underlying this tendency, many of which imply that it is culturally universal, perhaps even innate. Yet studies of lay people in non-Western cultures by anthropologists and cross-cultural psychologists have found an opposite tendency toward external situational attributions for certain kinds of events. Hence both the domain-generality and cultural-generality of the dispositionalist tendency are in question. For this reason we have chosen this dimension of attribution as the focus of our research.

VERBAL EXPLANATION OF CAUSALITY

Attribution theory in social psychology

An early report of a dispositionalist tendency in lay people's causal explanations came in Ichheiser's (1943, 1949, 1970) studies of social 'misunderstandings'. Ichheiser proposed that this tendency follows from an ideological framework of concepts:

We all have the tendency — conditioned . . . by the ideology of our society — to interpret in our everyday life the behavior of individuals in terms of specific personal qualities rather than in terms of specific situations. Our whole framework of concepts of 'merit' and 'blame', 'success' and 'failure', 'responsibility' and 'irresponsibility', as accepted in everyday life, is based on the presupposition of personal determination of behavior (as opposed to the situation or social determination of behavior). Ichheiser (1943, p. 151)

How general is the attributional mechanism? Such concepts would apply to a broad range of social behaviour. Ichheiser suggests that these concepts are widely distributed in our society but makes no claims about other societies.

Heider's (1958) treatise on attribution in interpersonal relations integrated Ichheiser's observations with ideas and findings from social perception research. He presented the dispositionalist tendency as a product of *Gestalt* perceptual processes rather than a product of culturally bound concepts: 'Behavior . . . tends to engulf the total field, rather than be confined to its proper position as a local stimulus whose interpretation requires the additional data of a surrounding field — the situation in social perception' (Heider 1958, p. 54). In effect, Heider proposed a more general mechanism than Ichheiser. The perceptual processes that Heider described would apply to any behavioural event and would be general across cultures.

Heider's proposals led to an enormous amount of experimental research on the determinants and consequents of dispositional attributions — a wave that 'engulfed the field' of social psychology for many years. Researchers found that subjects make more dispositional attributions for the behaviour of a powerful person (Thibaut and Riecken 1955) and for behaviour that contradicts a person's social role (Jones *et al.* 1961). Surprisingly, researchers found that for some behaviours subjects attribute to dispositions even when informed that a situational cause was present (Jones and Harris 1967). Jones and Nisbett (1972) found that dispositional attributions are made more often for others' behaviour than for one's own behaviour, an actor–observer difference. They explained that in an observer's perceptual field, the person is 'figural' against the 'ground' of the social situation. But the actor cannot see himself as he acts. Thus in the perceptual field of the actor, it is the situation, and not the person, which is figural. Taylor and Fiske (1975) further varied perspectives on behaviour and found dispositional attribution to be a function of perceptual point of view.

Kelley's (1967, 1972) influential models of attribution emphasized judgemental rather than perceptual mechanisms. In Kelley's view, a dispositional cause is judged more likely when a behaviour covaries with a person across situations than when a behaviour covaries with a situation across persons. Drawing on advances in judgement research (Kahneman and Tversky 1973; Tversky and Kahneman 1973, 1974), subsequent theorists explained attributional patterns in terms of heuristics, such as selecting causes which are high in 'availability' 'representativeness', or 'consistency'. For example, Ross (1977) and Nisbett and Ross (1980) accounted for the prevalence of attributions to personal dispositions in terms of their high availability (i.e. proximity of actor to act) and representativeness (i.e. similarity to the acts that they are adduced to explain). Because studies (of Western subjects) pointed to a widespread and consequential 'tendency to underestimate the impact of situational factors and to overestimate the role of dispositional factors in controlling behavior', Ross designated this the 'fundamental attribution error' (Ross 1977, p. 183).

Researchers have branded the tendency toward dispositional attribution a 'bias' or an 'error' based on evidence that this tendency leads people away from the actual non-dispositional causes of behaviour. Specific evidence of errors come from experiments in which subjects made dispositional attributions for behaviour which was, in fact, induced situationally by the experimenter (Jones and Harris 1967; Nisbett *et al.* 1973; Ross *et al.* 1977). Further evidence that the actual role of dispositional causes is smaller than that popularly believed are findings that personality traits do not substantially predict a person's behaviour across situations (Mischel 1968; Ross and Nisbett 1991). The level of honesty of elementary school children is not highly correlated across situations (Hartshorne and May 1928). Behaviour of adolescents related to basic personality traits is not highly correlated across different situations (Newcomb 1929). Pre-school children's level of dependence is barely correlated across situations (Sears 1963). Similarly, there is little evidence that there exist personal dispositions (e.g. needs, values, attitudes, or personalities) that predict behaviour or attitudes in organizations, despite the widespread belief in such qualities, the vast effort expended to recruit people on the basis on these qualities, and the continuing popularity of theories about these qualities (Davis-Blake and Pfeffer 1989).

Anthropological observations

Anthropologists have long argued that cultures differ in attributions for both physical and social events. In early ethnographies, causal attribution is one of the many abilities on which 'primitive' cultures are compared with Europeans and found wanting. An early and ungenerous account was simply that non-Europeans lack mechanisms for attribution: 'the whole mental furniture of the Kaffir's mind differs from that of a European. . . . His conceptions of cause and effect are hopelessly at sea' (Kidd 1905). Levy-Bruhl (1910) argued that a 'pre-logical' mentality in primitive cultures accounts for attributions of natural events to moral or supernatural forces. More generously Evans-Pritchard (1937) proposed that a theory of dual causation underlies the Zandean tendency to attribute an event to both natural and 'mystical' causes. This proposed mechanism is broad in scope as it applies to both physical events (e.g. a pot breaking in the kiln) and social events (e.g. a murder).

More recent proposals about cultural differences have avoided the connotation that attributions in one culture are inferior to those in another. Horton (1970) proposed that modern Western cultures and traditional African cultures make the same common-sense attributions but different theory-based attributions, in that Western scientific theory is 'open' and non-Western religious theory is 'closed' (Horton 1970). On this view, the 'mystical' attributions observed by Levy-Bruhl and Evans Pritchard were merely theory-based attributions, reflecting the same cognitive mechanism as Newton's attribution of an apple's fall to the unseen force of gravity. Other theorists take a relativist stance that cultures cognize the world in utterly different but equally valid ways. On this view, the apparent mysticism of another culture's attributions reflects the impossibility of translation between encapsulated cultural world views (Douglas 1975). Whereas for Horton the mechanism is general in scope and distribution, for Douglas it is general in scope but strictly limited in distribution.

Another anthropological stance has been that cultures are generally alike in cognition, but differ in particular concepts that affect social attribution. Mauss (1938) proposed that seemingly natural and self-evident concepts of 'person' and 'self' are, in fact, artefacts of social history and reflections of social organization. He traced an evolution from an early notion of role or character (*personnage*), which he finds in ethnographic descriptions of Native American and Chinese cultures, to the 'modern' notion of inner personality and personal civic identity (*personne*). This line of theorizing has been tremendously influential, although the notion of evolutionary priority is out of favour (Carrithers *et al.* 1985). Hsu (1953) proposed that person-centred conceptions of society guide American social thought, whereas situation-centred conceptions guide Chinese social thought; he linked these conceptions to social orders based on individualism versus interdependence. Dumont (1970) argued that the European conception of the individual does not apply in India, where society is seen as primary. Cultural differences in social concepts would affect attributions for social behaviour but not for other kinds of events. As for the generality of these concepts across the world's cultures, many have taken the stance of Geertz that 'the Western conception of the person as a bounded, unique, more or less integrated motivational and cognitive universe, a dynamic center of awareness, emotion, judgment, and action . . . is, however incorrigible it may seem to us, a rather peculiar idea within the context of the world's cultures' (Geertz 1975, p. 48).

Ethnographers in native American cultures have also described sociocentric folk theories and tendencies to attribute behaviour to the social situation or context (Gearing 1970; Strauss 1973; Selby 1974). Selby describes the Zapotec theory that behaviour is to be explained in 'sociological, rather than psychological, concepts' and that internal traits have no 'explanatory power for understanding social relations' (Selby 1975, p. 21), expressed in their proverb 'We see the face, but do not know what is in the heart', which is not (as it would be to us) an expression of despair. This Zapotec theory underlies their tendency to attribute deviant behaviour to a person's social situation rather than to personal dispositions. Even rare and deviant behaviour, such as murder, is explained in terms of situational causes. Moreover, Selby documented that Zapotec situationalism runs deeper than verbal discourse with the case of a murderer who was judged to be non-dangerous in a different situation: 'within four years of his conviction for premeditated murder, he was holding a political post in the village, and ironically, it involved looking after all the children during fiestas' (Selby 1974, p. 66). Selby proposed that this situational theory applies to all social behaviour by fellow villagers and that this theory may be 'general for small-scale, traditional societies, where face-to-face interaction is the dominant mode of social intercourse' (Selby 1974, p. 12).

Cross-cultural studies

In recent years, psychologists have conducted cross-cultural studies to test hypotheses suggested by ethnographic observations of cultural differences in person perception and attribution. Shweder and Bourne (1982) proposed that cultures with a 'holistic world view' tend towards 'context-dependent, occasion-bound thinking'. They tested this proposal by comparing American and Hindu Indians descriptions of people. Descriptions of acquaintances were collected from subjects, transcribed, and divided into clauses, which were then coded as references to various personal and situational factors. Hindus more frequently described behaviour as situated in a particular time, place, and social relationship, whereas Americans decontextualized behaviour by describing it in terms of general cross-situational dispositions. This situationalist tendency in Hindu person descriptions held across levels of education and social class. How general is the proposed mechanism? A world view would apply to events across domains (although only social events were studied) and would be shared within Hindu culture and across other holistic cultures (although it is not specified which cultures are holistic).

Continuing this line of research, Miller studied attributions for behaviour by Americans and Hindus, proposing the following hypothesis about causal attribution:

The Western cultural emphasis on the agent's autonomy from contextual influences and on individual responsibility for action, for example, is viewed as encouraging attributors to search for internal factors predicting behavior across contexts and distinguishing one agent's behavior from that of another. In contrast, it is posited that individuals' acquisition of more relational conceptions of the person in non-Western cultures may lead them to give less weight than Western attributors to general dispositions of the agent when making social inferences ... heightening non-Western attributors' sensitivity to the contextual determinants of action (Miller 1984, p. 964).

Miller asked Americans and Hindus of various ages to narrate and explain several types of behaviour by acquaintances and then analyzed the proportion of references to dispositional and situational (or contextual) causes. She found that explanations by children in the two cultures were alike, yet with development to adulthood Americans became increasingly dispositionalist and Indians increasingly situationalist. Situationalist attribution among Hindus was found across levels of education and social class.

These cross-cultural studies have greatly strengthened the case that attributional tendencies vary importantly across cultures, at least for events in the social domain. In the past, many psychologists tried to reduce purported cultural differences to cognitive developmental factors or to factors having to do with societal complexity. Shweder and Bourne (1982) and Miller (1984) have ruled out these alternative explanations by demonstrating situationalist social thinking in highly educated Hindus living in socially complex communities. However, some alternative explanations can still be suggested. A limitation in both their studies is that the behaviour explained was not held constant (American subjects talked about the behaviour of their American acquaintances; Indian subjects talked about Indian acquaintances). Hence it is unclear where the cultural difference lies — in subjects' cognitions or in their acquaintances' behaviour. To address this concern, Miller ran a second study in which she read to American subjects descriptions of behaviour which had originally been generated by Hindu subjects. She compared explanations by Americans with the original explanations by Hindu subjects and found, as predicted, that Americans were more dispositionalist. However, in this study culture is confounded with another factor known to increase dispositional attribution. Explanations based on descriptions of behaviour are more dispositional than those based on first-hand observation of behaviour (Gilovich 1987). Also, another limitation is that these studies only measured the behaviour of acquaintances. It might be argued that Hindu subjects are more inclined than Americans to know their acquaintance's social context, which would bring them closer to the actor's situationalist perspective. Evidence that non-Western attributors are situationalist even about strangers or people from the outgroup would rule out this alternative account. Ethnographic studies of cultural differences in attribution, such as those of Selby, share these evidential shortcomings.

A proposal about implicit theories of domains

We propose that attributions are guided by implicit theories. Previous psychologists have proposed that lay people have implicit theories about causes of physical events (McCloskey 1983; McCloskey and Kaiser 1984) and social events (Nisbett 1980; Ross 1989). However, few have been concerned with the generality of theories across both cultures and kinds of events (for an exception, see Fiske (1992)).

We propose that lay people have implicit theories that are specific to basic domains of events. The construct of domain theories has been refined by researchers of cognitive development, who have increasingly discovered that children's concepts are structured by skeletal theories of certain basic domains. Although the precise contours of such domains is unclear, some basic distinctions between domains are well supported by evidence. Gelman and colleagues have distinguished the development of thoughts about inanimate physical objects from those about animate creatures (Gelman and Spelke 1981; Gelman 1990) (see also Keil 1986, 1989). Others have distinguished the conceptual domain of psychological events, which involve intentions, as a subset of the animate domain (Shultz 1980; Wellman 1990; Wellman and Gelman 1992). A subset of these may be social events, which involve more than one intentional being (Shultz 1982; Chapter 7 of this volume). Drawing on these constructs, we posit that attributions are guided by domain-specific theories, particularly physical and social theories. The proposed 'theories' are attributional mechanisms narrower in scope than Shweder's 'world views' but broader than the specific 'concepts' proposed by Ichheiser and many anthropologists.

How widely shared across cultures are implicit theories? We argue that implicit theories are acquired from individual experiences with events and from collective representations of events. Cultures offer similar experiences and representations of physical events, but cultures offer very different experiences and representations of social events, as these are often culturally constituted (D'Andrade 1981, 1984). As Ichheiser put it:

Our conceptions about social reality are determined by two sets of factors: on the one hand, by the individual experiences we have in the course of our lives (which experiences, by the way, are actually not so individual as they might appear); and, on the other hand, by ideas which we simply take over from other people in imitating them or learning from them. . . . Not only our ideas and conceptions but even our perceptions and experiences are influenced by cultural patterns and social frames of reference. We perceive, we experience, often only those facts, or only those aspects of social reality, which fit into the scheme of our socially and culturally preformed and prepared dispositions of perceiving (or not perceiving), of having (or not having) certain experiences. (Ichheiser 1970, pp. 45-6)

Our proposal about how implicit social theories vary cross-culturally draws on the research of Hofstede (1980, 1983, 1991) which identified major dimensions of variation among the world's national cultures.* An individualist–collectivist dimension accounted for greatest variation in many aspects of social experience.[†] In highly individualist cultures (e.g. the USA) persons are primary. They leave groups (including family) as they wish, and behaviour expresses personal preferences. In highly collectivist cultures (e.g. China) groups are primary. Persons are not always free to detach themselves from groups, and behaviour expresses group norms and situational scripts. Recent cross-cultural studies comparing Americans and Chinese has demonstrated that some of the most basic social psychological principles (identified in individualistic cultures) are inverted in collectivist China, such as social loafing (Earley 1989), preference for adjudicatory justice procedures (Leung 1987), perception of the out-group as more

---

* Hofstede (1980) analysed predictors of attitudes and values among IBM employees (117 000 protocols) in 66 countries, and found, unexpectedly, that national culture was a stronger predictor of responses than occupation, income, age, or gender. Taking advantage of his large sample, he calculated means for each country on several indices and conducted factor analyses to explore the major dimensions of variance among the world's cultures. Four factors showed reliably across various indices and have since replicated with other variables and samples (Hofstede and Bond 1984; Triandis et al. 1986; Bond 1988).

[†] Although Hofstede's formulation has provided the catalyst for psychological research on individualism versus collectivism, related constructs have been used previously by many social thinkers such de Toqueville (1840), Tawny (1926), Weber (1930), and Lukes (1973) as well as social scientists, including those concerned with culture (Hsu 1953, 1971; Triandis 1972, 1980), values (Kluckhorn and Strodtbeck 1961), character (Riesman 1950, 1954), social systems (Parsons and Shils 1951), religion (Bakan 1966), cognitive differentiation (Witkin and Berry 1975), ecology and child-rearing patterns (Barry et al. 1959; Berry 1979), economic development (Adelman and Morris 1967), modernity (Berger et al. 1973; Inkeles and Smith 1974), and so forth.

homogeneous than the in-group, and so forth (Triandis *et al.*, 1988, 1990; Triandis 1989).

The individualism–collectivism dimension also contrasts starkly divergent social representations. Here it is important to make the distinction (after Sperber 1985, 1991) between **mental representations** (e.g. cognitions in the minds of the culture's members, such as implicit theories) and **public representations** (e.g. religious, legal, and philosophical texts, works of art and science, etc.). Public representations of the social domain in American culture are rooted in the Judaeo-Christian religious tradition, which emphasizes the individual soul, and the English legal tradition, which emphasizes free will. These notions were articulated in seventeenth-century English philosophical defences of individual rights, such as that by Locke, which start with an ontologically prior individual alone in a 'state of nature' and derive society as coming into existence through the voluntary contracts of individuals trying to maximize their own self-interest. These social conceptions saturate the *Declaration of Independence* and the *Bill of Rights*. Public representations of the social domain in Chinese culture are rooted in the Confucian tradition, which holds that humans exist primarily in relation to society (King and Bond 1985). In Confucian doctrine (and in traditional Chinese culture generally) there is no concept for an individual's internal dispositional personality; the closest is that for 'personage' (*jen*) which denotes the 'individual's transactions with his fellow human beings' (Hsu 1971, p. 29, 1981*b*; King 1981). Some of Mao's anti-individualist themes resonate with earlier social representations.*

Thus there is a good reason for believing that the implicit social theory in individualist cultures is person-centred and that the theory in collectivist cultures is situation-centred. The individualist theory is based on a category of person which isolates the individual from relationships, roles, and social contexts, and depicts the person as a container for internal stable dispositions (Markus and Kitayama 1991). According to this theory, social behaviour is primarily determined by such dispositions, and hence is consistent across time, across locations, and across relationships, roles, and social contexts. The collectivist theory is based on a category of person which centres on relationships to external social factors rather than internal dispositions. According to this theory, social behaviour is primarily shaped by

---

* We do not attempt to review but only to mention a few examples of the American and Chinese traditions, each of which obviously comprises enormous internal diversity. Nor do we argue that the mentioned texts cited are reflective of American and Chinese 'mentalities'. Clearly, cultures do not have minds; individuals do. Clearly, also, determinism between social experience and social representations is reciprocal and complex. Texts reflect the mental representations of their authors, which in turn reflect the authors' social (including political) experiences as well as their exposure to pre-existing public representations and systems of interpersonal exchange. For an analysis of how different forms of argument in Greek and Chinese texts may reflect different socio-political conditions, see Lloyd (1990).

relationships, roles, and situational pressures, and hence behaviour varies across situations. In sum, we posited that attributors in highly individualist cultures hold person-centred social theories which bias them towards personal dispositions as causes of behaviour, whereas attributors in highly collectivist cultures hold situation-centred theories which bias them towards social situations as causes of behaviour.

Murder studies

Although some previous evidence for cultural differences in causal explanation (ethnographies by Hsu (1953) and Selby (1974), and studies by Shweder and Bourne (1982) and Miller (1984)) are consistent with our proposal, we designed several cross-cultural studies to provide more direct and unequivocal evidence. First, we wanted to demonstrate that, for the same behaviour, Americans make dispositional attributions and Chinese make situational attributions. In previous data, it is unclear whether the cultural difference lay in the attributor's cognitions or in the behaviours under explanation. Second, we wanted to test whether Chinese make situational attributions even for the kinds of behaviour about which Americans are most dispositionalist — rare, negative, and deviant behaviour (Jones and Harris 1967). Third, we wanted to test whether differences are also found in attributions for out-group as well as in-group behaviour. Findings that non-Westerners are more situationalist about acquaintances are open to alternative interpretations. Finally, we sought to demonstrate differences in how Americans and Chinese genuinely model events rather than merely in how they verbally label events. To accomplish these aims, we conducted two studies comparing American and Chinese attributions for mass murders.

In one study (Morris 1993, Study 2), we compared attributions made in American and Chinese newspapers. Attributional patterns observed in this natural context (Lau and Russel 1980; Schoeneman and Rubanowitz 1985) can be safely assumed to be real tendencies rather than spurious reactions to unfamiliar research tasks (a crucial concern in cross-cultural studies). Two recent murders were selected and all articles about them in leading English language (*New York Times*) and Chinese language (*World Journal*) newspapers were collected. By selecting roughly parallel incidents committed by American and Chinese murderers, we also varied the actor's culture as well.

1. Gang Lu was a Chinese physics student who had recently lost an award competition, unsuccessfully appealed, and subsequently failed to obtain an academic job. On 31 October 1991, he entered the University of Iowa Physics Department and shot his advisor, the person who handled his appeal, several fellow students and bystanders, and then himself.

2. Thomas McIlvane was an Irish-American postal worker who had recently lost his job, unsuccessfully appealed the decision with his union, and failed to find a full-time replacement job. On 14 November 1991, he entered the Royal Oak, Michigan, Post Office and shot his supervisor, the person who handled his appeal, several fellow workers and bystanders, and then himself.

Five bilingual coders (three Chinese and two American) coded every clause of every article according to whether it was an attribution to a *personal disposition* of the murderer, *a situational factor*, or neither (non-attribution or non-classifiable attribution), which they were able to do with a high degree of reliability. Coders were instructed that a personal disposition is a property that the murderer carries across *time*, *place*, and *social context* (such as a personality trait, temperament, stable value or attitude, long-standing aim, habit, chronic pathology, general capability, physical characteristic, character flaw, etc.) and that it had to be a disposition of the person rather than a group norm to which the person adheres (such as class, gender, generational, or cultural norm). In contrast, a situational factor was a cause tied to a particular *time* (such as an emotional crisis, mood, temporary mental state, etc.) or tied to a particular *place* (such as stress at the workplace, homesickness, discomfort in an environment, etc.) or tied to a particular *social context* (such as a relationship, social role, institutional requirement, personal grudge, group norm, etc.).

As predicted, American reporters attributed more to personal dispositions and Chinese reporters attributed more to situational factors for both murders. For example, causes of the Lu murder emphasized by American reporters were personality traits (e.g. 'very bad temper', 'sinister edge to Mr Lu's character well before the shootings'), attitudes (e.g. 'personal belief that guns were an important means to redress grievances'), and psychological problems (e.g. 'darkly disturbed man who drove himself to success and destruction', 'a psychological problem with being challenged', 'whatever went wrong was internal'). Causes emphasized by Chinese reporters were Lu's relationships (e.g. 'did not get along with his advisor', 'rivalry with slain student', 'isolation from Chinese community'), pressures in Chinese society (e.g. 'victim of the "Top Student" Educational Policy', 'tragedy reflects the lack of religion in contemporary Chinese culture'), and aspects of American society (e.g. 'murder can be traced to the availability of guns'). Likewise, American reporters emphasized McIlvane's personal dispositions (e.g. 'repeatedly threatened violence', 'had a short fuse', 'was a martial arts enthusiast', 'mentally unstable'), whereas Chinese reporters stressed situational factors (e.g. 'gunman had been recently fired', 'post office supervisor was his enemy', 'influenced by example of a recent mass slaying in Texas').

In a second study (Morris 1993, Study 3), we surveyed matched samples of American and Chinese graduate students about the Lu and McIlvane murders. Under the guise of a national survey about homicide, we presented subjects with a brief report about one of the murders based on descriptions given in the English and Chinese language media, which was followed by a causal weighting task. Instructions stated 'We want to know your opinion about *to what extent* each of these factors was a *cause* of the shooting'. Below was a list of dispositional and situational explanations. Parallel items were used for the Lu and McIlvane murders, tailored as necessary to fit each case. As predicted, Americans placed more weight on dispositional causes and Chinese more weight on situational causes. Examples of explanations that evoked the strongest cultural differences are given in Table 19.1.

To test that Chinese genuinely model behaviour as situationally determined rather than merely favouring situational explanations for semantic or socio-linguistic reasons, we also included a counterfactual judgment task. Recent research (e.g. Kahneman and Tversky 1982; Kahneman and Miller 1986; Wells and Gavanski 1989) has explored links between attribution (thoughts that X was the cause of certain behaviour) and counterfactual reasoning (thoughts that if only X had not been present the behaviour would not have occurred). We predicted that when thinking about the murders both Americans and Chinese would reach conclusions of the form—*if only X had been different, the murder would not have happened*—but that Americans would replace X with a personal disposition whereas Chinese would replace X with a situational factor. Instructions stated, 'We want your opinion about some hypothetical questions — questions about whether this person would have murdered had things been slightly different'. Below this appeared a list of 'if only' scenarios describing a counterfactual disposition or situation. Results with dispositional counterfactuals were inconclusive, but results with situational counterfactuals strongly supported the prediction—Chinese were more likely to judge that if only the situation had been slightly different, the murder would not have occurred. Table 19.2 lists examples of scenarios which evoked the strongest cultural differences.

In sum, the murder studies furthered the evidence for cultural differences in four ways: (1) attributors made different attributions for the same behaviour; (2) cultural differences were obtained even with the kinds of behaviour most evocative of dispositional attributions; (3) cultural differences were obtained for out-group as well as in-group behaviour; (4) cultural differences were found not only in generation and evaluation of verbal explanations but also in counterfactual reasoning about causality.

Table 19.1. *Examples of causal explanations evaluated differently across cultures*

Lu murder	McIlvane murder
Dispositional causes given more weight by Americans than Chinese	
Lu was mentally imbalanced because his life consisted only of work, without other activities which relieve stress	McIlvane was mentally imbalanced because his life consisted only of violent activities such as hunting and martial arts
Lu drove himself crazy by putting too much pressure on himself	McIlvane drove himself crazy by worrying too much about getting his job back
Lu had chronic personality problems	McIlvane had chronic personality problems
Lu was a psychological time bomb — someone with a hidden mental illness that suddenly explodes	McIlvane was a psychological time bomb — someone with a hidden mental illness that suddenly explodes
If Lu could not win, he did not care about anything else	If McIlvane could not get his way, he did not care about anything else
Situational causes given more weight by Chinese than Americans	
America's extremely individualistic selfish values corrupt foreign students	This was an extreme example of behaviour that follows from America's individualistic selfish values
American films and television glorify violent revenge tactics	American films and television glorify violent revenge tactics
The advisor failed in his duties to help Gang Lu and respond to his increasing frustration	The supervisor and labour relations specialist failed in their duties to respect McIlvane and respond to his increasing frustration
The ruthless and brutal behaviour of Chinese Communists set an example for him	The daily violence of the Detroit area set an example him
The recession has hurt the job market, which places stress on people seeking a new job	The recession has hurt the job market, which places stress on people seeking a new job

Table 19.2. *Examples of counterfactual scenarious simulated differently across cultures*

Lu murder	McIlvane murder
Counterfactual situations judged more likely to avert murder by Chinese than Americans (i.e. Chinese judged that if only X, murder would not have occurred)	
Lu's advisor had worked harder to prepare him for his defence and for the job market	McIlvane's supervisor had worked harder to motivate him and explain the post office rules to him
Lu had belonged to a religious group	McIlvane had belonged to a religious group
Lu had had many friends or relatives also studying in Iowa	McIlvane had had many friends or relatives in Royal Oak
Lu had received a job	McIlvane had won his appeal and received his job back
Lu had stayed in China for his Ph.D. studies	McIlvane had stayed in the Marines (and been removed from a job there)
Lu was married and had children	McIlvane was married and had children

VISUAL PERCEPTION OF CAUSALITY

Research on the perception of causality from visual information began with attempts to apply methods of *Gestalt* theory to the problem of causation. *Gestalt* theorists argued that we perceive structure and pattern not by learning to interpret our sensations from the world but because evolution has provided configured brain processes that respond to important recurrent patterns (Koffka 1935). Accordingly, Michotte (1952) proposed that forms of mechanical or physical causation may be directly perceived from patterns of motion of objects A and B, not necessarily derived from experience of succession of A and B, as Hume (1734) had argued. Michotte experimented with hundreds of patterns and concluded that two evoke 'universal' and 'immediate' impressions of causality: 'entraining' in which A collides with stationary B and they move off together, and 'launching' in which A collides with stationary B and B alone moves off. However, evidence for universality is weakened by the fact that, in many experiments, he and his co-workers were the only subjects, and evidence for immediacy is weakened by the fact that displays were often shown repeatedly before the subject's response was recorded.* Moreover, in replications, as few as 50 per cent of subjects have perceived causality immediately (Gruber *et al*. 1957; Gemelli and Cappellini 1958; Powesland 1959; Boyle 1960; Beasely 1968).

Heider and Simmel (1944) (see also Heider 1944) investigated perception of social causality in patterns of motion. Like Michotte, they identified patterns which evoked causal perception: 'Simultaneous movements with prolonged contact [like entraining]. . . . Successive movements with momentary contact [like launching]. . . . Simultaneous movements without contact. . . . Successive movements without contact' (Heider and Simmel 1944, pp. 252–5). Yet perception of causal relations was also shaped constructively by perceivers' social representations: When shape movements resembled behaviour in a familiar social dynamic — two rival suitors vying over a beloved — subjects made more consistently social interpretations. However, most importantly, Heider and Simmel observed a general tendency to perceive internal dispositions as causes: 'Just as . . . a landscape seen through the window of a moving train can only be 'resolved', or made to yield a meaningful unit, by reference to distant objects laid out in space, so acts of persons have to be viewed in terms of motives' (Heider and Simmel 1944, p. 258).

There has recently been a resurgence of causal perception research among psychologists who take a modular view of mind. Modular theorists posit innate hard-wired mechanisms for perceiving causality from an object's trajectory through space and time. The evidence that humans are equipped with a module for perceiving physical causality from motion comes from findings that young children, and even infants, distinguish trajectories that are consistent with movement driven by a physical force (e.g. one object moves when another collides with it) from highly similar but physically anomalous trajectories (e.g. one object moves *before* another collides with it). Experiments have established that infants make this distinction before they could have induced knowledge of causality from experience (Leslie 1982, 1987; Leslie and Keeble 1987) (see also Ball 1973; Borton 1979). However, alternative non-modular explanations of this finding have been offered (White 1988). Also, research shows that perception of physical causality from object trajectory improves through childhood and adolescence, which suggests that any rudimentary innate process is substantially modified by acquired knowledge (Kaiser and Proffitt 1984).

* In a footnote, Michotte revealed that 'It sometimes happens, however, that the causal impression does not appear at the first presentation of the experiment, especially when it is tried on "new" subjects who are not accustomed to observing in the artificial conditions of the laboratory . . . they are all "mixed up" and do not realize what is going on at all, and their impression is chaotic and unorganized. Provided that the experiment is repeated a few times, however, a structuring in favour of causality will arise spontaneously' (Michotte 1952, p. 20).

Similar experiments provide evidence about modular perception of social causality. Adults and children can distinguish trajectories that are consistent with movement driven by an intention (Bassili 1976; Dasser *et al.* 1989). Modular theorists have concluded that this aspect of social perception is not influenced by experience or representations: 'perception of intention, like that of causality, is a hard-wired perception based not on repeated experience but on appropriate stimulation' (Premack 1990, p. 2). But the current evidence falls far short of proving this, since subjects were not too young to have induced a theory from experience. More compelling evidence for modularity would be cross-cultural data, like that which has been garnered in support of proposed modules for speech. We know of no such data, although there are findings that perception of emotional dynamics (e.g. 'hostility', 'warmth', etc.) in displays of moving shapes is common across several cultures (Rime *et al.* 1985).

Other researchers who study causal perception have proposed implicit theories. McCloskey (1983) proposed that lay people interpret the causes of object motion with an implicit theory reminiscent of the largely Aristotelian medieval theory of 'impetus'. His evidence came from errors that subjects made in the task of predicting the continued trajectories of objects. For example, subjects misinterpret the deceleration of a rolling ball as being due to the dissipation of this internal force (impetus) rather than as being due to external force (resistance). Stewart (1984) proposed that lay people perceive whether an object is animate and whether its cause is internal or external according to an implicit theory akin to Newton's laws of motion (i.e. conservation of rest, velocity, and direction). An object which deviates from these contraints (e.g. by changing its state from rest to motion) is seen as animate and as caused by internal force; an object which does not deviate is seen as inanimate and as caused by external force. She presented subjects with stimuli like those of Michotte and measured their perceptions of animacy and causality, finding support for her hypotheses. Of course, both Stewart and McCloskey may be partially correct despite their analogies with different historical scientific theories; that is, lay people may systematically relate internal force to an object's trajectory while still generally overestimating its role.

A proposal about implicit theories and perception

Our stance is that visual perception of causality, like verbal explanation of causality, is guided by implicit domain theories. Although the research on causal perception has largely been conducted to support *Gestalt* and modular mechanisms, we drew on its concepts and methods to refine and test our proposal. One aim was to establish that cultures differ not merely at the level of their after-the-fact discourse about social behaviour but also at the level of on-line causal perception of events. We reasoned that individualistic and collectivist cultures would vary in the tendency towards perceiving internal causes of behaviour (i.e. the tendency that Heider identified), but not in the tendency towards perceiving internal causes of physical events (i.e. the tendency that McCloskey identified). On our view, the only group of people expected to differ in their implicit physical theory would be physical scientists, who may have internalized basic Newtonian laws into their implicit theory.

Concepts from causal perception research helped us to clarify the boundary conditions for the application of domain theories. We hypothesized that implicit theories are triggered by trajectories in an event rather than by intrinsic features of objects. For example, a leaf blowing in the wind may be perceived as animate, a school of swimming fish as social. Trajectories, in fact, may distinguish each successive domain by revealing its distinctive forms of causation: physical objects can only move when caused to do so by external forces; animate creatures can move themselves; intentional creatures can direct their movement towards a goal; social creatures can direct their movement according to intentions about others' intentions (see Bassili 1976; Dennett 1983; 1987). Our hypotheses focused on the boundaries of the physical and social domains. We predicted that an object moving within certain trajectory constraints would be processed with a physical theory and attributed primarily to external force, whereas one deviating from such constraints would be perceived as animate and attributed more to internal force. We expected that this boundary between domains would be culturally invariant (see Jeyifous 1985; Atran 1989; Gelman 1990). Also, we predicted that multiple objects on contingent trajectories will tend to be perceived as a social group, and that this social perception will be strongest when trajectories resemble those of important social dynamics of the perceiver's culture.

Cartoon studies

To test our hypothesis that cultures differ in causal perception of social but not physical events, we showed cartoons of various kinds of events to American and Chinese subjects and measured their causal perceptions. In our primary study, large samples of high school students were tested at their schools in the USA and the People's Republic of China, with instructions and questions in their respective languages. In a second study, small samples of science graduate students were tested at a US university, with instructions and questions in English. Our cartoons were designed to test the hypothesis that domain theories are applied to events on the basis of object trajectories. Cartoons testing perceptions of physical causality featured an object moving across a soccer field; its trajectory varied.

The object's shape left ambiguous whether it was a soccer ball or an animal. We predicted that *physical* theories would be applied to cartoons in which the object essentially conserved rest and velocity, but *animate* theories would be applied to those in which its trajectory deviated from these constraints. We expected no cultural differences in perceptions of the object's movement as internally or externally caused. Cartoons testing perceptions of social causality featured five fish swimming in a lake on contingent trajectories. We predicted that *social* theories would be applied to these. Hence we expected a cultural difference—specifically, that Americans would perceive a fish's movement as more internally caused and Chinese perceive it as more externally caused. For example, one fish swimming in front of the others might be perceived by Americans as leading (i.e. its movement would be due to an internal disposition) and by Chinese as being chased (i.e. its movement would be due to an external situational pressure).

Physical event cartoons were designed to test the hypothesis that animacy and internal causality would be perceived as a function of an object's deviation from certain trajectory constraints. Figure 19.1 shows the COLLISION set (based on Michotte's displays) which varied the object's deviation from conservation of rest. There is no deviation in the 'entraining' and 'launching' displays, slight deviation in the 'time gap' and 'space gap' displays, and marked deviation in the 'starting' display. Another display set varied the deviation from, essentially conservation of velocity. After viewing each display, subjects indicated to what extent the round object seemed animate, seemed influenced by internal force, and seemed influenced by external force. As can be seen in Fig. 19.2, perceived internal force rose, perceived external force fell, and perceived animacy rose with increasing deviation from this trajectory constraint. It should also be noticed that perceptions of American and Chinese subjects were similar overall. The same pattern of results was obtained in perceptions of displays increasing in deviation from conservation of velocity. Differences between cultures were not significant with either display set. This lack of cultural difference in the physical domain suggests that any differences observed with this method in the social domain are due to differences in perception, not to artefacts such as mistranslation of questions (Campbell 1964). We did observe a consistent difference between high school students and science graduate students. As would be expected of scientists compared with lay people, graduate students' perceptions were more sensitive to object trajectory, which can be seen in Fig. 19.2 in the steeper slopes of their perceptions as a function of object trajectory.

Social event cartoons were designed to test the hypothesis that social theories are applied on the basis of trajectories in an event and thus cultural differences in causal perception will extend to events other than human

COLLISION

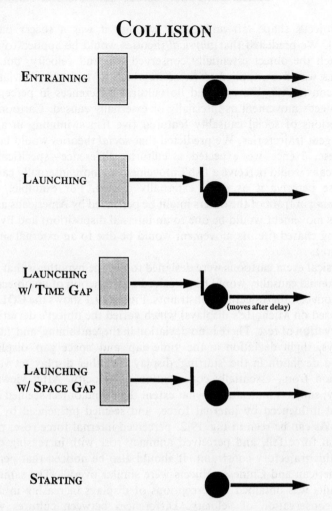

Fig. 19.1. Diagrams representing trajectories of objects in COLLISION displays. Arrowed lines show direction of movement; vertical lines show stops.

social behaviour. Three sets of displays were created of five coloured fish swimming on contingent intentional trajectories in various positions and directions. Within each set, we varied a factor predicted to make the event correspond more closely to an American versus Chinese social dynamic. For example, Fig. 19.3 shows the COMPULSION set which depicted 'social collisions' between individual and group and varied whether compulsion was a harmonious bonding event or a discordant divisive event. Other sets varied whether an individual joined or left a group and whether a group

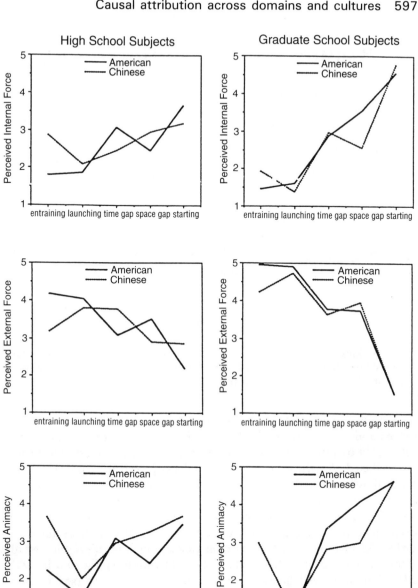

Fig. 19.2. Causal perceptions of American and Chinese high school students (left panel) and science graduate students (right panel) across the five COLLISION displays.

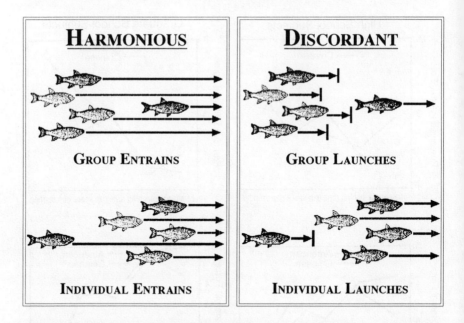

Fig. 19.3. Diagrams representing trajectories of fish in COMPULSION displays. Arrowed lines show direction of movement; vertical lines show stops. The blue fish is the one that appears darkest in this diagram.

converged or dispersed. Subjects indicated to what extent the blue fish (which appears darkest in Fig. 19.3) seemed a member of a group, seemed influenced by internal factors, and seemed influenced by external factors. As predicted, American high school students perceived significantly more internal influence and Chinese students perceived significantly more external influence on the fish's movements in the COMPULSION displays. In the other display sets, the Chinese consistently perceived significantly more external influence, but perception of internal influence did not significantly differ. As might be expected based on Heider and Simmel's results, we also found that perceiver culture interacted with trajectory factors: in COMPULSION displays Chinese were relatively more likely to perceive social influence in harmonious events, akin to dynamics of social influence in their culture, and Americans were more likely to perceive social influence in discordant events, akin to dynamics more familiar in their culture. Some, but not all, cultural differences were replicated in the comparison of American and Chinese graduate students.

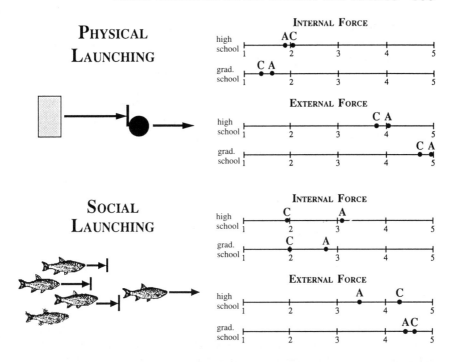

Fig. 19.4. Perceptions of internal and external force in launching events in the physical and social domains. Points A and C mark the mean American and Chinese ratings respectively on each scale.

GENERAL DISCUSSION

Causal representations at different levels of generality

Previous psychologists and anthropologists have proposed attributional mechanisms at various levels of generality. We have proposed that mechanisms at one level—domain theories—can account for most of our results and for many previous findings concerned with the important dimension of internal dispositional versus external situational causes. However, we believe that cognitive mechanisms at other levels of generality also guide causal attribution. In fact, patterns in our data are consistent with attributional mechanisms that differ in scope (across domains) and distribution (across cultures).

Domain-general and *cultural general* mechanisms are often discussed under the rubric of basic 'cues to causation', such as causes are temporally prior to effects (Taylor 1982; Kassin and Prior 1985; Einhorn and Hogarth 1986). By comparing responses to analogous launching displays in physical and social domains in Fig. 19.4, we can see a pattern at this level of generality. External force was rated higher than internal force for both physical and social displays by all groups of subjects (see Fig. 19.4). Perhaps the launching pattern cues a very general representation of externally caused motion. Since infant studies suggest a possible hard-wired mechanism for physical launching, cultural generality in the physical domain is unsurprising. But the fact that it extends to the social domain is interesting because it may suggest that either (a) the hard-wired mechanism is actually domain-general or (b) the hard-wired representation of physical launching is extended metaphorically to represent causality in other domains — see related proposals by Lakoff and Johnson (1980), Talmy (1988), and M. W. Morris and E. E. Smith (unpublished manuscript). Hence it would be interesting to test whether infants habituate to social launching and to test whether infants who have habituated to physical launching dishabituate to social launching, and vice versa.

Domain-specific but *culturally general* representations are proposed by modular theorists and others. A pattern at this level in our data is that more internal force is perceived in the social than in the physical domain. Internal force was rated relatively higher for social launching than for physical launching by both American and Chinese subjects (compare lower and upper panels of Fig. 19.4). These results are consistent with proposals that internally caused or self-propelled movement is a feature that characterizes or defines a domain (Stewart 1984; Premack 1990; Mandler 1992). Since we also found (for both cultures) that perception of internal force tracked perception of animacy, the best conclusion seems to be that a representation of *internally caused motion* is specific to the animate domain, of which the social domain is a subset. This is consistent with Gelman's (1990) thesis that the animate–inanimate distinction is a culturally invariant first principle in cognitive development.

At the level of *domain-specific culturally specific* representations are the implicit social theories we have proposed. In the social domain, Americans perceived relatively more internal force and less external force than Chinese. The predicted pattern of responses can be seen clearly in Fig. 19.4 by the differences between points A and C in the social domain but not the physical domain. We have already discussed this level of causal representation extensively; the only further point illustrated by Fig. 19.4 is that these cultural differences come against a background of cultural commonality in causal perception.

Those who consider science to be a culture (e.g. Snow 1963) would argue that our results also point to a culturally specific representation in the physical domain. Across cultures, graduate science students perceived the launched soccer ball to be influenced less by internal force and more by external force than high school students, as can be seen in the upper panel of Fig. 19.4. This finding provides cross-cultural evidence that the lay person's implicit physics attributes object motion partially to an internal force (like 'impetus') (McCloskey 1983), and that science education reduces this tendency (Clement 1982). However, scientific physics is a 'reflective belief' rather than an 'intuitive belief' and hence it is distributed across individuals differently than a representation like the dispositional theory of social behaviour (Sperber 1985, 1991). In epidemiological terms, physical theories are transmitted through formal education, and the susceptible population is small; social theories are transmitted through everyday practices and informal communication, and the susceptible population is large.

Public representations of social theories

The hypotheses that we have tested concerned **mental representations** of social causality, i.e. cognitive structures in the minds of individuals. Yet we proposed that such mental representations are acquired in part from **public representations** of social causality, and we drew on contrasting American and Chinese religious, legal, or philosophical texts to formulate hypotheses about mental representations. Although these public representations (e.g. the *Bill of Rights*, *Confucian Analects*) applied only to human behaviour, we predicted that mental representations (i.e implicit theories of social causality) would extend in application to non-human events. As predicted, we found that American dispositionalist and Chinese situationalist biases affected their perceptions of fish behaviour in cartoons. The strongest cultural difference was that Chinese subjects perceived more influence on an individual fish from its social group. Also, we found that subjects perceive social influence — perceive fish anthropomorphically — when fish trajectories resembled dynamics from their culture. It may be that the tendency to project one's cultural representations onto natural events bolsters the tendency to think of culturally sanctioned events as 'natural'. Each culture re-makes 'nature' in its own image: 'People have a tendency to treat culturally created things as if they were natural things . . . because it gives greater moral force to the idea that one should act in some certain way if it is thought that it is natural to act in that particular way' (D'Andrade 1984, p. 92).

Hence an interesting question is whether cultural differences in public representations extend to the behaviour of animals. A form of public representation close to visual perception is painting. A comparison of prominent American and Chinese painters who have chosen fish as their subject reveals a difference much like the one we observed in perceptions (see Fig. 19.5). Winslow Homer (right panel) perceived 'individualist' fish, swimming alone ruggedly, leaping in defiant self-expression. Wang Ch'ing-fang (left panel) perceived 'collectivist' fish, swimming in harmonious

Fig. 19.5. On the left are *Fish* and *Three Fish* by Wang Ch'ing-fang (1900–1956), a Chinese painter best known for depictions of fish, whose watercolours are admired for capturing the group's 'rhythms of movement' (Hejzlar 1978). On the right are *Leaping Trout*, *Trout*, and *Adirondack Catch* by Winslow Homer (1836–1910), perhaps the most prominent American painter of fish, whose watercolours are noted for capturing the fish's 'magnificent struggle' against nature, man, and 'impending death'—and only in death are fish portrayed in a group (Cooper 1986).

groups, responding to the social context. A parallel difference between American and Chinese conventions of painting human beings has been discussed by Hsu:

Paintings that circulate widely in the West . . . reveal, more than anything else, the mental state of the subject. . . . In the majority these paintings, the background on the canvas — such as a house, furniture, trees, or sky — is important only insofar as it adds color to the human beings portrayed. . . .

Even when Chinese artists do portray the human form, they either treat it as a minute dot in a vast landscape, or so heavily clothe it that the body is hidden. The facial expression of such figures is nil. The viewer obtains a much better idea of the status, rank, prestige, and other social characteristics of the subjects portrayed than he does of their personalities. The two lifestyles are thus reflected clearly in the two nations' paintings. In Western art the focus is on man or woman as an individual. In Chinese art the important thing is the individual's place in the external scheme of things. In addition, American art often reflects the inner tension of the individual; this concern is practically absent from Chinese art. (Hsu 1981a, pp. 20-1)

A form of public representation close to verbal explanation is the novel. Classic American novels, such as *Moby Dick*, focus on a few lead characters (bipedal or finned) and describe deep psychological interiors, replete with traits, drives, obsessions, tastes, etc. Classic Chinese novels encompass many more characters and describe their external contextualized behaviour. For example, *Dream of the red chamber* copiously describes the Chia family's history, status, and wealth; it describes family members' interactions and feelings in many contexts on many occasions, but it does *not* describe decontextualized personal dispositions. In Hsu's words, 'Chinese traditional novels as a rule concentrate upon what the characters do in their roles as emperors or common men, while American novels are much more concerned with what the characters *do*, *think*, or *feel* as individuals. . . . The absence in Chinese novels of introspective excursions into the mind of the character is as pronounced as its relative abundance in American fiction' (Hsu 1953, p. 24).

Perhaps cultural representations affect not only lay persons' perceptions and artists' portrayals of animal behaviour but even scientists' theories. Heider (1958) reported the case of a primate research laboratory which tried to institute a ban on anthropomorphic description and found that without it they could not collect orderly data or train workers. Only by applying social representations could workers make sense of primate behaviour. Perhaps Chinese researchers working with the same primates would also need to anthropomorphize, but would do so drawing on different social representations leading to different research results. Such differences were noted in results of animal learning studies by Bertrand Russell.

The manner in which animals learn has been much studied in recent years, with a great deal of patient observation and experiment. . . . One may say broadly that all the animals that have been carefully observed have ... displayed the national characteristics of the observers. Animals studied by Americans rush about frantically, with an incredible display of hustle and pep, and at last achieve the desired result by chance. Animals observed by Germans sit still and think, and at last evolve the solution out of their inner consciousness. To the plain man, such as the present writer, this situation is discouraging. (Russell 1960, pp. 32–3)

Which culture is right?

The finding that American and Chinese attributors disagree raises the question of *who is right?* Since we have employed the terms 'bias' and 'error', which connote inaccuracy, it is worth denoting what can and cannot be concluded about accuracy. An accurate attribution for an event is one that refers to the actual objective cause of that event. Since we do not know the actual causes of the Lu and McIlvane murders, we cannot say whether it was the Americans, the Chinese, or both who were inaccurate. Since the fish behaviours were cartoons, not actual events with actual causes, the question of accuracy does not apply. Hence we can conclude that each culture was biased relative to the other culture, but not that either was biased relative to the truth. American attributions followed the dispositionalist tendency which leads to errors in many contexts (Ross 1977), but we cannot conclude whether or not these attributions were inaccurate in the context of our studies.

Of course, experiments could be designed to probe the issue of accuracy in attribution across cultures. It would be necessary to collect attributions about a behaviour for which the actual cause is known, such as a behaviour manipulated previously in an experiment. Cross-cultural studies of this sort would probably reveal that accuracy of attributions depends on several factors. One factor might be the culture of the actor. It may be that Chinese behaviour is actually caused by situational factors more than is the case with American behaviour, and vice versa. If so, then Chinese attributors will be relatively more accurate about Chinese actors than American actors, and vice versa. Another factor might be the type of behaviour. Situation-driven behaviour, such as compliance, conformity, and contagion, may fall in the blind spot of American attributors. For example, college students shown a film of Milgram's (1963) experiment on obedience to authority mistakenly attributed the 'shocking' behaviour of Milgram's subjects to personal dispositions rather than to the situational pressure (Safer 1980). Our prediction is that Chinese students shown this film would be more inclined to attribute to the situational pressure, which Milgram demonstrated to be the actual cause. Future research may discover blind spots of collectivist attributors, but at present much more is known about the errors made by attributors in highly individualist cultures.

Which biases are most useful?

The question of utility can be distinguished from the question of accuracy. We found that Chinese subjects were more likely to attribute murder to situational factors and more likely to reason counterfactually that murder would have been averted in a changed situation.* Cultural differences in counterfactual reasoning may lead to cultural differences in problem-solving. In particular, if Chinese are more likely to react to a problematic behaviour by mentally simulating counterfactual situations in which the behaviour does not occur, then they should be more aware of situational interventions for the problematic behaviour. Some evidence for this can be seen in Chinese versus American approaches to mathematics education. Americans attribute mathematics performance primarily to a disposition (ability), whereas Chinese attribute it primarily to a situational factor (effort of student and family) (Stevenson, Lee and Stigler 1986; Hess *et al.* 1987). Hence, American counterfactual reasoning about a student's failure in mathematics would run as follows: *if only this student had better genes, he would not have failed the mathematics test.* Whereas Chinese counter-factual reasoning would run as follows: *If only this student and his family had put in more effort, he would not have failed the mathematics test.* Unlike the American line of reasoning, the Chinese line of reasoning suggests an approach to solve the problem, and there is evidence that they take this approach. Chinese children are assigned more homework, do more homework, and receive more assistance from family members with home-work than American children (Chen and Stevenson 1989). Moreover, there is evidence that this difference is consequential: Chinese children show higher achievement than American children of similar intellectual capacity (Stevenson *et al.* 1986). In this case, a situationalist bias, whether or not it provides a 'correct' account of mathematics achievement, almost surely serves to increase it. Of course, in other cases there may be unique utilities associated with a dispositionalist bias in attribution of behaviour.

In sum, traditional social psychological research in highly individualist cultures has identified regions of the social domain in which perception is myopic and judgement flawed. Yet recent cross-cultural research suggests that subjects looking through different cultural lenses and basing judge-ments on different implicit theories may have acuity and acumen for those regions of social experience where individualists flounder. Future research may identify distinct cultural biases in social judgement which bring accuracy and utility in certain kinds of social problem-solving. Of course,

---

* This finding adds to the evidence against Bloom's (1981, 1984) thesis that Chinese speakers engage in less counterfactual reasoning than English speakers (Au 1983, 1984; Cheng 1985).

such comparative research could only proceed by the collaboration of researchers deeply familiar with different cultures, and this collaboration seems the best defence against ethnocentric conclusions. Our hunch is that there is more in common across cultures in social experience than in understanding of that experience, and that each culture has local regions of expertise. Ultimately, researchers may be able to offer a different kind of prescription for social judgement: adopting an implicit theory from a culture with relevant expertise — thinking through cultures (Shweder 1991).

REFERENCES

Adelman, I. and Morris, C. T. (1967). *Society, politics and economic development: a quantitative approach*. Johns Hopkins University Press, Baltimore, MD.

Atran, S. (1989). Basic conceptual domains. *Mind and Language* **4**, 5–16.

Au, T. K. (1983). Chinese and English counterfactuals: the Sapir–Whorf hypothesis revisited. *Cognition* **15**, 162–3.

Au, T. K. (1984). Counterfactuals: in reply to Alfred Bloom. *Cognition* **17**, 289–302.

Bakan, D. (1966). *The duality of human existence*. Rand McNally, Chicago, IL.

Ball, W. A. (1973). *The perception of causality in the infant*. Report 37, Department of Psychology, Developmental Program, University of Michigan, Ann Arber, MI.

Barry, H., Child, I. and Balcon, M. (1959). Relation of child training to subsistence economy. *American Anthropologist* **61**, 51–63.

Bassili, J. N. (1976). Temporal and spatial contingencies in the perception of social events. *Journal of Personality and Social Psychology* **33**, 680–5.

Beasley, N. E. (1968). The extent of individual differences in the perception of causality. *Canadian Journal of Psychology* **22**, 399–407.

Berger, P., Berger, P. and Kelner, H. (1973). *The homeless mind*. Random House, New York.

Berry, J. W. (1979). A cultural ecology of social behavior. In *Advances in experimental social psychology* Vol. 12, (ed. L. Berkowitz), pp. 177–207. Academic Press, New York.

Bloom, A. (1981). *The linguistic shaping of thought*. Erlbaum, Hillsdale, NJ.

Bloom, A. (1984). Caution — the words you use may affect what you say: a reply to Au. *Cognition* **17**, 281.

Bond, M. H. (1988). Invitation to a wedding: Chinese values and global economic gowth. In *Handbook of cross-cultural psychology* (ed. D. Sinha and H. S. R. Kao), pp. 197–209. Sage India, New Delhi.

Borton, R. W. (1979). The perception of causality in infants. Presented at the Meeting of the Society for Research in Child Development, San Francisco, CA.

Boyle, D. G. (1960). A contribution to the study of phenomenal causality. *Quarterly Journal of Experimental Psychology* **12**, 171–9.

Campbell, D. T. (1964). Distinguishing differences of perception from failures of communication in cross-cultural studies. In *Cross-cultural understanding: epistemology in anthropology* (ed. F. S. C. Northrop and H. H. Livingsten). Harper and Row, New York.

Carrithers, M., Collins, S. and Lukes, S. (1985). *The category of the person: anthropology philosophy, history.* Cambridge University Press.

Chen, C. and Stevenson, H. W. (1989). Homework: a cross-cultural examination. *Child Development* **60**, 551–61.

Cheng, P. W. (1985). Pictures of ghosts: a critique of Alfred Bloom's *The linguistic shaping of thought. American Anthropologist* **87**.

Clement, J. (1982). Students' preconceptions in introductory mechanics. *American Journal of Physics* **50**, 66–71.

Cooper, H. A. (1986). *Winslow Homer watercolors.* Yale University Press, New Haven.

D'Andrade, R. (1981). The cultural part of cognition. *Cognitive Science* **5**, 179–85.

D'Andrade, R. (1984). Cultural meaning systems. In *Culture theory: essays on mind, self, and emotion* (ed. R. A. Shweder and R. A. Levine). Cambridge University Press.

Dasser, V., Ulbaek, I. and Premack, D. (1989). Perception of intention. *Science* **243**, 365–367.

Davis-Blake, A. and Pfeffer, J. (1989). Just a mirage: the search for dispositional effects in organizational research. *Academy of Management Review* **14**, 385–400.

Dennett, D. (1983). Intentional systems in cognitive ethology: the 'Panglossian paradigm' defended. *Behavioral and Brain Sciences* **6**, 343–88.

Dennett, D. (1987). Evolution, error, and intentionality. In *The intentional stance* (ed. D. Dennett), University Press, Cambridge, MA.

de Tocqueville, A. [1840] (1946). Democracy in America. Knopf, New York.

Douglas, M. (1975). *Implicit meanings: essays in anthropology.* Routledge and Kegan Paul, London.

Dumont, L. (1970). *Homo hierarchicus.* University of Chicago Press.

Earley, P. C. (1989). Social loafing and collectivism. *Administrative Science Quarterly* **34**, 565–81.

Einhorn, H. J. and Hogarth, R. M. (1986). Judging probable cause. *Psychological Bulletin* **99**, 3–19.

Evans-Pritchard, E. E. (1937). *Witchcraft, oracles, and magic among the Azande.* Oxford University Press.

Fiske, A. P. (1992). Four elementary forms of sociality. *Psychological Review* **99**, 689–723.

Gearing, F. (1970). *The face of the fox.* Aldine, Chicago, IL.

Geertz, C. (1975). On the nature of anthropological understanding. *American Scientist* **63**, 47–53.

Gelman, R. (1990). First principles organize attention to and learning about relevant data: Number and the animate-inanimate distinction as examples. *Cognitive Science* **14**, 79–106.

Gelman, R. and Spelke, E. (1981). The development of thoughts about animate and inanimate objects: implications for research on social cognition. In *Social cognitive development: frontiers and possible futures* (ed. J. H. Flavell and L. Ross). Cambridge University Press.

Gemelli, A. and Cappellini, A. (1958). The influence of the subject's attitude in perception. *Acta Psychologia* **14**, 171–9.

Gilovich, T. (1987). Secondhand information and social judgment. *Journal of Experimental Social Psychology* **23**, 59–74.

Gruber, H. E., Fink, C. D. and Damm, V. (1957). Effects of experience on perception of causality. *Journal of Experimental Psychology* **53**, 89–93.

Hartshorne, H. and May, M. A. (1928). *Studies in the nature of character*, Vol. 1, *Studies in deceit*. Macmillan, New York.

Heider, F. (1944). Social perception and phenomenal causality. *Psychological Review* **51**, 358–74.

Heider, F. (1958). *The psychology of interpersonal relations*. Wiley, New York.

Heider, F. and Simmel, M. (1944). An experimental study of apparent behavior. *American Journal of Psychology* **57**, 243–59.

Hejzlar, J. (1978). *Chinese watercolors*. W. H. Smith, New York.

Hess, R. D., Chang, C.-M. and McDevitt, T. M. (1987). Cultural variations in family beliefs about children's performance in mathematics: comparisons among People's Republic of China, Chinese-Americans, and Caucasian-American families. *Journal of Educational Psychology* **79**, 179–88.

Hofstede, G. (1980). *Culture's consequences: international differences in work-related values*. Sage, Beverly Hills, CA.

Hofstede, G. (1983). National cultures revisited. *Behavior Science Research* **18**, 285–305.

Hofstede, G. (1991). *Culture and organizations*. Sage, Beverly Hills, CA.

Hofstede, G. and Bond, M. (1984). Hofstede's culture dimensions: an independent validation using Rokeach's value survey. *Journal of Cross Cultural Psychology* **15**, 417–33.

Horton, R. (1970). African traditional thought and Western science. In *Rationality* (ed. B. R. Wilsen), pp. 131–71. Blackwell, Oxford.

Hsu, F. L. K. (1953). *Americans and Chinese: two ways of life*. Schuman, New York.

Hsu, F. L. K. (1971). Psychological homeostasis and *jen*: conceptual tools for advancing psychological anthropology. *American Anthropologist* **73**, 23–44.

Hsu, F. L. K. (1981*a*). *American and Chinese: passage to differences* (3rd edn). University of Hawaii Press, Honolulu, HI.

Hsu, F. L. K. (1981*b*). The self in cross-cultural perspective. In *Culture and self* (ed. F. L. K. Hsu), pp. 24–55. Tavistock, London.

Hume, D. [1739] (1987). *A treatise of human nature*. Clarendon Press, Oxford.

Ichheiser, G. (1943). Misinterpretations of personality in everyday life and the psychologist's frame of reference. *Character and Personality* **12**, 145–60.

Ichheiser, G. (1949). Misunderstandings in human relations: a study in false social perception. *American Journal of Sociology* (Suppl.), **55**, 1–70.

Ichheiser, G. (1970). *Appearances and realities: misunderstanding in human relations*. Jossey-Bass, San Francisco, CA.

Inkeles, A. and Smith, D. H. (1974). *Becoming modern*. Harvard University Press, Cambridge, MA.

Jeyifous, S. (1985). Atimodemo: semantic conceptual development among the Yoruba. Ph.D. Dissertation, Cornell University.

Jones, E. E and Harris, V. A. (1967). The attribution of attitudes. *Journal of Experimental Social Psychology* **3**, 1–24.

Jones, E. E. and Nisbett, R. E. (1972). The actor and the observer: divergent perceptions of the causes of behavior. In *Attribution: perceiving the causes of behavior* (ed. E. E. Jones *et al.*). General Learning Press, Morristown, NJ.

Jones, E. E., Davis, K. E. and Gergen, K. J. (1961). Role playing variations and their informational value for person perception. *Journal of Abnormal and Social Psychology* 63, 302–10.

Kahneman, D. and Miller, D. T. (1986). Norm theory: comparing reality to its alternatives. *Psychological Review* 93, 136–53.

Kahneman, D. and Tversky, A. (1973). On the psychology of prediction. *Psychological Review* 80, 237–51.

Kahneman, D. and Tversky, A. (1982). The simulation heuristic. In *Judgment under uncertainty: heuristics and biases* (ed. D. Kahneman, P. Slovic and A. Tversky). Cambridge University Press, New York.

Kaiser, M. K. and Proffitt, D. R. (1984). The development of sensitivity to causally relevant dynamic information. *Child Development* 55, 1614–24.

Kassin, S. M. and Pryor, J. B. (1985). The development of attribution processes. In *The development of social cognition* (ed. J. Pryor and J. Day). Springer Verlag, New York.

Keil, F. (1986). The acquisition of natural kind and artifact terms. In *Conceptual change* (ed. A. Marrar and W. Demopoulus). Ablex, Norwood, NJ.

Keil, F. (1989). *Concepts, kinds, and cognitive development*. MIT Press, Cambridge, MA.

Kelley, H. H. (1967). Attribution theory in social psychology. In *Nebraska Symposium on Motivation* (ed. D. Levine). University of Nebraska Press, Lincoln, NB.

Kelley, H. H. (1972). Causal schemata and the attribution process. In *Attribution: perceiving the causes of behavior* (ed. E. E. Jones *et al.*). General Learning Press, Morristown, NJ.

Kidd, D. (1905). *The essential Kaffir*. A&C Black, London.

King, A. Y. C. (1981). The individual and group in Confucianism: a relational perspective. Presented at the Conference on Individualism and Wholism, York, Me.

King, A. Y. C. and Bond, M. H. (1985). The Confucian paradigm of man: a sociological view. In *Chinese culture and mental health* (ed. W. S. Tseng and D. Y. H. Wu), pp. 29–46. Academic Press, New York.

Kluckhorn, F. and Strodbeck, F. (1961). *Variations in value orientations*. Row, Peterson, Evanston, IL.

Koffka, K. (1935). *Principles of Gestalt psychology*. Harcourt Brace, New York.

Lakoff, G. and Johnson, M. (1980). *Metaphors we live by*. University of Chicago Press.

Lau, R. R. and Russel, D. (1980). Attributions in the sports pages. *Journal of Personality and Social Psychology* 39, 29–38.

Leslie, A. M. (1982). The perception of causality in infants. *Perception* 11, 173–86.

Leslie, A. M. (1987). Do infants perceive causality? *Cognition* 22, 127–39.

Leslie, A. M and Keeble, S. (1987). Do six-month-old infants perceive causality? *Cognition* 25, 265–87.

Leung (1987). Some determinants of reaction to procedural models for conflict resolution: a cross-national study. *Journal of Personality and Social Psychology*, 53, 898–908.

Levy-Bruhl, L. [1910] (1926). *Les fonctions mentales dans les coieties inferieures*. Presses Universitaires de France, Paris. Translation: *How natives think*. Allen and Unwin, London.

Lewin, K. (1935). *Dynamic theory of personality*. McGraw Hill, New York.

Lloyd, G. E. R. (1990). *Demystifying mentalities*. Cambridge University Press.

Lukes, S. (1973). *Individualism*. Blackwell, Oxford.

Mandler, J. (1992). How to build a baby: II. Conceptual primitives. *Psychological Review* **99**, 587–604.

McCloskey, M. (1983). Intuitive physics. *Scientific American* **24**, 122–30.

McCloskey, M. and Kaiser, M. K. (1984). Children's intuitive physics. *Sciences* **24**, 40–5.

Markus, H. R. and Kitayama, S. (1991). Culture and the self: implications for cognition, emotion, and motivation. *Psychological Review* **98**, 224–53.

Mauss, M. [1938] (1985). A category of the human mind: The notion of person; the notion of self. In *The category of the person: anthropology, philosophy, history* (ed. M. Carrithers, S. Collins and S. Lukes), pp. 1–25.

Michotte, A. E. (1952). *The perception of causality*. Basic Books, New York.

Milgram, S. (1963). Behavioral study of obedience. *Journal of Abnormal and Social Psychology* **67**, 371–8.

Miller, J. G. (1984). Culture and the development of everyday social explanation. *Journal of Personality and Social Psychology* **46**, 961–78.

Mischel, W. (1968). *Personality and assessment*. Wiley, New York.

Morris, M. W. (1993). Culture and cause: American and Chinese understandings of physical and social causality. Ph.D. Dissertation, University of Michigan.

Morris, M. W. and Smith, E. E. (1992). How much explanation does behavior require? The role of causal force in discounting and conjunction effects. Unpublished manuscript, University of Michigan Psychology Department.

Newcomb, T. M. (1929). *Consistency of certain extrovert-introvert behavior patterns in 51 problem boys*. Columbia University Teachers College Bureau of Publications, New York.

Nisbett, R. E. (1980). The trait construct in lay and professional psychology. In *Retrospections on social psychology* (ed. L. Festinger). Oxford University Press, New York.

Nisbett, R. E. and Ross, L. (1980). *Human inference: strategies and shortcomings of social judgment*. Prentice-Hall, Englewood Cliffs, NJ.

Nisbett, R. E., Caputo, C., Legant, P. and Maracek, J. (1973). Behavior as seen by the actor and as seen by the observer. *Journal of Personality and Social Psychology* **27**, 154–64.

Parsons, T. and Shils, E. A. (1951). *Toward a general theory of action*. Harvard University Press, Cambridge, MA.

Powesland, P. F. (1959). The effect of practice upon the perception of causality. *Canadian Journal of Psychology* **13**, 155–68.

Premack, D. (1990). The infant's theory of self-propelled objects. *Cognition* **36**, 1–16.

Riesman, D. (1950). *The lonely crowd*. Doubleday, New York.

Riesman, D. (1954). *Individualism reconsidered*. Free Press, Glencoe.

Rime, B., Boulanger, B., Laubin, P., Richir, M. and Stroobants, K. (1985). *Motivation and Emotion* **9**, 241–60.

Ross, L. D. (1977). The intuitive psychologist and his shortcomings: distortions in the attribution process. In *Advances in experimental social psychology*, Vol. 10 (ed. L. Berkowitz) pp. 173–220. Random House, New York.

Ross, L. and Nisbett, R. (1991). *The person and the situation: perspectives of social psychology*. McGraw-Hill, New York.

Ross, L., Amabile, T. M. and Steinmetz, J. L. (1977). Social roles, social control, and biases in social-perception processes. *Journal of Personality and Social Psychology* **35**, 485–94.

Ross, M. (1989) Relation of implicit theories to the construction of personal histories. *Psychological Review* **96**, 34–57.

Russell, B. (1960). *An outline of philosophy*. Meridian, New York.

Safer, M. A. (1980). Attributing evil to the subject, not the situation: student reaction to Milgram's film on obedience. *Personality and Social Psychology Bulletin* **6**, 205–9.

Schoeneman, T. J. and Rubanowitz, D. E. (1985). Attributions in the advice columns: actors and observers, causes and reasons. *Personality and Social Psychology Bulletin* **11**, 315–25.

Sears, R. (1963). Dependency motivation. In *Nebraska Symposium on Motivation* (ed. M. R. Jones). University of Nebraska Press, Lincoln, NB.

Selby, H. A. (1974). *Zapotec deviance: the convergence of folk and modern sociology*. University of Texas Press, Austin, TX.

Selby, H. A. (1975). Semantics and causality in the study of deviance. In *Sociocultural dimensions of language use* (ed. M. Sanches and B. Blount), pp. 11–24. Academic Press, New York.

Shultz, T. R. (1980). Development of the concept of intention. In *The Minnesota Symposium on Child Psychology*, Vol. 13 (ed. W. A. Collins). Erlbaum, Hillsdale, NJ.

Shultz, T. R. (1982). Causal reasoning the social and non-social realms. *Canadian Journal of Behavioral Science* **14**, 307–22.

Shweder, R. A. (1991). Cultural psychology — what is it? In *Thinking through cultures' expeditions in cultural psychology* (ed. R. A. Shweder). Harvard University Press, Cambridge, MA.

Shweder, R. A. and Bourne, E. J. (1982). Does the concept of the person vary cross-culturally? In *Cultural conceptions of mental health and therapy* (ed. A. J. Marsella and G. White). Riedel, Boston, MA.

Snow, C. P. (1959). *The two cultures: and a second look*. Cambridge University Press, New York.

Sperber, D. (1985). Anthropology and psychology: towards an epidemiology of representations. *Man* **20**, 73–90.

Sperber, D. (1991). The epidemiology of belief. In *Psychological studies of widespread belief* (ed. C. Fraser). Oxford University Press.

Stevenson, H. W., Lee, S. Y. and Stigler, J. W. (1986). Mathematics achievements of Chinese, Japanese, and American children. *Science* **236**, 693–8.

Stevenson, H. W., Stigler, J. W., Lee, S.-Y., Lucker, G. W., *et al.* (1986). Cognitive performance and academic achievement of Japanese, Chinese, American children. *Annual Progress in Child Psychiatry and Child Development*, 324–450.

Stewart, J. (1984). Object motion and the perception of animacy. Presented at the meeting of the Psychonomic Society, San Antonio, TX.

Strauss, A. S. (1973). Northern Cheyenne ethnosociology. *Ethos* **1**, 326–57.

Talmy, L. (1988). Force dynamics in language and cognition. *Cognitive Science* **12**, 49–100.

Tawney, R. H. (1926). *Religion and the rise of capitalism*. Penguin, Harmondsworth.

Taylor, S. E. (1982). Social cognition and health. *Personality and Social Psychology Bulletin* **8**, 549–62.

Taylor, S. E. and Fiske, A. (1975). Point-of-view and perceptions of causality. *Journal of Personality and Society Psychology* **8**, 426–32.

Thibaut, J. W. and Riecken, H. W. (1955). Some determinants and consequences of the perception of social causality. *Journal of Personality* **24**, 113–33.

Triandis, H. C. (1972). *The analysis of subjective culture*. Wiley, New York.

Triandis, H. C. (1989). Cross-cultural studies of individualism and collectivism. *Nebraska Symposium on Motivation*. University of Nebraska Press, Lincoln NB.

Triandis, H. C., Bontempo, R., Betancourt H., Bond, M., Leung K., Brenes, A., *et al.* (1986). The measurement of 'etic' aspects of individualism and collectivism across cultures. *Austrialian Journal of Psychology* **38**, 257–67.

Triandis, H. C., Bontempo, R., Villareal, M. J., Asai, M. and Lucca, N. (1988). Individualism and collectivism: cross-cultural perspectives on self-ingroup relationships. *Journal of Personality and Social Psychology* **54**, 323–38.

Triandis, H. C., McCusker, C. and Hui, C. H. (1990). Multimethod probes of individualism and collectivism. *Journal of Personality and Social Psychology* **59**, 1006–20.

Tversky, A. and Kahneman, D. (1973). Availability: a heuristic for judging frequency and probability. *Cognitive Psychology* **5**, 207–32.

Tversky, A. and Kahneman, D. (1974). Judgment under uncertainty: heuristics and biases. *Science* **185**, 1124–31.

Weber, M. (1930). *The protestant ethic and the spirit of capitalism*. Allen and Unwin, London.

Wellman, H. (1990). *Children's theories of mind*. MIT Press, Cambridge, MA.

Wellman, H. and Gelman, S. (1992). Cognitive development: foundational theories of core domains. *Annual Review of Psychology* **43**, 337–75.

Wells, G. L. and Gavanksi, I. (1989). Mental simulation of causality. *Journal of Personality and Social Psychology* **56**, 161–9.

White, P. A. (1988). Causal processing: origins and development. *Psychological Bulletin* **104**, 36–52.

Witken, H. A. and Berry, J. W. (1975). Psychological differentiation in cross-cultural perspective. *Journal of Cross-cultural Psychology* **6**, 4–87.

DISCUSSION

Participants: F. Keil, D. Premack

Keil: If you, were to describe an artefact metaphorically as behaving socially (using clear theory of mind format) do you think that attributions for this behaviour woud differ across cultures? For example, a subject would hear a description of my car's behaviour: 'My old car and I got along very well together, but my new car and I have a very difficult relationship. The two of us don't get along at all. Yesterday the car got stuck in the snow, etc.'. . . .

Morris: Given equivalent stories, Americans might be somewhat more inclined to attribute automobile behaviour to a disposition (something is wrong with the new car) and Chinese to the situation (something is wrong with your relationship to this car, perhaps its 'newness'). However, my guess is that metaphorical language is not necessary for social perception of cars. We perceive cars as social creatures because they walk and talk like social creatures: they move on mutually contingent goal-directed trajectories; they compel each other to move; they congregate and disperse. Only in accidents do cars exemplify the physical 'launching effect', and only after accident do they exhibit the physical 'entraining effect'.

Consistent with this prediction, I can offer anecdotal evidence that Americans attribute car behaviour to dispositions more than is warranted. In the 'verbal protocols' of fellow drivers in San Francisco traffic jams, my car's lack of forward motion is often attributed to an internal disposition rather than to its situation of being blocked by other cars in front. Also, in consumer discourse comparing vehicles, situational causes of performance are underweighted. For example, statistics such as average longevity and repair costs are used to argue that a particular jeep is of inferior quality to a particular car without taking into account that jeeps are driven over harsher terrain, which contributes to their earlier demise.

Premack: Is individualism — collectivism the best interpretation? Perhaps it has to do with different views of individual differences and/or with differences in obligation of all individuals to meet a standard. Suppose that you charged an individual with growing a garden and offered him a choice of seeds, on the one hand, or manipulating temperature, on the other. Similarly, suppose that you charged an individual with building a railroad and offered a choice between selecting crew members and manipulating pay.

Morris: Both these interpretations are closely related to the interpretation that we propose, which is a distinction between person-centred and situation-centred implicit social theories. A person-centred theory, which holds that personal dispositions are and ought to be the determinants of behaviour emphasizes individual differences and de-emphasizes external obligations.

The choice problems you suggest would be an interesting and novel paradigm for investigating causal understandings. My guess is that social theories would not be applied to plants, because plants do not have social trajectories, but social theories would be applied to railroad workers. Hence a cultural difference would be predicted for the latter but not the former.

20

Causal understandings in cultural representations: cognitive constraints on inferences from cultural input

PASCAL BOYER

Cultural environments differ, in obvious and often striking ways, in the repertoire of causal understandings conveyed explicitly as well as implicitly. In cultural anthropology, it has often been assumed that this variability is unbounded, and that cognitive constraints have only marginal, generally trivial, effects on the range of causal representations and beliefs entertained in different cultural environments. Here, the opposite view, according to which important aspects of cultural representations are constrained by universal features of the mind–brain, will be defended. It is argued that causal judgements, however culturally variable, are constrained by a series of universal intuitive principles. These early developed principles, which are not acquired through social interaction, constrain cultural representations in two different ways. First, they give the developing mind definite presumptions about what kinds of objects there are in the world, how they are likely to behave, and how one can learn about them. Second, culturally transmitted representations are likely to be acquired and memorized only if they are connected to those intuitive principles in a particular way, which will be described. The argument stems from a general framework which places particular emphasis on universal cognitive constraints in order to account for the cross-cultural recurrence of certain features of cultural representations (Boyer 1992a, 1993a, 1994).

My argument focuses on a domain which has always been central to anthropological discussions of causation and causal concepts, that of religious and 'magical' assumptions. This domain constitutes, in a sense, a limiting case. Religious concepts and assumptions seem to display obvious cross-cultural variation, perhaps in a more salient way than other types of cultural representations. Moreover, for obvious reasons, they are not constrained by objective features of the environment. These two facts have led anthropologists to consider religious representations as constrained only by the cultural input. Therefore it is particularly important to show that, even in this apparently unconstrained domain, the range of cultural representations likely to be transmitted is in fact limited by universal intuitive principles.

In this chapter anthropological and psychological data are used to provide an answer to a series of five questions, with each answer being the starting point for the next. The first question is: *Are concepts of causation culturally specific?* It will be argued that this is not the case. Arguments for relativity are not supported by any compelling evidence, and in fact are often theoretically incoherent. The main source of incoherence is that most models ignore early conceptual development and the constraints that it imposes on further cultural acquisition. This naturally leads to the question: *What is the structure of early causal understandings?* This is answered by summarizing some salient points of recent developmental research. In order to go further, and understand the consequences of these developmental facts for cultural acquisition, one must have a precise description of the cultural input in the domain considered. Thus the next question turns specifically to the domain of religious representations: *What is the structure of the causal understandings implied by religious categories?* This is described as a particular combination of culturally transmitted counter-intuitive assumptions and spontaneous intuitive inferences. This leads to the question: *What is the role of early intuitive principles in the treatment of the cultural input?* The answer is that, in certain domains, cultural input provides under-specified causal scenarios, which are then 'filled' abductively by available intuitive principles. The final question is: *What does this tell us about causal understandings in culture?* The answer is that the present model allows us to make definite predictions about the recurrence of particular types of representations in cultural systems.

CAUSATION AND ANTHROPOLOGICAL MODELS

The argument of this section is mainly critical. Anthropological theory is often misguided in the way that it describes causal thinking. As this argument has been presented in detail elsewhere (Boyer 1992*b*), only the main points are summarized here. The cognitive processes underlying causal judgements are generally seen in anthropology as both *culture-specific* and *domain-general*. Influential models state that people brought up in different places are likely to have very different conceptions of what causes and effects are, presumably by virtue of having different 'cultural schemes' or 'world views'. Conversely, these models assume that causal judgements in a given cultural environment are produced by applying a unified and coherent concept of causation to a variety of empirical situations. I think that both assumptions are wrong: anthropological data do not really support the former, and the latter is refuted by psychological evidence.

The idea of culture-bound concepts of causation

Causal understandings seem to differ dramatically between any two societies. In any human group, one can find explanations of natural and social occurrences which are held to be true or plausible, yet would strike members of other groups as particularly odd or naive. From that observation, a number of anthropologists have concluded that causal judgements differ, not just in their empirical content, but also in the underlying concepts of 'cause' and 'causal connection'. For instance, Lee (1949) argued that Trobriand islanders have no notion of causation at all (see Hutchins (1981) for a detailed refutation). In a more sober and also more sophisticated manner, Needham (1976) has contended that in some societies people may be using a concept of 'direct causation' that has no counterpart in Western mentality. In a systematic study of 'primitive thought', Hallpike (1979) described the 'collective representations' reported by anthropologists, in such domains as magic and religion, as very similar to Piaget's pre-operatory stage, in many respects including causal understanding.* For Hallpike, the 'primitive notions of causation', like those of pre-operatory children, are 'absolutist, phenomenalist, psychologistic, irreversible and static, lacking a real grasp of process' (Hallpike 1979, p. 451).

It may seem economical to assume that radical differences in judgements are the outcome of a deeper misunderstanding about what is expressed by 'A caused B'. Additional arguments are sometimes given in support of this interpretation. The **rationality argument**, for instance, states that, given the evidence available, it would be irrational for people to think that 'A caused B', unless of course the term 'cause' is interpreted in a special way. A **Whorfian argument**, in contrast, emphasizes the fact that some languages have no term, or conversely several terms, to translate the English word 'cause'. Finally, the **'explicit theory' argument** focuses on the fact that, in some literate traditions, there are explicit conceptions of the nature of causes and effects. This argument is often found in the study of exotic cultures with a 'high' scholarly tradition, such as those of Greece, China, or India. In such cultural contexts, some people put forward explicit theories about the nature of causes and effects, about the conditions for

---

* For instance, 'primitives' are said to have animistic beliefs, to endow inanimate objects with intentionality. Also, they are said to believe in the power of words (e.g. in magical incantations supposed to bring about a desired state of affairs just by describing it), they hold certain causal connections true without bothering to inquire by what mechanisms they could work, they project onto an object aspects of its relation to the person who handles it, and they think that all features of an object (e.g. its shape and colour) can enter into causal connections.

causal connectedness. These local theories, which often differ considerably, are assumed to reflect corresponding differences in the way that people represent the concept of causation. However, all these additional 'arguments' can be arguments only if we have evidence that the principles of causation are indeed different.

Causal principles and causal judgements

There is no such positive evidence, however. Most of the evidence that is mentioned in support of this idea can be interpreted, more prosaically, as resulting from differences in the empirical principles that underpin causal judgements. A clear distinction must be made between the concept of cause or causal connection on the one hand, and the assumptions describing the causal propensities of various objects or entities on the other. To see the relevance of this point, take a limiting case. Claims to radical differences are typically made in the description of what are loosely described as 'magical' beliefs. For instance, some people state that stealing a lock of hair from someone and reciting special incantations over it will make the person ill. Such a belief implies assumptions which would seem odd or impossible to people from other cultural environments. But the odd or shocking assumptions are assumptions about hair, incantations, and illness, not assumptions about causation. The only assumptions about causation which are implied by such a belief are (i) that certain objects have particular causal powers, (ii) that those powers can be activated by particular recipes, and (iii) that the objects will have the intended effects after the relevant causal powers have been activated. Such innocuous principles are implied by a variety of causal judgements, in all sorts of contexts, and in all sorts of places. Strictly speaking, two subjects can be said to have two different 'conceptions of causation' only if the following conditions obtain: (i) they are presented with the same situation; (ii) they are operating on the same description of the causal powers of the objects considered; (iii) they have different interpretations of the causal connections involved. Given the obvious differences in assumptions about causal propensities, it is not surprising that people from different cultural environments should make different causal judgements about the same objects. But this, by itself, does not support the claim of different concepts of cause.

The additional 'arguments' mentioned above do not support this claim either. For instance, it is possible to show that typical examples of strange or apparently irrational beliefs are in fact amenable to a rationalistic description, once they are understood as speculative assumptions about particular objects and entities (Sperber 1982). The linguistic facts do not allow us to makes inferences to underlying conceptual structure in any domain unless we have positive evidence for that structure. The polysemy of the word 'because' in ordinary English should remind us that direct inferences of this kind are particularly dangerous. Finally, one cannot take for granted the relevance of 'explicit theories' as a source of underlying notions of causation. The 'explicit theory' argument is founded on the assumption that we can take the principles and notions of which people are aware as direct evidence for the causal concepts and causal assumptions that they actually entertain. In other words, it consists in confusing the *explicit reflective* notions that people have about their cognitive processes with those cognitive processes themselves. Explicit theories are not used by people as a way of producing causal judgements. Rather, they are a posteriori attempts to quantify over the domain of causal judgements produced spontaneously. As a number of authors have pointed out (Harris and Heelas 1979), many anthropological claims to relativity are based on this confusion between mental representations on the one hand, and what anthropology misleadingly calls 'collective representations' on the other.*

Obviously, many anthropologists are aware of these and other empirical flaws in the notion of culturally specific concepts of causation. One particular problem is that, in such claims, what is in fact a particular exceptional way of thinking is unduly extended to the whole mental life of certain societies. People who state that reciting a certain spell can bring about someone's death, nevertheless stick to rather 'normal' ideas of causation as concerns trivial everyday events such as stones breaking windows or kicks inducing pain. This is why many anthropologists are led to assume that people engaged in magic or other such activities are in fact 'suspending' the constraints of their common-sense everyday conception of causality. As pointed out above, however, there is no clear indication that specific 'principles of causation' are implied by magical or religious claims. It follows that there is no special reason to 'suspend' ordinary principles unless one confuses these principles with empirical expectations. There is certainly a tension between ordinary expectations and what is described in magical or religious representations; this point will be examined in detail below. The tension concerns what can be expected from particular objects or kinds of objects in particular circumstances, not the characterization of causes and effects in general. Indeed, I will now go further and argue that, in an

---

* This vague label often lumps together different categories of phenomena, none of which give us direct access to mentally represented assumptions or categories. They include such publicly available manifestations as myths and anecdotes, as well as assumptions and ideas which are *inferred* by anthropologists on the basis of their informants' statements. The resulting mixture, although it sometimes gives a coherent account of a particular cultural environment, hardly counts as direct evidence for cognitive processes. This is why Hallpike's comparisons of pre-operatory causation and 'primitive' causal judgements seem particularly inadequate. The material culled from anthropological descriptions was taken from authors who were not concerned with the direct study or description of mental representations.

important sense, the very notion of 'principles of causation' is inadequate in a description of causal thinking.

Is there a domain-general concept of causation?

So far, I have argued that anthropologists tend to see differences where there are none, mistakenly inferring from empirical assumptions to principles of causation. I will now argue, conversely, that there *are* differences in causal principles, which are systematically ignored in anthropology, between the types of causal understandings applied to different ontological domains. Most anthropological ideas about causation take it as unproblematic that a single coherent notion of causation is applied to all conceptual domains. However, this assumption seems less than perfectly evident given the difficulties that philosophers and psychologists have encountered in the description of the 'principles of causation' actually used by people in causal judgements. Even in domains where there *should* be a coherent concept of causation, actual judgements seem to be based on a variety of weakly related notions 'bringing about'. This was demonstrated, for instance, by Hart and Honore's (1959) study of causation in legal judgement. If such explicit, rationally argued, and coherence-seeking judgements as legal attributions of responsibility rely on a variety of causal concepts, then *a fortiori* common-sense judgements should not be expected to display unity and coherence in causal concepts. Such difficulties are familiar to philosophers engaged in the conceptual analysis of the notion of cause.

There are several ways of dealing with this problem. One is to assume that the concept of cause is represented in a prototypical way. In this account, singular causal connections are judged on the basis of their resemblance with certain core cases, such as the intuitive link between contiguous physical events (Lakoff 1987, pp. 54 ff.; Miller 1987, pp. 121 ff.). Another, not necessarily incompatible, solution is to abandon the very notion of 'principles of causation', at least in the constraining sense used here. The notion of general principles of causation, however intuitively self-evident, is by no means the only conceivable account of causal thinking. It is perfectly conceivable that causal judgements in different domains, even if they share certain properties, are based on different principles. Whatever 'causal principles' are involved in causal judgements might be 'decentralized' principles, which apply to only certain types of connections. Some of these principles would extend to whole ontological domains, for example specifying special conditions for causation in **animate beings** as opposed to **inanimate objects**. Other such empirical generalizations would be more specific and concern *kinds* of natural objects or *types* of artefacts (e.g. fluids as opposed to solid objects). In such a view, the very notion of 'principles of causation' is dissolved; whatever principles make causal judgements plausible are part and parcel of empirical knowledge. Indeed, as we shall see below, this is precisely what the psychological evidence seems to indicate.

EARLY DEVELOPMENT OF CAUSAL UNDERSTANDINGS

Discussions of causality and culture rarely pay much attention to the actual principles used in the production of causal judgements. One may add that the cognitive, particularly developmental, aspects of those principles are also neglected. This results in psychologically implausible descriptions. Subjects are said to receive and somehow assimilate 'cultural models', including cultural models of causation, but we have no description of what is received and how it could be transmitted. Some recent results in developmental psychology, which tend to correct the anthropological picture on a number of crucial points, are discussed below.

Constructivism and its limits

Anthropological reflections on causation tend to take for granted the hypothesis of a single cross-domain coherent notion of causation. This hypothesis is consistent with (and in Hallpike's case directly inspired by) a Piagetian developmental framework. The child is described as applying a number of structural domain-general principles to a variety of situations. Different formal principles characterize successive stages of development; once a principle is available to the child, it is applied to all domains. This domain-general approach is particularly clear in the description of causal thinking (Piaget 1930, 1954, 1974; Laurendau and Pinard 1962). The child is said to shift from an 'animistic' notion of causality to a more differentiated conception, in which intentional and mechanistic causation are adequately distinguished. For instance, 4-year-old children generally use an intentional vocabulary to account for the course of the clouds in the sky: the clouds 'want to go' somewhere or 'want to stay put', etc. However, 8-year-old children tend to prefer some mechanistic 'push–pull' type of explanation (Laurendau and Pinard 1962).* But even children at this stage of 'concrete operations' tend to invoke intentional causation in the

---

* According to Piaget, more subtle effects of the animistic principle can be seen in other domains. For instance, 6-year-old children seem generally unaware of the purely physical nature of shadows, and appear to construe them as things 'emanating' from objects and persons. The subjects state that shadows are things 'made' by people and objects; they also maintain that people 'make' shadows even at night, although it is too dark to see them (Piaget 1930, p. 187).

explanation of physical phenomena. It is only with the formal operational stage (about 11–12 years old) that the child develops a full understanding of causal connections.

This classical account has been criticized for a number of reasons. First, it does not make a precise enough distinction between the development of causal principles and the development of empirical knowledge. For instance, Piaget tends to score the child's explanations as 'non-causal' if they are causal but empirically wrong (Bullock *et al.* 1982; p. 219). The child's intentional descriptions of clouds and shadows may have more to do with his or her poor knowledge of those domains than with an intrinsically 'animistic' understanding of causation (Bullock 1985).* As Bullock *et al.* conclude, 'the development of causal understanding is more a process of learning where, when and how to apply the rules of [causal] reasoning rather than figuring out what these rules might be' (Bullock 1982, p. 216).

Moreover, the Piagetian description ignores the amount of information about causal relations that can be extracted from perceptual cues. Experiments show that these perceptual cues are crucial even at the earliest stages of causal thinking. In a series of classical studies, Michotte (1963) demonstrated that adult subjects can have strong stable intuitions about the 'causal' nature of the connections between the relative movements of dots on a screen, depending on precise variables in the relative movements. As Leslie puts it, 'all that is required on this account is the ability to detect certain formal properties of stimulation which "specify" a causal concept' (Leslie 1982, p. 185). In a series of dishabituation experiments with infants, Leslie and colleagues (Leslie 1979, 1982; Leslie and Keeble 1987) were able to show that such physical criteria for singling out causal events are present in children from early infancy.†

Two assumptions are crucial to the Piagetian account, and both are taken

---

* When tested on more familiar domains, children do not seem to exhibit an animistic bias. For instance, Bullock *et al.* (1982, p. 211) give a rough description of the common-sense notion of physical causation in terms of three abstract principles: **determinism**, following which no event can happen without a cause; **priority**, which states that causes precede effects; **mechanism**, the assumption that there must be a 'transfer of causal impetus', direct or indirect, between cause and effect. In all experiments concerning physical objects and simple mechanical processes, the children's explanations are invariably consistent with those three principles. In other words, the 'principle' of mechanical causation, if there is such a thing, cannot be acquired at the stage of 'concrete operations, since the child had it long before.
† From 18 weeks infants can indeed single out the specific spatio-temporal conditions which lead adults to interpret certain events as 'causal', and by 27 weeks they can distinguish between causal and non-causal versions of such events (see also Watson (1984) on the parameters of causal events in infants). Leslie and Keeble conclude that there is 'a visual mechanism, already operating at 27 weeks, which is responsible for organising a causal percept [. . .] Instead of causality being entirely a result of the gradual development of thought [. . .] an important and perhaps crucial contribution is made by the operation of a fairly low-level perceptual mechanism'. (Leslie and Keeble 1987, p. 285)

for granted in anthropological accounts of causal thinking. The first is that causal judgements are produced by applying a formally or abstractly defined domain-general notion of causation to domain-specific descriptions of events. The second is that the child's understanding of those abstract principles of causation is gradually modified by experience. Experimental research now tends to show that the child's causal concepts may be perceptually grounded (long before the child has any relevant practical experience of the events considered) and much more 'decentralized' in its principles than the Piagetian account assumed. Indeed, such research indicates that a whole variety of early-developed, intuitive principles constrain conceptual development, and that these principles constitute domain-specific understandings of particular ontological domains.

Intuitive domain-specific principles

The starting point of the 'domain-specific' approach is that, contrary to what a Piagetian framework would require, different conceptual domains are structured by different principles which (i) carry information about the types of stimuli that are likely to correspond to particular ontological categories, (ii) convey expectations about non-obvious properties of objects in the different domains, and (iii) constrain the manner in which spontaneous inductive inferences are made about objects from different domains. The fact that the availability of a given structural principle in one conceptual domain does not entail its application to other domains was demonstrated by Keil, for instance, in his studies of the 'characteristic to defining shift' (Keil and Batterman 1984; Keil 1986). Between the pre-school age and middle childhood, subjects tend to shift from an understanding of concepts based on characteristic properties (e.g. an uncle being an adult relative, friendly to parents) to an understanding based mainly on defining traits (uncles being siblings of parents, whatever their age). Now this shift occurs at different times for different ontological categories (kinship categories, artefacts, natural kinds, etc.). The fact that a given structural principle is available in one domain does *not* imply that it is applied to any other domain. The notion of formally defined stages, characterized by principles which apply across conceptual domains, has been replaced by a series of domain-specific developmental schedules, constrained by corresponding domain-specific principles.

These principles constitute the skeleton of 'intuitive' or 'naive' theories for these different domains. They are generally implicit, and seem to play a crucial role in the development of later, partly explicit, representations of the domains concerned, such as a theory of physical objects (Spelke 1990), a biology (Keil 1986, 1989), an understanding of mental processes (Astington *et al.* 1988; Wellmann 1990; Perner 1991; Whiten 1991), and an early understanding of number (Gelman and Greeno 1989) or of principles that structure social categorization (Hirschfeld 1988, 1989). These principles establish boundaries for each domain, which single out stimuli that are relevant to conceptual development in that domain. As Rochel Gelman puts it, 'different sets of principles guide the generation of different plans of action as well as the assimilation and structuring of experiences' (Gelman 1990; p. 80). It may be of help to illustrate these general points in the domains of intuitive physics, biology, and psychology.

Intuitive physical principles, notably concerning the properties of solid objects, orient the child's understanding of the physical environment from infancy. For instance, principles specifying that solid objects are cohesive and continuous, and are not susceptible to action at a distance, seem to emerge before 4 months (Leslie 1988; Baillargeon and Hanko-Summers 1990; Spelke 1990). Later developments (around 6 months) include the principle of support — that objects fall if they are not supported (Spelke 1990). Also, the child's sensitivity to specific patterns of movement allows him or her to make ontological distinctions from early stages of cognitive development. There is ample evidence, for instance, that a distinction between self-generated and non-self-generated movement is made by infants (Massey and Gelman 1988). This distinction gives an initial skeleton to a differentiation between **animate** and **inanimate** kinds of objects, which has important consequences for causal reasoning as we shall see presently.

The domain of biological reasoning is also the object of early developed principles, which orient the child's intuition of which objects are likely to have biological properties, and what kinds of unobservable features are likely to be present in such objects (Carey 1995). For instance, 4-year-old children seem confident that one can make inductive generalizations about living kinds on the basis of one exemplar, whilst this is not as 'safe' for artefacts. Moreover, they tend to think that not all properties of living kinds can be induced on the basis of one exemplar; they make such instance-based inductive generalizations more easily if the properties chosen are 'inherent' properties of the exemplars (ways of breathing and feeding) rather than properties like the weight of a given animal or its mobility (Gelman and Markman 1987; Gelman 1988). These theoretical assumptions are also manifest in children's reactions to putative scenarios of transformation from one kind to another. Such transformations are judged more plausible between types of artefacts than from one living kind to another, even in cases where an animal is described as having acquired the other's outside appearance or behaviour (Keil 1986). At a very early stage, children seem to be already reasoning on the basis of what Medin and Ortony (1989) call the principle of 'psychological essentialism', i.e. the belief that 'category membership [depends] upon the possession of some "hidden" [. . .]

properties of which observable properties are but typical signs' (Medin and Ortony 1989; p. 84).

In the same way, the psychological interpretation of other people's behaviour, in terms of their perceptions, beliefs, and intentions, is the object of early developed specific principles. In adults, routine ascriptions of beliefs and intentions are made on the basis of a number of tacit principles that describe mental entities and their functional relations. For instance, everyday 'belief–desire psychology' assumes that thoughts are not material entities—that they are caused by external states of affairs (which they may misdescribe) but do not cause them. It is also assumed that causal connections lead from perceptions to beliefs to intentions to actions, not the other way round. Such principles appear between the ages of 2 and 5. For instance, 3-year-old children know that thoughts are not mental entities, and they have a rudimentary causal framework to account for their occurence, including false beliefs (Wellmann and Estes 1986; Wellmann 1990). This goes against Piaget's notion of 'childhood realism', following which the child cannot represent the difference between mental and material entities. Also, the developmental schedule of these 'naive' psychological principles seems obviously underdetermined by the child's experience. For instance, children seem to develop an understanding of the consequences of false beliefs (i.e. the possibility that people are acting on the basis of mistaken descriptions of a state of affairs) from the age of 4 (Perner *et al.* 1987), although they have some of the necessary conceptual tools before that age (Leslie 1987), and this change does not seem to correlate with any significant changes in the child's social environment.

Causal understandings in intuitive principles

Intuitive domain-specific principles not only specify what properties distinguish ontological categories, but also postulate a causal structure to account for the stability of these categories. If the account is correct, it implies that, from the earliest stages of cognitive development, children use intrinsically *diverse* principles of causation. Take for instance the distinction between animate and inanimate objects. In a conjectural essay on causal perception in infants, Premack (1990) argues that the distinction between self- and non-self-propelled movement may constitute the basis of a conceptual distinction between physical and intentional types of causal connection.* Premack's hypothesis is that this perception-based distinction

---

* As Premack puts it, 'motion *per se* is not the critical parameter [. . .] change is what is critical, in velocity or direction [. . .] Induced changes in movement in non-self-propelled objects is what the infant perceives as physical causation [. . .] Changes in the movement of self-propelled objects are what, I suggest, the infant perceives as intentional' (Premack 1990, p. 3).

constitutes a skeleton, which is then conceptually enriched and partly modified as an **animate** versus **inanimate** distinction. Now the difference between **animate** and **inanimate** objects lies not only in the specific content of the causal hypotheses entertained by the child about these different categories, but also in the structure of explanations. Whilst the behaviour of inanimate objects is explained in terms of forces, thrust, obstacles, and resistance, that of animate objects is likely to be explained in terms of beliefs and intentions. In another domain, the development of early biological understandings for such processes as ageing, feeding, breathing, etc. shows the emergence of explanations focusing on the *normal function* of particular organs as the explanation for their existence and structure. To sum up, a distinction between three forms of causal explanation (mechanical, functional, intentional) seems to be grounded in the intuitive distinction between three ontological domains: **solid objects**, **living beings**, and **persons**. The ontological taxonomy and the differentiation between types Of causal propensities (and types of relevant explanations) are just different aspects of the same development of domain-specific principles. Classical models gave a unified concept of **cause** pride of place in cognitive development, as an originally unbiased correlation-sensitive device. However, this is not really the picture that emerges from domain-specific research. Causal understandings appear to be specialized at the onset of development, and to isolate certain types of connections as salient for a certain domain.

Experience and enrichment

One aspect of intuitive domain-specific principles is particularly important for the study of cultural representations. A central theme in the studies cited here is that prior principles provide the child with a series of definite *expectations* about the boundaries of ontological domains, and about certain properties of the objects that fall within these domains. The principles constitute a skeleton that is then completed by a process of *enrichment*. Enrichment leads from the broad initial distinctions between domains, provided by intuitive principles, to the complex theoretical structures that can be observed at a later stage. However, the principles themselves, together with the expectations that they trigger, cannot be described as the result of any specific tuition, and their developmental schedule is relatively independent from particular changes in the experienced environment. This should imply that they are not directly constrained by changes in the *cultural* environment. Indeed, there is ample evidence to show that important variations in cultural settings do not affect the content of intuitive presumptions or their developmental schedule in a significant way. Take for instance the question of the defining-to-characteristic shift, as described by Keil in

American children. In a series of field studies in Nigeria, Jeyifous (1985, 1992a, b) was able to show that the shift occurs in the same form at the same age in Yoruba subjects, with the same domain-specific characteristics. If anything, more variation can be found between rural and urban Yoruba subjects than between the Yoruba average and the American results. As regards biological knowledge, the universality of its basic principles is a familiar point (Berlin et al. 1973; Atran 1987, 1989, 1990). Together with the formal apparatus of taxonomic ranking, children in all cultural environments seem to develop an early understanding of the implicit 'essentialism' that is characteristic of common-sense understandings of living kinds. Finally, other aspects of conceptual development appear to be similar, even in domains which could give rise to strong cultural influences. For instance, Avis and Harris (1991) were able to show that early principles in the child's 'theory of mind' appear in much the same way in Pygmy children in Cameroon as in classical American conditions. The developmental schedule for an awareness of the possibility of false belief in other subjects is similar. Given the enormous differences in socio-cultural settings, it would of course require some quasi-miraculous coincidence for such shifts to occur at the same age and in the same way in the cultural environments compared.* In the remainder of this chapter I shall try to show how these facts can help us reformulate anthropological hypotheses as regards the acquisition of causal understandings, even in domains that may seem far removed from such intuitive structures.

RELIGIOUS ASSUMPTIONS AND THEIR INTUITIVE BACKGROUND

Let us now return to cultural representations proper. As mentioned above, it makes little sense to evaluate the contribution of cultural input and cognitive constraints to a particular domain unless we have a precise description of the representations actually entertained. There is no reason to think that cognitive constraints operate in the same way in all domains of cultural representations, so that most generalizations on the subject may turn out to be vacuous. Here I focus on the loosely defined domain of 'religious' and 'magical' representations, which has often been at the core of anthropological reflections on causation. After all, religious assumptions

---

* However, this is true only of the basic principles of belief–desire intuitive psychology. It does not apply to more complex structures, such as the explanation of behaviour in terms of traits and dispositions (see Chapter 11). Although children in all cultures seem to have the conceptual tools for such explanations, not all environments make such types of explanatory concepts equally salient.

in general seem to imply particularly strange notions as concerns the causal propensensities of particular objects or entities. Therefore we must understand how people are led to entertain thoughts which rely on those particular causal understandings. Here, again, I will be summarizing a general framework, the details of which can be found elsewhere (Boyer 1993a, 1994). The main point of this framework is that ordinary anthropological descriptions of religious and 'magical' categories and beliefs are essentially fragmentary. They focus on what is only a part of the assumptions involved in the representations in question. Once we have a proper description of the assumptions involved in the acquisition and representation of these categories, we can understand what makes certain types of causal judgements particularly likely to be entertained.

Recurrent counter-intuitive assumptions

Religious ontologies typically centre on a number of counter-intuitive assumptions which describe religious entities or objects in ways that clearly mark them off from the domain of everyday experience. For instance, spirits, ghosts, and gods are described as entities whose material properties are strikingly different from those of familiar objects. They are generally invisible and intangible, yet can produce physical effects in the observable world. Ghosts in the Western world are known to knock on walls and move heavy objects; in a more sinister way, in many human groups malevolent spirits are said to provoke illnesses or destroy crops. Gods and similar beings often have other counter-intuitive properties: for instance, they are immune to ordinary biological processes of growth, death, and decay. This notion of an invisible intangible being with remarkable material powers is so common that anthropologists like Tylor (1871) construed it as the defining criterion of 'religion'. However, there are many other counter-intuitive assumptions to be found in religious ontologies. Parts of a landscape (e.g. mountains or trees) can be said to have mental capacities, so that they 'watch' humans and have to be placated. In some cases, rocks or mountains are described as live beings, who need to be 'fed' by humans through ritual offerings (Bastien 1978).

I described these assumptions as 'counter-intuitive' and this point needs some explanation. In describing certain religious assumptions as counter-intuitive, I only claim that they violate people's *intuitive expectations* about what commonly takes place in their environment. For instance, some entities are described as invisible, yet located in space, and intangible, yet capable of mechanical action on physical objects; things fly in the air instead of falling to the ground; ageing and death do not affect certain beings, and so on. Representing such events or states as special and non-ordinary, because they are counter-intuitive, does not require a 'conception of nature'. It only requires intuitive expectations about the behaviour of physical objects in space, the biological processes which lead to death and decay, the mental processes underlying intentional behaviour, etc. Intuitive principles should not be confused with whatever explicit representations people entertain about what 'nature' is or what is 'natural' or what theoretical account can be given of observed regularities in the environment.* As will be shown in the following sections, there is some experimental evidence to show that such expectations are produced by universal cognitive structures, so that expectations do not vary with cultural environments. Against the background of these principles, of which only a small subset is accessible to the subject's consciousness, certain events and representations stand out as intuitively 'unnatural', to use a handy term.

The widespread anthropological notion, that apparently 'un-natural' religious representations are in fact perfectly natural in the appropriate 'cultural context', is in fact implausible. Remember that we are dealing with assumptions, inferences, and actions which elicit considerable interest in the groups concerned. For want of a better term, we can describe these religious representations as highly salient or *attention-demanding*. They focus people's attention (and often generate emotional responses) to an extent that is remarkable, and certainly deserves some explanation. Now, whatever that explanation is, it seems difficult to base it on the idea that religious assumptions are held as perfectly natural. Imagine, as a thought experiment, trying to found a religious system on assumptions like the following: objects dropped will fall downwards, people have thoughts and feelings, mountains are solid objects, dead men do not talk, and so on. The attention-demanding nature of religious representations is a necessary characteristic, for which their counter-intuitive nature may be the simplest sufficient explanation.†

Counter-intuitive assumptions and the rest: an example

The counter-intuitive claims are extensively documented in anthropological descriptions. However, these descriptions are essentially fragmentary; they

---

* In many societies, there is simply no such explicit conception. In some places, however, either isolated individual reasonings or whole traditions are elaborated, the point of which is to reflect on the regularities of the environment. Such elaborations display great cross-cultural variations. As Lloyd (1991, pp. 417–34) points out, nothing could seem more straightforward, but nothing is in fact more distant from modern Western science than the Greek notion of *physis*.

† In view of some anthropological confusion on this problem, it must be emphasized that intuitive naturalness and intuitive 'realness' are distinct features. People may find it unnatural to think that corpses can talk, yet have the representation that in certain contexts they *really* do talk. It is precisely to the extent that such events are represented as real that their unnaturalness is attention-demanding.

make no mention of a host of additional assumptions which are crucial to a description of the cognitive processes involved. This will be easier to show using a particular example, and since the notion of 'spirits' is traditionally taken as central to religious ideas, I shall briefly describe one such conception from Lambek's description of spirit possession on the island of Mayotte (Lambek 1981).

The religious life of Mayotte islanders combines adherence to Sunni Islam with a variety of activities centred on spirit possession. The spirits in question are conceived as wandering, generally inopportune, but not necessarily malevolent invisible beings. The spirits have, as spirits generally do, strange physical characteristics. They are of course invisible, they are not hampered by physical obstacles, and they can travel extremely fast (however, the islanders are adamant that they cannot be in two places at the same time, so that two people cannot be possessed by the same spirit). There are many different kinds of spirits, conceived as different species 'identified not on the basis of abstract principles . . . but by concrete signs, by the peculiar customs and habits ascribed to the class' (Lambek 1981, p. 34). For instance, the *patros* spirits are said to dwell in underwater villages, the location which is imprecise. One of their striking characteristics is their diet, made manifest by their demands during possession; they typically ingest handfuls of sugar and liver, and drink cologne as well as the blood of chickens or goats. Their main contact with humans occurs during possession; in the local terms, they 'rise to the head' of a particular individual. According to the islanders, the spirits take 'temporary control of all bodily and human functions . . . A rigorous distinction is maintained between the identity of the individual who enters and leaves the trance state and the individual who is actually present during the former's trance . . . During the trance the human host is absent, no one can say where, and is temporarily replaced by the spirit' (Lambek 1981, p. 40). During the possession, the spirit makes all sorts of excessive demands, in terms of foods and offerings, against the 'releases' of the possessed person. The relatives try to persuade the spirit to settle for a reasonable agreement.

Lambek gives several examples of such possession episodes, and of the difficult negotiations with spirits. In one of those cases (Lambek 1981, p. 71 ff.), a spirit 'rises' to the head of a woman, Mohedja, ostensibly to warn the family of an impending illness, and recommends that a blessing ritual should be performed to avoid it. The spirit identifies himself and declares that he has been regularly 'rising' in people of the village for some years now, to warn them of various dangers. He claims to have a particular connection with Tumbu, another member of the family: 'Tumbu had given the spirit many gifts over the years, and in return the spirit liked to help him out whenever he could'. The spirit states that he has tried to warn Mohedja 'directly', i.e. through her dreams, but she did not heed the warnings. Also, he blames Mohedja for being overconfident; this is an allusion to an incident in which she had starkly rebuked a man who wanted to sleep with her; the spirit states that Mohedja should have shown more tact in her refusal, if only to avoid angering the man. He points out that Mohedia should not complain about possession because he is only trying to help her. After having drunk some cologne, the spirit finally departs, and Mohedja regains consciousness. The family communicates to her the spirit's warnings, which she hears with great interest and some surprise, having no recollection of what happened during the possession episode.

The tacit intuitive background

These ideas about spirits and their efforts to communicate with people may seem like an accumulation of conceptual oddities, of counter-intuitive claims. As stated above, our description would be essentially incomplete if we stopped at this point. In order to understand what people believe about these spirits, and how they are led to form those beliefs, we must also describe a number of implicit, often tacit, assumptions which constitute the background of these ideas. Counterintuitive exchanges, with an invisible being that temporarily 'dislodges' a person from his or her body, are based on a host of implicit, but definite and constraining, assumptions. To begin with, each spirit is supposed to belong to a certain *kind*, with essential characteristics and typical causal propensities. As Lambek (1981, p. 35) points out, there are several *kbila* or types of spirits; although *kbila* derives from the Arabic *qbila*, 'tribe', these are in fact conceived as different *species*. A consequence of this principle is that identifying the spirit as belonging to a particular *kbila* entails particular expectations about its powers and typical behaviour. Conversely, once a spirit is identified as belonging to a particular type, most features of his behaviour can be generalized inductively as potential features of the type as a whole. The importance of this type of essentialist understanding for the acquisition of religious categories has been emphasized (Boyer 1993*b*). In most cultural environments, people do not build their understanding of supernatural entities on the sole basis of explicit tuition. They (often by necessity) also rely on ostensive presentations, in situations where there is a clear indication that spirits, ancestors, etc. are involved. The tacit essentialist assumption entails that particular aspects of those situations can figure as potential instance-based generalizations in an understanding of the causal powers of the entities in question. As will be argued below, such essence-based understandings need not be culturally transmitted; they belong to spontaneous hypotheses which are triggered by cultural cues.

Another set of background assumptions, perhaps more directly relevant to the example, is made manifest by the fact that the exchanges with spirits would not be possible if the participants did not project onto the spirits a set of precise *psychological* assumptions concerning the spirits' mental states and mental processes. As Lambek (1981, p. 43) points out, the spirits 'have desires, they calculate, they may study and be learned'. The spirits are assumed to *know* certain facts, to have *beliefs*; they are also described as *wanting* certain events to happen. To be more precise, it is assumed that spirits form beliefs on the basis of perceptions, and intentions on the basis of their beliefs, and that they act on the basis of their intentions. If they are said to want P, and are assumed to know that P cannot obtain unless Q, then they are assumed to want Q. These complex hypotheses never made explicit, and most participants in these possession episodes are not even aware of them, yet they form a necessary background to all the 'conversations' that take place in these counter-intuitive circumstances.

All these assumptions may seem trivial or self-evident. This is probably the reason why they are not the object of much attention in anthropological theory. Indeed, they *are* self-evident or, rather, transparent to most human subjects because they confirm the intuitive expectations that we constantly apply to the understanding of everyday situations, without necessarily being aware of their content. The fact that such assumptions are self-evident to common sense does not mean that they are theoretically unimportant. On the contrary, I would argue that we cannot understand the cognitive processes involved in the acquisition of religious ideas unless we focus on the content and consequences of those intuitive expectations.

Violations, confirmation, and inferences

The hypothesis here was illustrated by a single example, that of Lambek's account of spirit possession in Mayotte. However, the main point is not directly dependent on the particular case, but applies more generally to a variety of religious categories (for other examples, see Boyer (1992*a*, 1993*a*, *b*, 1994). The general hypothesis is that religious ontologies and their causal implications comprise two types of assumptions. On the one hand, some assumptions constitute direct *violations* of intuitive expectations. On the other assumptions constitute direct *confirmations* of these expectations. These two types differ in terms of (i) origin, (ii) representational status, and (iii) functional properties.

Counter-intuitive assumptions are generally part of the cultural input; they are acquired in the context of social interaction, in most cases through direct stimulation from cultural peers and elders. In contrast, I have tried to show above that detailed expectations concerning ontological domains appear in similar forms in very different cultural environments, and are not greatly affected by differences in the environment experienced. Indeed, some of these basic principles could not be acquired through experience, simply because they are necessary for experience, i.e. for a structured apprehension of stimuli.

As a consequence, the assumptions also differ in representational status. Most counter-intuitive assumptions described here are the object of explicit representations. It should be noticed that they need not be explicitly transmitted, as long as they are directly entailed by cultural transmission. For instance, it is possible to convey the idea that spirits are invisible without ever uttering the generalizing statement that 'spirits are invisible'. The important point is that the counter-intuitive part of religious assumptions is always *available* as an explicit explanatory principle. By contrast, the intuitive expectations are implicit, and indeed tacit, in the course of most cognitive activities. Obviously, some individuals are perceptive enough to grasp some of the tacit intuitions on which most of their thinking is based, but this is clearly exceptional. In the same way, some institutionalized groups (e.g. philosophers or experimental psychologists) devote some of their time to the description of intuitive expectations. But again, this is not necessary for, and has little effect on, the usual inferential processes based on such intuitive expectations.

The difference in functional role is particularly striking. On the whole, counter-intuitive assumptions often have a particularly weak inferential potential. That is to say, to accept them as descriptions of particular entities or events does not lead to rich or richly structured chains of inferences. If we admit that spirits are invisible, this obviously has some direct consequences for people who try to detect their presence or locate them. Beyond such direct entailments, however, it is difficult to determine what could be expected from spirits on the basis of the counter-intuitive description. In contrast, the confirming assumptions typically have a strong inferential potential. To pursue the same example, to accept that spirits have minds which form beliefs out of perceptions, intentions out of beliefs and desires, and so on, gives the subject a grip on a rich explanatory framework for their behaviour. The statements accepted as a description of the spirits can then be the object of a variety of non-demonstrative inferences, for example inferring intentions from behaviour, beliefs from intentions, and so on.

The main hypothesis here is that only religious representations which combine such violations and confirmations of intuitive expectations are likely to be acquired and transmitted in such a way that they become the widely distributed representations that we usually call 'cultural'. Obviously, the conceptual structure described here is not a sufficient condition for distribution and stability, on which a variety of extraneous factors are likely to impinge. However, the claim is that all else being equal, we should not be surprised if most widespread religious representations combine (i) a high degree of attention-demanding potential, as a consequence of the counter-intuitive assumptions, with (ii) a high inferential potential, resulting from the confirmation of intuitive expectations.

Underspecified conceptual structures

A consequence of the hypothesis presented above is that religious categories are based on *underspecified* conceptual structures. This point deserves some explanation, as it has important consequences for the representation of causal judgements. Most anthropological models imply that religious understandings are based on some kind of 'theory' of religious entities and events. This is obviously true, if it only means that there is a loosely organized set of assumptions directing people's expectations in that domain. However, this vague description cannot be sufficient as an account of the representation of religious categories.

Most ordinary concepts correspond to stable clusters of interconnected assumptions (Murphy and Medin 1985; Medin and Wattenmaker 1987)* These not only establish the relative relevance of different attributes for categorization, but they also provide explanations for the presence of the attributes: 'people not only notice feature correlations, but they can deduce reasons for them based on their knowledge of the way the world works' (Medin and Wattenmaker 1987, p. 36). For certain categories, however, the clusters seem to be indeterminate at certain crucial junctures, and this is typically (although not exclusively) the case for religious categories. Take for instance the case of the Mayotte spirits, mentioned above. The cohesiveness of the category is given in this case by a series of definite assumptions about the special properties of the spirits, as well as a host of tacit default assumptions. However, it must be noticed that there are obvious gaps in the network of assumptions. For instance, the spirits are described as living underwater, but there is no description of the properties that would allow them to do so. Of course, pople are familiar with under-water animals, but it does not seem that they apply any of their knowledge of those species to their understanding of the spirits. In the same way, spirits are said to 'rise to people's heads' during possession, but there is no understanding of this process beyond this metaphorical description. Again, to take less salient aspects of the phenomenon, the possessed person's mind is said to be 'somewhere else' during possession, but no one seems to have precise hypotheses about what happens. More generally, one can say that all such religious categories display this underspecified structure. Religious

---

* Obviously, such assumptions and their links do not exhaust the features of conceptual structures. Concepts also include such features as (typically) a verbal label, semantic indicators (such as countability), etc. These features are irrelevant to the points made here.

entities are given counter-intuitive properties, which are not integrated in a network of causal assumptions to the same degree as assumptions describing ordinary concepts. Spirits can go through walls, but it is not clear whether they can go through one another. Spirits are said to have 'beliefs' and 'memories', and usually such mental entities are supposed to be stored in people's heads, but the seemingly obvious inference to draw from this, namely that spirits must have (suitably special) heads, is simply not made, not even implicitly. One reason why such inferences and assumptions are missing is simply that they are irrelevant to the kind of inferential and speculative reasonings that people are engaged in as far as spirits are concerned. To return to the case of the *patros* spirits, what matters is the tenor and consequences of their relationship with particular people. Of course, this relationship is affected by the spirits' special capacities and properties. But the technicalities of those capacities, the precise ways in which disembodied beings can store memories and beliefs, do not matter, and therefore are left unspecified.*

CAUSAL SCENARIOS AND ABDUCTION

Some consequences of this model are now examined in more detail for an understanding of the acquisition and development of causal understandings. What we have shown so far is that the fundamental principles underlying causal understandings (i) are not culturally specific, (ii) are domain-specific in a way that can be found in all cultural environments, and (iii) are activated even in domains which seem mainly structured around counter-intuitive assumptions such as religious representations. However, it is not enough to show that intuitive domain-specific principles constitute part of the representation of religious ontologies. We must also show how they happen to be activated in the interpretation of a fragmentary, not entirely coherent, cultural input. In the description of these processes, I shall mainly consider religious and 'magical' assumptions again, although the argument also applies to other domains of cultural representations.

Empty causal schemes and abductive filling

The fact that religious categories are based on underspecified conceptual structures has important consequences for the type of causal judgements

---

* These underspecified conceptual structures correspond to what Kant (1790, §59) described as 'symbolic presentations', in contrast with 'schematic' representations. The relevance of this point for cultural elaborations is stressed by Atran (1990, p. 215), who calls such representations 'non-schematized'. In a similar way, Sperber (1982) has argued that most religious symbolism is directed as 'semi-propositional' objects.

that can be made on the basis of such categories. In order to examine this point, let me first describe briefly what is wrong with ordinary anthropological analyses of causal claims in the domains of religion and 'magic'. The anthropological interpretation tends to assume that, for each and every causal judgement, 'A caused B', there is an implicit general principle or theoretical statement to the effect that 'As cause Bs'. People who claim that reciting a spell can make crops grow are assumed to entertain general theories about spells and crops, which would warrant the particular causal connections that they hold valid. In other words, the anthropological view here is a straightforward statement of the **covering-law** account of causal judgements.

As it happens, the domain of 'magical' or religious judgements is probably one where such a covering-law account is particularly inadequate. The connection between putative general principles and the singular causal judgement is not that between a theoretical principle and a deductive application to a singular case. This is because (i) there is no certainty about the identification of the current situation as precisely an example of A and B, and (ii) because the principle itself ('As cause Bs') is generally represented as a plausible conjecture, not as a certain fact (Boyer 1992*b*). To sum up, the process that leads to accepting 'magical' claims seems to be essentially characterized by *abductive* inferences. The principles are tentatively accepted as explanation of the current situation, in so far as they can provide a context in which the connection between A and B is made less surprising.

This has important consequences. The connection between the singular states or events A and B in such cases is represented as a **causal scenario**, i.e. as the single assumption that 'A caused B'. An important property of causal scenarios, as opposed to deductions from a theoretical principle, is that they may be *underspecified* in both their content and their logical structure. Take the example of the representation that 'reciting the spell XYZ killed so-and-so'. People who hold this as a true description of what happened to so-and-so may have no definite representations about which general principle is involved here: Is it all magical spells that kill or only this one? Is it the case that any magical spells would have killed him, or only this precise one? What are the other necessary conditions? etc. Accepting the causal scenario commits one to accepting a counterfactual, but it is not exactly clear which counterfactual is being accepted. Indeed, in most cases of 'magical' connections, it is clear that what is accepted is, as it were, an **empty causal scenario**, to the effect that 'there is a state C, such that it made it possible for A to cause B'. Finding good candidates for the abductive explanation surely makes the connection between A and B more plausible, but again we must keep in mind that representing 'A caused B, because of C' does not necessarily depend on having *any* candidate for C.

Epistemic states

This notion of 'candidates' introduces an aspect of these processes which is crucial to a description of cultural acquisition. In the context of abductive inferences, a proposition (or any other form of representation, henceforth called an 'assumption') is entertained as a conjectural description of the current state of affairs. Assumptions which are activated in this way can vary in their credal status or **strength**. They command graded commitment between possible conjectures and certain truths. Second, these assumptions can vary in **salience**, i.e. in the probability that they will be activated, given a certain situation. Credal status and salience must be distinguished because there are many situations in which an assumption can have a low credal status and a high salience. The study of cultural acquisition is hampered by the absence of a proper understanding of **epistemic states**, which describe mechanisms underlying the dynamics of strength and salience. There is a considerable literature on 'degrees of belief' and on states that can be characterized by uncertainty or by less than complete commitment to a particular belief (see general surveys in Cohen (1977) and Smithson (1989). However, this literature does not really give us the theoretical basis for a satisfactory description of cognitive strength and salience.* These reservations explain why the present argument has to remain speculative. Although it is quite clear that a range of cognitive phenomena must be described in terms of epistemic states, there is simply no framework to account, in a descriptive way, for the functional properties of those states in qualitatively rich ways. However, the particular properties of certain conceptual domains make it possible to put forward speculative descriptions of strengthening, and this is what I shall try to do as concerns religious representations, particularly the limiting case of 'magical' connections.

---

* On the whole, the study of epistemic states has focused on aspects of the question which are irrelevant to our problems, for three reasons. First and foremost, most studies of partial belief have been conducted within a *normative* framework. The point of such studies was to describe the conditions under which a rational agent should evaluate and revise belief, typically in situations of uncertainty. Second, even the non-normative literature generally construes credal states as an explicit *reflective* evaluation, by the subject, of his or her own degree of belief. In studies of 'judgement under uncertainty' (Tversky and Kahnemann 1974; Kahnemann *et al.* 1982), degrees of belief are still conceived in terms of subjective probability. However, this only measures one possible outcome of cognitive strength and salience, but not those properties themselves. Third, even studies which focus on the actual non-normative properties of epistemic states, and do not consider them only in terms of subjective probability (Holland *et al.* 1986), are based on the assumption that all phenomena of cognitive salience are unidimensional. That is to say, there is a metric of strength or commitment that ranks beliefs in terms of certainty, and is the *only* relevant dimension of epistemic states. Although such models are of great interest (and most of my remarks about salience are in fact inspired by Holland *et al.*'s 'induction theory'), we should not neglect the possibility that epistemic states are in fact richer, from a qualitative viewpoint, than such models assume.

Taxonomy, intuitive principles, and strengthening

As stated above, it is possible for people to represent a causal connection as an empty scenario which includes an existential hypothesis of the form 'there is an unspecified state C, such that A caused B' ('there is something going on, that allowed this spell to cause that illness'). In some cases, the scenario can remain underspecified and become stronger because of straightforward correlations, for instance if most occurrences of curses are actually followed by the effect that they predict. In such cases, people's epistemic state towards the scenario that 'curses do have the effect they predict' will be predictably strengthened. However, this phenomenon is certainly not the most important aspect of strengthening, particularly not in the domain of magical claims where positive evidence is not really relevant. Far more important, from a cognitive viewpoint, are the processes whereby an empty causal scenario is filled with abductive assumptions. In the above description, I simply said that abductive inferences would provide whatever material is relevant to the causal scenario entertained. But we can in fact go further, and describe certain regular features of this phenomenon.

For instance, a central feature of 'magical techniques', i.e. techniques in which 'recipes' are followed in order to attain a particular goal, is that the technician's attention is focused on various manipulations supposed to make particular ingredients 'special'. This is indeed why those ritual techniques are generally called 'recipes'. Now, an interesting property of such recipes is that they are supposed to modify the identity of the ingredients. A particular item (e.g. a stone, a lock of hair, a piece of clothing) is 'prepared' in such a way that it is no longer exactly the same as any other stone, lock of hair, or piece of clothing. It has acquired particular causal propensities. In these ritual preparations, one can see a demonstration of a familiar principle, following which taxonomic identification and the description of causal propensities are two aspects of the same process. Things belong to the same category only inasmuch as they share causal propensities, and to different categories inasmuch as they differ in causal propensities. In the magical preparations, a series of elements leads to representation of the prepared object as belonging to another, special, category which in most cases is left unnamed. This in turn is likely to make the assumption of particular causal powers more salient.

This makes it possible to describe the constraints imposed by intuitive domain-specific principles on magical claims. The explicit point of a magical claim is to make a certain connection which violates intuitive ontologies. This type of connection has some initial salience, simply by virtue of being counter-intuitive (this is what was described above as 'attention-demanding'). However, the scenarios are unlikely to gain strength unless they are filled with abductive assumptions which themselves have considerable strength. The fact that different kinds of objects, notably different *natural* kinds, correspond to different causal propensities, is one of those strong principles. Therefore a causal scenario based on the special use of a transformed object will be made stronger, inasmuch as some assumptions are available which would make it plausible that the object belongs to a particular kind, by virtue of the transformations. This constitutes a general illustration of the principle described above in the case of the Mayotte spirits. Causal propensities are assumed to be typically similar within a particular kind of object, so that category membership and causal expectations reinforce each other. This is also a reason why magical claims are often strengthened by the fact that they are made by particular people, supposed to be endowed with particular capacities. Again, the hypothesis of such 'pseudo-natural kinds' of people strengthen the expectation of specific causal powers. The strength of the causal scenarios involving these persons is a function of the salience of the assumption that makes them naturally different from others.

CONCLUSION: SALIENCE, RECURRENCE, AND CULTURAL REPRESENTATION

Some consequences of these hypotheses for a general understandings of causal understandings in cultural representations are now outlined. This chapter started with the observations that the repertoire of causal judgements held valid is, obviously, culturally variable. However, this does not exclude that this variability is constrained by universal cognitive mechanisms, and a description of these constraints is the main aim of the present theory. A number of early-developed cognitive structures correspond to maturational properties of the mind-brain, and are only weakly influenced, if at all, by the experienced environment, including the social environment. Developmental studies show that such structures are much more specific, and constraining, than anthropological theories would assume. They orient the subject's attention towards certain types of cues, but also constitute definite presumptions about the existence of various ontological categories, as well as what can be expected from objects belonging to those different categories. Moreover, they provide the subject with what Keil (Chapter 9) calls 'modes of construal', i.e. formally different ways of recognizing similarities in the environment and making inferences from them. As we saw above, intuitive domain-specific principles inevitably include precise expectations about different types of causal processes projected onto different ontological domains. Thus the explanation of physical movement in terms of impetus, obstacles, and support does not require particular experience, but allows the development of an enriched set of causal expectations about physical objects. In the same way, the explanation of behaviour in terms of mental entities (beliefs and intentions) is not inferred from experience or tuition, but provides the background for more sophisticated causal expectations directed at people's behaviour.

Another source of information about causal processes is cultural input. In cultural anthropology, this input is generally described in terms of integrated sets of assumptions, such as cultural 'theories' or 'conceptions'. In contrast, the main conclusion to draw from the hypotheses presented here is that, in a fundamental sense, religious representations (and, more generally, cultural representations) are *underdetermined* by cultural transmission. Anthropological models generally tend to emphasize the extent to which in any specific group, representations receive their content and structure through social interaction. This is certainly true in the trivial sense that all cultural representations are acquired in the context of social interaction of some sort. However, this claim for cultural determination cannot be maintained if we pay closer attention to the actual processes whereby people gradually build adult 'competence' in most cultural domains. Subjects are not given theorized or explicit models of the cultural representations that they finally develop. Rather, they are given a number of disordered and fragmentary cultural cues, on the basis of which they build conceptual structures by accretion and stabilization of non-demonstrative inferences.

This is why I have tried here to emphasize the fact that cultural acquisition is an *inferential* process in which subjects develop categories by producing various types of non-demonstrative inferences on the basis of cultural cues. To insist on the inferential nature of this process has important consequences. Non-demonstrative inferences, by definition, are not entirely constrained by the cues that trigger them. Therefore the question of whether a given subject does or does not make a given inference by necessity probabilistic. This implies that we cannot talk about cultural acquisition as a simple process of *transmission* of established 'systems of representations'. All we can describe are the various factors that increase (or decrease) the probability of certain inferences being actually made by a members of a given goup.

Among these constraints, the domain-specific intuitive principles that appear in early conceptual development are particularly important. These principles influence the subjects' inferences as regards other types of cultural cues concerning, for instance, the causal properties of religious entities. As I have tried to show here, inferences in this domain are constrained by intuitive principles in two different ways. First, the cues can focus attention, and therefore become the object of inferences, only in so far as they imply recognizable violations of *some* intuitive expectations; second, they must permit the application of other intuitive expectations. The main prediction here is that cues which combine these features are more likely than others to be the object of strong chains of inferences. They are more likely to be used as the starting-point for abductive inferential reasonings. Consequently, they are more likely to appear in the relatively stable, relatively shared representations that we usually call 'cultural'.

Obviously, these are not the only constraints imposed on representations. The frequency of a cue, its apparent consistency with other cues, and the support given to it by external factors (such as the presence of literacy or the existence of transmission institutions such as schools) are among the obvious factors that constrain transmission. The point of this account, however, is that, all else being equal, the transmission process will, in the long run, favour counter-intuitive cues that allow for abductive inferences supported by intuitive principles. This is indeed what seems to happen, in the sense that cross-culturally recurrent features of religious representations are precisely of that type.

ACKNOWLEDGEMENTS

This chapter benefited greatly from suggestions and criticisms of an earlier version notably by Frank Keil, Alan Leslie, Geoffrey Lloyd, and Leonard Talmy.

REFERENCES

Astington, J. W., Harris, P. and Olson, D. R. (eds). (1988). *Developing theories of mind*. Cambridge University Press.

Atran, S. (1987). Ordinary contraints on the semantics of living kinds. A commonsense alternative to recent treatments of natural-object terms. *Mind and Language* 2, 27–63.

Atran, S. (1989). Basic conceptual domains. *Mind and Language* 4, 5–16.

Atran, S. (1990). *Cognitive foundations of natural history: towards an anthropology of science*. Cambridge University Press.

Avis, J. and Harris, P. L. (1991). Belief–desire reasoning among Baka children: evidence for a universal conception of mind. *Child Development* 62, 460–67.

Baillargeon, R. and Hanko-Summers, S. (1990). Is the object adequately supported by the bottom object? Young infants' understanding of support relations. *Cognitive Development* 5, 29–54.

Bastien, J. W. (1978). *Mountain of the condor. Metaphor and ritual in an Andean Ayllu*. West Publishing Co., St Paul, MN.

Berlin, B., Breedlove, D. and Raven, P. (1973). General principles of classification and nomenclature in folk-biology. *American Anthropologist* 75, 214–42.

Boyer, P. (1992a). Explaining religious ideas: outline of a cognitive approach. *Numen* 39, 27–57.

Boyer, P. (1992b). Causal thinking and its anthropological misrepresentation. *Philosophy of Social Science* 22, 187–213.

Boyer, P. (1993a). Introduction: cognitive aspects of religious symbolism. In *Cognitive aspects of religious symbolism* (ed P. Boyer). Cambridge University Press.
Boyer, P. (1993b). Pseudo-natural kinds. In *Cognitive aspects of religious symbolism*. (ed P. Boyer). Cambridge University Press.
Boyer, P. (1994). *The naturalness of religious ideas: outline of a cognitive theory of religion*. University of California Press, Los Angeles, CA.
Bullock, M. (1985). Animism in childhood thinking: a new look at an old question. *Developmental Psychology* **21**, 217-25.
Bullock, M., Gelman, R. and Baillargeon, R. (1982). The development of causal reasoning. In *The developmental psychology of time* (ed W. J. Friedman). Academic Press, New York.
Carey, S. (1985). *Conceptual change in childhood*. MIT Press, Cambridge, MA.
Cohen, L. J. (1977). *The probable and the provable*. Clarendon Press, Oxford.
Gelman, R. (1990). First principles organize attention to and learning about relevant data: number and the animate–inanimate distinction as examples. *Cognitive Science* **14**, 79-106.
Gelman, R. and Greeno, J. (1989). On the nature of competence: principles for understanding in a domain. In *Knowing and learning: essays in honor of Robert Glaser* (ed L. B. Resnick). Erlbaum, Hillsdale, NJ.
Gelman, S. (1988). The development of induction within natural kind and artefact categories. *Cognitive Psychology* **20**, 65-95.
Gelman, S. and Markman, E. (1987). Young children's inductions from natural kinds: the role of categories and appearances. *Child Development* **58**, 32-41.
Hallpike, C. R. (1979). *The foundations of primitive thought*. Clarendon Press, Oxford.
Harris, P. and Heelas, P. (1979). Cognitive processes and collective representations. *European Journal of Sociology* **20**, 211-41.
Hart, H. L. A. and Honoré, T. (1959). *Causation in the law*. Clarendon Press, Oxford.
Hirschfeld, L. A. (1988). On acquiring social categories. Cognitive development and anthropological wisdom. *Man* **23**, 611-38.
Hirschfeld, L. A. (1989). Rethinking the acquisition of kinship terms. *International Journal of Behavioural Development* **12**, 541-68.
Holland, J. H., Holyoak, K. J., Nisbett, R. E. and Thagard, P. R. (1986). *Induction. Process of inference, learning and discovery*. MIT Press, Cambridge, MA.
Hutchins, E. (1981). Reasoning in Trobriand discourse. In *Language, culture and cognition* (ed R. W. Casson). MacMillan, New York.
Jeyifous, S. (1985). Atimodemo: semantic conceptual development among the Yoruba. PhD Thesis, Cornell University.
Jeyifous, S. (1992a). Supernatural beliefs, natural kinds and conceptual structure. *Memory and Cognition* **20**, 655-62.
Jeyifous, S. (1992b). Developmental changes in the representation of word-meaning: cross-cultural findings. *British Journal of Devlopmental Psychology* **10**, 285-99.
Kahnemann, D., Slovic, P. and Tversky, A. (ed). (1982). *Judgement under uncertainty: heuristics and biases*. Cambridge University Press.
Kant, I. (1790). *Kritik der Urteilskraft*. Königsberg.
Keil, F. C. (1986). On the structure-depdendent nature of stages of cognitive development. In *Stage and structure: reopening the debate* (ed I. Levin). Ablex, Hillsdale, NJ.

Keil, F. C. (1989). *Concepts, kinds and conceptual development*. MIT Press, Cambridge, MA.

Keil, F. C. and Batterman, N. (1984). A characteristic-to-defining shift in the development of word meaning. *Journal of Verbal Learning and Verbal Behaviour* **23**, 221–36.

Lakoff, G. (1987). *Women, fire and dangerous things. What categories reveal about the mind*. University of Chicago Press.

Lambek, M. (1981). *Human spirits: A cultural account of trance in Mayotte*. Cambridge University Press.

Laurendau, M. and Pinard, A. (1962). *Causal thinking in the child*. International Universities Press, New York.

Lee, D. D. (1949). Being and value in a primitive culture. *Journal of Philosophy* **8**(13), 401–15.

Leslie, A. (1979). The representation of perceived causal connection. D.Phil. Thesis, University of Oxford.

Leslie, A. (1982). The perception of causality in infants. *Perception* **11**, 173–86.

Leslie, A. (1987). Pretense and representation: the origins of 'theory of mind'. *Psychological Review* **94**, 412–26.

Leslie, A. (1988). The necessity of illusion: perception and thought in infancy. In *Thought without language* (ed L. Weizkrantz). Clarendon Press, Oxford.

Leslie, A. and Keeble, S. (1987). Do six-months old infants perceive causality? *Cognition* **25**, 265–88.

Lloyd, G. E. R. (1991). *Methods and problems in Greek science*. Cambridge University Press.

Massey, C. and Gelman, R. (1988). Preschoolers' ability to decide whether pictured unfamiliar objects can move themselves. *Developmental Psychology* **24**, 307–17.

Medin, D. L. and Ortony, A. (1989) Psychological essentialism. In *Similarity and analogical reasoning*. (ed S. Vosniadou and A. Ortony). Cambridge University Press.

Medin, D. L. and Wattenmaker, D. (1987). Category cohesiveness, theories and cognitive archaeology. In *Concepts and conceptual development: ecological and intellectual factors in categorization* (ed U. Neisser). Cambridge University Press.

Michotte, A. E. (1963). *The perception of causality*. Basic Books, New York.

Miller, R. (1987). *Fact and method. Explanation, confirmation and reality in the natural and the social sciences*. Princeton University Press.

Murphy, G. L. and Medin, D. L. (1985). The role of theories in conceptual coherence. *Psychological Review* **92**, 289–316.

Needham, R. (1976). Skulls and causality. *Man* (NS) **11**, 71–88.

Perner, J. (1991). *Understanding the representation mind*. MIT Press, Cambridge, MA.

Perner, J., Leekham, S. R. and Wimmer, H. (1987). Three year olds' difficulties with false belief: the case for a conceptual deficit. *British Journal of Developmental Psychology* **5**, 125–37.

Piaget, J. (1930). *The child's conception of physical causality*. Routledge & Kegan Paul, London.

Piaget, J. (1954). *The child's construction of reality*. Basic Books, New York.

Piaget, J. (1974). *Understanding causality*. Norton, New York.

Premack, D. (1990). The infant's theory of self-propelled objects. *Cognition* **36**, 1–16.

Smithson, M. (1989). *Ignorance and uncertainty. Emerging paradigms*. Springer-Verlag, New York.

Spelke, E. S. (1990). Principles of object perception. *Cognitive Science* 14, 29–56.

Sperber, D. (1982). Apparently irrational beliefs. In *Rationality and relativism* (ed M. Hollis and S. Lukes). Blackwell, Oxford.

Tversky, A. and Kahnemann, D. (1974). Judgement under uncertainty: heuristics and biases. *Science* 185, 1124–31.

Tylor, E. B. (1871). *Primitive culture*. John Murray, London.

Watson, J. S. (1984). Bases of causal inference in infancy: time, space and sensory relations. In *Advances in infancy research* (ed L. P. Lipsit and C. Rovee-Collier). Ablax, Hillsdale, NJ.

Wellmann, H. M. (1990). *The child's theory of mind*. MIT Press, Cambridge, MA.

Wellmann, H. and Estes, D. (1986). Early understanding of mental entities: a re-examination of childhood realism. *Child Development* 57: 910–23.

Whiten, A. (ed). (1991). *Natural theories of mind: the evolution, development and simulation of everyday mindreading*. Blackwell, Oxford.

DISCUSSION

Participants: F. Keil, A. Leslie, G. Lloyd, L. Talmy

Leslie: The conservatism you described in religious thought is a feature of all counterfactual thought, in which the 'possible world' that one creates is minimally different from what one assumes is true of the real world. Furthermore, each point of divergence must be made explicit or inferable from what is made explicit. This same conservatism shows up in very early counterfactual reasoning, i.e. in pretend play in 2-year-old children. For example, a 2-year-old child will pretend to fill an empty cup and then pretend to upturn the cup. I showed that, under these circumstances, the child will infer that an object or surface below the cup will now be 'wet'. In other words, the child will spontaneously infer that the pretend liquid will go downwards rather than up. Now, it is possible to persuade the child to pretend that the liquid will go up, but then the idea has to be marked in some way and will not be employed by default. Therefore I would think that the kind of conservatism you discussed is a cognitive universal and this a cultural universal also.

Boyer: There are, in fact, a whole range of situations in which people activate assumptions in this way, typically when producing inferences on the basis of some underspecified set of assumptions. Most analogies are only partly specified, in the sense that the extent to which one should operate a transfer of properties from source to target is not necessarily explicit. In a similar way, the understanding of metaphorical utterances requires a transfer of assumptions, from vehicle to tenor, whose scope is often left underspecified and must be established by pragmatic inference. The understanding of fiction also requires a partial transfer of assumptions, whose limits are not always determined by the features of text. Obviously, the understanding of any counterfactual scenario requires that the subject accept, for the sake of speculation, a number of assumptions whose consequences are only partly specified (imagining for instance that 'kangaroos would not jump so far if they had shorter legs' does not require any precise hypothesis about their posture or gait under those conditions). This is exactly what happens in the understanding of religious categories, in the sense that tacit assumptions are activated only to the extent that they are relevant to the particular inferences that the subject is making about the religious entity. However, there is a major difference between such situations and religious categories, in that the latter constitute *stable* conceptual structures as opposed to transient speculative representations. The particular mix of intuitive and counter-intuitive assumptions, which leaves some aspects of the entity underspecified, actually constitutes a labelled category. This may not be special to religious categories, of course, but means that we are dealing with a particular extension of this speculative mechanism, which I agree is certainly a cognitive and cultural universal.

Keil: There are two quite different ways of suspending belief. First, one can violate just one very specific principle and be particularly zealous at keeping the rest of the belief system intact so as to continue to render things sensible and comprehensible, and it cannot be a principle that figures so centrally that its suspension alone undermines a domain. Even the most fanciful science fiction takes care to be scrupulous, with most of its novel worlds being like ours, or else nothing makes sense. Alternatively, one can completely shift all assumptions briefly in a specific context, such as saying that ghosts are just like normal physical objects in their interactions with each other and other things in the world, except that we shall treat them like shadows in their interactions with our world. Which method of suspension is more likely? If you think that both are, where is each type more common and why?

Boyer: There is simply no empirical evidence at the moment that would allow us to answer this in anything but a very speculative way. There is probably no definite answer in any case. As I said in the paper, we are dealing here with partly specified conceptual structures. As a result, the acquisition and pertinent use of these categories do not require that all subjects in a given group fill the gaps in that structure in the same way. It is not even necessary that they all have some assumptions to fill them. However, what is given by the cultural input would probably orient people towards the understanding described in your first alternative. This is simply because, as we said above (see Leslie's question and my answer), this potential activation of all default assumptions, except the ones that are directly contradicted by the situation imagined, is a prevalent mode of speculation that is necessarily exercised in many contexts in addition to the the representation of religious ontologies.

Talmy: You say that ghost and spirit phenomena obey all the usual causal expectations for physical or social entities, with only a few exceptions intended as attention-attractors, and you imply that these exceptions could be fully random. However, it appears to me that there is much structure to the exceptions. First, it can be noted that certain kinds of exceptions, such as invisibility and passing through walls, are recurrent, whereas other kinds of exceptions, which on other grounds might have equally seemed to be candidates for conceptualization, appear, by your own account, never to occur. An example of this is temporally backwards causality. If it is true that there is structure governing which exceptions may and may not occur, then the next question is what principles govern such allowed and disallowed occurrences.

Let me offer a possible explanation for the exceptional phenomena that do occur. They may well constitute conceptual phenomena that already exist in other cognitive systems—cognitive phenomena which are then tapped for service in cultural spirit ascriptions. As one example, languages extensively manifest what I term the 'fictive motion' system whereby phenomena which on other grounds are static are treated in terms of motion or other kinds of change. One example of such fictive motion is what I call 'orientation paths', evident for example in English sentences like 'The cliff wall faces into/towards/past/away from the valley', which syntactically seems to depict a conceptualized situation in which some kind of fictive line of sight emerges from the wall of the cliff and moves in the direction specified by the path prepositions. A comparable fictive motion type is that of 'demonstrative' paths, seen for example in 'The arrow points into/towards/past/away from the city', again as if there were some kind of line emerging from the front end of the arrow. Indeed, all forms of human pointing work in the same way, as seen in 'I pointed into/towards/past/away from the city'.

Now, this linguistic expression of fictive motion and its non-linguistic conceptual counterpart have certain properties. For example, if I am inside a windowless building and am asked to point towards the town centre, I shall not indicate a path which begins at my finger, leads through the open doorway, out of the exit of the building, turns around, and then moves in the direction of the city. On the contrary, I will simply extend my arm with pointed finger in the direction of the city, regardless of the structure around me. That is to say, the line of sight, effectively conceptualized as emerging from the finger, itself has the following crucial properties: it is (1) invisible and (2) passes through walls. These are the very same properties that are ascribed to spirits and ghosts. It seems quite likely that various cognitive systems which generate imaginal entities with their own conceptual properties are tapped so as to feed conceptual phenomena occurring in such other domains as spirit conceptions. In other words, the structure of spirit phenomena is not random or its own mode of construal, or domain of constructions; rather, it is probably the confluence and product of conceptual organization, already extant in other cognitive domains.

Boyer: One can certainly make a comparison between the counter-intuitive physical properties ascribed to ghosts and other such entities on the one hand, and partly metaphorical understandings of other domains on the other. The parallel between the physics of the ghosts and the 'fictive motion' of gaze, for instance, is indeed striking, and certainly explains the recurrence of assumptions concerning straight-line motion and movement through solid obstacles. Obviously, the salience of a counter-intuitive assumption must be higher if that assumption is taken as an intuitive description for another domain. In other papers (Boyer 1992a, 1993b) I have examined a similar case, that of the transfer of essentialist understandings, taken from the domain of living beings to the construction of social categories for religious roles (such as the shaman for instance). However, a number of counter-intuitive assumptions have no such intuitive origin. For instance, ancestors or gods are construed as beings that are immune to ordinary biological processes of growth and decay, an assumption which has no counterpart in ordinary intuitive understandings. In a general account of religious ontologies, the putative origin of such assumptions is only part of the problem; what remain to be explained are the processes whereby counter-intuitive assumptions are made more salient.

Lloyd: First, as a matter of the history of the term 'magic' in Greece, it was used often as a term of abuse, and what passed as magic for the actors themselves varied considerably. Much of what was passed as magic to commentators seemed natural to the actors. Second, much work is done by the notion of 'attention-demanding' in your argument. This needs elaborating.

Boyer: Your first point is well taken. What is magic and myth to you may be technology and religion to me. However, two remarks are in order. First, I was trying to argue from the point of view of 'our' anthropological understanding of the domain of 'magic' and to say that, whatever we think of the cohesion of that domain, one thing that does *not* hold it together is the acceptance of strange 'principles of causation' or the suspension of 'everyday' principles of causation. Second, I do not think that magical techniques ever seemed 'natural' to any practitioner, if we understand natural in the precise sense of 'in conformity with intuitive expectations'. If this were the case, such techniques would not be worth commenting or reporting. That they seem effective, that their effects seem real enough to some of the people who use them, is beyond doubt. However, this is not the same as being 'natural'. With regard to your second point, the intuitive notion of 'attention-demanding' ideas is meant to label, if not to explain, a property of the subjects' epistemic states as regards particular assumptions. These states are characterized by the fact that the assumption is more likely to be remembered than others, because it violates certain intuitive expectations. As a result, any assumption that strengthens this counter-intuitive representation is likely to be strengthened itself. This mechanism is described elsewhere in more detail (Boyer 1994, ch. 8), as precisely as possible, given the absence of a general cognitive theory of epistemic states and their dynamics.

Afterword

DAVID PREMACK AND ANN JAMES PREMACK

Let us imagine a mind lacking in causality. The basic device of such a mind is what we will call a Hume machine, a device that deals in contiguity not causality. If two items qualifying as events occur contiguously, they will be recorded by paramecia no less than primates. These events are recorded by the Hume machine, a domain-general device that accepts all contiguous events and is found in all species.

The Hume machine does not distinguish cause and effect. The first event in a contiguous pair does not correspond to cause, nor the second to effect. Either the device does not record order — pairs being represented as contiguous but not ordered events — or order is present but is not marked with cause-effect.

Unfortunately, psychology neither studied nor seriously contemplated the Hume device. From Pavlov to the present, conditioning theory has insisted that temporal contiguity is not a sufficient condition for connecting events. Conditioning, it was said, required stimuli of a special kind, presented in a special order (but see Gallistel (1994) for recent exception).

A neutral or unimportant event (CS) must be paired with an important one (US), the important one preceding the unimportant one, so that in negative conditioning an electric shock is preceded by a tone or light and in positive conditioning food is preceded by the same. 'Backward conditioning', shock or food followed by tone or light, was said not to work. In fact, backward conditioning works just as well as forward conditioning; there is no priviledged order (R. Rescorla, personal communication).

Similar erroneous reasoning was applied to instrumental conditioning where an individual's act produces an outcome. An instrumental or neutral act was to be followed by a goal act, for example bar pressing followed by eating or running followed by drinking; the reverse it was said would not work. In fact, eating before bar pressing or drinking before running works perfectly well (Premack 1962).

Both of the original formulations were derived from mistaken conceptions based on misguided evolutionary theory. The purpose of conditioning, it was universally agreed, was to signal the impending occurrence of important events — food, mate, danger — thereby enabling an individual to prepare him/herself for these events. This putative advantage was said to explain why both backward conditioning would not work and why conditioning evolved. Not only is this not the purpose of conditioning but, strictly speaking, the purpose of conditioning remains unknown. What we do know is that erroneous guesses about 'purpose' fostered mistaken conceptions that have yet to be eradicated.

VOLITION AND CAUSALITY

What is needed to turn a Hume machine into a causal one? A causal machine is, of course, capable of voluntary action, as a Hume machine is not. Voluntary action requires a condition of want, and a Hume machine lacks this condition. When stimulated, it may or not react depending on whether or not it is habituated. But when habituated it does not compare its present state to a former one and prefer the latter, i.e. it does not want to respond.

A Hume machine is further incapable of voluntary action, for in recording the occurrence of contiguous events, it cannot form separate lists, one for contiguous events in the world, another for contiguous events in which at least one member is its own reaction. It cannot form lists that distinguish between what it does and what is done to it—a prerequisite for voluntary action.

The evolution of voluntary behaviour entails a distinction between act and outcome. This could introduce cause and effect—a distinction that could then map onto the temporal order of the contiguous pairs in the Hume machine. Although we cannot, of course, observe the evolution of voluntary action, we can on occasion observe its ontogenesis in the infant. An infant who grimaced involuntarily when a bitter substance was placed on its lips, later grimaced though nothing was placed on its lips (Premack and Premack 1983). The infant made this transition in the context of a game that began traditionally, with the infant imitating the adult, but ended nontraditionally, with the infant causing the adult to imitate him or her; moreover, when he or she succeeded, the infant registered great delight. Cause, as Watson (1966) was among the first to emphasize, is not something infants take lightly. The adult's desire to explain causality is largely foreshadowed by the infant's wish to participate in causality.

ONTOGENETIC PRIORITY OF INTENTIONAL CAUSE

There is a mistaken tendency, we believe, to relegate the intentional construal of causality to a secondary status, to treat push–pull as primary. In the first place, one seldom sees the pure physical case, for example lightning felling a tree or wind blowing a boat; one is more likely to see the mixed case, an agent producing a physical outcome, for example an agent using an axe to cut a tree or using oars to row a boat.

Furthermore, only a few species, a handful of primates, are likely to be specialists in push–pull, for only a few pick up the objects in the world

(Chapter 2), strike them together, push them into holes, pile them, throw them, and perhaps even look at them.

Finally, the infant can causally affect its social world as in the example above, well before it can affect its physical world (Watson 1966). At 6 weeks the infant returns smiles and may also initiate them, using them (whether recognized by the adult or not) to cause the adult to smile back. The smiles need not be contiguous in order that the infant recognize a causal connection between them. In this respect, intentional causality represents a significant departure from the Hume machine.

ON RECONCILING HUME AND MICHOTTE

The two conflicting traditions of causality in psychology are both represented in the book: the **arbitrary** tradition of Hume (in which causality is learned) and the **natural** tradition of Michotte (in which causality is directly perceived) (Premack 1994). The bar pressing–food delivery case perfectly represents Hume's view (bar pressing and delivery of food are not connected by any natural mechanism, the relation between them is arbitrary); the object-launching case perfectly represents Michotte's view (collision and launching are connected by a known mechanism, the relation between them is natural). Given the patent difference between causal belief that is produced by learning in one case (Hume) and perception in the other (Michotte), one may well ask: Is the representation of causality the same in the two cases?

The answer apparently is 'no' to judge from recent data from Schlottman and Shanks (1992). Humans were shown two variations on a Michotte display (in which one object appears to collide with and launch another). A variation, contiguity, contrasted immediate and delayed collision. A second variation, contingency, contrasted an object launched by collision with an object launched despite the absence of a collision.

In this display humans rated separately their **perception** of a causal relation between launching and collision and their **judgement** that a causal relation obtained between the two events. Perception and judgement were affected in entirely different ways. While not affecting judgement, delay had a detrimental effect on perception. Lack of contingency did not affect perception but had a detrimental effect on judgement.

The complexity does not end there. Delay evidently affects arbitrary and natural causality differently. Although not affecting judgement in the natural case, in an arbitrary case when humans pressed a lever to produce a light, delay weakened both instrumental responding and judgement of a causal relationship (Chapter 1). While the judgement of natural causal relations remains untouched, delay weakens the judgement of arbitrary causal relations.

Can we make sense of this jumble of relations? Consider the following hypothesis. Although in pre-causal creatures, contiguous events are merely entered on the Hume machine list, in post-causal creatures they are interpreted causally; contiguity is a sufficient condition for causality. We could test this somewhat counter-intuitive hypothesis by adding a control condition to the Leslie–Keeble (Chapter 5) procedure.

These writers habituated infants on either a direct or a delayed launching case, and then reversed the order of the launching, object B now colliding with object A rather than vice versa. Since infants in the direct group showed more recovery, they argued that these infants perceived a causal relation. But did the infants perceive a causal relation because launching is a natural case, or because they interpret all contiguous events in this manner?

We can distinguish the two alternatives by repeating the Leslie–Keeble procedure but with an arbitrary case rather than a natural one, say a tone followed by a color change. After habituating infants to this pair of events with and without delay, we reverse the order of the two events. If the results are not the same as those of Leslie–Keeble, we could retain their interpretation, taking it to indicate that infants perceive causality in the natural case but not in the arbitrary one.

On the other hand, if delay has the same effect in both arbitrary and natural cases, we could not retain their interpretation. For although collisions cause launchings, tones do not cause color changes. The infant's reaction might then be seen as indicating that contiguity is interpreted causally.

Finally, if the hypothesis is not confirmed, if infants react differently to natural and arbitrary cases, we cannot reconcile Hume and Michotte, but must admit that the representation for causality is not the same when one directly perceives the relation (natural) and when one learns it (arbitrary). This dims one's hopes for finding an integrated view of causality. It may still be possible to unify Hume and Michotte at some deeper level of analysis at some future date, for it would be heartening to conclude on a note of reconciliation of differences. But whether this note can be heard remains uncertain.

REFERENCES

Gallistel, C. R. (1994). Interview *Journal of Cognitive Neuroscience* 6, 174–9.

Premack, D. (1962). Reversability of the reinforcement relation. *Science* 136, 255–7.

Premack, D. (1995). Induced motion/cause: spontaneous motion/intention. In *The origins of the human brain*, (ed. J. P. Changeux and J. Chavillion), Chapter 18. Oxford University Press, Oxford.

Premack, D. and Premack, A. J. (1983). *The mind of an ape*. Norton, New York.

Schlottman, A. and Shanks, D. R. (1992). Evidence for a distinction between judged and perceived causality. *Quarterly Journal of Exeprimental Psychology* 44A, 321–42.

Watson, J. S. (1966). The development and generalization of 'Contingency awareness' in early infancy: hypotheses. *Merrill-Palmer Quarterly of Behavior and Development*. 12(2).

Contributors

Scott Atran holds positions as a research scientist at the CNRS (CREA-Ecole Polytechnique) in Paris and at the University of Michigan (Department of Anthropology, Institute for Social Research). Born in 1952, he studied at Columbia University (BA 1972, PhD 1984). He has been a researcher at the Museum National d'Histoire Naturelle de Paris (Laboratoire d'Ethnobiologie-Biogeographie 1981–87), a senior SSRC-MacArthur Fellow in International Peace and Security (1987–90), and has lectured at Cambridge (1984) and the Hebrew University (1988–89). He has done long-term field research in the Middle East and is presently co-ordinating a multidisciplinary project on Maya natural history. He is the author of *Cognitive foundations of natural history: towards an anthropology of science* (Cambridge University Press 1990).

Renée Baillargeon was born and raised in Quebec City, Canada. She obtained her BA from McGill University in 1975, and her PhD from the University of Pennsylvania in 1981. After spending a year as a postdoctoral fellow at the Cognitive Science Center at MIT, she joined the faculty of the Department of Psychology of the University of Texas at Austin. In 1984 she moved to the University of Illinois at Urbana–Champaign, where she still resides. She has received fellowships from the Guggenheim Foundation the Natural Sciences and Engineering Research Council of Canada, the Center for Advanced Study of the University of Illinois, and the Center for Advanced Study in the Behavioral Sciences at Stanford. In 1989 she received a Boyd R. McCandless Young Scientist award from the American Psychological Association (Division 7), and a University Scholar award from the University of Illinois. In 1993 she was elected a fellow of the American Psychological Society. Her research seeks to establish what infants know about the physical world and how they attain this knowledge; she is preparing a book on this topic for the 'Oxford Psychology Series'.

Pascal Boyer is a senior research fellow in anthropology at King's College, Cambridge. He has written on the cognitive aspects of cultural transmission, and is now doing experimental research on intuitive ontological principles and their effects on the acquisition of cultural representations, particularly religious categories. He is the author of *Tradition as truth and communication* (1990), and *The naturalness of religious ideas*

(1994), as well as the editor of *Cognitive aspects of religious symbolism* (1992).

Susan Carey is professor of psychology in MIT's Department of Brain and Cognitive Sciences. She received her education at Harvard, as a member of J. Bruner's and G. Miller's Center for Cognitive Studies, both as an undergraduate and as a graduate student. Carey works on a variety of problems within cognitive science, including face recognition, lexical development, and conceptual development. This latter research includes case studies of conceptual change, both within the history of science (thermal concepts in the seventeenth century) and within middle childhood (intuitive biology and intuitive physics).

Patricia Cheng is an associate professor of psychology at the University of California at Los Angeles. She received her PhD degree in cognitive psychology from the University of Michigan at Ann Arbor. Her research has investigated the processes by which people infer the causes of events. In addition to work on causal inference, she has conducted research on deductive reasoning and on attention.

Anthony Dickinson received his first degree in psychology from the University of Manchester and a doctorate in behavioural neuroscience from the University of Sussex. Following a postdoctoral fellowship at Sussex, he moved to the University of Cambridge as a lecturer in the Department of Experimental Psychology. During the last 15 years he has published research papers on the basic associative learning mechanisms in conditioning, and the cognitive and motivational processes underlying goal-directed action in both humans and animals.

Rochel Gelman, a professor of psychology at UCLA, is working on a rational-constructivist theory of concept acquisition. She studies first principles about number, causality, and the animate–inanimate distinction, their effects on early leanings, the acquisition of domain-specific symbol systems, and learning about new principles. These efforts relate to her collaboration with cognitive scientists on science learning in formal and informal learning environments. She has been a Guggenheim Fellow, and a fellow at the Center for Advanced Study in the Behavioral Sciences.

Ian Hacking is a philosopher who was born in Vancouver in 1936, and completed a first degree in mathematics and physics at the University of British Columbia in 1956. His subsequent education in philosophy was at Cambridge University, with a doctorate in 1962. He has taught in Vancouver, Kampala, Cambridge, Stanford, and Toronto where he is now University Professor. His books include *Logic of statistical inference* (1965), *Why does language matter to philosophy?* (1975), *The emergence of probability* (1975), *Representing and intervening* (1983), *The taming of chance* (1990), and *Le plus pur nominalisme* (1993). He is completing a book to be called *Multiple personality and the politics of memory*.

Denis J. Hilton, born in 1955, received his BA in developmental psychology from the University of Sussex in 1977, and his doctorate in psychology from the University of Oxford in 1984 for his work on causal attribution processes. Since then he has taught and done research in Great Britain, the United States, and Germany. Since September 1991 he has been associate professor of marketing at ESSEC, in Cergy-Pontoise, France. His current research interests include causal explanation processes, conversational pragmatics, and decision-making.

Lawrence A. Hirschfeld is assistant professor of anthropology and of social work, and faculty associate, Research Center for Group Dynamics, Institute for Social Research, University of Michigan. He received his PhD from Columbia University. His primary research interest is the mental representation of human groupings, particularly by children. He has explored children's conceptual understanding of various social categories, including race, kinship, and language, conducting long-term field work among the Toba Batak of Indonesia and the Kuna of Panama, and experimental work with children and adults in France and the United States. Recent publications include 'Discovering social difference: the role of appearance in the development of racial awareness' *Cognitive Psychology* (1993); *Mapping the mind: domain specificity in cognition and culture* (co-editor Susan Gelman) (Cambridge University Press 1994); and 'The child's representation of human groups', *The psychology of learning and motivation: advances in research and theory* (ed. D. Medin) (Academic Press 1994).

Born in 1949, **Pierre Jacob** has a position in philosophy at CNRS. He is a member of CREA (Ecole Polytechnique, Paris). In 1978 he received his PhD from the History of Science Department at Harvard University for work on the philosophy of science. He is the author of *L'Empirisme logique* (Minuit, Paris 1980), and *De Vienne à Cambridge, l'heéritage du positivisme logique de 1950 à nos jours* (Gallimard, Paris 1980). Since then he has published papers on philosophy of language and philosophy of mind. His current work focuses on mental causation, particularly on the role of mental content in the causal explanation of intentional behaviour.

Frank C. Keil, born in 1952, received a BA in molecular biology from MIT in 1973, an MA in Psychology from Stanford in 1975, and a PhD in psychology from the University of Pennsylvania in 1977. He has been a member of the Psychology Department at Cornell University since 1977 where he is now the Willian R. Kenan, Jr Professor of Psychology and Co-Director of Cornell's Cognitive Studies Program. He has been a

Guggenheim Fellow, a fellow at the Center for Advanced Study in the Behavioral Sciences, and has received two national awards from the American Psychological Association for his work in cognitive development. His recent work focuses on the roles of explanation and causal understanding in structuring concepts and guiding their acquisition. He is the author of *Semantic and conceptual development: an ontological perspective* (Harvard University Press 1979) and *Concepts, kinds and cognitive development* (MIT Press 1989).

Hans Kummer was born in 1930. He studied zoology in Zurich and took his doctorate in developmental physiology. His early research, which focused on social organization in nonhuman primates (including the development and function of dyadic and triadic relationships), involved both field studies in Ethiopia and experimental studies of captive animals at the Delta Regional Primate Research Center in the United States. More recently he has been interested in how monkeys represent their own social relationships. He is professor of ethology at the University of Zurich, and from 1972 to 1976 served as president of the International Primatological Society. His recently published *Vies de singes* (Odile Jacob 1993) is a popular account of the social organization of hamadryas baboons.

Alan M. Leslie. A native of Scotland, he took his first degree at Edinburgh University and his doctorate at Oxford University. He spent a year as a Leverhulme European Scholar at the Max-Planck-Institut fur Psycholinguistik while it was still a Projektgruppe, and joined the MRC Cognitive Development Unit, University College London at its inception, remaining there for 11 happy years. He recently joined the new Center for Cognitive Science (and Psychology Department) at Rutgers University.

Gilbert Lewis lectures in social anthropology at the University of Cambridge. He qualified first in medicine at Oxford University and received a PhD in social anthropology from the London School of Economics for research in Papua, New Guinea. He has done field research on medical and anthropological topics in Papua, New Guinea and, more recently, in the Gambia and in Guinea Bissau in West Africa. His publications include *Knowledge of illness in Sepik society* (Athlone Press and Humanities Press Inc. 1975) and *Day of shining red* (Cambridge University Press 1980).

Geoffrey Lloyd is Master of Darwin College, Cambridge; since 1983 he has also been professor of ancient philosophy and science. He was born in 1933 and educated at Charterhouse and Cambridge (King's College, gaining BA, MA, PhD). He has published extensively in the area of Greek philosophy and science. His most recent books are *The revolutions of wisdom* (University of California Press 1987), *Demystifying mentalities* (Cambridge University Press 1990), and *Methods and problems in Greek science* (Cambridge University Press 1991). He is currently engaged in comparative studies on Greek and Chinese science in collaboration with Nathan Sivin.

Michael W. Morris, born in New York in 1964, is an assistant professor of organizational behavior at Stanford University (GSB). He obtained a BA in english literature and in cognitive science from Brown University in 1986, where he began research on event perception and conceptualization. As a doctoral student in social psychology at the University of Michigan, he studied causal reasoning and inference. His dissertation, which investigated cultural differences in causal attribution, received the 1993 award from the Society for Experimental Social Psychology. Among his current research interests is the role of causal attributions in the escalation of social conflict and in its resolution.

Richard Nisbett received his PhD from Columbia University in 1966. He is the Theodore M. Newcomb Distinguished Professor of Psychology and Director of the Research Center for Group Dynamics of the Institute for Social Research at the University of Michigan. In 1991, he was given the Distinguished Scientific Contribution award by the American Psychological Association and in 1992 he was elected to the American Academy of Arts and Sciences. He is the author of *Rules of reasoning* (1992), co-author with Lee Ross of *The person and the situation: perspectives of social psychology* (1991), and co-author with J. H. Holland, K. J. Holyoak, and P. Thagard of *Induction: processes of inference, learning, and discovery* (1986) among a number of other books.

Philip Pettit is professor of social and political theory at the Research School of Social Sciences, Australian National University. He is a philosopher and works in two main areas: the foundation of the psychological and social sciences; and moral and political theory. He is co-author with John Braithwaite of *Not just deserts: a republican theory of criminal justice* (Oxford 1990), and author of *The common mind: an essay on psychology, society, and politics* (Oxford 1993). In 1992 he was Centennial Visiting Professor at the London School of Economics, and Professeur Invité at the Ecole des Hautes Etudes en Sciences Sociales in Paris.

Ann James Premack graduated from the University of Minnesota, and is now a science writer whose work has appeared in many journals and magazines, including *Scientific American*, *La Recherche*, *Le Débat*, *National Geographic*, and *Geo*. Her book, *Why chimps can read* (1975), has appeared in four foreign-language translations. With D. Premack, she has published *The mind of an ape* (1983).

David Premack received his PhD from the University of Minnesota in 1955, and is presently a visiting member of CREA Ecole Polytechnique, Paris. He has been a Guggenheim Fellow, and a fellow at the Institute for

Advanced Thought in the Behavioral Sciences, Stanford; Wissenschaftskollege, Berlin; Van Leer Jerusalem Institute; Japan Society for Promotion of Science. He was awarded the Francis Craik Research Award, St John's College, Cambridge 1987, and the Fyssen Foundation Research Prize, Paris 1988. His recent work, in collaboration with A. J. Premack, concerns the phylogenetic and ontogenetic bases of human social competence. He is the author of *Intelligence in ape and man* (1976); *Mind of an ape* (1983), with A. J. Premack; and *Gavagai! Or the future history of the animal language controversy* (1986).

Elizabeth S. Spelke, born in 1949, was educated at Harvard, Yale, and studied for her PhD at Cornell with Ulric Neisser and Eleanor Gibson. She has taught at the University of Pennsylvania, and is presently at Cornell University. For some 20 years her research has focused primarily on explorations of the perceptual and cognitive capacities of human infants. She has studied infant ability to perceive objects; and to relate events they see to events they hear. In addition, she has studied infant understanding of the behaviour of physical objects, and representation of space and number. She has been a Guggenheim Fellow, a Fulbright Fellow, and was a recipient of the American Psychological Association's Boyd McCandless award.

Dan Sperber is a French cognitive and social scientist. Born in 1942, he studied at the Sorbonne and at Oxford. He is the author of *Rethinking symbolism* (Cambridge University Press 1975), *On anthropological knowledge* (Cambridge University Press 1985), *Relevance: communication and cognition* (with Deirdre Wilson, Blackwell 1986), and papers in anthropology, philosophy, psychology, and linguistics. He holds a permanent research position at the Centre National de la Recherche Scientifique and at the CREA of the Ecole Polytechnique (Paris), and has held visiting positions at Cambridge University, the British Academy, the London School of Economics, the Van Leer Institute in Jerusalem, the Institute for Advanced Study in Princeton, and Princeton University.

Amanda L. Woodward earned her doctorate at Stanford University in 1992. She was a Sloan Foundation Fellow at Stanford, a postdoctoral fellow at Cornell University and is now an assistant professor of psychology at the University of Chicago.

Index

Note: bold denotes illustrations; italic denotes tables.